P9-EDS-961

Best Places
to Stay
in California

THE BEST PLACES TO STAY SERIES

Best Places to Stay in California
Fourth Edition/Marilyn McFarlane and Anne E. Wright

Best Places to Stay in the Caribbean
Third Edition/Bill Jamison and Cheryl Alters Jamison

Best Places to Stay in Florida
Third Edition/Christine Davidson

Best Places to Stay in Mexico
Third Edition/Bill Jamison and Cheryl Alters Jamison

Best Places to Stay in the Mid-Atlantic States
Second Edition/ Dana Nadel Foley

Best Places to Stay in the Midwest
Second Edition/John Monaghan

Best Places to Stay in New England
Sixth Edition/Christina Tree and Kimberly Grant

Best Places to Stay in the Pacific Northwest
Fourth Edition/Marilyn McFarlane

Best Places to Stay in the Rockies
Second Edition/Roger Cox

Best Places to Stay in the South
Second Edition/Carol Timblin

Best Places to Stay in the Southwest
Fourth Edition/Anne E. Wright

Best Places
to Stay
in California

FOURTH EDITION

Marilyn McFarlane
and Anne E. Wright

Bruce Shaw, Editorial Director

HOUGHTON MIFFLIN COMPANY
BOSTON • NEW YORK

For information about this and other Houghton Mifflin trade and
reference books and multimedia products, visit The
Bookstore at Houghton Mifflin on the World Wide Web at
http://www.hmco.com/trade/.

Fourth Edition

ISSN: 1048-5422
ISBN: 0-395-73520-3

Printed in the United States of America

Maps by Charles Bahne
Design by Robert Overholtzer
Illustrations provided by included establishments
and by Lynn M. Michaud.

This book was prepared in conjunction
with Harvard Common Press.

CRW 10 9 8 7 6 5 4 3 2 1

To my daughters, who also love California — M. M.

For my family and friends, may they enjoy California as much as I have — A. E. W.

Contents

Introduction

Places to stay in California are as diverse as the state. They range from rustic cabins in the woods to luxurious city hotels, with an astounding variety in between. You can lodge at a luxurious resort, a homey bed-and-breakfast inn, a Victorian mansion, or a romantic retreat in the county. You'll find the best of them all here in this book.

The fourth edition of *Best Places to Stay in California* is divided by region and, within the region, by the city or town where each hotel or inn is located. There are new lodgings, a few deletions, and numerous changes. These are the result of months of personally investigating hundreds of inns. Again, the best were selected. That does not mean they're the most elegant or expensive. What we look for are comfortable accommodations, cleanliness, a commitment to hospitality, an interesting setting, and personality. These criteria apply to every lodging in the book.

In addition to entries divided by location, the hotels and inns are also listed under the categories that help you decide if this is the type of place you're looking for. The book also has brief descriptions of each region, maps, and a recommended reading list.

The Appendix is a handy reference to help you select your preferences in sports, dining, business services, and other interests. It indicates which inns are accessible to wheelchairs and which have cooking facilities.

The inns are not rated, as each has its own merits, and your choice depends upon the type of place you want. If it's in this book you can assume it is among the best of its kind. None of the inns paid to be included.

You may not agree with all the choices. Some fine places were excluded, not as a reflection on their quality, but by necessity (the inn may be changing ownership, for example, with its future in doubt). You won't find many chain hotels in the book because, with a few outstanding exceptions, they differ very little among locales.

Your comments are welcome. If you know of a special place that is not described here, or if you've had an unsatisfactory experience at an inn listed, please let us know. Your suggestions will help with future editions and allow us to provide you and other travelers with accurate information. Send your comments to:

Chris Paddock
Best Places to Stay in California
The Harvard Common Press
535 Albany Street
Boston, Massachusetts 02118

Rates

Please note that all the rates given applied at press time and are subject to change without notice. Unless otherwise noted, the rates cited are for one night. "Single" is the cost for one person, "double" the cost for two. Be sure to ask about discount packages, corporate and family rates, and off-season and midweek discounts. These are frequently offered, and you may save a substantial amount.

Meals

Breakfasts are described as Full, Continental, or Expanded Continental. A full breakfast connotes a hot entrée; a Continental meal is a light repast, usually coffee or tea, rolls, and fruit; while expanded Continental falls between the two, often including cereal, yogurt, or an assortment of cheeses.

Children

By law, California hotels may not refuse to accept children. However, young children aren't appropriate at some lodgings. Bringing a lively three-year-old to a quiet, antique-filled romantic hideaway can be a frustrating experience for everyone. Common sense is your best guide. Some of the larger hotels welcome children, even providing toys and special menus, and many allow children to occupy the same room as their parents at no charge.

Booking A Room

If you explain your needs clearly when you make a room reservation (do you prefer a private bath, a view, quiet surroundings, a firm bed?), they are likely to be met. If you are not satisfied, request a change. Every hotel has less desirable rooms, but you should never have to accept a room you don't like.

The information in this guidebook is as current and accurate as possible, but changes inevitably occur. We recommend asking about rates and policies before you check in. We also strongly urge making reservations ahead. But if you haven't made reservations, try anyway! Innkeepers are delighted to fill rooms that are suddenly empty because of cancellations.

Best Places to Stay in California is the most comprehensive compilation of outstanding lodgings in the state. We hope you enjoy reading and using it as much as we've enjoyed the research and writing. Happy travels!

Categories

Intimate City Stops

This category reviews small hotels and bed-and-breakfast inns that combine sophisticated urban amenities with personal style and attention to detail. They may have as few as four rooms; none has more than 100.

Grand City Hotels

Famous historic landmarks and hotels of contemporary opulence are included in this category.

Country Inns and B&Bs

When you're looking for a peaceful retreat from city noise and bustle, a country inn or homey bed-and-breakfast is the ideal choice. Those described here are not all in rural areas, but each has a distinct country inn atmosphere and offers a chance to enjoy a change of pace.

Family Favorites

If you've wondered where to find a vacation spot for the whole family, possibly offering complete programs for children, these inns, lodges, and ranches are your answer. They fit other categories, too, but they have perfected the art of providing fun for every age, and their rates often favor families.

Inns by the Sea

Resorts, condominiums, lodges, private homes, and old-fashioned beach hotels are the inns described here. Most are right on the shore, with views of the broad Pacific, while some are a few blocks inland in seaside towns. Each has a setting that focuses on the ocean.

On a Budget

These inns are included not only for their unusually low rates, but for other appealing qualities such as an outstanding view, a quaint atmosphere, or a prime location.

Resorts

If a resort offers a wide variety of recreational activities and all meals, and if it is a destination rather than a stopover, we consider it a full-service resort that belongs first in this category.

Romantic Hideaways

No matter what your romantic preferences, you'll find a special place among these choices. They all offer privacy and an enchanting atmosphere.

Spas

When you're ready for a vacation that combines health, fitness, good food, companionship and pampering in a tranquil atmosphere, these are the places to try.

California

First there were the mountains and the desert, the roaring surf and animals, vast redwood forests and condors wheeling above silent canyons. Then came the Indians, following the sun after crossing the Bering Strait from Asia. Their clans and communities had been deeply settled along the Pacific for untold generations by the time Spanish explorers arrived, seeking a fabled golden island. The English and the Russians laid claim, and in the 18th century the Franciscans established missions, some of them still standing, along the Camino Real (King's Highway). In 1848, after three centuries of Spanish and then Mexican rule, California became a U.S. territory.

In the same year, gold was discovered in Sutter's Mill, near Sacramento. California's future was assured. Thousands of prospectors, struck by gold fever, swarmed in with settlers and merchants on their heels. Immigrants began moving west, dreaming of gold or a new life. California has become the most populated state in the nation, with an ethnic mixture that borders on the bewildering.

As a visitor in this state of diversity, you too will find gold. It may not glitter in a creek bed, but you'll see it in other ways: oranges gleaming against glossy green leaves . . . hillsides aflame with poppies . . . gold-flecked sands on miles of beaches . . . the sun-burnished hair of surfers and swimmers . . . clusters of ripening dates hanging high in palm trees. And the memories you take home will be pure gold, whether you find them in the sun-dappled depths of a redwood forest, on a lively city street, along a sandy beach, or on a white-cloaked mountain.

Because of California's incredible diversity and size, the tourism department divides The Golden State into twelve regions, "The Californias." They are Shasta-Cascade, the Central Coast, Deserts, the Central Valley, San Diego County, the Inland Empire, Greater Los Angeles, Orange County, the

Gold Country, the North Coast, the San Francisco Bay Area, and the High Sierra.

For maps and information on any or all of the twelve regions, contact the California Office of Tourism, 1121 L Street, Suite 103, Sacramento, California 45814; phone 916-322-1396.

Mt. Shasta

Northern
California

Mendocino

Wine Country

South Lake Tahoe

Healdsburg

Bodega
Bay

Sacramento

Sierra Country

Inverness

Napa

Oakland

San Francisco

San Jose

Yosemite

Bay Area

Santa Cruz

Central
Coast

Death
Valley

Desert
Country

Santa Barbara

Big Bear
Lake

Los Angeles

Palm Springs

Southern Calif.

Borrego
Springs

San Diego

Bay Area

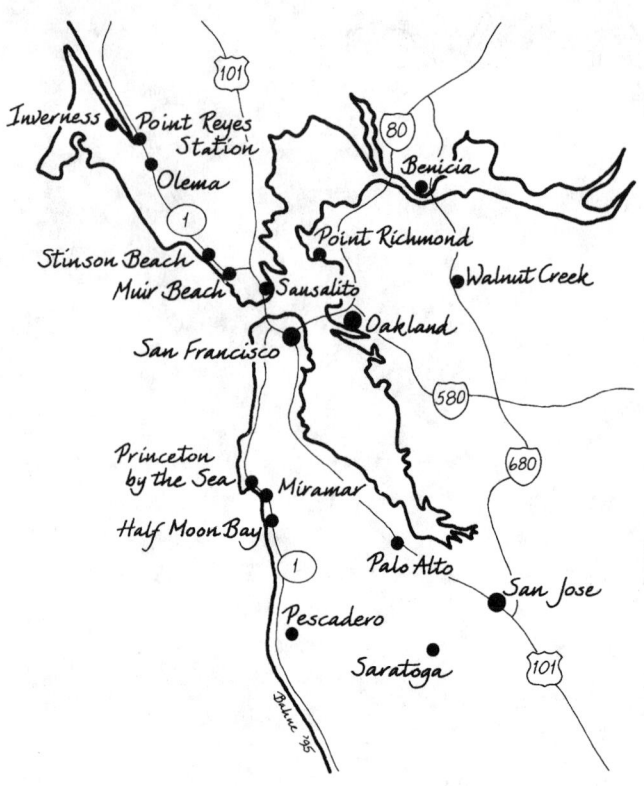

Best Country Inns and B&Bs

Inverness
  Blackthorne Inn
  Holly Tree Inn
  Ten Inverness Way
Muir Beach
  The Pelican Inn
Olema
  Point Reyes Seashore Lodge
  Roundstone Farm
Point Reyes Station
  Thirty-nine Cypress
Saratoga
  The Inn at Saratoga
Walnut Creek
  The Mansion at Lakewood

Best Family Favorites

Point Reyes Station
  Gray's Retreat
San Francisco
  Seal Rock Inn

Best Grand City Hotels

San Francisco
  The Fairmont Hotel
  Four Seasons Clift Hotel
  Hotel Nikko
  The Huntington Hotel
  Mandarin Oriental
  The Mark Hopkins Intercontinental
  The Pan Pacific Hotel
  The Ritz-Carlton San Francisco
  Sheraton Palace Hotel
  Renaissance Stanford Court Hotel
  The Westin St. Francis

Best Inns by the Sea

Half Moon Bay
  Old Thyme Inn
  Cypress Inn
Oakland
  Dockside Boat & Bed
Point Richmond
  East Brother Light Station
Princeton-by-the-Sea
  The Pillar Point Inn
Stinson Beach
  Casa del Mar

Best Intimate City Stops

Benicia
  The Union Hotel
Palo Alto
  Garden Court Hotel
  The Victorian on Lytton
San Francisco
  The Archbishops Mansion
  Campton Place
  Casa Arguello
  Country Cottage
  Galleria Park Hotel
  Harbor Court Hotel
  Hotel Griffon
  Hotel Juliana
  Hotel Triton
  Hotel Vintage Court
  Inn at the Opera
  The Inn at Union Square
  Jackson Court
  The Majestic
  The Mansions
  Petite Auberge
  The Red Victorian
  Victorian Inn on the Park
  The Villa Florence Hotel
  The White Swan Inn
San Jose
  Hotel De Anza

Best On A Budget

Pescadero
   Pigeon Point Lighthouse Hostel
San Francisco
   Golden Gate Hotel
   Hotel Sheehan
   The San Remo Hotel

Best Resorts

Oakland
   The Claremont Resort and Spa

Best Romantic Hideaways

Point Reyes Station
   Jasmine Cottage
Sausalito
   Casa Madrona Hotel

San Francisco, an elegant gem of verve and grace, is everybody's favorite city. Despite earthquakes, fires, and ceaseless change, it remains a place of beauty, from the buttercup-strewn meadows of Golden Gate Park to the chic shops on Nob Hill. The hotels and restaurants in San Francisco are, appropriately, among the best in the world.

It is not only San Francisco's striking location on the bay that brings tourists by the drove each year, but the city has so much to offer the visitor that it deserves its reputation as one of the top destinations in the country. What better pleasure than to ride the clanking cable cars over the hilly city streets, zigzag down curving Lombard Street, or dine in the Italian cafés of North Beach or the chic bistros of SOMO and Russian Hill. You can get a bird's-eye view of the city and bay from the top of Coit Tower, then there are the neighborhoods to explore such as exclusive Nob Hill and Pacific Heights, the 1960s revolutionary enclave of Haight-Ashbury, or bustling Chinatown. In Golden Gate Park there are acres of gardens to enjoy, including the Botanical Gardens, the Conservatory of Flowers, and the famed Japanese Tea garden, as well as the

M. H. deYoung Museum, Asian Art Museum, and California Academy of Sciences with its natural history museum, planetarium, and small aquarium to visit when misty weather drives one indoors. Shops abound at Pier 39, the Embarcadero, and in Ghirardelli and Union Squares; and the abandoned prison on the island of Alcatraz has its own spooky allure. The newly reopened San Francisco Museum of Modern Art in the revitalized SOMA (for South of Market) district is further evidence of the city's ongoing appeal.

Yet with all there is to see in San Francisco, the Bay Area has a far wider reach than Marin County and the communities immediately fronting San Francisco Bay. In this context, it extends north as far as the Point Reyes area along the coast, and down the peninsula to San Jose and Saratoga. Immediately north of San Francisco are the waterfront boutiques of **Sausalito;** farther north, in the hilly ranch country close to the ocean and Tomales Bay, lies Point Reyes National Seashore, bordered by charming, unpretentious villages — **Inverness, Point Reyes Station,** and **Olema**.

East Bay visitors like to amble by the marina at Jack London's Waterfront, in **Oakland,** and taste the fresh seafood offered in waterfront restaurants. Boaters, joggers, and bicyclists enjoy Lake Merritt, the country's largest salt water lake within a city.

Up in **Benicia,** an art colony has formed, with glass-blowing studios selling works of fine quality. The town, which was California's capital from 1853 to 1854, has antiques shops and 19th-century architecture. Not far from here is the famous Marine World Africa USA, which has more than a thousand animals. If you travel west on the peninsula south of San Francisco, you'll come to the charming seaside towns of **Princeton-by-the-Sea** and **Half Moon Bay.** Surrounded by farmland, Half Moon Bay calls itself the pumpkin capital of the world and holds a popular Pumpkin Festival in October. Princeton Harbor offers charter fishing and whale-watching cruises.

Inland from the coast, the Santa Clara Valley — nicknamed the Silicon Valley for its electronic technology industry — has California's third largest city, **San Jose.** Its best-known attraction is the Winchester Mystery House, a 160-room mansion built by the eccentric heiress of the Winchester rifle fortune. It is said that she believed she would live as long as she kept building — so the house has ten thousand windows and forty staircases, some leading nowhere.

San Jose also has the Rosicrucian Egyptian Museum, with

an impressive collection of ancient artifacts from Egypt and Assyria. The San Jose Historical Museum displays items of more recent vintage: buildings and relics from turn-of-the-century California. The Chinese Cultural Gardens are in Overfelt Botanical Gardens, a 37-acre wildlife sanctuary.

Nearby Saratoga is known for its fine cuisine; Palo Alto, the home of Stanford University, has a collegiate air.

BENICIA

The Union Hotel

401 First Street
Benicia, CA 94510
707-746-0100
800-544-2278
Fax: 707-746-6458

> *A historic hotel*
> *in a quaint town*
> *on the bay*

Manager: Bill Berg. **Accommodations:** 12 rooms (all with private bath) in main building, 9 rooms in annex. **Rates:** $79–$135 single or double. **Included:** Continental breakfast. **Added:** 9% tax. **Payment:** Major credit cards. **Children:** Welcome. **Pets:** Not allowed. **Smoking:** Allowed.

It's a cheerful, whimsically furnished hostelry today, without a tinge of scandal, but the historic Union Hotel has a risqué past. It was established in 1882 as a 20-room bordello, back when Benicia was a bustling port town on the edge of the Carquinez Strait. You can still see the peephole in one of the doors — just about the only piece left of the original building. The trim, three-story hotel was restored in 1981, with each guest room decorated individually. Although they are furnished with antiques, the rooms have modern features like television, phones, desks, air conditioning, and whirlpool tubs. The rooms bear names rather than numbers. Mei Ling, on the third floor, has an Oriental decor. Four-Poster, as the name suggests, contains a high, antique bed with a curved canopy.

Beautiful prism chandeliers sparkle in The Ritz, which has a matching carved bedframe and armoire. This room has a view of the Carquinez Strait, where the boats head upriver to Sacramento or southwest toward the bay. For the best view in the hotel, request one of the most glamorous rooms, Louis Le Mad.

Massachusetts Bay hints of Cape Cod, with its spindle bed, wooden rocker, and braided rug. White wicker chairs and fresh flowers give Summer Skies a country garden theme, enhanced by the pretty sky-blue ceiling afloat with white painted clouds. There's an art deco motif in 1932, while Victoriana fits the image of a fine English hotel room a century ago.

> **Benicia served as a U.S. Army arsenal and fort in the mid-19th century, and was the first state capital. Here, in an adobe saloon, the discovery of gold was announced to the world. California's first public school was also in Benicia.**

The main floor of the Union contains a noted restaurant. The management takes pride in the fact that everything it serves is fresh. The menu offers daily specials and changes seasonally. Diners are served in a room that evokes the hotel's original period, with a stained glass skylight, green lincrusta walls, and historic photographs. A hand-carved mahogany backbar dominates the lounge.

In keeping with this step into the past are the antiques shops and historic buildings on First Street. Victorian and false-front western architecture dates from the 1850s to the early 1900s.

Today the quiet little town on the bay, a 45-minute drive northeast of San Francisco, honors its heritage and thrives on old-fashioned celebrations such as a Fourth of July parade and picnic. The Peddler's Fair in August is the largest antiques and handicraft fair in northern California.

HALF MOON BAY

Cypress Inn on Miramar Beach

407 Mirada Road
Half Moon Bay, CA 94019
415-726-6002
800-83-BEACH
Fax: 415-712-0380

A small seaside inn with a festive atmosphere

Innkeepers: Suzie Lankes and Dan Floyd. **Accommodations:** 12 rooms (all with private bath). **Rates:** $150–$275, $20 additional person, off-season discounts. **Included:** Full breakfast and wine, hors d'oeuvres, and dessert. **Added:** 10% tax. **Payment:** Major credit cards. **Children:** Not appropriate for small children. **Pets:** Not allowed. **Smoking:** Not allowed indoors

The Cypress Inn's exterior, in quiet sand and teal, gives no hint of the riot of color within. From the yellow parlor to the vividly painted guest rooms, the atmosphere is as bright as an artist's palette. Each room a different color, they all have a fireplace, wicker furniture, a deck or balcony, featherbeds, a fluffy comforter and pillow, and tiled baths. They're decorated with carved wooden animals from Mexico — colorful folk art that fits in perfectly with the inn's cheery style. The rooms have names from nature: La Estrella (Star), La Luna (Moon), El Viento (Wind), and El Mar (Sea) are examples. Las Nubes (Clouds) is a third-floor penthouse in white with an oversize whirlpool tub and a panoramic view.

Every room has an ocean view in this light and breezy, contemporary inn on a quiet frontage road two miles north of Half Moon Bay. Step out the door and you're facing a five-mile stretch of sandy beach with public access.

The Cypress has a conference room for small groups, and four additional rooms are located in a separate home behind the inn. Called the Beach House, rooms are named for area beaches (Dunes, Moss, Venice, and Naples), and are more luxurious than those in the main inn. Most have whirlpool tubs for two and all have fireplaces. Dunes is the grandest, with a terrific view, large deck, and an in-room spa in front of the fireplace.

Breakfast, served in your room or in the dining area next to the skylighted parlor, is outstanding. In addition to a granola-yogurt-berry parfait, you'll have juice, fresh croissants, and an entrée such as peaches-and-cream French toast or an omelette with tomatoes. Consult the inn's information-packed notebook for nearby attractions and restaurant recommendations. One deservedly popular and festive spot is Pasta Moon, which serves wonderful pasta and cheesecake.

Old Thyme Inn

779 Main Street
Half Moon Bay, CA 94019
415-726-1616

A bed-and-breakfast in a seaside village

Innkeepers: George and Marcia Dempsey. **Accommodations:** 7 rooms (all with private bath). **Rates:** $75–$160 single, $85–$160 double, $25 additional person, suite $165–220. **Included:** Full breakfast. **Added:** 10% tax. **Payment:** MasterCard, Visa, and personal checks. **Children:** Over age 10 welcome. **Pets:** Not allowed. **Smoking:** Restricted.

An English herb garden gives this charming bed-and-breakfast inn its name. More than eighty varieties of herbs grow in the garden, spicing the air with their scents and providing dash to breakfast dishes. The Queen Anne home is a comfortable, relaxing place to visit. The hosts offer afternoon wines, restaurant recommendations, information on the sights of Half Moon Bay, and directions to the nine state beaches nearby, the tidepools at the Fitzgerald Marine Reserve, art galleries, and nearby pumpkin patches.

> This may be the pumpkin capital of the world.
> Every October thousands of people drive 30 miles south from the Bay area to buy their jack-o'-lanterns.

Old Thyme Inn was built in 1897 and restored as a bed-and-breakfast ninety years later. The guest rooms have antique furnishings, colorful wallpapers, and several contain fireplaces and whirl-pool tubs.

All but Oregon Room have queen-size beds; it has an antique French double bed.

Rosemary, on the main floor, is furnished with a curved white iron bed, Oriental carpet, wicker chair and rocker, and lace curtains. Behind a stained glass window is a blue and white bath with a two-person whirlpool.

Wild Thyme, also on the main floor, has a coronet canopy bed and down comforter, a gas fireplace, and a double whirlpool in the bathroom. An armoire holds padded hangers for clothing. Lavender, a small room upstairs, is the only one with a detached bath.

The Garden Suite offers secluded, quiet, romantic lodgings in a separate building behind the herb garden. Its four-poster pine and oak bed is canopied in violet and blue floral fabric to match the balloon shades and complement the room's rose decor.

The suite includes a fireplace, a TV and VCR, a refrigerator with complimentary wine, and a double whirlpool under a skylight. In the Garden Suite you may have breakfast in bed or if you are in a sociable mood, join the other guests at a single table in the dining room.

Breakfast includes juice, fruit, usually banana bread, and a main dish such as quiche or a frittata. A different breakfast is served every day for five days before repeating the menu. You might be served Italian bread with herbed cream cheese and tomatoes, a lemon bread, nut bread, scones with marmalade, or a homemade French cherry flan, along with a tray of cold meats and English cheeses.

INVERNESS

Blackthorne Inn

P.O. Box 712
266 Vallejo Avenue
Inverness, CA 94937
415-663-8621
Fax: 415-663-8635

*A whimsical,
handbuilt home
on Tomales Bay*

Innkeeper: Susan Wigert. **Accommodations:** 5 rooms (3 with private bath). **Rates:** $105–$195 double; $25 less for single during the week. **Included:** Full breakfast. **Minimum stay:** 2 nights weekends. **Payment:** Major credit cards. **Children:** Not appropriate **Pets:** Not allowed. **Smoking:** Not allowed.

North of San Francisco, in the wooded hills of the quiet town of Inverness, the Blackthorne Inn offers a unique retreat. It's been called a "carpenter's fantasy" and "an architectural extravaganza," well-deserved labels for a four-story rambling home that resembles an oversize treehouse. It used to be a one-room cabin surrounded by fir, bay and oak trees. Then Susan and Bill Wigert decided to add a deck. Their plans expanded, local carpenters and woodworkers became involved, and "the project got out of control," says Susan. Now it's a delightfully quirky construction with towers, alcoves, nooks, balconies, skylights, and a spiral staircase winding to the top.

Stones from seven counties were collected for the big fireplace in the living room on the main floor. Local artisans did the stonework, built fir plank walls, and put in rustic beams that came from San Francisco wharves. In this inviting room are books, games, a tape deck, and stereo. Alcoves with windows that look into the forest are ideal for curling up with a book and nibbling the brownies and cookies Susan offers in the afternoons.

There's also a wet bar with a refrigerator for guests' use. A 3,500-square-foot deck, complete with fire pole to the ground, circles the house on the second level.

In the adjacent dining room, breakfast is served buffet style Some choices are fresh fruit, baked apples, orange juice, granola and other cereals, quiche, and pastries.

Stairs wind up to two guest rooms on the third level and

one at the top. Lupine has a queen-size bed under a gable, a private bath in the room, and an outside deck. From the deck, stairs lead to the upper level and a hot tub under the trees.

> An interesting shop in Inverness is Shaker Workshops West, which sells handmade boxes, baskets, rocking chairs, and other Shaker furniture and crafts.

Overlook is a light, airy room with a peacock chair, and stained glass windows in artful thistle, poppy, and iris designs. Its bath is down the hall. Overlook also has two balconies, one with a view of the treetops and the other above the living room.

Eagle's Nest is the most enchanting (and the most expensive) space. An octagonal room at the top of the staircase, it's enclosed by glass to give you a fine view of the California buckeye trees and starry sky.

Outside, a ladder will take you to a private deck at the uppermost level. Cross a walkway and bridge from your private entrance, and you reach the deck, with a hot tub and bath.

The drawback to Eagle's Nest (if you don't mind all the climbing) is that you must go outside to the bathroom, and share it with hot-tubbers. However, it's a big favorite with those looking for a truly special romantic spot.

The inn's other two rooms are on the lowest level. Studio and Hideaway are spacious suites, each with a private entrance and sitting room. Both are nicely furnished with wicker and pastels; they share a bath with a shower. The advantage of these rooms is their proximity to the parking area, with few stairs to negotiate. The disadvantage is the view of the deck's underside. However, you do get forest glimpses as well.

The atmosphere is relaxed and casual, befitting Inverness's homey style. Susan enjoys her guests and is happy to sit down for a chat or to discuss the merits of local restaurants and beaches. You'll want to explore Point Reyes for its outstanding scenery, flowery meadows, steep headlands, and ocean views.

Holly Tree Inn

3 Silverhills Road
Inverness Park
Mailing address:
Box 642
Point Reyes Station, CA 94956
415-663-1554
800-286-4655
Fax: 415-663-8566

> *A wooded retreat*
> *near Point Reyes*
> *National Seashore*

Innkeepers: Diane and Tom Balogh. **Accommodations:** 4 rooms and 3 cottage (all with private bath). **Rates:** $90 single, $115–$150 double, cottages $170–$225. **Included:** Full breakfast. **Added:** 10% tax. **Minimum stay:** 2 nights weekends. **Payment:** Major credit cards. **Children:** $10–$15 additional per day. **Pets:** Not allowed. **Smoking:** Not allowed indoors.

An abundance of holly trees gives this bed-and-breakfast inn its name. Surrounded by lawns and flowers, it stands on 19 hilly, wooded acres outside Inverness and next to Point Reyes National Seashore, just north of San Francisco.

Holly Tree Inn is a dwelling of quiet comfort, a place for reflection. The heart of the inn is its spacious living room, where overstuffed chairs and sofas face a copper-hooded brick fireplace. Soft music plays and a fire glows on foggy days, a perfect setting for sipping a cup of tea, reading, or visiting.

Each of the guest rooms has its own character. Holly Room features a 1930s bedstead with hand-painted flowers on the headboard. A private balcony overlooks the front lawn, creek, and garden of daisies and golden lilies.

Mary's Garden, the smallest room, is off the kitchen but has soundproof walls and a private entrance. Its long windows overlook the rose garden.

Ivy, decorated in pale green, has a spool bed and ruffled curtains. Laurel's corner windows, hung with white Priscilla curtains, overlook the crab apple tree in the side garden. This spacious blue and white room has a sitting area with a wing chair and a king-size bed.

Cottage in the Woods is a few yards up the driveway from the main house. Built in 1987, it is simple, light and airy, a wonderfully inviting retreat. Bare wood floors are of warm, polished pine, and walls have a wash of pink-toned white.

The Cottage is furnished with pearwood antiques from Austria — note the carved pear baskets on the headboards and armoire. There is a toaster oven, and refrigerator in the kitchenette. There's a sitting room with a woodstove and a clawfoot tub in the bathroom, where you'll catch a whiff of bayberry and lemon verbena from the soaps on the counter. Making the room picture-perfect is the greenhouse window by the tub framing a view of the fern-covered hill just outside.

> The nearest beach is Limintaur, a 15-minute drive. You can walk for miles on its firm sand. The waters of Tomales Bay are warm enough for swimming in summer. In the winter, watch for gray whales from the lighthouse at the tip of Point Reyes. The entire peninsula is a bird-watcher's delight in all seasons.

Sea Star Cottage, situated on its own pier over the tidal waters of Tomales Bay, and Vision Cottage, discreetly tucked away among the pines, are two recent additions to the inn.

Sea Star has a queen-size four-poster bed, living room with a wood-burning stove, and fully equipped kitchen.

Vision Cottage, named for its view of Mount Vision, is a good option for families as the cottage has two bedrooms as well as a full kitchen. A 1.3 mile long trail leads from Vision Cottage to the swimming beaches in Tomales Bay State Park. Both cottages have their own private hot tubs.

For cottage guests, breakfast is placed in their refrigerators the night before; other guests eat in the inn's dining room by the brick fireplace. Orange juice, fruit, eggs Benedict, quiche, and French toast are among the dishes Diane prepares. After breakfast, guests can relax in the inn's hot tub or visit nearby attractions.

Point Reyes National Seashore has some of the most spectacular scenery and is one of the great hiking areas of the California coast. The inn is a mile from the visitors' center, the starting point for trails that wind to the sea over the woodlands and grassy meadows, often gold with California poppies. The most popular trail is Bear Valley, a 4.1-mile hike to Arch Rock.

Ten Inverness Way

P.O. Box 63
10 Inverness Way
Inverness, CA 94937
415-669-1648

> *A turn-of-the-century redwood home on Point Reyes peninsula*

Innkeeper: Mary Davies. **Accommodations:** 4 rooms, 1 suite (all with private bath). **Rates:** $100–$140 single, $110–$150 double, suite $160. **Added:** 10% tax. **Included:** Full breakfast. **Minimum stay:** 2 nights weekends, 3 nights on holiday weekends. **Payment:** MasterCard, Visa, personal checks. **Children:** Welcome in suite. **Pets:** Not allowed. **Smoking:** Not allowed indoors.

Mary Davies has written the book on innkeeping, literally. She's the author of a how-to guide for prospective bed-and-breakfast owners. Fortunately for her guests, she follows her own advice, resulting in a delightfully homey, comfortable inn where the energetic hostess knows how to welcome you, provide for your needs, and leave your privacy intact.

> **Mary's an avid reader who's happy to trade book suggestions; she even publishes a summer reading list of her ten favorites for the year. "This is an inn for hikers and readers," she says.**

Inverness, a quiet village on Tomales Bay, was formed a century ago as a resort development by James McMillan Shafter, who hoped to recoup his railway investment losses. The town and its streets were given Scottish names such as Hawthornden Way, Dundee Way, and Cameron Street, based on the family's Scottish background. The promotion wasn't successful, but today the town is a popular tourist destination.

The redwood shingle home that is now Ten Inverness Way was built in 1904. In 1980, Mary Davies bought it, converted it to an inn, and filled it with antiques, Oriental rugs, and handmade quilts. She planted an English country garden of nasturtiums, iris, penstemon, roses, and geraniums, under fruit trees, with paths winding around to the back of the house and the hot tub. Robes are provided for guests to wear to the hot tub.

The suite, entered through a private entrance from the garden, has a kitchen and a sitting area, a queen-size bed in an alcove, and a sofa bed. As a suite guest, you may have breakfast in your room or in the private garden.

In the main part of the house, unusual box windows allow plenty of light. In the big living room, a fire burns on cool evenings. There's a phone here and a sideboard where sherry and hot tea and coffee are always available. Guests enjoy the piano, a guitar, puzzles, and games, but the many books are the main draw.

The common room is upstairs from the inn's entrance, and guest rooms are a flight above that. Each room has something special — a skylight over the bed, an old wicker table, a bright patchwork quilt, or a daybed piled with pillows. Room 2, at the top of the stairs, is a favorite for its view of the bay from the high bed.

The innkeeper maintains a basket with such items as aspirin, dental floss, a hair dryer, heating pad, and Band-Aids. Other thoughtful touches are the assortment of books in each room, good reading lamps, and numerous hooks, hangers, and pegs.

The light-filled sunroom next to the living room has a cheery red woodstove, original art on the walls, and pots of bright flowers. Breakfast here includes toasted homemade bread with blackberry jam, juice, fresh fruit, and scrambled eggs with basil and cheese or Mary's specialty, banana buttermilk buckwheat pancakes — and plenty of strong hot coffee.

You can keep very busy on the Point Reyes Peninsula. Mary will give you pages of ideas, along with a trailhead guide for hiking in the area. She recommends Heart's Desire Beach in Tomales Bay State Park for swimming and picnics, walking at Abbott's Lagoon on a foggy day, whale-watching from Chimney Rock, and hiking Tomales Point Trail, where you may see Tule elk.

MUIR BEACH

The Pelican Inn

10 Pacific Way
Muir Beach, CA 94965-9729
415-383-6000

A touch of old England near the California coast

Innkeeper: Barry Stock. **Accommodations:** 7 rooms (all with private bath). **Rates:** $150–$170 single or double. **Included:** Full breakfast. **Added:** 10% tax. **Payment:** MasterCard, Visa. **Children:** Welcome ($20 for rollaway bed). **Pets:** Not allowed. **Smoking:** Allowed.

The Pelican nestles among pine and alder trees in the hills a short distance from the ocean (there is no water view). The Tudor-style inn, surrounded by lawns and flowers, looks like a manor house from Elizabethan England though it was built in 1979. Inside, it's even more British.

In 1579, when Sir Francis Drake beached the Pelican (later renamed the Golden Hinde) here on the Marin coast a few miles north of the Golden Gate Bridge, there were no country inns offering a warm bed, a mug of ale, and a game of darts. He might have enjoyed this one in Muir Beach, but this bit of Britain arrived four hundred years late.

The restaurant and pub are on the ground floor. Leaded glass windows, heavy beams, worn Oriental carpets on brick flooring, and a menu that offers Devonshire chicken, bangers, cottage pie, and would have made Sir Francis feel right at home. Benches against dark wood walls, tall candles on trencher tables, and a crackling fire in the fireplace create a cozy atmosphere on the foggiest of nights. Open to the public for other meals, the dining room serves guests only, for a breakfast of toast, marmalade, English sausage, and eggs. There's also a sitting area — the Snug — for guests' use, with a decor that continues the English-country theme.

The guest rooms have low doors with wrought-iron hardware. Room 1 features a half tester with a white eyelet quilt, lined tapestry curtains, an upholstered couch, and an old chest so battered it could have been left behind by the crew of the Pelican. Room 5 is smaller, its mullioned windows overlooking a balcony. One bedpost is an aged beam into which honeymooning guests often carve their initials; the obliging innkeeper will provide a knife if you ask. Room 2 is the smallest, though it has plenty of room for two. Here you ascend a stepladder to the high bed and fall asleep to the scent of jasmine, which climbs to the roof outside your window.

Barry Stock, who hails from Devonshire, Sir Francis' home port, sees that a decanter of sherry and fresh flowers are placed by your bedside. Ask him about the stone hanging from a ribbon over the bed and he'll tell you it is to ensure against rickets in case of pregnancy and keeps the evil eye at bay.

Barry's humor and hospitality, the inn's charm, and the proximity to Muir Woods and Muir Beach make rooms at the Pelican in great demand. You'll need reservations far in advance, especially for summer weekends. Spring and fall weekdays are more peaceful — and every bit as beautiful.

OAKLAND

The Claremont Resort and Spa

P.O. Box 23363
Ashby and Domingo Avenues
Oakland, CA 94623
510-843-3000
800-551-7266
Fax: 510-843-6239

A contemporary spa resort in a convenient East Bay location

General manager: Henry Feldman.
Accommodations: 211 rooms and 28 suites. **Rates:** $150–$209 single, $150–$229 double; suites $275–$720. **Added:** 10% tax.
Payment: Major credit cards. **Children:** Under age 18 free in room with parents. **Pets:** Not allowed. **Smoking:** Nonsmoking rooms available.

Across the bay from San Francisco, the Claremont has been a hilltop landmark on the Oakland-Berkeley border since 1915. The original castlelike home on the site, built by a farmer from Kansas who struck it rich in the gold mines, burned to the ground in 1901. A sprawling, many-gabled resort hotel was erected in its place, opening in time for the 1915 Panama-Pacific Exposition.

It has undergone several refurbishments, including a $30 million overhaul started in 1971. Today the Claremont reigns over 22 landscaped acres and a lofty view of San Francisco Bay, its bridges, and the glimmering skyline.

The location is a plus. It's convenient to the city, yet offers resort facilities. The Claremont boasts ten tennis courts, an Olympic-size pool and an exercise pool, saunas, whirlpools, and a luxurious, European-style health spa, added in 1989. It offers a full program of spa treatments, personal training and wellness services. Both spa cuisine and traditional fare are featured on the menu of the poolside café.

The Pavilion is the resort's showcase restaurant, with a menu that changes daily. The wine collection is extensive and rated highly, and the restaurant is noted for its lavish Sunday brunch. The Terrace Bar offers entertainment and dancing Tuesday through Saturday, and there are gift and florist shops, car rentals, and easy parking. A free shuttle is provided to the Oakland airport, BART stations, and the Tilden Golf Course. If you're driving to San Francisco, where parking is at a premium, you'll be given a voucher for three hours of free parking near Union Square.

Because the hotel's owners (the Schnitzers of Harsh Investment Corp.) are art devotees from the Pacific Northwest, the long, wide lobby and halls are filled with superb examples of contemporary art by Northwest artists — it's considered to be the largest private collection of its kind. Outside, sculptures are set among the palms, roses, marigolds, and pampas.

The guest rooms at the front of the hotel overlook the city and bay; the back rooms look toward the Berkeley hills and eucalyptus groves. The colors and designs are different in all the rooms, and every six months another block is refurbished. Suite 606 (with adjoining 605) is the Tower Suite, featuring long, low windows with great views of the bay and city sky-line. The secluded suite is reached by a short flight of stairs. More stairs lead to a private balcony in the tower itself, at the top of the hotel, where a sauna awaits. Suite 409 has the widest picture window in the hotel. The view is spectacular.

There's a wet bar and, under a skylight in the bath, a tub big enough for two.

The Claremont offers several weekend packages and an array of activities. Downtown San Francisco is only twenty minutes away, and other attractions lie close at hand. The East Bay regional park system, with walking and bridle trails, lakes, forests, and panoramic viewpoints, is just out the back door. The campus of the University of California is a few minutes' drive away. Oakland and Berkeley have excellent restaurants and shopping and interesting historic districts to explore.

> **Highly recommended for dining are Chez Panisse, as good as its stratospheric reputation, and Santa Fe Bar and Grill, where the chef performs magic with the mesquite grill. Citron and Bay Wolf are also notable eateries.**

If you're a walker, pick up a guide to walks in the area, and you'll find dozens of byways through gardens and residential neighborhoods.

Dockside Boat & Bed

77 Jack London Square
Oakland, CA 94607
510-444-5858
800-4-DOCKSIDE
Fax: 510-444-0420

> *A bed-and-breakfast afloat in the bay*

Proprietors: Rob and Mollie Harris.
Accommodations: Approximately 10 yachts. **Rates:** $95–$275 single or double, $50–$100 additional person. **Included:** Continental breakfast. **Payment:** Major credit cards. **Children:** Additional $50–$100. **Pets:** Not allowed. **Smoking:** Not allowed indoors.

Hundreds of yachts and sailboats bob at the marina off Jack London Square in Oakland and Pier 39 in San Francisco. Dockside Boat & Bed makes few of them available to guests looking for unusual lodgings. The vessels Dockside handles range from thirty-five feet to sixty-eight feet long. All are equipped with showers, television, coffeemakers, stereos, refrigeration, and microwaves. Some have VCRs and complete entertainment centers.

Arnie's Ark is a 35-foot boat with narrow gangways, a snug salon, a small modern bathroom, and a queen-size bed in the master stateroom. The boat is available for charter trips at a rate of $30 per hour, and three hours is the suggested minimum time to get a good, exhilarating sail on the bay.

> **From the deck of a sailboat or motor yacht, you can watch the sunset over the San Francisco skyline while you listen to the gulls' cries and water lapping against the hull of the boat.**

The Voyager, a 46-foot motor sailer, is a good option for families because it has three staterooms and sleeps up to six people. Dockside also rents out several yachts at Pier 39 in San Francisco. The 51-foot *Athena* is docked at the Pier 39 location, and with three staterooms, it is available for overnight accommodations as well as private cruises.

Breakfast — orange juice and a basket of muffins — is brought to your boat in the morning along with the local paper. Dockside can also arrange for catered candlelight dinners on board some of the yachts by prior arrangement. Concierge services such as limousines, gourmet picnic baskets, floral bouquets, and massages can also be arranged.

Most guests board their yacht-for-a-day looking for relaxation in a romantic setting, but there are other diversions nearby. Jack London Square, a gangplank walk away from boats at the Oakland dock, has a dozen restaurants and shops including the largest Barnes & Noble bookstore in northern California. The U.S.S. *Potomac*, formerly used by President Franklin D. Roosevelt, is docked at the marina and can be toured by the public. Ferry service connects Oakland with San Francisco.

Overnight guests staying in Dockside's San Francisco boats will find themselves adjacent to Pier 39, popular with tourists because of its many shops and restaurants. Fisherman's Wharf and the Hyde Street Maritime Museum are nearby.

OLEMA

Point Reyes Seashore Lodge

P.O. Box 39
10021 Coastal Highway 1
Olema, CA 94950
415-663-9000

> *A country lodge by*
> *a magnificent park*

Innkeepers: Jeff and Nancy Harriman, Jean and Scott Taylor. **Accommodations:** 22 rooms and suites. **Rates:** $85–$140 single or double, suites $165–$185, cottage $195–$250, $15 additional person. **Included:** Continental breakfast. **Added:** 10% tax. **Payment:** Major credit cards. **Children:** Under age 12 additional $5 per day, over age 12 additional $15 per day. **Pets:** Not allowed. **Smoking:** Restricted.

The entire Point Reyes National Seashore, 65,000 acres of scenic parkland, abuts the backyard of this attractive luxury lodge. It stands on an acre of landscaped grounds in Olema, thirty-five miles north of San Francisco. Though the three-story cedar inn resembles a turn-of-the-century country lodge, it was built and opened in 1988. The owners wanted to combine the elegance and comfort of a hotel with the personal warmth of a bed-and-breakfast; for the most part they've succeeded admirably.

You enter to an open lobby of light, natural wood and excessive lighting. Directly above, up a few steps, is a cozy library with books and games; a few steps down is the fireplace room, where a buffet breakfast of fruit, muffins, and croissants is served. You may take a tray to your room, if you prefer, or breakfast will be brought to you.

Off to the side is a game room with pool table. Walls are hung with old photographs of the area, reflecting Jeff Harriman's interest in local history. There are four guest rooms on this lower floor, each with a private entrance from the flagstone terrace. Sloping west is a lawn down to Olema Creek where willows and eucalyptus grow. A bridge across the creek leads to a path to Bear Valley Visitor Center, the park headquarters and starting point for numerous hiking trails.

Other guest rooms are located on two floors in the main lodge and wings on either side. They all have direct-dial phones, digital clocks, and contemporary colors of mauve, green, blue, and aqua. The quality is excellent, though the mixture of rough woods with European fixtures,

> **Everyone at the inn offers a friendly welcome and is happy to tell you about outstanding beaches and viewpoints in the neighboring park. They'll make reservations at restaurants, arrange for horseback rides or bicycle rentals, tell you about the park's naturalist activities, and help you find shops with special handicrafts.**

shoji screens, and modern brass is occasionally jarring.

Some rooms have a fireplace, whirlpool tub, and magnificent views of the pastoral surroundings and Mount Wittenberg. An unusual feature of the rooms is the sliding screen in an arched opening between sitting room and bathroom; from the tub you can see the trees of the park. The three suites have wet bars, refrigerators, and bedroom lofts with feather beds.

Birds are the theme of the Audubon Suite. An Audubon egret print hangs above the sofa bed and Roger Tory Peterson's book on the famed ornithologist lies on the fireplace mantel. White walls extend up to a high ceiling and loft. A balcony overlooks the grounds and park.

The Garcia Suite is named for the original owner of the land grant on the hotel's site and contains artifacts that were found in his old barn. The Sir Francis Drake Suite has books on the early sea voyager, a world globe, and a painting of Drake's ship, *The Golden Hinde.* Sir Francis Drake landed on these shores in 1579 and named the area Nova Albion (New England), perhaps because the pale cliffs that rise steeply above the beach reminded him of the coast of Dover.

Roundstone Farm

9940 Sir Francis Drake Blvd.
Olema, CA 94950
415-663-1020

*A ten-acre farm
with a view
near Point Reyes
National Seashore*

Innkeeper: Inger Fisher. **Accommodations:** 5 rooms (all with private bath). **Rates:** $95 single, $135 double. **Included:** Full breakfast. **Added:** 10% tax. **Minimum stay:** 2 nights weekends. **Payment:** MasterCard, Visa. **Children:** Over age 6 welcome, additional $25 per day. **Pets:** Not allowed. **Smoking:** Not allowed indoors.

Roundstone Farm occupies ten acres of hilly ranchland above Olema, a village on the Point Reyes Peninsula. From the deck of the cedar board-and-batten farmhouse, you can see Mount Wittenberg and Mount Vision, Inverness Ridge, Olema Valley, and Tomales Bay.

Point Reyes National Seashore is an immense seaside park north of San Francisco Bay. Within its boundaries — Tomales Bay and Sir Francis Drake Boulevard on the east and the Pacific Ocean on the west — are miles of hiking trails, sand dunes, rolling moors, forests of oak and pine, and far-reaching views of the sea.

The solar home was built in 1987 specifically as a bed-and-breakfast. Inger Fisher used her skills as an interior designer to create a haven for visitors. Each soundproof guest room is on a different level. The furnishings and color schemes vary, but all have fireplaces, thick carpeting, and white goose down comforters.

Fresh flowers or plants lend color to the understated decor. The quality is first rate, with bathroom fixtures from Copenhagen, Swiss linens, and armoires from England and Denmark providing Old World charm and workmanship. Wooden headboards, patterned after ranch gates, were made by a local craftsperson.

The large living room has a 16-foot ceiling, with skylights

in the pitched roof and sliding doors along one glass wall that open to a deck and a magnificent view. Guests enjoy reading by the fire, playing board games, listening to the CD player, and admiring the broad expanse of forest, meadow, and ranchland. From here you can see the farm's pond, where waterfowl and red-winged blackbirds nest. A few steps up is the dining area, where a substantial breakfast is served at one seating. Inger believes that part of the B&B experience is getting acquainted with fellow guests over the breakfast table. "People will sit down at 9:15 and not get up until 11:00, they're so relaxed," she says.

Early morning coffee is on the sideboard. Later, Inger comes in with juice, fresh fruit, and an unusual dish such as an apple puff pancake with sausage. "No quiche or croissants," she says. "I try to do things no one else does." The meal is always hearty, to prepare you for a day of hiking, bicycling, and exploring the Point Reyes National Seashore. Tea and coffee are available all day.

The farm was named after the village of Roundstone in the Connemara district of western Ireland, where Connemara ponies first lived in the wild. Inger has raised Connemara and Arabian horses for years. There are several on the property now, and guests are welcome to visit them.

The Bear Valley Visitor Center, the headquarters for the Point Reyes National Seashore, is just a few minutes away. It has extensive displays of natural and historic highlights of the park. From here, trails lead over ridges and cliffs to protected beaches.

Inger can recommend several good restaurants a short distance from Roundstone Farm. Visitors give the Olema Inn high praise for its light, pleasant atmosphere and excellent food.

PALO ALTO

Garden Court Hotel

520 Cowper Street
Palo Alto, CA 94301
415-322-9000
800-824-9028
Fax: 415-324-3609

*A small hotel
with a
Mediterranean
atmosphere*

General Manager: Lorilee Houston.
Accommodations: 62 rooms and suites. Rooms $195–$350 single or double, $15 additional person, suites $200–$400. **Added:** 8.5% tax. **Payment:** Major credit cards. **Children:** Welcome. **Pets:** Not allowed. **Smoking:** Nonsmoking rooms available.

In cozy little Palo Alto, on the peninsula twenty minutes south of the San Francisco airport, the Garden Court nestles snugly in the heart of the downtown district. The four-story Mediterranean-style building, of ochre stucco with dark green wrought iron trim and curving archways, has a casual, inviting look.

When you arrive, you're greeted by the parking valet and the fragrance of freshly baked bread wafting from Il Fornaio, a handsome ground-floor restaurant serving fine Italian food.

The hotel's residential ambience is apparent in the small, second-floor lobby, where soft chairs and a couch face a fireplace, a big bowl of apples sits on a table, and a window alcove has benches filled with pillows.

Off to one side are the check-in counter and concierge desk. The staff here is patient and helpful, ready to decipher a foreign accent or lend an umbrella.

Each of the spacious, pastel rooms has a small balcony with just enough room for two chairs and a trellised, potted vine. Palo Alto is quiet at night, but to ensure peace, request an inside room above the courtyard. You'll look down upon an array of colorful flowers and the restaurant terrace. All rooms have phones, mini-bars, fresh flowers, and four-poster beds. Some include fireplaces and whirlpool tubs. The newspaper of your choice is delivered to the door in the morning.

The Garden Court, which has banquet and meeting rooms that accommodate up to 250, caters to business travelers, visitors to Stanford University, and those looking for a relaxing getaway. It has no exercise facilities, no pool, and no coffee shop. This hotel concentrates only on fine-quality accommodations. Several cafés in the district are open for breakfast — a good excuse for a stroll into the Palo Alto lifestyle.

On a larger scale, the Stanford Shopping Center is a short distance away, along with more typical roadside development.

The Victorian on Lytton

555 Lytton Avenue
Palo Alto, CA 94301
415-322-8555
Fax: 415-322-7141

A Victorian inn with modern style, near Stanford University

Proprietors: Maxwell and Susan Hall. **Accommodations:** 10 rooms. **Rates:** $112–$200 single or double. **Included:** Continental breakfast. **Added:** 10% tax. **Payment:** Major credit cards. **Children:** Additional $10 charge, no cribs are available. **Pets:** Not Allowed. **Smoking:** Not allowed.

This pretty Victorian inn in downtown Palo Alto has served many purposes since it was built in 1895 as the home of a schoolteacher. It was a commune, a bookstore, and an apartment house before it became a registered historical landmark and a bed-and-breakfast inn. Susan and Max Hall, who bought the crumbling home in 1985, transformed it into a place of charm and comfort. Five guest rooms are in the main house and five are in another building behind it, set off by a colorful English garden. Parking spaces are tucked away at the edge of the property.

Each oversize room has a down comforter on a four-poster or canopy bed, and antiques that reflect the home's Victorian period, yet details important to today's travelers such as good lighting and modern bathrooms, have not been overlooked.

The artistic skills of the innkeeper, who was once an art director for an advertising agency, are evident in the stylish, understated decor. The Halls gutted and rebuilt the interior of

> **The first things you notice when you step in the door are the soft strains of classical music and the mouthwatering scent of Susan's just-baked cookies.**

the newer building in back, now called the Carriage House. This is where they placed the honeymoon suite, which has a fireplace, bo-tanical prints on the wall, a four-poster bed with embroidered pillows, and a claw-foot tub in an alcove.

A breakfast of fruit, croissants, and coffee or tea is brought to each room on a tray. In the evenings, while guests ponder which of Palo Alto's restaurants to try, the port and sherry come out.

PESCADERO

Pigeon Point Lighthouse Hostel

210 Pigeon Point Road
Pescadero, CA 94060
415-879-0633

> *An inexpensive place to stay in a spectacular setting*

Managed by: Hostelling International. **Accommodations:** 52 beds. **Rates:** $11 per person American Youth Hostel members, $14 non-members, $10 additional for private room. **Maximum stay:** 3 nights. **Payment:** MasterCard, Visa, and personal checks. **Children:** Half price in room with parents. **Pets:** Not allowed. **Smoking:** Not allowed.

Between San Francisco and Monterey Bay, where the rocky shore curves into the sea, the lighthouse at Pigeon Point stands at the edge of a steep, rugged cliff. Below it, breakers crash and foam against the rocks, and seals bob in the surf. It's a dramatic location for a lodging on scenic Highway 1.

American Youth Hostels owns and operates this and other hostels in California, which are open to all ages.

The accommodations are next to the lighthouse, in four low, white bungalows surrounded by geraniums and ice plant. Each building has a carpeted living room, kitchen, two bathrooms, a couple's bedroom, and dorm rooms with six bunk beds each. Furnishings are basic: plain pine beds with covered mattresses, lamps, closets, and carpeting. But, the rooms and baths, which have showers, are well maintained. Bring your own food to cook in the worn but clean kitchen. The view from the window over the sink is a knockout, placing this hostel far above the simple category of low-cost lodging.

> At Año Nuevo State Reserve, six miles south of Pigeon Point, you can see elephant seals. This is the only mainland breeding colony of the 3,500-pound mammals.

At the edge of the bluff is the former Fog Signal Building, now a recreation and meeting room with table tennis, couches, and a woodstove. Here you'll find brochures on area attractions and other hostels. There's also an outdoor hot tub that can be rented in the evening. A boardwalk and steps extend over the cliff to a fenced viewpoint where you gain a closer look at the Pacific panorama.

When you stay at a hostel, you're assigned an easy cleanup chore (vacuuming, dusting, etc.), and you bring your own bedding, linen, and food. Alcohol is not allowed. The hostel is closed during the day, from 9:30 A.M. to 4:30 P.M.; check in after four-thirty in the afternoon.

This is open coastal country, and there are no facilities or shops nearby, though in Pescadero, five miles north and two miles inland, there are gift and clothing stores, a gas station, and a restaurant, Duarte's, that serves lunch. Pigeon Point Lighthouse, 115 feet tall, has been guiding mariners since 1872. It's open for tours on Sundays, May through August. A small donation is requested.

Watch for migrating whales and explore tidepools along the coast, or you can drive six miles inland to Butano State Park, where you may hike through redwood forests.

POINT REYES STATION

Gray's Retreat

P.O. Box 56
Point Reyes Station, CA 94956
415-663-1166
Fax: 415-663-1390

A country home for a couple or family

Innkeeper: Karen Gray. **Accommodations:** 1 cottage. **Rates:** $115 night for 2, $15 additional person, weekly rates available. **Added:** 10% tax. **Payment:** MasterCard, Visa, personal checks. **Children:** Over age 2 welcome; $15 charge if third person in cottage. **Pets:** Allowed by arrangement, $15 charge. **Smoking:** Not allowed.

If you're bringing the family to Point Reyes Peninsula for a few days of rest, birdwatching, hiking, and enjoying the scenic beauty, Gray's Retreat is an excellent lodging choice.

The town of Point Reyes Station is within walking distance and has a popular family restaurant, Station House Café. Another recommended dining spot is Tony's, on the water in Marshall.

Set in an open pasture and sheltered by a cypress windbreak, the rough cedar home overlooks Inverness Peninsula. Built as a guest house for the owners' parents, it has an occupied apartment on the upper floor and an apartment on the ground level where overnight visitors stay. Furnished with wicker and assorted wooden chests and chairs, the living room is bright and homey. Sunlight streams through western windows on honey-colored walls and big bouquets of flowers.

Beyond the living room is a full kitchen, and beyond that a dining area that opens to an enclosed patio.

Gray's Retreat accommodates six, with a trundle bed, a sofa bed, and a queen-size four-poster. Cribs, high chairs, and laundry facilities are available. Other helpful features for those traveling with children are soundproof walls, fenced front and back patios, shelves with games and puzzles, and a playground across the road.

Jasmine Cottage

P.O. Box 56
Point Reyes Station, CA 94956
415-663-1166
Fax: 415-663-1390

A romantic cottage in the country

Innkeeper: Karen Gray. **Accommodations:** 1 cottage. **Rates:** $115 single or double, $15 additional person; $650 per week. **Included:** Full make-your-own breakfast. **Added:** 10% tax. **Payment:** MasterCard, Visa, personal checks. **Children:** Over age 2 $15 charge if third person in cottage. **Pets:** Welcome with permission, $15 charge. **Smoking:** Not allowed indoors.

Set apart from the innkeeper's home by vegetable, flower, and herb plantings, Jasmine Cottage is for the exclusive use of one group of guests, from one to four people. There are two cabinet beds in the light-drenched sitting room and a queen-size bed in an alcove. A crib and high chair are provided. The refrigerator in the fully equipped kitchen contains breakfast makings: coffee, jam, granola, milk, fruit, cheese, and eggs from the chickens that

This cozy cottage is the quintessential romantic hideaway in the country. It's sequestered in a pretty garden near Point Reyes National Seashore.

live in the yard. Flowered quilts, posters of native flora, fresh flowers, and Karen Gray's fabric art complete the gardenlike ambience, enhanced by the sweet fragrance of jasmine and window views of fruit trees, geraniums, and roses.

The shed outside is well stocked with wood for the fireplace. Linens and housekeeping supplies are provided. The shelves are full of books about birds and Point Reyes, and there's an album full of information on local points of interest. There is no telephone and no television to intrude upon the tranquil scene, but if you can't live without TV during your visit, cable TV can be provided upon request.

Outside the gate is a brick patio with a hot tub and a view across rolling pastureland to Inverness Ridge. In the cottage you'll find a picnic basket, complete with dishes and a thermos bottle, ready to pack with a lunch and take into the park or to the seashore; but Jasmine's setting is so irresistible you may get no further than the picnic table on your own patio.

Thirty-nine Cypress

Box 176
39 Cypress
Point Reyes, CA 94956
415-663-1709
Fax: 415-663-1709

*A charming
country cottage
above
Tomales Bay*

Innkeeper: Julia Bartlett. **Accommodations:** 3 rooms (all with private half or full bath). **Rates:** $100–$135. **Included:** Full breakfast. **Added:** 10% tax. **Minimum stay:** 2 nights on weekends. **Payment:** MasterCard, Visa, personal checks. **Children:** Welcome by arrangement, $20 additional. **Pets:** Allowed by arrangement. **Smoking:** Not allowed indoors.

When you're looking for a cozy, rustic hideaway with a pastoral view, lovely gardens, and a cliffside hot tub, book a room at Thirty-nine Cypress. The single-story weathered gray inn opened in 1981, one of the first in the Point Reyes National Seashore area north of San Francisco. It was Julia Bartlett's home, but now she lives across the neighboring field and comes over

Staying at this B&B is like visiting a friend who has a guest house in the country. You're welcome to use the tape deck, books, and wine glasses; fix popcorn in the kitchen; and light a fire in the fireplace on foggy days.

in the mornings to fix a hearty breakfast for her guests.

Wild flowers fill a jar on the table, and binoculars hang from a nail by the sliding glass doors. The terrace, bordered by rosemary shrubs, overlooks part of a 500-acre ranch by Tomales Bay.

The rooms are furnished in a country style. The north bedroom is the most private. It has a full bath, skylights, and a private patio. The two south rooms each have a tiny half bath. All the rooms have outdoor showers — step outside your door and there's a protected, sunlit shower. Robes are provided. The house is often taken by three couples; it's ideal for a retreat, a reunion, or a vacation with friends.

Flora Borealis, Julia's friendly Australian cattle dog, will try to accompany you on walks. There are some outstanding hikes in the area, and you can go mountain biking or to the beach.

POINT RICHMOND

East Brother Light Station

117 Park Place
Point Richmond, CA 94801
510-233-2385

A cozy lighthouse on an island

Managers: John Barnett and Lore Hogan. **Accommodations:** 4 rooms (2 with private bath). **Rates:** $295 double. **Included:** Breakfast and dinner; transportation from harbor. **Payment:** No credit cards. **Children:** Welcome if reserving all rooms. **Pets:** Not allowed. **Smoking:** Not allowed indoors. **Open:** Thursday, Friday, Saturday, Sunday.

When his grandfather was the lighthouse keeper, between 1914 and 1921, Walter Fanning used to come to the tiny island to visit. Today, East Brother Light Station looks just as Walter remembers it — a trim and tidy, well-kept lighthouse of the Victorian era, with carved railings and gingerbread. Volunteers (Walter among them) worked long hours to restore and maintain the lighthouse, which was built in 1873 and automated in 1969. It's owned by the U.S. Coast Guard and is on the National Register of Historic Places.

There are two rooms on the ground floor, each with a brass bed and period furnishings, and a cozy parlor that guests share. The best views are upstairs. The Marin Room faces west toward the Marin County hills and Mount Tamalpais. It's romantic in rose and pink, with lace-edged pillows on the brass bed. The San Francisco Room, in blue and white, has a view of the bay and the city beyond San Pablo Bridge. There's a parlor upstairs, too, which has a woodstove and a nautical theme.

To get to East Brother, a one-acre island in San Pablo Bay, you take an exhilarating, 15-minute boat ride from Point San Pablo Yacht Harbor. Once on the island, you're surrounded by peace and quiet. This is a place to visit when you want to do nothing but watch the cormorants and seagulls.

The enthusiastic managers enjoy showing the lighthouse and preparing hearty meals, which are served in the dining room at a single table for eight. Wine and apéritifs are included. They sell T-shirts and a few gift items in the office that was once Walter Fanning's grandmother's parlor.

PRINCETON-BY-THE-SEA

The Pillar Point Inn

380 Capistrano Road
Princeton-by-the-Sea, CA
Mailing address:
  P.O. Box 388,
  El Granada, CA 94018
415-728-7377
800-400-8281
Fax: 415-728-8345

> *A New England–
> style inn on the
> harbor*

Manager: Sarah Woodruff. **Accommodations:** 11 rooms (all with private bath). **Rates:** $150–$185 single or double, $20 additional person. **Included:** Full breakfast. **Added:** 10% tax. **Payment:** Major credit cards. **Children:** Additional $20 if third person in room. **Pets:** Not allowed. **Smoking**: Not allowed.

Halfway between San Francisco and Santa Cruz, facing the only harbor for seventy-five miles, Pillar Point Inn provides a touch of Cape Cod on the West Coast. The gray, solidly built hotel trimmed in white and nautical blue sits behind a white picket fence, its curved and gabled windows looking toward the boats bobbing a few yards away.

    Princeton-by-the-Sea is an idyllic setting for relaxing, boating, and fishing. An unpretentious little town with a livelihood that comes from the sea, it has a waterfront busy with boat building and repairs, charters, fishing, pleasure boats, and whale-watching excursions. There are a few shops, galleries, and restaurants, but this working port has nothing like the tourist activity of its neighbor, Half Moon Bay. It does have a romantic inn offering warm hospitality and luxurious accommodations, however.

In the small living room, guests relax on loveseats by the double-sided fireplace and peruse the shelves of books and movies. You can watch old-time favorites such as Robin Hood, Abbott & Costello, and even Hopalong Cassidy on your video player; there's one in every room. The rooms also have European-style feather beds, radios, telephones, and refrigerators, and ten have views of the water. Themes from local history provide a different decor in each room.

> **The inn has menus for the few nearby restaurants. Across the street is Barbara's Fish Trap, a casual spot by the water. Moss Beach Distillery is a dinner house, and Shore Bird is a favorite for brunch before going whale-watching.**

El Granada, a second-floor room that faces the road and harbor, holds photographic reminders of 1909, when a developer tried to turn the region into a major resort. Nobody was interested in buying, but many took the offer of a free lunch and a train ride to and from the beach. El Granada has a brass and white iron bed and a white rocker by the high, arched window. A writing table stands in one corner and a tiled gas fireplace with raised hearth in another. Sounds of traffic and restaurant noise from across the street fade in the late evening, as the village settles down, until finally all you hear is the moan of the buoy in the harbor. The Whaling Room, also called the Hideaway, is extra large, very quiet, and has a view of the mountains and a partial harbor view.

A full breakfast with egg dishes and homemade granola and muffins is served by the fireplace in the dining room.

SAN FRANCISCO

The Archbishops Mansion

1000 Fulton Street
San Francisco, CA 94117
415-563-7872
800-543-5820
Fax: 415-885-3193

*A romantic,
historic home on
Alama Square*

Owners: Jonathan Shannon and Jeffrey Ross. **Manager:** Rick Janvier. **Accommodations:** 15 rooms (all with private bath). **Rates:** $129–$385 single or double, $20 additional each person. **Included:** Continental breakfast. **Added:** 12% tax. **Minimum stay:** 2 nights weekends. **Payment:** Major credit cards. **Children:** Welcome. **Pets:** Not allowed. **Smoking:** Allowed in designated areas only.

If you want lodgings in San Francisco that remind you of home, don't stay at this inn unless you live in an opera set. The opulence of The Archbishops Mansion is best enjoyed by those who revel in the lavish, the lush, and the extravagant — all carried off with great taste and a sense of humor.

The inn is across the street from Alamo Square, a hillside park eight blocks from Golden Gate Park and six blocks from the Civic Center, Davies Symphony Hall, the Opera House, and the Museum of Modern Art. The Alamo Square area, its streets lined with lovely Victorian houses, has been designated a City Historic District, thanks in large part to the efforts of Jeffrey Ross and Jonathan Shannon. They have also worked to preserve other parts of the city. In 1980, they began the painstaking task of restoring their time-battered mansion.

The three-story home, built in 1904 as a residence for Archbishop Patrick Riordan, was based on Second Empire French styling, so the new owners gathered furnishings from around the world to reflect that period. When they were through, they had created a La Belle Époque French château and, because it is so grand (and so close to the Opera House), named the rooms after romantic 19th-century operas.

The rooms, all with impressive antiques or reproductions, are furnished with comfort and flair. The smallest is La Bohème, which has a partial canopy above a bed that is as elaborate as the tent of a fabled sheik. Romeo and Juliet is another elegant little room, with flowers and garlands. Cosi Fan Tutti is a suite with antique lace, gilded molding, and French pine doors separating the bed and sitting areas.

Don Giovanni is an expansive suite with cher-ubs carved in the four-poster bed. There's a dramatic fireplace (one of several in the inn), and in the bath a seven-headed shower. La Traviata, on the main floor, features a sitting room with a glazed tile fireplace, head-high wain-scoting, and a gilded chandelier hanging from a high, coffered ceiling. In the white tiled bathroom are robes, a shower, a pedestal sink, and a lighted makeup mirror.

> The owners have been careful to encourage a lively, friendly ambience. "I've been in historic inns where you're afraid to sit on the sofa," says Jonathan Shannon. "Antiques are wonderful, but I want people to be comfortable. I like to see them in jeans and shorts, being casual."

The main hall is another example of the owners' sense of atmosphere. It has chairs inlaid with mother of pearl, a gilt-framed mirror from Abraham Lincoln's home in Illinois, and columns of polished redwood and mahogany. At one end is a grand piano — playable, but also computerized, so you may hear a tune without a piano player. A pair of 17th-century Venetian figures guard the wide staircase; above the stairs is a large stained glass dome.

Morning coffee and complimentary newspapers are offered in the front parlor, and wine in the evening. Breakfast, brought to your room in a picnic basket, includes juice, croissants, granola, and eggs, with tea or coffee. You may have breakfast in the formal dining room if you prefer.

The innkeepers will make restaurant reservations and help with tour ideas. Parking is available in a tiny area beside the house, but it's less than convenient, as cars must stack up and then be moved.

Campton Place

340 Stockton Street
San Francisco, CA 94108
415-781-5555
800-235-4300
Fax: 415-955-5536

> *A small central
> hotel known for
> its high quality*

General Manager: Herman R. von Treskou. **Accommodations:** 117. **Rates:** Rooms $195–$330, suites $395–$850. **Added:** 12% tax. **Payment:** Major credit cards. **Children:** Welcome. **Pets:** Allowed. **Smoking:** Non-smoking rooms available.

Campton Place is a jewel. Around the corner from Union Square, in busy downtown San Francisco, it offers extraordinary luxury, superb service, and a fine restaurant.

When you arrive, uniformed doormen usher you into a marble lobby with a theme both French and Oriental. Carved Buddhas, antique jars, and a 16th-century Japanese sumi screen accent the graceful curves of French furniture. An antique Swedish chandelier hangs above a glass table supported by four swans. Off the lobby is a sunken lounge, divided from the dining room by a curving sweep of glass etched with a swan, the hotel's emblem.

Since the restaurant opened in 1983, it has consistently received rave reviews for complex flavors in an outstanding cuisine. Both California and European wines are available.

Service throughout the hotel is cheerful, personal, and efficient. There are no VIP floors or differing levels of attention. A valet will unpack your luggage and, when you leave, repack it in tissue paper. The valet will run your bath at just the right temperature (each tub has a thermometer) and assist you with tours, or, if you prefer, set up your entire visit.

Other routine services include a choice among four complimentary morning newspapers, overnight shoeshine, immediate pressing, same-day laundry and dry cleaning (if you spot your jacket during lunch it will be cleaned and returned to you before the bill for your meal arrives), twice-daily housekeeping, and a full concierge service. Valet parking is available.

The guest rooms, decorated in soothing pale gold, peach, and tan tones, have a residential ambiance. Furnishings are both contemporary and traditional, with attractive Oriental print fabrics. There are oversize beds with comforters, Henredon armoires housing remote control television sets, Louis XVI writing tables, mini-bars, and limited-edition art on the pastel walls. Double-glazed windows keep street noise at a distance, but they open if you prefer the city's sea breezes to air conditioning. Marble baths with brass fixtures contain vanities, scales, night lights, phones, hair dryers, and terrycloth robes. Luxurious French milled soaps and a supply of cotton balls are among the toiletries provided.

> In a pastel setting of peach and apricot walls, white Wedgwood china, and Swiss linens, diners feast on foods presented as works of art.

The hotel is actually two buildings, one of seventeen stories and the other, eight stories. On the lower rooftop is a garden with potted petunias and citrus trees and a view of Union Square. This is a pleasant little oasis for enjoying the morning sun, despite the noise from machinery hidden behind a lattice.

Campton Place used to be the Drake-Wiltshire Hotel, dating from the early 1900s. Changed and remodeled several times, it lapsed into decline until 1981, when Ayala International acquired and rebuilt the property turning it into the fine charming hotel it is today.

Casa Arguello

225 Arguello Boulevard
San Francisco, CA 94118
415-752-9482

> *A classic San Francisco home in a city neighborhood*

Innkeepers: Emma Baires and Marina McKenzie. **Accommodations:** 5 rooms (2 with private bath). **Rates:** $50–$79 double, $15 additional person. **Included:** Expanded Continental breakfast. **Added:** 12% tax. **Minimum stay:** 2 nights. **Payment:** Cash or check. **Children:** Over age 7 welcome. **Pets:** Not allowed. **Smoking:** Not allowed.

As you walk and drive the hilly streets of San Francisco, you pass hundreds of stucco rowhouses, each with a bay window and, usually, a trim box of geraniums in front. Casa Arguello is one of them, located in a neighborhood of similar homes, apartments, and shops. Clement Street restaurants and the boutiques on Sacramento are nearby; Golden Gate Park is five blocks away. The beautiful Temple Emmanuel is across the street.

> **An international clientele comes to Casa Arguello, so you're likely to meet people from all over the world — especially from Switzerland, Germany, and England.**

This bed-and-breakfast is larger than it seems from the outside, extending back to a courtyard and up some stairs. Owning such an inn was Emma Baires's childhood dream, when her father had a hotel in El Salvador. Emma and her daughter opened their B&B in 1978.

As in many similar homes, the main floor is up a flight of stairs from the entrance. The walls are white, hung with prints of San Francisco scenes and in the living room are lavish floral couches, rosy carpeting, and arched windows. Antique and contemporary furnishings have been tastefully combined. Coved ceilings and the original wall sconces and moldings date the building to the 1920s.

All the guest rooms have TV. Room 1 is a small corner room with a western view; Room 2 has a king-size brass bed. Room 3, overlooking Lincoln and Golden Gate parks, has a king-size bed in white iron. Room 4 is spacious enough to include three armchairs and a refrigerator. Sheer curtains topped by floral swags lend soft color and style to this airy room, which has a view of the University of San Francisco campus. Room 5, for one person, has a twin bed and shares a bath with Rooms 1 and 2.

Breakfast is served family-style in the dining room. Fresh fruit, a choice of cereals, muffins, croissants, scones, and coffee and tea are the usual offerings. The breakfast table is a fine place to meet and talk with other guests, trading sightseeing ideas and restaurant discoveries.

The Clift

495 Geary Street
San Francisco, CA 94102
415-775-4700
800-65-CLIFT
Fax: 415-441-4621

*A top-quality
historic hotel near
Union Square*

General Manager: George Terpilowski. **Accommodations:** 329 rooms and suites. **Rates:** $225–$340 single, $225–$370 double, suites $315–$825. **Added:** 12% tax. **Payment:** Major credit cards. **Children:** Welcome. **Pets:** Small dogs allowed. **Smoking:** Nonsmoking rooms available.

When you want the very best city lodgings — accommodations that are absolutely top quality in every regard — check in at the Clift, two blocks from Union Square. Its atmosphere, furnishings, amenities, and above all its service make the updated Clift one of California's finest hotels.

The 1915 Clift has always been a luxury hotel of dignity that attracted the celebrated and the elite. But it didn't keep up with the times, and by the early 1970s the grand old place seemed a relic of a bygone era. After a multi-million renovation, the Clift had surpassed its initial luster and was on its way to becoming the jewel it is today. Its sense of history and elegance remained, while its facilities were modernized.

The staff will remember your name, see you quickly through check-in and check-out, provide near-instant 24-hour room service, polish your shoes, bring in a computer, launder your jeans, and place a flower on your pillow at night.

From the buff brick exterior and snazzy glass and brass entry, you step into a wood-paneled lobby. Not imposing or grand, it's a gracious, welcoming place where businesspeople with briefcases and kids with lollipops are equally at home.

One of the main attractions of the Clift, and of San Francisco, is the Redwood Room. Built in 1934, it is an art deco masterpiece that shouldn't be missed, whether you stay at the hotel or not. The walls of the lounge, reaching twenty-two feet to a ceiling of pressed metal, are paneled in aged redwood, taken from toppled giants that had lain in Northern California stream beds and gullies for years. The inner wood from these ancient tree trunks, when polished, takes on a deep patina of bronze and topaz. Frosted glass sconces, pyramid chandeliers, and black Italian marble tables continue the art deco motif. The most striking element, other than the redwood itself, is the mural above the 75-foot bar, a stylized forest scene of inlaid woods.

Breakfast is served in the French Room, while in the Redwood Room, diners enjoy fine Continental cuisine featuring regional foods with entrées such as baked Pacific salmon in filo with shiitake mushrooms ($19) or San Francisco Dungeness crab cakes ($15). California labels dominate the award-winning wine list, which also offers European vintages.

The guest rooms in the 16-story hotel are spacious and luxurious with large windows. Request a room on one of the higher floors to avoid traffic noise. They all have numerous amenities: mini-bars, two-line phones with modem access, remote control TV, hair dryers in marble bathrooms, and tiny booklights for bedtime reading. A Petite Suite has a sitting room with Henredon furniture, window drapes in sophisticated gray and white stripes accented with peach, pearly gray walls, and windows that view Nob Hill on one side and Twin Peaks on the other. Theatre Suites have two baths so that more than two people trying to make a curtain can get ready at the same time.

A typical corner Deluxe Suite has plush rose carpeting, a wet bar in the living room, a CD player, a VCR, a glass coffee table, and a dining table for six, lighted from above by a teardrop chandelier. There are potted palms, original artwork, soft robes, an array of toiletries in a white ceramic basket, and a dressing room bigger than many San Francisco apartments.

The Clift offers unmitigated luxury, but it's the impeccable service that draws the most admiration. Each person seems genuinely glad to be of help.

Children ("Clift dwellers") receive equally happy treatment. The hotel provides supplies for infants, games, comic books, balloons, and treats, as well as baby-sitting services and a whole program of activities.

Several function rooms provide space for meetings, receptions, and parties of 8 to 250. Many a bride and groom have chosen to be married at the Clift before slipping upstairs to celebrate with champagne for two in a sybaritic honeymoon retreat. The hotel is within walking distance of the shops near Union Square, fine restaurants, Theater Row, museums, and art galleries; and it's a cable-car ride away from other San Francisco attractions.

Country Cottage

Mailing address:
Bed & Breakfast San Francisco
P.O. Box 420009
San Francisco, CA 94142
415-931-3083
800-452-8249
Fax: 415-921-2273

> *A cozy cottage*
> *in the city*

Contact: Bed and Breakfast San Francisco. **Accommodations:** 4 rooms (all with shared baths). **Rates:** $59 single, $69 double. **Included:** Full breakfast. **Payment:** Major credit cards. **Children:** $10 additional if third guest in room. **Pets:** Not allowed. **Smoking:** Not allowed.

You wouldn't expect to find country charm in the heart of San Francisco, but the city is full of surprises. This pretty cottage nestles behind a wrought-iron gate on a cul-de-sac in a quiet, sunny neighborhood near Mission Dolores.

> **Built in 1791, Mission Dolores has been completely restored down to the ornate altar and the hand-hewn redwood timbers lashed with rawhide.**

Country Cottage has a parlor with a bentwood rocker beside a brick fireplace and a wicker basket full of pine cones. Muslin curtains hang at the window panes. The furnishings are American primitives.

The tiled kitchen, also with a skylight, has a gas stove and refrigerator and is well equipped with dishes, spices, teas, coffee — even a toaster. The innkeeper comes in to make breakfast each morning. Fresh flowers and greenery in the kitchen and throughout the house add color and charm. Open the casement window and you'll smell the sweet scent of jasmine from the courtyard.

One bedroom, off the parlor, has a pineapple motif and a high four-poster bed. The skylighted bath is across the hall. The other bedrooms are downstairs. One has a brass bed and a door to the flowery little courtyard with a picnic table. Another darker room has a four-poster bed and the third has a carved wooden bed and blue ruffled curtains at the windows. There's a phone for guests' use in a sitting room next to the kitchen, along with an informative letter of welcome.

The Fairmont Hotel

950 Mason Street
San Francisco, CA 94106
415-772-5000
800-527-4727
Fax: 415-837-0587

A Nob Hill classic overlooking the city and bay

General Manager: John Ceriale. **Accommodations:** 535 rooms and 60 suites. **Rates:** $139–$299 single, $20 additional person, suites $450–$6,000. **Added:** 12% tax. **Payment:** Major credit cards. **Children:** Under age 18 free. **Pets:** Not allowed. **Smoking:** Nonsmoking rooms available.

Opulence on the grand scale in a historic building at the top of one of the world's great cities — that's the Fairmont. When it opened in 1907 (after a delay caused by the 1906 earthquake and fire), the community was impressed by its resemblance to a European royal palace. It's still impressing locals and visitors alike with its ornate facade, magnificent lobby, fine accommodations, and panoramic views of the city and San Francisco Bay.

The Fairmont, long known for its luxury and upper-income clientele, was used as the location of the television series *Hotel*. Television and film celebrities show up regularly, both as guests and performers.

The Fairmont has several restaurants. Off the lobby, the

plush Squire features seafood and an extensive wine list. Masons is downstairs, as is Bella Voce, where you'll hear operatic arias as you dine on pizza, pasta, and seafood. From Chinese food in the Polynesian-style Tonga to chocolate sundaes in Sweet Corner, you can find just about anything your tastebuds yearn for in this hotel. The Fairmont Crown, reached by a glass enclosed elevator, is as noted for its stunning views as well as its lavish buffets.

> Guests were entertained in the darkly rich Venetian Room from 1947 until 1989, when Tony Bennett sang "I Left My Heart In San Francisco" for the last time in that room and the supper club closed. Now it's used for private banquets.

If it's people-watching you want, just sit in the lobby for awhile. Fascinating crowds come and go between the gold marble pillars that soar to an ornamented ceiling.

Ten of the hotel's suites overlook the rooftop garden and terrace, a green oasis of palm trees and flowers. There is no pool, but a fitness center with weight machines, sauna, whirlpool, steam room, and massage service is available.

The guest rooms feature simple, elegant furnishings. Down pillows, 200-count cotton sheets, a TV with a movie channel, electric shoe buffers, and daily maid and turndown service are some of their luxuries. To assist the corporate traveler, multiline, modem phones are in each room. Voice mail and a business center are available.

The rooms in the main building vary, but in general they are larger and have more spacious baths and closets than those in the adjoining 23-story tower. The architecture of the tower, which went up in 1963, is outlandishly inappropriate to the imposing original building, but there's no denying the beauty of the views from the inside out. Some suites feature balconies that overlook the garden or downtown to the Financial District.

The suites vary in decor. You may see a classical Roman theme, with off-white colors and low tables made to resemble temple columns, or a more traditional look with dark woods and antique reproductions. For the ultimate in luxury, reserve the penthouse, probably the most expensive hotel suite in the nation. The eighth-floor, eight-room suite, reached by a private elevator, rents for $6,000 a night, which includes an around-the-clock butler, maid, and private limousine to and from the airport.

Galleria Park Hotel

191 Sutter Street
San Francisco, CA 94104
415-781-3060
800-792-9639
Fax: 415-433-4409

A stylish hotel in the heart of the city

General Manager: David C. Smith.
Accommodations: 177 rooms and suites. **Rates:** $149–$185 single or double, suites $235–$400; weekend and corporate rates available. **Added:** 12% tax. **Payment:** Major credit cards. **Children:** Welcome. **Pets:** Not allowed. **Smoking:** Nonsmoking rooms available.

Urbane and sophisticated, the eight-story Galleria Park is one block from the financial district and two blocks from Union Square. One of the Kimco boutique hotels, it offers incentives designed for the business traveler. There are conference and reception rooms, a full array of support equipment for meetings, and a catering service. A full-time program coordinator will handle arrangements with professional care. Parlor suites are suitable for small and informal meetings.

The hotel offers same-day laundry and valet service and a parking garage. Runners appreciate the track on the rooftop terrace. Each room has large soundproof windows, well-lighted writing desks, direct-dial telephones with long cords, television, and digital clock radios.

Both leisure and business travelers (along with a good many San Franciscans) like Bentley's, an oyster bar and restaurant off the lobby, through etched glass doors. On the street side, windows etched in shell and lobster designs fill the wall. With tiled flooring, a zinc bar, and brasserie tables, the mood is of a classic oyster bar — always crowded and usually noisy. A jazz pianist plays most evenings.

Up on the carpeted mezzanine, overlooking the curved bar

where delectable oysters nestle in their shells on ice, the atmosphere is softer. Bentley's seafood menu has received superlative reviews, especially for its shellfish. Other highlights include grilled yellowfin tuna and salmon, blackened rock cod with garlic lemon sauce, and egg and spinach fettuccine with bay scallops.

> **The Galleria Park offers several packages and special rates. Ask for the Romantic Rendezvous and you'll stay in a park studio and receive champagne, Godiva chocolates, and a rose, as well as Continental breakfast in bed.**

The hotel's small lobby has a distinctive art nouveau decor. Beyond the glass and marble entrance are padded green fabric walls and soft couches under a frosted glass skylight. The wall fixtures are opaque glass in tulip shapes; in a corner there's a curving, hand-sculpted white fireplace. Complimentary wine is served by the fire on Friday and Saturday evenings.

Guest rooms are decorated with appealing botanical print fabrics in cool greens, blues, and pinks, and baths tend to be on the small side but are clean and have hair dryers. The guest room configurations vary, because a restoration in 1988 worked within the existing spaces. The Galleria Park is an extensive remake of the Sutter Hotel, which was built on the site in 1911. The seven park studios are large rooms with sitting areas. There are seven hospitality suites, plus the popular two-bedroom Grand Suite, with a fireplace and a whirlpool tub.

A typical hospitality suite has a sitting room with a large TV (making it a good gathering place for a small group wanting to watch a ball game together) and, in a few, a white brick fireplace on a raised hearth. In the bedroom are a king-size bed and small television. The suite's comfortable furniture and assortment of potted plants and flowers create the ambience of a city apartment. As in most Kimco suites, the space is in the sitting area.

The hotel is next to Crocker Galleria, three levels of shops and restaurants under a vaulted glass dome. Two rooftop parks in the shopping center have benches and greenery, pleasant sites for a picnic lunch or rest.

Golden Gate Hotel

775 Bush Street
San Francisco, CA 94108
415-392-3702
800-835-1118
Fax: 415-392-3702

A European-style hotel at bargain prices

Innkeepers: John and Renate Kenaston. **Accommodations:** 23 rooms (some with shared bath). **Rates:** $59–$99 single or double. **Added:** 12% tax. **Included:** Continental breakfast. **Payment:** Major credit cards. **Children:** Welcome. **Pets:** Allowed with permission; $10 charge. **Smoking:** Discouraged; nonsmoking rooms available.

In the heart of downtown San Francisco just north of Union Square, this hotel is more than a terrific bargain. It has several extras you wouldn't expect at these prices. The narrow white Edwardian building was built in 1913 and has been carefully maintained by the Kenastons, who manage it with warmth and enthusiasm. Half their guests are experienced travelers from abroad, and many are return visitors.

Bright geraniums bloom at bay windows in front, where an awning marks the marble entrance. In the little parlor with windows overlooking the rush of Bush Street traffic, coffee (the city's strongest, Renate claims), tea, and croissants are served in the mornings. Afternoon tea and cookies are also offered by the fireplace. It's a relaxing spot to read, chat, and listen to classical music.

An old-fashioned birdcage elevator, operated by the original drums and relays, connects four floors of guest rooms. The more expensive rooms have private baths; the others have washbasins and share bathrooms nearby. All the rooms have television and phones, and some have bay windows that overlook a tree-filled courtyard. Renate sees that each has fresh flowers. Some accommodations are quite small, but they are clean, have a European charm, and are nicely furnished with antique armoires, floral wallpaper, and wicker pieces. Some have brass beds.

> **Golden Gate Hotel is not a luxury establishment, but it offers excellent quality for the price. It's a good San Francisco find.**

The friendly, multilingual (German, Chinese, French, and Spanish) hosts are delighted to help with sightseeing tours. The hotel is within walking distance of the city's great shops, many of its best restaurants, and Chinatown. The cable car stops at the corner and follows Powell Street to Fisherman's Wharf and North Beach.

Guests can park at the garage across the street where the fee for 24 hours with in and out privileges is $12.

Harbor Court Hotel

165 Steuart Street
San Francisco, CA 94105
415-882-1300
800-346-0555
Fax: 415-882-1313

> *A bayview hotel with top-quality fitness facilities*

Manager: Jay Slattery. **Accommodations:** 130 rooms, 1 penthouse suite. **Rates:** $155–$165 single or double, suite $295. **Added:** 12% tax. **Payment:** Major credit cards. **Children:** Welcome (cribs available). **Pets:** Not allowed. **Smoking:** Nonsmoking rooms available.

At last the Embarcadero freeway is gone and the view toward East Bay is open again. The Harbor Court Hotel is a prime viewing spot, as half of its guest rooms overlook the bay. The eight-story hotel was built in 1907 and was once a YMCA. The Harbor Court, which opened as a European-style hotel in 1991 as one of the Kimco group, now adjoins a renovated YMCA. Guests may use all the Y facilities — an Olympic-size pool, weight room, racquetball courts, a basketball court, exercise machines, steam room, sauna, and rooftop running track.

Another bonus, especially for business travelers, is the Harbor Court's location, close to the financial district as well as to the Embarcadero Center.

> Menu offerings at the popular Harry Denton's restaurant are as basic as Yankee pot roast with mashed potatoes and as imaginative as grilled filet mignon with cracked peppercorns and warm new potato salad, seasonal vegetables, and a cognac sauce.

The hotel provides limo service twice each morning to the financial district. The hotel also has a business center with fax, photocopying and typing services; same day valet service; and complimentary coffee, tea, fruit, and evening wine in the lobby.

Nautical prints adorn the walls of the guest rooms, which are on the top four floors. Comfortably elegant bay-view rooms, decorated in shades of olive, are small but adequate — it's the panoramic view that makes them so popular. Half-canopy beds with matching European shams are elevated so that guests can lie in bed and still see the view. Space-savers include under-the-bed storage drawers, built-in ironing boards hidden behind mirrors, and wardrobes that hold closet space, TVs, and honor bars. Wide mirrors add an illusion of expanse. Interior rooms, which view a flowery courtyard, are larger. Baths in all rooms are modern, and in-room extras include hair dryers, voice mail, computer hook-ups, and Nintendo.

For relaxation, the Harbor Court has a sizable lobby lounge with sofas and chairs in intimate groupings in front of a fire that blazes in the hearth behind a frosted glass screen. For fine dining and entertainment, Harry Denton's adjoining the lobby is considered a hot spot in the Bay Area. A festive restaurant with a beautiful mahogany bar, rich wood columns, and red velvet booths, Harry Denton's is open for breakfast, lunch, and dinner seven days a week. It has live music nightly (generally jazz and rhythm and blues), with dancing on Thursday, Friday, and Saturday nights.

Hotel Griffon

155 Steuart Street
San Francisco, CA 94105
415-495-2100
800-321-2201
Fax: 415-495-3522

A sophisticated waterfront hotel with a Bay Bridge view

General manager: Alice Morris. **Accommodations:** 59 rooms, 3 suites. **Rates:** $155–$165 single or double, penthouse suite $250. **Included:** Continental breakfast. **Added:** 12% tax. **Payment:** Major credit cards. **Children:** Welcome (cribs available). **Pets:** Not allowed. **Smoking:** Nonsmoking rooms available.

With the dismantling of the Embarcadero Freeway, the view from the back of this small hotel near the waterfront has improved dramatically. Now you can see boats scudding across the water and the Bay Bridge stretching to the East Bay (eight guest rooms have views of the Bay Bridge). The front of the hotel faces San Francisco's busy financial district.

As you enter the hotel, which was built in 1906 but was refurbished and opened as the Griffon in 1989, you notice its namesake, a papier-mâché griffon standing beside the fireplace in the small lobby. Hotel guests partake of pastries and coffee here between 6:00 A.M. and 10:00 A.M. Marble floors, tapestry print sofas in front of a fireplace, and built-in bookcases give the lobby a residential feel, but a lively buzz from the Rôti restaurant, divided from the lobby by an etched glass partition, often predominates. One of the city's popular bistros, game and fowl are spit-roasted on an open wood-fired rotisserie. Light jazz plays in the background.

Upstairs, the fresh, light rooms have mahogany, cherry, or rosewood headboards, custom-carved with the Griffon motif, and marble baths. Most suites have a sleeping and sitting area in one room rather than separate spaces. Lots of style went into appointing these rooms. Exposed brick behind the beds contrasts with the creamy alabaster-toned walls, 12-foot high ceilings, tapestry-covered pillows, writing desks, original artwork, and inviting window seats. In keeping with the European flavor, vanities with sinks are located in the bedroom, separate from the bathroom. Among the items in the stocked mini-bars are bottles of Sonoma Valley chardonnay with the hotel's own label. The entire fifth floor was built during the 1989 renovation, and suites there have extras such as private terraces, coffeemakers, bathrobes, and stereos.

> **The hotel is close to the BART system and the Bay Bridge and is a few steps from Embarcadero Center, cable car stops, and ferry service.**

An alternative to the big, central hotels, the Griffon has become a favorite with business travelers and tourists for its atmosphere, service, and convenient location. Business travelers especially appreciate the dual-line telephones in the guest rooms which have voice mail, and data ports for fax machines and PCs. All guests have complimentary use of the fitness facilities at the YMCA a couple of doors away. Parking is available, with 24-hour in-and-out privileges.

Hotel Juliana

590 Bush Street
San Francisco, CA 94108
415-392-2540
800-382-8800
Fax: 415-391-8447

*A small urban
hotel with
European charm*

Manager: Jan Misch. **Accommodations:** 106 rooms, 22 suites. **Rates:** $129–$159 single, $139–$169 double, suites $159–$295. **Added:** 12% tax. **Payment:** Major credit cards. **Children:** Under age 12 free in room with parents. **Pets:** Allowed with $100 charge. **Smoking:** Nonsmoking rooms available.

During the past several years, a number of affordable little first-class hotels have opened in San Francisco, filling a niche between small economy and big luxury hotels. Bill Kimpton, founder of Kimco Hotels, has opened several such European-style hostelries since 1981; one of the best is the charming Juliana.

The nine-story beige brick building with burgundy and blue trim is on a busy corner on the Nob Hill side of Union Square. Built in 1903, it has been completely renovated and boasts modern comforts with the atmosphere of a Continental pensione.

The strains of taped viola music play as you enter the lobby, handsome, in rusts and blacks. Soft chairs and couches covered with Egyptian print fabrics are grouped by the pink marble fireplace. Against one wall is a table with always-hot coffee, tea, and a tray of fresh fruit. Complimentary wines are served every evening. On the walls in the lobby and throughout the hotel hang artworks provided by local galleries. The rotating collection showcases contemporary pieces that are available for purchase.

Classical music plays softly in the background as you enter your guest room. Attractively decorated in pastels with coordinating flowered drapes and bedspreads, the atmosphere is that of a nicely furnished private apartment with a French flair, befitting this traditionally French area of San Francisco. The Juliana is next to Notre Dame de Victoire, where Mass is still spoken in French. All the rooms have direct-dial telephones with voice mail, built-in ironing boards, well-lighted desks, honor bars, large baths with hair dryers, and televisions with HBO. VCRs and movies are available.

With guest rooms named for famous San Francisco women, corporate packages designed to cater to women travelers, and soothing decor, Hotel Juliana is an especially hospitable lodging for women traveling on their own.

Complimentary limousine service is provided to the financial district in the mornings. These and other services, such as same-day laundry and valet service, put the Juliana in the category of the city's better hotels, while its budget-minded aspects (room service is available only part of the day; the bellman doubles as concierge) keep it affordable.

Hotel Nikko

222 Mason Street
San Francisco, CA 94102
415-394-1111
800-NIKKO US
Fax: 415-421-0455

*A touch of Japan
near Union Square*

Assistant General Managers: Fumio Moroi and Alain Ané.
Accommodations: 500 rooms and 22 suites. **Rates:** $185–$245

single, $215–$275 double, suites $375–$1,300. **Added:** 12% tax. **Payment:** Major credit cards. **Children:** Under age 18 free in room with parents. **Pets:** Seeing Eye dogs allowed. **Smoking:** Nonsmoking rooms available.

In angular simplicity, the Nikko rises 300 feet above Mason and O'Farrell streets, two blocks from Union Square and four blocks from the Moscone Center. The hotel's sleek, modern look has been modified in recent years with warm jewel tones and sheer curtains in the marble lobby. Cascading water, recessed lighting, and elegant floral arrangements create a soothing effect and welcoming atmosphere.

Prosperous-looking business travelers, many of them Japanese, patronize the Nikko, which Japan Air Lines opened in 1987. Business and leisure travelers alike receive the best of care, from a computerized key system for security to a fitness center where you can relax under a shiatsu massage. You never have to stand three-deep waiting for an elevator at the Nikko. Swift Mitsubishi elevators whisk you to your floor at 700 feet per minute. The ride is said to be so smooth that a nickel placed on end will remain in place throughout the trip.

The guest rooms and suites, serene in shades of gray, are furnished in a contemporary style. Conveniences include a stocked refrigerator that automatically charges your bill when an item is dispensed, a switch by the king-size bed that turns on all room lights, and speedy in-room television checkout. Rooms on the Nikko floors are slightly larger and have extras such as silk drapes, bathrobes, irons and ironing boards, coffeemakers, and CD players with CDs featuring local musicians.

For a rare treat, book one of the Nikko's two Japanese suites. With tatami rooms, silk futons, western baths with huge soaking tubs as well as a traditional Japanese bath, and even the accoutrements to perform a Japanese tea ceremony, the suites are truly special.

Business travelers may prefer one of the four business suites on the sixth floor; they have meeting rooms and the latest audiovisual equipment. Other conference rooms are available — the Nikko offers 18,000 square feet of meeting space. It also has a business center providing fax, FedEx, translation, xeroxing, and other office services, including computers that have word processing software in Japanese.

On the fifth floor there's a health facility with an inviting swimming pool under a glass-enclosed atrium, a whirlpool tub, tanning machine, saunas (one is a Kamaburo — a Japanese dry sauna), massage service, exercise equipment, and two "Ofuros" which are soaking tubs in the Japanese tradition. The center is attractive and useful — just bring your tennis shoes — everything else is provided, even swimsuits. The shiatsu massage is a refreshing way to unwind after a business meeting or day's sightseeing. Outside on the rooftop, there's a sunning area with lounge chairs, and a Japanese garden.

> **The Nikko's restaurant, Café 222, serves California cuisine with Pacific Rim influences, as well as Japanese dishes. However, sushi lovers needn't leave their rooms to dine if they don't want to, as the hand-rolled delicacy is available on the hotel's room service menu as well.**

To lure vacationers, the Nikko offers special weekend packages that include deluxe accommodations, use of the fitness center, and free valet parking.

Hotel Sheehan

620 Sutter Street
San Francisco, CA 94102
415-775-6500
800-848-1529
Fax: 415-775-3271

> *A comfortable budget hotel in a great location*

Manager: Don Hayden. **Accommodations:** 69 rooms (5 with shared bath). Rates: $69–$89 single, $79–$99 double, $10 additional person. **Included:** Continental breakfast. **Payment:** Major credit cards. **Children:** Under 12 free in room with parent. **Pets:** Not allowed with the exception of guide dogs. **Smoking:** Nonsmoking rooms available.

It's unusual to find clean, quiet lodgings for two in an excellent downtown San Francisco district, for $79 a night — especially when it includes breakfast. Not only are the Sheehan's room rates are a bargain, the staff is friendly, the hotel has a swimming pool, workout facilities, and a café where you can buy snacks, caffé latté, beer, wine, espresso, cappucino, and afternoon tea.

> If you'd rather spend your money on San Francisco's wonderful restaurants than on fancy digs, this is a good choice. The location (just two blocks from Union Square) and the price are unbeatable.

Admittedly, the amenities are basic. Most rooms are simple, with carpeting, a dresser, a closet, and, usually, a washbasin. All have cable TV, direct-dial phones, and clock radios. A few rooms are as well appointed as those in any good hotel. All the shared bathrooms are well maintained and clean and have several showers.

If you're traveling alone and want to spend the minimum, the $69 room is decent, if small. The most expensive accommodations are larger and have a private bath. Breakfast is usually juice, coffee or tea, and homemade scones, muffins, or brown soda bread. Cereal for children is free, for adults it's $1.50.

The swimming pool, the largest hotel pool in the city, dates from the days when this was a YWCA, a favored lodging for many young women in San Francisco. The new owners remodeled the building in 1988.

In the large, open lobby you'll hear a dozen languages spoken as world travelers come and go. At one side of the lobby is a box office selling tickets to the Lorraine Hansberry Theater next door. Parking is available in a garage across the street.

There's nothing luxurious about the Sheehan, but the Ferdon brothers, while planning to keep their hotel in the budget range, have more improvements under way.

Hotel Triton

342 Grant Avenue
San Francisco, CA 94108
415-394-0500
800-433-6611
Fax: 415-394-0555

*A sophisticated
small hotel with
a sense of fun*

General manager: Jan McCormick.
Accommodations: 140 rooms. **Rates:** $125–$175 single or double, suites $255–$295. **Included:** Complimentary wine in the afternoon. **Added:** 12% tax. **Payment:** Major credit cards. **Children:** Welcome. **Pets:** Not allowed. **Smoking:** Nonsmoking rooms available.

Whimsical designs and bright colors of deep hues set the tone for the Triton's mood. It's playful, creative, and sophisticated, but firmly based in the needs of its guests for comfort and efficiency.

The hotel, which opened in 1991 as part of the Kimpton group of small hotels, is conveniently located across from the gate to Chinatown and close to Union Square and the financial district. Entering guests first notice the dramatic, curving columns in vivid gold, teal, and purple, and the gold chairs with undulating backs. The walls are painted with a dreamlike, mythological mural, while seagrass-green stars stud the royal blue carpet. Soft couches are arranged in conversation nests, one by the fireplace is built into a purple wall and surrounded with painted flames.

Guest rooms are equally interesting. The smallest, called Salon Rooms, were designed to maximize limited space and appeal particularly to the business traveler. The full-size bed fits into a corner and used as a couch during the day, is covered with a handsome striped spread. There are cleverly angled drawers, mirrors to visually enlarge the space, and theater-style curtains at the windows. Other rooms are larger and more traditionally furnished, though they too have unusual elements such as curved fixtures and walls painted with big blue and yellow diamonds or pastel swirls. Among the services and features are honor bars with reasonably priced items, on demand first-run movies, Nintendo, and individual heat control. For the ecology minded, the Triton has an "eco-floor" where linens are made from organically grown cotton, garbage is recycled, the water is filtered, natural soaps and shampoos are dispensed from reusable containers, and baths are outfitted with low-flow plumbing fixtures.

For a hotel room that you won't soon forget, splurge and rent one of the Triton's designer suites. The Jerry Garcia suite, dedicated to the late rocker, is decorated with colorful fabrics Garcia designed (if you've seen his ties and scarves you'll know the look). The featherbed, covered in a Garcia silk print comforter, is so plump it resembles an over-puffed soufflé, and the bath has a lively silk shower curtain. In the Wyland suite on the eco-floor, Wyland's aquatic art adorns the walls, the coffee table is a dolphin sculpture topped with glass, and live fish swim in a nearby tank. Stuffed animal lovers will be in teddy bear heaven in the Joe Boxer suite where teddy bears reign supreme — they are even affixed to the canopy over the bed. The suites have coffeemakers, stereos with CD players, and adding to the whimsy, each has a rubber duckie in the bath.

> **In keeping with the Triton's creative tone, Aioli's menu is innovative with dishes such as wild boar ravioli, or braised monkfish served in a curry sauce flavored with orange peel and ginger. Meals are casual at Café de la Presse, also on the premises.**

Lined with black and white photographs of actors and rock stars, even hallways are distinctive at the Triton. On the mezzanine level the artwork changes every three months, and there's a meeting room called the "Creative Zone" with an adjacent patio.

Hotel Vintage Court

650 Bush Street
San Francisco, CA 94108
415-392-4666
800-654-1100
Fax: 415-433-4065

*A boutique hotel
with one of the
city's best
restaurants*

Manager: Jim McPartlin. **Accommodations:** 106 rooms, 1 suite.
Rates: $119–$169 single or double, suite $300. **Included:** Continental breakfast. **Added:** 12% tax. **Payment:** Major credit
cards. **Children:** Under age 16 free in room with parents. **Pets:**
Not allowed. **Smoking:** Nonsmoking rooms available.

A restful environment, reasonable rates, and one of the city's
best French restaurants draw increasing numbers of travelers
to this attractive downtown hostelry. The Vintage Court is a
part of the collection of boutique hotels that have provided a
new lodging option in San Francisco in recent years. Bill
Kimpton, with his highly successful Kimpton Group Hotels,
is a leading figure in the move to renovate old buildings and
turn them into distinctive, stylish hotels with rooms at comparatively low prices.

The Vintage Court opened in 1983, built in an eight-story
hotel originally constructed in 1913. Its wine theme is evident each evening when complimentary Napa Valley wines
are served in the lobby living room near the marble fireplace,
while classical music plays in the background.

Guest rooms, which are spacious for an older hotel, are attractively decorated with contemporary furnishings, rose
motif comforters, coordinating drapes, and complementing
striped bedskirts and padded fabric headboards. Cabinets
house stocked refrigerators, and additional comforts, many
geared to the business traveler, include writing tables with
good lighting, direct-dial phones, and digital clock radios.
Some rooms have bay windows with window seats, and there
are comfortable sitting areas on each floor for guests seeking
even more room to lounge. A single corner suite on the eighth
floor has a separate living room with a sleeper sofa and wood-burning fireplace, a bath with Jacuzzi tub and brass fixtures,
an original 1913 stained glass skylight, and views of the city
skyline.

Complimentary morning transport to the financial district

is provided, and coffee and tea are available around the clock in the lobby. Same-day laundry service and express check-out are also available. In the mornings, guests help themselves to a complimentary French Continental breakfast, with more substantial breakfast items available at a nominal charge.

At Masa's, etched mirrors reflect tables set with crisp, burgundy and white linens, Christofle silver, and fresh flowers, all under a coved ceiling with moldings of polished oak. The lighting is subdued and the music soft.

The hotel's restaurant, Masa's is mentioned in tones of hushed reverence by San Francisco gastronomes. Exquisite food is served in the small, flawless restaurant. The chef, Julian Serrano, from Spain, follows the tradition established by the late Masataka Kobayashi, the restaurant's founder. Serrano combines fresh ingredients with classic sauces to create dishes that are works of art. The prix fixe menu changes regularly but entrées such as grilled Maine lobster with herbed butter and shrimp quenelles, or Sonoma milk-fed spring lamb with tomatoes confit and cumin potatoes are examples of the restaurant's choice cuisine. The wine list, with more than five hundred fine French and California selections, is extraordinary. Desserts include a silky lemon charlotte with raspberry sauce, feather-light puff pastries, thick wedges of chocolate with hazelnuts, and fruity mango sorbet in a praline cone.

Predictably, reservations at Masa's can be difficult to come by — Tuesday or Wednesday night are your best chances of getting a table in the dining room, which seats one hundred. If you can't get into Masa's, you can order room service from a variety of restaurants offering everything from Indian to Italian, and Mexican to Japanese.

The Huntington Hotel

1075 CA Street
San Francisco, CA 94108
415-474-5400
800-227-4683 in U.S.
Fax: 415-474-6227

A Nob Hill hotel of elegance and luxury

General manager: Gail Nishikawa.
Accommodations: 100 rooms and 38 suites. **Rates:** $170–$220 single, $190–$240 double, suites start at $290. **Added:** 12% tax. **Payment:** Major credit cards. **Children:** Under age 4 free in room with parents. **Pets:** Not allowed. **Smoking:** Non-smoking rooms available.

This dignified, 12-story red brick hotel at the top of Nob Hill thrives on tradition and a reputation for excellence. Almost since the day it opened in 1924 as an apartment building, it has been owned by the same family. John Cope, president of the ownership company, is the great-grandson of the developer who bought the property the year it was built. Many on the staff have been with the Huntington for years. Whether you're a repeat guest or a newcomer, you are greeted by name, and the concierge always calls to be sure you're comfortably settled in.

Off the gracious lobby is the hotel's dining room, the Big Four. It's named for the early San Francisco railroad tycoons Collis P. Huntington, Leland Stanford, Charles Crocker, and Mark Hopkins, and displays a collection of railroad memorabilia. The impressive room has dark woods, etched mirrors, and reflective walls. The menu, under the skilled direction of Gloria Ciccarone-Nehls, offers innovative American and Continental dishes, with seafood and game specials. The chef's spectacular chocolate creations give new meaning to dessert. Wines are California and French vintages. A pianist performs nightly in the Big Four's lounge.

The guest rooms and suites are all larger than average, a legacy from their former years as residential apartments. Each was individually decorated by Anthony Hail, Lee Radziwill, Elizabeth Bernhardt, and Charles Gruwell, using differing color schemes and furnishings that include a generous smattering of antiques and original art. Suites have refrigerators and wet bars, and some contain kitchenettes.

Every room has large windows that open to gorgeous views

of San Francisco Bay, the city, or Huntington Park and stately Grace Cathedral. Accouterments include fluffy down cushions, hair dryers, plush bath towels, and linen hand towels.

Twice-daily housekeeping, overnight laundry service, valet parking, and your choice among three daily newspapers are some of the services provided. One block away is the Nob Hill Club fitness center; guests are welcome.

> **Understated elegance, unobtrusive service, and assurance of privacy make this San Francisco landmark a romantic retreat and a favorite with a demanding clientele that includes many famous names.**

The hotel has several handsome meeting rooms suitable for board meetings and receptions. The concierge is on duty all day and will arrange for tours, theater and restaurant bookings, secretarial services, and babysitters. A Cadillac limousine will take you to the financial district and Union Square at no charge, and the cable car stops at the hotel's front door.

The Huntington is a member of Small Luxury Hotels of the World and Preferred Hotels and Resorts.

Inn at the Opera

333 Fulton Street
San Francisco, CA 94102
415-863-8400
800-325-2708
Fax: 415-861-0821

> *A small, elegant hotel close to the Civic Center*

Managing Director: Tom Noonan.
Accommodations: 30 rooms and 18 suites. **Rates:** $125–$175 single, $140–$190 double, $15 additional person, suites $200–$265. **Added:** 12% tax. **Included:** Continental breakfast. **Payment:** Major credit cards. **Children:** Under age 12 free in room with parent. **Pets:** Not allowed. **Smoking:** Nonsmoking rooms available.

Although San Francisco's Civic Center has long been the cultural and governmental focus for the city, with the Opera House, Davies Music Hall, San Francisco Ballet School, Civic Auditorium, Museum of Modern Art, and City Hall grouped closely together, the area has lacked a first-class hotel. With the restoration of the seven-story Inn at the Opera, it gained a gem. The hotel was built in 1927 as the Alden, to house visiting opera performers. Over time it fell into disrepair and was eventually purchased in 1983; after a $7 million renovation it reopened in 1985, again hosting internationally acclaimed singers and conductors as well as patrons and tourists.

Entering the inn is like stepping into the parlor of a gracious private home. Classical music flows around French armchairs in silk and damask, past tall mullioned windows, potted palms, and porcelain jardinieres painted with curling dragons. At the end of a short hallway lined with Paul Renouard sketches of Paris Opera Ballet dancers is the focal point of the hotel: Act IV. This intimate lounge and restaurant is rich in texture and color. Its dark woods, muted jewel tones, subdued lighting, and exotic fabric wallcoverings patterned with jungle birds create a sensuous, elegant mood. Green velvet sofas, facing a fireplace in the bar, are favored seats for enjoying post-performance liqueurs or steaming espresso.

A pianist plays every night in Act IV. The restaurant's menu, which changes regularly, features California cuisine and wines. Act IV is one of the city's few restaurants offering after-theater dinner.

You may choose to have breakfast delivered to your room or eat in the restaurant, where orchids grace tables with white linens. The buffet includes fresh fruit, yogurt, cereals, muffins, quiche, and a cheese tray.

There's only one elevator, but it takes you swiftly to guest rooms in the boutique hotel. Accommodations include six junior suites, six one-bedroom suites, and six two-bedroom/two-bath suites. All rooms and suites have half-canopy queen-size beds, microwave ovens, stocked mini-bars, and oversize baths. They're furnished with dark mahogany and color schemes of blue, green, and peach that exude a soft and welcoming warmth.

The least expensive and smallest are Standard rooms; Superiors are larger, but all have the same amenities — a basket of apples, plenty of pillows, fresh flowers, and evening turndown. You'll find a different sweet treat (chocolate truffles, strawberries dipped in chocolate, almond marzipan cakes) in your room each night.

You may park on the street, but it's not recommended in this urban neighborhood. Valet parking is available for $19 per day.

The Inn at Union Square

440 Post Street
San Francisco, CA 94102
415-397-3510
800-288-4346
Fax: 415-989-0529

> *A small urban hotel of comfort and style*

Manager: Brooks Bayly. **Accommodations:** 30 rooms. **Rates:** $130–$190 single or double, suites $180–$300. **Added:** 12% tax. **Included:** Continental breakfast; afternoon tea and wine; evening hors d'oeuvres. **Payment:** Major credit cards. **Children:** Additional $15 per night. **Pets:** Not allowed. **Smoking:** Not allowed.

In the heart of downtown San Francisco, half a block from Union Square, this little urban retreat is a delight. Behind the green and white awning that extends over the sidewalk is a narrow lobby, made to appear larger by the trompe l'oeil effect of wallpaper resembling open windows and shelves of books. A lovely floral display stands behind the front desk.

Guests receive two keys — one to the room and the other, for added security, to the single elevator. Intimate in size and tone, each floor of seven rooms has its own sitting area with a fireplace where morning muffins, fresh juices, and fruit are served (or breakfast will be brought to your room if you prefer). Afternoon tea is set out, complete with cucumber sandwiches and delectable cakes, and even as the teapots are whisked away, evening wine and hors d'oeuvres are brought. All this is complimentary, along with a daily paper.

The rooms are attractively furnished with Georgian furniture, canopy beds, and appealing fabrics. Ultra-soft sheets, downy pillows, wide windows that open, fresh flowers, a desk, wicker wastebaskets — these are the ingredients of a small and worthy hotel. Bathrooms are not immense marble affairs; they are simple and white-tiled, with brass water taps, shaded lamps, hair dryers, night lights, and mirrored medicine chests.

> **If you like European charm and attention to detail combined with the atmosphere of old San Francisco, the Inn at Union Square is an excellent choice.**

The larger rooms have sitting areas; one has a fireplace. There are two-room suites with fold-out love seats, a large two-room suite with a living room, and a penthouse suite with a king-size canopy bed, whirlpool bath, sauna, fireplace, and wet bar.

Jackson Court

2198 Jackson Street
San Francisco, CA 94115
415-929-7670

> *A residential-style lodging in a quiet neighborhood*

Manager: Pat Cremer. **Accommodations:** 10 rooms (all with private bath). **Rates:** $113–$160. **Included:** Expanded Continental breakfast. **Added:** 12% tax. **Minimum stay:** 2 nights on weekends. **Payment:** Major credit cards. **Children:** Not appropriate. **Pets:** Not allowed. **Smoking:** Not allowed.

A mining engineer who made his fortune in Australia at the turn of the century built this solid mansion in fashionable Pacific Heights. It withstood the 1906 earthquake and fire and now offers lodging to San Francisco visitors who prefer a quiet but convenient retreat away from the downtown bustle.

Parking is easy in this hilly neighborhood of lovely old residences. You can leave your car on the street or in a garage two blocks away. Marble stairs under a curved arch of red stone lead to a courtyard with greenery and a skylight at the entrance to Jackson Court. Inside, there's an intimate parlor furnished like a fine salon. Velvet couches sit on an Oriental carpet beside the fireplace, which is carved with cherubs, their mouths pursed as if to blow on the hearth. Ceiling beams and wainscoting are of dark woods. Fresh flowers are arranged on the coffee table, an encyclopedia is handy, and game boards are set for dominoes and backgammon. Sherry is served by the fire in the late afternoon.

The largest rooms are just off the parlor. The Executive Room has a brass bed and a large sitting area with an Italian marble fireplace (nonworking) and built-in bookcases. The

Garden Court, originally the dining room, features hand-crafted paneling, a bed with a curved brass headboard, a black marble fireplace, and a private patio filled with flowers.

The other rooms, on the second and third floors, convey the ambience of a well-appointed apartment. Two have working fireplaces. Room 1, once the library, is a big favorite for its quiet atmosphere, brass bed, and gray marble fireplace. All the rooms have TV and private phones.

> **Jackson Court is more like a home than a hotel because its accommodations are all time-share studios.**

Off the wide landing is a breakfast nook where fruit, croissants, and various cereals are available in the mornings. Guests are welcome to use the cooking facilities for heating foods or preparing light snacks.

Jackson Court is managed by the capable Pat Cremer, who will recommend good restaurants, give you a map and the morning newspaper, and answer questions about the city. "It's very informal here," she says. "This is a casual place. No one ever wants to leave."

The Majestic

1500 Sutter Street
San Francisco, CA 94109
415-441-1100
800-869-8966
Fax: 415-673-7331

> *A restored land-mark, the essence of old San Francisco*

General manager: Michael Nocula. **Accommodations:** 50 rooms and 7 suites. **Rates:** $135–$250 single or double, $15 additional person, midweek and group discounts. **Added:** 12% tax. **Payment:** Major credit cards. **Children:** Welcome (no charge for use of a crib). **Pets:** Not allowed. **Smoking:** Nonsmoking rooms available.

San Francisco's turn-of-the-century golden era is brought to life at the Majestic, a beautifully restored, five-story Edwardian structure. It's just outside the bustling downtown area, about six blocks from Union Square.

Entering the glass-paned double doors of the hotel takes you even farther from the modern rush and city noise. Wide stairs of green marble lead to a carpeted lobby where a chandelier with torch globes gives a warm glow to the antiques-filled room. A fire burns in the fireplace and Oriental vases hold bunches of golden lilies. Fringed lampshades and cushions, lace-curtained windows, and glass-fronted bookcases add atmosphere.

To the left of the lobby are the Café Majestic and bar, the latter a clubby spot with a nineteenth-century mahogany bar from France.

Some guest rooms have four-poster canopy beds, boudoir chairs, and velvet or plush couches. It's easy to imagine yourself in an old San Francisco residence — an updated one, however, with TVs, clock radios, and direct-dial telephones. Several rooms have gas fireplaces. If you'd like to step into a long-gone era, you'll enjoy the Majestic's charm. Soak in the clawfoot tub or sit at your desk in the bay window overlooking the trees and strollers on Sutter Street, and you might be a guest visiting in 1902, when the hotel was built. It has received state recognition for historic and architectural preservation.

> The Café Majestic — actually a full-scale dining room with a pleasantly French ambience — is noted for its combination of classic San Francisco dishes with California nouvelle cuisine. Among the memorable desserts are orange crème brûlée and chocolate cake with jalapeño chiles.

More of today's services include valet parking, complimentary limousine service to the financial district and Union Square, afternoon sherry in the library, and nightly turndown service. The concierge will arrange for restaurant reservations and wine country tours. During the off-season (November through March) the Majestic offers packages at lower rates.

Mandarin Oriental

222 Sansome Street
San Francisco, CA 94104
415-885-0999
800-622-0404
Fax: 415-433-0289

*A service
oriented hotel
with grand city
views*

General manager: Wolfgang K. Hultner. **Accommodations:** 158 rooms and suites. **Rates:** $275–$395 single or double; suites $595–$1,295. **Added:** 12% tax. **Payment:** Major credit cards. **Children:** Welcome. **Pets:** Not allowed. **Smoking:** Nonsmoking rooms available.

Located in the heart of the financial district, the Mandarin Oriental continually gets high marks for its service, and its award-winning restaurant. Opened in the mid-1980s as the prestigious Mandarin Oriental Hotel group's first U.S. hotel, the Mandarin Oriental San Francisco has only enhanced the chain's stateside reputation.

Guests register in the hotel's sleek, modern, marble lobby on the ground floor. Guest rooms are located on the top ten floors (floors 38–48) of the First Interstate Center — the third tallest building in the city. Glass enclosed skybridges lead from elevators to guest rooms, and although many may be tempted to stop and take in the incredible views of the city and the Golden Gate Bridge beyond, there is no need as views from the rooms are equally spectacular.

Rooms are spacious and attractive in creamy yellow, beige, and rosy brick tones. Comforters with complementing shams are striking — Oriental scenes appear to be etched on an ivory background. With rose-colored marble, a separate tub and oversize shower, the baths are luxurious. They feature a scale, clock, makeup mirror, hair dryer, English toiletries, Oriental silk slippers, an emergency flashlight, terry robes, and in the eastern tradition, a lightweight cotton robe is also provided. Room amenities include two-line phones with pc/modem hookups, writing desks, a clothesbrush, and a built-in luggage bench — a welcome change from the more precarious fold-up luggage racks often found in hotels.

Junior suites, called Mandarin Kings, have 100 more square feet of space than standard rooms, and their sitting area with a sofa and easy chair, is partially partitioned off from the sleeping area. Best of all their roomy tubs are set below large windows strategically placed to take full advantage of the view. For a real splurge, the Oriental suite has two bedrooms, a living room with a dining area, a Jacuzzi bath, and a 2,000-square-foot private terrace.

In keeping with the chain's eastern emphasis on service, thoughtful provisions have been made with the guest in mind. Doorbells at each room lend an air of distinction, while twice-daily housekeeping service keeps the rooms looking fresh. As part of nightly turndown, cookies at the bedside provide a comforting touch, while the room service kitchen, located just one floor below the guest rooms, ensures that meals are still oven-warm when they arrive.

Services at the Mandarin Oriental include a fully equipped business center, guest privileges at a nearby health club, and meeting rooms.

Silk's is the hotel's top-rated restaurant. Under the skilled direction of young chef Ken Oringer, the cuisine is billed as Californian, but entrées such as grilled lobster with Thai spices, or grilled squab with soybean, asparagus, and lily flowers belie the hotel's Asian origin. The Mandarin Lounge, adjacent to the lobby, serves Continental breakfast in the morning, appetizers and desserts from 3:00 P.M. to 8:00 P.M., and evening cocktails.

The Mansions

2220 Sacramento Street
San Francisco, CA 94115
415-929-9444
800-826-9398
Fax: 415-567-9391

> *A pair of mansions featuring luxurious style and a sense of fun*

Owner: Robert C. Pritikin. **Accommodations:** 21 rooms. **Rates:** rooms $129–$179 single or double, suites $189–$350. **Included:** Full breakfast and magic show. **Added:** 12% tax. **Payment:** Major credit cards. **Children:** Additional $18 per night. **Pets:** Allowed. **Smoking:** Allowed.

Two long-time San Francisco hotels, side by side in a neighborhood of apartments, homes, and a medical center, form an unlikely lodging combination. The Mansion Hotel, a twin-towered Queen Anne structure, is known for its sense of fun and eclectic mixture of whimsy and Victoriana. The Hermitage House is a serene, urban refuge. Connected by a hallway, they are The Mansions.

Robert Pritikin is a hotelier of boundless energy and many interests. He writes books (*Christ Was an Ad Man*), collects sculpture (he has a major Benjamin Bufano collection), keeps a macaw in the hotel parlor, and plays the musical saw. A few of his original hotel's features are a "hauntress" named Claudia who plays the piano, a billiards room with a wall-size mural of pigs, caged white doves, and priceless Joseph Turner and Joshua Reynolds paintings.

One of the world's largest examples of stained glass stands in the dining room. The colorful mural, first created for a villa in Spain, is nine feet high and stretches the length of the room. Prix fixe dinners are served nightly.

The grand home was built in 1887 by a senator from Utah, Charles Chambers, who earned a fortune in silver mines and moved to San Francisco. It's a historic landmark now, filled with museum-quality art and antiques.

> **With all its trappings, the hotel has a lighthearted atmosphere. Even the ghost seems to have a good time, concluding her evening concerts with a rousing march or ragtime tune, while bubbles float to the ceiling. A magic show is presented nightly.**

Accommodations, divided among three floors, are sumptuous, with four-poster beds, potted palms, and elaborately trimmed wardrobes. They all have piped-in classical music, fresh flowers, candy, velvet quilts, and red carpets. The Lillie Coit Room, once a third-floor hideaway, has been combined with the De-Young Room to form a small suite with windows that look out on the Golden Gate Bridge and Mount Tamalpais. Tom Thumb, on the second floor, is the smallest room, good for a single traveler or a cozy twosome.

Breakfast is served in the country kitchen. Fresh coffee ground in an antique grinder, cereal, fruit, crumpets, eggs, English sausage, and potatoes are on the wide-ranging menu.

The west wing (formerly Hermitage House) has a different flavor. Tasteful Laura Ashley prints and fabrics grace most rooms with a French country decor. High coffered ceilings, mullioned windows, antiques, and flowers give this side of the hotel a European flavor. Most suites have fireplaces. This building houses the Bufano Conference Center, the hotel's meeting space.

The Mark Hopkins Intercontinental

999 California Street
Number One Nob Hill
San Francisco, CA 94108
415-392-3434
800-327-0200
Fax: 415-421-3302

> *A 1920s land-mark on the crest of Nob Hill*

General manager: Sandor Stangl. **Accommodations:** 360 rooms, 30 suites. **Rates:** $190–$270 single or double, suites $375–$1200. **Added:** 12% tax. **Payment:** Major credit cards. **Children:** Under age 14 free in room with parents. **Pets:** Not allowed. **Smoking:** Nonsmoking rooms available.

In the devastating earthquake and fire of 1906, the fabulous Mark Hopkins mansion at the top of Nob Hill burned to the ground. The more modest structure that followed was moved in 1925 by a mining engineer, George D. Smith, who then began building the luxury hotel that stands today.

The 19-story Mark Hopkins, a combination of French château and Spanish Renaissance architecture, has been a world-famed city landmark since it opened in 1926 and was proclaimed "perfect, flawless." Ownership has changed several times (in early 1989 it was acquired by a Japanese firm), but its traditional style and quality of service remain. A recent major renovation updated the tired lobby, restaurant, and all the guest rooms and suites, so the hotel is again a place of grandeur, with marble floors and Persian carpets in the light-filled lobby. Off the lobby is the Lower Bar, where cocktails, high tea, and light meals are served under a Tiffany-style skylight.

Because the hotel comprises a central tower and two wings, every room has a view of San Francisco Bay and the city skyline. Even the lowest rooms, on the second floor, overlook machinery-screening flower boxes to the city below. The public spaces are grand and gilded, befitting a hotel of such prestige. Only its neighbor, the Fairmont, vies with the Mark Hopkins for compelling views and an air of festivity.

> **The Top of the Mark is obligatory on every San Francisco tourist's must-see list. As a result, the rooftop lounge is crammed every night with imbibers trying to catch a glimpse of the breathtaking views. Everyone is in a celebratory mood.**

In the hotel restaurant, Andre Zotoff prepares creative contemporary cuisine. Among his specialties are sautéed escalope of foie gras with lentils, apple purée and olive oil and roast loin of lamb in a fresh herb coulis. The herbs come from what is probably the most expensive herb garden in the world: a little plot of land the hotel owns on nearby Mason Street, valued at $4,000 a square foot. The wine list includes labels from thirty-four out of forty-one wine-producing states.

The guest rooms have been redone in neoclassic style, with color schemes of gray or khaki and gold. The quilted chintz bedspreads, thick carpeting, and damask wallcoverings were all designed for the hotel. The nightstands have tortuma tops made with crushed South American gourds in black resin. Televisions and mini-bars are encased in cherrywood armoires.

The best of the preferred accommodations are the corner terrace suites. Each features an enclosed solarium with a closeup of the hotel's elaborate architectural ornamentation and the spectacular panorama beyond. Each suite has three phones, a desk, and a white marble bath with pedestal sink, hair dryer, oversize towels, robes, and assorted toiletries.

The service at the Mark Hopkins is excellent, and the presence of groups (the hotel has a conference capacity of 750) does not seem to detract from its appeal to the individual traveler. The concierge will handle most requests. An additional level of service, Guest Relations, provides for special needs — language interpreters, VIPs, group assistance.

Several seasonal and honeymoon packages and special rates are offered.

The Pan Pacific Hotel

500 Post Street
San Francisco, CA 94102
415-771-8600
800-533-6465
Fax: 415-398-0267

A contemporary hotel of cool elegance

Managing director: Volker Ulrich.
Accommodations: 311 rooms, 19 suites. **Rates:** $205–$315 single or double, $25 each additional person, suites $475–$1,700. **Added:** 12% tax. **Payment:** Major credit cards. **Children:** Welcome. **Pets:** Small pets allowed by arrangement. **Smoking:** 8 nonsmoking floors.

The Pan Pacific rises 21 stories above the corner of Post and Mason streets, a block west of Union Square. Famed for its elegant, contemporary style, the hotel was designed by architect John Portman, who is known for introducing the open atrium to large convention hotels. This is a smaller, more opulent version of the Portman trademark.

In the porte-cochere, you are met by a white-gloved attendant who welcomes you effusively and whisks your car away. Inside, on the third-floor lobby level, a 17-story glass and brass atrium soars above a dazzling array of lights, and the focal point of the lobby area — a wonderful Elbert Weinberg fountain sculpture of women dancing called Joie de Danse. Sitting areas atop Oriental carpets on either side of the sculpture provide intimate gathering spots in the otherwise vast atrium.

Nearby the Pacific restaurant offers French-accented California cuisine. Representing the French side of things, the pastry chef once worked for Prince Ranier. Fittingly, Chocolate Napoleon is one of his specialties. Mustard roasted rabbit, and filet of salmon with Niçoise-style salad are just some of the main courses offered. Room service also features dishes from the restaurant's menu.

The floor below the entry level has an executive conference center, the only one like it in downtown San Francisco, containing four conference suites and a dining room. There's a large ballroom on the second floor.

> **The hotel is noted for its impeccable service, a continuation of the tradition established by the Portman Hotel when it opened in 1987.**

Each room has a personal valet call button which summons a valet to unpack luggage, press clothing, shine shoes, draw a bath, or bring fresh ice. The valet can even bring exercise equipment if you want to workout in the privacy of your own room. The guest rooms include sixteen Pacific Suites and three specialty suites: The Penthouse, The Olympic, and The California. The Penthouse occupies 3,000 square feet on the 21st floor. It has two bedrooms with canopy beds, two baths (and a huge whirlpool tub), powder room, living room with working fireplace, dining room, study, access to an open-air terrace, valet's room, and pantry.

Standard guest rooms, which have a contemporary Oriental look, are decorated in gray on gray with accents of pale mauve. The rooms are reminders of the sea fog that swirls through this coastal city's streets. Lavish Portuguese marble in the baths mirror the colors of the bedroom. Rooms have two TVs (one in the bath), phones with voice mail, Neutrogena toiletries, makeup mirrors, hair dryers, and terry robes.

There is an on-site fitness facility with cardiovascular and weight-training equipment, or you can arrange to use a larger health club nearby. The check-out system is flexible, and the hotel will provide in-city transportation in a Rolls Royce. Other hotel services include nightly turndown, and a foreign currency exchange.

Petite Auberge

863 Bush Street
San Francisco, CA 94108
415-928-6000

> *A city hotel with country charm*

Manager: Rich Revaz. **Accommodations:** 25 rooms, 1 suite. **Rates:** $110–$160 single or double, $15 additional person, suite $220. **Included:** Full breakfast. **Added:** 12% tax. **Payment:** Major credit cards. **Children:** Under age 2 free in room with parents. **Pets:** Not allowed. **Smoking:** Not allowed.

A French country inn in the heart of San Francisco, between Nob Hill and Union Square, Petite Auberge offers the best of both romantic worlds. It has flower-filled window boxes on every floor, and French and American flags fly over a green awning.

Inside the five-story, narrow hotel, light and breezy pastels, floral fabrics, comfortable antiques, and French landscapes set the tone. The registration desk is just inside the front beveled glass doors, but the gathering place for guests is belowstairs, where couches are pulled up to the fireplace, daily newspapers lie on the tables, and afternoon tea is served.

> **The inn has a quiet breakfast area where guests have their juice, cereals, egg dish, croissants and coffee at round tables, viewing a little garden full of well-tended shrubs and delicate ferns.**

The guest rooms line pale cream halls with paneled wainscoting. The rooms on the first floor tend to be dark; those above are more attractive. They vary in size and are decorated individually, but all carry through the French country theme with striped and flowered wallpapers, pastel comforters, muslin curtains, handmade pillows, and fresh flowers and fruit. Most have gas fireplaces.

Every room has a teddy bear, one of the signature touches in all Four Sisters Inns. The company, which owns a collection of inns, was begun by Roger and Sally Post in Pacific Grove, when they opened their own 19th-century home to guests. The Posts' four daughters helped make it a family venture and gave the new innkeeping company its name. The sisters are still involved in the operation of the inns. Sally Post, who decorates with flair, worked with other designers to create inns modeled on those in Europe. Each inn has bits of whimsy. At Petite Auberge they include an antique carousel horse by the front door, floppy-eared ceramic rabbits, and the ubiquitous bears, which may be purchased.

The staff at Petite Auberge is helpful in arranging for dinner reservations or tickets to the symphony or other events. Valet parking is available.

If you're looking for flowery charm, downtown convenience, and warm hospitality, this little inn is an excellent choice.

Prescott Hotel

545 Post Street
San Francisco, CA 94102
415-563-0303
800-283-7322
Fax: 415-563-6831

A sophisticated hotel with an urban mood

Manager: Michael Anderson. **Accommodations:** 166 rooms including 34 suites. **Rates:** $195–$215 single or double, suites $245–$265. **Added:** 12% tax. **Payment:** Major credit cards. **Children:** Welcome. **Pets:** Not allowed. **Smoking:** Nonsmoking rooms available.

Here's another boutique hotel with the winning Kimpton Group combination: small but attractive rooms, reasonable rates, and a top-quality restaurant. Curved copper awnings mark the entrance to the hotel, which is close to Union Square. Inside you'll find a quiet sitting area with couches and wingback chairs in the lobby, and curving staircases leading to the mezzanine's meeting rooms and guest rooms above.

The smartly appointed rooms, more elaborate than the other Kimpton hotels, have hair dryers and robes in the modern, well-lighted baths. The compact suites make efficient use of the space and are more like urban apartments than hotel lodgings.

On the Club Level (the fourth through seventh floors), guests have their own concierge and lounge where appetizers — catered by the Prescott's restaurant, Postrio — are served in the evenings. A complimentary buffet breakfast is provided, along with the morning papers.

Pizza is a specialty at Postrio, but you won't go wrong ordering anything on the menu. Please be sure to reserve a dinner table when you make your room reservation; Postrio is usually booked weeks in advance, though a few tables are held for hotel guests.

> **When the hotel opened in 1990, Postrio earned immediate raves. Lavish bouquets, Robert Rauschenberg paintings, and handblown light fixtures hung with copper spirals create a bright and whimsical setting for the outstanding California cuisine.**

The Red Victorian

1665 Haight Street
San Francisco, CA 94117
415-864-1978

> *An offbeat inn
> in the heart of
> the Haight*

Owner: Sami Sunchild. **Accommodations:** 18 rooms (4 with private bath; others share 4 baths). **Rates:** $76–$126 double, suite $200; discounts available for stays of three days or more. **Included:** Expanded Continental breakfast. **Added:** 12% tax. **Minimum stay:** 2 nights on weekends. **Payment:** Major credit cards. **Children:** Welcome. **Pets:** Not allowed. **Smoking:** Not allowed.

Exuberant colors, good-humored hospitality, and touches of whimsy characterize this delightful turn-of-the-century hotel in the famous Haight-Ashbury district. Sami Sunchild's paintings, which incorporate affirmations and positive thoughts, hang in the halls and guest rooms and are for sale. You'll see them on display in the art gallery/breakfast room on the ground floor, next to the Global Village Center, where products that help environmental causes are sold.

The hotel rooms range from modest to luxurious and are filled with creative artworks and furnishings. The Rainbow Room, where bay windows overlook Haight Street, has a bed swathed in netting of rainbow hues; the Conservatory is like a garden with its fresh greenery and white wicker. The Peacock Suite has stained glass windows, a moon window between the tub and sitting room, and a king-size bed with an exotic canopy.

Others include the Japanese Tea Garden Room, the Sunshine Room, the Butterfly Room, the Redwood Forest Room, and the Skylight Room. Each room has a washbasin. The shared baths are artistic ventures of their own, with mirrored walls, an aquarium, skylights, and colored lights.

In tune with the times,

> **It wouldn't be Haight-Ashbury without the Flower Child Room and the Peace Room, reminiscent of the district's renown in the 1960s.**

the Red Victorian has Macintosh computers available for rent. There's a café where light fare is available. German, French, and Spanish are spoken in this European-style, friendly hotel just two blocks from Golden Gate Park.

Renaissance Stanford Court Hotel

905 California Street
San Francisco, CA 94108
415-989-3500
800-227-4736
Fax: 415-391-0513

> *A historic luxury hotel on the Nob Hill cable car line*

General manager: Christian J. Mari. **Accommodations:** 402 rooms. **Rates:** $205–$295 single, $235–$325 double, $30 additional person; suites $450–$2000. **Payment:** Major credit cards. **Children:** Under age 18 free in room with adult. **Pets:** Allowed by arrangement. **Smoking:** Nonsmoking rooms available.

The Stanford Court has been a Nob Hill landmark for years, with its stained glass domes above the entry courtyard and lobby, antiques and art collection, and outstanding restaurant. Recent enhancements include a full-service business center, fitness facility (complimentary for guests), redecorated guest rooms, and renovated function space including a 5,000-square-foot grand ballroom.

The hotel was first a fashionable apartment building, constructed in 1912 on the site of Leland Stanford's 1876 Italianate mansion (which went up in flames in 1906). The apartment building was remodeled in the early 1970s as an elegant hostelry overlooking the city and the bay. In recent years the Hotel has been entirely refurbished.

> **Unusual and thoughtful touches in the rooms at the Renaissance Stanford Court include dictionaries, prethreaded sewing kits, and heated towel racks.**

In the marble and wood-paneled lobby are Baccarat chandeliers, Oriental carpets, and fine antiques such as ornately framed 18th-century mirrors and a grandfather clock that was a gift from Napoleon Bonaparte to his minister of war in 1806.

The guest rooms in the eight-story hotel are comfortable and, for the most part, spacious, with a blend of 19th century European reproductions and antique or Oriental pieces. Each room has television, two or more phones with call-waiting feature, clock radios, and desks. Rooms facing the street get traffic noise, so if you want quiet and are willing to forego the spectacular views, request an inner courtyard room.

Business travelers appreciate the hotel's complimentary limousine rides to the financial district and downtown, the on-site business center, and the 24-hour room and laundry service.

Fournou's Ovens is the Stanford Court's award-winning restaurant, featuring contemporary cuisine with a Mediterranean flair. It serves three meals a day. There are little dining alcoves, private rooms, and a section by the 54-square-foot roasting ovens covered with Portuguese tiles. The other main area has conservatory-style windows overlooking the cable cars and city skyline. The wine cellar is remarkable, with more than 20,000 bottles.

The Ritz-Carlton San Francisco

600 Stockton Street
San Francisco, CA 94108
415-296-7465
800-241-3333
Fax: 415-296-8559

*A luxury hotel in
a historic building*

Hotel Manager: Mark DeCocinis. **Accommodations:** 292
rooms, 44 suites. **Rates:** rooms $205–$350, suites $550–$700.
Added: 12% tax. **Payment:** All major cards. **Children:** Welcome. **Pets:** Not allowed. **Smoking:** Nonsmoking rooms available.

One of the city's best examples of neoclassical architecture is
part of the Ritz-Carlton group of luxury hotels. Built in 1909
for the Metropolitan Life Insurance Company, the stately
structure on Nob Hill was restored and opened in 1991. Like
the other Ritz-Carlton hotels, it offers sumptuous accommodations in a conservative setting. As evidence, the staff
dresses in navy or black, however, this being San Francisco,
there's a light-hearted quality that keeps pretension at bay.
Heavy, dark woods have been kept to a minimum.

Oriental rugs are spread on marble floors in the lobby, and
crystal chandeliers are elegant but not ostentatious. The
walls are adorned with museum-quality 18th-and 19th-cen-
tury paintings, while a grandfather clock and china cupboard
add a residential flavor. Across from the main entrance, afternoon tea is served in the lobby lounge — a Ritz-Carlton tradition.

One of the most appealing places in the imposing hotel is
its sunny outdoor Terrace restaurant, with its fountain and
umbrella tables. Roasted Tuscan baby chicken with braised
swiss chard, and orzo, and grilled veal chops with eggplant
fennel gratin, soft polenta, and sweet pepper compote, are examples of the restaurant's contemporary Mediterranean cuisine. You may also dine in the more formal, yet intimate and
elegant Dining Room, where French inspired dishes such as
filet of beef with pancetta oysters are served, and the wine list
is lengthy.

Guest rooms are handsomely decorated in classic residential style, with rich wood furniture, botanical or hunt prints
on the walls, and dashes of color. The marble bathrooms are
lovely, down to the orchids on the counter and white eyelet

shower curtains, though you may notice minor flaws such as no shelf in the oversize shower and only a single hook on the door. Amenities include bathrobes, irons and ironing boards, hair dryers, makeup mirrors, European toiletries, and scales.

Rooms and suites on the eighth and ninth floors are designated the Ritz-Carlton Club. Guests have the use of a concierge, a private lounge with a subdued atmosphere, and complimentary snacks and cocktails. All rooms have numerous useful features: remote control TVs (VCRs and a video library are available), stocked honor bars, clock radios,

> **The hotel bustles with activity, as many functions take place at the Ritz, but the halls, padded in gray damask, are quiet.**

safes. Some have bay views, but if you prefer a quiet room, follow the example of frequent San Francisco visitors and request one on the courtyard side.

Services by the multilingual staff include twice-daily maid service, valet parking, a 24-hour concierge, child care, and newspaper delivery. Swimwear is available in the fitness center, where you'll find a swimming pool, whirlpool, sauna, and weight machines.

The San Remo Hotel

2237 Mason Street
San Francisco, CA 94133
415-776-8688
800-352-REMO
Fax: 415-776-2811

> *A bargain-priced pensione near North Beach and Fisherman's Wharf*

Owners: Tom and Robert Field.
Accommodations: 62 rooms (share 6 baths). **Rates:** $45–$55 single, $55–$65 double; suite $85; $10 additional person. **Payment:** Major credit cards. **Children:** Welcome. **Pets:** Not allowed. **Smoking:** Allowed.

The 1906 earthquake left San Francisco in desperate need of hotel rooms, so A. P. Giannini, the founder of the Bank of America, built the New California Hotel. Close to the wharf and Embarcadero, the hotel was convenient for sailors and waterfront workers. Today, after extensive restoration, it's the San Remo, a warm, European-style inn with narrow halls, comfortable rooms, and ferns hanging below stained glass skylights.

> **The San Remo, renovated with taste and loving care by two brothers, is a block from a cable car stop and within walking distance of Fisherman's Wharf and North Beach.**

A restaurant open for private parties, weddings, and banquets is on the ground floor. The hotel's reception area and rooms are on the floors above. Down the hall, which has walls of white wainscoting and a pressed-paper design, are a phone, laundry room, and soft-drink machine.

The guest rooms, each one different, have two twin beds or a twin and a double, white walls, flowered quilts, tables, and extra touches such as an interesting piece of art, a wicker chair, or throw rugs. Each has a washbasin. The shared tiled bathrooms are immaculate. The separate shower room has black and white tile and corner sinks painted with flowers.

The shingle-sided penthouse suite has a private bath, television, refrigerator, and a rooftop deck with a view of Coit Tower and Telegraph Hill. If there are no guests in the penthouse, others may use the deck.

Seal Rock Inn

545 Point Lobos Avenue
San Francisco, CA 94121
415-752-8000

> *A family-oriented motel on a hill near the ocean*

Proprietors: Larry and Barbara Elam. **Manager:** Cecilia Downer. **Accommodations:** 27 rooms. **Rates:** $68–$94 single, $76–$102 double, $8 additional adult, $4 children. **Minimum stay:** 2 nights on weekends. **Payment:** Major credit cards. **Children:** Welcome. **Pets:** Not allowed. **Smoking:** Nonsmoking rooms available.

This three-story hotel with free covered parking is in San Francisco's northwest corner, across the street from Sutro Heights Park. It overlooks Seal Rocks, famous for their sea lions, and is just two blocks up the hill from a venerable name in restaurants, Cliff House.

> Sutro Heights Park, overlooking Cliff House and the ocean, was once the estate of Adolph Sutro. Now the buildings are gone, but you can see bits of statuary among the groves of eucalyptus, cypress and pine. It's a pleasant place to stroll and watch the sunset.

Seal Rock Inn is a wise lodging choice when you're bringing children to the city. It's removed from the downtown hubbub (though the street does get a lot of city and tourist buses) and has a casual atmosphere. Some rooms have a kitchenette, which you can use for an additional $4; it comes in handy when you want a snack or when the kids tire of restaurants. Dishes and utensils are supplied, along with a refrigerator and two-burner stovetop.

The furnishings are plain and serviceable. You won't worry about rambunctious youngsters destroying fragile antiques here, yet the comfortable sitting areas, earthtone carpeting and grasscloth walls are attractive and clean. Each room has a television and direct-dial phone, refrigerator, and complimentary coffee. Many include fireplaces with gas starters; oak logs are supplied. These units are the most popular and should be reserved far in advance. The rooms with ocean views are also big favorites.

Ideal if you're traveling with children is a unit with a queen-size bed and two studio twins. A folding vinyl wall can be pulled out to separate the two sleeping areas. Other rooms contain two double beds.

The coffee shop at the inn can be crowded and steamy, but is known for its omelettes and pancakes. It's open for breakfast and lunch only. The inner patio is set up for table tennis and badminton and has a small swimming pool.

In addition to Sutro Heights Park, a nearby attraction that intrigues kids and adults alike is Musée Mécanique, down the street at Cliff House. It showcases a collection of antique amusement machines, including coin-operated musical instruments. Golden Gate Park, one of the world's great urban oases, is four blocks south of the hotel.

Sheraton Palace Hotel

2 New Montgomery Street
San Francisco, CA 94105
415-392-8600
800-325-3535
Fax: 415-543-0671

> *A glamorous old hotel near the convention center*

General manager: Donald N. Timbie. **Accommodations:** 552 rooms, includes 78 suites. **Rates:** $245–$325 single, $265–$345 double, suites $600–$2,800, $20 additional person. **Added:** 12% tax. **Payment:** Major credit cards. **Children:** Under age 18 free in room with parents. **Pets:** Not allowed (though actress Sarah Bernhardt brought her pet tiger and parrot in 1887). **Smoking:** Nonsmoking rooms available.

With names such as Winston Churchill, Franklin D. Roosevelt, Warren G. Harding (who died in the hotel's Presidential Suite while still in office in 1923), and Nikita Khrushchev appearing on the roster over the years, the Palace Hotel's guest list reads like a who's who of the twentieth century and with good reason. After a 27-month, $150 million restoration that returned the historic hotel to its former glory, the Palace opened again in April of 1991. The original Palace Hotel was built on the site in 1875 as the first hotel west of the Mississippi, and was designed to be the most luxurious lodging in the world at that time. The hotel's sturdy construction survived the 1906 earthquake, but guest Enrico Caruso's nerves didn't — running from his room in only a towel he promised never to visit San Francisco again. The Palace, however, did not survive the subsequent fire that swept through the city immediately following the famous earthquake, so the hotel was rebuilt; it is the 1909 structure that remains today.

> **Take a trip back to the Gilded Age in the Sheraton's palatial Garden Court. It's a beloved lunch, tea, and Sunday brunch spot for San Franciscans who remember the old days, as well as for awed newcomers.**

The glamour has returned to the aptly named Palace with the 1991 renovation, and the exquisite Garden Court is its centerpiece. A frequent setting for many a grand banquet over the years (Woodrow Wilson gave two luncheons here in 1919 in celebration of the signing of the Treaty of Versailles), the Garden Court now serves classically inspired American cuisine, but it's the room's sheer beauty and grandeur that diners remember long after their meal. A magnificent leaded glass dome (over 80,000 pieces of glass were used) covers the famous restaurant, where ten chandeliers sparkle above the potted palms, and marble columns. Linen-covered tables are set with purple irises complementing deep royal carpeting adding to the overall lavish ambience.

Other public spaces in the Palace are also appealing, if not on such a grand scale as the Garden Court. A large mural of the Pied Piper of Hamilin by Maxfield Parish hangs over the polished wood bar in the pub named for the painting. The painting was especially commissioned to commemorate the hotel's 1909 reopening and is currently valued at over two million dollars. From the Pied Piper Bar diners walk through a wine display to Maxfield's restaurant named for the renowned artist. Maxfield's is a handsome eatery with green leather backed chairs and booths, and a lovely stained glass ceiling and tiled mosaic floor that were discovered in the 1991 restoration. Maxfield's, a San Francisco-style grill, features steaks, seafood, and pasta. Kyo-Ya, the Palace's third restaurant, is attractive in the Japanese tradition, and serves award-winning sushi and Japanese cuisine at both lunch and dinner.

Acres of marble, high ceilings, polished wood reproduction furniture, and numerous amenities characterize the classically elegant guest rooms and suites. There are hair dryers and magnifying mirrors in the marble and brass baths, irons and ironing boards, safes, refrigerators, movies, robes, and hookups for personal computers. Overnight valet service, nightly turndown, and 24-hour room service are offered. Business travelers like the telephones with custom message, conference call, voice mail, and call waiting features.

Recent additions to the hotel include a conference area and business center, a health spa, and a sunny skylighted swimming pool pleasantly surrounded by striped chaises and glass tables. The hotel's location is convenient for both business and pleasure. It's adjacent to the financial district and within walking distance of Moscone Center and the Embarcadero Center. Theaters and shops are nearby.

The Sherman House

2160 Green Street
San Francisco, CA 94123
415-563-3600
800-424-5777
Fax: 415-563-1882

An elegant mansion offering distinctive service and fine views of the bay

Owner: Manou Mobedshahi. **Accommodations:** 8 rooms, 6 suites. **Rates:** $250–$375 single or double, suites $575–$825. **Added:** 12% tax. **Payment:** Major credit cards. **Children:** Welcome. **Pets:** Not allowed. **Smoking:** Allowed in designated areas.

This intimate, exclusive hostelry in one of the city's most fashionable districts is an 1876 French-Italianate mansion. Once the home of Leander Sherman, founder of the Sherman Clay Music Company, it is now a princely enclave catering to a discriminating clientele. The rich and famous find it a haven, as do those looking for service far above the ordinary.

Manou Mobedshahi, an Iranian economist turned San Francisco entrepreneur, bought the historic landmark in 1981 and, with his wife, an art preservationist, carefully restored the house and its formal gardens.

The gallery above the Music Room provides a pleasant sitting room, with cushioned seats at five bay windows, a fireplace, and French provincial armchairs and sofa. It is here that wine is served in the afternoon, and occasionally there's a wine-tasting or a music recital.

> **In the Music Room, where finches trill in a birdcage that is a miniature of Château Chenonceau in France, it's easy to imagine Paderewski playing the grand piano in the corner, as he did in years past.**

The guest rooms are in the main house and former carriage house. One of the suites has its own garden with a deck and arbor. Furnishings in all rooms are antique or custom-made. Hand-loomed carpets, Coromandel screens, Belgian tapestries, marble fireplaces, brass fixtures, crystal chandeliers, and original art fill the interiors, planned by the late great designer, William Gaylord. Most rooms adhere to a French Second Empire theme, popular in Leander Sherman's day, with a few in a Biedermeier or Jacobean motif. All have a sense of solidity and permanence.

Some rooms have sweeping views of the bay, Golden Gate Bridge, and Alcatraz. The Garden Suite, set among the multi-level lawns and cobblestoned pathways, is the largest and has the most contemporary decor. It has a spacious living room with a free-standing fireplace, lattice walls, slate floors, and wide windows overlooking shrubs and flowers, a gazebo, and a pond. Hollow core rattan wraps the four-poster bed. The suites upstairs in the carriage house are equally light and bright. The top-floor suite features a sunken living room with French doors to a balcony overlooking the bay.

In the main house, the Biedermeier Suite, with its window seat invitingly set with plump pillows in a bay window offering glorious views of the Golden Gate Bridge, is a personal favorite. If you can tear your eyes away from the view, you'll find a cozy suite tastefully appointed in cranberries and golds with fringed velvet chairs, round ottomans, reading lamps, botanical prints, and a king-size canopy bed draped in tapestry fabric. The Pacific Heights room, so named because it faces the fashionable neighborhood, has high ceilings, yellow-washed walls, and a marble fireplace. Heavy drapes separate the bedroom from the parlor where an antique trunk doubles as a coffee table, and the tan leather sofa matches the bed's headboard. Amenities in all of the rooms include down comforters, dimmer light switches, thick fabric shades to keep out early daylight, elegant black marble baths with small TVs and a second telephone, plush white towels and robes, and Crabtree and Evelyn toiletries.

Three meals a day are served in the intimate dining room, which is open to guests only. French cuisine with California accents is served, under the direction of David Salvatore. Custom meals can be designed for guests and served in the privacy of their suite for special occasions, and because of the inn's distinctive service and ambience, many guests do make the Sherman House their lodging of choice for important personal anniversaries.

Needless to say, the service and attention to detail at this hotel are impeccable. Whether it's room service at any hour, immediate shoe repairs, secretarial services, a tour of the Napa Valley, or a ride to the airport in a vintage automobile, the staff of Sherman House is willing and able to oblige. This is a lodging of polish, privilege, and ease.

Victorian Inn on the Park

301 Lyon Street
San Francisco, CA 94117
415-931-1830
800-435-1967
Fax: 415-931-1830

A Queen Anne mansion overlooking Golden Gate Park

Innkeepers: Lisa and William Benau. **Accommodations:** 12 rooms and suites (all with private bath). **Rates:** $99–$164, suites $164–$320. **Included:** Expanded Continental breakfast. **Added:** 12% tax. **Minimum stay:** 2 nights on weekends. **Payment:** Major credit cards. **Children:** Welcome. **Pets:** Not allowed. **Smoking:** Nonsmoking rooms available.

Directly across the street from the Panhandle of Golden Gate Park, in an area of noble Victorian homes, the hospitable Benaus welcome guests to this Queen Anne mansion. It was built in 1897 for Thomas Jefferson Clunie, a prominent lawyer and legislator, who piled on the gingerbread and fretwork and added an open belvedere tower. Only two homes in the city still boast such towers.

After the Clunies were gone, the gray brick house underwent a steady stream of changes, going from private residence to a haven for '60s flower children and rock bands, to rebirthing center. In the early 1980s, Shirley and Paul Weber took over and began a handsome restoration. Shirley's daughter and son-in-law now run the inn with casual, good-humored style.

> A cozy fire burns in the parlor's white tiled fireplace on foggy afternoons, and a game table with a backgammon set stands by the curved windows. A tapestry-covered fainting couch, baskets of flowers, fringed lamps, and a red settee make the parlor a place of comfort and charm.

Marble steps lead to a front door with stained glass side panels and a foyer beautifully paneled in mahogany. Up the carpeted stairs, past 19th-century opera posters, you come to six guest rooms on the second floor and four on the floor above. Each bedroom has special characteristics — a brass bed, a freestanding mirror, a fireplace, a sunken tub. Each has a phone, and television and a fax machine are available upon request.

The tower room has French doors that open onto the belvedere porch overlooking the bay and eucalyptus trees of the Panhandle. In the pleasant little room you can lie in the bathtub and watch flames flicker in the marble fireplace, their reflections dancing in stained glass. The tower room connects with the larger one next to it to form a suite.

The rooms on the garden level, below the main floor, face the sidewalk and passersby through curved, lace-curtained windows. One large room, which has a brass bed and a working fireplace of ceramic tile, combines both antique and contemporary furnishings. The inn's location is ideal for jogging — it's both flat and scenic. You can run without interruption through the Panhandle and Golden Gate Park, all the way to the ocean. After your morning jog, you'll be served breakfast in the bay-windowed dining room — baskets of scones, croissants, and freshly baked poppyseed or strawberry bread, along with juice and platters of fresh fruits and cheeses. It all comes with full pots of coffee or tea and the morning paper.

The innkeepers know the local restaurants and will steer you in the right direction for sightseeing, dining, and recreation. Limited parking is available. Two bus lines run within one or two blocks, leading downtown or to the Marina district, near the Golden Gate Bridge.

The Villa Florence Hotel

225 Powell Street
San Francisco, CA 94102
415-397-7700
800-243-5700
Fax: 415-397-1006

A boutique hotel with an Italian flavor

General manager: Steve Miller. Accommodations: 180 rooms, including 36 suites. Rates: $115–$175 single or double, suites $165–$285. Added: 12% tax. Payment: Major credit cards. Children: Under age 17 free in room with parents. Pets: Not allowed. Smoking: Nonsmoking rooms available.

The Villa Florence is one of the city's distinctive small hotels offering stylish lodgings in a historic building to cost-conscious travelers. Bill Kimpton helped to lead the way for these boutique hotels when he saw a niche to be filled and began renovating a few of San Francisco's rundown but usable structures.

Formerly the Manx Hotel, built in 1916, the Villa Florence was remodeled with an Italian Renaissance theme and opened as one of the Kimpton Hotels in 1986. In the busy lobby are a marble fireplace and a gauzy mural depicting 16th-century Florence. Indirect lighting on the marble columns highlights ceiling detail.

Separated from the lobby by etched glass walls is Kuleto's Restaurant, which is known for its Italian food with a California perspective. Baked goods and desserts such as pumpkin tarts and rich chocolate decadence on raspberry sauce are made daily on the premises. The restaurant's ambience combines an aura of old San Francisco with Italian vitality. Dark wood, warm lighting, and strings of peppers, herbs, sausages and garlic hanging above the bar add to the atmosphere. Ficus trees grow to the ceiling under three stained glass skylights in the light and airy dining section.

> **Highlights in Kuleto's are the pastas, innovative salads, and grilled fish and meats. A specialty is the excellent antipasto bar.**

Guest rooms, which include junior and deluxe suites, have a pastel decor, with flowered fabrics and pale furniture. All include honor bars, concealed televisions, direct-dial phones with long cords, and soundproof walls and windows. Desk space is on the skimpy side — adequate for writing postcards. Some bathrooms are very small. Much roomier are those in the junior suites, which also have sitting areas, though not divided rooms. The deluxe suites have two rooms.

The hotel offers morning and evening room service, complimentary limousine service to the financial district, and same-day laundry and valet service. There are three meeting rooms and a full range of audiovisual equipment. Room keys are coded for security.

Villa Florence is just south of Union Square on the main cable car line, not a poor location but highly touristed, with many trinket shops and hordes of people. With new developments such as the snazzy shops of San Francisco Centre, the tenor of the neighborhood may change.

The Westin St. Francis

335 Powell Street
San Francisco, CA 94012
415-397-7000
800-228-3000
Fax: 415-774-0124

> *A historic hotel
> on Union Square*

Managing Director: Gerald D. Wolsborn. **Accommodations:** 1,200 rooms and suites. **Rates:** $185–$305 single or double; suites $225–$1,000. **Added:** 12% tax. **Payment:** Major credit cards. **Children:** Under age 18 free in room with parents. **Pets:** Small, well-trained dogs allowed. **Smoking:** Nonsmoking rooms available.

The St. Francis has been a landmark on Union Square since it first opened in 1904. The interior had to be redone following the fire which swept through the city immediately after the great earthquake of 1906, and when the hotel reopened in 1907 a third wing was added along with the renovation. In 1913 a fourth wing was built on to what is now considered the historic section of the hotel, and a 32-story tower was constructed behind the main hotel in the early 1970s bringing the total number of rooms to 1,200 — making the St. Francis one of the largest hotels in the city.

The St. Francis certainly has its share of history. Every President since Taft has visited the hotel, as have dignitaries such as Queen Elizabeth, two Japanese Emperors, and King Juan Carlos of Spain. It is said that a strike by the hotel's wait-staff may have swayed the 1916 presidential election, and President Gerald Ford successfully evaded a second assassination attempt while at the hotel. Because of the interest in the hotel's past, the St. Francis has instituted free historical tours that take place about once a month.

Because of the hotel's size and location, its lobby is almost always buzzing with activity. Here the walls have hand-painted murals, and chandeliers dripping with crystal beads hang from the high ceilings, while an ornately carved rosewood grandfather clock, which has been holding court in the lobby since the hotel's reopening in 1907, stands as a reminder of an earlier era. Mirrored columns shield sofas arranged in intimate groups to provide a quiet respite from the bustle beyond.

Down the hall the Compass Rose is grand with gold leaf topped marble columns, carved wooden ceilings and Oriental screens. Evocative of a slower time, it is the spot to linger over champagne and caviar. Victor's, on the thirty-second floor of the tower building, is the hotel's fine dining restaurant. Named for a renowned chef who worked for the hotel in its first two decades (and who had once been chef to the King of Portugal), the restaurant specializes in innovative interpretations of traditional favorites such as pan-seared veal sweetbread served with crispy polenta, bacon, fava beans, and truffle, or ratatouille stuffed game hen with herb risotto and lemon thyme jus. Other dining choices at the St. Francis include a Mediterranean café, the St. Francis Grill on the lobby level (where you can get everything from Dungeness crab cakes to prime rib), and Dewey's with its sports bar, lunch buffets, espresso bar, and good beer selection. Club Oz on the third floor is the place to go for dancing and views of Coit Tower and the Transamerica building.

Guest rooms in the main section of the hotel have sleigh beds, writing desks, armoires, end tables, and small crystal chandeliers. The small baths have marble vanities and Caswell and Massey toiletries. Glass elevators, with views of the city and bay, transport guests to their rooms in the tower. In teals, beiges, and salmons, with satiny fabrics, the tower rooms have an Oriental flavor. They have marble topped honor bars, and their baths, which are larger than those in the main building, have extra amenities such as hair dryers, safes, irons and ironing boards.

With the Westin Kids Club, the youngest members of your family will be treated as a special guest with their own room registration card, a sports bottle with free refills, maps of the hotel and San Francisco, coloring books, and crayons. In-room refreshment centers are stocked with kid favorites, and the restaurants and room service have special children's menus. The hotel's fitness room is small but adequate for light workouts. More extensive facilities are available at a nearby health club.

With 1,200 rooms the hotel naturally caters to groups, and there is a business center with secretarial services on property. Other services include a concierge, valet parking, an on-site florist, foreign currency exchange, a barber and beauty salon, and menus in Braille.

The St. Francis has the cleanest coins in town. The hotel possesses a "money laundering" machine that was brought to the hotel in the late 1930s by a general manager in order to keep dirty coins from soiling ladies' white gloves.

Although the St. Francis tends to be group oriented, there is still much to draw the leisure traveler. The hotel's Union Square location means that Macy's, Neiman Marcus, Saks Fifth Avenue, Tiffany's, and Nordstrom, among others, are just steps away, as is the cable car line. The kid-friendly programs offered by the hotel also make it an appealing choice for families.

The White Swan Inn

845 Bush Street
San Francisco, CA 94108
415-775-1755
800-999-9570
Fax: 415-775-5717

An English garden theme in a city hotel

Innkeeper: Celeste Lytle. **Accommodations:** 23 rooms, 3 suites. **Rates:** $145–$160 single or double, $15 additional person, suites $195–$250. **Included:** Full breakfast. **Added:** 12% tax. **Payment:** Major credit cards.

Children: Under age 5 free in room with parent. **Pets:** Not allowed. **Smoking:** Not allowed.

Once this four-story hotel with a marble facade and bay windows was the Hotel Louise, built after the great earthquake of 1906. Renovated in 1986, it now provides a tranquil downtown retreat from the busy city. This is one of the more expensive of the Four Sisters inns and has the most amenities.

Beveled glass doors open to a large reception area with granite floors, an antique carousel horse, and English art. Downstairs is the guests' lounge, where breakfast and a full afternoon tea, with scones, cheeses, fondues or other hearty snacks, are served. In the parlor and library are inviting chairs before the granite fireplace, shelves full of books, and a standing world globe — a peaceful setting with a manor house motif.

The terrace outside, shaded by an avocado tree, is next to a conference room that can accommodate up to thirty people. The White Swan also does catering upon request. A few of the hotel's special services are one-day laundry and pressing, complimentary cookies and fruit all day, business equipment, and complimentary wine and roses in every guest room.

All rooms have wet bars, a television, fireplaces, and phones. The hotel's two-bedroom suite has two fireplaces. Four-posters, antique reproductions, and books in the rooms lend a residential ambience. The baths are modern, with basins set in granite counters, but contain some original tiles.

Valet parking is available, and the front desk provides concierge services, booking restaurant tables and tickets to events. Several fine restaurants are close to the hotel. Recommended are Fleur de Lys, L'Epic, and Café Mozart. Kuleto's and Trattoria Contadina serve excellent northern Italian cuisine, and Fratelli's is noted for its dishes of southern Italy.

SAN JOSE

Hotel De Anza

233 W. Santa Clara Street
San Jose, CA 95113
408-286-1000
800-843-3700
Fax: 408-286-0500

*An updated
historic hotel in
Silicon Valley*

General manager: Judy Young. **Accommodations:** 94 rooms, 6 suites. **Rates:** $125–$250 single or double, $15 additional person (special packages available), penthouse suite $795. **Added:** 10% tax. **Payment:** Major credit cards. **Children:** Under age 18 free with parent. **Pets:** Not allowed. **Smoking:** Allowed on 1 floor only.

Originally opened in the 1930s, this art deco landmark fell into decay. Restored and reopened in 1990, the De Anza again offers fine accommodations with a sophisticated flavor. This architectural classic, a few blocks from the Convention Center, the Center for the Performing Arts, and the Civic Arena, is a part of San Jose's revitalized downtown area.

You won't find resort amenities here — there's no pool, the health club is tiny and seldom used, and the views are mainly of freeways and buildings. But the distinctive character and in-room conveniences make up for any deficiencies. In keeping with its Silicon Valley location, state-of-the-art technology is provided. Each room has two TVs, a VCR (movies are complimentary), three phones, a two-line desk phone with fax capabilities, and voice mail message service. Other services include the use of a computer, a portable cellular phone, a video camera, and a beeper and pager.

Business is the mainstay on weekdays, but romance takes over on weekends at the De Anza. With the Remember the Romance package, you'll receive champagne, a red rose, dinner for two at La Pastaia, chocolates, a night in a standard room or suite, and a generous breakfast.

Meeting more leisurely needs are honor bars, ice machines on every floor, terrycloth robes, turndown service, and an unusual offering called Raid Our Pantry. Your room key opens a fully stocked bar on the second floor where you can help yourself to drinks and snacks (salads, fruits, muffins) at any time. Most of the rooms are unusually large for a city hotel and have king-size beds. In a small suite you'll find a foyer with wet bar, a cozy sitting area with puffy cushions on the couch, and a green granite and tiled bath with a whirlpool tub. Most elaborate is the penthouse suite, an apartment with two rooftop patios. Furnished in an Egyptian theme and featuring two rooftop patios, it has a black tiled fireplace, a glass-topped bar, and a luxurious bathroom.

Off the lobby on the main floor are La Pastaia, a restaurant noted for its Italian food, and The Hedley Club lounge. The lounge, named for an architect who was influential in South Bay building design, is an inviting spot to enjoy cocktails and listen to opera on Sundays. The Hedley Club's painted ceiling is one of the few pieces remaining from the original hotel.

The De Anza has several meeting rooms and an enclosed outdoor patio, The Patio Court Terrace.

SARATOGA

The Inn at Saratoga

20645 Fourth Street
Saratoga, CA 95070
408-867-5020
800-543-5020 in California
800-338-5020 in U.S.
Fax: 408-741-0981

An inn of contemporary comfort in the Santa Cruz Mountains

Manager: Jack Hickling. **Accommodations:** 39 rooms, 7 suites. **Rates:** $145–$245 single or double, suites $390–$440. **Added:** 10% tax. **Included:** Continental breakfast. **Payment:** Major credit cards. **Children:** Free in room with parents. **Pets:** Not allowed. **Smoking:** Nonsmoking rooms available.

Saratoga is a special place. A hidden village tucked away among the redwoods on a hillside south of San Jose, Santa Clara and Silicon Valley, Saratoga offers a retreat from high tech, an escape from high rise.

This historic resort area in the Santa Cruz Mountains first began to lure visitors in the 1860s because the waters of its hot springs were said to be as therapeutic as those in Saratoga, New York. For nearly fifty years the springs (long since abandoned) attracted city-weary Bay Area residents for a few days of relaxation and rejuvenation.

> **In this shady spot you feel miles from anything remotely resembling a city. Yet you're just a few steps from Saratoga's main street, Big Basin Way, which is lined with excellent restaurants, chic boutiques, and galleries.**

Today, Saratoga has become a fashionable dining spot, with an array of award-winning restaurants, and it's a good base for exploring some of California's most interesting wineries. Outdoor enthusiasts enjoy Big Basin Redwoods State Park and its miles of hiking trails. Via Montalvo and Hakone Gardens invite visitors to stroll their manicured pathways.

When the Inn at Saratoga opened on the site of the old Toll Gate in 1987, it fit in well with this relaxing environment. Intended as a retreat for the executives of Silicon Valley, the inn offers quiet, privacy, proximity to fine dining, and rooms appointed to meet the needs of business travelers.

Nestled in a glen overlooking Saratoga Creek, the inn is surrounded by elm, sycamore and eucalyptus trees and colorful gardens, giving it a sense of seclusion. All the guest rooms are spacious, with separate sitting areas, balconies, and views of Saratoga Creek and the gardens. The appointments include two phones, robes, double sinks, hair dryers, cable television, and honor bars.

The suites serve as midweek meeting sites for businesspeople as well as romantic weekend retreats. These elegant two- and three-room arrangements have separate living rooms with a wet bar, refrigerator, and a television with VCR. The bathrooms are large, with double whirlpool baths and — a nice touch — European towel warmers. Two suites are named for the actresses Olivia de Havilland and Joan Fontaine, sisters who grew up in Saratoga. These suites include formal dining rooms that can accommodate up to six people for private dining.

The Inn at Saratoga places a premium on personal service. A light breakfast is served in the lobby. Tea, complimentary wine, and hors d'oeuvres are set out every evening. The newspaper is delivered to your room and the inn offers nightly turndown service. Secretarial and valet service are available.

Like Saratoga itself, this inn offers a touch of tranquility in a stressful world.

SAUSALITO

Casa Madrona Hotel

801 Brideway
Sausalito, CA 94965
415-332-0502
800-567-9524
Fax: 415-332-2527

*A romantic inn
with a bay view*

Proprietor: John Mays. **Accommodations:** 35 rooms (all with private bath). **Rates:** $105–$245 single or double, $10 additional person. **Included:** Breakfast and afternoon wine and cheese. **Added:** 10% tax. **Minimum stay:** 2 nights on weekends. **Payment:** Major credit cards. **Children:** Free in room with parents. **Pets:** Not allowed. **Smoking:** Not allowed in restaurant.

Few inns are as romantic in atmosphere and style as the lovely Casa Madrona. Terraced on a hillside above the chic town of Sausalito, just across the Golden Gate Bridge from San Francisco, the hotel offers comfortable accommodations, excellent food, and superb views. Every room has a view, sometimes breathtaking, of the harbor, San Francisco Bay, and the city, or the bridge and headlands. Brick paths and stairs separate the rooms (there are elevators, too) winding up the hill to a Victorian mansion, the oldest building in Sausalito.

Built in 1885 by William Barrett, a wealthy San Franciscan, the Italianate villa later became a boarding house, an inn, a

'50s crash pad, and a fine country inn and restaurant. In the late 1970s, the now-historic landmark was purchased by John Mays, a lawyer with a vision. He renovated and expanded on the property, creating an exceptional hotel.

The retreats range from a Parisian artist's loft, complete with easel, paints, and brushes, to a tribute to Hollywood, which has a harbor view from the elevated canopy bed, epic movie prints, a neon flamingo, and classic films. Kathmandu is a regal room of paisley fabrics, huge cushions, and alcoves. It has a fireplace, a deck, and tub for two. A 19th-century English merchant would feel at home in Lord Ashley's Look-

> During the day you can watch the boats come and go over the moody bay waters; at night the lights of the city sparkle against the horizon or are diffused by drifting fog.

out, where he could keep an eye on the ships in the harbor from sunny bay windows in this oak and brass-filled room.

In the gardenlike Renoir Room, an inviting window seat set with pillows is ideal for gazing at the sails in the bay below. Summer House, with wicker furniture, white oak walls, high bed and array of books, is reminiscent of a New England vacation home. Ascot suite has an English tone and separate sitting room. Casa Cabana is southwestern in style with a crown canopy bed and marble fireplace. Salon Nouveau is fittingly art nouveau in decoration and 1000 Cranes has a contemporary Oriental look.

Cottages with kitchenettes are Calico Cottage, cozy with a rocking chair by the fireplace; English Gate House, which has two bedrooms and a sunporch; and La Tonnelle, a little hideaway with a panoramic view. It has a tiled tub for two and a garden deck.

In the main house, rooms have period decor, with brass beds, flowered quilts, greenery, and wicker furniture. Perhaps most romantic is the soft blue Belle Vista Suite, two rooms divided by a partition. It has a tub for two near a window overlooking Angel Island and the San Francisco skyline.

In Mikayla, the hillside restaurant, you may eat indoors or on a deck with retractable glass walls and roof. A buffet breakfast of fruit, cheese, scones, and juice is served here. Dinner specialties are charred prime sirloin with asparagus, roasted potatoes and sauce Foyot, or potato-wrapped striped sea bass with leek fondue in a red wine sauce.

Casa Madrona also has a private Jacuzzi available to guests by reservation.

STINSON BEACH

Casa del Mar

P.O. Box 238
37 Belvedere Avenue
Stinson Beach, CA 94970
415-868-2124

> *A hillside villa
> near the shore*

Innkeeper: Rick Klein. **Accommo-dations:** 6 rooms (all with private bath). **Rates:** $100–$210. **Included:** Full breakfast. **Minimum stay:** 2 nights on weekends. **Payment:** MasterCard, Visa. **Children:** Age 6 and older welcome. **Pets:** Not allowed. **Smoking:** Not allowed.

Like a Mediterranean villa, this peach stucco home with a red tile roof rises above a blue sea and masses of flowers in a terraced garden. This hillside, though, is on the Pacific shore, in a village north of San Francisco. It's a 35-minute drive from the Golden Gate Bridge to Stinson Beach, which lies at the foot of Tamalpais State Park.

Casa del Mar is slightly inland from the beach. Wooded trails extend from the back door up Mount Tamalpais, through meadows of wildflowers to wide ocean views. Rick Klein moved to the area in the mid-1980s, planning to settle down after a checkered background as a restaurateur, fisher, treasure hunter, builder, and attorney. Gardening was to become his next passion, along with rebuilding the house he purchased and turning it into a bed-and-breakfast. His efforts have created an inn that is a work of art and a lovely sanctuary.

Light streams through many windows in the open, white interior, where Rick's collection of works by Marin County artists is displayed. Guests share two breakfast tables in the informal, sun-splashed dining area, getting acquainted as they feast on fresh fruit, granola, yogurt, pastries, and a main dish. The guest rooms, varied in size, are named for the hand-painted ceramic designs in the showers: Shell, Passion Flower, Hummingbird, and Heron. Each has a queen-size bed covered with a duvet, fine cotton linens, and a private balcony with a view of the woods or ocean.

The penthouse on the third floor contains an additional single bed. Decorated in blue and white, this sky-lighted room has a big bathroom with a two-person tub. The Garden Room, below the kitchen, has its own entrance and patio.

The softspoken, hospitable innkeeper has numerous suggestions for things to do during your visit. You're close to Point Reyes National

> **Meandering the rocky paths of the Casa del Mar garden, with the sound of the surf in the background, is a special pleasure. Herbs and wisteria scent the air, while jacarandas, palm trees, and cacti lend exotic appeal.**

Seashore, the giant redwoods in Muir Woods, and Audubon Canyon Ranch, where, in spring, you can watch herons nesting in the treetops. Stinson Beach has three miles of white sand to stroll.

WALNUT CREEK

The Mansion at Lakewood

1056 Hacienda Drive
Walnut Creek, CA 94598
510-945-3600
800-477-7898

> *A historic estate in East Bay*

Innkeepers: Sharyn and Mike McCoy. **Accommodations:** 7 rooms (all with private bath). **Rates:** $135–$300 weekends, $20 less midweek, $15 additional person. **Included:** Full breakfast. **Payment:** Major credit cards. **Children:** Discouraged. **Pets:** Not allowed. **Smoking:** Not allowed.

The oldest home still standing in Walnut Creek is on a three-acre estate that is a tranquil oasis in the fast-developing East

Bay area. This 1860 manor home is on the site of a Mexican land grant, a 50-minute drive from the Oakland airport.

After the electric gate is opened, you enter landscaped grounds with a fountain, lush lawn, and flowers (the property has its own well, so even in times of drought the gardens remain green).

> The well-furnished library and parlor are open to guests in this lovely, romantic inn. It's a popular spot for weddings and as a getaway for area residents.

The rooms are large and cool, with high ceilings and windows. There are four rooms on the main floor, each decorated individually.

The Terrace Suite has an antique bed, a fireplace, and lace at the windows. Country Manor contains a heavy four-poster and a double-headed, white tiled shower. The Estate Suite is lavish and romantic, with a white fireplace and white carpet, padded fabric walls, and a high brass bed. There's a private deck overlooking the lawn and gazebo, and a Jacuzzi for two in black and ivory. Upstairs is the Attic Hideaway, a cozy retreat in winter, when you can hear rain pattering on the roof. It has antique furniture, greenery tucked into a corner by an eyebrow window, and puffy pillows on the window seat.

A breakfast of fresh fruit, home-baked quick breads, fresh-squeezed juice, and Dutch baby pancakes (puff pancakes filled with fruit and topped with fruit syrup) or quiche is served in the dining room, on the veranda, the garden tea room, or is brought to your suite. On some afternoons tea luncheons are served to interested guests ($18.50), and the well-furnished library and parlor are open to guests in this lovely, romantic inn. The Mansion is a popular spot for weddings and as a getaway for area residents.

Central Coast

Davenport
Soquel
Capitola
Santa Cruz
Pacific Grove
Gilroy
Aptos
Pebble
Beach
Monterey
Carmel Valley
Carmel
Big Sur
1
101
Cambria
Shell Beach
Arroyo Grande
Los Alamos
Ballard
Montecito
Solvang
101
Ojai
Goleta
Santa Barbara

Best Intimate City Stops

Carmel
  Cobblestone Inn
  Cypress Inn
  La Playa Hotel
  The Stonehouse Inn
  Sundial Lodge
Montecito
  Montecito Inn
Santa Barbara
  The Upham Hotel

Best Country Inns and B&Bs

Aptos
  Apple Lane Inn
  Mangels House
Arroyo Grande
  Crystal Rose Inn
Ballard
  The Ballard Inn
Cambria
  Olallieberry Inn
  The Squibb House
Carmel Valley
  Robles del Rio Lodge
New Davenport
  Davenport Bed & Breakfast Inn
Gilroy
  Country Rose Inn and Bed and Breakfast
Los Alamos
  Union Hotel
Montecito
  San Ysidro Ranch
Santa Barbara
  The Glenborough Inn
Soquel
  The Blue Spruce Inn

Best Family Favorites

Goleta
  Circle Bar B Guest Ranch

Best Inns by the Sea

Big Sur
Deetjen's Big Sur Inn
Post Ranch Inn
Ventana
Cambria
Beach House
Carmel
Highlands Inn
The Sandpiper Inn
Monterey
The Jabberwock
Monterey Plaza Hotel
Spindrift Inn
Pacific Grove
The Centrella
Gatehouse Inn
The Green Gables Inn
Seven Gables Inn
Santa Barbara
Four Seasons Biltmore
The Old Yacht Club Inn
Shell Beach
The Cliffs at Shell Beach

Best Resorts

Carmel Valley
Carmel Valley Ranch
Quail Lodge Resort and Golf Club
Ojai
Ojai Valley Inn
Pebble Beach
The Inn at Spanish Bay
The Lodge at Pebble Beach
Santa Cruz
Chaminade
Solvang
The Alisal Guest Ranch

Romantic Hideaways

Capitola
 The Inn at Depot Hill
Carmel
 Happy Landing Inn
 Vagabond's House
Los Alamos
 Victorian Mansion
Monterey
 Old Monterey Inn
Pacific Grove
 The Martine Inn
Santa Barbara
 The Bayberry Inn
 Secret Garden Inn and Cottages
 Villa Rosa
Santa Cruz
 The Babbling Brook Inn

From **Santa Cruz** to **Santa Barbara,** the California coastline is a constant and changing panorama of ocean vistas. With the spectacular, 90-mile exception of Big Sur, the shore is less rugged here than in the northern part of the state. Numerous public parks along the way make broad sandy beaches and gentle waves easily accessible. Around the long crescent of Monterey Bay is some of the world's most celebrated scenery wind-twisted cypress trees, hidden coves, and inviting towns with sophisticated shops and restaurants. World-class golf courses, grand estates, and a forest of pine cover the southern peninsula to the resort town of **Carmel**.

 South of quaint Carmel and the resorts and pastoral land- scape of **Carmel Valley,** past the wooded bluffs of Point Lobos State Reserve, is **Big Sur.** Here Highway 1 winds through the western slopes of the Santa Lucia Mountains as they tilt to- ward the Pacific. Streams rush down ravines, tawny cliffs drop steeply to the sea, and spindrift plumes above waves that rush to break against jagged rocks far below. Under the glare of the sun, a silvery sea glints, occasionally turning a brilliant green in the eddies of a shallow cove.

 The mountains move inland as you near San Simeon and **Cambria,** and the crumpled ridges soften to grassy rolling hills, green in winter, seared dry in summer. On a hill above San Simeon is the Hearst Castle, a state historic monument open to the public. The palatial estate is filled with fabulous antiques and art treasures.

Development crowds the shoreline as you continue south to **Shell Beach** and **Arroyo Grande,** then fades to miles of ranches and vineyards as the main highway travels inland toward the Santa Ynez valley.

The city of **Santa Barbara** lies beside the sea and climbs the steep slopes of the Santa Ynez Mountains, which form a dramatic backdrop to one of California's loveliest communities. The white walls of the city's Spanish mission style architecture gleam in the ever-present sun, palm trees wave in gentle breezes, and a civilized attitude prevails. Every visitor plans to tour the beautifully restored mission. Fewer see the county courthouse, but it's well worth a visit for its outstanding architecture, colorful tiles and artwork reminiscent of Old California.

Inland from Santa Barbara, near the Topatopa Mountains and Los Padres National Forest, are vineyards, sprawling horse ranches, and the small town of **Ojai**.

APTOS

Apple Lane Inn

6265 Soquel Drive
Aptos, CA 95003
408-475-6868
800-649-8988
Fax: 408-475-6868

A 19th-century farmhouse close to Santa Cruz

Innkeepers: Douglas and Diane Groom. **Accommodations:** 5 rooms. **Rates:** $85–$175 single or double, $25 additional person. **Included:** Full breakfast. **Added:** 8.5% tax. **Payment:** Major credit cards. **Children:** Welcome by arrangement. **Pets:** Allowed by prior arrangement; $200 refundable deposit required. **Smoking:** Not allowed indoors.

Three acres of fields and gardens surround this Victorian farmhouse just south of Santa Cruz. The house was built in the 1870s, and though it's now close to a busy town and you can hear traffic in the distance, it retains the sense of seclusion and quiet you'd expect from a country home of decades past.

Velvet ties hold parlor drapes, a red settee faces the fireplace, and a player piano stands against the wall. Shelves filled with books on art and local history reach to the ceiling. A mantel clock chimes the hour. A bay window overlooks the garden, wisteria vines, and gazebo.

The guest rooms are furnished with antiques, many of them the Grooms' family heirlooms. Blossom has a ring-patterned quilt on a 14th-century French canopy bed and a flowery bathroom as big as the bedroom. It has a wicker lounge, a rocker, and a clawfoot tub with hand shower. Uncle Chester's room contains a 260-year-old Spanish mahogany four-poster. The Pineapple room is dominated by a four-poster pineapple bed and features a pineapple motif. Arbor and Orchard, in the attic, make a good family suite. The inn's wine cellar has been turned into spacious guest room with a wine theme.

> **After driving up the hillside lane from the highway, you park under the grape arbor and walk a brick path bordered by jade plants and rosemary to the front porch. Inside, the present day recedes; you've entered the Victorian era.**

There is little space for hanging clothes in the small rooms, but they're comfortable, light, and quiet. On the second floor landing there's a sitting area with a phone, a television, and a little refrigerator of juices. Morning coffee is set out here for early risers to take back to their rooms. Breakfast, served in the dining room, includes fresh fruit, a pitcher of juice, homemade granola, Diane's blue-ribbon baked goods, and a hot dish with eggs from the farm's chickens. When you leave, take an apple from the basketful in the front hall to feed the horse named Rio, or the cows, Bonnie and Lucky.

Mangels House

P.O. Box 302
570 Aptos Creek Road
Aptos, CA 95001
408-688-7982

*A country home
by a forested park*

Innkeepers: Jacqueline and Ron
Fisher. **Accommodations:** 6 rooms (all with private bath).
Rates: $110–$145 single or double, $20 additional person. **Included:** Full breakfast. **Minimum stay:** 2 nights weekends.
Payment: American Express, MasterCard, Visa accepted,
check or cash preferred. **Children:** Over age 12 welcome; additional $20 if third person in room. **Pets:** Not allowed in
rooms. **Smoking:** Allowed in restricted areas only.

Aptos is a small community just south of Santa Cruz, in the
northern curve of Monterey Bay. It was here, in the woods
along Aptos Creek, that Claus Mangels built his vacation
home in the 1880s. Mangels and his brother-in-law, Claus
Spreckels, founded the sugar beet industry in California. The
home in Aptos stayed in the family until 1979, when the
Fishers purchased the country estate and turned it into a bed-and-breakfast.

The two-story white frame house bears some resemblance
to an imposing antebellum mansion, but it's comfortably
rather than lavishly furnished. This is a large, airy, country
home with verandas, four acres of lawns and gardens, and two
creeks nearby. English antiques and contemporary decor are
combined to pleasing effect. In the immense living room, a

rough marble fireplace stands eight feet wide and reaches from floor to ceiling, with high windows beside it. Books fill the built-in shelves and there's a grand piano at one end of the room.

The dining room has a long table where breakfast is served if the house is full, but if only a few guests are present, they eat in the kitchen. Juice, scones, muffins, persimmon bread, fruit, and an egg entrée are a few of the dishes Jackie likes to serve her guests. Coffee is always set out early on an antique oak sideboard on the upstairs landing.

The large upstairs guest rooms have views of the orchards, the garden, or the wooded canyon. The smallest is the cozy Mediterranean room decorated in bright red, blue, and green prints. Nicholas's Room, named for the Fishers' son, is exotic with African artifacts, mementoes of Nicholas' two years in Zaire. The Mauve Room, with a daybed, sleeps three people. It has a marble fireplace, stencils on the pink walls, and tall windows.

In the Guest Room, you can raise one of the floor-to-ceiling windows to get to the balcony overlooking the English garden. This room has a cheery country look, with a wicker couch, white lattice headboard, and fresh roses on the table.

Mangels House is on a quiet road on the edge of the Forest of Nisene Marks State Park, 9,600 acres of wooded wilderness. The park was donated to the state by the Marks family in memory of their mother in 1963.

> Once the canyons and ridges were covered with redwoods, but by 1923 the last stand of old-growth forest was gone. When the loggers left Aptos Canyon, the forest gradually began to heal. That process continues today as new redwoods grow and wildlife returns. There are thirty miles of hiking and biking trails in this peaceful refuge.

ARROYO GRANDE

Crystal Rose Inn

789 Valley Road
Arroyo Grande, CA 93420
805-481-5566
800-ROSE-INN
Fax: 805-481-9541

*An ornate
pink home a
mile from the sea*

Innkeepers: Dona Nolan and Bonnie Royster. **Accommodations:** 9 rooms (all with private bath). **Rates:** $85–$175 single or double, $25 additional person. **Included:** Full breakfast, afternoon tea, and evening hors d'oeuvres. **Added:** Tax. **Minimum stay:** 2 nights on weekends. **Payment:** Major credit cards. **Children:** Under age 16 not appropriate. **Pets:** Not allowed. **Smoking:** Allowed outside only.

Rose is the theme of this inn on the coast halfway between San Francisco and Los Angeles. The four-story home is painted in four shades of pink, each guest room is named for a type of rose, and the garden is full of roses that are picked to adorn every room.

The ornate house, built in 1885 as a homestead for a walnut farm, is surrounded by farmland, with a sprinkling of houses here and there. Development is encroaching, but for now the fields of green beans, lettuce, and celery provide a rural context. The ocean is a mile away, as the crow flies. You can see the sand dunes from the upper floors of the Crystal Rose.

The inn also has a successful restaurant called the Hunt Club. In the garden-level eatery, pink and white linens grace the tables, and windows overlook the gazebo and rose arbor. Items on the menu include Asian-style chicken breast or sautéed shrimp with lemon butter, linguine, tomatoes and parsley. At lunch you can order everything from a steak-and-ale pie to a lamb curry rice bowl, while southern-style crab cakes and frittata Paisano are available at Sunday brunch.

In the afternoons high tea is served in the tea room. Scones topped by Dona's homemade rose petal jam made from roses on the property is the specialty. Later there are hors d'oeuvres and wine. Breakfast is served in the tea room, your guest room, or in the garden. The menu varies but there is always a fresh fruit plate, pastry basket, coffee, tea, and juice. Guests then choose an entrée, which may be the inn's own granola, a vegetable and sausage strata, or wild rose pancakes with applesauce and country bacon.

At the front of the mansion is a parlor with a fireplace, a pump organ, and a bay window. Another sitting room, a favorite of guests, features a square grand piano and table with an ongoing jigsaw puzzle.

> **There are more than forty wineries in San Luis Obispo County, many of them open for tours and tastings. Lopez Lake, the valley's water source, is ten miles inland; a popular site for water sports.**

The guest rooms are furnished with a combination of antiques and period reproductions. Each is named for a rose, with decor and a color scheme that are representative of its namesake. In Intrigue, the queen size brass bed is covered with a plum velvet bedspread. The spacious Queen Elizabeth Tower Suite has a separate sitting area; the Tiffany Suite overlooks the gardens; and the Honor Suite is decorated in white lace. Peace, located in the garden cottage, is cozy and has its own private deck.

For recreation the inn has an exercise room, bicycles, croquet, badminton, darts, bocce ball, and horseshoes. For a romantic bike ride there's even a tandem bicycle handy. Massages are available by appointment.

BALLARD

The Ballard Inn

2436 Baseline
Ballard, CA 93463
805-688-7770
800-638-BINN
Fax: 805-688-9560

*A peaceful
retreat in a
frontier village*

Owners: Steve Hyslop and Larry Stone. **Manager:** Kelly Robinson. **Accommodations:** 15 rooms. **Rates:** $160–$195 single or double; $50 additional person. **Included:** Full breakfast. **Minimum stay:** 2 nights on weekends. **Payment:** Major credit cards. **Children:** Welcome. **Pets:** Not allowed. **Smoking:** Not allowed.

Some forty miles east of Santa Barbara in the scenic Santa Ynez Valley is a village with a frontier history. It's the valley's oldest town, with a quaint church and an 1883 red schoolhouse still in operation.

On the main road, behind a white picket fence bordered with roses, is the Ballard, the image of a genteel country inn. From a long porch with white rocking chairs, double doors lead to a foyer with a vaulted white ceiling and a three-sided green marble fireplace. On the right is a dining room where a sumptuous breakfast is served. Omelettes, French toast with sautéed bananas and cinnamon, muffins, and fruit are a few of the morning offerings, and at night the dining room becomes Café Chardonnay, serving creative wine country cuisine. If you're musically inclined, you may play the black grand piano in the corner. The Vineyard Room is on the other side of the lobby. Here a carved cabinet holds games and puzzles, local wines are on display, and hors d'oeuvres and wines are set out in the evening. In keeping with the wine theme are the burgundy wallpaper in a trellis pattern, an oak bar with legs carved in grapevines, and displays of wine labels.

Sofas by the fireplace and a case of books and antiques make the living room an inviting place to relax and contemplate the portrait of William Ballard. The bearded patriarch built and operated a stagecoach stop here for the two-day run from San Luis Obispo to Santa Barbara. His adobe home has been preserved and is still in use.

The Stagecoach Room, dark with black leather chairs and a braided rug on a polished floor, is done in the colors of the original stage: burgundy, black, and gold. A painting of the Ballard Stage Station and coach hangs on the wall, along with coach lanterns and photographs of other valley coaches.

All the rooms, named for places and people important in Ballard's history, have phone jacks, air conditioning, and soundproof walls. Oak bathroom cabinets are stocked with wine soap, wine hand lotion, and champagne shampoo. Welcoming baskets of fruit, cheese, and wine are provided.

> **If you really want to get in the spirit of the place, go to the antique trunk in the corner of the Stagecoach Room and pull out a hat with trailing boa, a coonskin cap, or a shawl, and imagine yourself just stepping off the stage.**

Western Room is a tribute to the cowboys who worked the cattle ranches. It has a log cabin quilt, old-fashioned rockers, a fireplace, and a collection of western hats.

Davy Brown's Room, in honor of a rugged frontiersman who rode with the Texas Rangers, also has a rustic charm. It has a fireplace made of native stone, a wagon-wheel quilt, and American antiques.

Quite different is the Valley Room, commemorating five little valley towns with scenes from each on walls bright with California poppies. There is a Belgian armoire and matching dresser and a friendship quilt made by local quilters. Jarado's Room takes its theme from a Chumash Indian who helped construct the Ballard Station. It contains the red, white, and black designs of Chumash cave paintings. Pine furniture and arrowheads add to the atmosphere.

Cynthia's Room recalls a pioneer who came west to marry her sweetheart, William Ballard, on his deathbed. Ballard's last wish was that she marry his friend George Lewis, which she did. The room holds a portrait of the youthful widow; the handmade quilt on the bed is, appropriately, in a double wedding band pattern.

When you wish to explore the picturesque countryside, with its highly regarded wineries and thoroughbred horse ranches, the innkeepers can help you plan your route. They'll also arrange for a hot air balloon ride, a romantic way to see the valley. To the south is Solvang, a tourist-oriented village in quaint Danish style. Los Olivos, north of Ballard, has numerous art galleries.

BIG SUR

Deetjen's Big Sur Inn

Highway 1
Big Sur, CA 93920
408-667-2377
Fax: 408-667-0466

A rustic group of cabins among the trees

Manager: Andy Gagarin. **Accommodations:** 20 rooms (14 with private bath). **Rates:** $65–$175 single or double, $11 additional person (includes tax). **Payment:** Major credit cards. **Children:** Under age 12 not appropriate. **Pets:** Not allowed. **Smoking:** Not allowed.

In the early 1930s, when the coastal highway was a dirt road, Helmuth Deetjen, a Norwegian immigrant, built a homestead by the road in Castro Canyon. He and his wife, Helen, welcomed overnight guests, and they gradually added more simple frame buildings until the home became the Big Sur Inn.

There is no real town of Big Sur, though there is a post office, but you feel a sense of community in the group of homes and shops that extends for six miles along the highway. Its heart is the Big Sur Inn, where locals and tourists alike come for coffee, meals, and conversation.

The restaurant is in Helmuth Deetjen's original house. With windows that look out to wisteria vines, low-beamed ceilings, low lighting, and dark walls, the restaurant has several rooms and rustic charm. Woodstoves help to ease the chill of an early morning or cool evening, and excellent breakfasts and dinners are served. The morning menu offers pancakes, oatmeal, eggs Benedict, French toast and other dishes at reasonable prices. Dinner, by reservation, is served by candlelight with classical music in the background. Roasted New Zealand rack of lamb with a honey-mustard pecan crust, filet mignon with sautéed shiitake and oyster mushrooms, and fresh herb-marinated oak grilled chicken breast topped with a virgin olive oil and caper sauce and herb salsa served with a grilled risotto cake, are some of the tempting dishes you may find on the ever-changing menu.

> Big Sur is an 80-mile stretch of wild coastline that runs from Carmel south to San Simeon. Rugged cliffs and wooded ridges rise steeply from the shore, and every curve of the snaking road presents another astounding view of green coves, blue ocean flecked with white, and rocky headlands and beaches.

The guest rooms are back among the trees in various buildings lining a dirt path that extends above the canyon creek. No two rooms are alike, but in general, with unpainted plank walls, and rough-hewn doors, they are dark and rustic, but comfortable and clean. Amenities are few and simple such as wind up alarm clocks and doors that can only be locked from the inside (none of the rooms have keys). Despite the rustic environment, the beds are firm and cozy under down comforters. In Grampa's, across from the restaurant, an old radio rests on the big desk and an antique pump organ stands against a wall. In Château Fiasco behind the restaurant, you feel as if you're in a treehouse. It has a writing desk, private porch, and a small but modern bath with a shower. There's a wood-burning stove and a handsome coverlet on the bed in Antique Apartment, and the adjoining room, called the Hostelry, has a twin bed topped by a teddy bear.

Not all the rooms have a backwoods atmosphere. Faraway,

perched at the edge of the canyon, has an all redwood interior, a small porch, and a private fenced area with ferns and fuchsias. Chalet, a personal favorite, is brighter than many of the rooms due to white walls and plentiful windows. The front room, which looks out to towering redwoods and a running stream below, has a queen-size bed and an attractive antique vanity. In the adjoining room, two twin beds with French country print coverlets, a stuffed bunny on the pillow, and framed illustrations from children's books on the wall will take you back to your childhood.

Post Ranch Inn

P.O. Box 219
Big Sur, CA 93920
408-667-2200
800-527-2200
Fax: 408-667-2824

A unique contemporary inn above the Pacific

Manager: Larry Callahan. **Accommodations:** 30 suites, 1 bedroom suite, 1 house. **Rates:** $265–$525, $50 additional person, 1 bedroom suite $425 for 4 people, Post House $900. **Included:** Expanded Continental breakfast. **Added:** 10% tax. **Minimum:** 2 nights on weekends. **Payment:** Major credit cards. **Children:** Discouraged. **Pets:** Not allowed. **Smoking:** Allowed in restricted areas only.

Tucked against a cliff 1,200 feet above the spectacular Big Sur coast, this is the resort that critics have raved about since it opened in 1992. Imaginative and whimsical, yet filled with the practical comforts travelers appreciate, Post Ranch deserves all its accolades. Great care was lavished on the planning and construction, and it shows in almost every detail.

> In building this resort, only one tree went down, an example of a concern for the environment that is apparent at every turn. Some call the construction "politically correct"; more astute observers note that this commitment to protecting the land is more than merely political.

Five of the redwood guest units are Ocean Houses. Overlooking the Pacific, they have sod roofs covered with grass and wildflowers. Others, just as round as giant tree trunks, are Coast Houses and Mountain Houses. The seven Tree Houses stand on stilts, designed to protect the roots of the surrounding redwood trees. When these houses are wreathed in the mists that often move along the coast, the houses seem to float in the branches. One building, the Butterfly House, has six units and is shaped like a butterfly with its wings outstretched.

Inside, the rooms have character and style, as well as the usual luxury hotel features: coffeemakers, mini-bars, phones, music systems, fireplaces, and Jacuzzi tubs. The floors are of slate and the angled and curved walls of natural wood. The decor is spare, with nothing to detract from the dramatic views. Quiet and privacy are paramount.

Also on the 98-acre property, once part of a 1,600-acre cattle ranch, are groves of madrone and oak trees, trails, grassy meadows, and a fish pond.

Guests are invited to enjoy the panorama from the outdoor basking pool, swim in the lap pool, get a massage or tarot card reading, select a book from the little library, and, especially, dine in the exquisite Sierra Mar restaurant. Perched at the edge of a cliff, it looks out over the riveting ocean view. Raised sections allow every table to have a view. A buffet breakfast is set out here (or breakfast will be brought to your room if you prefer). Sierra Mar also serves lunch and memorable dinners.

Wendy Little, the chef, came to Sierra Mar from the renowned Mustard's Grill in Napa. Her fresh California cuisine features simple but interesting dishes on a fixed price menu that changes regularly, but might include sautéed baby abalone with almonds and basil, rack of venison with chanterelles and smoked bacon, and albacore with sesame, shiitake, and wasabi butter. The restaurant's organic garden provides much of the produce. The broad wine list offers more than 2,000 selections.

Ventana

Highway 1
Big Sur, CA 93920
408-667-2331, 408-624-4812
800-628-6500
Fax: 408-667-0573

A contemporary inn with a grand view and quiet location

General manager: Randy Smith. **Accommodations:** 59 rooms and suites, and 3 houses. **Rates:** $175–$195 single or double, $50 additional person; suites $360–$400. **Included:** Expanded Continental breakfast and wine and cheese buffet. **Added:** 10.5% tax. **Minimum stay:** 2 nights on weekends. **Payment:** Major credit cards. **Children:** Discouraged. **Pets:** Not allowed. **Smoking:** Not allowed in restaurant; nonsmoking rooms are available.

A thousand feet above the sea, where the Santa Lucia Mountains rise in steep folds and ridges along the dramatic Big Sur coast, Ventana's weathered cedar buildings blend with their environment of rocky canyons, meadows, and redwood groves.

The inn, built in 1975, is one hundred fifty miles south of San Francisco. Monterey Peninsula Airport, thirty-five miles north, has rental cars. Contemporary buildings, latticed against the sun, are dispersed among groves of redwood, oak, and bay laurel. In the main lodge is an airy glass and cedar lobby with a large stone fireplace. Every afternoon complimentary wines and cheeses are presented, and breakfast with pastries made on the premises is served here or delivered to your room.

The guest rooms are decorated tastefully in Swedish country style, all light woods and wide windows. Most of them have wood-burning fireplaces and hot tubs, or dining alcoves with wet bars and refrigerators. All the rooms are furnished with wicker and rush chairs, natural wood paneling, hand-painted headboards with complementing handmade quilts, fine pastel linens, honor bars, and televisions with VCRs. The large tiled baths have separate vanities, coffeemakers, hair dryers, and make-up mirrors. Every room has a private balcony or patio with an ocean or mountain view.

> **This is country lodging at its best, offering relaxation and tranquility in a setting of stunning beauty. There are no tennis courts or golf courses within miles; Ventana is a place to relax, unwind, go for walks, go for a swim, take a sauna, and read in the sun or by the fire.**

The rooms in the Pacific House have window seats and canopy beds set with fluffy pillows.

A library and lounge, which serves as another breakfast room, are near the second swimming pool and a Japanese hot tub complex. With a casual, European attitude toward sunbathing, nudity is allowed in some areas and swimwear is optional in the coed hot tub.

Ventana's dining room, a delightful walk up lighted paths from the inn, is noted for its extraordinary cuisine. With the much-acclaimed Joachim Splichal as consulting chef, many travelers come just for the imaginatively prepared food. The menu features fresh local fish, herbs and vegetables grown on the grounds, wild mushrooms and berries, and breads from the inn's own bakery. There's an extensive wine list of California and imported labels.

The food may be exceptional, but the setting is incomparable. The 50-mile view of the misty Big Sur coast from above is breathtaking, worthy of hours of admiration from the restaurant windows or from the broad, flowery terrace where lunch and cocktails are served.

Ventana, which means "window" in Spanish, offers many vistas of mountains, sea, and sky, and given its peace and serenity, it can also be a window to renewed inner perspectives.

CAMBRIA

Beach House

6360 Moonstone Beach Drive
Cambria, CA 93428
805-927-3136

A bed-and-breakfast by the sea

Innkeepers: Penny Hitch and Kernn McKinnon. **Accommodations:** 7 rooms (all with private bath). **Rates:** $125–$140 single or double. **Included:** Full breakfast. **Added:** Tax. **Payment:** MasterCard, Visa; no personal checks. **Children:** Welcome (limit of 2 persons per room). **Pets:** Not allowed. **Smoking:** Not allowed.

The village of Cambria is best known for its proximity to the San Simeon Historical Monument, often called the Hearst Castle.

Beach House, just outside Cambria, is on a quiet road by the shore. The sound of rumbling breakers can be heard from every room. The modern blue house with angles and dormers and tall windows opened as a bed-and-breakfast in 1986. Penny Hitch and her daughter operate the little inn, though the rest of the family helps too. They provide such hospitable touches as umbrellas in the entryway, wine and cheese in the evenings, and bicycles to lend if you'd like to ride the level roads in the area.

The guest rooms are spread over three floors and a two-room bungalow in back. All have television with a cable movie channel. They're decorated in a contemporary country style, with white wicker furnishings and light shades of plum, gray, blue, and white.

From the common room, on the second floor, sliding glass doors open to a large deck and an expansive ocean view. Binoculars and a telescope are provided for spotting birds and boats and deciding whether that black shape in the water is a rock or a whale. It's a casual and inviting space, with bentwood rockers by a tiled fireplace, books, games, and a long table where breakfast is served. Fruit, salmon quiche, stuffed French toast, muffins, and granola are some of the morning choices. Guests have the use of a microwave oven and a coffeemaker.

Above the common room on the third-floor loft, closed off by smoked-glass sliding doors, is a large room that is everybody's favorite. It has a king-size platform bed, great views on three sides, a cavernous walk-in closet, and a wall-length mirror in the bathroom. You might have a noise problem here, as the common room is just below, but Penny says no one has complained so far. Another favorite is in the back cottage. This light and airy room has only a partial ocean view, but the white walls flood with morning sun. There's a small bath and a wicker lounge. Family photos create a homey atmosphere.

> Hearst Castle, near Cambria, is a magnificent estate that is a major tourist attraction. Daily tours allow visitors to see the opulence and fine art that William Randolph Hearst and his friends enjoyed in the '20s and '30s.

Guests enjoy perusing menus by the upstairs fire, for Cambria has several good restaurants. Penny owns the Moonstone Beach Bar and Grill which serves seafood, steaks, and pastas. Fish tacos are a popular favorite at lunch. Other recommended restaurants include Ian's, Rigdon Hall, Robin's, and Sow's Ear.

Penny also owns the Cambria Landing Inn up the street from the Beach House which you may want to inquire about if you prefer a more traditional hotel style atmosphere to a bed-and-breakfast environment. Guest rooms in the two-story main building have sleigh beds, reproduction furniture, ceiling fans, TVs in armoires, and floral decor. Guests staying in the Jacuzzi suites receive a complimentary bottle of champagne every day they stay, and the suites have private entrances, four-poster beds, gas fireplaces, and TVs with VCRs.

Olallieberry Inn

2476 Main Street
Cambria, CA 93428
805-927-3222
Fax: 805-927-0202

> *A congenial bed-
> and-breakfast
> on the edge of
> Cambria*

Innkeepers: Peter and Carol Ann Irsfeld. **Accommodations:** 6 rooms (all with private bath). **Rates:** $85–$175. **Included:** Full breakfast and afternoon hors d'oeuvres. **Added:** Tax. **Payment:** MasterCard and Visa. **Children:** Not appropriate. **Pets:** Not allowed. **Smoking:** Allowed outside only.

This pleasant beige clapboard house, with white and plum trim, sits on the edge of the coastal town of Cambria. Built in 1873, when the town was in its infancy, the home is a registered historic landmark. Planted in 1885, the giant redwood that towers over the front yard garden and is nearly as old as the home.

Just inside the front door there's a formal Victorian parlor with a grandfather clock and handsome china display case. Yet despite the formal first impression, the mood is casual at this homey inn. You'll be welcomed by one of the convivial innkeepers, and be taught a fetching trick by their friendly black cocker named Niki.

Beyond the front parlor there's the considerably less formal gathering room with blue and white checked country fabrics, and a long Pennsylvanian farmhouse table made from barn siding where breakfast is served. Guests are welcome to use the refrigerator, stereo, telephone, and books located in an adjoining alcove. French doors lead from the gathering room out to a back porch set with wicker chairs and sofas where you can watch a game of croquet on the back lawn, or wander down to Santa Rosa Creek which borders the property.

Three guest rooms are on the first floor. San Simeon has a tub for two, a fireplace, petit rose wallpaper, and a king-size bed with embroidered pillows, a rose print coverlet, and matching curtains. Cambria, with a fireplace and sunken tub, is the most popular room for honeymooners. Wheelchair accessible, it has a queen-size iron bed draped in pink taffeta, and a mirrored armoire. Of all the guest rooms, Santa Rosa has the most Victorian decor.

> Take some time to enjoy the inn's gardens. Artichokes, colorful red and green Swiss chard, rosemary, marjoram, thyme, lettuce, and mint are just a few of the plants found in the bountiful herb garden. The adjoining "Secret Garden" has a central fountain and a white wrought iron bench, inviting visitors to linger.

There are three additional guest rooms upstairs. Olallieberry, under slanted ceilings, is a riot of violet with a lavender velvet fainting couch and a violet motif coverlet atop the queen-size bed. Olallieberry's clawfoot tub for two is well known among repeat guests. Harmony room, in lace, has a hall bath; and in Room at the Top you can enjoy the wicker furnishings, a gas fireplace, and a Nancy Drew mystery (there's a complete set), while curled up in the window seat overlooking the garden.

In keeping with Peter and Carol Ann's emphasis on hospitality, they provide ample meals. In the morning, crêpes filled with almond custard, fresh strawberries, kiwi, and banana; eggs baked in a hash brown potato crust topped with cheddar and salsa; or stuffed French toast are served. Freshly baked muffins, granola, yogurt, seasonal fruit, freshly squeezed juice, and gourmet coffees and teas are also offered. Afternoon hors d'oeuvres may be goat cheese and roasted garlic served with freshly baked focaccia, or a black olive, roasted garlic, and rosemary pizza garnished with herbs from the garden. If you're still hungry, Cambria's shops and restaurants are nearby.

At press time plans were under way to turn the Irsfeld's former residence adjacent to the inn into additional guest rooms. Several rooms with antique furnishings, fireplaces, and modern baths are planned, so you may wish to inquire about the status of these rooms when you book your reservation.

The Squibb House

4063 Burton Drive
Cambria, CA 93428
805-927-9600

A beautifully restored Victorian in the heart of Cambria

Owner: Bruce Black. **Accommodations:** 5 rooms (all with private bath; outhouse available upon request). **Rates:** $95–$125. **Included:** Continental breakfast. **Added:** Tax. **Payment:** MasterCard and Visa. **Children:** Not appropriate. **Pets:** Not allowed. **Smoking:** Not allowed.

Guests are not the only ones to pause in front of this cheerful yellow Gothic-style Victorian home in downtown Cambria. On one of the main streets in the shopping district, tourists are often seen stopping to enjoy its gingerbread trim and colorful garden abloom with hollyhocks, nasturtium, snapdragons, daisies, pansies, and geraniums.

Named for the Squibb family who were former owners, the home was built in 1877. Over the years the home was occupied by many of Cambria's most active citizens, until Bruce Black took over ownership in the early 1990s, saving the splendid structure from an uncertain fate. A master craftsman, Bruce restored the home with loving care, and furnished the bed and breakfast with many pieces he built himself.

Throughout, the inn has a crisp, clean look. There are two bedrooms on the first floor and three on the second. The Village Room looks out to charming Burton Street, lined with shops and restaurants. Gray-washed furniture, wicker chairs, a wooden washstand, floral wreath, and a queen-size bed topped by a patchwork quilt give the room a fresh country flavor.

> **Because of its in-town location, the Squibb House is convenient to many shops and restaurants. Cambria beach is about a mile from the inn, and the incredible Hearst Castle is less than ten miles away.**

In the Gothic Room is a lovely pine wardrobe with matching bedside tables, and a gas-lit stove. On the ground floor, the Garden Room has its own entrance, and the bed's headboard matches the gingerbread scrollwork on its private porch. Televisions and telephones are not provided, but are available upon request.

Breakfast, which consists of fresh pastries from a neighboring bakery and fruit, is served in the formal parlor downstairs, or in bed if you prefer. In the afternoon, coffee, tea, fruit, cheese, and a sweet treat are offered to guests. Offstreet parking is available behind the inn.

CAPITOLA

The Inn at Depot Hill

250 Monterey Avenue
Capitola, CA 95010
408-462-3376
800-572-2632
Fax: 408-462-3697

> *An opulent hillside inn near the sea*

Innkeepers: Suzanne Lankes and Dan Floyd. **Accommodations:** 8 suites (all with private bath). **Rates:** $165–$250 single or double. **Included:** Full breakfast, afternoon tea and evening dessert. **Minimum stay:** 2 nights on weekends when Saturday included. **Payment:** Major credit cards. **Children:** Not suitable. **Pets:** Not allowed. **Smoking:** Not allowed indoors.

Sumptuous and sophisticated, the Inn at Depot Hill is one of the most romantic lodgings on the coast. It's come a long way from its origins as a 1901 train depot on a hill above Capitola, a charming seaside village south of Santa Cruz. The depot lobby is now a parlor with polished floors, a baby grand piano, and built-in bookshelves.

Each suite has been painstakingly furnished and decorated to evoke the mood of a train destination. The Paris room is an elegant study in black and white. It has fabric walls, a double fireplace, French doors to a patio, and a bath in black and white marble. Sissinghurst is like a garden room in a traditional English country inn, with a canopy bed and raised fireplace.

> **The inn holds a few reminders of turn-of-the-century rail travel. The original columns and ticket windows are there, and the dining room, once the ticket office, is decorated with a rack of old-fashioned baggage and a trompe l'oeil scene that creates the illusion of countryside seen from a train window.**

Delft is exquisite in blue and white; Stratford-on-Avon is cozy with a window seat and trellis wallpaper; Portofino has the frescoed walls of an Italian villa; and Cote d'Azur, once the depot's baggage room, has a Mediterranean theme with tiled floors, whitewashed columns, and an iron bed draped in chintz.

Capitola Beach is casual and contemporary, with a metal four-poster bed. The Railroad Baron's Room, in red, is the grandest, with ornate moldings, thick draperies, a domed ceiling, and damask and silk fabrics.

Each room has a television with VCR, a stereo system, phones with modem and fax capability, a marble bath with a two-person shower, and such luxurious extras as a hair dryer, clothes steamer, Egyptian cotton towels, robes, fresh roses, and embroidered Belgian linens. Some rooms have private brick patios with hot tubs and separate entrances.

Breakfast is served in the dining room, on the terrace, or in your own room. Entrées such as frittatas make up the international menu, and Depot Hill eggs is the inn's specialty dish. For other meals, Santa Cruz and Capitola have several excellent restaurants. The inn provides afternoon tea or wine, after-dinner dessert, and off-street parking.

At press time, plans were under way to add four more guest rooms to the inn. You may want to inquire about these rooms as well when you book your reservation.

CARMEL

Cobblestone Inn

P.O. Box 3185
Carmel, CA 93921
408-625-5222
800-833-8836
Fax: 408-625-0478

*An inn with
English charm
in the heart
of Carmel*

Owners: Roger and Sally Post. **Innkeeper:** Ray Farnsworth. **Accommodations:** 24 rooms. **Rates:** $95–$150 single or double; suites $160–$175. **Included:** Full breakfast and afternoon refreshments. **Added:** Tax. **Payment:** Major credit cards. **Children:** Welcome. **Pets:** Not allowed. **Smoking:** Not allowed.

It could be said that the Cobblestone Inn is Carmel to the core, as the rocks that make up its stone exterior and stony interior fireplaces all came from the Carmel river. On Ocean Avenue on the edge of the downtown shopping district, the inn is perfectly situated for exploring the charming seaside town.

A carousel horse in the lobby alerts well-traveled guests that they are checking in to a Four Sisters Inn. For those not familiar with the small, well-run inn group owned by Roger and Sally Post, they are about to be treated to the quality service and accommodations common to all Four Sisters Inns. Teddy Bears in the comfortable main living room are another trademark of the respected inn group.

> **The Cobblestone offers services often found only at luxury hotels, such as twice-daily housekeeping and a morning newspaper.**

The horse-shoe shaped inn wraps around a central slate courtyard where guests often choose to eat their breakfast of muesli, home-baked breads, fresh fruit, cereal, and a hot entrée. When the weather does not permit patio dining, breakfast is served in the dining room, or you can request breakfast in bed if you prefer. In the afternoons guests gather for tea or wine, and later retire to their rooms with homemade cookies in hand.

Each room in the two-story inn is individually decorated. Some have canopy beds, others have pine furnishings and dried floral arrangements. Mauve carpeting, floral wallpaper, and a cobblestone fireplace are common to each, and all rooms have an English country flavor. Although the rooms vary in size, all have telephones, televisions, private baths, terry robes, and small refrigerators stocked with cold drinks. Suites have sitting areas and wet bars.

The shops and restaurants of Carmel are in easy walking distance from the inn. For those wishing to venture farther, the inn has bicycles that guests can use to explore the area's glorious coastal terrain.

Cypress Inn

P.O. Box Y
Lincoln & 7th
Carmel, CA 93921
408-624-3871
800-443-7443
Fax: 408-624-8216

*A small hotel
with a light,
bright atmosphere*

General manager: David Wolf. **Accommodations:** 33 rooms. **Rates:** $98–$265 single or double, $15 additional person, off-season rates available. **Included:** Continental breakfast. **Added:** 10.5% tax. **Minimum stay:** 2 nights on weekends. **Payment:** Major credit cards. **Children:** Welcome (no cribs or rollaways available). **Pets:** Allowed with permission. **Smoking:** Nonsmoking rooms available.

In the heart of quaint Carmel-by-the-Sea on the Monterey Peninsula, the Cypress first captures your eye with its white Moorish Mediterranean facade and red Spanish tile roof. When the hotel opened in 1929, it was hailed as a landmark for its classic exterior and stately interior. That charm has been restored, and it is again a fine and quiet place to stay, gracious in its tasteful simplicity. With the updated accommodations are hints of the hotel's origins in ceramic tiles, arched windows, oak flooring, and a few antiques.

This is one of the few hotels where pets are welcome, thanks to the influence of animal lover Doris Day. You will often see pampered pets being paraded through the lobby by adoring owners, and there's a photo album of pet guests in the living room.

The Cypress abuts the sidewalk on Lincoln Street (there's no number — Carmel doesn't allow street addresses), facing the Church of the Wayfarer and its garden across the street. A few brick steps lead to the reception area. On the right is a sitting room, light with peach walls, a large white fireplace, and white beamed ceiling. Tall windows face the street on one side; on the other are three sets of double glass doors leading to a serene courtyard with blooming fuchsia and morning sun. Garden furniture is placed among the shrubs and topiary ivy, and an outdoor fire-place blazes on cool evenings.

Guest rooms, on two floors, are cheerful, and are decorated in peaches and silvers. They look out to the garden courtyard, flowering alley, or to town. Each room has fresh fruit and flowers, sherry, a telephone, a television, and a tiled bath. Different configurations are available; some have two twin beds, others have a double or a king, and some include fire-places.

Six specialty rooms are noted for their size and amenities — sitting areas, wet bars, balconies, and ocean views. One has a pleasant terrace with blooming bougainvillea and gerani-ums and an ocean view. Another has a canopy king-size bed, fireplace, and a Jacuzzi. The Tower Suite has a bedroom up-stairs surrounded by arched windows with ocean views and a living room and bath downstairs. Room 219 is reached by climbing a flight of stairs from the courtyard. It has comfy seating in front of its fireplace, and French doors open onto a small patio.

The concierge and staff are uniformly obliging about pro-viding information on nearby attractions and restaurants. Menus are available to help you choose a spot for dinner. Breakfast is served in the courtyard, in your room, or in the li-brary bar where Doris Day movie posters grace the walls. (Day is one of the owners of the inn.)

Happy Landing Inn

P.O. Box 2619
Monte Verde Between 5th and 6th
Carmel, CA 93921
408-624-7917

*A quaint,
relaxing inn with
a garden setting*

Innkeepers: Robert Ballard and Richard Stewart. **Accommodations:** 5 rooms and 2 suites. **Rates:** $90–$155. **Included:** Expanded Continental breakfast. **Added:** 10% tax. **Minimum stay:** 2 nights on weekends. **Payment:** MasterCard, Visa. **Children:** Welcome. **Pets:** Not allowed. **Smoking:** Nonsmoking rooms available.

The focus of this pretty inn is its central garden. If you like ponds and fountains, lush vines, garden gnomes, and pots overflowing with geraniums and fuchsias, you will love this spot. It's a beautiful retreat where you can sit under a white trellis with hanging plants or watch the goldfish dart among the water lilies.

Although it is a few blocks from the sea and you can glimpse the water from some windows, Happy Landing is not the place to go for panoramic views of the Pacific. "We get glimpses, not ocean views," says Robert Ballard. "Carmel is really an urban forest, full of trees."

Most of the guest rooms are in three pink, one-story buildings that form a U around the garden; their private entrances are blue doors under curved arches, each painted with birds and vines — quintessentially quaint Carmel. On the fourth side of the garden, the street side, is the main building with the office and common room. Here guests may relax, read, or have tea and cookies.

The rooms are furnished individually with antiques and modern comforts such as hair dryers and thick pink towels. There are brass beds, balloon shades or cottage curtains, iron latches on the built-in drawers, casement windows, and fresh flowers.

Room 1, in yellows, has a queen-size brass bed and a Mexican tiled fireplace. Room 7 is pretty and feminine, and has charming animal lithographs on the walls. Room 4 is a suite with a fireplace and sofa bed in the living room, a king-size bed in the bedroom, and a lovely hand-painted sink and floral wallpaper in the cheerful bath.

Gorgeous foxglove grows just outside the door of Room 3. Also a suite, it has a hand-painted floral design on its ceiling, wicker furnishings, and stained glass windows in the bath. The cottages, in darker colors than the standard guests' rooms, are more like private homes with fully equipped kitchens, private parking, and decor that includes Brazilian artifacts.

When you're ready for breakfast, you part the curtains or raise the shades — that's the signal for the innkeeper to bring your tray. You'll have fruit, fresh orange juice, muffins or scones, and quiche or strata for breakfast.

Happy Landing has menus for nearby restaurants. Among those recommended are Flaherty's for good seafood and a casual atmosphere, and Piatti's for flavorful Italian cookery.

Highlands Inn

P.O. Box 1700
Carmel, CA 93921
408-624-3801
800-682-4811
Fax: 408-626-1574

*A contemporary
resort with an
ocean view*

General manager: David Fink. **Accommodations:** 142 rooms and suites. **Rates:** $265 and up single or double in Sur rooms, $25 additional person; suites $325–$600. **Added:** Tax. **Payment:** Major credit cards. **Children:** Under age 18 free in room with parent. **Pets:** Dogs allowed if 10 pounds or less. **Smoking:** Allowed.

Terraced against the hillside above the rocky, rugged cliffs south of Carmel, this contemporary inn of stone and wood offers grand views, fine food, and luxurious accommodations. Completely transformed in the 1980s from a humbler lodging, the main building now has a skylighted promenade, bleached oak floors, a big lobby with a beamed ceiling and two granite fireplaces, and a snazzy restaurant, Pacific's Edge.

It's a curious blend of formal (jackets and ties are requested in the restaurant) and casual (the friendly parking valets wear shorts), of natural beauty and corporate sleekness.

In the lounge, wide windows overlook spectacular vistas of sea and sky, and entertainment is offered in the evenings. Around the corner is the two-tiered restaurant, known for its outstanding thirty-one-page wine list, Continental cuisine, and fresh seafood. Chilean sea bass with a white bean vinaigrette, braised leeks and bacon potatoes; or grilled Atlantic salmon wrapped in pancetta with local baby artichokes, garlic, and a tangy onion rosemary sauce are examples of the main courses you may wish to try. You can eat more casually and on the terrace at the California Market, a combined deli, tavern, and boutique.

Although the views of the Monterey pines and the ocean are striking, there is no immediate access to the shore. The action is at the resort itself. There are three whirlpool tubs, a swimming pool, a VCR library of movies, board games, and dancing to the music of a jazz combo in the lounge. Mountain bikes are available, and tennis, golf, and horseback riding are nearby.

The Highlands's guest rooms are scattered among twenty-two buildings and the main lodge. They're all furnished in a contemporary style, and amenities include binoculars for looking at the view, televisions with built-in VCRs, bathrobes, coffeemakers, and refrigerators. Most have fireplaces and kitchens. Some are equipped with CD players and spa baths. Sizes and views vary; you can get a single room or a two-bedroom townhouse, a view of the road or a panoramic ocean view. Generally, the higher up the hill you go, the better the room. Some of the rooms close to the pool are good choices, too.

La Playa Hotel

P.O. Box 900
Camino Real & 8th
Carmel, CA 93921
408-624-6476
800-582-8900 in California
Fax: 408-624-7966

> *A Mediterranean hotel with ocean views*

Owner: Newton A. Cope, Sr. **General manager:** Tom Glidden. **Accommodations:** 75 rooms and 5 cottages. **Rates:** $115–$210 single or double, $15 additional person; suites and cottages $210–$495. **Added:** Tax. **Payment:** Major credit cards. **Children:** Under age 12 free in room with parents. **Pets:** Not allowed. **Smoking:** Nonsmoking rooms available.

Two blocks from Carmel's beach is a hotel that is a lovely find. La Playa has a classic Mediterranean look, with pink walls, red tiled roofs, and terraced gardens. In the gardens are a heated swimming pool, a fountain, a filigreed black iron gazebo, and a brick patio. There are hundreds of colorful flowers and beds of pungent herbs, many used in the kitchen.

The hotel grew from a rockwork mansion built in 1904 by artist Chris Jorgensen for his bride, a daughter of San Francisco's Ghirardelli family. Later, the property was turned into a hotel and in 1983 sold to the Cope family and completely restored. Newton Cope is a historian who concentrates on turn-of-the-century California and the

> "Our concierges are human encyclopedias," the desk clerk declares proudly, citing a few of the requests they fill with ease — from getting postage stamps or a recipe to assisting you with golf reservations.

Old West. Photographs and memorabilia from his collections hang on the walls of La Playa's public spaces.

Parts of the original mansion still exist — mainly the rockwork at the entrance of the L-shaped building, and the curving staircase that leads up from the lobby.

The hotel's restaurant, the Terrace Grill, is open for three meals a day and Sunday brunch. Continental cuisine, using local seafood and produce, is served in this room above the gardens. The wine list includes California, French, and Italian labels and several rare old ports and sherries. If you wish to eat outdoors while you watch the sunset, the terrace is a romantic spot.

About a third of the guest rooms have ocean views, three are beside the pool, and nine have private walled patios. Those without an ocean view overlook the fragrant garden, the patio, or residential Carmel. The hotel's mermaid motif is seen in unexpected places — embroidered on the towels and carved into the driftwood-like headboards. The decor is a mix of heavy, Spanish-style furniture and plain white walls and louvered shutters. Porcelain lamps, rawhide chairs, and brass tables mingle to create an effect that works best in the larger rooms; the smaller ones feel crowded. The views, especially from the upstairs rooms that face west, are stunning.

In a separate building on Camino Real, the executive suite is a good choice for entertaining a group. It has a meeting room, a kitchen, a living room with a gas fireplace, and an angled glass wall that opens to broad patios. There's a large bedroom with solid carved furniture, a vaulted beam ceiling, and two closets.

La Playa's five cottages are a block away from the hotel, toward the beach. Tucked away amid their own gardens, they are much more private than the hotel rooms, yet cottage guests are welcome to use the swimming pool and all of the other facilities at the hotel. Room service delivery is available to the cottages during the day. You can hear the ocean's roar from the one-bedroom Skyway Cottage, and the sunny yellow shingled Moongate Cottage also has one bedroom. Loghaven, named for its log exterior, is the largest. A good choice for a family, it contains three bedrooms, 2½ baths, and a full kitchen, living room, and dining room. Four cottages have kitchens.

The Sandpiper Inn

2408 Bay View Avenue
Carmel, CA 93923
408-624-6433
800-633-6433
Fax: 408-624-5964

> *An ocean-view*
> *home with warm*
> *hospitality*

Owners: Graeme and Irene MacKenzie. **Accommodations:** 16 rooms (all with private bath). **Rates:** $95–$190 single or double, $20 additional person. **Included:** Expanded Continental breakfast. **Added:** 10% tax. **Minimum stay:** 2 nights on weekends, 3–4 nights on some holidays. **Payment:** Major credit cards. **Children:** Age 12 and older welcome. **Pets:** Not allowed. **Smoking:** Not allowed indoors.

One hundred yards from Carmel Beach, the Sandpiper has some of the best ocean views in town. The beige stucco house with brown shutters and green awnings stands on a residential corner, surrounded by green hedges and pots of bright flowers. It's a welcoming place, and the innkeepers take care to keep it that way.

The MacKenzies, who've owned the house since 1975, had a strong background in the resort business when they opened the Sandpiper. Originally from Scotland, they worked in the Orient and Bermuda before settling in Carmel. Memorabilia from their travels is displayed throughout the house, along with traditional and contemporary furniture and some rare antiques.

A dark beamed ceiling and small chandeliers grace the living room, where a fire is usually crackling in the stone hearth. A breakfast of natural cereal, freshly baked muffins (almond raspberry filled are a favorite), croissants, and fruit is served buffet-style, by windows that overlook the front garden and glimpse the sea.

Graeme and Irene are well aware of travelers' preferences; their expertise has pleased visitors from seventy countries. They have numerous menus from nearby restaurants and will make reservations for dinner, tennis, and golf. Guests may make tea in the kitchen and use the refrigerator to store drinks and snacks. Sherry is served every evening.

> **The Sandpiper is close to a path that winds above the shore. If Carmel Beach is crowded, go south to Carmel River State Beach, which is less frequented. It has a lagoon and natural preserve where you may see herons, brown pelicans, and other wildlife and birds.**

Guest room furnishings vary, ranging from standard contemporary to European antiques and reproductions. Fresh flowers, walk-in closets in the largest rooms, modern baths with Crabtree & Evelyn toiletries, and hair dryers and makeup mirrors are among their features. Some have fireplaces. Several rooms have views of the ocean and Pebble Beach. None have television or phones, but there's a pay phone in the hall for guests. Behind the fragrant garden are three charming cottage rooms with skylights.

Among Carmel's noted restaurants are Flaherty's, serving good fresh seafood, Rio Grill in Crossroads shopping center, and Sans Souci.

The Stonehouse Inn

P.O. Box 2517
8th below Monte Verde
Carmel, CA 93921
408-624-4569
800-748-6618

A bed-and-breakfast retreat a few blocks from the beach

Innkeeper: A. Navailles. **Accommodations:** 6 rooms (share 3 baths). **Rates:** $90–$145 single or double. **Included:** Full breakfast and evening wine and hors d'oeuvres. **Payment:** MasterCard, Visa. **Children:** Age 12 and older welcome. **Pets:** Not allowed. **Smoking:** Not allowed.

This handsome stone inn, built in 1906, offers a peaceful retreat in a residential neighborhood of quaint Carmel-by-the-Sea. Its first owner was Josephine ("Nana") Foster, an eccentric and beloved patron of the arts, whose many guests included important artists and writers of the day.

In recognition of this history, the guest rooms are named for her notable visitors, as well as for Nana herself. Jack London, one of the larger rooms, has a daybed as well as a white iron and brass bed. Another large

For the best clam chowder on the peninsula, local residents will refer you to the Monterey Aquarium, which you'll undoubtedly want to see anyway. Just schedule your visit for lunchtime.

room, and the most expensive, is George Sterling, which has an unusual king-size canopy bed draped in lace, a distant view of the ocean, a walk-in closet, and a reading area with an antique desk.

Lola Montez is quaint, with a high antique four-poster bed under the eaves. Nana's room is quite small — a good choice for one person. It's a hideaway with an antique armoire and a cotton duvet on the double bed. Natural light floods the room through a skylight. This room has a tiny washbasin in one corner. In peaches and deep greens, Mary Austin is cute and comfy. Soft colors, fresh flowers, and comfortable quilts make the guest rooms welcoming havens.

In the European style, all the rooms share three baths. One, done in white tile, has a pedestal sink, a shower, and a skylight with a view of the dark green branches of a Monterey cypress tree. Another also has a skylight and a shower, as well as a clawfoot tub.

In the morning there's a full breakfast of breads and jams, perhaps a sweet muffin, cereal, fruit cocktail or grapefruit, oatmeal, juice, coffee, tea, and meat and eggs, French toast or hot cakes. You can eat in the small, sunny dining room or on the patio. The living room is a big, informal gathering place where hors d'oeuvres — hot in winter, cold in summer — are available every evening and a fire burns steadily in the big stone fireplace (ask about the secret hiding place in the stone).

Sundial Lodge

P.O. Box J
Monte Verde and 7th Avenue
Carmel, CA 93921
408-624-8578
Fax: 408-626-1018

A small hotel surrounding a flower-filled courtyard

Manager: Robbin Imus. **Rates:** $105–$170 single or double, $15 additional person; off season discounts available. **Included:** Continental breakfast. **Minimum stay:** 2 nights on weekends. **Added:** 10% tax. **Payment:** Major credit cards. **Children:** Over age 5 welcome. **Pets:** Not allowed. **Smoking:** Nonsmoking rooms available.

Two hours south of San Francisco, the little town of Carmel lies on a long, gradual slope between Highway 1 and the Pacific. Sundial Lodge is on Monte Verde Street, a few blocks above the beach. The two-story building with gray shutters and a blue awning has tidy boxes of privet in front. Red geraniums tumble from window boxes, and bright yellow marigolds bloom against the wall.

> **Despite its heavily congested tourist traffic in summer, Carmel-by-the-Sea retains its charm. The shops are a delight, the restaurants excellent, and the beaches inviting.**

The flowery entrance hints at what you'll see as you step through a vine-covered trellis to a central brick courtyard. It's a bower of daisies, fuchsias, begonias, ferns, and honeysuckle, with an old-fashioned rusty metal sundial in the center. Peeking from among the flowers and ivy are Chinese animal sculptures. White chairs and glass-topped tables are set about the two-level terrace; in warm weather, you might enjoy breakfast here.

The guest rooms surround the courtyard and have garden or ocean views over the rooftops. They all have cable television and direct dial phones. Ten rooms include kitchens, useful for preparing light snacks. Silverware and dishes are provided; ask at the office for pots and pans. A breakfast of juice, toast, muffins, and coffee or tea is served in the small lobby, or you can take your repast to an outdoor table.

The rooms, in French country or Victorian styles, are furnished in wicker and brass and have Italian marble in the baths. Room 17, on the ground level, has a garden view and a four-poster bed with a canopy. An armoire serves as closet and a curtained alcove holds an extra bed. In the trim little kitchen there's a fold-down ironing board and a table for two. Room 28 has an ocean view through the trees. Decorated in light blues and ivories, it has a brass king-size bed set against long windows, a loveseat covered in satin damask, a small kitchen, and a twin bed in an adjoining room perfect for child.

Sundial Lodge has no off-street parking, but you can easily find long-term parking on the street within two blocks.

Vagabond's House

P.O. Box 2747
4th & Dolores
Carmel, CA 93921
408-624-7738
800-262-1262
Fax: 408-626-1243

A quiet inn surrounding a courtyard garden

Proprietor: Dennis LeVett. **Accommodations:** 11 rooms (all with private bath). **Rates:** $85–$235 single or double, $20 additional person. **Included:** Continental breakfast. **Added:** 10.5% tax. **Minimum stay:** 2 nights on weekends. **Payment:** Major credit cards. **Children:** Over age 12 welcome; additional $20 if third person in room. **Pets:** Allowed with permission; additional $10 per night. **Smoking:** Discouraged in rooms.

This cluster of half-timbered, shingled cottages blends perfectly with the quaint ambience of Carmel-by-the-Sea, as the village of Carmel is often called. The main building, which was a private home in the 1940s, and the one- and two-story guest accommodations face a flagstone courtyard with a waterfall. Centered by an immense old oak tree, the courtyard is lush with color and greenery: camellias, rhododendrons, and trailing vines fill every nook, ferns grow against the oak tree and fuchsias hang from its branches. On December nights, the tree twinkles with hundreds of tiny lights. The effect is magical.

Vagabond's House was named for a poem written by Don Blandings in 1928, in which the poet, who stayed at the inn in years past, describes his dream house. Several copies of a book of Blanding's poetry are on display in the parlor, where you may also see the owner's intriguing collections of British lead soldiers and Big Little Books.

All the guest rooms have fireplaces with wood supplied, and most have kitchens. Those rooms without full kitchens have small refrigerators. Most of the guest rooms have been redone in the past few years. A few still have individual themes, such as a nautical decor and an English hunt motif, but most are now in a comfortable residential style, with flowered comforters, easy chairs, and balloon shades. They have

> **Vagabond's House is a 5-minute drive from Carmel's beautiful mission, which dates from 1793 and is one of only two Basilicas in the western United States. The annual Carmel Bach Festival is held at the mission during the summer.**

roomy closets, luggage racks, full baths with tubs and showers (or shower only), and good reading lamps. Some have white wicker furnishings and beds with a partial canopy. Breakfast (breads, fresh fruit, orange juice, a hot beverage, and an egg dish) is delivered to your room within minutes after you call the office.

Treasure-filled shops, art and antiques galleries, and restaurants are within a short walk of the inn, and a long curve of surf-lapped sandy beach lies at the bottom of the hill.

CARMEL VALLEY

Carmel Valley Ranch

One Old Ranch Road
Carmel, CA 93923
408-625-9500
800-4-CARMEL
Fax: 408-624-2858

A hillside golf resort with grand valley views

General manager: Cal Jepson. **Accommodations:** 100 suites. **Rates:** $235–$575 single or double, $20 additional person; luxury suites $875. **Added:** 10.5% tax. **Payment:** Major credit cards. **Children:** Under age 17 free in room with parents. **Pets:** Not allowed. **Smoking:** Nonsmoking rooms available.

Carmel Valley Ranch is six miles east of Carmel on the Monterey Peninsula. The only resort in the area with a private, guarded gate, it is sequestered on 1,700 hilly acres above the valley.

Once admitted, you drive up a hillside, past fairways and greens, to the main lodge and twenty-three buildings of suites clustered among the oak trees. You immediately notice the striking display of color. Hundreds of flowers — geraniums, dahlias, roses, irises, day lilies, rhododendrons, petunias, zinnias — surround the contemporary ranch-style lodge, maintained by the chief gardener and artist Doris Ewing. Her creative skills are also evident in the resort's floral arrangements, and in the watercolors which hang in the suites and lodge.

The lobby and lounge have gray-stained redwood walls and a blend of antiques and early California furnishings. Floor-to-ceiling windows overlook the golf course on one side, and a terrace and freeform swimming pool on the other. Tucked against one corner of the terrace is a whirlpool spa, one of five on the property.

The intimate, formal dining room (jackets are suggested for men) is warm with earth tones, a natural wood ceiling, and a rough stone fireplace. Bruce Silverblatt, the executive chef, uses regional foods in dishes such as pan seared Santa Barbara abalone with herb polenta cakes, and grilled Pacific salmon with oven-roasted portabello and shiitake mushrooms. There's a varied wine list, and a pianist plays light jazz every evening. The kitchen will also pack a picnic basket if you request it.

Some suites are near the lodge; the rest are above it, in buildings with sweeping views of the valley. The commodious suites, redecorated in 1995, are tastefully furnished and comfortably elegant with sofas, easy chairs, and two poster beds in tapestry and tweed fabrics. Standard features include a stocked wet bar, two TVs (VCRs are available), three two-line phones, robes, and gas fireplaces. Some suites have two fireplaces and a private hot tub out on the deck. Cookies are left at turndown, and coffee, tea, and cocoa are in every room.

Each of the one- and two-bedroom accommodations has a large deck with a view of the oak groves, golf course, gardens, or valley. A luxury master suite has a dining room often used for business hospitality or executive conferences. There are granite fireplaces in both bedroom and living room, a pink granite bar between the dining room and kitchen, and a deck on two sides jutting into the tops of oak trees.

> **The 18-hole golf course, designed by Pete Dye, is known for its challenges and beauty. Five fairways climb the mountainside, offering wide views of the valley floor. Three manmade lakes, the Carmel River, and numerous sand and grass bunkers provide opportunities to test all levels of skill.**

Country club facilities are open to resort guests. The clubhouse restaurant is down the hill from the main lodge and overlooks the front nine holes of the golf course. Poolside dining is also available. In addition, the resort has ten hard-surface and two clay tennis courts, along with a pro shop and instructors who will arrange matches, lessons, special events, and tournaments. Bikes are available for rental, and horseback riding can also be arranged.

For a luxurious golf or tennis vacation in a serene setting, Carmel Valley Ranch is an excellent choice. The service and staff are excellent, and the security of a guarded entrance is important to many guests, who like knowing that the only visitors who wander around uninvited are the deer that come to nibble the begonias hanging from oak tree branches by the front door.

Quail Lodge Resort and Golf Club

8205 Valley Greens Drive
Carmel, CA 93923
408-624-1581
800-538-9516
Fax: 408-624-3726

A luxurious resort on a golf course

General manager: Csaba Ajan. **Accommodations:** 100 rooms and villas. **Rates:** $210–$285 single or double, $25 additional person; suites $325 and up. **Added:** 10.5% tax. **Payment:** Major credit cards. **Children:** Under age 12 free in room with parents. **Pets:** Allowed with permission. **Smoking:** Nonsmoking rooms available.

A few miles east of Highway 1, off Carmel Valley Road two hours south of San Francisco, this resort stands on ten landscaped acres of a private country club. Ten small lakes, the habitat of wildlife and waterfowl, dot the grounds, and an 18-hole golf course sprawls across the valley floor.

You drive down a road lined with pepper trees to a scattering of buildings behind winding paths. Inside the main lodge, there's a two-story atrium with dark beams and skylights above the mezzanine. Around the corner are the Covey restaurant and a cocktail lounge. In the plant-filled sunroom, a few steps down from the lounge, the glass walls offer views of the lake and lush grounds.

Candlelit and romantic, with dark, polished woods, rose upholstery, and white linens, the two-level dining room overlooks Mallard Lake and its lighted fountain. A pianist plays in the small bar five nights a week.

Breakfast and lunch are available at the Club, a casual restaurant overlooking the driving range just across the Carmel River, which divides Quail Lodge from the country club.

The guest rooms are beside walks with trellises that bloom with trumpet vines. Fragrant blossoms and expensive perfume scent the air as you walk or ride in a golf cart to your room. Every room has either a patio or a balcony. All have phones and television, and VCRs can be requested. A typical room, in rusts, greens, and ivories, will have two queen-size beds, a dressing area, and a tiled bath with a lighted makeup mirror, hair dryer, coffeemaker, and separate vanities. A pants press and a complimentary bottle of wine are also provided, but the rooms are not air conditioned.

The light cottage suite has a sitting-bedroom combination with a wet bar, gas fireplace, and vaulted ceiling with track lighting and skylights. The windows overlook the curving lakeshore, and from the patio you see ducks swimming on the lake and the arching bridge under graceful trees.

The California Suite is dramatic, in a dark, shadowy mood. Black tables, brass lamps, indirect lighting, an Oriental cabinet, and a bed set on a platform accentuate the striking decor. All the rooms have stereo systems; this one has a VCR as well. A pocket door leads to a bath in deep red tile, with tub and shower. On the private deck, behind vine-covered walls, is a wooden hot tub. The suite has a dining room, which can be rented separately if you wish to host a meeting or dinner for eight. It too has dramatic flair, with its dark bamboo chairs, an Oriental screen, and low couches.

Most of the guests at Quail Lodge are repeat visitors. Among the recreational diversions are four tennis courts, two swimming pools, and guest privileges on the golf course. The generally well-heeled patrons make occasional use of the helicopter landing next to the country club's driving range.

Robles del Rio Lodge

200 Punta del Monte
Carmel Valley, CA 93924
408-659-3705
800-833-0843
Fax: 408-659-5157

*A casual
country lodge*

Proprietors: Adreena and Glen Gurries. **Accommodations:** 33
rooms and cottages. **Rates:** $89–$130 single or double, $10 additional person; cottages $160–$250; weekday and winter discounts available. **Included:** Expanded Continental breakfast.
Added: Tax. **Minimum stay:** 2 nights on weekends. **Payment:**
MasterCard, Visa. **Children:** Welcome (infants free). **Pets:** Not
allowed. **Smoking:** Not allowed.

Oak trees stud the rolling hills around Carmel Valley, thirteen miles inland from coastal Highway 1, and centuries-old
oaks shade the flagstone terrace of Robles del Rio. Hence the
lodge's name, which is Spanish for "oaks of the river."

The lodge, the oldest in the area, covers nine acres of a hillside off a winding road above the valley. A swimming pool
lies behind trimmed hedges, oak trees, and beds of daisies.
Potted pink geraniums add color to the lovely terrace, where
dozens of tiny birds in the trees keep the leaves fluttering. In
the low, main building are the Cantina bar and The Ridge, a
restaurant with a view of the valley. The Continental menu
includes seafood, chicken, and beef. The avocado soup, fresh
salmon, and rack of lamb are commendable. Also overlooking
the valley is a lounge with a stone fireplace, where a buffet
breakfast of fresh fruit, cereals, boiled eggs, and juice is set
out.

Accommodations are in one- and two-story buildings (Oak

Leaf, Cypress, Cherry, Knotty Pine, and El Roblar) and cottages set against the hillside below the lodge. The cottages are rustic, and the standard rooms have thin walls and outmoded decor, but the suites offer excellent lodging for the price. Roblar Suite C, for example, is a second-floor apartment in crisp blue and white. The living room holds a sofa-bed, TV, several chairs and tables, and a white cabinet decorated with painted flowers. Trim curtains frame a fine view. There's a clean, well-equipped kitchen and a bedroom

> **The lodge was built in 1928 as a private golf club and turned into a public resort in 1939. Now run by the Gurries family, it's a casual, low-key place far removed from the busy, shop-lined streets of Carmel.**

with two white iron queen-size beds. Double doors open to a private deck above the lawn and slope covered with painted daisies. With the use of a kitchen and breakfast included, the suite is well priced for four people.

Stonepine

150 East Carmel Valley Road
Carmel Valley, CA 93924
408-659-2245
Fax: 408-659-5160

> *An exclusive inn in the country*

General manager: Daniel Barduzzi.
Accommodations: 13 suites. **Rates:** $250–$900 single or double, $50 additional person. **Included:** Expanded Continental breakfast. **Minimum stay:** 2 nights on weekends, 3 nights on holidays. **Added:** 10% tax. **Payment:** Major credit cards. **Children:** Welcome (age 12 and older in main château). **Pets:** Not allowed. **Smoking:** Not allowed.

This luxurious retreat began in the 1930s as a thoroughbred racing farm in the hills east of Carmel. Called the Double H Ranch by its owners, Helen and Henry Potter Russell of the

Crocker banking family, it covered 7,000 acres of the valley. No effort was spared in creating the perfect estate, from the Mediterranean main house to the carefully designed gardens and orchards.

By 1983, when it was purchased by Noel and Gordon Hentschel, the property had dwindled to 330 acres. Its new owners renamed the place after the Italian pines that Helen Russell had planted as saplings, and began an extensive restoration that would turn the estate into an opulent inn and equestrian retreat.

> Enter through the triple-arched porch and you're greeted by a gracious staff member who will invite you to have cognac in the living room after dinner, or perhaps attend the performance of a string ensemble on a summer afternoon.

Eight suites comprise Château Noel, a pink French country mansion with a tower, black iron-work, and red tiled roof. The château is at the end of a mile-long road that winds up a hill past meadows and trees and over a creek to a circular gravel drive punctuated with oak trees and low stone walls.

The living room is furnished in a combination of contemporary and traditional styles. Its seven-foot carved limestone fireplace is from 19th-century Italy; the French tapestries above it date from the 1700s. The theme is light and restful, and the mood tranquil.

French doors lead to a loggia with stone arches supported by carved columns from ancient Rome. Tall stone pines edge the sheltered lawn and garden beside it. Flowering shrubs scent the air, and vines and gnarled olive trees cast leafy shadows over the chairs and tables where breakfast may be served. Around the corner, below walls cascading with white wisteria and purple bougainvillea, is the pool level, reached by descending broad stairs.

Indoors, in the dark, elegant dining room, guests who choose to dine here sit at a single table set with fine china, crystal, and sterling silver. The oak paneling is from 19th-century France — a wedding gift to Helen Russell from her family. The same burnished paneling is in the library, a comfortable nook for reading, chess, and conversation by the marble fireplace.

The only lodging on the main floor is the Don Quixote Suite, which has a private patio garden. Up time-worn stairs are the other suites, all lavishly appointed with antiques, down comforters, and luxurious baths. Each room has cable television and VCR, fresh flowers, lounging robes, and shelves of books. Several have fireplaces laid with wood and ready to light.

Wedgwood, in blue, has a king-size bed and Wedgwood china on display. The big bathroom contains a two-person whirlpool tub. Chanel is a favorite of many guests, with its soft gray satins, a fireplace, antiques, and a whirlpool tub. The bedroom has two double beds. Taittinger is the largest and most expensive suite. A chilled bottle of Taittinger champagne awaits your arrival, and a champagne satin decor sets the tone. There are two bathrooms (one with a whirlpool tub and bidet) and dressing rooms.

Four more suites are down the hill in the Paddock House, an old-fashioned green and white country ranch house with a large veranda and lawn. If you bring young children, this is where you'll stay. Guests in the informal but well-furnished inn can use its kitchen and dining room. A third building is Briar Rose Cottage, which has two suites, a kitchen, a fireplace, and a garden with a gazebo. It's a good choice for two couples traveling together.

Horseback riding lessons and trail rides are offered at the equestrian center. Stonepine also has a soccer field, an archery range, a croquet lawn, tennis courts, and a horseshoe pitch. There's also an exercise room, and mountain bikes are available.

DAVENPORT

New Davenport Bed & Breakfast Inn

31 Davenport Avenue
P.O. Box J
Davenport, CA 95017
408-425-1818
800-870-1817 in California
Fax: 408-423-1160

> *A seaside inn
> with artistic flair*

Innkeepers: Bruce and Marcia McDougal. **Accommodations:** 12 rooms (all with private bath). **Rates:** $75–$125 single or double, $10 additional person. **Included:** Full breakfast and complimentary drink. **Added:** 10% tax. **Payment:** Major credit cards. **Children:** Allowed in some rooms; over age 5 charged as an additional person. **Pets:** Not allowed. **Smoking:** Not allowed.

The seaside community of Davenport, halfway between San Francisco and Carmel on Highway 1, was an active port at the turn of the century. When a cement plant went up in 1906, it grew into a town with blacksmith shops, a general store, and half a dozen hotels.

Over time, Davenport gradually declined, but in recent years new homes and business have sprung up. On the site of the former Cash Store, which burned down in 1953, Bruce and Marcia McDougal built the New Davenport Cash Store and opened it in 1978 as a pottery gallery, restaurant, and lodging. Next to the two-story brick structure is the area's oldest remaining building, which has served as a public bath, bar, restaurant, dance hall, and private home. The McDougals renovated this cottage and opened it to guests.

They brought a background of hospitality to their venture, for they had fed and housed hundreds of people at Big Creek Pottery, their studio and school. The present gallery, on the ground floor of the inn, has become a center for folk art, textiles, pottery, and jewelry from around the world.

Across the room is the rustic restaurant, with brick walls hung with masks and carvings. Here you may sit at wooden tables on mismatched chairs or benches — there are even a few church pews — and dine on inventive pasta and seafood dishes such as grilled filet of salmon served with salmon ravioli and a warm ginger and scallion vinaigrette sauce. Hotel guests are given a $7 credit for breakfast on weekdays; one weekends, breakfast is served in the cottage. In the evenings inn guests are welcome to a complimentary cocktail from the bar.

Above the Cash Store and Restaurant are eight guest rooms with a sheltered balcony that stretches around two sides of the building, overlooking the highway and, beyond it, a bluff above the ocean. Wide doors open to rooms furnished with antiques and ethnic art from the McDougals' extensive collection. The rooms have telephones but no television, and armoires or pegs rather than closets.

China Ladder has an Oriental theme. Pigeon Point is small, cool, and blue, decorated with a New England flavor. Captain Davenport's Retreat, on the corner, is the largest room. It has a sitting area with four double doors opening to the balcony, peacock wicker chairs, and an ocean view.

> **Within walking distance are several studios and showrooms where local craftspeople display their works. The historic St. Vincent de Paul Church and the restored jail are interesting photographic subjects.**

If you're willing to sacrifice the view for quiet (Highway 1 can be noisy, though it's usually peaceful at night), request one of the four rooms in the cottage around the corner. It has a common area, decorated with Indian wall hangings where guests may relax, read, and visit. There are games, a sideboard with coffee, tea, mugs and plates for breakfast, and a small kitchen. As one visitor wrote in the guest book, "All the comforts of home — or the home you'd like to have — and yet you're on a holiday."

The decor in the cottage is light and bright, with country furnishings. Grandma's Room, small and serene, has a white iron bed, and eyelet curtains at a high window. It faces east to a small garden and patio. The other three — Nellie's Sewing Room, The Guest Room, and Mike's Room — are also furnished in white wicker and have cotton print quilts on white iron beds. You may find scuff marks and peeling paint, but the inn is clean and comfortable and generally well maintained.

Across the highway there's a secluded beach to stroll, and from the ocean cliffs you may see migrating gray whales spouting just offshore.

GILROY

Country Rose Inn Bed and Breakfast

P.O. Box 2500
Gilroy, CA 95021-2500
408-842-0441

A serene home in garlic-growing country

Innkeeper: Rose Hernandez. **Accommodations:** 5 rooms (all with private bath). **Rates:** $89–$179. **Included:** Full breakfast. **Added:** 8% tax. **Minimum stay:** 2 nights on summer weekends. **Payment:** Major credit cards. **Children:** Not appropriate. **Pets:** Not allowed. **Smoking:** Not allowed.

Roses dominate this charming inn, from the flowers in the rooms to the innkeeper's name. Carefully tended gardens and shade trees grow by the white Dutch Colonial home, which was built in the 1920s on a chicken ranch. The chickens are gone, but the sense of rural tranquility remains on these five acres surrounded by farmland. Gilroy, the garlic capital of the world, is a few miles away, and San Jose is a 30-minute drive.

Rose, a former teacher, is a conscientious hostess. She will offer information on accessible attractions such as San Juan Bautista and Pinnacles National Monument and recommend good restaurants in the area.

There are two parlors in the simply furnished inn. One has a brick fireplace and a baby grand piano. The dining room has a view of the front veranda and rosebed. Also on the main floor is the Garden Room, the home's original living room. It reflects Rose Hernandez's interests and family, with its carved antique bed and trunk, a photograph of her parents' 1916 wedding, and her mother's treasured wedding dress in the armoire.

The upstairs rooms have views of the big valley oaks and in the distance, the Gabilan Hills. Imperial Rose is secluded behind two doors; Sterling Rose is a corner room with a window seat and a view of the magnolia tree and its birds' nests. Usually the magnolia blooms in time for Rose's annual Valentine tea.

Double Delight has a window seat and a walk-in closet. Rambling Rose is a large suite with French doors between the sleeping and sitting areas. Its balcony extends to the branches of a 300-year-old oak tree.

GOLETA

Circle Bar B Guest Ranch

1800 Refugio Road
Goleta, CA 93117
805-968-1113

A family ranch for relaxing and horseback riding

General Manager: Pat Brown. **Accommodations:** 13 rooms (all with private bath). **Rates:** $186–$225 double, $60–$75 additional person. **Included:** All meals. **Added:** 9% tax. **Minimum stay:** 2 nights on weekends, 3 nights on holidays. **Payment:** MasterCard, Visa. **Children:** Under age 3 free in room with parents. **Pets:** Not allowed. **Smoking:** Allowed outside only.

The Circle Bar B, twenty miles north of Santa Barbara, combines a rustic atmosphere with contemporary comforts. Tucked in a wooded canyon in the Santa Ynez Mountains, the ranch has stables, a chicken coop, and assorted animals, including peacocks that wander the grounds and peer from the branches of the walnut trees. The atmosphere is down-home casual, befitting a place that opened fifty years ago as a children's camp.

Yet along with the rusticity are rooms with down comforters on the beds and free-standing fireplaces. Five are small, attached rooms; the rest are in separate cabins. All are set against a hillside of olive trees and reached by brick baths bordered by large jade plants.

A typical cabin resembles a spacious hotel room with a raised brick hearth, high beamed ceiling, white walls, and southwestern art. It has a king-size bed with padded headboard, a dresser and closet, good reading lamps, and a bath with a tiled shower stall.

> On nearly 1,000 acres of hilly, coastal countryside, the ranch offers great scenery and good food and lodging, but for many guests its major appeal is the horses. Experienced wranglers take riders of all levels of ability on daily rides. They'll give individual instruction, too.

A recent addition is a two-bedroom cabin, useful for families. The kids' favorites though, are the two cabins with pull-down stairs that lead to lofts with double beds. Linens are changed daily, and full cleaning is provided on alternate days.

The ranch, begun by the Brown family in the 1930s, is still a family operation. Pat Brown runs the stables, and Jim, his father, handles maintenance and the Friday and Saturday night cookouts. Weekend barbecue buffets feature country-style ribs, steak, chicken, baked beans, three kinds of salad, garlic bread, and carrot cake. Afterward, those who've come for the dinner theater mosey down to the Old Barn to watch a Circle Bar B production. The theater, which has been operating since the early 1980s, presents comedies, mysteries, and musicals that are usually (though not always) suitable for the whole family.

Meals are eaten at common tables in the dining room of the main ranch house or under the grape arbor. Breakfast is hearty country fare — fruit, eggs from ranch chickens, pancakes, potatoes, and strong coffee. After breakfast, you may want to take a picnic lunch on a hike to the swimming hole beneath a waterfall or a trail ride to a scenic vista above the coast. The ranch is three and a half miles inland from Refugio State Beach. When you return you can wash off the trail dust with a dip in the pool, play croquet or table tennis, or soak in the hot tub. The living room — also the lobby, office, and game room — has books and games.

LOS ALAMOS

Union Hotel

P.O. Box 616
362 Bell Street
Los Alamos, CA 93440
805-344-2744
800-230-2744
Fax: 805-344-3125

> *An Old West
> hotel with a
> frontier flavor*

General Manager: Bill Bubbel. **Accommodations:** 13 rooms (3 with private bath). **Rates:** $66–$182 single or double. **Included:** Full breakfast. **Payment:** Major credit cards. **Children:** Not appropriate. **Pets:** Not allowed. **Smoking:** Allowed.

It took the wood from twelve old barns to restore the original appearance of the Union Hotel. That was just a part of the work that was done to turn it into an exaggerated version of a 19th-century lodging. With the potted palms and Victorian furniture in the lobby are a fireplace mantel taken from a Pasadena mansion, a clawfoot copper bathtub topped with beveled glass, a pair of 200-year-old Egyptian burial urns, and a *Gone with the Wind* lamp.

Saloon doors swing open to a 150-year-old mahogany bar. Headlights from a 1914 Oldsmobile hang on the side wall, along with washboards, saws, boots, well-used tools, horseshoes, and a moose head. There are two jukeboxes, an upright piano, a pay phone encircled with a red velvet curtain, and a carved mahogany ping pong table. The ceiling was once the wall of the oldest store in town.

The dining room has chandeliers made from gas lights and an oak dining set that once graced a Mississippi plantation home. Here, dinner is served in the evenings Wednesday through Sunday. The menu includes filet mignon, scallops, chicken, and lamb.

The first Union Hotel was built in 1880 as a stagecoach stop. It went up in flames in 1886, and was rebuilt of eighteen-inch-thick adobe and renamed the Los Alamos. When the late Dick Langdon found a picture of the hotel as it was in 1884, he determined to restore it. So the old barns were dismantled to create the dark facade it has today.

The hotel stands behind an old-fashioned boardwalk on the

main street of tiny Los Alamos, fourteen miles from Solvang, a Danish-style village. Formerly from Los Angeles, Dick Langdon was in the meat business when he dreamed of escaping the city's fast pace. In 1972 he stumbled upon the hotel and found a master craftsman, Jim Radhe, who constructed the entire front of the building by hand.

> **Each room has something special: a bearskin rug, an unusual Murphy bed, a curtained alcove, a fireplace. There's even a secret passage. Ask to be shown the hidden room behind a retreating bookcase.**

Upstairs, you can wile away an evening in the large, skylighted parlor that has an 1880 Brunswick pool table, game tables, and shelves filled with books. The guest rooms contain antique furniture, sleigh beds, handmade quilts, ceiling fans, pedestal sinks, and authentic Victorian wallpapers. The three rooms with private baths have clawfoot tubs. The bridal suite has its own secret entrance behind a sliding bookcase. This huge room lined by French doors, which open onto a terrace overlooking the pool, has a sunken whirlpool tub.

In this quiet place your sleep will be undisturbed. Come morning, the scent of freshly brewed coffee will lure you downstairs to breakfast. As you linger over bacon and eggs, you can chat with other guests and plan the day. Not that there's much to plan in Los Alamos (which is Spanish for "the cottonwoods"). This is a sleepy agricultural town, with no resort activity or nightlife.

However, you may get to take a ride in a 1918 White touring car, originally used in Yellowstone National Park that is now parked in front of the hotel. And you may be given a tour of the Mansion, the amazing Victorian house next door run by the same owners (see Victorian Mansion, next page). Lounging on the brick terrace by the swimming pool and soaking in the hot tub, which sits under a heart-shaped trellis in a gazebo entwined with night-blooming jasmine, or finding your way through the backyard maze, are probably the favorite pastimes.

Victorian Mansion

P.O. Box 616
Los Alamos, CA 93440
805-344-2744
800-230-2744
Fax: 805-344-3125

*A one-of-a-kind
hotel with
fantasy themes*

General Manager: Bill Bubbel. **Accommodations:** 6 rooms. **Rates:** $198–$242. **Included:** Full breakfast. **Payment:** Major credit cards. **Children:** Not appropriate. **Pets:** Not allowed. **Smoking:** Allowed.

From the outside, this yellow Victorian with white gingerbread trim looks like a perfectly preserved, quaint example of a 19th-century home. Step inside and you enter a unique world that is far from anything remotely Victorian. It bears no resemblance to the rest of southern California, either, or the little agricultural town of Los Alamos. Each room is a fantasy, a dream brought to life by the late Dick Langdon's fertile imagination and the two hundred artisans who turned his ideas into reality. The immortilization of some of the artisans' faces crafted into the inn's hallway wall should be some hint of the tremendous creativity to come.

For starters, there's the 50s Drive-In room. Enter the black leather padded door, and you see a yellow 1956 Cadillac convertible. That's the bed, facing a screen where a movie from the '50s will be shown later. The rear of another Cadillac forms a magazine table, and the trunk of yet another holds a black porcelain wash basin. In the room is a sunken tub, operated by remote control. A neon sign reads "Snack Bar." There are no visible windows — here or in any of the rooms. The walls are meticulously painted with scenes of the Hollywood hills and Mickey and Minnie Mouse dancing to a jukebox. In the cedar closet, hidden behind the scenery, are Mickey and Minnie robes.

That's just the beginning. In the Roman Room, you sleep in a silver Ben Hur chariot that holds a queen-size bed. You're surrounded by paintings of arbors, arches, busts, ruins, and Rome burning in the distance. The bathroom, behind a bookcase, has ancient battle scenes handpainted on the tiles. A remote control operates the lights, television, fireplace, and Roman tub. Wide marble stairs lead to the sunken tub. The robes are togas.

The Egyptian room, behind a stone door, is a sheik's oasis with a canopy bed on a platform, a fabric ceiling, Oriental carpets, and a tiled fireplace. A low table, set with silver teapots from Arabia, is surrounded with plush cushions. Pull the beard of a life-size King Tut, and the mummy pulls from the wall to reveal a bathroom with an Egyptian motif.

> The whole house is an illusion. It lets you step into another world for a day. The place could be hopelessly hokey, but because of the exceptional quality of the workmanship, the clever ideas, and the playful approach, it's highly successful.

If you've ever wanted to be a swashbuckling buccaneer, Pirate is the room for you. Shaped like the interior of a Spanish galleon, it has a bed tucked into a corner, an open treasure chest full of sparkling booty, a low table set on a 700-pound cannon, and a stone fireplace carved with dragons. Ship's lanterns sway from the ceiling mocking the movement of the ocean, and best of all is the small leaded glass window, with scenes of battling ships behind it. Open the window, and you hear the sounds of creaking masts and a stormy sea. A map covers the door which slides open to reveal a tiled bathroom where painted parrots watch pirates at work, a rum cask is used for the sink, and Blackbeard hides in the shower.

The French Room was Dick's idea of an 18th-century Parisian artist's studio. It includes a spiral staircase leading to a curtained bed, an alcove with a view of the French countryside, a tiny French fireplace, a fainting couch, and a partially completed canvas of a nude. The walls are painted with views of Paris, on the high pitched ceiling a hot air balloon appears to be floating in the sky. Over the deep two person soaking tub there's a mural of Marie Antoinette's cottage, and Toulouse Lautrec would have been pleased with the tiled shower.

Picture a gypsy encampment in the forest, and you have the Gypsy Room. Portières hang over the bed, which appears to be a Gypsy wagon, embellished with carved mythological horses. Every season in the woodland is painted on the walls, from the blossoms of spring to the snow-clad trees of winter. There's a stone fireplace, a sunken pool, and a bear rug. At the touch of a button, a hidden TV swings out; another button operates the whirlpool tub.

Guests are offered champagne on arrival, and can dine at the Union Hotel where the menu offers steak, seafood, and pasta entrées. More unusual items such as armadillo eggs and buffalo burgers can also be menu staples.

MONTECITO

Montecito Inn

1295 Coast Village Road
Santa Barbara, CA 93108
805-969-7854
800-843-2017
Fax: 805-969-0623

*A cheerful hotel
in the heart of
Montecito*

General manager: Linda Spann. **Accommodations:** 53 rooms and suites. **Rates:** $150–$195 single or double; suites $225–$695. **Included:** Continental breakfast. **Added:** 10% tax. **Minimum Stay:** 2 nights on weekends and holidays. **Payment:** Major credit cards. **Children:** Under age 17 free in room with parents. **Pets:** Not allowed. **Smoking:** Nonsmoking rooms available.

The Montecito Inn, located on Montecito's main street, has been welcoming guests since 1928. The three-story Mediterranean-style hotel, with its earthquake-resistant red tile roof, whitewashed exterior walls, and overflowing flower boxes, was funded by Charlie Chaplin (among others), and Chaplin's image can still be seen throughout the hotel. A Chaplin figure stands by the elevator, there are Chaplin movie posters behind the front desk and in the hallways, and the hotel maintains a Chaplin film library.

However, you don't need to be a Chaplin aficionado to enjoy a stay at the Montecito. Rooms, which range in size from small rooms with queen-size beds to luxury suites with living rooms, are attractive with French Provincial furnishings. All rooms have cable television and alarm clock radios. King rooms and suites have added amenities such as refrigerators and VCRs. The split-level Tower Suite was Charlie's favorite, and is often requested by honeymooners today.

> Montecito's shops and restaurants are just a few steps from the inn, but many guests are drawn by the fabulous smells emanating from the lively Montecito Café adjacent to the lobby, and decide to dine close to home. Seafood dishes are highlighted at this popular café.

The hotel has a small fitness room, and an outdoor swimming pool and spa surrounded by potted bougainvillea. Beautiful wooden game tables are laid out for checkers in a downstairs hallway, and bicycles are available on loan. The friendly and helpful front desk staff can steer you in the direction of additional recreation, as both the beach and downtown Santa Barbara are nearby. In the morning Continental breakfast is served in the lobby, and hot coffee is always available.

San Ysidro Ranch

900 San Ysidro Lane
Montecito, CA 93108
805-969-5046
800-368-6788
Fax: 805-565-1995

> *An exclusive
> cottage resort in
> the coastal hills*

General manager: Janice Clapoff.
Accommodations: 44 cottages. **Rates:** $235–$750 2 to 4 people. **Minimum Stay:** 2 nights on weekend, 3–4 nights on holidays. **Payment:** MasterCard, Visa. **Children:** Welcome. **Pets:**
Allowed; $45 additional. **Smoking:** Discouraged.

This cottage resort in the hills above the sea has been like a
second home to famous names and discerning travelers since
it opened in 1893. Somerset Maugham, Sinclair Lewis, and
John Galsworthy stayed in bungalows and wrote; Laurence
Olivier and Vivien Leigh were married in the garden. John
Huston stayed for three months, writing the screenplay for
The African Queen; John F. and Jacqueline Kennedy honey-
mooned here, and celebrities from Jean Harlow to Julia Child
have lauded the breathtaking views.

Once the 550 acres just south of Santa Barbara served as a
way station for Franciscan friars. It was later a cattle ranch
and citrus tree farm, and now a resort that attempts to preserve San Ysidro's traditional calm, beauty, and history while
providing contemporary luxury. A friendly staff insures a
comfortable, casual feeling throughout the resort.

The single-story white cottages with peaked roofs are
spread across the hillside under stately palms, eucalyptus,
oak, and sycamore trees. Most of the cottages contain one,
two, or three units; one has eight. They all have views of the
distant sea or wooded foothills of the Santa Ynez mountains.

Each room is decorated differently and with traditional
good taste. All the rooms have fireplaces or wood-burning
stoves, wet bars, coffeemakers, hair dryers, makeup mirrors,
down comforters, and terrycloth robes. Several feature private
outdoor Jacuzzis. Canyon Cottage, surrounding an oak-
shaded terrace, has some of the smallest rooms and best
views. Behind it is Lilac, highest on the hill and closest to the
tennis courts and heated swimming pool. With high vaulted
ceilings, Lilac 2 has a king-size brass bed set back in an alcove, a cowboy print sofa in front of a wood-burning stove, a

marble-topped antique washbasin in the bath, and an outdoor hot tub on a large deck. Sycamore 1 has a country look with a four-poster bed topped by a patchwork quilt. Geranium is one of the original cottages. It's been refurbished with a country flavor in white and natural wood, and has an outdoor Jacuzzi under flowering vines.

The Stonehouse is the Ranch's fine dining rest-aurant, and there is a stunning view from the terrace. Ancho pepper-honey glazed lamb shank with herbed cornmeal john-nycake and fire-roasted peppers and onions, and lobster and sweet corn tamale with chipolte chile and citrus cream, are examples of the rest-aurant's Mexican- and Southwestern-influenced American cuisine. Downstairs in the basement is the cozy Plow and Angel Pub. With sautéed white-fish and grilled asparagus, and warm smoked duck on Parmesan cheese grits with red chile and cilantro, the menu is a cut above traditional pub fare.

> A part of San Ysidro's history is an 1825 adobe building, once the home of a pioneer family. Another is a former citrus fruit-packing house that is now Stonehouse, an award-winning restaurant.

Most admired are San Ysidro's grounds. Scarlet-blooming bottle brush trees, brilliant lantana, natal plum and roses grow in profusion around lawns and paths. Vines cover a trellis in the wedding garden — a gorgeous garden terrace with a spectacular mountain backdrop. The air is fragrant with honeysuckle, jasmine, and orange blossoms, and birds can be heard singing from atop stately trees. Tidy herb and vegetable gardens keep the Stonehouse kitchen well stocked.

The Hacienda Lounge is in the main building, next to the registration office. Here you'll find a stone fireplace and pool table, and chess and backgammon are set up for play. For more active recreation, the ranch keeps horses for horseback riding. There's also an exercise room and a children's playground. Groups and small conferences are welcome at the ranch. Catering and audiovisual and meeting materials are available.

MONTEREY

The Jabberwock

598 Laine
Monterey, CA 93940
408-372-4777
Fax 408-655-2946

A well-located bed-and-breakfast with warm hospitality

Innkeepers: Jim and Barbara Allen. **Accommodations:** 7 rooms (3 with private bath). **Rates:** $105–$185 single or double. **Included:** Full breakfast and afternoon refreshments. **Added:** 11% tax. **Minimum Stay:** 2 nights on weekends, 3 nights on some holidays. **Payment:** MasterCard, Visa. **Children:** Older children welcome (rooms accommodate two persons). **Pets:** Not allowed. **Smoking:** Outdoors only.

" 'Twas brillig, and the slithy toves did gyre and gimble in the wabe." So begins "Jabberwocky," Lewis Carroll's poem in *Through the Looking Glass.* The Allens decided that it provided the perfect theme for their bed-and-breakfast, so every room has a Jabberwocky name, and bits of Lewis Carroll whimsy are found throughout the house. Be assured, however, that it's not overdone; the decor is charming but never precious.

The pleasant home, on a residential corner away from seaside tourist traffic, was built in 1911. Used as a convent for years, it was purchased by the Allens and opened to guests in 1982. Jim, a retired firefighter and a skilled gardener, landscaped the property, putting in gardens of impatiens, fuchsia, geraniums, gaillardia, and roses; flowerboxes bursting with pansies, ponds, waterfalls, a sundial; and red gravel paths traversing green lawns — as well as a brick parking lot.

Barbara, formerly in the hotel business, is the cook, and her breakfasts are noteworthy. You'll find early morning coffee on the dining room table, and later dishes with such names as "snarkleberry flumpsious" and "razzleberry flabjous" are served by the fireplace in the dining room or on the sunporch. Sherry and hors d'oeuvres are served on the sunporch at 5:00 P.M. Bedtime cookies and milk are the final treats of the day. Soft drinks and juices are always available in the refrigerator (called the Tum Tum Tree) on the upper stair landing, and you may store your own snacks and wine there.

The comfortable living room is available for relaxing, reading, listening to the stereo and tape deck, and looking through local menus and other guests' restaurant critiques. Beyond is the cheerful sunroom, filled with plants, overlooking the side gardens.

> Some recommended restaurants in Monterey are Domenico's, on the wharf, for its view and bouillabaisse, Gianni's for the best pizza in town, and the nearby Gallery, known for its Continental menu.

The Toves, the only guest room on the main floor, has an eight-foot carved walnut Victorian bed, a private bath with a clawfoot tub and shower, a little patio, and a white rabbit sized closet. High on the third floor are two garret rooms, The Mimsey and The Wabe, which share a bathroom and sitting room with an ocean view. Mimsey is a hideaway overlooking the bay and town, and binoculars are provided for looking at the view. A crisp eyelet lace coverlet tops the lovely queen-size bed. Peach-toned Wabe gets afternoon sun and has an Austrian carved bed.

The other rooms are on the second floor. Each is furnished distinctively and includes thoughtful accents such as fresh flowers, sachets, bathrobes, and fruit liqueurs. You may feel that you, like Alice, have stumbled through the looking glass when you see the card on your bedside table. It must be held to a mirror to be read.

Brillig is a small room, but its large closet and cupboards have plenty of storage space. The antique rolled oak bed with crocheted afghan gives it an old-fashioned country atmosphere. Mome Rath is dramatic and the most masculine of all the rooms. Borogrove is the largest and best room, running the width of the house and overlooking Monterey Bay and the garden through three walls of windows. It has a white brick fireplace, a king-size bed, and a bath with a shower. Despite its classic elegance, Borogrove has not escaped the Allens' lighthearted touch. A stuffed wool goose stands in one corner, a book of gnomes lies on the table, and a Victorian children's book reminds you of the era you've joined briefly.

Barbara and Jim go out of their way to assure that you have a good time in their home and in Monterey. They'll give you lists of sightseeing suggestions, sell admission tickets to the aquarium so that you won't have to wait in line, introduce you to their lovable English bull terrier, and provide you with dozens of restaurant recommendations.

Monterey Plaza Hotel

400 Cannery Row
Monterey, CA 93940
408-646-1700
800-334-3999 in California
800-631-1339 outside California
Fax: 408-646-5937

> *An elegant hotel
> above the bay*

General manager: John Narigi. **Accommodations:** 285 rooms and suites. **Rates:** $150–$250 single or double, $20 additional person. **Added:** Tax. **Minimum Stay:** 2 nights on holiday weekends. **Payment:** Major credit cards. **Children:** Age 17 and under free in room with parents. **Pets:** Not allowed. **Smoking:** Nonsmoking rooms available.

This is the snazziest hotel of size in Monterey, so grand and sophisticated it seems slightly out of place on Cannery Row, where seedy remnants of John Steinbeck's colorful stories still cling. Fish processing was the main activity here until the bay was fished out and the sardine canneries deserted. Now they house art galleries, shops, and restaurants, and tourism brings in new life.

> **The hotel is not merely close to the ocean, it's virtually on it. Waves crash, the surf splashes, and sea lions bark right below your balcony and beside the terrace where lunch and cocktails are served.**

Like a transplant from San Francisco, 120 miles to the north, the Monterey Plaza boasts white-uniformed valets who greet you in the porte cochere, take your car, and open the doors to a marble lobby. The exterior resembles Spanish

Colonial buildings, but inside, all is Oriental and Mediterranean luxury. Custom carpets, 18th-century Chinese and Italian Empire furnishings, sweeping staircases, and dramatic flower arrangements create an elegant mood.

Directly across the lobby is a wall of windows framing the water and mainland mountains across from this western hook of the bay. Downstairs, the Duck Club restaurant has an even closer proximity to the kelp-covered surf. The restaurant menu features duck, grilled meats, pasta, and seafood.

Some guest rooms are in another building across Cannery Row, but since the main attraction here is the stunning view, the oceanside rooms are far superior. The best are the "02" rooms on the corners. The rooms and suites have carpeting and light-colored walls, brass lamps by the beds, round tables with rattan chairs by the windows, and television with HBO. You can rent VCRs and movies.

A deluxe suite with a view offers a spacious, light-filled sitting area and two balconies from which you can watch the ducks, seagulls, kayakers, fishing boats, and sailboats. As you sniff the salt air, watch the sea otters cracking oyster shells, and listen to the sea lions beg for sardines at Fisherman's Wharf, you'll know this is unmistakably Monterey Bay.

Old Monterey Inn

500 Martin Street
Monterey, CA 93940
408-375-8284
800-350-2344
Fax: 408-375-6730

> *A tranquil bed-and-breakfast in a luxurious setting*

Innkeepers: Ann and Gene Swett. **Accommodations:** 8 rooms, 1 cottage, 1 suite. **Rates:** $170–$240 single or double. **Included:** Full breakfast. **Added:** 10% tax. **Minimum Stay:** 2 nights on weekends. **Payment:** MasterCard, Visa. **Children:** Not appropriate. **Pets:** Not allowed. **Smoking:** Not allowed.

Tucked away on a side street in a residential district of Monterey is Old Monterey Inn, a world removed from the crowds of Cannery Row.

Brick paths wind past bird baths under oak trees, ferns, a trickling fountain, blooming begonias, and drought-resistant succulents. Outside the dining room window, baskets of impatiens hang from the branches of an immense oak tree. Around the corner are painted carts from Costa Rica and other pieces of folk art collected during the Swetts' travels. The fragrant rose garden is Gene's labor of love; he has duplicated the garden planted by the home's original owner, Carmel Martin, and dedicated it to him.

In the large common room, tea and cookies are set out in the afternoon. They're replaced by wine and hors d'oeuvres in the evening, when the gracious hosts encourage mingling and getting acquainted. This is a good time to check through an assortment of local restaurant menus and consult with other visitors or ask the Swetts for a recommendation.

> For years the big, half-timbered house was the Swetts' family home, where they raised six children. In 1977, it opened to guests and now is one of the gems of the Monterey Peninsula, a thoroughly charming, peaceful retreat set on more than an acre of lovely grounds and gardens.

On the other side of the foyer is the dining room, which still has the original metal fireplace, built in 1929, and a stucco ceiling with hand-painted designs. A gourmand's breakfast is served here at one 9 A.M. seating. The dishes are different every day. You may feast on California quiche with chiles and pimentos, poached pears, crêpes, or Belgian waffles with Gene's special syrups. Takahashi china, painted with delicate birds and flowers, graces the table, centered by flowers from the garden.

The romantic rooms have no TV or phone to interrupt the mood. The beds are puffy with down comforters and pillows and hand-crafted natural woods and family antiques furnish the rooms. Most have featherbeds, wood-burning fireplaces, skylights, and stained glass windows.

The most spacious is the Ashford Suite, once the master bedroom. The sitting area has a tiled fireplace, an antique pine daybed, and bay windows overlooking the gardens. In the bedroom is a king-size bed and more windows above the flowers.

Appropriately named, the Library Room boasts walls of books and a stone fireplace. It also has a private sundeck. Third-floor hideaways are Dovecote, a built-in loveseat by the hearth, and Rookery, sunny with a skylight and wicker chairs.

Some rooms are in a cottage with private entrances behind the house. Shuttered windows, wicker furniture, and colors of white and green complement the inn's English country garden theme. The most secluded is wisteria-vined Garden Cottage, a suite with three skylights for stargazing, a private patio, and bay windows. Soft yellows and greens and a bed with a partial canopy of antique lace add to the romantic mood. Offstreet parking is available.

Spindrift Inn

652 Cannery Row
Monterey, CA 93940
408-646-8900
800-841-1879
Fax: 408-646-5342

*A romantic
retreat on the bay*

General manager: Randy Venard. **Accommodations:** 41 rooms. **Rates:** $159–$399 per room. **Included:** Continental breakfast and afternoon wine and cheese reception. **Added:** 10% tax. **Minimum Stay:** 2 nights some weekends. **Payment:** Major credit cards. **Children:** Welcome. **Pets:** Not allowed. **Smoking:** Nonsmoking rooms available.

The Spindrift Inn stands between Cannery Row and the Pacific — aloof from the souvenir shops — its focus is on the rumbling sea. The hotel's history is as storied as its Cannery Row locale, and the building once housed everything from a Chinese hotel in the 1920s and 1930s, to a bordello. Later it was abandoned until the mid-1970s when an impressive restoration was begun. The hotel reopened as the Spindrift in 1984, and today the elegant four-story hotel possesses residential charm in a turn-of-the-century environment. Fine reproductions of period furniture are enhanced by Italian and French influences.

Valet parking takes care of your car, and you step into an atrium lobby with a skylight above. Just past it is an intimate, carpeted sitting area with soft chairs and a couch facing a fireplace where wine and cheese are served in the afternoons. The concierge desk is nearby, where you can obtain information about sightseeing, restaurants, and tickets to peninsula attractions from a helpful member of the staff.

> There's an additional romantic retreat in the rooftop garden. Flowerboxes and lounges behind a white railing provide a relaxing place to enjoy the sun and Monterey's blue sea and sky.

Upstairs, the guest rooms are romantic and inviting, with walls in soft peach, hardwood floors topped by Chinese carpets, wood-burning fireplaces, feather mattresses, down comforters, and marble baths with brass fixtures, bath salts, and botanical toiletries. Many have queen-size beds with full or partial canopies.

Plush terrycloth robes, nightly turndown service with Swiss chocolates, and breakfast on a silver tray in your room are a few of the special touches. A television and a mini-bar stocked with soft drinks are in the armoire. Room service is provided by a local Italian restaurant.

Your room is likely to have a cushioned window seat piled with pillows, an ideal spot for contemplating the bay in sun and fog and watching for whales, sea lions, and the endlessly fascinating sea otters (oceanside rooms have binoculars). The corner rooms are the largest and have the best views, but no room lacks for space.

OJAI

Ojai Valley Inn

Country Club Road
Ojai, CA 93023
805-646-5511
800-422-OJAI
Fax: 805-646-9622

A golf resort in a tranquil valley

General manager: Thad Hyland. **Accommodations:** 207 rooms and suites. **Rates:** $195–$260 single or double, $25 additional person, suites $345–$850. **Payment:** Major credit cards. **Children:** Free in room with parents. **Pets:** Not allowed. **Smoking:** Nonsmoking rooms available.

In 1923, the wealthy glass manufacturer Edward Drummond Libbey began turning a long-held dream into reality: building a private club in the idyllic Ojai Valley. Libbey commissioned Pasadena architect Wallace Neff to design a classic resort that would harmonize with the tranquil valley's oak and orange groves and the encircling mountains. The result was an enduring example of southern California architecture — a low, rambling adobe hacienda with a red tile roof and flagstone terrace.

Over the years the inn and country club expanded, changed hands several times, and had a $35 million renovation. Now, spread over half a mile of the property's 220 hilly acres, it offers modern luxury accommodations, four dining areas and a bar, and many kinds of recreation.

An 18-hole golf course plays 6,252 yards across green hills

edged with oak trees. There are eight hard-surface tennis courts, four of them lighted; clinics and private lessons are available. Two swimming pools are appealing on summer days that may reach 100 degrees in Ojai, some fourteen miles inland from the ocean. Bikes can be rented for touring the countryside, and the inn grounds are connected to a bicycle path and equestrian trail. There's also a year-round Jacuzzi and a putting green, while a steamroom, sauna, and exercise equipment are located at the fitness center. Children will see nuzzling turkeys, pygmy goats, bunnies, and Tiffany the pot-bellied pig at the ranch's petting zoo.

> The finish materials used in the inn's renovation are of indigenous materials, with a strong influence of Southwest Indian art. Rose and lavender touches are in the shades of the valley's remarkable "pink moment," when sunset hues bathe the mountains in color.

Breezeways, arcades, and a fountain in the circular entrance freshen and cool the air during the day. In the evening, fireplaces in some rooms and in the lounge ward off the chill. The original lobby is now the lounge, where a ceiling of heavy, rough beams and white walls give it a southwestern flavor. It's a relaxing place for conversation, a game of chess, or snacking from the cookie tray. The new lobby is open and light, with a beamed ceiling three stories high a wrought-iron chandelier, and palms in terra cotta pots.

Vista, the main dining room, emphasizes light, healthy fare, with a special focus on fish of the central California coast and wines from small nearby vineyards. Mexican, southwestern, and classic Continental cuisine are also on the menu that includes dishes such as seared ahi tuna and crispy roast duck in an orange chipolte sauce with red wild rice. In the formal restaurant, the light bamboo decor is cheerful, and jackets are recommended.

The Oak Grill & Terrace, serving steaks, chicken, salads, sandwiches, and Sunday brunch is more casual. The restaurant has a Mexican look, and good views, but the Terrace offering al fresco dining under live oaks, provides the best mealtime views of Ojai's pastoral valley, golf course, and mountains.

The larger-than-average guest rooms have sofa beds and private patios or balconies with golf course or mountain views. Amenities include two separate vanities, scales, night-lights, irons and ironing boards, terry robes, coffeemakers, mini-bars, and televisions in armoires. New suites have two working fireplaces.

One section's four connecting rooms make it a good choice for several couples traveling together. If you're looking for the romance of the past, the oldest rooms, which are smaller and cozier, are the most appealing. Arched ceilings over the halls, solid doors, and baths in blue and white tiles of the period give these rooms character.

The Honeymoon Suite, in the old section, has just one room but is popular for its view and its private terrace. Shangri-La is a good choice for a family. It has three bedrooms, each with a king-size bed, and room for rollaways in the large parlor. It's named after the Shangri-La mountain view, filmed in the Topa Mountain Range for the 1937 movie, Lost Horizons. The same spectacular view of the rocky massif can be seen from the terraces of the ballroom in the Topa Center, which accommodates groups and meetings.

PACIFIC GROVE

The Centrella

612 Central Avenue
Pacific Grove, CA 93950
408-372-3372
800-233-3372
Fax: 408-372-2036

*A hotel
with comfort
and character
on the Monterey
Peninsula*

Manager: Maureen Diaz. **Accommodations:** 21 rooms and suites (19 with private baths) and 5 cottages. **Rates:** $90–$175 single or double, $15 additional person. **Included:** Buffet breakfast. **Added:** 10% tax. **Minimum Stay:** 2 nights on weekends. **Payment:** Major credit cards. **Children:** Welcome in cottages. **Pets:** Not allowed. **Smoking:** Not allowed.

Once a boarding house, this attractively restored inn on the Monterey Peninsula, a two-hour drive south of San Francisco, adds personal, homey touches to its hotel amenities. In the reception area and parlor, bright flames burn in the fireplace, and trays of afternoon cookies, sherry, and hors d'oeuvres sit on an old oak table. Against a wall, a framed stitchery is in progress. It's a design of the hotel, and any guest so moved may add a few stitches to it; eventually it will join a similar picture on the corridor wall.

> **Take the historic walk through old Monterey, play golf on some of the world's best courses, or go to the Monarch Natural Preserve to marvel at the thousands of butterflies that return every year.**

Up the open, skylit staircase are the guest rooms, each with a brass number on fabric in the colors of the room. Furnished with antiques, down comforters, and armoires, they have starched lace curtains at the windows and baths with showers or tubs with handheld showers. Preferred rooms are those overlooking the lovely gardens abloom with camellias and gardenias. These are the most quiet, away from the street.

In the Attic Suite on the third floor, you may watch the stars through a skylight above the white iron and brass bed. The suite has a television, wicker chairs, a standing full-length mirror, and a tub with a brass hand shower. From the window, you may catch a peek of the ocean two blocks away.

The cottages are reached by brick paths that wind through the courtyard gardens of calla lilies, palm trees, and Norfolk pines. Their rooms are furnished with a mixture of antiques and modern pieces. Each has a fireplace, wet bar, television, and phone.

A buffet breakfast of fresh fruit, juice, pastries, eggs, yogurt, and granola is presented in the parlor. Sometimes the old-fashioned waffle iron is put to use and you'll have crisp, buttery waffles to enjoy at an alcove table by the garden.

The Centrella is close to many of the Monterey Peninsula's attractions. You can stroll two blocks to Lover's Point for a view of the bay or drive to Monterey to meet sea creatures face to face in the highly acclaimed aquarium.

Gatehouse Inn

225 Central Avenue
Pacific Grove, CA 93950
408-649-8436
800-753-1881
Fax: 408-648-8044

> *A historic home
> within walking
> distance of
> Monterey Bay*

Manager: Lois DeFord. **Accommodations:** 8 rooms (all with private bath). **Rates:** $110–$150 single or double, $20 additional person. **Included:** Full breakfast. **Added:** 10% tax. **Payment:** Major credit cards. **Children:** Over age 12 welcome, additional $15. **Pets:** Not allowed. **Smoking:** Not allowed indoors.

The Gatehouse has an interesting history. It was built in 1884 by a state senator, Benjamin Langford, as a seaside retreat for his family. In those days, Pacific Grove was a religious meeting ground surrounded by a white picket fence. If the senator came home late when the gates were locked, he had to hunt up the keys and then return them. One night in 1885, tired of this ordeal, he chopped the gate down; it was never rebuilt.

There's no barrier now to this lovely old home on a residential corner. Guests are welcomed into the parlor, which retains the atmosphere of a Victorian summer house, with its white wicker, pale green walls, stained glass windows, and ferns. Several of the rooms have views of Monterey Bay, which is a short walk down the hill from the inn. The Langford Room, which has a fireplace and a sitting room, has the best water view. The small Sun Room, cheery in white and green, is flooded with morning sun through its two walls of windows. On the ground floor are the Steinbeck Room and Otter's Cove Room. Each has its own entrance and latticed patio.

Behind the main house, in a separate building, are the Cannery Row and Wicker rooms. Cannery Row has a king-size bed topped with floral pillows, a wood stove, and a claw-foot tub. Wicker has a Victorian garden theme, with a white lattice fence on the wall and exuberant flower displays.

> **In the kitchen of the main house, coffee, tea, cookies, and fruit are always available. The informal buffet breakfast may be taken to your room or eaten in the dining room or parlor, and some guests choose the table in the kitchen.**

The only drawback to this charming inn is the noise. In the main house you're likely to hear traffic from the busy street, early morning street cleaners, the clatter of dishes, and footsteps. If you're a light sleeper, the rooms in the back building are preferable.

The Green Gables Inn

104 Fifth Street
Pacific Grove, CA 93950
408-375-2095
800-722-1774
Fax: 408-375-5437

*A restored
Victorian with
contemporary
comfort*

Innkeeper: Tess Desmond. **Accommodations:** 11 rooms (6 with private bath). **Rates:** $100–$160 single or double, $15 additional person. **Included:** Full breakfast and afternoon tea and hors d'oeuvres. **Added:** Tax. **Payment:** Major credit cards. **Children:** Welcome in Carriage House. **Pets:** Not allowed. **Smoking:** Not allowed.

This half-timbered Queen Anne mansion, built in 1888, stands on a corner across the street from beautiful Monterey Bay. Soft music plays as you enter the house, and prisms dance against the wall from the stained glass window in the front door. Flowered carpeting, pale peach walls, and carved molding details create a warm setting in the living room. Here guests sit by the white fireplace and play chess, or retire to the alcove window to browse through restaurant menus. There are numerous reading lamps, but oddly, no books or magazines. Through double doors is the dining room, where a buffet breakfast is set out. After helping yourself to juice, fruits, cereal, a hot egg dish, muffins, and coffee, you may sit at the main table under a crystal chandelier or at a table for two by the window overlooking the sea.

The five upstairs rooms are furnished with antiques, soft quilts, and ruffled curtains. They all feature typical Four Sisters Inns decor: coordinated fabrics and wallpapers, fresh flowers, lavish greenery, and the occasional ceramic rabbit, teddy bear, or stuffed goose. Most of the rooms have ocean views and six have fireplaces.

> Pacific Grove is a fine place to relax, walk, and enjoy the sea views and tidepools. At Natural Bridges State Beach, you may see thousands of wintering Monarch butterflies in the Monarch Natural Preserve.

Chapel Room is reminiscent of a chapel on a private estate, with its mullioned windows, heavy woodwork, beamed ceiling, and straight-back benches. The room is full of cupboards and nooks and the bed is a hand-carved antique topped with a white cotton spread, lacy pillows, and a teddy bear. Floral wallpaper with a rose motif and matching curtains add a feminine touch.

The Lacey Suite can accommodate four people. It has a sitting room with a fireplace and an antique tub in the bath. Balcony Room, which has the best ocean view, accommodates three and shares a bath. In back, behind the main house and a tiny garden, is the Carriage House, with five rooms on three levels. All have fireplaces, king-size beds, television, and private entrances.

The staff at Green Gables seeks to please and enjoys the extras that make a stay memorable. Holiday celebrations, birthday and honeymoon specials, and arranging reservations at golf courses, concerts, theatrical events, and restaurants are among the services they provide.

Recommended restaurants in Pacific Grove include Fandango's, Taste Bistro, The Old Bath House, and, for Victorian atmosphere, Gernot.

The Martine Inn

255 Ocean View Boulevard
Pacific Grove, CA 93950
408-373-3388
800-852-5588
Fax: 408-373-3896

*A castlelike home
overlooking
the sea*

Innkeepers: Don and Marion Martine. **Accommodations:** 19 rooms (all with private bath). **Rates:** $125–$230 single or double, $35 additional person; suites $250–$280. **Included:** Full breakfast. **Added:** 10% tax. **Minimum Stay:** 2 nights on weekends, 3 nights on holidays. **Payment:** MasterCard, Visa. **Children:** $35 additional if third person in room. **Pets:** Not allowed. **Smoking:** Allowed in fireplace rooms.

Like a little Mediterranean castle, this rose-colored stucco mansion stands on a cliff above Monterey Bay. The first thing you notice when you enter the parlor is the irresistible view; from the picture window you see a panorama of surf and rocks, sea and sky. You may catch glimpses of the sea otters, seals, and whales that frequent these waters.

The next eye-catcher is the gleam of silver from the innkeepers' collection of ornate teapots, trays, vases and other museum-quality pieces. The Martines have myriad interests, as a quick glance around their home reveals. Their antique collection fills the common rooms and guest rooms.

The home was built in 1899 and purchased in 1901 by Laura and James Parke, of Parke-Davis Pharmaceuticals. Many dignitaries were entertained here over the years, and some major remodeling took place. Eventually the cupola and dormers were removed and the house was converted from a Victorian to Mediterranean style. Don Martine and his parents bought it in 1972.

Later, Don and Marion fully renovated the mansion, adding modern plumbing and heating but replacing the fixtures, wallcoverings, colors, and furniture with authentic turn-of-the-century pieces. Some are particularly outstanding: a mahogany suite from the 1893 Chicago World's Fair, an Eastlake suite from the estate of C. K. McClatchy (it's in the McClatchy Room), Edith Head's bedroom suite, and an 1860 Chippendale Revival four-poster bed with a canopy and side curtains.

> The Martines' goal is, Don says, "to recreate the experience you would have had ninety years ago if you'd been a personal guest of the Parkes."

The four-poster is in the original master bedroom, the Parke Room, now the most expensive and most popular at the inn. It has a spectacular bay view, a white brick fireplace, a ceiling-high armoire with a beveled mirror, and bathroom doors that open to an iron railing.

The Early American Room has a rope bed of solid burled walnut, dated 1800. Behind the main house, on the other side of a courtyard with a dragon fountain, is the Carriage House, which has six rooms. The Captain's Room is furnished with a carved, inlaid American bedroom set, a rare standing mirror from 1840, peacock wallpaper, and a view through double doors to the breezeway and courtyard.

Guests gravitate to the courtyard, bright with potted flowers, to see the marble bar with stained glass windows and the Coinola player piano. There's a pool table behind the bar, and a whirlpool tub around the corner.

Intriguing collectibles are only part of what makes the Martine Inn superior. The service and hospitality are exceptional, drawing visitors back again and again.

The Martines offer hors d'oeuvres with wine and sparkling cider, and will bring champagne in a silver ice bucket to your room upon request. Breakfast, which is served on Sheffield china with sterling silver and crystal, is different every day. Fresh orange juice, muffins, quiche, eggs with artichoke sauce, and fruit in a spicy sauce are a few of the dishes.

A page of suggestions of things to see and do on the Monterey Peninsula is given to each guest, and the Martines will arrange for tours and restaurant reservations. They also handle conferences, seminars, and weddings.

Seven Gables Inn

555 Ocean View Boulevard
Pacific Grove, CA 93950
408-372-4341

A Victorian mansion overlooking Monterey Bay

Innkeepers: Susan, Ed, and John Flatley. **Accommodations:** 14 rooms (all with private bath). **Rates:** $125–$225 single or double. **Included:** Full breakfast. **Added:** 10% tax. **Payment:** Master-Card, Visa. **Children:** Not appropriate. **Pets:** Not allowed. **Smoking:** Not allowed

When this showy, yellow and white Victorian was built in 1886, it was one of a series of mansions fronting Monterey Bay. Few are left today, but the panorama of sea and surf and rocky bluffs remains much the same. Lucie Chase, a wealthy widow and civic leader, owned Seven Gables at the turn of the century; she added the sun porches and gables that give the home such distinctive style.

The Flatley family, who restored the old home and opened it as a bed-and-breakfast in 1982, maintain it with loving care. It's a gingerbread delight on the outside and a treasure chest within, full of the fine antiques the Flatleys have collected. Chinese carpets, ornate chandeliers, marble pedestals, gilded tables and armoires mingle in tastefully furnished rooms. A mirror with a gilded frame reaches to the ceiling in the dining room, where a silver bowl filled with roses rests on the table. Tea is served here in the afternoon, and in the morning guests get acquainted over a generous breakfast.

Off the dining room is a sunroom with a wall of lace-curtained windows and a view of the bay and coastal mountains to the north. The guest rooms are divided among four buildings: the main house, a guest house, and two cottages, one a separate unit and the other with rooms on two levels. All are furnished with antiques and a romantic but not fussy decor.

The Gable room is tucked under a high gable in the main house. With windows on four sides, it has views from the village streets to the horizon of sea and sky. The room is at the top of narrow, steep steps and has a low ceiling and slanted walls — cozy, but not for tall visitors.

The guest house in back, off the flowery courtyard, has four rooms, all with refrigerators. There's a pay phone in the hall and a television in a sunroom. The Cypress Room, one of the most expensive and most elaborate, is in a corner with wide windows and a window seat, a gilded couch, fabric walls, and Oriental pillows.

Spacious Ocean Mist has inlaid wood antiques, stained glass, and a bay window; Mayfair views the brick courtyard and cottage and catches a glimpse of the sea. Baskets of candies and fruit are provided in every room.

> Anyone at the inn will make golf reservations for you, recommend restaurants and entertainment, and tell you about nearby attractions such as Cannery Row, the Monterey Bay Aquarium, and Lover's Point Beach, a sheltered stretch of white sand that's just a 2-minute walk from the inn.

Despite all the gilt and marble elegance, you won't feel surrounded by formality at Seven Gables. The Flatley family is eager to see that you're comfortable. "We want to keep things homey," they say.

The Flatleys have recently opened up another inn in the Edwardian home next door. Called the Grand View Inn, it has ten guest rooms, and was built by the town's first woman mayor. You may want to inquire if the Grand View has space available if the Seven Gables is already booked.

PEBBLE BEACH

The Inn at Spanish Bay

2700 Seventeen Mile Drive
Pebble Beach, CA 93953
408-647-7500
800-654-9300
Fax: 408-644-7960

> *A seaside resort with a world-class golf course*

General manager: Gary Davis. **Accommodations:** 270 rooms and suites. **Rates:** $245–$350 single or double, $25 additional person; suites $550–$1,875. **Added:** 10% tax and $17 per night gratuity. **Payment:** Major credit cards. **Children:** Under age 18 free in room with parents. **Pets:** Not allowed. **Smoking:** Allowed in bar only.

The Inn at Spanish Bay and its 18-hole, par 72 golf course opened in late 1987, at the northern end of the sand dunes of Spanish Bay. The low-profile, red-roofed buildings of the complex blend with the setting, their walls the color of the dunes around them. Accommodations, located in two wings off the central lobby area, are spacious and well-appointed, with blond woods, gas fireplaces, wall-to-wall carpeting, and small decks or balconies that overlook the forest, golf course, or ocean.

Stocked refrigerators, television, large baths with deep soaking tubs, terrycloth robes, and assorted toiletries (including sewing kits and clothes steamers) are among the amenities. Abstract paintings and landscapes add a dash of color to the off-white and neutral tones of the rooms.

The resort has eight tennis courts, two with lights for night play, as well as a swimming pool and spa, but the main attraction is the golf course. The Links at Spanish Bay was modeled after the demanding seaside courses of Scotland and Ireland, with the game played close to the ground to avoid the wind. Fescue grasses, native to Scotland, provide a hard, fast surface. There's even a kilted bagpiper who plays at dusk as he strides across the fairway.

Several meeting rooms and a ballroom big enough to hold a banquet for four hundred give the resort a conference orientation. When a group is on the site, the lobby is often filled with name-tagged crowds, all enjoying the country club atmosphere.

Monterey Peninsula, 120 miles south of San Francisco, boasts some of the world's most spectacular coastal scenery. Winding above its rugged headlands, the renowned Seventeen Mile Drive is contained entirely within the Del Monte Forest Preserve, which covers some 5,300 acres.

Past the large, busy lobby is a lounge where appetizers and cocktails are served in the evenings by the stone fireplace and musicians play nightly. Just outside is the Grill, open in summer. The Dunes is Spanish Bay's two-level dining room, offering California cuisine in a light, bright, casual atmosphere. The crab cakes and the lamb noisettes are especially commendable in this restaurant of noteworthy food and service. More intimate, elegant, and dressy than the Dunes is the Bay Club, featuring a Mediterranean menu and fine wine list.

One of Spanish Bay's greatest attractions, after its location and golf course, is its service and attention to detail. A concierge and thirteen assistants are on hand to help you register, escort you to your room, and deal with special needs, such as finding a dentist, making tour reservations — or dressing up as elves for your group's Christmas party.

A $17 gratuity is charged each day. Room service is available 24 hours a day. You'll receive twice-daily housekeeping and a morning newspaper. Convenient racks are available to store your golf clubs, and you may have one-hour shoe shines and pressing, and same-day dry cleaning. A complimentary airport shuttle from Monterey is provided. If you don't want to head in to Carmel for shopping, there are several shops off the breezeway by the main entrance.

The Lodge at Pebble Beach

P.O. Box 1128
Seventeen Mile Drive
Pebble Beach, CA 93953
408-624-3811
800-654-9300 in California
Fax: 408-644-7960

A classic golf resort overlooking the Pacific

Manager: Gary Davis. **Accommodations:** 155 rooms, 6 suites. **Rates:** $295–$485, $25 additional person, suites $800–$1,800. **Added:** 10% tax and a $15 gratuity per night. **Payment:** Major credit cards. **Children:** Under age 18 free in room with parents. **Pets:** Allowed with permission. **Smoking:** Nonsmoking rooms available.

Since 1919, the Lodge at Pebble Beach has catered to travelers seeking luxurious accommodations in one of nature's most spellbinding and magnificent settings. Some 120 miles south of San Francisco, in the heart of the Del Monte Forest Preserve along the rocky coast, the sprawling resort stands on a bluff, under towering pines and gnarled cypress trees. Between the main lodge and the sea lies hallowed ground to golfers: the famed Pebble Beach fairways.

Until 1977 the hotel was known as Del Monte Lodge, after Charles Crocker's original resort; then the name was changed, but the superior hospitality and accommodations remained. Eleven guest rooms are in the original lodge. The rest are in rambling, low-rise buildings laced throughout the six acres of grounds and golf links.

Each room has its own patio or balcony with a view of the gardens, fairways, or the surf-pounded shore. The traditional, residential furnishings feature natural fabrics and light woods. There are fireplaces ready to light, stocked bars, television, and gracious accents such as fresh flowers and original art. The one- and two-bedroom suites are lavishly decorated and have grand views of the golf course and sea. Most in demand are the 18th fairway suites, with their marble fireplaces and unobstructed, spectacular ocean vistas.

A $15-per-night gratuity is added to all room rates. This is intended, say staff members, "to cover housekeeping, baggage handling, shuttle transportation, and airport pickup." So tipping in these areas is not expected.

If you're unable to get a reservation at the famed main course, guests do receive preferential tee times at the resort group's other golf courses: Spyglass Hill, the Links at Spanish Bay, and Del Monte Golf Course. If you prefer other sports, the lodge has some options. There are fourteen tennis courts, and games and lessons can be arranged. You may swim in a pool above the surf, hike or jog the trails in the Del Monte Forest, play polo or soccer, bicycle, sail, or fish. Horseback riding on thirty-four miles of scenic trails is offered; the Pebble Beach Equestrian Center is considered one of the finest on the West Coast.

> **The Pebble Beach Golf Links is often called the premier golf course in the world open to the public; you'll need a reservation far in advance to play. The site of many tournaments, it is both challenging and beautiful, perched at the edge of a seaside cliff.**

There is no good beach at the resort. For strolling on the sand, go next door to Stillwater Cove. Four restaurants give you a choice of cuisine. In the glass-walled Cypress Room, the menu favors California creativity and mesquite-grilled meats and seafood. The Tap Room is an informal spot for sandwiches and pub specials while you check the display of golfing memorabilia and photographs.

Club XIX overlooks the golf course and sea. During the day it's an al fresco café serving sandwiches and salads at outdoor tables hedged by cascading flowers; at night you dress up and dine by candlelight on classic French cuisine. The Gallery, above an arcade of a dozen shops across from the main lodge, is a bar and grill serving breakfast and lunch. It accommodates early birds eager to head for the first tee.

The Terrace Lounge is the place for cocktails, conversation, and gazing through wide windows at the seascape framed by cypress trees. A pianist plays during the day, and jazz artists or guest combos perform evenings and weekends. In this calm room, with its glass chandelier, two fireplaces, and soft couches in neutral colors, there's a sense of stability and tradition — an atmosphere that permeates the resort. It's too sporty for elegance, but the Lodge at Pebble Beach has been catering to elite crowds for some time, and it clearly intends to maintain the quality it takes to continue doing so.

SANTA BARBARA

The Bayberry Inn

111 West Valerio Street
Santa Barbara, CA 93101
805-682-3199
800-528-9691

A tranquil B&B with an atmosphere of luxury

Innkeeper: Bharti Singh. **Accommodations:** 8 rooms (all with private bath). **Rates:** $85–$135 single or double. **Included:** Full breakfast. **Added:** 10% tax. **Minimum Stay:** 2 nights on weekends. **Payment:** Major credit cards. **Children:** Not appropriate. **Pets:** Dogs occasionally allowed with permission; additional $10 per day. **Smoking:** Not allowed.

Pure enchantment is what you'll find at The Bayberry. From the cherub fountain in the entrance to the fresh flowers in every room, not a detail has been overlooked in creating an inn of beauty and comfort. The owners' backgrounds of art, catering, psychology, and interior design help them to create a fantasy home in a residential neighborhood. They have filled the restored, 1886 house with imported antiques, beveled mirrors, lush fabrics, and glistening crystal.

The dining room probably draws the most immediate admiration. From a ceiling of shirred pink silk hangs an elaborate chandelier, its prisms reflected in the room's crown of mirrors. Antique walnut chairs covered with hand-loomed tapestry from Italy, sit at a long table set with sterling silver, Royal Doulton china, tall candlesticks, and colorful flowers. Your first glimpse tells you that breakfast will be interesting.

And so it is. Bharti prepares different dishes daily. Orange juice and a fresh fruit bowl, often including oranges from the inn's own prolific tree, are always part of the meal. Early morning coffee, tea, and newspapers are available in the sunporch, where Letitia and Lawrence, the resident zebra finches, greet your arrival with soft chirping.

> Several eating places are within walking distance, and the innkeeper is happy to make recommendations. She'll also lend bicycles, provide maps for walking and shopping tours, and share her knowledge of Santa Barbara.

Beyond the light and sunny porch is a deck with glass tables, where breakfast may be served in warm weather. The deck faces an expansive lawn (fine for croquet and badminton) with the bountiful orange tree standing against a white lattice fence.

All of the guest rooms, five upstairs and three down, have queen-size beds, some with romantic canopies. Down comforters, fine linens, and opulent furnishings make these retreats luxurious. The inn is on a busy street corner, but outside sounds have been muted by upholstering the halls. There are no common walls between bedrooms; closets or baths divide them, keeping neighboring noise to a minimum.

Each room is named for a berry. Bayberry, the largest, has a dramatically draped canopy bed with a chandelier hanging from the center, a brick fireplace, and a tiny bath in green and white. Hollyberry is the quietest room and is cozy with a small, wood-burning fireplace. On a platform in the green tiled bath is an old weight scale from a long-gone hotel. Learn your weight for a penny (a tray of pennies has been provided). Blueberry is a showpiece in blue and pink and lace. Its highlight is a bath/sitting room with white recamier sofa and a Victorian clawfoot tub and hand-held shower. A plentiful supply of bubble bath is included.

Raspberry, one of the downstairs rooms, has French wallpaper handprinted with tiny berries. There are built-in shelves of books, a fireplace, and a private, elm-shaded deck fragrant with jasmine vines. Cranberry has a wood-burning fireplace, and camellia blossoms outside the window complement the room's decor. Although Strawberry is the least expensive, it's a sunny room and a personal favorite, with rose print wallpaper and a lace canopy.

Complimentary afternoon tea, cider, and snacks are served in the living room. It's a fine time to peruse the Bayberry's restaurant guide, or visit with other guests or the friendly innkeeper, who encourages an informal atmosphere despite the elegant surroundings.

Four Seasons Biltmore

1260 Channel Drive
Santa Barbara, CA 93108
805-969-2261
800-332-3442
Fax: 805-969-4682

*A Mediterranean
hotel with
Pacific views*

General manager: Chris Hart. **Accommodations:** 234 rooms, suites, and cottages. **Rates:** $199–$350 double, $30 additional person, suites and cottages $625–$1,700. **Payment:** Major credit cards. **Children:** Under 18 free in room with parents. **Pets:** Allowed with permission. **Smoking:** Nonsmoking rooms available.

Directly facing the Pacific Ocean and backed by the Santa Ynez Mountains, the Four Seasons Biltmore has a magnificent location. The accommodations live up to the setting. Elegance, serenity, and luxury come to mind when touring the 19 acres of landscaped gardens and white buildings with red tile roofs. The restored hotel dates from 1927, when the Bowman Biltmore chain planned it as the chain's crown jewel. The romantic structure has thick walls, Moorish arches, Portuguese tiles, and little balconies above intimate patios. Recent renovations left the richly designed tile work, carved lamps, and high entry ceiling, but the dark woods were lightened and a more open mood created.

Walkways edged with impatiens and fuchsia lead to guest rooms in two-story buildings and cottages tucked among the shrubs and palm trees of the lovely grounds that keep a crew of gardeners busy. Each room has a view of the ocean, the mountains, the lush gardens, or a pool. Many have balconies or private patios, fireplaces, vaulted ceilings, and oak ceiling fans. Walk-in closets and louvered shutters add to the sense of spaciousness. Botanical prints and tapestry fabric create an attractive look, while comforts include terry robes, hair dryers, safes, makeup mirrors, TVs with VCRs, bath phones, and two sinks — one in the bath and one in a separate vanity in the dressing area.

> **California style in a Mediterranean resort, with a superb location on the southern edge of Santa Barbara: the Four Seasons Biltmore combines it all with verve and a sense of history. This is a resort for the discriminating traveler who expects fine service in beautiful surroundings.**

In junglelike gardens, the nine cottages vary in size — up to five bedrooms. The larger units have two executive suites. Each cottage has a parlor with fireplace and floral-patterned chairs and soft couches. The most luxurious is the Odell Suite, with four baths, three bedrooms, three fireplaces, and a parlor furnished with antiques.

On the property are an 18-hole putting green, a croquet field, three lighted tennis courts, and a small health club where fitness equipment and massages are available. A swimming pool shimmers under tall palms and an immense fig tree. The concierge staff can arrange for sportfishing, sailing, horseback riding, polo, scenic tours, and golfing.

The service at the Biltmore, as at all Four Seasons hotels, is far above average. The staff is well trained in the art of pampering guests — even the youngest ones. During the summer and on winter weekends, children can participate in Kids For All Seasons, a free program of activities.

La Marina is the Biltmore's formal dining room. Its high arched windows look toward the front lawn and across the road to the sea. California cuisine is served in a candlelit setting, with fresh flowers and Wedgwood china.

You may also dine under the stars in The Patio, where the roof rolls back to reveal the sky. The café has an informal garden atmosphere, complete with tropical blooms, rattan furniture, and pink linens. Specialty meals such as a Mediterranean buffet are sometimes offered, otherwise the menus leans toward California cuisine, gourmet pizzas, pastas, and veal and lamb chops. In La Sala Lounge, a cozy library with a fireplace, English tea is served. At sunset guests spill out onto the terrace for cocktails, and later there is nightly entertainment.

Several meeting and banquet rooms make the hotel popular with groups, but even large numbers of people don't disturb the serene ambience.

Across the road, on the beach side, is the Coral Casino Beach and Cabana Club, which is open to hotel guests. It has a private beach, cabanas, and a 50-meter pool so close to the sea wall that, at high tide, swimmers may be splashed with sea spray.

The Glenborough Inn

1327 Bath Street
Santa Barbara, CA 93101
805-966-0589
800-962-0589
Fax: 805-564-8610

Friendly innkeepers make this lodging a good choice while visiting Santa Barbara

Innkeepers: Cathi Nystrom, Michael Diaz, Steve Ryan, and Ken Armstrong. **Accommodations:** 11 rooms in 3 homes. **Rates:** $90–$190 single or double, $25 per additional person per night. **Included:** Full breakfast. **Added:** Tax. **Minimum Stay:** 2 nights on weekends and most holidays. **Children:** Welcome in 2 suites; $25 additional. **Pets:** Not allowed. **Smoking:** Allowed outdoors only.

The Glenborough Inn consists of not one but three separate buildings on a residential street near downtown Santa Barbara. Eleven guest rooms are distributed between the Main House, a two-story Craftsman bungalow that was built in 1906, the White House, and a gray 1885 Victorian cottage bordered by a lovely side garden.

The Main House serves as the focal point for guest activities. It is here guests gather each afternoon between five and six o'clock for a social hour with wine and hors d'oeuvres while classical music plays in the background. There's a central guest refrigerator, and a tea caddy and home-baked cookies are always available. In the quiet yard, the outdoor hot tub can be used by all guests on a sign up basis. (Spa towels and robes are provided in each of the guest rooms.)

A selection of menus from area restaurants can be browsed through in the living room of the Main House. The downtown shopping district is just a few blocks from the inn.

There are five guest rooms in the Main House, four upstairs, and the deluxe Nouveau Suite with its own private garden and hot tub downstairs. The upstairs rooms presently share baths, but plans are in the works to create private baths in each. Garden, as one might expect, overlooks the garden, and has a white iron bed. Aurelia's Fancy features Norman Rockwell prints, slanted ceilings, and a fireplace. French Rose is romantic with inlaid furnishings, valentines, a fireplace, and a Jacuzzi tub.

In the Cottage, the Grand Suite has a canopy bed, while the decor in the nautically themed Captain's Quarters includes an antique cloth map. In the White House, Mountain View has a mirrored wardrobe and big walk-in closet. Inn View is a cheerful room with lace curtains and a wicker sofa topped with chintz cushions. The two rooms share a Victorian bath complete with a pull-chain toilet and clawfoot tub.

Breakfast is delivered to each room in a picnic basket in the morning. Frittatas, blintzes, or stuffed French toast accompanied by scones and fruit smoothies are typical, and accommodations are also made for those with dietary restrictions. In fact, it is the innkeepers' sincere desire to make their guests feel welcome that sets this bed-and-breakfast apart from other establishments.

The Old Yacht Club Inn

431 Corona Del Mar Drive
Santa Barbara, CA 93103
805-962-1277
800-676-1676 in California
800-549-1676 in U.S.
Fax: 805-962-3989

> *A bed-and-
> breakfast inn
> close to the beach*

Innkeepers: Nancy Donaldson and Sandy Hunt. **Accommodations:** 9 rooms (all with private bath). **Rates:** $90–$155 single, $95–$165 double, $30 additional person. **Included:** Full breakfast. **Added:** 10% tax. **Minimum Stay:** 2 nights on weekends. **Payment:** Major credit cards. **Children:** Additional $30 if third person in room. **Pets:** Not allowed. **Smoking:** Not allowed indoors.

Once upon a time this really was a yacht club. It had been built as a private home in 1912, but served as the boaters' headquarters when the first clubhouse was swept out to sea. Then it was moved inland a few yards, and in 1980 opened as an inn.

The capable owners are friends who met as school administrators in Los Angeles and were eager to try something different. They bought and restored the clubhouse, filled it with turn-of-the-century furnishings, and invited visitors to Santa Barbara to stay. It was the city's first bed-and-breakfast and is still the only one close to the beach.

The casual, friendly warmth of the inn is evident from the moment you walk in the door and are welcomed by one of the partners — and perhaps by the tiny poodle with the big name, Bella Mia Barboni. The front room of the stucco Craftsman home feels lived-in and homey. Dozens of guidebooks and travel books fill the bookshelves, fresh flowers grace the tables, and a ceramic cat rests on the hearth of the white brick fireplace. Notes from grateful visitors spill from an album on the piano.

On the other side of the room, tables are set for breakfast or for Nancy's famous Saturday night dinners. Coffee is on the sideboard by 6:30 A.M., followed by breakfast served course by course. Orange juice, fruit with flavored yogurt, muffins, a Spanish omelette, and sour cream coffeecake are part of a typical meal.

Dinners, presented three Saturdays a month, are usually

booked far in advance. They start with champagne by the fire and move on to a fixed menu that might include mushroom soup, salmon in a raspberry beurre blanc sauce, and asparagus wrapped in phyllo topped with a cheese sauce. A tempting dessert such as straw-berry cream pie and cof-fee follow. Several wines are available. Popular de-mand brought about a collection of Nancy's fa-vorite recipes called *The Old Yacht Club Inn Cookbook.*

> **After one of Nancy's superb dinners, you may wish to visit on into the night with other guests — this is a get-acquainted sort of place — or stroll to the beach to see the waves in the moonlight.**

Captain's Corner, the only main floor room, has twin four poster beds that can be made up as a king if requested, and a private deck. Upstairs, where the walls hold pictures of yachts and sailing vessels, are four rooms. Castellammare is light, done in lace and shades of rose. It has a two-person whirlpool tub and French doors that open to a balcony. Portofino is cool in blue and has a built-in window seat and dresser and a bath with shower.

The other part of the inn is next door: Hitchcock House, stucco with a red tile roof and a broad deck (made by the tal-ented Nancy) in back. Grapevines climb over the lattice fence and a lemon tree lends bright color to the deck, a pleasant place for lounging.

Hitchcock's four rooms are all on the ground floor and have separate entrances. They bear names of the innkeepers' fam-ily members. There's a childhood portrait of Nancy in the Gallaher Room as well as a picture of her ninety-something mother in younger years. The comforter, pillows, and cur-tains all complement one another in light shades of blue, pink, and green, and the bath has a whirlpool tub. The most expensive is the Belle Caruso Suite. It has a king-size bed draped in gauze, and a separate living room on a sunporch with a wicker daybed. Julia Metelmann, the largest room, is furnished in an eclectic assortment of antiques. A narrow ar-moire, a black and gold dresser, and a red and black Chinese dragon carpet are a few of the interesting collectibles.

Every guest room has a phone, but there's no radio or tele-vision (though one will be provided in Hitchcock House upon request). This is a place to sip sherry by the fire, relax on the flowery front porch, or chat with the innkeepers, who know a great deal about Santa Barbara and are happy to lend a beach chair or a bicycle and send you in the right direction.

Secret Garden Inn and Cottages

1908 Bath Street
Santa Barbara, CA 93101
805-687-2300
800-676-1622 in U.S.
Fax: 805-687-4576

A romantic bed-and-breakfast in central Santa Barbara

Innkeepers: Christine Dunstan and Jack Greenwald. **Accommodations:** 9 rooms (all with private bath). **Rates:** $95–$155 single or double, $20 additional person; weekday discounts November to mid-May. **Included:** Full breakfast. **Added:** Tax. **Minimum Stay:** 2 nights on weekends and holidays. **Payment:** Major credit cards. **Children:** Welcome. **Pets:** Not allowed. **Smoking:** Not allowed indoors.

All the rooms and cottages at the Secret Garden Inn have a pleasant country charm and offer comfortable lodging close to the center of Santa Barbara. Especially appealing and romantic is Wood Thrush Cottage, a quaint and private little brown home behind the main house. Wood Thrush has two sitting rooms and a bedroom furnished in French country style with warm colors. It has a refrigerator, a small bath with a clawfoot tub and shower, and a daybed that allows the cottage to hold a third person. Outside, oleander grows by the front porch and around the lawn where lounges await sunbathers.

The main house, a one-story family home with big oak and fragrant pittosporum trees in front, has two cheery rooms, Meadowlark and Bobwhite. The other guest rooms are in three more cottages in back. Cardinal, a pretty suite with a deck overlooking the garden, has English decor in hunter green and cardinal red. Mockingbird, in pale yellows, has a chintz coverlet and a country atmosphere. Nightingale has a fireplace and canopy bed. Whippoorwill and Hummingbird are in a cottage tucked away in back under eugenia and orange trees, and Hummingbird has a hot tub on its very private patio. Still farther back, off-street parking is provided.

The innkeeper serves breakfast specialties of popovers and muffins in the dining room of the main house or outdoors under the avocado tree. Breakfast includes a baked entrée such as quiche or an egg casserole, a bread basket, and fruit.

If you like Victorian decor and the luxury of Jacuzzi tubs, the owners of the Secret Garden also operate another inn in Santa Barbara. Called the Cheshire Cat, the well-run, tastefully furnished inn is about four blocks from the downtown business district.

> **The innkeeper places morning newspapers on the dining room window seat (guarded by Quincy, the quilted bear), offers wine or hot spiced cider and hors d'oeuvres in the afternoon, and lends you one of the inn's bicycles for your Santa Barbara excursion if you request it.**

Simpson House Inn

121 East Arrellaga Street
Santa Barbara, CA 93101
805-963-7067
800-676-1280
Fax: 805-564-4811

> *A historic mansion near the heart of Santa Barbara*

Owners: Glyn and Linda Davies. **Manager:** Gillean Wilson. **Accommodations:** 14 rooms (all with private bath). **Rates:** $105–$250 single or double. **Included:** Full breakfast, hors d'oeuvres, and local wines. **Minimum Stay:** 2 nights on weekends, 3 nights on holidays. **Payment:** Major credit cards. **Children:** Welcome. **Pets:** Not allowed. **Smoking:** Not allowed indoors.

This extraordinary inn is one of the loveliest places to stay in Santa Barbara. Though it's very close to the downtown area, it stands secluded behind wrought-iron gates and high hedges on nearly an acre of lawn under majestic oak, pittosporum, and magnolia trees.

The grand Eastlake-style Victorian, built in 1874, came perilously close to demolition, to make way for condominiums or office units, but was saved by Glyn and Linda Davies. Their extensive renovation brought the home back to its original splendor, with some updated comforts, and earned it a Structure of Merit award for its architecture and period setting. Now a historic landmark, the house was built for Mary and Margaret Simpson, the daughters of Scottish immigrants Robert and Julia Simpson, and it remained in the family until 1921. By then, Santa Barbara had been a winter resort favored by the wealthy for decades.

Today guests are welcomed into a Victorian parlor with rose velvet sofas and chairs, Oriental rugs, and bookshelves holding volumes of Shakespeare as well as guidebooks. An art book stands open on an easel at one of the windows. Afternoon hors d'oeuvres are set out on the sideboard in the adjoining dining room where there's a chintz covered chaise and potted orchids. Soft music plays in the background.

The guest rooms, several named in honor of the Simpson family, have down comforters under lace coverlets, antique furniture, and fresh flowers from the garden. In the main house, the largest room is the Robert and Julia Simpson Room, which has an antique queen-size bed, clawfoot tub, and French doors to a deck above the rose garden. The Parlor Room has an ornamental gas fireplace, shelves full of books, an iron and brass queen-size bed covered in lace, fringed lamps, a lovely Oriental vase, and two easy chairs set in a bay window covered with rose damask fabric. Even the small but sunny bath has a Victorian flavor with the same Victorian replica wallpaper, an inlaid wooden toilet seat cover, and an old-fashioned sewing machine table serving as a base for the marble-topped washbasin with brass fixtures. Smaller and cozier are the Sun Room, light with white wicker and a private sundeck, and Katherine McCormick, in deep red and blue, with a queen-size spool bed.

In recent years the Davies have expanded the inn's accommodations beyond the six rooms in the main house. Now there are the Old Barn Suites and three cottages. The 1874 barn was dismantled and rebuilt with the original wood on the interior. It now houses four attractive suites — Weathervane, Hayloft, Tack Room, and Carriage Room. The decor in

Weathervane — Oriental rugs atop antique pine floors, a king-size bed, wood-burning fireplace, a tapestry-covered chaise, a damask loveseat, pine furnishings including a blanket chest, a television, VCR, stereo system, private deck, and skylit Italian marble bath, is typical of the barn suites. The most expensive rooms are the cottages, furnished with understated elegance. They have fireplaces, Jacuzzi tubs, and private gates that open to an intimate courtyard.

> **The innkeepers suggest visiting Santa Barbara in fall or winter, when the skies are usually clear and sunny, restaurants and shops are uncrowded, and the calendar is full of cultural events.**

Breakfast is served on the veranda near the garden, or in the dining room if the weather prohibits outdoor dining. The meal generally includes fresh fruit and juices, an array of cereals, yogurt, homemade muffins, and a main dish such as apple-baked French toast, huevos Santa Barbara, or scones with savory eggs. After breakfast you may wish to enjoy the inn's lovely gardens where stone walkways wind past beds of lavender, lilies, roses, impatiens, and snapdragons. Benches are provided for relaxing and listening to the sounds of the birds or water splashing in a nearby fountain.

Although this distinguished inn has a stately quality, it offers a warm welcome from the affable owners, who know how to make you feel at home. They've put vast amounts of time and energy into restoring the old place, but managed to do so without losing their sense of humor. And your comfort always comes first. If you want to chat, one of the Davies or their charming assistant, Gillean Wilson, is available; if you prefer to be left alone with the complimentary morning and evening newspapers provided, you will be. The innkeepers know Santa Barbara, too, and will tell you about restaurants, shopping, scenic drives, and attractions not to be missed. All guests receive a free pass to the Santa Barbara trolley in addition to complimentary usage of a neighborhood gym.

The Upham Hotel

1404 De la Vina Street
Santa Barbara, CA 93101
805-962-0058
800-727-0876
Fax: 805-963-2825

*A historic hotel
with gardens and
cottages*

General manager: Jan Martin Winn.
Accommodations: 49 rooms and cottages. **Rates:** $120–$185
single or double, $10 additional person; suites $250–$350. **Included:** Continental breakfast. **Minimum Stay:** 2 nights on
some weekends and holidays. **Payment:** Major credit cards.
Children: Age 12 and under free in room with parents. **Pets:**
Not allowed. **Smoking:** Nonsmoking rooms available.

The Upham offers a sense of history and charm. The angular,
beige frame building with a long veranda holds comfortable,
well-kept rooms, a warm and welcoming lobby, and a restaurant, Louie's. In back of
the old hotel are surprises not seen from the
street: annexes, cottages,
gardens, and a deck with
a gazebo sprawl over the
property. At the far end is
a parking lot.

**In the early years, the
cupola was frequented
most often by the inn's
cooks who would climb up
to see the signals from an
arriving ship which would
tell them the number of
guests to expect, and
therefore the number of
meals they needed to
prepare.**

The hotel was built in
1871 by an adventurous
Boston banker, Amasa
Lyman Lincoln, who
sailed to California to
build a New England inn.
Using redwood timbers
and square-head nails,
he crowned his hostelry
with a cupola. Cyrus Upham bought the place a few years later, and it has carried his
name since.

The lobby is small, with two sitting areas. One is a sunny
corner with rattan furniture and potted plants; the other, a
quiet retreat by a fireplace flanked with built-in bookshelves.
Evening milk and cookies are served here. In the mornings,
guests help themselves from a breakfast buffet of pastries,

juice, tea and coffee and then repair to the lobby tables or drift to the little terrace, the gazebo, or their own porches.

The cottages are the nicest accommodations, though all the rooms are clean and decorated with taste. A typical duplex suite has a small porch and, inside, dark gray walls and dim lighting to soothe the eyes after Santa Barbara's white buildings and bright sun. A couch faces a gas fireplace; a large armoire holds a television set. The four-poster bed is covered with a down comforter. You might hear the outside ice maker during the night; otherwise a cottage is quiet hideaway at the edge of the pretty gardens where roses, lantana, and fuchsias bloom along winding paths.

The most expensive cottage is the very private Master Suite. Tucked in a corner behind a hibiscus-covered fence, it has a patio with an umbrella table. An inviting hammock sways gently under a palm tree. The suite features a brick fireplace, a bed, a walk-in closet bigger than some bathrooms, and a two-person whirlpool tub.

The rooms in the main hotel have antique touches such as clawfoot tubs in some baths and televisions hidden in antique armoires, but most have modern queen- and king-size beds. Other rooms are scattered among three additional buildings behind the hotel and gardens. The Carriage House contains five guest rooms and two meeting rooms.

Louie's Restaurant, in the Upham but under separate ownership, is well known for its fine food. The menu is not lengthy, but it offers a variety of entrées and changes several times a year. Pasta and pizza are available, along with beef, lamb, duck, and chicken dishes, a fresh fish of the day and a good Caesar salad.

Villa Rosa

15 Chapala Street
Santa Barbara, CA 93101
805-966-0851
Fax: 805-962-7159

A small, cozy inn within walking distance of the beach

General manager: Annie Puetz. **Accommodations:** 18 rooms. **Rates:** $80–$190 single or double; winter weekday discounts. **Included:** Continental breakfast. **Minimum Stay:** 2 nights on weekends. **Payment:** Major credit cards. **Children:** Over age 14 welcome. **Pets:** Not allowed. **Smoking:** Not allowed.

Built in 1931, this two-story hotel was renovated in 1981 and designed to offer the amenities of a larger resort with the intimacy of a small inn. A few of those amenities are breakfast in the lounge or in your room, the *Los Angeles Times* delivered to your door, complimentary wine and hors d'oeuvres in the afternoon, port and sherry in the evening, same-day dry cleaning, and a turn-down service with roses on your pillow. The staff pays careful attention to guests' needs. Whether

In the heart of beautiful Santa Barbara, just 84 steps from the sea (somebody counted), Villa Rosa welcomes guests to a Spanish Colonial Revival inn of style and warmth.

you request an iron, an aspirin, or a Band-Aid, the desk clerk will get it for you and ask if you need anything more.

The inn is decorated in southwestern style, with earth and clay colors and rough-hewn beams in the lobby. Here tables are covered with magazines, daily newspapers, and menus from local restaurants. A fire crackles on cool evenings on the tiled hearth. Double doors lead from the lobby and lounge to a pretty courtyard with a small swimming pool and a whirlpool under pepper, banana, and palm trees.

The guest rooms have different configurations but similar decor. They are done in colors of muted putty, blues, and rose; accessories are minimal, but their texture and tone are warm. Heavy, weathered pine from New Mexico, weavings on the walls, and rawhide chairs continue the desert-country theme, as do the beehive fireplaces in four rooms. Four of the rooms have partially equipped kitchens and a small dining area tucked back in a semi-circular alcove. Two have oval tubs under a window that looks out to a small garden.

The views vary, from glimpses of the ocean to mountains or the courtyard and gardens. Room 18 offers views of both ocean and pool, a sitting area, a kitchen, and a fireplace.

The inn's courtyard conference room is available to groups (up to twenty people) and there is a full range of audiovisual equipment.

SANTA CRUZ

The Babbling Brook Inn

1025 Laurel Street
Santa Cruz, CA 95060
408-427-2437
800-866-1131
Fax: 408-427-2457

A romantic inn set in a landscaped garden

Innkeeper: Helen King. **Accommodations:** 12 rooms (all with private bath). **Rates:** $85–$165 single or double, $21.50 additional person. **Included:** Full breakfast and afternoon wine and cheese. **Added:** 11% tax. **Minimum Stay:** 2 nights on weekends if Saturday included. **Payment:** Major credit cards. **Children:** Over age 12 welcome. **Pets:** Not allowed. **Smoking:** Not allowed in rooms.

This garden retreat sits on an acre of flowers, pines, redwoods, and waterfalls in the shadow of a cliff by Laurel Creek. The creek, which runs from spring-fed lakes on a hill by the university, meanders through the garden, under bridges and past guest room windows.

Helen King brings a wealth of experience in the travel industry to her inn in the city. Although its logs and shingles give it a rustic appearance, the accommodations are pure luxury. The original inn was built in 1909 on the foundation of an 1870s tannery and 1790s grist mill. It became a restaurant in 1942 and, in 1981, the first bed-and-breakfast in Santa Cruz.

Now it offers lodging in rooms with a French country

theme, most named for impressionist painters and decorated in the colors they used. All have phones, and most have a fireplace, private deck and outside entrance; two feature deep soaking jet bathtubs. There's a small television set in each closet.

> Below the deck, brick paths wind through the garden. Water cascades down the rocky cliff, and calla lilies bloom by the edge of the stream. Benches and a gazebo provide resting spots to contemplate this beautifully kept refuge, which is often used for weddings.

Toulouse Lautrec, with one of the whirlpool tubs, is flooded with light from the curved alcove windows. Monet, in a remote corner of the property and shielded from view, is in Delft blue and white, with a beamed ceiling and private deck across from the waterfall and footbridge. Degas is decorated with blue and white Laura Ashley wallpaper as a backdrop for prints of the artist's favorite subject, dancers. Secluded Cézanne is one of the largest rooms and is wheelchair-accessible. It has a corner fireplace and private deck above the brook. The smallest is Jonquil, a sunny yellow and white bedroom in the original house. It has a gas fireplace and a bed canopied with white eyelet lace. It's the only interior room, just off the reception area and kitchen.

From the kitchen come wondrous smells and tastes. Helen, the mother of six, is a superb cook who prepares an elaborate buffet breakfast with dishes that change daily. Fresh fruit, granola, yogurt, muffins, croissants, and a hot entrée are always served. You may have breakfast in your room, in the garden, or in the dining area at round tables under a glass roof.

Tea, coffee, and cookies are available all day, and wine and sherry are offered in the evenings. Guests enjoy sipping their wine on the Babbling Brook's wide deck, listening to the trickling fountains and rushing brook. Redwood trees grow through the deck, and pots of impatiens and cyclamen stand in the nooks and corners. Helen has menus of nearby restaurants and can provide recommendations. A few favorites are the Salmon Poacher, Theo's, Casablanca, and Shadowbrook.

Chaminade

One Chaminade Lane
Santa Cruz, CA 95065
408-475-5600
800-283-6569
Fax: 408-476-4942

*A country resort
in the hills above
Santa Cruz*

General manager: Tom O'Shea. **Accommodations:** 152 rooms. **Rates:** $149 Sunday–Thursday, $179 weekends, $35 additional person. **Payment:** Major credit cards. **Children:** Under age 14 free in room with parents. **Pets:** Not allowed. **Smoking:** Nonsmoking rooms available.

Chaminade, once a religious retreat, is now a retreat of a different nature. The two-story buildings, roofed with Spanish red tile, sprawl across 80 acres of landscaped grounds in the wooded foothills of the Santa Cruz Mountains. The resort, a quiet getaway favored as a conference site, is on a hilltop overlooking the city of Santa Cruz and the Pacific Ocean.

A row of windows curves around the front of the main building, and a translucent roof arches over the entry hall and up the stairs to a meeting room area. Modern works by California artists adorn the walls. The entire atmosphere is one of open space and light.

On the lower level are two restaurants. The Library offers formal dining, and casual meals are served in the Sunset Dining Room, which has views of the sea over the treetops. Meals for children under age five are free. Light buffet lunches are available in the Bayview Lounge.

The Library, one of the best restaurants in the area, offers six-course à la carte dinners on Friday and Saturday. Examples of the California-style Continental cuisine are medallions of free-range veal in a tangerine demi-glaze, grilled sea scallops with squid ink pasta and saffron cream, and roasted pheasant breast with honey chestnut glaze.

The guest rooms are in smaller, outlying buildings, most of them around the landscaped pool area. A typical room has a redwood balcony with a view of the eucalyptus and pine forest. There are two queen-size beds, two private phone lines, a TV, a loveseat, and a table and chairs.

Because 85 percent of the hotel's midweek business consists of conference groups, the facilities are geared to the businessperson — private phones, writing tables, convenient extender reading lamps, one-day valet service, a large parking lot. Leisure travelers are more evident on weekends, enjoying the swimming pool and whirlpool spas, the four tennis courts, the miles of jogging trails that wind through the forest, and the 14,000-square-foot Fitness Center.

The spacious center has a weight training system, sauna and steam rooms, yoga and aerobics classes, basketball, and locker rooms. Upstairs is the Game Room Lounge, with big-screen TV over the bar. It's open evenings for table tennis, pool, and backgammon. Windows on one side overlook the Santa Cruz Mountains, and on the other allow spectators to watch games in the short basketball court below.

Chaminade takes its name from a French priest and educator, Father William Joseph Chaminade. Father Chaminade founded the Society of Mary (Marianists) in the late 1700s. In 1929, the Marianist Brothers constructed the Chaminade boys' school in Santa Cruz and opened it in 1930. That building, renovated, now forms the core of the conference center's meeting rooms. Later the school was turned into a site for religious retreats and then, in the 1970s, remodeled as the present resort and executive conference center.

SHELL BEACH

The Cliffs at Shell Beach

2757 Shell Beach Road
Shell Beach, CA 93449
805-773-5000
800-826-7827 in California
800-826-5838 in U.S.
Fax: 805-773-0764

*A light, breezy,
oceanside resort*

General manager: John Dempsey. **Accommodations:** 165 rooms and 27 suites. **Rates:** $130–$325. **Payment:** Major credit cards. **Children:** Under age 12 free ($10 for roll-away bed). **Pets:** Not allowed. **Smoking:** Nonsmoking rooms available.

Shell Beach is just north of Pismo Beach, the only shore's edge town on Highway 101 between Santa Barbara and San Francisco. The view from the Cliffs, a white and blue, five-story resort on a bluff, is of the wide beach and rolling surf.

The Cliffs mixes luxury and the informality of a beach resort with ease. You're greeted at the door by a bellman in a gray and burgundy uniform and then enter an open, light lobby with white walls and high windows. Across the way is a terrace with white umbrella tables, next to the dramatic restaurant with a tropical theme. Birds of paradise are etched on glass parti-

The list of things to see and do in this area is a long one. You can rent horses, fish from the Pismo Beach pier or ask the concierge about a charter boat, tour Hearst Castle (55 miles north), go skin diving, watch the sea otters at play, dig clams, and taste regional wines.

tions; tall palms grow beside anthuriums and other exotic plants. There's also a cocktail lounge with music for dancing nightly. On the other side of the terrace is the pool and spa, on an island surrounded by a waterfall. Beyond it is a lawn and paths at the edge of the bluff.

The guest rooms are furnished in traditional style, some

with English reproductions and others in imitation French Provincial. The suites have white marble baths, balconies with views of the sea, and Jacuzzi tubs.

The Cliffs has complimentary valet parking, a fitness center, gift shop, beauty salon, meeting rooms, catering, room service — all the features of a modern resort, plus a stunning location and a helpful staff.

SOLVANG

The Alisal Guest Ranch

1054 Alisal Road
Solvang, CA 93463
805-688-6411
800-4-ALISAL
Fax: 805-688-2510

A country retreat in the Santa Ynez Valley

General manager: David Lautensack. **Accommodations:** 73 rooms. **Rates:** Studio: $280 single, $320 double, $65 additional person; suites $320–$360. **Included:** Breakfast and dinner. **Added:** 8.75% tax. **Minimum Stay:** 2 nights. **Payment:** Major credit cards. **Children:** Under age 2 free, age 3–5 $40 per day, over 6 $65 per day. **Pets:** Not allowed. **Smoking:** Not allowed in public spaces.

Some visitors come to this extraordinary, 10,000-acre retreat just for the horses. Experienced wranglers take guests out on daily trail rides, winding through the meadows, loping along ridgetops, and ambling beside a 96-acre manmade lake where fish leap and deer graze on the shore. It's far from the urban world most guests have left behind.

The Alisal, a three-hour drive from Los Angeles, is in the hills of the Santa Ynez Valley, near the imitation Danish village of Solvang. The resort has been open to guests since 1946, after a long history of cattle ranching. In addition to horseback riding, it offers golf on an 18-hole course, seven tennis courts and a pro shop, swimming in a freeform heated pool, boating, fishing, and sailing. Recreational activities are included in room rates on weekdays. There's an additional charge on weekends for golf, tennis, and horseback riding.

Meals (lunch is available at extra cost) are served in a restaurant with a ranch atmosphere. Dinner choices include three entrées plus appetizers, hot bread, salad or soup, and dessert and coffee. Imported and domestic wines, some with Santa Ynez labels, are available.

Musicians perform in the Oak Room Lounge, where a fire crackles on cool evenings. Leathery furnishings and western accessories add to the casual, welcoming ambience.

The guest rooms are in single-story cottages under the sycamore trees (alisal means "sycamore" in Spanish). They're furnished in Old West ranch style, with rough-paneled walls, oak beds and tables, working fireplaces, and paintings of horses. There are no phones, TVs, or radios. Executive suites sleep up to four people and have a patio with an outside fireplace.

> **If you wish to explore, you have many options in this valley of majestic oaks, vineyards, horse ranches, grassy meadows, and little towns. Visit quaint Solvang, tour and taste at nearby wineries, browse the art galleries of Los Olivos, or step into the Old West in Santa Ynez. Guided tours of the area are available.**

The real interest at Alisal lies in the outdoor activities and beautiful surroundings. Horseshoes, croquet, shuffleboard, badminton, and volleyball are a few sports to enjoy on the wide green lawns. The golf course, lush and secluded, is reserved for ranch guests. The resident tennis pro will provide lessons. You may go for a breakfast haywagon ride, jog a half-mile course, play pool or table tennis in the recreation room, soak in a bubbling hot water spa, or relax poolside in a lounge chair. In summer, counselors direct arts and crafts projects for children.

SOQUEL

The Blue Spruce Inn

2815 South Main Street
Soquel, CA 95073
408-464-1137
800-559-1137 (in California)
Fax: 408-475-0608

*A homey
bed-and-breakfast
south of
Santa Cruz*

Innkeepers: Patricia and Tom O'Brien. **Accommodations:** 6 rooms (all with private bath). **Rates:** $85–$135 single or double, $25 additional person. **Included:** Full breakfast. **Added:** 10% tax. **Minimum Stay:** 2 nights on weekends. **Payment:** Major credit cards. **Children:** $25 additional. **Pets:** Not allowed. **Smoking:** Not allowed indoors.

Each room in this pleasant bed-and-breakfast is named for its own work of art, painted by a local artist. The theme is an indication of the owners' love of art and the care that has gone into the selection of colors, fabrics, and furnishings at the Blue Spruce.

The 120-year-old home stands behind a white picket fence and a blue spruce in a community just south of Santa Cruz. It's a short distance from the beaches of Capitola and Santa Cruz. The O'Briens purchased the home in 1990 and renovated it in addition to working at their regular jobs — Pat as a school principal, Tom in the mental health profession.

If you're new to B&B lodgings, the Blue Spruce is a good choice because of the options available. You may prefer to have breakfast with other guests in the dining area, eat at a table for two by the fireplace, or take breakfast to your own room or patio. If you wish to sit in silence behind the morning newspaper, that's all right too. Breakfast always includes juice, fruit, and an entrée such as baked ham strata or enchiladas.

There are three rooms in the main house. The least expensive, romantic in red and white with a queen-size canopy bed and heart motif, is Two Hearts. Seascape has a gas fireplace, wicker furniture, a small deck and a whirlpool tub. Bloomin' Farm boasts a whirlpool.

In back of the main house, by the little pond and flower

garden, is the Carriage House, which has a carved oak bed and armoire, and a shower with a stained glass mural. Around the corner, somewhat removed from the others, Summer Afternoon offers the most privacy in an airy pastel nest.

A small room, Gazebo, is charming, with a picket fence headboard behind the feather bed. Lavish Waverly fabrics, boudoir chairs, a gas fireplace, a television behind shutters, and a phone and small desk furnish this room.

Just outside the door, on the deck by the garden, is a hot tub which all guests may use, a relaxing end to a day of exploring the beach or the many local antique shops and sampling the area's notable restaurants.

Fifteen restaurants are within walking distance of the inn. Theo's is known for its fine French cuisine, and the casual Star of Siam for flavorful Thai meals and swift service.

Desert Country

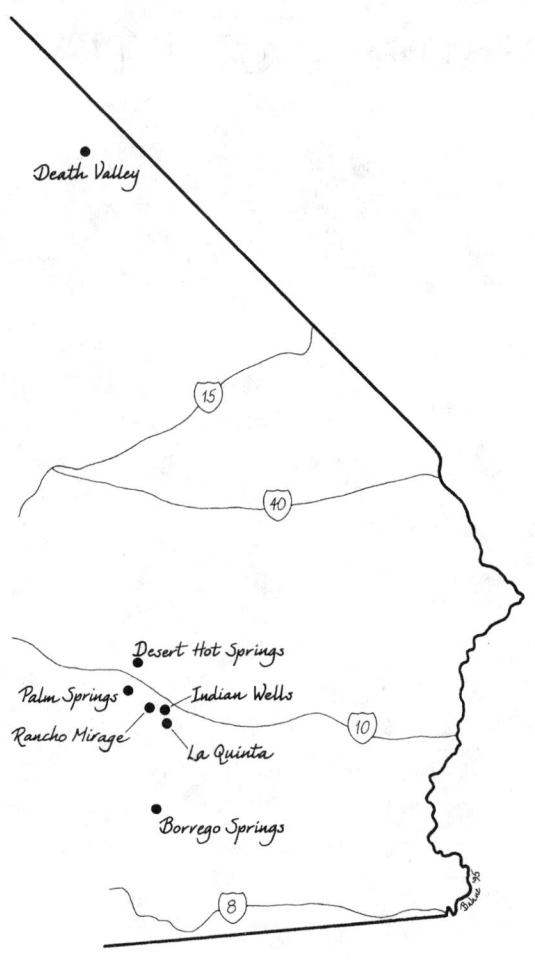

Best Country Inns and B&Bs

Desert Hot Springs
  Travellers Repose
Palm Springs
  Korakia Pensione
  L'Horizon

Best Family Favorites

Palm Springs
  Oasis Water Resort Villa Hotel

Best Resorts

Borrego Springs
  La Casa del Zorro
Death Valley
  Furnace Creek Inn
Indian Wells
  Renaissance Esmeralda Resort
La Quinta
  La Quinta Resort and Club
Rancho Mirage
  The Ritz-Carlton Rancho Mirage
  The Westin Mission Hills Resort

Best Romantic Hideaways

Palm Springs
  Ingleside Inn
  La Mancha
  Orchid Tree Inn
  Villa Royale

The deserts of California range from the dry expanses of Death Valley National Monument to the rugged mountains and green golf courses of the Palm Springs area.

Death Valley lies in the northeastern Mojave Desert, where great canyons, salt flats, ancient lake beds, and cliffs washed in a multitude of colors draw thousands of tourists yearly. This seemingly desolate land shelters a surprising amount of life — snakes and desert animals, bighorn sheep, a few burros, and, in protected pools, the desert pupfish.

The valley has resorts, campgrounds, swimming pools, a ghost town, a borax museum that records the old mining days, and a grand mansion. Scotty's Castle is a Mediterranean-style structure with three towers and twenty-five rooms filled with artworks and fine furniture, including a grand piano and pipe organ. Once the home of a sometime miner and teller of tall tales, it's now open for tours.

Far to the south of the great desert lies the Coachella Valley, where Mount San Jacinto rises a steep 10,000 feet from the sandy sea-level floor, a backdrop to Palm Springs. The valley sits atop a huge underground lake, and so the popular resort oasis uses water lavishly. There are more than 10,000 swimming pools and 85 golf courses in the region — and there's even a pool with waves big enough for surfing.

Lodgings in the valley, from simple motels to opulent and expensive resorts, are spread through seven adjoining cities; among them are **Palm Springs, Desert Hot Springs, La Quinta,** and **Rancho Mirage**. They're famous for their lush golf courses, boutiques, and celebrity homes; but the region has many lesser known attractions. In the Palm Springs Desert Museum you can view outstanding art and natural science collections and at the Living Desert you'll see animals and plants of the desert. The 1,200-acre park has hundreds of cactus varieties as well as gila monsters, foxes, and gazelles.

Beyond the fountains and green lawns of Palm Springs, the desert has its own haunting, quiet beauty, with rocky outcroppings and cliffs in a multitude of hues and cacti that blossom bright with color in the spring. In nearby Joshua Tree National Monument, you can see cacti, underground springs, palm trees, yucca plants, wildlife and the spring-blooming Joshua tree among the granite monoliths. One of the best ways to see it is by touring with Desert Adventures. The company's knowledgeable guides will tell you about the botany, wildlife, geology and history of the fascinating park.

In stark contrast to the rocky gorges and open desert in much of the valley are the Indian Canyons, a series of canyons with palm trees and streams. Some of the canyons are listed on the National Register of Historic Places, as the Agua Caliente Cahuilla Indians had complex communities here.

For a panoramic view of the valley, ride the Palm Springs

Aerial Tramway up San Jacinto Mountain. The cable cars climb through five climatic zones, from the desert floor to the cool mountaintop, in fifteen minutes.

California's largest state park is another desert landscape and geological wonder, Anza-Borrego Desert State Park. Known for its diversity, with rocky canyons, dry lake beds, palm groves, and year-round springs, it's a favorite in the spring when the wildflowers turn the desert to fields of color. The park is close to the quiet, pleasant town of **Borrego Springs.**

BORREGO SPRINGS

La Casa del Zorro

3845 Yaqui Pass Road
Borrego Springs, CA 92004
619-767-5323
800-824-1884
Fax: 619-767-4782

A luxury hideaway in the Anza-Borrego desert

General manager: Dori Holladay.
Accommodations: 77 rooms. **Rates:** $65–$325 in summer, $90–$505 in winter single or double, $10 additional person. **Added:** 11.5% tax. **Payment:** Major credit cards. **Children:** Welcome. **Pets:** Not allowed. **Smoking:** Nonsmoking rooms available.

Clear air and the silence of the desert surround this pleasant resort, spread over 32 acres of landscaped grounds. The resort is close to Anza-Borrego Desert State Park, California's largest state park, with 600,000 acres of canyons, palm groves, wildflowers, and rugged backcountry. The first structure, built in 1937, was an adobe ranch house that expanded over the decades into La Casa del Zorro; some of the original walls and beams remain as part of the lobby and lounge.

> **An unusual and delightful feature at La Casa del Zorro is its evening treat: instead of a mint on your pillow, you're given a booklet of short stories just right for bedtime reading.**

On the grounds, sprinkled with lawns, palm trees, and a fountain, are three night-lit swimming pools and spas, tennis courts, and a putting green. The rose garden and gazebo provide a pretty setting for parties and weddings. Guests can attend aerobics classes, rent bicycles, dance to live music, rent movies, shop in a boutique, hike nearby trails, play volleyball and table tennis, and dine on steaks, seafood, and pastas in the Presido Room, or have more casual meals in the Fox Pub surrounded by playful fox murals. As this is the type of resort that appeals to families as well as couples, parents will be happy to know that child care can be arranged, and the staff is warm and friendly.

Despite all the activity, the atmosphere is serene at La Casa del Zorro, with casitas spread over the property. Standard rooms and suites are located in two-story stucco buildings with red tile roofs. Guest rooms have a crisp southwestern look. Cheerful in blues and tans, they have lightly washed or blue stained wood furnishings and high ceilings. All rooms are supplied with coffee and coffeemakers, and a morning paper is delivered to your door.

Standard suites are attractively decorated, and have a separate living room and shuttered windows. A deluxe suite features a fireplace edged with colorful tiles, artwork and books in lighted niches, a wet bar, and a private patio. Most spacious are the adobe casitas, which are set off on their own surrounded by a native dessert landscape. One-bedroom casitas have outdoor hot tubs, and the three-bedroom casita has a large tiled patio and private swimming pool.

DEATH VALLEY

Furnace Creek Inn

P.O. Box 187
Death Valley, CA 92328
619-786-2345

> *A resort oasis in the desert*

Manager: Jim Heptner. **Accommodations:** 68 rooms. **Rates:** European Plan: $165 single, $175 double, $275 suite; Modified American Plan: $225 single, $275 double, $375 suite. **Added:** Tax. **Payment:** Major credit cards. **Children:** Under age 5 free in room with parents; $14 for rollaway or crib. **Pets:** Not allowed. **Smoking:** Nonsmoking rooms available. **Open:** October through mid-May.

Death Valley is the hottest, driest place in the world. Ground temperatures higher than 200 degrees Fahrenheit have been recorded here in summer. The landscape is stark, almost surreal in its contorted shapes, stretches of salty floor, brilliantly colored rocks, and high mountains.

In the midst of this desert on the Nevada border, 300 miles northeast of Los Angeles, Furnace Creek shimmers like a green mirage. Underground springs feed a garden of tropical flowers and palm trees, a swimming pool, and an 18-hole golf course. The rambling stone inn looks like a Spanish villa among the palms, with its red tile roof and Moorish arches.

Furnace Creek Inn was built in the late 1920s in response to public interest in Death Valley. Visitors were eager to see the strange and desolate beauty of a desert 200 feet below sea level. It had long been known for its rich mineral deposits, especially borax, which was brought out by the famous 20-mule team wagons. The Pacific Coast Borax Company built the resort and promoted it as a train destination, in connection with the company's own railroads.

Today the yellow, Spanish-style inn commands the desert valley from its hillside perch, and guest rooms have modern amenities such as air conditioning, television, refrigerators, irons and ironing boards, ceiling fans, and whirlpool tubs. The three categories of rooms — Deluxe, Desert, and Garden View — are furnished in a contemporary style. In desert tones of sand, salmon, and aqua, they have brass beds, floral comforters, and views of the desert or gardens. In the evening, from your room or patio, you can hear the coyotes howl.

The inn has two restaurants. Jackets are required in the more formal dining room where Mojave mixed

Most visitors take excursions to Death Valley landmarks. You can go on your own or with a guide who will explain the geology and history of Artist's Palette, Zabriskie Point, Dante's View, the jagged salt crystals of Devil's Golf Course, and Badwater, the lowest spot in the United States. Along the way you'll see wild burros, sand dunes, dried lake beds, and wide craters.

grill, and veal Zabriskie with escargots in a chardonnay beurre blanc sauce are examples of entrées served. Fresh seafood is also available. Caesar salads, flambés, tableside presentations, Italian fare, dancing, and entertainment is what you'll find at L'Ottimo's on the lower level.

From the inn, paths wind down the hillside through green lawns and a palm oasis to a spring-fed swimming pool. In addition to the 18-hole golf course, other recreational facilities include four tennis courts, shuffleboard, croquet, and horseback riding. There's no charge for tennis; a round of golf costs $36.

Manmade attractions are as unique as the landscape. Marta Becket's Amargosa Opera House, up a remote canyon, is a remarkable one-woman show. The artist and dancer from New

York has been performing for twenty years in the theater she restored in a former ghost town. Scotty's Castle is a Mediterranean-style structure with three towers and twenty-five rooms filled with artworks and fine furniture and china. Once the home of a sometime miner and teller of tall tales, it's now open to the public and well worth a tour.

DESERT HOT SPRINGS

Travellers Repose

P.O. Box 655
66920 First Street
Desert Hot Springs, CA 92240
619-329-9584

A charming bed-and-breakfast in the desert

Innkeeper: Marian Relkoff. **Accommodations:** 3 rooms (1 with private bath). **Rates:** $60–$80 double, 10% less for singles. **Included:** Expanded Continental breakfast. **Added:** 10% tax. **Payment:** Cash, personal checks, or travelers checks. **Children:** Over age 12 welcome. **Pets:** Not allowed. **Smoking:** Not allowed indoors. **Open:** September through June.

About twelve miles from the resorts of Palm Springs, Desert Hot Springs is a small, quiet community. On a slope above town, stands the Victorian-style Travellers Repose. It's unusual to find a Victorian home in the desert, and this one, gray, with dark blue and white trim, is not really of Victorian vintage — it was built in 1985 by Marian and Sam Relkoff as their dream home. Sam, formerly a contractor in Los Angeles, made much of the wood furniture and incorporated such details as heart cut-outs in the window shutters. Ask Marian about the heart-shaped shadow that appears on the front walkway after dark that the Relkoffs did not discover until the home was completely built. Obvious care went into the construction of the home, and it is immaculately maintained by Marian.

In front, by the white picket fence and vine-covered trellis, masses of flowers grow. There's a garden in back, too, by the swimming pool and spa. Just inside the front door there's a comfy parlor where guests can play board games or relax with a book. Breakfast, usually fruit, homemade granola, and home-baked rolls such as scones, cinnamon rolls, or muffins, is sometimes served on the patio by the pool. Marian also provides afternoon refreshments.

For unusual views of the desert, take a covered wagon tour or a jeep ride with a Desert Adentures naturalist into the canyons or Joshua Tree National Monument.

The guest rooms are spotless and attractive, and each is individually furnished in a country style. Buttons & Bows, on the main floor, is romantic in lavender and lace. It has antique oak furniture, a mirrored armoire, and an iron and brass queen-size bed; a velvet hat, beaded bag, and old pair of shoes hang on a wooden rack in the corner. You can see San Jacinto Peak from the bay window. The private bath has a wooden water closet and brass fixtures.

Upstairs the Pine Room is handsome in mint greens, and also has views of the peak. Sam made the cannonball bed, and dresser and armoire of honey pine. It shares a bath with the Heart Room across the hall. Cheerful in its decor, hearts are everywhere, and Marian quilted the heart-patterned quilt.

An added plus to staying at Travellers Repose is the price. For as little as $60 (plus tax), two people can enjoy pleasant accommodations, breakfast, afternoon tea, the use of a pool (which is not heated), spa, and the hospitality of the kindly innkeeper — a true bargain in the often expensive Palm Springs area.

INDIAN WELLS

Renaissance Esmeralda Resort

44–440 Indian Wells Lane
Indian Wells, CA 92210
619-773-4444
800-552-4FUN
Fax: 619-346-9308

*A golfer's paradise
in the desert*

Accommodations: 560 rooms and suites. **Rates:** $145–$380 single or double; suites $320–$600; $25 per additional adult. **Added:** 9.25% tax. **Payment:** Major credit cards. **Children:** Under age 18 free in room with parents; $15 charge for roll-away. **Pets:** Not allowed. **Smoking:** Nonsmoking rooms available.

About twenty minutes from Palm Springs, Indian Wells is a quiet community with date-bearing palm groves and some of the best golf courses in the area. As available land became more and more scarce in Palm Springs, a long-time winter destination, developments and resorts began to spring up all along the valley, and the Renaissance Esmeralda Resort, which opened in 1989 just off Highway 111 in Indian Wells, is one such resort.

Lanky palms trees line the driveway that leads from the highway to the resort. Like a fortress, the six-story peach colored stucco hotel, contrasted by green tinged oxidized copper balcony railings, is surrounded by a moat. Inside an impressive curved double staircase made from anagre (a rare African wood) winds down one flight to the polished marble base of the atrium lobby. Strains of music from a ghostly pianist at the grand player piano fill the air, and restaurants border both sides of the lofty hall. At the far end, opposite the staircase, doors open out to the pool area.

Guests check in at a registration counter down a hallway on the entry level. Rooms surround the central atrium or are located in outlying wings. Decorated in pleasant pastels and contemporary furnishings, they have balconies that offer pool, golf course, or mountain views. Two-poster beds are painted in pale yellows, Impressionist prints adorn the walls, and TVs are hidden in armoires (in-room movies are complimentary). Other amenities include stocked refreshment centers, bathrobes, and irons and ironing boards. Baths have marble vanities, a small television, phone, hair dryer, and Bath & Bodyworks toiletries.

Corner rooms, with large windows on two sides, are sunny and cheerful. They are more spacious than standard rooms so there's room enough for a sofa, easy chair, and two closets. For those needing even more space, spa and one-bedroom executive suites are also available.

Active guests will find there is plenty to do at the resort. Beyond the lobby is an extensive pool complex with a waterfall pavilion, gazebo bar, and sandy beach. There's a fitness center with a professional masseuse on staff, two outdoor spas, steam rooms, and a sauna. Two of the resort's seven tennis courts are lighted for nighttime play. For golf lovers, there are two 18-hole championship golf courses designed by Ted Robinson.

> **Las Estrellas Bar is dark and comfortably elegant with sofas and rounded easy chairs placed in cozy groupings. Just outside the lounge's windows, the moat cascades into a long pool.**

Sirocco's Mediterranean cuisine, such as basil lemon linguine with clams, shrimp, scallops, white wine, and tomatoes or broiled tenderloin of beef with roasted garlic and thyme butter with smoked mushroom sauce, gets high marks from diners in the valley. Charisma is more casual and has a contemporary Californian slant, although its southwestern buffet on Saturday night is quite popular.

LA QUINTA

La Quinta Resort and Club

P.O. Box 69
49–499 Eisenhower Drive
La Quinta, CA 92253
619-564-4111
800-598-3828
Fax: 619-564-5718

*A village-style
resort known for
its privacy and
recreation*

General manager: Scott Dalecio.
Accommodations: 640 rooms and suites. **Rates:** $89–$300 single or double; suites $155–$2600. **Added:** 11% tax. **Payment:** Major credit cards **Children:** Under age 18 free in room with parents **Pets:** Small pets allowed with permission, additional $25. **Smoking:** Nonsmoking rooms available.

In 1926, a Spanish hacienda-style hotel was built in the California desert twenty miles from the sleepy village of Palm Springs. From that day to this, La Quinta has been known for its hospitality and distinctive style. During the '30s, it was a haven for Hollywood stars such as Greta Garbo, Charlie Chaplin, Errol Flynn, Bette Davis, and Clark Gable. In 1932, Frank Capra first visited La Quinta; his stay inspired the creation of *It Happened One Night,* which won an Academy Award. Capra returned to the hotel later to write eight additional scripts.

Since then, the resort has expanded into a 45-acre compound of rooms and suites, twenty-five swimming pools, and thirty-eight spas. Yet, because of its careful design, there's no sense of overcrowding. Rather, you feel as though it's fiesta time in a village where shops, meeting rooms, and restaurants surround a colorful tiled plaza.

You reach the hotel by a cypress-lined drive and enter a small lobby with tiled floors, white walls, and Spanish wrought-iron accents. In the adjacent Santa Rosa Lounge, Mexican art objects — bright papier mâché fruits, Guerrero coconut masks, a tin-framed mirror — add to the Old California atmosphere. Here guests read the morning paper on overstuffed chairs and sofas, or gather before dinner. Afternoon tea is also available.

A champagne brunch is offered on the hotel's original patio from October to May. Montañas is the place to go for fine dining. Pancetta wrapped chicken breast and tiger shrimp ravioli with sea scallops are examples of the restaurant's Mediterranean cuisine. Morgan's, named for Walter Morgan the founder of La Quinta, is a casual 1920s American café with black and white checked tile floors, wood paneling, and an open kitchen. At the entrance to the restaurant there are photos of Frank Capra, and outside tables provide additional dining. The Adobe Grill offers elegant presentations of dishes such as grilled breast of duck with a tamarind chile sauce or Mexican molés. With talavera tile, leather-backed chairs, and jumbo margaritas, the mood is definitely old Mexico.

One thing you can't help but notice at La Quinta is the landscaping. The grounds are beautifully maintained all year long, and the plants in the flower beds are continually rotated providing maximum color in every season. So pleasant are the surroundings that Ginger Rogers held her wedding here in front of a courtyard waterfall.

One- and two-story bungalows, called casitas, are scattered over the property, many behind whitewashed walls espaliered with red-blooming bougainvillea, and some date to the 1920s when the hotel first opened. Each casita has from three to eight units. For the best views of the Santa Rosa Mountains, request a second-floor room.

A typical Double Deluxe room has two beds and a simple decor. The mood is cool, with white walls and white louvered shutters at the windows. The room has a television, a writing table, and a refrigerator. The large baths have double sinks and assorted toiletries that include sewing kits, loofahs, and sachets.

The suites are larger, with more amenities. Many have private wraparound patios with whirlpools. Wet bars are stocked with liquors and snacks, soft drinks and complimentary boxes of dates as this is date growing country, and baths have Crabtree and Evelyn toiletries. In one suite, louvered double doors divide the sitting room from a white and blue bedroom with a two-poster bed. A second TV is tucked into a niche beside a fireplace that passes through the wall to the bathroom. Firewood is provided in another niche. The Eisenhower Villa has a southwestern look with a large living room with a long dining table, a spacious bedroom with its own fireplace, and a kitchenette.

> **Water cascades in tiers to a fountain near the hotel entrance and the sweet scent of grapefruit blossoms wafts in the air.**

Yellow ribbons are placed on the doors of returning guests, and many come back to La Quinta year after year, but all guests get the same care. There's a private outdoor cubicle that has been available for massages in the sun since the 1930s. Twice-daily maid service, and same-day laundry and dry cleaning are provided. Though its main focus is tennis and golf, the resort has nightly entertainment, several gift shops on the central plaza including a wine shop with a wine tasting bar, and all kinds of meeting and conference space that includes a 17,000-square-foot ballroom.

There are thirty tennis courts; guests play free of charge. Clinics are offered regularly and include video analysis, programmable ball machines, and unlimited open play. Packages are available for both tennis and golf players. Between the resort and PGA West, four championship golf courses are available to La Quinta guests. The 18-hole Dunes course, adjacent to the resort, is especially demanding, with water on eight holes, rolling hills, and scrubby desert to skirt. Shuttle service is provided to the PGA West course.

PALM SPRINGS

Ingleside Inn

200 West Ramon Road
Palm Springs, CA 92264
619-325-0046
800-772-6655
Fax: 619-325-0710

> *A secluded inn
> frequented by
> movie stars*

Owner: Melvyn Haber. **Accommodations:** 29 rooms an suites. **Rates:** $95–$385 single or double in season, $20 additional person; discounts available in the off season. **Included:** Continental breakfast. **Added:** Tax. **Payment:** Major credit cards. **Children:** Not appropriate. **Smoking:** Allowed.

There's an air of exclusivity as you turn into the curved driveway of the Ingleside Inn. The parking lot is filled with fancy cars, and if you arrive at night the trees sparkle with lights — perhaps representing the hundreds of movie stars who have frequented the inn over the years. The list of celebrities that have visited the Ingleside is several pages long, and some Hollywood types have been known to fly into town just for a meal at Melvyn's, the inn's well-known restaurant.

A local historic site, the Ingleside was originally built in the 1920s as a private home for the Birge family who owned the Pierce Arrow Automobile Company. Later it was purchased by Ruth Hardy, the city's first councilwoman, and turned into an inn. In recent years the Ingleside has been in the hands of night-club owner Melvyn Haber.

Set back from the road, on two and a half tree-shaded acres almost at the foot of San Jacinto Mountain, the inn feels removed and secluded even though it is only a few blocks from the center of Palm Springs. It is this sense of privacy that no doubt appeals to beleaguered celebrities in search of some peace and quiet.

The inn's front porch, set with cushioned rattan chairs, a porch swing, and hummingbird feeders, is all but obscured by thick growing vines. Inside the lobby is an unusual mix of antiques. A romantic 100-year-old Belgian tapestry hangs above a sideboard that was once used as a vestment chest by priests in the 15th century. An intricately carved cherry screen with willow pattern china insets stands behind the concierge desk, and Oriental rugs and plush velvet sofas sit atop parquet floors. In one corner there's a unique iron light fixture in the shape of the sun topped by a cross that came from a church.

Two marble columns outside the lobby frame a courtyard with a cherub fountain. Here there is also a wonderful sculpture of Selene, the Goddess of the Moon. Some guest rooms are reached via this courtyard, while others are located in villas sprinkled over the grounds. One room accessed off the main building's front porch is called the Library because it was the room where guests used to gather for cocktails. It has Queen Anne furnishings, a brass bed, and wood-burning fireplace. Other suites in the main building include the Lily Pons Room (named in honor of the diva who was a regular guest at the inn for many years) with Louis XV furniture, and the Princess Room, which is romantic with a half-canopy bed, white tile floors, and two loveseats in front of a fireplace.

> Among the pictures on the lobby wall is one of June Allyson's 1976 wedding, which took place at the inn, along with her quote "Everyone should be married at the Ingleside Inn at least once in their lifetime."

Among the villas, Villa 2 is attractive and comfortable in cool blues and greens. It has stars on the ceiling, a fireplace, writing desk, and colorful prints evocative of the Riviera. Villas 7 and 8 can be rented together to create a large two-bedroom suite accommodating four people called the Royal Suite. The living room is formal with Oriental chests and chairs covered in pink damask. The bedroom in Villa 8 has a lovely hand-painted dressing screen that's over 350 years old, and both villas have sunken tubs. All guest rooms have steam baths with whirlpool tubs, refrigerators stocked with complimentary refreshments, coffeemakers, makeup mirrors, alarm-clock radios, telephones, TVs, air conditioning, and English toiletries. In the morning, a Continental breakfast is brought to your guest room along with the morning paper.

Most guests spend at least some time lounging around the pool or soaking in the outdoor Jacuzzi. There's also shuffleboard, darts, croquet, and Ping-Pong, and a gazebo is tucked back in a corner of the lawn beyond the swimming pool.

The shops and restaurants of downtown Palms Springs are within easy walking distance, although many guests choose to dine at Melvyn's, the inn's restaurant located next to the main building.

Mirrors, gold and black shimmering fabrics, and silver-plated chargers add more than a touch of glitz to Melvyn's main dining room and bar area, while diners in the adjoining glass enclosed "patio," with its white wrought iron chairs and lattice-covered ceiling, will find themselves in a more garden-like setting overlooking a fountain and ornamental pool. Veal Ingleside (veal medallions served with avocado and a mousseline sauce along with fettuccine) is the restaurant's signature dish, while other entrées include salmon Grand Marnier and steak au poivre. Of course caviar is on the appetizer menu, and the champagne Sunday brunch is extremely popular. Jackets are recommended for dinner, and jeans are discouraged.

Korakia Pensione

257 S. Patencio Road
Palm Springs, CA 92262
619-864-6411

A Mediterranean villa built in the 1920s

Proprietors: Joy and Douglas Smith. **Accommodations:** 15 rooms. **Rates:** $79–$229 double, $15 additional person. **Included:** Continental breakfast. **Added:** Tax. **Payment:** No credit cards. **Children:** Not appropriate. **Pets:** Welcome by arrangement. **Smoking:** Not allowed in rooms.

In 1924, the Scottish artist Gordon Coutts constructed a villa in the then-remote desert area adjacent to the village of Palm Springs. The architecture was reminiscent of Morocco, where the artist had spent some time, and a radical departure from the Spanish Colonial style favored in southern California.

Over the years, cultural leaders and dignitaries visited the castlelike home (Sir Winston Churchill painted in the upstairs studio), but after Gordon Coutts' death the villa deteriorated. In 1989, the Smiths purchased the building and began its restoration; Douglas is an architectural preservationist. Bougainvillea against the whitewashed walls give the inn an exotic look, and the atmosphere and furnishings throughout reflect the five years that Doug spent living in Greece.

A fanciful wooden entryway from Afghanistan leads from the parking lot to the inn which stands behind an oleander hedge. In the lobby, fabulous carved chests and Mediterranean music immediately set the tone. Beyond the lobby, you can see a courtyard with a small swimming pool, chaises, large pottery urns, and a stone wall with a spouting waterfall. Each guest room is different, but each feels as if it has been transported from somewhere along the Mediterranean coast. All have kitchens or refrigerators, fresh flowers, crisply ironed sheets, and individual charm. The rooms do not have phones or TVs, though those are available upon request.

> **The white, uncluttered rooms feature antiques, worn Oriental rugs, period lamps, leather-bound books, and artifacts from Mediterranean countries.**

Climb tiled steps to the Artist Studio, where Churchill painted. It is a big, open space with slanted windows and a telescope so you can better admire the view of Mt. San Jacinto and garner artistic inspiration. There's a Moorish trunk in the living room, and the bedroom has a feather bed. The Library, where literary discussions and chamber music concerts were held in decades past, has a beamed ceiling, cushioned bancos, a gas fireplace, French doors leading to a shaded patio, a queen-size handmade poster bed, and, of course, shelves full of books.

The Lower Guest House is a spacious suite with a living room, bedroom, kitchen, bath, and simply furnished dining room. There's a fireplace, a black futon sofa, and tapestry-backed chairs in the living room. Cement tiled floors help keep the rooms cool in hot weather.

The Adobe Room, once the villa's master bedroom, is the smallest and is different from the rest, with ochre adobe walls. In Garden Suite B in an adjacent building, there is little decoration on the walls, but furnishings such as the fantastic Middle Eastern sideboard, which was originally designed to be carried on the back of a camel, create enough visual interest on their own.

A Continental breakfast of fresh fruit and pastries is served in your room or on the flagstone terrace beside the antique Moorish fountain, where doves coo in antique bird cages under the fruit trees. A communal kitchen is available for preparing light fare.

La Mancha

P.O. Box 340
444 Avenida Caballeros
Palm Springs, CA 92262
619-323-1773
800-255-1773
Fax: 619-323-5928

A cluster of luxurious villas in central Palm Springs

Owner: Ken Irwin. **Accommodations:** 65 rooms and villas. **Rates:** $115–$895 single or double, $25 additional person. **Added:** 10% tax. **Payment:** Major credit cards. **Children:** Free in room with parents. **Pets:** Not allowed. **Smoking:** Nonsmoking rooms available.

One of the most extravagant, secluded, charming getaways in California is right in the middle of Palm Springs. Tucked behind walls and electronic security gates, La Mancha stands on twenty lushly landscaped acres, a Mediterranean-style village of stucco buildings with red tile roofs. Once inside the secured compound the rest of the world seems far removed even though the center of Palm Springs is just steps away.

The private villas range in size from one bedroom and one bath to three bedrooms with three baths. Some are one-story casitas, others loft villas with two levels. Every imaginable luxury is provided, depending upon the lodging you choose. Traditional hotel style guest rooms, mini-suites, or sections of the three-bedroom villas, are also available.

The most expensive are the four private tennis villas. Each boasts a tennis court, a walled courtyard patio, a private swimming pool, a therapy pool and bath, an outdoor wet bar with ice maker, a split-level living and dining room with a fireplace, an equipped kitchen, laundry facilities, and a state-of-the-art video and sound system.

The luxury estate villas have the same features without the tennis courts. They all resemble fine private homes in a well-to-do neighborhood, but even when the complex is full there's no sense of crowding. Some have their own security entrances and garages — favorites with celebrities who wish anonymity. Each is individually decorated, many have big-screen TVs, and all lodgings have VCRs — rentals are available from La Mancha's video library.

> **La Mancha has its own fleet of ten white Chrysler LeBaron convertibles, named for each of Ken Irwin's ten children, which can be rented by guests at quite reasonable rates. Bicycles are also available for jaunting about town.**

In addition to the private pools or spas (or both) in forty-seven villas, La Mancha has a centrally located freeform pool with a waterfall and stream, which is convenient for guests in the few rooms that don't have their own pool. On a raised deck beside it are yellow tent cabanas and a thatch-roofed bar. There are four tennis courts, two croquet courts (one is regulation size for tournaments), a golf green for chipping and putting, and facilities for small meetings. For workouts, there is a small fitness center over the lobby with exercise equipment and a sauna.

You may dine on a terrace near the pool or in La Mancha's tiny restaurant called the Don Quixote Room. It is only open to La Mancha guests so it has just seven tables — although a wall of mirrors makes the room appear twice as large as it really is. Continental favorites dominate the menu, which changes nightly.

Four stained glass windows depicting scenes from *Don Quixote* hang in the dining room, clues to the owner's interest in Cervantes' hero. Ken Irwin has long been fascinated with the legendary figure, and his own "impossible dream" is the resort he and his late wife made a reality.

La Mancha specializes in superb service that goes beyond daily maid service and cheese and fruit baskets. With advance notice you can request a private dinner in your villa that the chef will prepare for you in your own kitchen. If you want a violin serenade of your favorite song, you have only to ask. Or if you're in the mood for a Palm Springs shopping foray, you may ride in a limousine, compliments of La Mancha. Baby-sitting service is available, and there's a masseuse on call. Airport pickup is complimentary.

In short, La Mancha is an extraordinary hideaway. It's the place to go when you tire of those incessant autograph hunters — or when you simply want total privacy in a romantic dream.

L'Horizon

1050 East Palm Canyon Drive
Palm Springs, CA 92264
619-323-1858

> *A tranquil inn for sunshine and relaxation*

Manager: Zetta Castle. **Accommodations:** 22 rooms. **Rates:** $85–$125 single or double (rates vary according to season). **Added:** 10% tax. **Included:** Continental breakfast. **Payment:** Major credit cards. **Children:** Not appropriate. **Pets:** Not allowed. **Smoking:** Allowed. **Open:** October–July 4th weekend

This quiet enclave in the desert city of Palm Springs, has a crisp clean look to its lodgings and grounds. Behind walls covered with scarlet bougainvillea, three and a half acres of lawns, tall palm trees, and spicy-scented pepper trees provide the setting for seven low-lying buildings. Each building has three guest rooms and a kitchen. Generally the guest rooms are rented out separately, though groups can rent out an entire unit if they choose to do so.

The cheerful, sunny rooms, have interesting configurations. Decorated in light white and pastels, they are tastefully furnished in a contemporary style and have tall, shuttered windows and private patios. In the bathroom, a glass

> **Built in the 1950s and remodeled in the late 1980s, the rooms surround a swimming pool, Jacuzzi, and barbecue area with lounge chairs and umbrella tables. There's a fine view of San Jacinto Mountain.**

door leads to an atrium fragrant with the scent of orange blossoms. A basket of fruit and chocolates is in each room, and breakfast is brought to your door with a morning newspaper. The staff will bring lunch from a nearby eatery, and several restaurants are within walking distance.

L'Horizon lends bicycles and will make reservations for golf, tennis, and horseback riding. The inn also has a library and facilities for croquet, horseshoes, and bocce ball. Desert Adventures offers noteworthy, highly recommended tours to Indian Canyon and Joshua Tree National Monument.

Le Petit Château

1491 Via Soledad
Palm Springs, CA 92264
619-325-2686
Fax: 619-322-5054

A casual, quiet, clothing-optional inn for adults

Innkeepers: Don and Mary Robidoux. **Accommodations:** 10 rooms. **Rates:** $80–$90 single or double midweek, $110–$130 weekends. **Included:** Expanded Continental breakfast. **Added:** 10% tax. **Minimum stay:** 2 nights on weekends. **Payment:** Major credit cards. **Children:** Not appropriate. **Pets:** Not allowed. **Smoking:** Discouraged.

On the French Riviera, nudity or seminudity on public beaches is fully acceptable. That's not the custom in the United States, so those who like to swim or sunbathe au naturel turn to special places like Le Petit Château. Clothing is optional here, but this comfortable, low-key inn is definitely not a nudist camp. Rather, the guests are people who enjoy swimming, lounging poolside, or soaking in the outdoor whirlpool without a cover-up.

Rooms are in low-lying buildings that form a U around the pool and lounging area. Half the rooms have kitchens and all are individually decorated. They have attractive furnishings and a light, airy atmosphere. White wicker, flowered comforters, and greenery make them inviting. Hand-stenciled trim on the walls adds a personal touch. Your room will also have a clock radio, ceiling fan, a television with a movie channel, and a wallpapered bath with a shower. Pool towels are provided. Room keys open the front door to the walled courtyard, which is kept locked.

Don, a former salesman, and Mary, a teacher, came to Palm Springs from Los Angeles in 1983, determined to escape a hectic lifestyle. In opening an inn they combined several things they enjoyed: the outdoor life of the desert, nude sunbathing (discovered on a trip to St. Tropez), and meeting like-minded people. Their little inn, located on a quiet side street, is close to the resort town's fine shops and restaurants.

Personable hosts, Don and Mary are happy to share their knowledge of the area and will recommend eating places and attractions. Don is a hiker who welcomes company on the trails of the mountains that rise abruptly from the desert on the edge of town.

> **In the mornings guests gather around the breakfast buffet which is always laden with juices, cereals, bagels, yogurt, fruit, and pastries. Coffee, tea, and chocolate are available all day, and in the late afternoon wine and cheese are set out by the pool. The inn also has a putting green.**

Le Petit Château is one of the most relaxing places to stay in southern California; there's no pretense here, and you'll see all adult ages and shapes tanning by the pool. And what could be more pleasant than resting in a bubbling whirlpool under a moonlit sky, with the scent of lemon blossoms permeating the air?

Oasis Water Resort Villa Hotel

4190 East Palm Canyon Drive
Palm Springs, CA 92264
619-328-1499
800-247-4664

> *A resort community featuring water fun*

Resident manager: Terry Durst.
Accommodations: 110 villas. **Rates:** $179–$339 2–8 people (rates vary with season; weekly and monthly discounts available). **Included:** Expanded Continental breakfast. **Added:** 10% tax. **Payment:** Major credit cards. **Children:** Welcome. **Pets:** Not allowed. **Smoking:** Allowed.

The entrance to the Oasis is from a circular driveway where figures of dolphins spout in a tiered fountain. Crossing over ponds fed by a waterfall, you enter a small and usually busy lobby. On one side is the coffee shop where guests line up for breakfast; it's hectic in the morning, and noisy if the big TV is on. You can avoid this by coming in early or late and taking your tray to the terrace.

> **Oasis Waterpark has seven waterslides, a wave-action pool for surfing (boards may be rented), a 600-foot inner tube ride, and kiddy slides. Also on the property are restaurants, locker rooms, a sportswear shop, and a well-equipped health club.**

The 27-acre resort, resembles a suburban development, with its two-condominium villas grouped in clusters, lining curving streets that end in cul de sacs. There are separate areas for adults only and for families with children. The condos have two bedrooms and two baths, and some are sizable homes.

Typical of the deluxe units furnished in a contemporary style is one with a white tile foyer, grasscloth walls, and a queen-size sofa bed. The kitchen has a gas stove, a dishwasher, microwave, refrigerator/freezer, toaster, and coffeemaker. There's a table for four in the angled breakfast nook and a pass-through counter to the living room. From the balcony, which has a barbecue, there's a view of the Santa Rosa mountains. The bedrooms are clean, spacious, and for the most part well maintained, though you may see a few chips and scratches on the walls and furniture. Daily maid service is provided.

Facilities on the hotel property include eight swimming pools, nine spas and sunning decks, and five lighted tennis courts. The area's biggest attraction is the nearby Oasis Waterpark, a 21-acre playground open daily from March to Labor Day and on weekends in September and October. A fee is charged for admission to the park, but hotel guests receive up to four complimentary passes per unit.

Orchid Tree Inn

261 South Belardo Road
Palm Springs, CA 92262
619-325-2791
800-733-3435
Fax: 619-325-3855

A garden retreat with the tranquility of Old Palm Springs

Proprietors: Bob and Karen Weithorn. **Accommodations:** 40 rooms, suites, and cottages. **Rates:** $55–$300 depending upon season and type of accommodation. **Included:** Continental breakfast, Nov.1–May 31. **Added:** 10% tax. **Minimum stay:** 2 nights on most weekends November–May; longer stays may be required on holidays. **Payment:** Major credit cards. **Children:** Not appropriate. **Pets:** Not allowed. **Smoking:** Nonsmoking rooms available.

When old-timers wax nostalgic about the Palm Springs of the past, this is the kind of place they remember with fondness. At the Orchid Tree, the charm of Palm Springs in the 1920s and '30s still exists. The Spanish bungalows, built in 1934, are gray with red tile roofs and striped awnings. Inside they have been carefully restored and updated. They have ceramic tiles, hand-painted flower stencils, and a variety of furnishings, including Spanish Colonial, Queen Anne, lodgepole pine, wicker, Old West–style leather, and saddle blankets.

Arts and Crafts–style Unit 24 is spread over two floors. It has a patio that overlooks one of the swimming pools, oak paneling, a fireplace, dressing room, walk-in closet, large Jacuzzi tub, and an upstairs bedroom. Cahuilla House is one of the largest units with two bedrooms, two baths, a living room, and kitchen. Comfortable and rustic, the screened front porch is set with adirondack chairs.

Some rooms are located in a two-story building built in the 1950s by Albert Frey. Originally it stood across the street, but was moved in sections in recent years to its present location at the inn for additional lodging. Most rooms have kitchens available (for an extra fee) with gas stoves and dishware in prewar patterns. From private balconies and patios the rocky slopes of the mountains appear to rise up from right behind the bungalows, yet the heart of downtown Palm Springs is only a block away. Beautifully landscaped gardens, oleander shaded shuffleboard, two large pools, and a spa area round out the relaxed environment.

> **Trellised walkways around the complex are bordered with citrus and other trees, flowers, birdbaths, and bird-houses.**

Next to the spa is the Cahuilla Lodge building, a gathering place where breakfast is served, and guests can watch television, work on a jigsaw puzzle, enjoy a novel from the stocked bookshelves, or play a game of chess or checkers. Its '30s theme is enhanced by wall sconces with wrought iron cutouts, stained glass windows, and the saddle blanket cushions and cacti evocative of old California. Seminars and classes that focus on the arts and self-realization are often planned for this site.

No room service or meals (other than the winter breakfast) are offered at the Orchid Tree, but there are fifty restaurants within walking distance. For a nominal fee guests can use a nearby athletic club, and hiking trails are not far from the inn.

Villa Royale

1620 Indian Trail
Palm Springs, CA 92264
619-327-2314
800-245-2314
Fax: 619-322-3794

*A friendly inn
with an
international
theme*

Innkeeper: Bob Lee. **Accommodations:** 33 rooms. **Rates:** $75–$250 in winter, $59–$189 in summer, single or double, $25 each additional person. **Included:** Continental breakfast. **Added:** 10% tax. **Payment:** Major credit cards. **Children:** Not appropriate. **Pets:** Not allowed. **Smoking:** Nonsmoking rooms available.

This European-style country inn is a gem hidden among the flashier baubles around it. Behind its stucco walls and iron gates, Villa Royale holds many surprises. First is the series of interior tree-shaded courtyards, each bright with cascading bougainvillea and pots of flowers. There are two swimming pools; one is in the main courtyard where a light breakfast is served. You reach the other, smaller pool by following brick pathways that amble past fountains and vine-covered trellises to another courtyard. The atmosphere at Villa Royale is low-key and friendly. Most guests spend at least part of their time here relaxing and reading by the pools.

You may borrow bicycles, purchase a picnic lunch from the inn's restaurant, or join a tour of the boutiques and shopping centers on Palm Canyon Drive.

The Mediterranean-like compound covers three and a half acres. Each guest room has a different country theme: Morocco, France, Portugal, Germany, Italy, England, and Greece to name a few. The Spain Room has Spanish ceramic tile edging the curved brick hearth of the fireplace and dark carved furniture. Decorative plates hang over an arch to the full kitchen, and double doors open to a courtyard with a fountain.

The Monte Carlo Suite has red tile floors, a bleached-beam ceiling, and a fireplace. Its private patio faces a garden of roses and palm trees and, at night, the soft glow of filigreed Moroccan lamps hanging in the rubber trees. In another suite, a Grecian urn, blue tiled bath, and travel posters of the sun-splashed Mediterranean country let you know you're in a room dedicated to Greece.

Compared to recent developments in luxury hotels, amenities are basic: simple soaps, no hair dryers, few writing tables, no stationery. Television sets are hidden under tablecloths. But the charm of the place more than outweighs any such flaws; indeed, many guests view them as attributes. Even the smallest room, which has a Dutch theme, is appealing with slate floors, a brass bed, and Dutch doors. It's a bargain to boot (although it's too small for comfort if you're planning a lengthy stay).

In keeping with the international theme, the Europa restaurant features Continental cuisine, its antique bar came from a Parisian restaurant, and pottery from various European countries adorns its walls. Cozy and attractive, with brick floors and floral fabric tablecloths, the Europa is known as one of the best dining spots in Palm Springs. Examples of the excellent entrées include roasted duck with caramelized orange and sweet and sour cabbage and veal scallops sautéed with capers, lemon demi-glaze, and fresh thyme. California and European wines are available.

RANCHO MIRAGE

The Ritz-Carlton Rancho Mirage

68–900 Frank Sinatra Drive
Rancho Mirage, CA 92270
619-321-8282
800-241-3333
Fax: 619-321-6928

A traditional luxury hotel above the desert

General manager: Scott Nassar.
Accommodations: 219 rooms and 20 suites. **Rates:** $225–$300 single or double; suites $460–$750; reduced rates available in summer. **Added:** 10% tax. **Payment:** Major credit cards. **Children:** Under age 17 free in room with parents. **Pets:** Not allowed. **Smoking:** Nonsmoking rooms available

Above the desert valley and village of Rancho Mirage, on a 650-foot-high plateau south of Palm Springs, the beige-toned buildings of the Ritz-Carlton stand like great boulders against a rocky landscape. It's a stark setting, here in the rugged foothills of the Santa Rosa Mountains. At the entrance to the hotel a bronze bighorn sculpture stands at attention in deference to the wildlife that shares the surrounding terrain.

Inside the contrast is astounding — you enter a world of European antiques, marble floors, crystal chandeliers, heavy drapes, and museum-quality oil paintings on paneled walls. In the lobby, fine Meissen china is on display in a Dutch rococo walnut breakfront. There's also a handsome Regency sideboard in mahogany, an antique map of California (circa 1666) hanging on one wall, and a lovely Persian rug atop the marble floor before the registration desk. At the far end of the long, chandeliered hallway leading from the lobby is a scene that appears surreal in this context, but is in fact a picture window framing a view of the desert and mountains beyond a terrace with white canvas umbrellas.

All hotels with the Ritz-Carlton name specialize in a strong classical tradition of luxury, along with an emphasis on personal service. Rancho Mirage is no exception. Ignoring the desert surrounding it, the resort is all damask drapes, dark woods, and formal furniture.

The accommodations feature custom crown moldings, writing tables, balconies or patios, and marble baths with telephones. Plush terrycloth robes (or lightweight cotton robes in summertime), and Scottish Fine shampoos are among the amenities. The decor, in muted silver, tan, and gold, reflects the hills outside while damask fabrics set the tone of understated luxury. Television sets are tucked into antique reproduction highboys; stocked honor bars hide behind false drawers. Rooms have balconies overlooking the grounds, the pool, or have the mountains.

Standard rooms have two doubles or one king-size bed. Executive suites have a separate living room; the Presidential suites have a spacious living room with a baby grand piano, and a dining room. The Club Floor has its own concierge and a lounge where breakfast, lunch, tea, afternoon appetizers, cold beverages, beer, cordials, and desserts are served complimentary to Club Floor guests only.

The resort has a fitness center with workout equipment, steam and sauna rooms, and massage (a personal trainer can be provided upon request). The center is near the outdoor pool, which is in a grassy plateau above the Coachella Valley. Across the road are ten tennis courts, a pro shop, and an outdoor basketball court. There's a small pitch-and-putt course at the resort (you can borrow clubs from the fitness center), and several nearby golf courses are open to guests (the closest is Rancho Mirage Country Club). For families traveling with children, the hotel runs a "Ritz Kids" activity program.

> Some of the sky views are glorious. Ask for a west-facing room and you may see color-streaked skies at sunset and pastel reflections against Mount San Jacinto at sunrise.

The hotel restaurants vary in terms of decor and cuisine. For fine cuisine, diners reserve a table at the Dining Room, which has relaxed its previous stringent formality. In the 75-seat dining room, elegant with damask walls, light blue velvet chairs, and silver candle holders, Continental and American dishes such as roasted pink snapper served with warm couscous salad and sun-dried tomato tapenade are beautifully presented.

There are two more casual cafés. The Café, open for all three meals daily, serves soups, salads, pastas, and grilled pizzas at lunch, and has a menu that ranges from mahi-mahi to jerked New York steak in the evening. Mirada, right on the edge of the hillside, has outdoor dining and serves sandwiches and tropical drinks. In the afternoon, tea is served in the lobby lounge. The bar has the rich wood paneling and hunt scenes often found in a Gentlemen's club, and poolside snacks are served all day.

The friendly service in this atmosphere of refined gentility is pure West Coast. The bellman who carries your luggage may linger to lean on the balcony railing and chat about the desert sunset and life in Palm Springs. The desk clerk may grab your arm and point out an unusual sight he thinks you shouldn't miss, such as the bighorn sheep that wander in every day from the mountains to graze on the lawn or the roadrunners that also roam the property. This may be the Ritz, but it's still California.

The Westin Mission Hills Resort

Dinah Shore & Bob Hope Drive
Rancho Mirage, CA 92270
619-328-5955
800-228-3000
Fax: 619-321-2955

> *Recreational
> activities abound
> at this extensive
> resort*

General manager: Tom Cortabitarte.
Accommodations: 512 rooms including 40 suites. **Rates:** $219–$329 single or double, suites $420–$810, rates vary seasonally. **Added:** Tax. **Payment:** Major credit cards. **Children:** Welcome. **Pets:** Not allowed. **Smoking:** Nonsmoking rooms available.

An island of green grass with rows of flower beds, palms and citrus trees, accentuated by a granite pyramid fountain stands like an oasis in the desert at the entrance to the Westin Mission Hills Resort. Beyond it the pink Moorish structure of the main building is striking with its multiple arches, wings, and courtyards. Upon reaching the entrance a valet will whisk away your car, and you pass through a dramatic colonnade to the lobby. Outside the lobby is a rock waterfall with a 60-foot waterslide on the reverse side spilling into a small pool which adjoins the much larger meandering Las Brisas swimming pool. All of this is just a hint of what the resort has to offer.

The resort originally opened in 1987 with two hundred rooms. Westin Hotels took over the property in 1989, closed the hotel while they added convention space, a golf course, and more than three hundred additional guest rooms before reopening the resort in August of 1991. Now in addition to the impressive main building, there are sixteen separate pavilions housing about thirty guest rooms each, 57,000 square feet of meeting space, a 20-acre resort park (with a paved jogging and bike path), seven lighted tennis courts, and three swimming pools spread over 360 acres. There's also a fitness center, sand volleyball court, croquet, shuffleboard, and two 18-hole golf courses — one designed by Pete Dye the other by legendary Gary Player.

The two-story guest pavilions are grouped around courtyards with small gardens. Rooms in shades of mauve, taupe, and blue have contemporary and light wood furnishings and modern art prints on the walls. In some rooms the bed is placed at an angle to create a more interesting look. They have either a king or two queen-size beds, balconies or patios, alarm-clock radios, remote control televisions with in-room movies, stocked refreshment centers, coffeemakers, two direct-dial telephones with computer capability and voice mail, safes, and baths with double vanities, and hair dryers.

> **Landscaping at the resort will make you forget you're in the desert. Everywhere you look is the deep green of the lush golf-course fairways and the manicured lawns bordered by colorful annuals that lead to the guest pavilions. Lagoons wind between buildings, and sculptures add an artistic touch to the already pleasing grounds.**

Resort suites have a separate living room with a marble dining table and chaise lounge, and a separate tub and shower in the bath.

Chairman suites are the most deluxe with two bedrooms, two and a half baths, a fireplace, baby grand piano, a whirlpool, and three private patios. A $5 per day resort fee covers phone charges, daily newspaper delivery, in-room coffee, and use of the fitness center.

La Concha Pacific Bistro is the resort's fine dining restaurant. As its name suggests, Pacific Rim cuisine is the specialty, and seared tuna sashimi is one of the bistro's signature dishes. Bella Vista is more casual serving both Californian and southwestern favorites. Light meals are also available at each of the swimming pools.

Although there is plenty to do at the resort, many guests steal time away from the golf course or swimming pool to visit the attractions of nearby Palm Springs, or shop at the chic boutiques on El Paseo — Palm Desert's version of Rodeo Drive — about fifteen minutes from the resort. The hotel's excellent concierge can help you with sightseeing arrangements. For arrivals and departures, the Palm Springs airport is only seven miles from hotel.

Northern
California

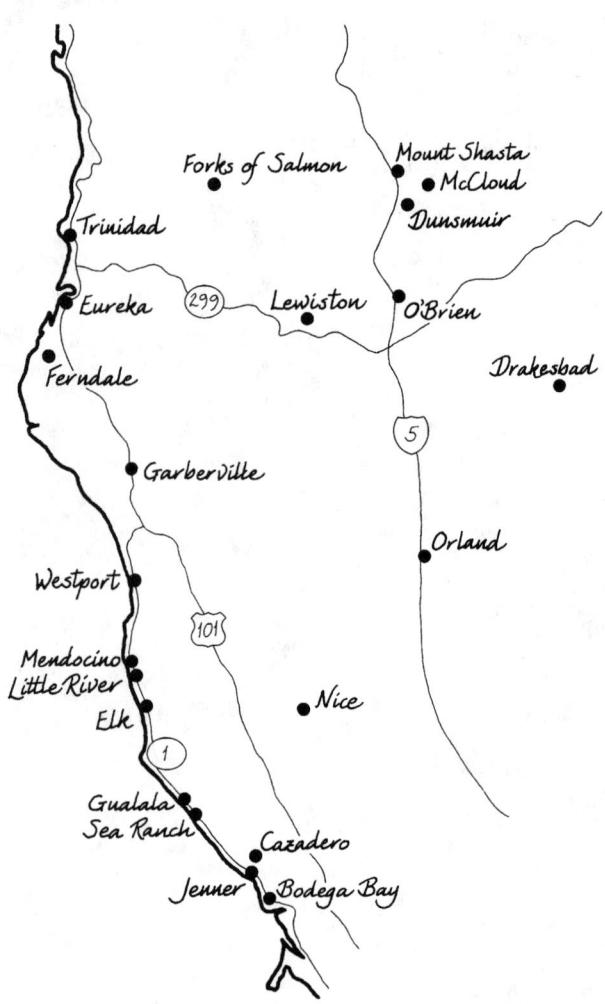

Best Intimate City Stops

Eureka
An Elegant Victorian Mansion
Carter House and Hotel Carter
Mendocino
Mendocino Hotel

Best Country Inns and B&Bs

Garberville
Benbow Inn
Little River
Glendeven
McCloud
McCloud Guest House
Mount Shasta
Ward's Big Foot Ranch
Nice
Featherbed Railroad Company, A Bed & Breakfast Resort
Orland
The Inn at Shallow Creek Farm
Westport
Howard Creek Ranch

Best Family Favorites

Dunsmuir
Railroad Park Resort
Lewiston
Trinity Alps Resort
Mendocino
Sea Haus
O'Brien
Holiday Harbor
Trinidad
The Lost Whale Bed & Breakfast Inn

Best Inns by the Sea

Bodega Bay
The Inn at the Tides

Elk
Elk Cove Inn
Greenwood Pier Inn
Harbor House
Gualala
The Old Milano Hotel
St. Orres
Little River
Heritage House
Little River Inn
Mendocino
The Headlands Inn
Hill House of Mendocino
Joshua Grindle Inn
MacCallum House
The Stanford Inn by the Sea
Trinidad
Trinidad Bay Bed & Breakfast

Best on a Budget

Jenner
Stillwater Cove Inn

Best Resorts

Sea Ranch
The Sea Ranch

Best Romantic Hideaways

Cazadero
Timberhill Ranch
Ferndale
The Gingerbread Mansion
Little River
Sea Arch
Mendocino
Hranrad House
Reed Manor

Best Wilderness Retreats

Drakesbad
   Drakesbad Guest Ranch
Forks of Salmon
   Otter Bar Lodge

For unspoiled, uncrowded wilderness, head for California's far north. The Klamath, Shasta, and Trinity regions are vast stretches of thick forestland, rugged mountains, alpine meadows, rushing rivers, and deep canyons. Towns are few and cities nonexistent.

Mount Shasta, rising 14,162 feet from the valley floor, dominates much of the landscape. South of the dormant volcano is Shasta Lake, fed by rivers and dammed to form an immense reservoir where every sort of freshwater recreation is available. East of Shasta and I-5 are trout-filled rivers, dark lava beds, and sanctuaries for birds and wildlife. In Lassen Volcanic National Park, deep craters and steaming sulfur vents are reminders of Mount Lassen's explosive past. The southernmost volcano in the Cascade chain, 10,000-foot Lassen last erupted in 1917.

West of I-5 lie the Trinity Alps, where angular peaks reach 8,000 feet above evergreen forests and steep ravines. This is prime fishing and backpacking country.

Still further west is, finally, the edge of the continent, the end of the American frontier. Here the redwoods grow, the tallest trees in the world. Most of the primeval forests are gone now, cut for lumber, but in Redwood National Park and the state parks along Highway 101, cathedral-like groves are preserved. The largest park is near the little town of **Trinidad.**

Continuing south past **Eureka,** a bay city known for its Victorian architecture, Highway 101 turns inland toward **Garberville** and then hugs the coastline again, offering spectacular scenes of rugged beauty. Ceaseless, wind-driven waves, with spindrift pluming, crash against craggy cliffs and sea arches; white surf curls against smooth sand. Coves and inlets, lagoons and tidepools wait to be explored. From any bluff along the way you may see gray whales spouting as they migrate between Alaska and the sheltered waters off Baja California.

Small communities such as **Mendocino, Little River,** and

Elk, separated by high cliffs and empty beaches, punctuate the winding ribbon of coastal road from Oregon to San Francisco Bay.

BODEGA BAY

The Inn at the Tides

P.O. Box 640
800 Pacific Coast Highway 1
Bodega Bay, CA 94923
707-875-2751
800-541-7788
Fax: 707-875-2669

*A hilltop resort in
a seaside village*

General manager: Carlo Galazzo. **Accommodations:** 86 rooms. **Rates:** $120–$195 weekdays, $145–$230 Saturdays, $20 additional person. **Included:** Continental breakfast. **Added:** 9% tax. **Payment:** Major credit cards. **Children:** Under age 12 free in room with a parent. **Pets:** Not allowed. **Smoking:** Nonsmoking rooms available.

This luxury resort on six hilltop acres faces the bay some sixty miles north of San Francisco. It offers visitors to the Sonoma coast a quiet, sophisticated retreat with a host of facilities.

The guest rooms are divided among twelve two-story shingled redwood lodges, every one with a view of the harbor. From your window you can watch the fishing fleet come and go and see the sun set over the Pacific, beyond lawns bordered by hardy native plants and blooming annuals.

Most of the rooms have fireplaces and vaulted ceilings. They feature a television with a movie channel, direct-dial phones, clock radios, refrigerators, and terrycloth robes in roomy closets. The baths have hair dryers, custom soaps and gels, and, convenient for wet swimsuits, a clothesline that stretches over the tub.

A typical room is furnished with a sturdy oak table and chairs and a gray couch with soft cushions. By the blue ceramic tiled fireplace is a basket of wood; more will be brought upon request, at a nominal charge. In this quiet retreat, nighttime sounds fade away until all you hear are the moans of a distant buoy and the crackle of your fire.

In the morning, a complimentary newspaper will be delivered to your door. When the mood strikes you can amble down to the Tides Wharf Restaurant for a breakfast of croissants, muffins, and fruit. A wall of windows offers fine views of the harbor and Bodega Head, and there's a terrace just outside where you can have breakfast in warm weather.

> **Bird-watching opportunities abound. Great blue herons, pelicans, cormorants, osprey, sandpipers, and scores more have been sighted here. Movie fans may remember that Alfred Hitchcock's *The Birds* was filmed at Bodega Bay.**

The restaurant has an à la carte dinner menu that features fresh seafood and local game, fowl, and produce. It also offers the Dinner with the Winemaker series, a chance to meet local winemakers and sample their wines.

On the property are a whirlpool spa, a sauna, and an indoor/outdoor heated lap pool protected from sea breezes by glass walls. For more outdoor recreation, you may golf at Bodega Harbour Golf Links, an 18-hole course a mile away, or go whale-watching, horseback riding, charter boat fishing, clamming, or beachcombing.

The annual Fishermen's Festival in April features a decorated boat parade, the blessing of the fleet, arts and crafts shows, food stalls, and races. Crabbing season runs from mid-November through April, and crab feasts are a Bodega Bay specialty. Try them at the Tide Wharf Restaurant's annual Crab Feed, or buy or catch your own and have a feast, accompanied with sourdough bread and chilled Sonoma County wine.

CAZADERO

Timberhill Ranch

35755 Hauser Bridge Road
Cazadero, CA 95421
707-847-3258
707-847-3342

*A luxurious
ridgetop ranch
and cottages*

Owner: Tarran McDaid. **Accommodations:** 15 cottages. **Rates:** $350 double weekends, $325 weekdays. **Included:** Breakfast and dinner. **Added:** 9% bed tax, 7.5% sales tax. **Minimum stay:** 2 nights on weekends, 3 nights on holiday weekends. **Payment:** MasterCard, Visa. **Children:** Not appropriate. **Pets:** Not allowed. **Smoking:** Restricted.

Timberhill is a mile inland as the crow flies from the rugged northern Sonoma coast, two and a half hours from San Francisco. But the road you take to get there twists five miles from the shoreline highway up into the hills.

The luxury ranch stands on a ridgetop more than a thousand feet above sea level. If you're in need of a soothing haven with no phone or television or harsh intrusions, the drive is worth it. Add superb meals to the peaceful ambience and pampering Timberhill offers, and you understand why it's in great demand. Hiking trails meander through 80 acres of grassy meadows, towering redwoods, and placid ponds, leading to wide views of Salt Point State Park and Kruse Rhododendron Reserve. The park and reserve cover 6,000 acres of wooded hills and ferny glens, extending to the sea.

Tennis courts are tucked away behind a hill overlooking a wooded canyon. A 40-foot swimming pool surrounded by decking is next to the main lodge, with a whirlpool spa in one corner.

In the lodge is an intimate little restaurant where six-course dinners are served nightly to guests in a romantic, candlelit setting. Local products are used to prepare the "California French" cuisine, which features specialties such as roasted quail with red and black currant sauce, Peking duck under a sour cherry sauce, and pan-grilled salmon with papaya chutney. The wine list has about thirty Sonoma County wines.

The cedar cottages are scattered over the property, some hidden among the redwoods and others on the edge of a meadow overlooking the duck pond. Handmade quilts grace the beds, tiled fireplaces are laid with wood, and traditional furniture stands against rustic walls. Fresh flowers add dashes of color, in pottery vases, on the pillows, and even placed carefully atop a stack of fluffy towels in the bathroom.

> If you want to tour the surrounding countryside during the day, the kitchen will pack a picnic basket for you. A good place to enjoy it is Salt Point, a beach park with convoluted lava formations, colorful tidepools, and high bluffs that are good for whale-watching.

The innkeepers have added a few unexpected touches such as flashlights for evening walks, matchbooks and napkins with your name in gilt lettering, and coffeemakers with Timberhill's own blend of coffee. The flaws are mere annoyances: no towel racks, no place to hang wet swimsuits, and little drawer space.

Privacy is respected in this rarefied atmosphere. The owners are available to answer questions and will show up at your cottage door with a breakfast tray (fruit, muffins, juice, and tea or coffee); otherwise, you're on your own for solitary rambles, tennis, sunning by the pool, or hot-tubbing. The skylighted common room in the main building has soft couches facing a big stone fireplace, but most appealing is the seclusion of your own cottage and crackling fire.

Long ago the property was a Pomo Indian encampment. After the redwood forest was logged, it became a working ranch and the site of an alternative school before the present owners took over in 1983. The two couples from the Bay Area decided to build the perfect country retreat with their own hands. With little help they constructed the lodge, the cottages, the pool, barns, and tennis courts. More cottages have been added in recent years.

DRAKESBAD

Drakesbad Guest Ranch

Chester, CA 96020
916-Drakesbad 2 via Susanville
  operator
Off-season:
California Guest Services
2150 North Main Street, #5
Red Bluff, CA 96080
916-529-1512
Fax: 916-529-4511

> *A woodsy lodge*
> *near Mount Lassen*

Owners: John and Pam Koeberer. **Accommodations:** 19 rooms. **Rates:** $82–$98 single, $87–$98 per person double, $72–$75 additional person, $57 child age 2–11, weekly rates available. **Included:** All meals. **Payment:** MasterCard, Visa. **Children:** Under age 2 free in room with parents. **Pets:** Discouraged. **Smoking:** Nonsmoking rooms available. **Open:** June to October.

The only lodge in Lassen Volcanic National Park in northern California, Drakesbad offers an extraordinary summer wilderness experience, combining basic comforts with outdoor leisure and backcountry exploration. Meadows, lakes, and trout streams surround the property. Hiking trails wind through 150 miles of verdant forest, glaciated canyons, and volcanic terrain. Horseback rides are scheduled daily to scenic spots in the park. And on the sprawling ranch there's a naturally heated swimming pool, open 24 hours a day.

The ranch, nestled in a scenic valley two and a half miles from the park's southeastern entrance, was founded by E. R. Drake a century ago. In 1900 he sold it to the Sifford family, who named it Drakesbad for the hot springs and pools on the property. For fifty years the Siffords operated the ranch much as it is today. The present owners have made improvements but have retained its rough texture.

> **Hiking trails cross areas of devastation with steaming fumaroles and boiling mud pots caused by past volcanic outbursts.**
> **Bumpass Hell Trail shows dramatic examples of geothermal activity. The hike with the most panoramic views is Lassen Peak Trail, which leads to the summit.**

All accommodations are modest but clean and well kept. Some share shower facilities, and most use kerosene lamps rather than electricity. The six rooms on the second floor of the main lodge have half-baths; tubs and showers are in a modern outdoor bathhouse. Housekeeping is provided daily.

The main floor of the lodge is where guests stop by to sit in the rocking chair by the stone fireplace, read, work on a jigsaw puzzle, or buy candy and film. In this big, knotty pine room with scuffed wooden floors, braided rugs, and rusted old farm tools hanging on the walls, there's a sense of timelessness. You know that although changes have been made, this is just how it must have looked years ago. Typical of the ranch's informality, if you are the last person to leave the lodge at night, you're asked to turn out the lanterns that hang from ceiling beams.

Outside, a long veranda faces a lawn with picnic tables, a volleyball net, a campfire pit, barbecues, and a path that leads through the adjacent field to the pool.

Across the way, under pine and fir trees, are three bungalows, each with two adjoining units with knotty pine walls and rustic furnishings. They have a propane heater and a private bath, and can connect to the next room to make two bedrooms and two baths. Similar rooms are in an annex, a duplex, and four cabins among the trees on the other side of the property, not far from the stables. There are no locks on the doors, so it's wise to lock valuables in your car.

Meals are served in the dining room, a separate building with pine walls, a potbellied woodstove, and wooden tables and chairs. Hearty ranch breakfasts and dinners are served to your table; lunch is buffet style. Beer and wine are available.

You can take guided horseback trips to lovely spots in the 106,000-acre park, such as Devil's Kitchen, Boiling Springs Lake, Terminal Geyser, Kings Creek Falls, and Willow Lakes. Along the way you may see bears, marmots, deer, and golden mantle squirrels, as well as wildflowers and birds.

DUNSMUIR

Railroad Park Resort

100 Railroad Park Road
Dunsmuir, CA 96025
916-235-4440
800-974-RAIL in California
Fax: 916-235-4470

A group of railroad cars, restored as lodgings

Proprietors: Bill and Delberta Murphy. **Accommodations:** 22 cabooses, 1 boxcar, 4 cabins. **Rates:** $60 single, $55–$85 double, $5 additional person. **Payment:** Major credit cards. **Children:** $5 additional if third person in unit. **Pets:** Welcome with approval; $2.50 additional. **Smoking:** Nonsmoking units available.

In the 19th century, the last car on a train was used for storage space and living quarters and, as time went on, it became the personal domain of the conductor. To live the life of such a railroader, visit Railroad Park Resort. It takes a leap of imagination, for these cabooses go nowhere. Each is anchored firmly to its own brief stretch of track just off I-5 south of the little town of Dunsmuir, in the mountains of northern California, but children and railroad buffs will enjoy the idea of sleeping in a caboose.

The cabooses bear fresh coats of paint — green, blue, yellow, and mostly, a familiar railroad red. The Santa Fe, Great

Northern, Southern Pacific, and the McCloud River are a few of the rail lines represented, and each has a different interior decor. Some are painted, others paneled in knotty cedar. A typical rectangular room has a brass bed, table and chairs, a dresser, a coffeemaker, telephone, refrigerator, and a TV (with satellite reception). Blue fluffy curtains hang at small windows. The effect is not unlike a mobile home except for the metal braces and pipes, the iron ladders and lofts, which are evidence of the car's railroading days. The only other mementoes are the photographs on the walls.

> **Bill and Delberta Murphy are proud of their region and of their resort in the Sacra-mento River Canyon. They lend mountain bikes and will direct you to hiking trails and their trout pond. Their unusual resort also has sixty campsites and RV sites.**

The circle of cabooses make a colorful railyard below the craggy peaks above, and they surround a freeform swimming pool, wooden deck, and spa. A stream runs by, winding through the property to a pond. Off to the side are four attached housekeeping cabins, which hold four people each.

The resort's office and gift shop are in a faded yellow building that resembles an old-fashioned train depot with a high boardwalk entrance. Near it is the showpiece of the resort, its restaurant. Made from antique dining cars, it's steeped in railroad history. Above the bar is a hand-built scale model of the Cascade, which ran from San Francisco to Portland in the 1930s. Antique hand tools, lamps, and steam gauges make this a railroad buff's delight.

Dinners are served in an equally nostalgic atmosphere, with a view of relics of the steam era. Among them are an 1893 Wells Fargo car, a gear-driven logging engine, and a restored water tower. The menu offers American fare — steak, chicken, pasta, and seafood dominate the dining scene. The restaurant is only open for dinner. For other meals, drive a mile north into Dunsmuir, where there are several good cafés (try Rosie's Ice Cream Parlor for homemade soups and sandwiches).

Outside the Patio Car, there's a deck for relaxing with a cocktail and enjoying the fine view of the gray spires of Castle

Crags State Park. In the shadow of these steep granite out-croppings, the last Indian battle fought with bows and arrows occurred in 1885.

ELK

Elk Cove Inn

P.O. Box 367
6300 South Highway 1
Elk Cove, CA 95432
707-877-3321
800-275-2967
Fax: 707-877-3321

*An ocean-view
inn and cottages*

Innkeeper: Elaine Bryant. **Accommodations:** 10 units (all with private bath). **Rates:** $98–$168 weekdays, $108–$188 weekends. **Included:** Full breakfast. **Added:** 10% tax. **Minimum stay:** 2 or 3 nights on weekends and holidays. **Payment:** Major credit cards. **Children:** Not appropriate. **Pets:** Not allowed. **Smoking:** Not allowed indoors.

The main house of this clifftop inn was built in 1883 by the L. E. White Lumber Company as an executive guest house. In 1968 it was reborn as a bed and breakfast. At Elk Cove, the energetic innkeeper will greet you with a smile, give you a hearty welcome, and treat you like an honored friend.

The guest rooms are in the main house, and four cabins stand at the edge of the cliff. They have fine views of the drift-wood-strewn sandy beach, offshore rock formations, and surf. The furnishings include antiques, down comforters, and bathrobes. Fresh flowers, potted greenery, and hand-embroidered linens add a personal touch, while port, chocolates, candles, and complimentary wine create a romantic ambience.

The rooms in the duplex addition feature large bay windows, high-beamed ceilings, skylights, and fireplaces. The windows in the Greenwood Room overlook Greenwood Creek and the beach below. Even the shower stall, its tiles bright with hand-painted folk art, has a long window with a view.

The large, bright rooms upstairs in the main house have

paneled wainscoting, window seats, and skylights. They share a sitting area and a redwood deck. The newest addition is the Swallow's Nest, a small corner room on the main floor that has access to the deck.

> Climbing roses, boxes of pink geraniums, and flower-beds under the cypress trees give this gabled white inn and its guest cottages a country atmosphere. The inn stands on 1½ acres on a cliff above the ocean.

Breakfast is served in the oceanfront dining room of the main house. Elaine is likely to prepare a soufflé served with her southern corn pudding and fresh-baked crois-sants, or a decadent car-amelized apple French toast. The main course is always preceded by a first course such as baked pear with almond cream cheese stuffing or baked grapefruit with a honey-raspberry sauce. A selection of juice and teas and the inn's own specially blended coffee round out the morning meal.

Many guests enjoy the inn's gazebo or taking a walk down the path that leads to the beach. Here great blue herons and snowy egrets often visit, and two ravens are such frequent visitors they are virtually pets. For exploring farther afield, the inn is close to a number of Anderson Valley wineries and fifteen miles south of the shops and art galleries of Mendocino.

Greenwood Pier Inn

Box 336
5928 South Highway 1
Elk, CA 95432
707-877-9997
Fax: 707-877-3439

An artistic inn
overlooking
the sea

Innkeepers: Isabel and Kendrick Petty. **Accommodations:** 11 rooms (all with private bath). **Rates:** $100–$225 single or double, $12 additional person. **Included:** Continental breakfast. **Added:** 10% tax. **Minimum stay:** 2 nights on weekends in most rooms. **Payment:** Major credit cards. **Children:** Additional $10. **Pets:** Allowed with prior arrangement; additional $10. **Smoking:** Allowed by prior arrangement.

A bower of flowers, an art gallery, a charming café, cliff-top views of the Pacific surf — all this and comfortable rooms make up the unique Greenwood Pier Inn. The energetic and talented innkeepers started their venture in 1980 with two cottages. Now they have a complex of lodgings, all connected by paths that wind through extravagant gardens, high above the sea.

It's a ten-minute walk to the beach from the inn. You can also go sea kayaking or horseback riding, and visit the giant redwoods in Hendy Woods State Park, nineteen miles inland.

The rooms have hand-painted tiles, stained glass by regional artists, leaded glass windows, skylights, and pieces collected by the Pettys on their world travels. In one corner you might see a huge vase filled with calla lilies four feet high; in another, a pink dressing table painted with flowers.

In Sea Castle North and Sea Castle South, Kendrick's seascapes hang on the walls and sliding glass doors open to a deck at the edge of a cliff, overlooking the ocean. A staircase spirals up to a tub for two next to a wide window. Books fill the shelves, and tapes are provided for the tape deck.

This is a place of exuberance, color, and quirky character. You'll see curtains askew, rough walls next to Oriental artifacts, and an eclectic mix of art and furniture. Isabel's artistic sense and enthusiasm make it all work. She sews the quilts, designs clothing and jewelry, paints portraits, bakes the breads and desserts served in the café — and if you need marriage counseling she can provide that, too.

The restaurant is open everyday for breakfast and lunch, and for dinner as well Thursday through Monday. Breakfast and dinner can be brought to your room on a tray if you wish (dinner is extra; Continental breakfast is included in the room rate). And while you're at the inn, don't miss a trip to Greenwood Pier's intriguing country store and garden shop.

Harbor House

P.O. Box 369
5600 South Highway 1
Elk, CA 95432
707-877-3203

*A seaside home
in the grand style*

Innkeepers: Dean and Helen Turner. **Accommodations:** 10 rooms (all with private bath). **Rates:** $140–$225 single, $175–$265 double, $50 additional person; winter discounts available. **Included:** Breakfast and dinner. **Added:** 10% tax on lodging; 7.25% on dining. Minimum stay: 2 nights on weekends. **Payment:** No credit cards; personal checks accepted. **Children:** Under age 12 not appropriate. **Pets:** Not allowed. **Smoking:** Not allowed indoors.

On a bluff facing a spectacular seascape is Harbor House, one of the finest examples of luxury lodging on the coast. The all-redwood inn stands above Greenwood Landing, once a busy port for lumber schooners.

The beamed ceiling and paneled walls in the living room glow with the rich patina of polish and age. A century-old Persian rug lies under deep cushioned couches grouped around the big fireplace. In one corner is a Steinway console piano; occasionally concerts are held in this room. A niche near the fire holds a telephone and shelves of books and games for guests to use.

Beyond is the dining room, where a wall of windows faces the irresistible view. Breakfast here is different every day: always fruit juice, homemade pastries and breads, and coffee; accompanying main dishes such as eggs Benedict, huevos rancheros, pancakes, and quiche. Eggs come from the inn's own chickens. Dinners feature home-grown produce, meats and cheeses from nearby farms, and fresh seafood. California wines are served.

> **The inn was built in 1916 by the Goodyear Redwood Lumber Company as a residence and a guest house for VIPs, and is a larger version of the Home of Redwood building at the Panama-Pacific International Exposition, held in San Francisco in 1915.**

The guest rooms, six of them in the main house, have antique furnishings and fireplaces. Harbor Room, one of the largest, has room for two beds, comfortable chairs, and an English library table. The views of the sea from this attractive, rose-colored room are stunning. Lookout is the smallest and most popular room in the house. It has a deck that is ideal for watching the sun set over the Pacific.

The other rooms are in four red and white cottages on the south side of the inn, under tall cypress trees. Seaview and Oceansong share a deck that juts dramatically over a ravine that descends to a cove. For privacy, the deck is divided by a lattice with an ivy vine. Shorepine and Edgewood have partial ocean views from their decks; Edgewood is closest to the highway and therefore least desirable (however, the busy road quiets at night).

Harbor House offers comfortable accommodations, beauteous surroundings, fine food, and, most important, superb service. Dean and Helen Turner, former school administrators in Los Angeles, took over the inn in 1985 and have added their personal style of friendly warmth to the well-appointed sanctuary. They'll point out the path that leads from the lawns and garden down to the cove, introduce you to the attractions of Elk and Mendocino, and join you by the fire for evening conversation and music. Winter is a good time to visit, they say. The weather is often clear, and the coastal storms are thrilling to watch.

EUREKA

An Elegant Victorian Mansion

1406 "C" Street
Eureka, CA 95501
707-444-3144 or 442-5594

*A historic home
with warm
hospitality*

Innkeepers: Doug and Lily Vieyra. **Accommodations:** 4 rooms (1 private bath, 3 share 3 baths). **Rates:** $75–$145 single or double (corporate and midweek rates available). **Included:** Full breakfast. **Added:** 10% tax. **Payment:** MasterCard, Visa. **Children:** "Precocious, well-behaved, older children welcome by prior arrangement." **Pets:** Not allowed. **Smoking:** Not allowed.

When you're greeted at the door by a smiling "butler" in formal dress who escorts you to an elegant parlor and then to a finely furnished guest room, you know you're in an unusual bed and breakfast. Doug Vieyra is the tuxedoed greeter. Full of enthusiasm, he and Lily will show you around the parlors, the library, the sitting room and garden, suggesting a game of croquet or a ride in an antique automobile.

The house was built in 1888 for William Clark, a successful businessman and Eureka's mayor. Now the home is on the National Register of Historic Places and is a California State Historic Site. It's considered a prime example of Queen Anne–influenced Eastlake Victorian architecture.

Authenticity was very important to the innkeepers when it came to furnishing their bed and breakfast. Lily made most of the drapes in the home from Victorian fabrics or from fine reproduction fabrics of Victorian prints. Wall coverings are reproductions of William Morris patterns, and some of the home's original carpeting is still intact and in remarkably good condition. Molded plaster ceiling medallions are colorfully painted as they would have been at the turn-of-the-century to protect the ceilings from the emissions of the gas light fixtures below. All the rooms contain period furnishings, and the walls are adorned with old family portraits.

Straw boaters, men's bowlers, and other vintage hats hanging on a wonderfully carved hat rack at the entrance immediately set the nostalgic tone. Then there are the parlors. One has a velvet fainting couch set with embroidered silk pillows. On a table nearby there's a *Ladies Home Journal* from 1890, and a *Saturday Evening Post* dated 1905. The fine china displayed in a sideboard has been in Lily's family since the 1800s. Another parlor has a pink and green tiled fireplace with intricate walnut fretwork, and an old fashioned gramophone set to play one of the inn's selection of 1920s LPs. One parlor has an open game of scrabble awaiting players, and a chess set in a window alcove; while the most informal sitting room is where guests gather in front of a wood burning stove to watch movie classics on the TV/VCR or listen to music.

Guests rooms are located on the second floor, and each room has a queen-size bed, a desk, and a sitting area. Some have views of Humboldt Bay and the Samoa Peninsula. A fringed drape divides the bed from the sitting area in the Van Gogh suite where books of the artist's works can be perused while sitting on tapestry upholstered chairs lighted by beaded lamps. The bedroom set and lacy black dress hanging on the wall belonged to Lily's mother.

Lily Langtry, a celebrated 19th-century actress, once performed in Eureka, so one room is named for her. It is highlighted by a dark oak four-poster bed and a Palladian window that overlooks Humboldt Bay. A lace umbrella and decorative fans add a feminine touch. French country furnishings create a warm, bright atmosphere in the Governor's Room. It has a private bath, queen-size bed, and a fine view. A daybed, easy chair, and writing desk make the small connecting room a perfect reading or writing nook, or sleeping quarters for a third person.

The least expensive is the Senator's Room, which contains another family heirloom — a marble-topped bedroom set that belonged to Lily's grandmother in Belgium. All rooms have bedside tables equipped with reading lamps. Of the three shared bathrooms, one is upstairs and two are on the main floor. Robes are provided for the trip down the hall and for visiting the Finnish sauna.

> One of the most ornate and well-preserved of Eureka's numerous Victorian homes, the inn is owned by people who delight in sharing its history and beauty with their guests.

The day begins in the formal dining room with breakfast at a single table set with placecards, and red and white china on a lace cloth. Served by Lily wearing a costume from her native Belgium, the meal may consist of poached pears in blackberry sauce followed by creamed eggs with red and green peppers, and smoked ham in a puff pastry topped with a light hollandaise, accompanied by delicious homemade almond stollen, zucchini bread, and orange juice. Other popular hot entrées include a spinach soufflé and French toast stuffed with bananas and walnuts, as the menu changes daily.

For other meals Doug and Lily are happy to provide dining suggestions. One of their favorites, the Sea Grill, is certainly worth a visit for its outstanding salad bar and fresh seafood dishes. Ask the Vieyras what there is to see and do in the area, and you'll be given a list that could keep you busy for days. Stroll through the shops, galleries, and restaurants of Old Town, see Eureka's architectural treasures, cruise on the bay or take a deep sea fishing charter. Don't miss the astonishing Carson Mansion, probably the most-photographed Victorian creation in California.

Doug and Lily have an array of books and magazines, lend tandem bicycles, and hold occasional musical events. In the afternoon they often serve ice cream sodas while guests play croquet in the side yard. These sociable hosts claim to provide "the lavish hospitality of a bygone era." With good cheer and charm, that's exactly what they do.

Carter House and Hotel Carter

1033 3rd Street
Eureka, CA 95501
707-445-1390
800-404-1390
Fax: 707-444-8067

> *Victorian style,
> contemporary
> flair, and fine
> cuisine are the
> highlights of this
> lodging group*

Innkeepers: Mark and Christi Carter. **Accommodations:** 32 rooms. **Rates:** $79–$295. **Included:** Full breakfast. **Added:** Tax. **Payment:** Major credit cards. **Children:** Not appropriate. **Pets:** Not allowed. **Smoking:** Not allowed in guest rooms.

The port city of Eureka boasts a wide variety of Victorian architecture, including what is probably the finest example in the country, the ornate Carson Mansion.

Another Victorian-style home is the Carter House — but this one was built in the 1980s, not the 1890s. Mark Carter, a long-time admirer of 19th-century design, had restored several houses before he found a book of drawings by Samuel and Joseph C. Newsom, architects of the Carson Mansion and other Eureka buildings. One drawing showed a house that had been built in San Francisco in 1884 and destroyed in the 1906 earthquake. Mark decided to recreate that house in Eureka. He and a crew of three hand-crafted the spacious four-story structure, following the Newsom plans in almost every intricate detail.

High, curtainless windows, polished oak floors, white

walls, and a collection of abstract art make a pleasing contrast to the rich, dark wainscoting and woodwork. Orchids add delicate color. A basket of apples stands on the sideboard in the front parlor; in the evenings you'll find decanters of after-dinner drinks and cookies. Wine and hors d'oeuvres are served in the afternoons.

> **The handsome redwood Carter House draws travelers who admire the quality of workmanship and Victorian structure, yet appreciate the light, uncluttered interior.**

Mark and Christi have furnished the guest rooms with a few well-chosen antiques, fresh flowers, clock radios, robes, and special soaps.

The two 2-bedroom suites are good choices for families or couples traveling together. The suite on the second floor is particularly spacious and has a fireplace, numerous windows, and a tiled bathroom with a whirlpool tub and a double-headed shower.

Three more rooms, plus kitchen facilities, are offered in the Bell Cottage, a remodeled turn-of-the-century home a few doors from the inn. The cottage guest rooms have a more contemporary look than those in the Carter House, and have modern amenities such as TVs, VCRs, CD players, and marble double Jacuzzis. All three rooms share a common living room and fully equipped kitchen.

Guests at each of the inns register at the Hotel Carter across the street from the Carter House. The hotel has 24 tastefully furnished rooms and romantic suites. Standard rooms are pleasant with light pine furniture, blanket chests, armoires, and woven rugs.

The luxury suites are more spacious and have extra amenities. The first thing you see when you enter suite 301 is a giant round Jacuzzi below a bay window with town and marina views. French doors separate the living room and bedroom, and the bath has an oversized shower with two shower heads. The suite also has its own CD player, VCR, and refrigerator, and robes are provided.

There are fine restaurants in Eureka, but the best by far is the Hotel Carter. The light and airy restaurant is superb, and it has earned a nationwide reputation. Here you'll find dishes based on fresh ingredients, a relaxed atmosphere, an exceptional wine list, and a talented chef. Dinner entrées might include grilled breast of Long Island duck with seasonal fruit and Zinfandel sauce, grilled Pacific salmon in a mustard rosemary sauce, or Burgundy-glazed filet mignon with cypress grove peppered fromage blanc. A lighter café menu is also available.

All overnight guests go to the restaurant for breakfast — one of the best breakfasts you'll ever have at an inn. The emphasis on quality is evident in the breads, pears poached in wine sauce, eggs Florentine, pasta, and strawberry cake (and that's just one flower-garnished meal).

The well-tended gardens that supply much of the produce and herbs for the restaurant intrigue guests almost as much as the food. The Carters offer garden tours and a lecture series. The hotel also has a wine shop where you can purchase some of the wines you may have sampled from the restaurant's 21-page wine list while dining.

FERNDALE

The Gingerbread Mansion

400 Berding Street
Ferndale, CA 95536
707-786-4000
800-952-4136
Fax: 707-786-4381

A historic home in a Victorian village

Innkeepers: Ken and Sandie Torbert. **Accommodations:** 11 rooms (all with private bath). **Rates:** $110–$140 single, $130–$160 double, $160–$350 suite. **Included:** Full breakfast. **Added:** 7.9% tax. **Minimum stay:** 2 nights on summer weekends and holidays. **Payment:** Major credit cards. **Children:** Welcome. **Pets:** Not allowed. **Smoking:** Not allowed indoors.

In the far northwestern corner of California, the little town of Ferndale lies steeped in the past. The entire village of restored Victorian buildings is a State Historical Landmark. Its Main Street is probably the brightest in the West, with facades painted in a rainbow palette of hues that lend welcome color to the often foggy area.

The most striking home in this quiet backwater is the Gingerbread Mansion. The ornate bed-and-breakfast inn is surrounded by English gardens with boxwood-edged paths that wind through archways and tulip beds, past topiary, fountains, and statuary. In the center is a silver reflecting ball on a pedestal.

The mansion, built in 1899, is a showcase of turn-of-the-century elegance. Five parlors are filled with antiques and settees where visitors may browse through travel books and magazines, play games, and enjoy an elaborate tea, with petits fours and chocolate-dipped strawberries, in the afternoons. A 1,000-piece jigsaw puzzle of the mansion lies partially completed on a separate table, while the third-floor parlor has a VCR where guests can view classic films.

Antiques, Egyptian cotton towels, and high-quality linens are common to all guest rooms, and several have old-fashioned clawfoot tubs. In fact, the Fountain and Gingerbread suites each have two such tubs for romantic "his and her" bubble baths. The twin tubs in the luxurious Fountain Suite are side-by-side, facing a mirrored wall. The bed has a canopy, and a bay window looks out on the village and garden. In the Gingerbread Suite, the tubs are in the bedroom on a raised platform surrounded by a Victorian railing.

Each room offers something special. The Rose Suite has two fireplaces and a tub in a flowery bower, with mirrors on the walls and ceiling. Strawberry Hill, in peach and green, has a fireplace and lots of windows and light; Garden overlooks a multitude of flowers; and Lilac has a burl maple bed with walnut trim draped in purple, a fainting couch, clawfoot tub, and a lovely stained glass window. Hideaway, one of the newer rooms at the back of the inn, has a country garden atmosphere, but is consistent with the mansion's style in its molding detail and carved wood.

On the top floor, the Empire Suite is the newest addition to the inn, and the most deluxe. From the marble entryway French doors open into a luxurious and spacious suite that any Emperor would approve of. There's a bed draped in black and gold Egyptian cotton, a clawfoot tub before one of the marble fireplaces, and an Empire sofa in front of the second fireplace. Other features include a Biedermeier-style antique armoire, a reading alcove, a dining area set back in another gable, and a bath with a two-sink vanity, bidet, and sit-in shower with three shower heads and five massage sprays.

One of the outstanding features here is the innkeeper's attention to detail. Sandie says she loves what she does, and her concern for her guests clearly shows. Nothing a guest could need has been overlooked. You'll find bathrobes in your dresser drawer, hand-dipped chocolates by the bed, and a tray of coffee or tea on the hall sideboard in the morning. Clock radios are discreetly hidden in nightstands, and two rooms have inconspicuous TVs.

> **The quiet roads around Ferndale pass acres of green fields and dairy farms that once formed the economic base of the region, which is why the Victorian mansions are called Butterfat Palaces.**

Breakfast, served at two tables in the formal dining room, includes fresh juice, homemade granola, local cheeses, various pastries, and a hot entrée such as cheese blintzes or an egg dish individually baked in a ramekin. Parking space is not provided, but there's plenty of curb parking in Ferndale, where rush hour consists of three cars and a truck on the same street at the same time.

Ferndale has shops, art galleries, a repertory theater, and a museum. Yearly events fit the small-town image: the Ice Cream Social in September, the County Fair and Horse Races in August, the Easter Egg Hunt. There are the Beef Bar-B-Que and the Firemen's Annual Main Street Games, and for something out of the ordinary, the Portuguese Holy Ghost Festival (many of the early settlers were Portuguese). In late May the Great Arcata-to-Ferndale Cross-Country Kinetic Sculpture Race takes place. In wild and crazy contraptions, racers from around the country compete for three days and two nights, ending in a grand finale on Main Street. Moviemakers felt so strongly that Ferndale was the quintessential small American town that they used it as a backdrop for the movie *Outbreak*. If you watch the film closely enough you can spot the Gingerbread Mansion's cheerful yellow and salmon exterior briefly in one scene.

FORKS OF SALMON

Otter Bar Lodge

Box 210
14026 Salmon River Road
Forks of Salmon, CA 96031
916-462-4772

> *A wilderness lodge offering rest and recreation*

Proprietors: Peter and Kristy Sturges.
Accommodations: 6 rooms (with 6 shared baths). **Rates:** $100 per person per day in fall, $1,290 per week in spring and summer. **Included:** All meals. **Payment:** No credit cards; personal checks accepted. **Children:** Welcome with prior arrangement. **Pets:** Not allowed. **Smoking:** Not allowed. **Open:** April–October.

If you want to be completely surrounded by remote, rugged wilderness where steelhead swim in emerald green waters, consider Otter Bar. It's a mountain refuge of comfort and style where you can fish, kayak, ride mountain bikes, and feast on excellent food.

The lodge takes only twelve guests at a time. "We want to keep it small, personal, and private," says Peter Sturges, who built the low, rambling ranch house to blend with the forested environment. A waterwheel generates power, and a woodstove and immense stone fireplace provide heat. Antiques and handmade furniture fill the rooms.

Outside are a redwood hot tub and a wood-fired sauna, and each guest room has a private deck. The beds all have down comforters. In the living room guests enjoy the stereo, VCR, and assorted books. Meals receive nothing but heartfelt praise. You'll be served five-course dinners (roast lamb, salads and vegetables from the garden, velvety cheesecake), buffet lunches, and full breakfasts (omelettes, fresh fruit, hot currant scones, coffee).

The original intention was to create a wilderness retreat and fishing lodge, but along the way Otter Bar Lodge also grew into one of the nation's foremost kayaking schools and mountain bicycling destinations.

Getting to Otter Bar is an adventure in itself. The lodge is a two-hour drive west from Yreka, or two and a half hours east of Eureka, along the Salmon River that cuts through the

Salmon Mountains, bounded on the north by the Marble Mountain Wilderness. The last few miles are on a tortuously winding, narrow road high above the river. Two miles beyond the village of Forks of Salmon, you reach the lodge, a welcome sight under the maple, oak, and madrone trees.

The activities are divided by season. Kayaking and bicycling are offered in summer and early fall. Later, fishing takes over. The Salmon is known for its runs of classic fly water, riffles, and deep, slow pools. You can fish from the bank, wade, or go out in a drift boat with Peter as a guide. Skilled instructors teach visitors to kayak, from beginning skills to advanced techniques in rough white water. All equipment is provided. The trails and fire roads that snake through the forests are ideal for mountain biking. At Otter Bar Lodge, you can enjoy a mountain bike holiday that includes instruction and plenty of riding over terrain as easy or challenging as you choose. Summer afternoons are usually too hot for serious riding, so those are the hours for swimming in the river, lounging on white sandy beaches, and rafting.

> **These vacations are for people looking for a place far off the beaten path with exceptional quality and beautiful scenery. There are no bars or restaurants anywhere in the area, so bring your own beverages and plan on good food and company, fine fishing, expert instruction, and adventurous thrills.**

GARBERVILLE

Benbow Inn

445 Lake Benbow Drive
Garberville, CA 95442
707-923-2124
800-355-3301
Fax: 707-923-2897

An old-fashioned atmosphere with contemporary touches

Proprietors: John and Teresa Porter.
Accommodations: 55 rooms. **Rates:** $110–$295 single or double, suites $225–$295, $15 additional person. **Added:** 10% tax. **Minimum stay:** 2 nights on weekends. **Payment:** MasterCard, Visa. **Children:** Welcome; $15 for rollaway. **Pets:** Allowed by prior arrangement. **Smoking:** Not allowed. **Open:** Late April through December.

This unusual inn in the north coast redwood country is a National Historic Landmark. The three-story, half-timbered hotel was built in 1926 and welcomed many famous people, including Herbert Hoover and Eleanor Roosevelt, before it gradually fell into disrepair. In recent years the inn has been restored to its original elegance. The Benbow stands just west of (and unfortunately close to) Highway 101, south of Garberville.

Inside the hotel is a lobby and lounge, paneled in dark woods, with an immense stone fireplace at one end. A jester holds court on one side of the fireplace, and a table in the center bears a swan vase filled with fresh flowers. The floors are covered with Oriental rugs and sofas, and alcoves hold partially completed jigsaw puzzles where every afternoon guests may be found pondering them as they enjoy their tea and scones or mulled wine.

Off the lobby is a bar with an antique fireplace and a tapestry-adorned half-timbered dining room that offers Continental cuisine. Meals are served on tables set with linens, candles, and fresh flowers. The menu emphasizes seafood, poultry, and pastas, featuring such dishes as roasted salmon filet, herb rigatoni, and daily fresh specials. For dessert don't miss the chocolate mousse pie.

> **The inn overlooks little Benbow Lake, which is filled only in summer, when the Eel River is dammed. You may swim in the lake, and canoes and paddle boats are available from the Park Service.**

In back of the hotel is a large, partially shaded terrace with several guest rooms beyond it, each with its own patio overlooking the lawn and river. The separate Garden Cottage boasts a four-poster canopy bed on a carpeted platform. Books on the mantel, a grandfather clock, and an Oriental rug fit the mood of rock-solid stability in a room that's big enough to dance in. It also has a whirlpool tub and separate shower in the bath.

The older guest accommodations in the main hotel are on the small side, but are tastefully furnished with antiques, four-poster reproduction beds, red velvet chairs, tiled baths, irons and ironing boards, sherry, fresh ground coffee and coffeemakers, reading lamps, and a basket of magazines and well-worn paperback mysteries. They're just right for an evening of reading by the crackling fire in the parlor — when you're not working on a puzzle or sipping sherry.

As the innkeeper is also a writer, Teresa tries to incorporate literary themes into inn activities whenever possible. There's a magnetic poetry board on a table near the fireplace in the lobby. In July the Benbow throws a Shakespeare-style poetry contest. In the past, the inn inspired artistic creativity of another sort. While *Bambi* was being made, some of the animators stayed at the inn while they sketched background drawings for the movie from area scenes.

GUALALA

The Old Milano Hotel

38300 Highway 1
Gualala, CA 95445
707-884-3256

*A landmark inn
with lush
gardens and a
panoramic view*

Innkeeper: Leslie Linscheid. **Accommodations:** 7 rooms (6 with shared baths), 1 cottage, 1 caboose **Rates:** $80–$175 single or double. **Included:** Full breakfast. **Added:** 7.25% tax. **Minimum stay:** 2 nights on weekends. **Payment:** Major credit cards. **Children:** Not appropriate. **Pets:** Not allowed. **Smoking:** Not allowed indoors.

The setting for this historic landmark hotel could not be more splendid — three acres of lawns and gardens bordered by tall cedar trees on the edge of a cliff. In the cove below, waves crash against boulders and slide over smoothly worn pebbles, with the sea stretching beyond to a misty horizon.

On this prime property a mile north of Gualala and 100 miles north of San Francisco, the hotel opened in 1905 as the Milano, noted for its Italian food and hospitality. Since 1984 it has been owned by Leslie Linscheid, who continues to offer excellent meals and comfortable accommodations to north coast travelers.

The house is furnished with rich Victorian pieces, set against floral wallpapers and red carpeting. Two guest rooms, a parlor, and a dining room occupy the main floor. The dining room is a full restaurant, open to the public Tuesday through Sunday, with a menu that changes seasonally. A prix fixe dinner might be quail stuffed with rice and plums, grilled pork tenderloin, or filet mignon in a cabernet demi-glaze. Seafood is fresh and local, as are most vegetables and herbs. There's an extensive wine list.

The small restaurant has a stone fireplace and the original back bar from the hotel's early days. Fringed lampshades, a candelabra, a gilt-framed mirror, and an old-fashioned cash register add to the period mood.

On the other side of the house is the Master Suite, the largest and most expensive room. It has a sitting room with a separate outside entrance, a bed of carved wood, and best of all, a superb ocean view. Of the five upstairs rooms, Room 3 is the smallest. It has a double bed, a little desk graced with fresh flowers, and a large closet where you'll find towels and a flashlight for night visits to the outdoor spa. This room overlooks the garden, with its huge dahlias and rose-covered trellis.

> **When you're ready for the ultimate in relaxation, sign up for a private sunset session in the spa, pick up your towel and flashlight, and amble down the path to the secluded hot tub. As you soak in bliss, you're gazing out at craggy Cathedral Rock and a blue-green sea.**

The other rooms all have sea views and individual furnishings — a big armchair by a window, a high armoire, built-in bookshelves, framed musical scores, and a high brass bed are a few examples. Most rooms have double beds (some are soft, so if you prefer a firm mattress, be sure to request it).

Outside, behind the circular herb garden and immense fuchsias, and under salmon-colored passion flowers, is Passion Vine Cottage. This cozy spot has a Jotul woodstove, a double bed, a full kitchen, and a reading loft. There's a shower stall in the tiny bathroom.

The Caboose, or Engine 9, is a railroader's dream, tucked among the cedars for privacy. A warm and rustic nest, it has a woodstove, a small bath, and a refrigerator. There's a deck at one end of the authentic car and an observation cupola on top. Breakfast is served in the dining room, in your own room, or on the patio. Leslie oversees the preparation of such morning delectables as fresh fruit turnovers, quiche, French toast, and baked eggs. After breakfast you might stroll through the gardens and down to a rocky beach at the foot of the cliff. You're likely to see seals, sea lions, numerous birds, and possibly whales on their annual migrations. Other activities include badminton and croquet. Nearby are tennis, golf, horseback riding, bicycling, hiking, and fishing.

St. Orres

P.O. Box 523
Gualala, CA 95445
707-884-3303

*A seaside hotel
and cottages
with unusual
architecture*

Owners: Rosemary Campiformio and Eric and Ted Black. **Accommodations:** 8 rooms (share 3 baths), 11 cottages. **Rates:** $60–$75 single or double in hotel, $85–$270 in cottages. **Included:** Full breakfast. **Added:** 7.25% tax. **Minimum stay:** 2 nights on weekends. **Payment:** MasterCard, Visa. **Children:** Welcome (rollaways available). **Pets:** Not allowed. **Smoking:** Allowed except in dining room.

You've probably heard that there was a Russian settlement on the coast in the late 1800s, so when you first see the St. Orres's onion-domed towers and weathered cedar exterior, you might think it's a remnant of the past. But it's not even a restoration. The inn was built in the mid-1970s by California master carpenters Richard Wasserman and Eric Black.

Their love of fine wood is evident throughout their handsome creation. The doors are of California oak; the redwood walls are paneled in intricate geometric patterns. They used the work of local craftspeople to furnish the inn, from the stained glass windows to the colorful velvet quilts on the beds. The colors and styles look a bit dated now, but the overall effect is impressive.

Across the road from the inn, at the bottom of grassy cliffs, are coves to explore and the inn's private beach, a bit of sheltered sand where St. Orres Creek joins the Pacific surf.

One tower holds a spiral staircase that winds up to the guest rooms on the second floor. In the other is a restaurant of renown, where meals are served in an octagonal room with three levels of windows rising to the dome. Diners can look across the highway to rugged bluffs above the sea.

The guest rooms in this building share three baths: "his," "hers," and "ours," which boasts an oversize dual shower. The rooms aren't large, but they're designed with care to avoid a cramped feeling.

The cottages are more spacious and modern. Three are off paths that wind up the hillside to the edge of a redwood forest where wild orchids grow. Tree House has an elevated sleeping area, a Franklin stove, and French doors that open onto a sundeck with a wide ocean view. Rose Cottage also has an elevated bed, and Wildflower is a rustic cabin with a sleeping loft.

In the newest area, Creekside, are seven more cottages with polished woods, skylights, and ocean or forest views. They have the use of a hot tub under multi-tiered glass domes, a sauna, and an expansive sun deck edged with flower boxes.

The most dramatic cottage is Pine Haven, which accommodates four. The two-bedroom, two-bath home has three copper domes, a beach stone fireplace, a breakfast nook with an ocean view, a wet bar, and a patio by the old apple tree.

All the cottages have refrigerators and coffeemakers. Breakfast will be delivered in a basket, or you may go to the dining room if you prefer.

St. Orres stands above the highway, outside the village of Gualala, three hours north of San Francisco.

JENNER

Stillwater Cove Ranch

22555 Coast Highway 1
Jenner, CA 95450
707-847-3227

A ranch with inexpensive cottages and an ocean view

Proprietor: Linda Rudy. **Accommodations:** 6 rooms and bunkhouse (some with shared bath). **Rates:** $40–$70, 2–4 people ($10 more per unit on weekends and holidays); bunkhouse $115 for 8, $7.50 additional person. **Added:** Tax. **Minimum stay:** 2 nights on weekends. **Payment:** No credit cards. **Children:** Age 3 and over charged as an additional person. **Pets:** Allowed with permission in some rooms, additional $5. **Smoking:** Allowed.

On the scenic north coast sixteen miles north of Jenner, a 150-acre ranch once sprawled across the rolling hills that rise from surf-splashed rocks. Now most of that ranch is parkland

and belongs to the state, but fifty acres remain as a destination for coastal travelers. Furnishings are simple, but the views of headlands, the kelp-strewn cove, and the ocean are fantastic. And the rates make it an extraordinary value.

Stillwater Cove is near Fort Ross, the historic site of a 19th-century Russian outpost and Kruse Rhododendron State Reserve.

In 1931, Clarinel Ione and Paul Rudy founded a boys' school on the site. They had cows, pigs, horses, a barn and a dairy, and boarded fifty boys at a time until 1966, when the school closed. Now the property is owned by the sons and daughter of the Rudys.

There are a few animals on the ranch and dozens of peacocks that roam the grounds, preening, displaying their colors, and dropping gorgeous feathers.

Four rooms are in an L-shaped building on a knoll, under eucalyptus and pine trees. The identical East and West rooms, side by side, face the sea. Each has linoleum floors, two beds, a stone fireplace, a bath with a tub and shower, and a kitchenette. They share a long front porch.

Behind them is King Room, a large room with director's chairs, a small desk, and views of the trees and rocky outcroppings. Next to King is the Science Room, with a soft bed, a daybed, a Berber carpet, and a Swedish fireplace. In recognition of the room's original use, there's a microscope on the table.

Teacher's is a separate cottage with two beds, a fireplace, a bath with a tub and shower, and big windows. Cook's Cottage is for romantics who want a private hideaway removed from the rest of the lodgings. This cozy unit has two beds, a stone fireplace, white wicker chairs, and cottage-style windows. The small bath shows signs of wear but is clean. It has a tub only, and with it a rubber ducky.

The Dairy Barn, at the top of the hill, offers the most basic accommodations. The concrete block building is a large bunkhouse with two shower rooms and a kitchen. Extra cots are available; bring your own bedding. The well-equipped kitchen includes a gas range. A woodstove heats the big, open space; wood is supplied for one night's use. The Dairy Barn is a good choice for groups, as eight people can cook, sleep, and shower for less than $15 per person per night. It's popular among divers who come to the area for its excellent diving sites.

A low, native stone building was used as a dorm and dining room during the ranch's days as a boys' school. Now it's available for seminars, meetings, conferences and retreats.

LEWISTON

Trinity Alps Resort

1750 Trinity Alps Road
Trinity Center, CA 96052
916-286-2205
Fax: 916-286-2205

*A family favorite
in the wilderness*

Owners: Morgan and Margo Langan. **Accommodations:** 40 cabins and 3 apartments. **Rates:** $435–$785 week, 2–10 people; $75 week additional person; off-season and group rates available. **Added:** 8% tax. **Minimum stay:** 1 week in June, July and August; 3 nights in May and September. **Payment:** No credit cards; personal checks accepted. **Children:** Welcome. **Pets:** Allowed with prior arrangement. **Smoking:** Discouraged. **Open:** May 15 through September.

This family resort has changed very little since it was built in the 1920s. Its rustic cabins stand on 90 acres of forest, surrounded by 500,000 acres of magnificent Trinity Alps Wilderness, west of Clair Engle (Trinity) Lake in northern California. High mountain peaks rise above tree-clad slopes, while the wild Stuart Fork flows through the property carrying rainbow and native brown trout.

Trinity Alps Resort is off a steep, winding road north of Weaverville, a village with an eventful logging and railroad history. The Langan family bought the resort in 1987 and quickly learned that their guests wanted nothing changed or "improved." Many had been coming here for years and considered it their place, perfect in all its quaint and woodsy charm. So the cabin doors are creaky and the furniture is worn. One improvement the Langans were forced to make was to replace the original iceboxes in the units with modern refrigerators, as the iceboxes no longer worked properly. Many regular guests miss the iceboxes, but the Langans felt that the modernization was a necessity.

The large, rambling general store is the community gathering place, where you're bound to meet everyone if you sit on the porch a while. In the store you can buy groceries (except for fresh produce and meat), fishing supplies, and locally hand-crafted gifts. There's a soda fountain and, toward the back, a recreation room with a pool table and video games (another concession to the modern age).

> In the evenings there are talent shows, square dancing, movies, and bingo. Singalongs around the campfire, rafting, backpacking, and doing nothing but relaxing are favorite activities.

A daily schedule of activities is posted on a bulletin board, along with the dinner entrée (in September only). During the summer, guests choose from a full menu. In September, the main course might be barbecued beef ribs or steak marinated in Margo's special vinaigrette. Children's portions are available. Most visitors prepare their own meals, planning to eat once or twice in the restaurant above the river.

Simple cabins are tucked among the wild lilacs and maple and alder trees along a mile of the Stuart Fork. Each has a sleeping veranda, one or two bedrooms, a bath with a shower, an outdoor barbecue, and an equipped kitchen.

Entering one of these cabins is like stepping sixty years back in time. The screen door slams, and you're in a kitchen with uneven painted floors, a gas stove, a linoleum-covered table, and a wooden counter at the sink. In the bedroom are a double and two single metal beds. A few steps further is the veranda overlooking the trees and river. Strung around it is a clothesline, where those seeking privacy hang sheets. You sleep well on the veranda, for you're surrounded by the world's most peaceful sounds: leaves rustling in the breeze and a rushing, gurgling river below.

The larger one-bedroom cabins sleep six. Some two-bedroom units have two bathrooms and can accommodate ten people. Bring your own linens and blankets, or rent them from the office at $20 per bed. Towels are not available, so be sure to bring them. A crib may be supplied for $15 per week.

The range of activities includes fishing, swimming, tennis, badminton, volleyball, horseshoes, gold panning, innertubing, and basketball. The stable has dependable trail horses. Children under age eight may ride ponies on paths around the resort. Hiking trails along the river lead to limpid pools and waterfalls, and wilderness trailheads are just two miles away.

In the height of summer the resort often books up quickly, often by families who return year after year, so be sure to make your reservations well in advance if you plan to visit during June, July, or August. In May and September things are quieter, and special sports and fishing weekends are offered. Packages including all horseback riding are also available.

LITTLE RIVER

Glendeven

8221 North Highway 1
Little River, CA 95456
707-937-0083
800-822-4536
Fax: 707-937-6108

A stylish, artistic country inn

Innkeepers: Jan deVries. **Accommodations:** 10 rooms (all with private bath) plus Barn Suite. **Rates:** $100–$140 single, $110–$160 double, $20 additional person. Barn suite: $220. **Included:** Expanded Continental breakfast. **Added:** 10% tax. **Minimum stay:** 2 nights on weekends, 3 nights on some holidays. **Payment:** Major credit cards. **Children:** Welcome. **Pets:** Not allowed. **Smoking:** Not allowed indoors.

Little River is a quiet village that scarcely causes a ripple in the twisting coastal road south of Mendocino. But the scenery around it is spectacular: giant redwoods, open fields dotted with wildflowers, rocky beaches, and high cliffs above the Pacific. Jan deVries owns a sturdy clapboard farmhouse, built in 1867 by one of the area's first settlers. Jan's artistic background and skills are evident throughout the old home overlooking Van Damme Bay. With the restoration of the home, Jan created a gracious, comfortable inn on a slope of Monterey cypress and eucalyptus trees, with brick walks, camellias, and pampas grass in the front garden.

Guests are housed in three buildings: the Main Farmhouse, Stevenscroft, and Barn Suite. The Eastlin Suite, on the ground floor of the main house, has a sitting room, French rosewood bed, fireplace, and French doors that open to a brick terrace and a view of the bay. Other farmhouse rooms are smaller but equally charming, furnished with an eclectic assortment of antiques and decorated with color and verve. A perennial favorite is the Garret, an extravagantly floral attic room with dormer windows framing meadow and ocean views. In the bathroom, a floor-to-ceiling window overlooks the front yard's greenery.

> **The Kelley House Museum in nearby Mendocino has a walking tour map, and the Mendocino Art Center shows some of the area's talented artistry. There are several good restaurants.**

Stevenscroft contains four rooms, all with fireplaces. Bayloft, colored in soft, muted tones and accented with redwood, has a cozy bed alcove with skylight above and a wide view from a bay window. On the second floor, Briar Rose is light and airy, with high-vaulted ceilings, a French country decor, and a private balcony. Pinewood and East Farmington are warm, sunny rooms, both with private decks.

The original barn, extensively remodeled, has two bedrooms and one and a half baths. The suite tastefully combines hand-crafted country furniture and contemporary and antique pieces. A cast-iron fireplace warms the redwood-detailed walls and sunlight filters through shuttered windows. The suite's deck faces east toward the gardens and hills. Pink roses climb the barn trellis, and window boxes are bright with pink geraniums. Gallery Glendeven, on the barn's ground floor, displays contemporary arts and crafts and chairs made by Jan deVries.

Breakfast is served in the dining area of the main house or brought to your room in a basket. Fresh fruit, coffee, juice, homemade muffins, apples baked with brown sugar and currants are some of the savory morning treats. Sherry is decanted in the evenings next to the fireplace in the parlor, where the company is convivial.

Glendeven is a quarter-mile north of 1,800-acre Van

Damme State Park, which extends from deep forest to the coast. Two miles north of the inn is the pretty town of Mendocino, founded by New Englanders who brought their distinctive style of architecture to the California coast more than a century ago.

Notify the Glendeven innkeepers in advance, and they will have a tidbit platter of French bread, cheese, fruits, and chocolates waiting when you arrive, at a cost of $35.

Heritage House

5200 North Highway 1
Little River, CA 95456
707-937-5885
800-235-5885
Fax: 937-0318

A romantic inn on a seaside cliff

Proprietor: Gay Dennen Jones. **General manager:** Candace Prairie. **Accommodations:** 68 rooms. **Rates:** $170–$330 single, $190–$350 double, $65 additional person; 15% weekday discounts sometimes available. **Included:** Breakfast and dinner. **Added:** 10% room tax, 7.25% meal tax. **Payment:** MasterCard, Visa. **Children:** Charged as an additional person if over age 6. **Pets:** Not allowed. **Smoking:** Allowed in rooms and bar; not allowed in dining rooms or lounge. **Open:** Early February through Thanksgiving as well as Christmas Week.

This romantic inn on the Mendocino coast began with a farmhouse, built in 1877 in the Maine style popular in the area at the time — probably because so many settlers came from Maine. The yellow farmhouse is still there, covered with ivy.

Loren and Hazel Dennen bought the place in 1949, run-down and abandoned, and transformed it into a top-quality inn. Opening with three rooms in the farmhouse, they expanded over the years until today most of the lodgings are in cottages with two to eight rooms spread over thirty-eight acres. The Dennens' daughter, Gay, now runs the inn, and Dennen family photos still hang on the lobby walls in the farmhouse.

The cottages, tucked unobtrusively into the landscape on a cliff above the sea, were given names associated with early buildings in the area, such as Country Store, Bonnet Shop, Barber Pole, and Ice Cream Parlor. Two cottages have a more recent history. Same Time and Next Year were a single cottage in 1978 and were used in the film *Same Time Next Year.* The cabin was split in two after the movie, with each half taking half of the movie title.

> The main activity here is walking the paths and brick steps that wind between cottages and around the cliff, while admiring the moody Pacific.

Furnishings vary from contemporary pieces to four-posters and antiques bought from local families. Many pieces were hand-crafted in the community and many more came around the Horn and up the coast by schooner a hundred years ago. The Carousel Suites, built in 1990, are the closest to the ocean and offer terrific ocean views as well as double Jacuzzi tubs, wet bars, dining tables for four, and wood-burning fireplaces (some have two-sided fireplaces). Because the inn is meant to be an escape, there are no telephones or televisions in any of the rooms.

The farmhouse is now used as the reception area, restaurant, and lounge, with three guest rooms upstairs. Meals are served in the dining room under an oval dome painted with fruits and flowers. Cane chairs stand at tables set with pale linens, candles, and flowers, all reflected in a wall of mirrors. (Jackets and ties are encouraged for dinner.) Beyond the main room is a smaller dining area; next to that is a deck with a stunning view of the cypress trees, a rocky headland, and the ocean.

Breakfast is a major event. First is the buffet with fruit, cereal, and juice. Then you order one of five hot dishes, such as eggs Benedict, French toast, pancakes, eggs, and bacon or sausage. The restaurant is open to the public for all three meals, if it's not filled by guests. There's a choice of entrées every night: braised tiger prawns, seared breast of muscovy duck, and free-range chicken roulade are examples. The menu changes with the seasons, but nightly specials are offered, most notably prime rib on Saturdays.

The lounge in the farmhouse is an addition made from an apple storage house that was dismantled and moved. Apple House is a comfortable place to relax by the huge brick walk-in fireplace, to read, play cards, or if the musical urge strikes, play the square grand piano. With prism chandeliers and rough-hewn walls, the atmosphere in the lounge successfully combines rusticity with elegance. And the view is breathtaking. If you're looking for more active pursuits, the town of Mendocino just five miles up the coast, has bicycle and canoe rentals, as well as many shops, galleries, and restaurants.

Little River Inn

Little River, CA 95456
707-937-5942
Fax: 707-937-3944

An ocean view homestead expanded into a resort

Innkeepers: Dan Hervilla and Susan McKinney. **Accommodations:** 65 rooms and cottages. **Rates:** $85–$255 double, $10 additional person; winter rates available on weekdays, November–March. **Added:** 10% tax. **Minimum stay:** 2 nights on weekends. **Payment:** MasterCard, Visa. **Children:** Under age 12 free in room with parents. **Pets:** Not allowed. **Smoking:** Nonsmoking rooms available.

In the mid-19th century, pioneers came to Little River from Maine to log the region's redwood forests that built the rowhouses and mansions of San Francisco. One of those pioneers was Silas Coombs who, in 1853, built his family a home that also served as a haven for stagecoach and lumber schooner travelers. Two generations later, Cora Coombs and Ole Hervilla were married, and the homestead was turned into the Little River Inn. The parlors became lobbies and dining rooms, and the conservatory was converted into a bar. Later, cattle pastures and apple orchards were cleared for a golf course. The inn is still owned by the same family — Dan Hervilla and Susan McKinney are brother and sister.

The main house, white with gables and window boxes and an old-fashioned veranda, is situated on a slope above the busy (and often noisy) highway. Its rooms are furnished in early California style, with antiques and double beds.

The other rooms are in a newer two-story motel annex, duplex units higher on the hillside near the golf course, and cottages across the road on low bluffs above the sea. More than half the rooms have fireplaces. The rooms in the annex are furnished with oak tables and chairs and sliding glass doors that open to a long, shared balcony. From the cottages here you can see the cove and beach across the highway and watch the skin divers bob in the sparkling surf. For sweeping, unrestricted views, request Hilltop Annex, near the 9-hole golf course.

> **The most private and luxurious lodgings are the cottages, in their own wooded enclave by the sea. They all have private decks with lounge chairs and good views of the crashing waves. Each unit has a brick fireplace and tiled bath with tub and shower. Two have Jacuzzis.**

Breakfast, dinner, and Sunday brunch are served in the dining room in the main house. The breads, soups, and desserts are all made on the premises; the restaurant specializes in seafood and flavorful country dining using fresh local products.

Two lighted tennis courts and the golf course are open to the public as well as to guests, so the inn bustles with activity, especially in the summer. For group meetings and small weddings the inn also has conference facilities in Abalone Hall.

Sea Arch

Little River, CA
Mailing Address:
Mendocino Coast Reservations
P.O. Box 1143
1000 Main Street
Mendocino, CA 95460
707-937-5033
800-262-7801 in California
Fax: 707-937-4236

*A private home on
an oceanside cliff*

Contact: Mendocino Coast Reservations. **Accommodations:** 2-bedroom private home. **Rates:** $175–$200 single or double plus $60 cleaning fee, plus $100 security deposit. **Minimum stay:** 2 nights. **Payment:** MasterCard, Visa. **Children:** Over age 12 welcome. **Pets:** Not allowed. **Smoking:** Allowed.

The agency that handles this home on the coast has a list of sixty-odd accommodations; Sea Arch is one of the best. Built in the early 1960s, the two-story, gray-shingled home stands at the edge of a cliff high above the ocean, surveying a panorama of sea and sky.

Sea Arch's many windows are designed to take advantage of the view, both upstairs and down. There's a massive stone chimney on one side, for the living room fireplace. Wood fills a basket by the

Kelp gardens float on the waves near the cove at the foot of the rocky cliff, and sea lions bark from their rocky perches in the surf. The blue Pacific shimmers as far as the eye can see.

hearth, and more cut wood is stacked outside. Cushions are piled on a bench along a glass wall, where guests can play games, work puzzles, listen to the large collection of classical records, or just admire the mesmerizing vista.

The well-stocked kitchen has every utensil a cook needs, a couple of cookbooks, a phone, a small TV, and battery lanterns and candles for emergency use. Doors from the small dining area lead to a patio under the pine trees.

The house has a three-quarter bath on the main floor, and a full bath upstairs with the two bedrooms. One carpeted room contains a twin bed with trundle that can be pulled out to make a king-size bed. It has a desk and closet and an eastern view that looks into the trees rather than toward the ocean. The main bedroom is larger and has a telephone and shelves of books. Paneled and decorated in earth tones, it provides a comfortable hideaway.

Sea Arch is for those who want to do nothing but watch the ever-changing ocean. You can follow the antics of the squirrels as they scamper among the pine trees, stroll to the pond in back, or thumb through the owners' numerous books about the Mendocino area. You can fire up the barbecue and grill some fresh seafood for supper, or drive a few miles north to the shops, restaurants, and beaches of Mendocino. But most guests prefer to settle by the fire for a quiet, romantic evening, with soft music accompanying the thunder of the distant surf.

McCLOUD

McCloud Guest House

P.O. Box 1510
606 West Colombero Drive
McCloud, CA 96057
916-964-3160

A comfortable country inn in rural Northern California

Innkeepers: Biil and Patti Leigh. **Accommodations:** 5 rooms (all with private bath). **Rates:** $75–$90 single or double. **Included:** Continental breakfast. **Added:** Tax. **Payment:** MasterCard and Visa. **Children:** Not appropriate. **Pets:** Not allowed. **Smoking:** Allowed outdoors only.

This gracious country inn on the lower slopes of Mount Shasta was built in 1907 as the summer residence of J. H. Queal, president of the McCloud River Lumber Company and employer of most of the townspeople. Queal would leave his Minnesota home in the spring, traveling west in a private railroad car to McCloud, and return to the Midwest in October, for in those days the mill shut down in the fall.

> **A Continental breakfast of muffins, fresh fruit, juice, and coffee is set out on the sideboard in the upstairs parlor and may be taken to your room if you prefer to dine in privacy.**

After Queal's death in 1921, the lumber company kept the house for visiting executives and dignitaries. Herbert Hoover stayed here while he was running for president, and many celebrities attended gala parties. That era ended, and the house stood idle until 1984 when four people decided to turn it into an inn and restaurant. Bill and Patti Leigh and Dennis and Pat Abreu put considerable effort into restoring the place — from replacing the roof to removing layers of aged wallpaper.

Nearly six acres of lawn and cedar and oak trees surround the house and its wide, wraparound veranda. Mount Shasta, 14,126 feet high, looms above — a snow-capped giant amidst a rural landscape. Cherry-stained southern pine panels the interior, richly detailed with coffered ceilings, beveled glass, and built-in cabinets. A massive, two-sided stone fireplace divides the lobby from the dining room, which has earned a reputation as one of the best restaurants in Siskiyou County.

The restaurant, serving dinner only, takes up the entire ground level of the inn with a number of intimate floral wallpapered dining rooms, and tables set with peach and green linens. Bill, who has been cooking for more than thirty years, prepares a variety of Continental dishes with an Italian slant. His specialty is chicken Piedmontese — chicken baked in a white wine, mushroom, and cheese sauce. Wines, stored in glass cabinets, are reasonably priced.

Overnight lodgings are upstairs off of a central parlor. The wall fixtures in the parlor are replicas of those in Queal's railroad car. A gray patterned velvet couch stands by a coffee table full of magazines, and a desk is available for writing. The focus of the room is the antique, hand-carved pool table with inlaid wood that is said to have come from the Hearst estate.

The large bedrooms off the parlor are well kept, and have air conditioning, antique furniture or reproductions, and private baths. Room 1 has an elegant lace bedspread, two wicker chairs, and a window seat overlooking the front lawn. In the bath a clawfoot tub sits atop hardwood floors. Room 5 is the smallest with a four-poster spool bed placed at an angle, and a shower only in the bath. In pale pastels, Room 2 is especially light and pleasant. It has a brass bed, eyelet trimmed pillows, a white wicker chair, and a spacious closet. There's a white and yellow clawfoot tub in the bright bathroom.

The inn is in a beautiful part of California. The area lacks crowds, noise, and heavy traffic. Although Siskiyou is the second largest county in the state, it has the lowest population. The Shasta-Cascade wilderness is replete with tall green forests, sparkling lakes and stream, and dancing waterfalls. Here, easily accessible from the inn, are downhill and Nordic skiing, trout fishing, bicycling, golfing, hiking, and swimming.

MENDOCINO

The Headlands Inn

P.O. Box 132
Corner of Howard and Albion
Mendocino, CA 95460
707-937-4431
800-354-4431

A historic home with views of a coastal town

Innkeepers: Sharon and David Hyman. **Accommodations:** 6 rooms and 1 cottage (all with private bath). **Rates:** $95–$189 single or double. **Included:** Full breakfast. **Added:** 10% tax. **Minimum stay:** 2 nights on weekends, 3–4 nights on holidays. **Payment:** No credit cards; personal checks accepted. **Children:** Over age 12 welcome. **Pets:** Not allowed. **Smoking:** Not allowed.

This attractive Victorian home was built in 1868 as a small barbershop on Main Street; a second story was added in 1873 to serve as living quarters for the barber and his family. Later it became a restaurant. In 1893 it was moved to its present location, on the corner of Howard and Albion streets, by horses pulling the house over logs used as rollers. From then on it was used as a private home. The Headlands has been a popular bed-and-breakfast inn for several years. The Hymans, who have owned it since late 1992, made few changes when they took over.

> Guests are welcome to relax by the fireplace in the little parlor or enjoy afternoon tea and cookies in the sitting area on the upstairs landing.

The guest rooms, named for former owners of the historic home, have fireplaces and antique furnishings. Nice touches include chocolate mints, featherbeds, and down comforters. Bessie Strauss, on the second floor, is a spacious room with a Victorian settee, pots of greenery, an oversize armoire and, the most outstanding feature, an ocean view from the bay window. The bed in W. J. Wilson is a four-poster. There's a private deck with an ocean view, pleasant for an alfresco breakfast.

George Switzer, on the third floor, is a many-angled hideaway with window seats at alcove windows. A green velvet chair stands by the fireplace where a fire is laid and extra wood is at the ready in a brass holder. John Barry, also on the third floor, is named for the home's original owner. It has a cushioned seat in a dormer window, and a view across the nasturtium beds and lawn to open fields, part of the town, and the sea. Yet another room is in a separate building, Casper Cottage, just right if you want complete privacy. It has a cannonball four-poster, a sitting area with a small refrigerator, and a large bath complete with bubbles and tub toys.

Breakfast is brought to your room on a tray, along with a San Francisco Chronicle. The artistically arranged meal may include baked pears in ginger sauce, Mexican artichoke soufflé, muffins, and a pitcher of hot coffee, tea, or cocoa.

The Hymans keep an array of menus, brochures, and maps on hand, and they're glad to help you with sightseeing plans. You'll want to browse in the shops and art galleries, many in historic buildings, and try Mendocino's excellent restaurants, such as Café Beaujolais and the Moose Cafe.

Hill House of Mendocino

P.O. Box 625
10701 Palette Drive
Mendocino, CA 95460
707-937-0554
800-422-0554 in northern
California
Fax: 707-937-1123

*A New England-
style inn
overlooking the
Pacific*

Proprietor: Robert Short. **Accommodations:** 44 rooms. **Rates:** $110–$175 single or double, $10 additional person. **Included:** Continental breakfast. **Added:** 10% tax. **Minimum stay:** 2 nights on weekends. **Payment:** Major credit cards. **Children:** Welcome. **Pets:** Not allowed. **Smoking:** Allowed.

If you watch *Murder, She Wrote*, this hotel may look familiar. The popular television program, which supposedly takes place in New England, has been filmed here, with Hill House as the backdrop. It fits well with Mendocino, a north coast town built mostly by settlers from Maine.

The theme is comfortable and casual in Spencer's Lounge, which has a large-screen TV and a sunken fireplace area — just the spot to relax with a warm brandy on a brisk fall evening.

The gray-green inn trimmed in white stands on a hill behind a white picket fence among neat gardens. With a jaunty whale weathervane on the pitched roof, it has the look of a classic hotel on the New England coast. In fact, the main house was built in 1978 with that architecture in mind. It has been expanded since to include a two-story wing with guest rooms off two courtyards.

In the main house there are two sitting areas, a lounge, a restaurant, and a chapel for meetings and weddings. In the spacious front parlor and lobby, chess is set up for the next group of players. With antiques, lace curtains, and a quiet atmosphere, the mood is of another time and another place. On the walls are photographs of the actors and crew of *Murder, She Wrote*, along with pictures of Mendocino in an earlier day.

Upstairs, diners enjoy sweeping coastal views while lingering over Continental cuisine. The atmosphere is romantic, with deep rose walls, crystal, and candlelight. Fresh fish, steak, chicken, and pasta dominate the menu. A number of wines have Mendocino County labels.

About half the guest rooms overlook the ocean. They all have television, direct dial phones, and baths with tubs and showers and assorted toiletries. A typical room with a view features brass beds with comforters, lace curtains, burgundy or deep green carpeting, and antique reproductions. An armoire holds hanging clothes. Through the windows you see the dark green of cypress trees on grassy bluffs and the Pacific beyond them. The second-story rooms have the best views. The fireplace suites are the most expensive and spacious with sitting areas in front of the hearth.

Hranrad House

Mendocino, CA
Mailing address:
Mendocino Coast Reservations
P.O. Box 1143
1000 Main Street
Mendocino, CA 95460
707-937-5033
800-262-7801 in California

A private guest house in a dramatic, secluded setting

Contact: Mendocino Coast Reservations. **Accommodations:** 2-bedroom private home. **Rates:** $225 for up to four people, $60 cleaning fee and $100 security deposit. **Added:** 10% tax. **Minimum stay:** 2 nights. **Payment:** MasterCard, Visa. **Children:** Over age 12 welcome. **Pets:** Not allowed. **Smoking:** Not allowed.

North of Mendocino, in a private community, Hranrad House is reached by a narrow, winding access road. There is another, almost identical house on the two-and-a-half-acre property, but the out-of-town owners do not use it when the guest house is occupied.

An immense, beveled copper roof covers Hranrad House,

which was built in 1980. Inside, the floors and a twelve-foot front door are of polished redwood. In one big room, with spaces divided by the central fireplace, are a living area with a wall of windows, a screened four-poster metal bed, and a kitchen with a walnut counter, Jenn-Air range, micro-wave, refrigerator, freezer, and all the tools a cook might need. There's a stereo with CDs, a TV in the kitchen, and shelves of books. Local phone calls are free. On the desk is a booklet of information on the house and nearby restaurants and attractions.

> Seclusion and privacy in a stunning, contemporary home overlooking the Pacific are what you find at Hranrad House (the Anglo-Saxon name means Whales' Road House).

In the glass-walled bathroom you may feel that you're showering in a goldfish bowl, but your privacy is assured, protected by cypress trees, streams, stretches of grass, and rocky headlands above the water. There are no near neighbors.

French doors open to a deck on the west. Beyond it are the rugged headlands, with chasms and caves to explore, and a panorama of sea and sky.

Joshua Grindle Inn

P.O. Box 647
44800 Little Lake Road
Mendocino, CA 95460
707-937-4143
800-GRINDLE

> *A 19th-century home with New England charm*

Innkeepers: Arlene and Jim Moorehead. **Accommodations:** 10 rooms (all with private bath). **Rates:** $90–$155 single or double. **Included:** Full breakfast. **Added:** 10% tax. **Minimum stay:** 2 nights on weekends. **Payment:** Major credit cards. **Children:** Not appropriate. **Pets:** Not allowed. **Smoking:** Not allowed.

This quiet New England–style home sits on a knoll overlooking Mendocino. The two-story white farmhouse was built in 1879 by an early settler who came from Maine to make his fortune in redwood lumber. Joshua Grindle prospered, becoming the town banker and primary owner of the Bank of Commerce, forerunner of the Bank of America. The home he built remained in the Grindle family until 1967.

In 1978, the house opened as the first small bed-and-breakfast in Mendocino. The inn and its two-acre property were purchased in 1989 by the Mooreheads, who came from San Francisco seeking a change. They have kept the furnishings and style established by the previous owners virtually intact.

> **You are welcome to play the antique pump organ, enjoy a game of backgammon or chess, relax in an Adirondack chair on the inn's two acres, read by the fire, or chat with the innkeepers about the exceptional attractions of the Mendocino area.**

There are five guest rooms in the main house, some with an ocean view and others with a wood-burning fireplace. Early American antiques in cherrywood and pine fill the rooms. The Grindle is the room Joshua built for himself, above the kitchen for warmth. It's a big, hearty room with a sitting area overlooking the town's distinctive water towers and the bay.

The Library, which was once a dining room, has a four-poster bed, country pine furniture, an old-fashioned typewriter on the floor-to-ceiling bookcase, and a fireplace with hand-painted tiles. Treeview is the inn's least expensive room. It's a light, airy space with such old-fashioned touches as a cut-paper lampshade and a sled now used to hold magazines. From the window you can see hundred-year-old cypress trees.

Behind the main house stands the redwood Water Tower, of recent vintage but architecturally designed to blend with the old water towers of Mendocino. It has three guest rooms on two floors furnished in antique country pine. An interesting detail is the lack of art on the walls of the second-story room; pictures will not hang flat, since the walls slant inward as the tower rises.

Two rooms are in the weathered saltbox cottage. North Cypress contains Early American antiques and a Franklin fireplace; South Cypress has Shaker furniture and a country flavor. The Salem rocker and wing club chair are inviting places to read by the fire as the coastal fog creeps in. There's no sea view from the cottage, but it has a pretty little garden.

Breakfast is taken in the main house at a long, narrow harvest table, which dates from the 1830s. The Mooreheads serve fresh fruit, a choice of cereals, homemade muffins, and a hot dish such as mushroom crust quiche. In the evening they place California cream sherry and fruit on the huntboard in the parlor.

MacCallum House

P.O. Box 206
45020 Albion Street
Mendocino, CA 95460
707-937-0289

A historic Victorian home in a picturesque town

Proprietors: Joe and Melanie Reding. **Accommodations:** 22 rooms (some with private bath). **Rates:** $75–$210 single or double, $15 additional person; suite for 3–4 people $260, midweek winter discounts available. **Included:** Continental breakfast. **Added:** 10% tax. **Minimum stay:** 2 nights on weekends, May through December; 3 nights over holidays. **Payment:** MasterCard, Visa; personal check preferred. **Children:** Under age 10 free in room with parents. **Pets:** Not allowed. **Smoking:** Not allowed.

When Daisy MacCallum was married in 1882, her parents, William and Eliza Kelley, gave her a house across the street from their own home as a wedding present. The Kelley house, a museum of Mendocino and coastal history and Daisy's home, where she lived until her death in 1953, is a busy and popular inn.

The Redings have put considerable effort into preserving the atmosphere Daisy created in her gracious Victorian home. Active socially and in civic affairs, Daisy entertained often, seeking to promote refinement in this lumber frontier town. She would have approved of the restored garden and the furnishings that were resurrected from the attic. She might have been less approving of the bar — she was a staunch temperance advocate — but today's visitors appreciate the friendly, casual Grey Whale Bar.

> **MacCallum House is noted for its restaurant, which serves Continental cuisine based on fresh regional ingredients. Books line the walls of the restaurant.**

There's a wide range of accommodations. Those in the main house, which share baths, have sleigh or iron and brass beds, floral comforters, country antiques, and windows that get morning sun or have an ocean view. Most of the rooms have sinks, but some mattresses are on the soft side, so request a firm one if you need it. The attic rooms, off a hall papered with the *San Francisco Chronicle* from the 1920s, look over the gardens or Mendocino's rooftops. You must go down a short flight of stairs to the bathroom.

The other rooms are in the former barn and cottages. Two rooms on the barn's ground floor share a bath; the suites have their own. One suite with a private entrance has hefty beams from the original barn and redwood slabs for the kitchen and bath counters. There's no view — in fact, the bed is set against a window facing the street — and the room is somewhat dark, but it's roomy and comfortable. From the bed you can watch the fire in the stone fireplace. In the kitchen are a small refrigerator, stove, and beaten copper sink. The bath has a Roman tub, a tiled shower, and a small and impractical copper basin.

Other barn accommodations are equally individual. An upstairs suite features a stone fireplace, a burl coffee table, and a similar rough-beamed style but with country antiques and a lighter atmosphere. In the bath are a shower with a skylight and the same pretty but small copper sink.

The units in the Carriage House are furnished with wicker and vintage pieces and have Franklin stoves and private baths. The Greenhouse has two platform beds, a rustic Franklin fireplace, and a private patio. The three-story Water Tower offers the best ocean view. The Gazebo, once a child's playhouse, has a double bed with a wicker headboard. There are two tiny windows, each barely a foot square. The outside bathhouse, a few steps away, has a stained glass window in the shower.

MacCallum House is not a hideaway. Crowds come and go, and tourists are forever wandering through the gardens and taking pictures of the picturesque home and its weathered picket fence. Also, the inn is done in a curious mixture of new and old that works well only part of the time. Yet, steeped in Mendocino history and reflecting the personality of the strong woman who lived here for most of her adult life, it has a special ambience that draws guests back again and again.

Mendocino Hotel

45080 Main Street
P.O. Box 587
Mendocino, CA 95460
707-937-0511
800-548-0513

A historic hotel on Mendocino's waterfront

General manager: Peter Ehrenberg.
Accommodations: 51 rooms. **Rates:** $50–$225 single or double; $20 each additional person. **Added:** 10% Tax. **Payment:** Major credit cards. **Children:** Welcome in garden cottages. **Pets:** Not allowed. **Smoking:** Allowed in three rooms only.

In the late 1800s, Mendocino was a busy logging town with some 20,000 residents and a rather active nightlife. In contrast to some of the more colorful establishments, the Mendocino Hotel opened in 1878 as the Temperance House offering those with "good Christian morals" a respite from the town's seamy saloons and pool halls. Today, Mendocino, with only about 1,000 residents, is frequented primarily by artists and tourists, and the Mendocino Hotel has been restored to reflect its Victorian origins.

The hotel's unassuming clapboard exterior does not adequately prepare you for the comfortable elegance that awaits within. The lobby is lovely with Oriental rugs, Victorian antiques, and lots of sofas and comfy chairs that are perfect for quiet conversation or curling up with a novel. A fire blazes in the fireplace, and some seating groups look out to the ocean across the street. An oval stained glass ceiling sets the tone in the bar where a piano player entertains in the evenings and light meals are served.

> **The hotel reputably has a resident ghost. The apparition of a Victorian woman is said to haunt the hotel dining room, and a number of staff members claim to have encountered the spirit.**

Separated from the lobby by 19th-century stained glass panels from British train stations (Cheltenham, Brighton, Southampton, etc.), the Victorian dining room offers gourmet meals such as fresh seafood poached in a savory fume with a white chocolate beurre blanc and Muscovy duck accompanied by French lentils and barley; tempting appetizers such as grape leaves filed with homemade lamb sausage and feta cheese dressed with a balsamic vinaigrette and roasted tomatoes stuffed with Gorgonzola served with baked garlic and Italian puff bread; and an extensive wine list that emphasizes local vintages. With meals by candlelight the mood is intimate in the dining room, while nearby green tile floors, floral seat cushions, fresh flowers, and a trellis lend a garden atmosphere to the aptly named Garden Room Bar and Café.

There are twenty-six rooms in the hotel's main building. They vary in size and decor, but all have period furnishings and crisp linens. Some of the interior rooms are quite small, and must share hall baths; but each has an in-room washbasin, and bathrobes are provided for those rooms without private baths. Suites contain old photographs and memorabilia from some of Mendocino's founding families. Suite 225A on the second floor is especially desirable because of the view from its balcony. There's a queen-size bed and fainting sofa in the bedroom, and an easy chair with an ottoman and a powder blue velvet Victorian loveseat in the sunny living room. Rooms in the historic section of the hotel do not have televisions, but all rooms have telephones.

The remaining twenty-five rooms are situated in garden cottages behind the hotel. Although they tend to be larger than some of the rooms in the main building, the cottages are still decorated with antiques, and some have modern luxury features such as Jacuzzi tubs. The gardens that surround the cottages include plants that date to the 1800s and a latticed gazebo.

Reed Manor

P.O. Box 127
Mendocino, CA 95460
707-937-5446
Fax: 707-937-5407

A luxurious mansion on a hilltop

Innkeepers: Monte and Barbara Reed. **Accommodations:** 5 suites. **Rates:** $175–$350 per room, 1–4 people. **Included:** Continental breakfast. **Added:** 10% tax. Minimum stay: 2 nights on weekends. **Payment:** MasterCard, Visa. **Children:** Not appropriate. **Pets:** Not allowed. **Smoking:** Not allowed.

Reed Manor, which opened in 1990, sits on the highest hill in Mendocino. Here the former owners of Hill House, a hotel across the road, have created a haven of luxury and intimacy. Behind a brick entrance and courtyard is an imposing house with slate floors, sofas covered with tapestry fabrics, crystal chandeliers, and lighted display cases showing the owners' numerous collections. There are celebrity dolls, wildlife sculptures and plates, paintings, and a remarkable array of model cars. There's even a stained glass window showing a 1955 Chevrolet convertible. The suites are spacious and tastefully furnished — never fussy or overly ornate. Each has a fireplace, TV with VCR, a refrigerator (where a light breakfast is stored), a phone with an answering machine, a coffee maker, and a private deck or patio. Baths have whirlpool tubs, hair dryers, makeup mirrors, and English herbal toiletries. Two rooms have wet bars.

> **Next to the inn is a windswept hillside cemetery ("We have quiet neighbors," Barbara jokes) that is an interesting place to stroll; its headstones date from 1852.**

You will truly feel like the lord of the manor in the luxurious Napoleon Room. Here the Reeds' Napoleon collection is on display, including books, plates, wine glasses, and a chess set. Decorated in soft colors, the room has light wood furnishings including a king-size four-poster bed and a writing desk. When you are not gazing at the stars through the telescope, or the grand view of Mendocino and the ocean beyond from your porch, you can soak in the deep whirlpool tub in front of the double-sided fireplace, which can be enjoyed from both the bedroom and the sumptuous bath.

The Morning Glory room, in ivory, seafoam, and pale pink florals, is on the main floor. It's slate patio also offers views of the village and the sea, and from the room's open-sided tub, you can see the TV and fireplace. Josephine's Garden Room, in country French style, has no view; it faces the gardens and has its own sunny, fenced deck. Imperial Garden is decorated with an Oriental motif. This suite has poppies touched with gilt in the wallpaper; it also has a bamboo mat ceiling, and Chinese and Japanese plates and figures. The Majestic Rose is a large two-room suite with a queen-size Murphy bed in the living room.

Nut bread, fruit, juice, and coffee are provided in the rooms. The Reeds have several classic movies, such as *Gone with the Wind*, to lend, along with the episodes of *Murder, She Wrote* that were filmed in Mendocino. They keep an album of restaurant menus and will make recommendations and reservations.

Sea Haus

P.O. Box 1143
Mendocino Coast Reservations
Mendocino, CA 95460
707-937-5033
800-262-7801 in California
Fax: 707-937-4236

A cozy family home in a residential area

Contact: Mendocino Coast Reservations. **Accommodations:** 3 bedrooms (1 bath). **Rates:** $135 for 2, $150 for up to 6 people, plus $60 cleaning fee and $100 security deposit. **Added:** 10% tax. **Minimum stay:** 2 nights. **Payment:** MasterCard, Visa. **Children:** Welcome. **Pets:** Not allowed. **Smoking:** Not allowed.

This comfortable two-story family home is on a quiet residential street in the heart of Mendocino. It's within walking distance of the town's myriad shops and Mendocino Headlands State Park. Roomy and private, it's an excellent choice for a family visiting the north coast, as it offers conveniences such as a washer and dryer and an ironing board. The dining area has seating for four at a round oak table.

Youngsters enjoy riding the Skunk Railroad, which runs for 40 miles through scenic redwood country, and clambering among the tidepools of MacKerricher State Park in Fort Bragg.

The immaculate kitchen is stocked with dishes, pans and utensils as well as a few spices and a cookbook from the renowned Mendocino restaurant, Café Beaujolais. From the window you catch glimpses of the bay beyond the trees.

A woodstove stands on a brick hearth in the carpeted living room; firewood is stacked neatly beside it. Shelves filled with books and a soft brown leather couch are invitations to relax and read by the fire.

Down the hall are a laundry room, a bath with a shower, and the master bedroom. Scenes of Mendocino hang on the walls of this pastel room, which is furnished with a queen-size bed, a couch, a phone, and a clock radio. An outside door opens to a deck and a fenced backyard where rosemary and fuchsia grow.

The other bedrooms are up steep stairs on the second floor. They're separated by an open arch. One contains a four-poster double bed and the other two twins, all with white chenille spreads. From the south room's long window there's a view of the sea (cobwebbed by a maze of telephone wires). The north room views rocky headlands, cliffs, and the blue water in the distance. This pleasant little room has a rocker and a small writing table.

Throughout the house you'll see such personal touches as family photos and exquisite needlepoint. The owners clearly take pride in their seaside haven and expect you to make yourself at home and take care of the place as they would.

Weekly and monthly rates are available. The cleaning fee is nonrefundable (and not taxed), but if the house is left in order, the security deposit will be returned to you.

Points of interest when you're bringing children to the Mendocino area include the beach and clifftop trails; Jughandle State Reserve, where five terraces, created by erosion and ocean waves, show 500,000 years of geological change; and Pygmy Forest, with its dwarfed pines and cypress trees.

The Stanford Inn by the Sea

P.O. Box 487
Coast Highway 1 and Comptche-
Ukiah Road
Mendocino, CA 95460
707-937-5025
Fax: 707-937-0305

*A country inn
with ocean views*

Innkeepers: Joan and Jeff Stanford. **Accommodations:** 24 rooms and suites and 1 cottage. **Rates:** $175–$210 single or double, suites $200–$275, $20 additional person. **Included:** Expanded Continental breakfast and afternoon refreshments. **Added:** 10% tax. **Minimum stay:** 2 nights on weekends, 3 nights on holiday weekends. **Payment:** Major credit cards. **Children:** Additional $15–$20 depending upon age. **Pets:** Allowed with permission; additional $15 per stay. **Smoking:** Not allowed indoors.

Where Big River meets Mendocino Bay, Stanford Inn faces the sea from a green hillside. Once this area grew produce for villagers and loggers during the redwood lumber boom. Today, llamas and horses graze under the old apple trees. The stagecoach road is now a hiking trail, and canoeists paddle the river where logs once floated to the mill.

Joan and Jeff Stanford took over a standard two-story motel and turned it into an outstanding hostelry in 1981. They now offer charming accommodations and a wide range of services. The long, dark shingle ranch house, set above pastures and ponds, has rooms off a loggia with ivy-covered columns. In the lobby are menus from area restaurants and a gift shop corner. A generous buffet breakfast, served in the adjoining parlor, includes champagne as well as fruit, yogurt, granola, muffins, and coffee. The guest rooms are individually decorated and furnished with country antiques, fresh plants, a decanter of wine, a coffeemaker with a supply of the inn's private blend of coffee, and cable television with a VCR (the inn has some 200 movies to rent). Most have a refrigerator and fireplace.

> Big River flows gently through a narrow canyon, winding between redwoods and firs, passing the habitat of osprey and the great blue heron.

The second-floor rooms are the best because of their balcony views. They overlook gardens, a pond with swans and geese, and the bay, ocean, and a corner of Mendocino. To the south, the view is of a sheltered, wooded headland that juts into the sea. There are two suites in a cottage by the river; one sleeps five people and the other two.

Don't miss a tour of the inn's bountiful organic gardens. The raised beds supply produce to area restaurants. The Stanfords also have mountain bikes that the guests can use free of charge, as well as canoes to rent, which provide an opportunity to explore the estuary filled with wildlife. Big River is tidal for eight miles, so you can float up on the incoming tide and back as it recedes.

Other activities include swimming in the indoor pool, hiking, fishing, beachcombing, and whale-watching. The best sites for spotting whales are the coastal headlands, Mendocino village headland, or the beach at Fort Bragg, six miles north.

MOUNT SHASTA

Ward's Big Foot Ranch

P.O. Box 585
1530 Hill Road
Mt. Shasta, CA 96067
916-926-5170
800-926-1272

A country bed-and-breakfast with a view of Mt. Shasta

Innkeepers: Barbara and Phil Ward. **Accommodations:** 3 rooms (with private baths). **Rates:** $55–$90. **Included:** Full breakfast. **Added:** 8% tax. **Payment:** No credit cards. **Children:** Welcome. **Pets:** Not allowed. **Smoking:** Not allowed indoors.

You may not see Big Foot, the elusive and possibly fictional hairy giant of the woods, but you'll never miss him; there's too much to keep you occupied here in the Mount Shasta foothills. Near the Wards' ranch there are two lakes for swimming, boating, and fishing, four golf courses, downhill and cross-country ski areas, and dozens of wilderness hiking trails.

A mile away, on Old Stage Road, there's a hatchery that produces 13.5 million trout yearly. When it was built a century ago, this was the largest hatchery in the world. Next door, a museum displays pioneer artifacts and a Model T Ford fire engine. If you just want to unwind on the deck and enjoy the quiet and the stunning view of majestic Mount Shasta, Ward's is the perfect place for it. Phil and Barbara, both former educators, bought the ten-acre property in 1980 and opened their bed-and-breakfast three years later. Avid gardeners, they have created a little paradise on a hill above a trout stream, with flower baskets hanging from oak trees, broad lawns, and vegetables and blooms in profusion.

When you arrive, you're welcomed not only by the Wards and their two friendly golden retrievers Baron and Buffer. Jasper the donkey and Bobbin the lovable llama will press their noses against the fence, hoping for a pat and a treat.

> **The Ward's have enjoyed their second career so much that Phil has recorded some of their more humorous experiences as innkeepers in his book *Life With Bigfoot*.**

The single-story red house with white trim, built in the early 1960s, is roomy and comfortable, with a living room containing a grand piano where guests can converse, and an adjacent family room for watching TV or listening to music. On sunny days, breakfast and afternoon refreshments are served on the big redwood deck, where barrels of pansies and petunias lend bright spots of color, and a tall cedar tree provides shade. From here you have glimpses of strutting ostriches (there's an ostrich farm on the adjoining property) and the cherry, apple, and peach orchard near the driveway.

One guest room has a king-size bed with a flowered comforter, a big closet, and a view of the deck and lacy cedar branches. A cabinet full of toys and shelves of books are reminders of the family atmosphere the Wards share. The other room, with a bath across the hall, features a queen-size bed with a handmade quilted coverlet and a soothing pastoral view.

When Phil rings the triangle in the morning, it's time for a "bodacious Big Foot breakfast" that includes ebleskivers (delicious Danish puff pancakes stuffed with chopped apple), Dutch babies or sourdough pancakes. Horseshoes, volleyball, table tennis, and croquet are among the ranch's activities, and because the indefatigable Barbara and Phil love kids, they've hung rope swings in the trees. If relaxation is what you're after, cross Wagon Creek to "Big Foot's Lair" where a hammock has been strung for afternoon naps.

NICE

Featherbed Railroad Company, A Bed & Breakfast Resort

P.O. Box 4016
2870 Lake Shore Boulevard
Nice, CA 95464
707-274-4434
800-966-6322
Fax: 707-274-4433

*A lakeside resort
of railroad cars*

Innkeepers: Lorraine and Len Bassignani. **Accommodations:** 9 cabooses. **Rates:** $90–$140. **Included:** Full breakfast. **Added:** 9% tax. **Payment:** Major credit cards. **Children:** Not appropriate. **Pets:** Not allowed. **Smoking:** Allowed outdoors only.

Railroad buffs and aficionados of the unusual are bound to fall in love with this assemblage of vintage cabooses. They are permanently stationed on five tree-shaded acres in Nice, close to the north shore of Clear Lake. The lakefront property is enhanced by turn-of-the-century street lamps, park benches, and an authentic Old English telephone booth.

The stationary railroad cars are a few yards from Clear Lake, which is popular with watersports enthusiasts. The Bassignanis rent boats and jet skis. The fishing is good; Clear Lake is noted for its big-mouth bass and crappie.

Effervescent Lorraine and affable Len Bassignani have impeccably restored the cabooses, a labor of love. Before opening in 1989, the couple and their partner-son removed thick layers of grime, soot and rust that had accumulated on the twenty-five- to fifty-year-old cars.

Why cabooses? "We were looking for something different to put our hearts into," explains Lorraine, "and both Len and I have always loved trains. It took several years to locate the cabooses to carry out our dream. This is a family endeavor."

Conductors never had it so good. The interior of each caboose has been decorated around a theme. The romantic Lovers Caboose has a hand-hewn four-poster featherbed draped with a lace canopy, and a whirlpool tub for two. The Rosebud, painted in Ashes of Roses, is abloom with roses on the floral bedspread, matching balloon valance curtains and hand-painted flowers (all done by Lorraine) on the walls. It has a Jacuzzi for two.

Mint Julep, as refreshing as its name, has mint-green walls and white wicker furniture. A cushioned cupola provides a retreat for sipping a cool drink, reading or conversing. Casey Jones, the only car with a railroad theme, features a red, cream, and navy blue decor, with a gleaming brass bed, authentic switchman's lanterns, and vintage railroad prints. Unlike the other cars, this caboose was left largely intact, which you can see in the original brass fittings, exposed pipes, and two padded conductor's chairs in the cupola. Other cars include Wine Country, Mardi Gras, Chocolate Moose, and the Loose Caboose.

Each caboose has a coffee pot, a television, books and games, fresh flowers and potpourri. Special touches include sewing kits, candies on the pillows, and newspapers delivered to the door. Breakfast is served in the Bassignanis' 100-year-old ranch house. You may choose to eat on the flagstone veranda or by the swimming pool. Breakfast includes juices, fresh fruit, assorted breads and quiches, and coffee and tea.

Lake County is an emerging wine-producing region, and tours of nearby wineries are available. Other attractions include Clear Lake State Park and Anderson Marsh State Park, a Native American archeological site and excellent bird-watching area. The Harbor Bar & Grill in Nice is recommended for its good food and interesting decor.

O'BRIEN

Holiday Harbor

P.O. Box 112
O'Brien, CA 96070
916-238-2383
800-776-2628
Fax: 916-238-2102

*A cruising
houseboat on
Lake Shasta*

Owners: Stephen and Ann Barry.
Accommodations: 70 houseboats. **Rates:** $1,120–$3,195 per
week in summer, 6–12 people; off-season rates available.
Minimum stay: 3 nights in summer, 2 nights in winter. **Payment:** MasterCard, Visa. **Children:** Welcome. **Pets:** Allowed
with permission. **Smoking:** Allowed.

Three rivers and a major creek are the main water sources of
Shasta Lake, at the northern end of the Sacramento Valley.
The Sacramento flows in from the northwest, the McCloud
from the northeast, and Squaw Creek and Pit River join on
the east side. A huge dam, with the highest center overflow
spillway in the world, forms the sprawling blue lake. It has
370 miles of shoreline, bounded by steep wooded hills. Majestic Mount Shasta, snowcapped in all but the driest of
weather, looms on the north. You'll find virtually every type
of fresh water recreation on this immense body of water. A
big favorite, especially with families and groups, is houseboating.

Holiday Harbor, tucked against Bailey Cove on the McCloud, is an easily accessible resort, fifteen minutes from
Redding and a mile off I-5. The Barrys take pride in keeping
their houseboats in peak condition. Theirs is one of the few
companies offering smaller sized houseboats suitable for six
or eight people. They also have 56-foot boats that can sleep
twelve.

The boats each have one or two sleeping areas, one or two
bathrooms with a tub or shower, an equipped kitchen, and an
eating space. All have roof decks. Furnishings are simple —
molded plastic chairs, some bunk beds, and benches that pull
out to become double beds. Pillows, soap, dishes, and pots
and pans are supplied. You bring your own groceries and blankets, linens, or sleeping bags.

"This is glorified camping," cautions Steve Barry, "and most people love it. They come in uptight and stressed out, and by the time they leave they're so relaxed they're practically comatose." The Barrys have owned Holiday Harbor since 1980, when they left a business life in San Francisco. "Now I'm hooked on this," Steve says.

Some houseboaters like simply to cruise on the lake and inlets, enjoying the slow pace and taking a dip now and then. Others fish, swim, visit Lake Shasta Caverns, and hike the numerous trails. Steve recommends the walk to an old iron mine on Bully Hill. For more fun on the water, you can rent anything that floats from Holiday Harbor's "Toy Box": canoes, kayaks, jet skis, sailboards, paddleboats, rowing sculls, ski boats (with water skis), sailboats, and more.

> **Running a houseboat is easy. If you can drive a car, you can handle one of these floating RVs. Moving slowly on pontoons, they never exceed a speed of six or seven knots. At night they tie up along the shore, usually in a protected cove.**

Bring your fishing rod, or go to one of the many sporting goods stores around the lake, and you can fish for rainbow and brown trout, salmon, small mouth bass, largemouth bass, crappie, and catfish. To catch the big trophies, fish the lake in cooler months. It gets hot here in summer — 90 to 100 degrees Fahrenheit and more. But temperatures can plummet thirty degrees at night.

ORLAND

The Inn at Shallow Creek Farm

4712 County Road DD
Orland, CA 95963
916-865-4093
800-865-4093

> *A relaxing retreat
> in the country*

Proprietors: Kurt and Mary Glaese-
man. **Accommodations:** 4 rooms (2 with private bath). **Rates:**
$55–$75 single or double, $15 for rollaway. **Included:** Full
breakfast. **Payment:** MasterCard, Visa. **Children:** Not appropriate. **Pets:** Not allowed. **Smoking:** Not allowed.

Behind a white picket fence, shaded by big walnut trees, this
turn-of-the-century ranchhouse offers comfortable lodging
and an atmosphere of serenity. On the three-acre farm, west
of I-5 and twenty miles from Chico, there are citrus orchards,
plums, persimmons, figs, and pomegranates. Squirrels scamper in the trees, roosters crow in the background, and chickens and geese scratch near the barn. Giant black walnut trees
in the yard, and sinewy ivy vines climbing over the front of
the house help to keep things shady and cool in the summer.

Kurt and Mary Glaeseman opened their place to guests in
early 1987, after visiting many B&Bs. "We modeled ours after
things we liked," Mary says. They have furnished the inn
with soft easy chairs, country antiques, books (they're both
teachers), and such conveniences as air conditioning and electric baseboard heat.

The common room, with TV, stereo, and a stone fireplace,
is for guests' exclusive use; the Glaesemans occupy separate,

attached quarters. Next to it is the dining room, its glass-paned windows overlooking the front lawn. Breakfast is served here at one table — fresh muffins, juice and fruit from the farm's trees, egg dishes, and homemade breads such as prune oatmeal bread or California polka dot bread with raisins and oranges from Shallow Creek's own orchards. There's a sun porch too, where breakfast is occasionally served.

> **The Glaesemans raise unusual birds such as Polish-crested chickens, buff orpingtons, and voiceless Muscovy ducks. One of the farm's most endearing creatures is Rutherford B. Squeak, the pet goose who considers Kurt his best friend.**

The Penfield Suite off the parlor is the former master bedroom. It has a queen-size bed, white walls and louvered shutters, and its own telephone and bath. The upstairs rooms have the use of a phone on the landing, and they share a bath with a tub and shower. The Heritage Room in the oldest part of the house, has an old-fashioned flavor, with its morning glory wallpaper, complementing lamps, priscilla curtains, an oak dresser from Kurt's family, and framed vintage valentines that once belonged to his aunt. The Brookdale Room has two twin beds, a nice antique oak dresser, and a big window overlooking the trees. The four-room caretaker's cottage, across the yard from the ranchhouse, has wicker furnishings, a fully equipped kitchen, a separate living room and bedroom, a wood-burning stove, and an enclosed sun porch.

At this casual, friendly place you can feed the chickens, go for walks, or relax with a book under a fragrant orange tree. You can also explore the little-known northern Sacramento Valley, where the fields turn gold and purple with poppies and lupine. In spring the undulating hills are a brilliant green and dotted with oak trees. You can pick kiwis and boysenberries, visit a pioneer cemetery, go boating and fishing on Black Butte Reservoir, birdwatch at the wildlife refuge, and attend the rodeo at Paskenta. Orland has a few coffee shops, and Chico a number of good ethnic restaurants.

SEA RANCH

The Sea Ranch

Lodge:
P.O. Box 44
The Sea Ranch, CA 95497
707-785-2371
Rental Homes:
Sea Ranch Escape
P.O. Box 238
The Sea Ranch, CA 95497
707-785-2426
800-SEARANCH (for information on all accommodations)

*A resort colony
and coastal retreat*

Innkeeper: Marianne Harder. **Accommodations:** 20 lodge rooms, 55 rental homes. **Rates:** lodge $125–$180 single or double, $15 additional person; rental homes $200–$620 for 2 nights, plus refundable deposit. **Added:** 9% tax. **Payment:** Major credit cards. **Minimum stay:** 2 nights on weekends in lodge, 2 nights in rental homes. **Children:** Over age 5 $15 per child. **Pets:** Not allowed. **Smoking:** Nonsmoking units available.

The Sea Ranch, twenty-nine miles north of Jenner on a wild and lovely stretch of the Sonoma County coast, is a second-home colony and resort on one of the last great Mexican land grants. The location, on 5,000 acres of bluffs and wooded slopes overlooking the Pacific, is outstanding.

The architecture blends unobtrusively into its surroundings. The vertical gray siding and fences are brightened by barrels of flowers, but most of the color here comes from wildflowers and natural vegetation, not from planted gardens.

The lodge is the center of social life for the 1,300 homes on the property. Its inviting lounge has a stone fireplace, grand piano, high rough-hewn walls, and wide windows overlooking the bluffs and sea. The dining room, open for three meals a day, serves American cuisine with an emphasis on fresh ingredients and seafood. Breads and desserts are baked on the premises, and the coffee is the ranch's special blend. The view from the picture windows is spectacular.

The guest rooms are in an L-shaped building north of the lodge. Two are family units, with two bedrooms. Several have fireplaces, with wood provided, and almost every room has an ocean view. There are no phones or television sets, though there's a TV in the bar and pay phones in the lodge. Carpeted and furnished in the style of a good-quality motel room, the accommodations are comfortable, but not outstanding.

Sea Ranch's privately owned rental homes, which sleep from two to eight people, offer the best variety of accommodations. Several agencies handle the rentals; Sea Ranch Escape carries many of the finest in the choicest locations. Among them are two of the original award-winning condominium units.

Set on bluffs directly above the ocean, in grassy meadows, or under the pines and redwoods east of the highway, the homes are, for the most part, furnished in a tasteful, contemporary style. Your rental might contain a dishwasher, washer and dryer, stereo, video player, pool or Ping-Pong table, or any combination of the above.

> **Sea Ranch has two swimming pools, tennis courts, and sauna, as well as private beaches and miles of trails through forest and meadows. As you walk the headlands, you may see blacktail deer, great blue heron, or even a bobcat or gray fox.**

You can bring your own bed linens, towels, and kindling for the fireplace, or the rental agency will provide them at extra cost. Sea Ranch Escape has three levels of service: you can bring supplies and do your own cleaning, have the agency make up the beds and clean, or choose to have everything, including the catering of meals, taken care of.

The most expensive rentals are the newest. One is a four-bedroom, three-bath home with a Jacuzzi in the master bath. It has a commanding ocean view from the edge of the bluff and is a five-minute walk from the recreation center and the beach.

On the property is a challenging, top-rated 9-hole golf course. Nearby are a clubhouse, snack bar, and pro shop.

TRINIDAD

The Lost Whale Bed & Breakfast Inn

3452 Patrick's Point Drive
Trinidad, CA 95570
707-677-3425
Fax: 707-677-0284

*An oceanfront
inn ideal for
family vacations*

Innkeepers: Susanne Lakin and Lee Miller. **Accommodations:** 6 rooms (all with private bath). **Rates:** November–April $95–$135, May–October and major holidays. $105–$150; $15 additional adult, $10 additional child age 3–16. **Included:** Full breakfast. **Added:** 10% tax. **Payment:** Major credit cards. **Children:** Under age 3 free. **Pets:** Not allowed. **Smoking:** Not allowed.

Adults and children alike are enchanted by this warm, spacious, Cape Cod style inn with plank floors and a modern country decor. High on a grassy bluff, it faces the Pacific and you can hear the sea lions that bask on Turtle Rock bark as you drive up.

The blue frame house, which stands behind a white picket fence covered with roses, was built in 1989 as a bed-and-breakfast. Originally from Los Angeles, Suzanne and Lee moved to Trinidad with their daughters ready to try a different way of life. Finding Trinidad to their liking, they purchased four acres of land, built their B&B, and have been welcoming visitors ever since.

Games are laid out on tables in the common room where comfy blue and white sofas are set on hardwood floors in front of a fire. Here guests have afternoon tea and cookies. Breakfast is served in a separate dining room on pine tables. A wall of windows brings sunshine and ocean views into the cheerful room. Spinach frittata, raspberry coffeecake, Parmesan potatoes, Dutch babies, and grapefruit, or sour cream pancakes, salmon eggs, currant scones, and fruit salad are typical of the bountiful morning meals.

Guest rooms are soundproof and practical, but a light decor, fresh flowers, greenery, and books and magazines lend sparkle as well. Two rooms have balconies and skylights, and five have stunning ocean views. Sea Lion on the main floor is crisp and airy with high ceilings and skylights. The decor, in

seafoam and plum, includes charming floral lamps and a dia-
mond patterned patchwork quilt with matching pillows. In
the Egret room a bird's-eye redwood egret stands in the corner, and a batik egret
hangs on one wall. The
Beluga Room has an up-
stairs sleeping loft with a
queen-size futon, and a
queen-size iron bed with
brass accents downstairs.
The Orca Whale Room,
with a four-poster pine
bed with heart cutouts
downstairs, also has a
sleeping loft. The Hump-
back Whale room has no
view, but a large overhead skylight makes the room sunny
and pleasant just the same.

> For dinner, try the nearby
> Larrupin's Café, which is
> famous for its barbecue
> sauce and excellent
> cooking. With advance
> notice, the innkeepers will
> arrange for childcare while
> you dine.

Youngsters love to amuse themselves in the charming
playhouse. You can walk a path to a private beach, relax in
the hot tub, go deep sea fishing, explore tidepools, windsurf in
fresh water lagoons, and walk in Redwood National Park, the
largest redwood forest in the world. It's a fifteen-minute drive
from the inn.

Trinidad Bay Bed & Breakfast

P.O. Box 849
560 Edwards
Trinidad, CA 95570-0849
707-677-0840

> *A casual home
> with panoramic
> ocean views*

Innkeepers: Carol and Paul Kirk.
Accommodations: 4 rooms (all
with private bath.). **Rates:** $105–$155 single or double, $30 ad-
ditional person; midweek discounts February–March. **Included:** Full breakfast. **Added:** 8% tax. **Minimum stay:** 2
nights weekends and holidays. **Payment:** MasterCard, Visa.
Children: Welcome (rooms accommodate 2 people). **Pets:** Not
allowed. **Smoking:** Not allowed. **Open:** February through November.

The most populous state in the union has a number of great vacation spots waiting to be discovered; Trinidad is one of them. This is not palm tree country. Trinidad Bay is on the far north coast, twenty-two miles above Eureka, just off Highway 101. Fog often drifts in, and the winter storms are wild. Nightlife consists of stargazing on clear nights or curling up with a good book and hot cider by a fire.

In ancient times, Trinidad was Tsurai, a village of the Yurok Indians, active until the early 1900s. Direct descendants of the tribe continue to live and work in the area. One Yurok builds dugout canoes for museums and gives seminars on the art of canoe construction.

If that prospect appeals, and you like gorgeous scenery, pristine beaches, good fishing, and intriguing history, you may enjoy Trinidad. You're close to wilderness here, with forests of redwood giants lining the highway. Redwood National Park is twenty miles to the north. Between it and I-5 on the east are many mountains and very few roads.

Overlooking Trinidad Bay, with broad views of the coastline and harbor, is a 1949 Cape Cod–style home with accommodations for travelers. When you arrive, Carol and Paul greet you with warmth and show you where to find the cider mix, cookies, and the refrigerator for chilling wine. It's clear that they want you to feel welcome in their pleasant home. Hot and cold beverages are available all day.

The guest rooms have a comfortable, casual atmosphere, traditional furnishings, and ocean views. The first floor suite has a fireplace and king-size bed. There's a telescope in the upstairs suite so you can watch the boats and whales go by. Both suites have microwave ovens, and popcorn is provided. If you are in one of the two rooms in the main house, you'll be served a family-style breakfast in the dining area; if you're staying in a suite with an outside entrance, breakfast will be brought to your room.

The house sits on a cliff directly above Indian Beach and the bay, facing south down the coast; you can see all the way to Mendocino Cape. Across the street is a little lighthouse, a memorial to those lost at sea. It's a replica of the working lighthouse around the corner.

Trinidad was named by a Spanish explorer, Don Bruno de Hezeta, in 1775. Landing on Trinity Sunday, he erected a wooden cross, christened the point of land Trinidad, and held the first mass in California's history. The Spanish cross remained on the head until 1913 when a granite cross replaced it.

The town became a port supplying gold-rush miners, a lumber town, and, in the 1920s, a whaling station. Lying in the path of the great gray whales' annual migration, it's an excellent place for viewing the whales. From the headlands, and even from the Kirks' front yard, you can see mother whales with their new youngsters heading north from Baja California.

Other activities are beachcombing for agates, walking the trails of Trinidad Head, and watching sea lions cavort on the rocks. You can charter a boat at the pier if you want to fish for salmon or cod or go crabbing. An excursion boat offers harbor cruises. At Telonicher Marine Lab you can see aquariums, touch intertidal animals, tour the research lab, and watch slide presentations on marine life.

WESTPORT

Howard Creek Ranch

P.O. Box 121
40501 North Highway 1
Westport, CA 95488
707-964-6725
Fax: 707-964-6725

An old-fashioned farmhouse near the sea

Innkeepers: Sally and Charles (Sonny) Grigg. **Accommodations:** 10 rooms. **Rates:** $55–$95 single or double; suites $95–$45. **Included:** Full breakfast. **Added:** 10% on lodging; 7.25% on food. **Minimum stay:** 2 nights on some summer weekends and holidays. **Payment:** Major credit cards. **Children:** Allowed by prior arrangement. **Pets:** Allowed by prior arrangement; $5 for small animals, $10 for larger pets. **Smoking:** Allowed outside only.

On the northern coast, where mists swirl around jagged headlands, coves protect sandy beaches, and every curve in the road presents another sweeping ocean view, there's a rural valley with a creek running through. On this idyllic site, a farmstead was built in 1871 by Alfred Howard, an early settler. The house, made entirely of heart redwood, still stands — the oldest home in the Westport area. Even today you can see the name of Lucy Howard, one of Alf's daughters, scratched in the wavy glass of an upstairs window pane.

Sally and Sonny Grigg are the third owners of the 40-acre ranch, a small portion of the land grant that once extended over 2000 acres of grassy slopes and wooded hills.

> A 75-foot swinging foot bridge spans Howard Creek, which flows past the big barn to the beach 200 yards away. Deer and elk roam the area, along with a resident porcupine.

Their restoration efforts have turned the historic home into a bed-and-breakfast for travelers looking for seclusion in the country several hundred feet from the sea.

The house stands in a colorful garden, the source of the fresh flowers in the rooms. On the hillside are a hot tub, a sauna, showers, and an ornamental pool fed by a creek. Horses and cows graze the pastures.

In the main house, the spicy scent of potpourri fills the air, while the original fireplace warms the parlor. The antique furnished parlor draws guests to Sally's extensive book collection, the chess set, and the Griggs' musical instruments. At a single table in the dining room, Sally serves a substantial morning meal. A typical breakfast includes baked apples with granola and whipped cream, a vegetarian omelette, strawberry banana pancakes, locally made sausage, eggs, fresh fruit topped with edible flowers, and a selection of beverages.

There are two guest rooms on the main floor. One opens to a patch of colorful flowers. Country antiques furnish the suite, which has a star quilt on the bed and scatter rugs on polished wood floors. In the sitting area is a small kitchen with a refrigerator and microwave oven. Upstairs, several more rooms offer comfortable accommodations; one has a cozy loft under a leaded glass skylight.

Other lodgings include a redwood cabin at the edge of the woods and quaint Meadow Cabin, covered with passion vine and nasturtiums. Meadow Cabin has a woodstove and a shower. Most unusual is the Boat House, which was constructed around the hull and galley of a boat. Sheltered by eucalyptus trees on the bank of Howard Creek, it holds a woodstove, microwave oven, and a refrigerator as well as its own bath. The Griggses also have a beach cabin with a king-size bed and ocean view.

Activities in the area are plentiful. You can stroll and beachcomb on miles of sand, explore tidepools, or go bird-watching (the innkeepers can give you a list of the types of birds you are likely to see during your visit). Sally and Sonny know all the nearby Nature Conservancy trails and panoramic viewpoints. Further afield, you may drive to Fort Bragg and Mendocino (about twenty-five miles south) for shopping and dining.

Sierra Country

Best Intimate City Stops

Sacramento
  Abigail's
  Amber House Bed & Breakfast Inn
  Delta King Hotel
  Hartley House
  The Sterling Hotel
  Vizcaya
Truckee
  The Truckee Hotel

Best Country Inns and B&Bs

Amador City
  Imperial Hotel
Bishop
  Chalfant House
Coloma
  The Coloma Country Inn
Columbia
  City Hotel
  Fallon Hotel
Coulterville
  The Hotel Jeffery
Georgetown
  American River Inn
Homewood
  Rockwood Lodge
Ione
  The Heirloom
Jackson
  Gate House Inn
  The Wedgewood Inn
Mammoth Lakes
  Edelweiss Lodge
Murphys
  Dunbar House, 1880
Nevada City
  Grandmere's Bed & Breakfast Inn
  Red Castle Inn
Sierra City
  Busch & Heringlake Country Inn

South Lake Tahoe
  Lakeland Village Beach & Ski Resort
Sutter Creek
  Grey Gables Inn
  Sutter Creek Inn

Best Family Favorites

Fish Camp
  Tenaya Lodge
Hope Valley
  Sorensen's
Sacramento
  Radisson Hotel Sacramento
Sonora
  Llamahall Guest Ranch

Best Resorts

Mammoth Lakes
  Mammoth Mountain Inn
Olympic Valley
  Resort at Squaw Creek
  Squaw Valley Lodge
South Lake Tahoe
  Lakeland Village Beach & Ski Resort
Truckee
  Northstar at Tahoe

Romantic Hideaways

Sutter Creek
  The Foxes Bed and Breakfast Inn

Wilderness Retreats

Crowley Lake
  Rainbow Tarns Bed & Breakfast
Kirkwood
  Caples Lake Resort

Mammoth Lakes
  Alpers' Owens River Ranch
  Tamarack Lodge Resort
Wawona
  Wawona Hotel
Yosemite
  The Ahwahnee

The broad Sacramento River delta holds the capital city of **Sacramento,** with its peaceful tree-shaded streets, lovely capitol grounds, art museums, and restored Old Town. Sutter's Fort, a state historic park, replicates the fort built in 1839 by John Sutter on the American and Sacramento rivers.

Not to be missed in Old Sacramento is the California State Railroad Museum, which exhibits restored locomotives, a luxurious private railroad car, and hundreds of items from train history. It's near the waterfront, where old-fashioned paddlewheelers cruise the river.

Sacramento is the gateway to the Gold Country in the foothills of the Sierra Nevada. Ghosts of the 49ers still linger in former mining communities like **Sutter Creek, Jackson,** and **Jamestown**. Some have more than a touch of the old frontier. **Nevada City** has carefully nurtured its heritage by restoring a 19th-century atmosphere. **Columbia,** a state park, is an authentic recreation of a mid-1800s mining town.

Reach deeper into the High Sierra and you find a lake-dotted wilderness with high cliffs, dancing waterfalls, and immense sequoia trees. The great granite mountains, called a "range of light" by the naturalist John Muir, extend from the Cascades on the north to the desert Tehachapis.

South of dazzlingly blue and clear Lake Tahoe, the largest alpine lake in North America, is California's crown jewel: **Yosemite** National Park. At its heart lies Yosemite Valley. Sculpted by glaciers eons ago, it's an awe-inspiring wonderland of vertical cliffs, massive granite domes, streaming waterfalls, and lush meadows. With three million visitors annually, Yosemite can seem as crowded as a San Francisco suburb. But a few steps away from the campgrounds, 750 miles of trails traverse pristine country where the only sounds you hear belong to the wild.

Tioga Pass Road leads through Yosemite's northern peaks and subalpine meadows and descends sharply to desert country on the east side. The road south then heads toward **Mammoth Lakes** and some of California's best skiing and High Sierra scenery.

In Owens Valley, between the Sierra Nevada and Inyo/White Mountain range, you can go hiking, fishing, bird watching, horseback riding, and boating. South of **Bishop,** in the Inyo National Forest, you can walk among the earth's oldest living trees, bristlecone pines. The oldest in this awe-inspiring forest of twisted trunks and weathered branches is 4,700 years.

Still farther south lie California's extreme points: Mount Whitney, at 14,494 feet the highest peak in the continental United States, and Badwater in Death Valley, 282 feet below sea level.

AMADOR CITY

Imperial Hotel

P.O. Box 195
Amador City, CA 95601
209-267-9172
800-242-5594
Fax: 209-267-9249

*A historic hotel
in gold country*

Proprietors: Bruce Sherrill and Dale Martin. **Accommodations:** 6 rooms (all with private bath). **Rates:** $60–$95. **Included:** Continental breakfast. **Payment:** Major credit cards. **Children:** Welcome. **Pets:** Not allowed. **Smoking:** Not allowed in guest rooms.

This brick hotel, which faces busy Highway 49, was first built as a mercantile store, and then redone and opened as a hotel in 1879 when Amador was a bustling town. It was made to last — the walls at its base are twelve bricks thick, and four bricks thick at the roof. The Imperial closed in 1927; the present owners restored it in 1988, adding bathrooms, air conditioning, a restaurant, and other modern niceties.

The Imperial's restaurant is open daily for dinner, Sunday brunch, and lunch Friday through Sunday. With exposed brick walls, white tablecloths, candlelight, and large, folksy, floral paintings, it has achieved distinction for its fine California cuisine. Asian pasta with pan-seared sea scallops in a sesame-ginger sauce and tossed with red chile linguine, or chicken breast sautéed with artichoke hearts, sun-dried tomatoes, capers, white wine, and lemon juice served with grilled polenta are typical items, although the menu changes four times a year. Guest breakfast is served in the restaurant, on a patio, or in your room. The original hotel bar is opposite the restaurant.

> **In the heart of the gold country, and once a major mining center, Amador City is known today for its numerous antiques shops and for the excellent restaurant in the Imperial Hotel.**

Upstairs, the guest rooms have such old-fashioned features as high ceilings, antique beds, and paddle fans. They have a delightfully whimsical decor, with designs by the talented John Johansen — the same artist who painted the colorful paintings downstairs in the restaurant. One room, for example, has a corner armoire with ties, socks, and a gown painted as if they're hung over the door. Another has a headboard made from Johansen's hand-painted murals.

Room 1 is bright, decorated in white with a canopy bed, sofa, and double doors that open out onto a balcony. Room 4 has a well-worn antique writing desk with a brass study lamp, and a mirrored armoire. Room 3 is sunny in pastels with wicker furnishings, and an iris patterned quilt. The baths are contemporary, in white and brass, and have hair dryers and towel warmers. As the Imperial is close to the highway, it's best to request a room at the back if you're a light sleeper.

A deck with flowerpots and chairs is at one end of the second floor hall. Across the front of the hotel there's a balcony accessible to guests. Inside, on the landing, are a desk and phone, shelves of books and games, and a basket of fruit. In back of the hotel there's a quiet garden patio to relax in.

BISHOP

Chalfant House

213 Academy Street
Bishop, CA 93514
619-872-1790

A cozy B&B in a town on the east side of the Sierra Nevada range

Innkeepers: Fred and Sally Manecke. **Accommodations:** 7 rooms (all with private bath). **Rates:** $55–$65 single, $65–$75 double, $75–$95 suite, $15 additional person. **Included:** Full breakfast. **Payment:** Major credit cards. **Children:** Over age 8 welcome; $15 additional. **Pets:** Not allowed. **Smoking:** Not allowed.

Chalfant House offers comfortable lodging while you explore the Owens Valley area. The turn-of-the-century inn, built for the publisher of the first newspaper in the valley, is a block from Main Street and within walking distance of shops, restaurants, and a pleasant park. After the Chalfants sold it in the 1920s, the house changed hands numerous times over the years, and was everything from a boarding house for "ladies of the night," referred to locally as the "Loose House," to a more respectable lodging called the Academy Hotel until it closed in 1983. Soon thereafter the house was left vacant, and was virtually in ruin when the Maneckes bought it in 1987. They turned it into the amiable bed-and-breakfast it is today.

Each guest room is named after a member of the Chalfant

family and is furnished with antiques and handmade quilts, and all are air-conditioned. Pleasant, named for Mr. Chalfant, has an inlaid oak armoire that came from Belgium, a queen-size white iron and brass bed, an exposed stone wall in the bath, and a private patio with a grape arbor. In Adeline, named for Pleasant's wife, the tub is draped in lace.

> Bishop is a small, peaceful town in the Owens Valley of the Eastern Sierra, halfway between Reno and Los Angeles. It provides easy access to mountain trails, lakes, the Mammoth Mountain ski area, and the ancient bristlecone pine forest.

Other guest rooms are named for the Chalfant children. There's a patchwork quilt on the bed under a slanted roof in Agnes; Willie has twin beds and is masculine, and Blanche suite has a Victorian parlor. A separate suite, above the Maneckes antiques store behind the house, has a carved walnut queen-size bed attractively set with a floral comforter and lots of pillows, a sofa bed in the living room, and a kitchen.

The Maneckes have restored the B&B with care, and put equal effort into creating a welcoming atmosphere for their guests. They'll greet you with a mug of hot cider in the cool months and a frosty drink in summer, take you to and from the Bishop airport at no charge, provide a sink for cleaning the fish you catch and a freezer to store it in, and invite you to join them for homemade ice cream sundaes in the evening. Before you leave they'll take your picture and send it along with the newsletter they publish.

Breakfast includes fruit, cinnamon rolls or homemade breads and jams, and a hot dish such as cream cheese French toast with apple cider syrup and turkey sausage or a baked omelette. It is served on fine table linens and china in the dining room, and you can take your coffee to the little side terrace under the grape arbor if you like. There's a piano and TV in the parlor, where guests gather to visit with each other and their hospitable hosts.

COLOMA

The Coloma Country Inn

P.O. Box 502
2 High Street
Coloma, CA 95613
916-622-6919

*A quiet
country home
in a historic park*

Innkeepers: Cindi and Alan Ehrgott. **Accommodations:** 5 rooms (3 with private bath) plus 2 suites in Carriage House. **Rates:** Rooms, $89–$99; Carriage House, $120–$165. **Included:** Full breakfast. **Added:** 10% tax. **Payment:** No credit cards; personal checks accepted. **Children:** Welcome. **Pets:** Not allowed. **Smoking:** Allowed outdoors only.

In 1848, gold was discovered in the American River, in the foothills of the Sierra Nevada. That event changed the face of the nation, helped the Union win the Civil War, and brought both fortune and disaster to thousands. By 1865, at least $750 million in gold had been mined in California.

It all started here, in the little town of Coloma, when James Marshall pulled a nugget from the tailrace of John Sutter's lumber mill. Richer diggings were soon found elsewhere, and Coloma became the commercial center for nearby mining camps. Saloon keepers prospered mightily from the newfound gold. Hugh Miller, who ran a saloon in Coloma, was able to build himself a fine home in 1852. This home, after several renovations, is now a delightful inn at Marshall Gold Discovery State Historic Park.

Coloma Country Inn has been open as a bed-and-breakfast since 1983. The inn stands behind a white picket fence on 5½ acres of beautifully landscaped grounds, with fruit trees, flowers, a gazebo, an old fashioned well, and a pond where bullfrogs croak among the cattails. The Ehrgotts offer warm hospitality and a touch of New England — plaid wingback chairs, patchwork quilts, hand-dipped candles, charming wall stencils — in the furnishings and decor of their inn. In the dining room there are shaker boxes, birdhouses, Oriental rugs, and a lace-draped mantel. Pewter mugs adorn the walls of the dining room where breakfast is served on an heirloom Duncan Phyfe table underneath a pewter chandelier.

In the main house, the Rose Room is bright with a rose motif decor, and has a private courtyard where roses bloom. Lavender Room is a light, cheerful space in lavender and white, with a white spool bed, lace curtains, stained glass windows, clawfoot tub, and an apple tree out the window and a view of the pond. The Blue Room has long, narrow windows hung with lace and framed with flowers. It shares a bathroom with the Garden Room, which is furnished in white wicker and pine. In the Eastlake room cushioned benches stand on either side of French doors which open out onto a small widow's balcony. The carved Eastlake bed is topped by a chenille spread. Each room has a small sitting area. A few yards away, behind a lavish country garden and brick courtyard, is the Carriage House, with two enchanting suites. Cottage Suite is a good choice for families, since it has two bedrooms and a kitchenette (not for cooking full meals, but quite adequate for storing snacks). Geranium Suite has a folk country feel and lives up to its name with a garden motif and geranium-patterned fabrics. It also has a kitchen where the red, white, and green color scheme is repeated down to a rooster egg cup set that was given to the inn by a guest who felt it just belonged there (and it does). Outside grapes and wisteria cover trellises on the large patio.

> **Alan Ehrgott is a veteran pilot and offers hot-air balloon flights over the American River Valley. First thing in the morning, balloonists are given a light snack and then a ride over the pine trees and oak-studded hills and the American River. The flight is followed by champagne and a full breakfast.**

You may have breakfast in your room, on the patio, or in the dining room, where French doors open to the grassy slope above the pond. You'll be served juice, fresh fruit, homemade baked goods, and a hot entrée such as scrambled eggs with salsa. Cookies, lemonade, and iced tea are in the kitchen, where guests are welcome.

The innkeepers have bicycles to lend and will arrange for whitewater rafting trips. When you tour the state park, you'll see a replica of Sutter's sawmill, James Marshall's cabin, tinsmith and blacksmith shops, and other historic structures.

For dining out in Coloma, the Ehrgotts recommend Vineyard House, which has a Continental menu and 19th-century atmosphere. They also urge guests to get into the spirit of the period at the Olde Coloma Theater, where melodramas are presented on weekends. Columbia

COLUMBIA

City Hotel

P.O. Box 1870
Main Street
Columbia, CA 95310
209-532-1479
Fax: 209-532-7027

*A frontier hotel
in an
Old West town*

Manager: Tom Bender. **Accommodations:** 10 rooms. **Rates:** $65–$90 single, $70–$95 double, $15 additional person. **Included:** Expanded Continental breakfast. **Added:** 8% tax. **Payment:** Major credit cards. **Children:** Age 2 and under free in room with parents. **Pets:** Not allowed. **Smoking:** Not allowed in guest rooms or parlor.

Horses clop down the street in Columbia, pulling stagecoaches to the Wells Fargo office. The blacksmith is in his shop repairing wagons. Melodramas are performed regularly at the theater. The barber cuts hair in an 1856 barber shop, and old-fashioned candies are sold in the sweet shop. And the same hotel that housed successful miners is open for business.

City Hotel is a two-story brick edifice that opened in 1856, fell into disrepair when the boom faded, and reopened in 1975 as a museum and hotel under state ownership. Now, just as in earlier days, lace curtains hang at glass-paneled doors and a ticking clock and heavy safe stand behind a wooden registration counter. The crowd in the What Cheer Saloon isn't quite as boisterous as in decades past, but the atmosphere is convivial around the cherrywood bar, which was shipped around the Horn from New England.

The frontier inn is well kept and comfortable, and the service attentive. The highly reputed restaurant serves a light French cuisine and has a wine list that includes labels from

Amador County, an area noted for its zinfandels. The restaurant and hotel are also a training ground for students in Hospitality Management at nearby Columbia College. Eager and enthusiastic, they assist a professional staff.

> **Columbia is the best-preserved gold rush town in the Mother Lode. Faithfully restored, it's now a state park where you can experience life as it was in the 1850s, when this was a boomtown of 15,000 people and 40 saloons. When you walk into town (no cars are allowed) you enter the mid-19th century.**

Guest rooms are upstairs, two in front (Balcony Rooms), four down the hall, and four off the large parlor (Parlor Rooms). In the Victorian parlor are games, playing cards, and a revolving bookcase of books and magazines. A breakfast of fresh juice, granola, fruits, and breads from the hotel kitchen is set out in the parlor and may be taken to your room.

The rooms are on display when they're not occupied. When you stay here, the chain across the door is unhooked and you're left to spend the night as a traveler of a century ago, in the finest accommodations the gold country had to offer. The rooms are larger than they were originally, when the hotel was strictly for gentlemen, with ladies allowed only in the parlor and dining areas. The addition of running water is another modern nicety. There's a half-bath in each room, but showers are down the hall. You're supplied with a basket containing robes, soft slippers, towels, soap, and shampoo.

Oriental rugs, 12-foot ceilings, lace curtains at high windows, and heavy carved furniture bring back the romance of another era. The two Balcony Rooms have private balconies with wrought-iron railings facing the trees above Main Street.

Room 1, a perennial favorite, is "the haunted room." It seems that a wealthy man from the Midwest bought a massive carved bedroom set for his bride and had it shipped to San Francisco. But the newlyweds never slept in the bed, for the bride died of a fever. The grieving husband shut the furniture in a warehouse. Later, after a stint in a museum, it ended up in a Balcony Room here, and occasionally visitors insist that they feel peculiar vibrations.

In Columbia State Historic Park, you can have your name stamped on a horseshoe or printed in headlines in a period newspaper, ride in a stagecoach, and pan for gold. Buy leather goods and wines, stop by the ice cream parlor, tour the museum, and have lunch or dinner at the best restaurant in town, the City Hotel. Miners who got lucky drank champagne here; you can too.

Fallon Hotel

P.O. Box 1870
11175 Washington Street
Columbia, CA 95310
209-532-1470
Fax: 209-532-7027

A Victorian hotel in a gold rush setting

Manager: Tom Bender. **Accommodations:** 14 rooms. **Rates:** $44–$85 single, $50–$90 double, $15 additional person. **Included:** Continental breakfast. **Added:** 8% tax. **Payment:** Major credit cards. **Children:** Age 2 and under free in room with parents. **Pets:** Not allowed. **Smoking:** Not allowed in rooms or parlor. **Open:** Weekends only during November, and January through April; Tuesdays through Sundays the rest of the year.

In Columbia State Historic Park, where gold rush days have been brought to life, the Fallon Hotel offers lodging just as it did when Columbia was a rip-roaring miners' town in 1857. Owned by the state, the hotel was authentically restored in 1986, using many of the antiques and furnishings discovered in the neglected, dilapidated building.

Now, when you enter the lobby, you're engulfed in the atmosphere of a fine Victorian hotel in the countryside. A green plush loveseat and burgundy velvet couch are set off by an

Oriental carpet and dark, carved moldings. When the restoration began, bits of the original wallpaper were found still clinging to the walls, so the noted firm of Bradbury and Bradbury was called in to recreate them. Elaborate, colorful designs cover the 15-foot walls and ceiling.

> Next to the hotel is a tree-shaded garden with a brick terrace. In the nearby Fallon Theater, the Columbia Actors' Repertory performs year-round.

Upstairs guest rooms contain double or twin beds and half-baths. Spacious and modern shared showers with skylights are down the hall. Baskets with soaps, towels, robes and slippers are provided. At the end of the hall, French doors open to a balcony overlooking the traffic-free street — no cars are permitted in Columbia — and some rooms have private balconies.

The best and largest rooms are toward the front of the hotel, but all are homey and comfortable, with carved or iron bedsteads, rocking chairs, and throw rugs on pine floors. Every morning, juice, coffee, assorted muffins and rolls, and jam are served in the ice cream parlor.

COULTERVILLE

The Hotel Jeffery

P.O. Box 440
1 Main Street
Coulterville, CA 95311
209-878-3471
800-464-3471
Fax: 209-878-3473

> *A former stagecoach stop in the Sierra foothills*

Proprietors: Karin Fielding, Gail Hystad, and Louis Bickford. **Accommodations:** 21 rooms (5 with private bath), 1 suite. **Rates:** $39–$74 single, $49–$74 double, $10 additional person, suites $99–$173 for up to 4 people. **Added:** 9% tax. **Minimum stay:** 2 nights on holiday weekends. **Payment:** MasterCard, Visa. **Children:** Under age

12 free in room with parents. **Pets:** Not allowed. **Smoking:** Allowed.

Travelers looking for the Old West love the Jeffery — it's the real thing, here in the foothills of the Sierras, thirty-one miles west of Yosemite National Park. The three-story, rock and adobe hotel was first built in 1850 as a store and fandango hall for the Mexican community. It burned down and was rebuilt three times over the years, but has been owned by the same family since 1851. Karin Fielding, one of the present owners, is a descendant.

> **The former stagecoach stop has a classic saloon with sawdust and peanut shells on the floor, lace at the windows, and a second story balcony with flags at the railing.**

There is little luxury at the Jeffery, but plenty of character and charm. In 1903 Theodore Roosevelt stayed in Room 1, one of two rooms with bay windows above the main street of this sleepy little village. Some windows overlook the county park across the street, which has a playground, swimming pool, and tennis courts.

The rooms are of different sizes, and there are a few cracks in the walls from the settling of the building. Pegs or rails with hangers take the place of closets. Big windows, transoms above the doors, and ceiling paddle fans provide air circulation. There are four bathrooms on each floor for the rooms that share baths.

The hotel was redone in 1988 and now has nicely decorated rooms large enough for families. The two most spacious rooms, done in blue and peach, are on the third floor. Like most old hotels, the Jeffery claims a ghost room where a spirit visits on occasion. You wouldn't know it to see the place; on the third floor, it's cheerful in bright red, with twin beds.

There is a meeting/banquet room with 1,600 square feet of space, and a nice courtyard in back. The plain and simple restaurant serves breakfast and dinner. Magnolia Saloon, with authentic frontier flavor, has pool tables and one of the oldest bars in the West. On display are military memorabilia and a whimsical, life-size scene of old-time poker players.

Coulterville has antique shops to browse and a historical museum that is well worth visiting.

CROWLEY LAKE

Rainbow Tarns Bed & Breakfast

Route 1, Box 1097
Crowley Lake, CA 93546
619-935-4556

> *An Old West
> farm home
> in the country*

Innkeeper: Lois Miles. **Accommodations:** 3 rooms (all with private bath). **Rates:** $95–$125. **Included:** Full breakfast and afternoon refreshments. **Minimum stay:** 2 nights, 3 nights on holidays. **Payment:** No credit cards. **Children:** Over age 12 welcome. **Pets:** Not allowed (except horses). **Smoking:** Not allowed indoors.

On the east side of the Sierra range, eighteen miles south of Mammoth Lakes, is a tiny community called Tom's Place. You can find it on your road map, but in reality it's little more than a restaurant and bar. About a mile further, on a dirt road, is Rainbow Tarns, a secluded, quiet, country home.

> **The restaurant at nearby Convict Lake is the place for dining by candlelight. Tom's Place, down-home and friendly, is where local residents go for good hamburgers and conviviality.**

The log and tan brick inn, built in the 1920s against granite boulders, has a rustic quality that is right out of the Old West. A battered wagon wheel leans against the veranda's log posts. The living room, with its log walls and high vaulted ceilings, has the feeling of a lodge. There's a deer over the stone fireplace, a wagon wheel light fixture, and sturdy woven rugs. Antiques, including a desk that predates the United States, a hand-cranked music box, and Lois' grandfather's cradle, decorate the room.

The guest rooms are furnished in country style, with lace curtains and down duvets to warm you on chilly mountain evenings (the elevation is 7,000 feet). Rainbow Room has a queen-size bed topped by a floral comforter and lace pillows, a beautiful 19th-century dresser, an oversize tile bath with a double Jacuzzi, and a deck. Gemini, with a view of the boulders and hillside, also has a whirlpool tub and a queen-size bed. Grandma's room is decorated with handsome hooked rugs and furnishings that belonged to Lois' mother.

This is a homey, casual spot where guests are welcome to use the kitchen and the innkeeper may join you for a family-style breakfast. She serves a hearty meal — fruit, eggs from the farm's chickens, pork chops, browned potatoes, and a basket of muffins and zucchini bread are typical. Since her son lives in Costa Rica, the coffee is a Costa Rican blend. A plate of cookies, a bowl of fruit, and beverages are always available, and in the afternoons Lois serves wine and cheese.

From the veranda or chairs on the grass you can watch the trout leap and ducks swim in the ponds. Bodie, Lois's lovable dog, will keep you company. Also on the farm are chickens, a cat, and Jamal, a white horse. Guests may bring their own horses, too, at no charge.

From Rainbow Tarns you can go bicycling or horseback riding, hiking on the John Muir Trail, cross-country skiing in open meadows, bathing in hot mineral springs, birdwatching, and star-gazing.

FISH CAMP

Tenaya Lodge

P.O. Box 159
1122 Highway 41
Fish Camp, CA 93623
209-683-6555
800-635-5807
Fax: 209-683-8684

A mountain lodge near Yosemite's border

Manager: Paul Ratchford. **Accommodations:** 242 rooms and 17 suites. **Rates:** summer $199–$249, winter $89–$135; $15 additional person, suites $249–$329. **Added:** Tax. **Payment:** Major credit cards. **Children:** Under age 17 free in room with parents. **Pets:** Allowed; $50 nonrefundable cleaning fee charged. **Smoking:** Nonsmoking rooms available.

Marriott's Tenaya Lodge opened in 1990, the only major resort built in the area in more than fifty years. Set on thirty-five hilly, wooded acres just two miles south of the entrance to Yosemite National Park, it's different from most Marriott hotels.

> **The Tenaya has two restaurants: the Sierra which features northern Italian dishes, and the Parkside Deli, an all-day coffee shop, will package a picnic lunch upon request. The rustic Lobby Bar, with a three-story stone fireplace, is a lively saloon that serves drinks and light fare.**

The three-story resort is like a mountain lodge with an American Indian and Southwest theme. In the spacious lobby are stucco walls, chairs fashioned from twigs and branches, and earthtone fabrics. All the amenities of a modern hotel are here, and the staff is enthusiastic and helpful.

There's an institutional tinge to the hotel, which you'll notice in the crowds, the bland music in the restaurant, and the convention groups. However, it does not detract from the cheerful ambience, and for family travel it can be a plus: you know what to expect. The big parking lot and minimal landscaping have a purpose — all that concrete is a required firebreak.

The comfortable, well-furnished rooms are soundproof and have mini-bars, TV, direct-dial phones, and individual climate control. Some suites have dining rooms and balconies. Cribs and babysitters are available.

Tenaya Lodge welcomes families with a variety of activities and services. There are indoor and outdoor swimming pools, sauna and steam rooms, mountain bikes, horseback riding, croquet, nature walks, and a summer day camp for youngsters ages five to twelve. The camp offers arts and crafts, nature hikes, meals, and movies. The morning forest walks, led by a knowledgeable guide, are worthwhile for all ages.

The main attraction, though, is Yosemite. You can admire the magnificent park from the valley floor, but to fully appreciate its wonders, hike away from the hordes of visitors, perhaps to Nevada Falls or Yosemite Falls. Or come in the winter, when the meadows and great granite domes are blanketed in snow and the park is not crowded.

GEORGETOWN

American River Inn

P.O. Box 43
Main at Orleans
Georgetown, CA 95634
916-333-4499
800-245-6566 in California
Fax: 916-333-9253

> *A casual, quiet
> inn near a former
> mining camp*

Innkeepers: Will and Maria Collin. **Accommodations:** 20 rooms (11 with private bath), 6 suites. **Rates:** $85–$115. **Included:** Full breakfast. **Payment:** Major credit cards. **Children:** Over age 7 welcome; additional $15 per child. **Pets:** Not allowed. **Smoking:** Nonsmoking rooms available.

Georgetown is a quiet backwater between the middle and south forks of the American River, about an hour's drive east of Sacramento. There are few tourist attractions here — just scenic surroundings of mountains, lakes, and streams.

The original American Hotel, built in 1853, was all but lost to flames forty-six years later. Fire was commonplace in those days, often destroying entire towns. One Georgetown blaze raced up Main Street to a cache of miners' dynamite, which exploded and tossed debris for two miles.

Today's American River Inn, a complex covering a square block, is on the same site as its forebear. Three buildings are set among lovely gardens, along with a dove aviary and a swimming pool. The main building, with a veranda and a long balcony, houses fifteen guest rooms.

The comfortable accommodations have a flowery charm and furnishings that include unusual brass beds, patchwork quilts, feather beds, ceiling fans, antique lamps and armoires, and clawfoot tubs. At the end of the upstairs hall, lighted by red glass lamps, a door opens to the front balcony overlooking the quiet road.

Each room has a different decor, ranging from country calico to Victorian grandeur. There are two suites on the third level, one with a canopy bed and fireplace. The main house also has a gift shop and a parlor with a potbellied woodstove, wingback chairs, and a bar in the corner. Classical music plays in the afternoon while guests enjoy wine and appetizers and thumb through the album of local history. On the walls are historic prints of naval heroes and, of course, a "God Bless America" sampler.

A substantial breakfast is served at small tables in the dining room. Belgian waffles with bananas, spinach quiche, sausage, and ham are some of the dishes prepared, always with muffins, fruit cup, coffee and tea.

> The promise of gold drew prospectors to Georgetown, in the foothills of the Sierra Nevada, in the mid-1800s. The mining camp, then called Growlersburg, was a rich source of the precious stuff. By 1853, an estimated $2 million in gold had been found; one famous nugget weighed in at 126 ounces.

In back of the hotel, down brick steps and past a big magnolia tree, are the fig-shaded pool and the aviary. Next to the patio, the Queen Anne House has five guest rooms, two with private baths. The big living room has a brick fireplace, Oriental carpets, and double doors to the deck. The most romantic of the light and airy rooms is the upstairs suite, with a partially canopied bed, white brick fireplace, and a balcony with a wrought-iron railing.

A third building holds the five Woodside Mine Suites, which have living rooms, wet bars, and one or two bedrooms. Attractively furnished in wicker and brass and decorated with stenciled designs, they have private entrances from the garden and the parking area.

The innkeepers can help you plan sightseeing tours of the gold country and will arrange for whitewater rafting trips or hot-air balloon rides over the American River. They'll lend mountain bikes for biking the backroads that wind through masses of purple iris and brilliant yellow daffodils and scotch broom.

Hiking, fishing, and golf are nearby. The hotel has a putting green and driving range, and facilities for horseshoes, badminton, table tennis, and croquet. The kitchen will prepare a luxury picnic basket for a day of exploring, at $100 for two. It includes a bottle of wine, and you may keep the basket and all its accessories for future picnics.

HOMEWOOD

Rockwood Lodge

P.O. Box 226
5295 West Lake Boulevard
Homewood, CA 96141-0226
916-525-5273
800-LETAHOE
Fax: 916-525-5949

*A comfortable
bed-and-breakfast
near the lake*

Innkeepers: Constance Stevens and Louis Reinkens. **Accommodations:** 4 rooms (2 with private bath). **Rates:** $100–$200. **Included:** Full breakfast. **Added:** 8% tax. **Minimum stay:** 2 nights on weekends, 3 nights on holidays. **Payment:** No credit cards; personal checks accepted. **Children:** Under age 18 not appropriate. **Pets:** Not allowed indoors. **Smoking:** Not allowed indoors.

"Skiing down Homewood Run feels as if you're flying right into the lake." Connie Stevens is enthusiastic when she's talking about skiing and Lake Tahoe, two of her favorite subjects. She and her husband, Louis Reinkens, live in an ideal area to enjoy them both. Their bed-and-breakfast is just across the road from the lake and within walking distance of downhill ski slopes.

Homewood is a quiet community on the northwestern shore. Rockwood Lodge was built in 1939, in old Tahoe style of stone and knotty pine, as a vacation home for a dairyman from Vallejo. Forty-five years later, Connie and Louis left their Bay Area home and bought Rockwood, renovated it, and opened it to guests. Longtime travelers, they know the comforts travelers look for. There are walk-in closets with thick velour bathrobes, wines and appetizers by the fire or on the patio, cordials in the evenings, sweets by the bed, and books to read. The innkeepers can lend beach towels and chairs in the summer, and gloves and scarves in the winter. There are ski and bicycle storage areas, backpacks and walking sticks to borrow, and flashlights for evening walks.

Once inside the lodge — even on August weekends, when Tahoe traffic and crowds reach temper-fraying levels — the atmosphere is one of peace, soft music, and good taste. Wing-back chairs and fender benches provide seating comfort in the living room, where a fire on the stone hearth takes away the chill of winter evenings. On the mantel is a miniature of the Tahoe steam train that once ran to the lake.

French doors open to the dining room and breakfast table. Connie and Louis prepare fresh juice, croissants and preserves, quantities of fruit, Dutch babies with blueberries, Belgian waffles, and other delectable items, which they serve here or on the patio.

> There are several excellent restaurants along Tahoe's shores. In the summer, you may rent or charter a boat for fishing. Brown and Mackinaw trout inhabit the clear waters of the lake.

The guest rooms are named for places around the lake: Zephyr Cove, Emerald Bay, Secret Harbor, and Carnelian Bay. Zephyr Cove, the only room on the third floor, contains an extra-long double bed and pedestal sink. From its windows you look into the green branches of a 100-year-old pine tree. This room shares a bath-and-a-half with Emerald Bay, on the second floor. Secret Harbor, overlooking the lake, is the largest room and has extra appeal: a four-poster bed, an 18th-century cobbler's bench, and a bath with a double shower. All the rooms feature feather beds, down comforters, and sitting areas.

HOPE VALLEY

Sorensen's

14255 Highway 88
Hope Valley, CA 96120
916-694-2203
800-423-9949

> *A group of wilderness cabins near Carson Pass*

Proprietors: John and Patty Brissenden. **Accommodations:** 29 cabins (all but 2 have private baths). **Rates:** $65–$350. **Added:** 10% tax. **Minimum stay:** 2 nights on weekends, 3–4 nights on some holidays. **Payment:** Major credit cards. **Children:** Welcome (crib charge $10). **Pets:** Allowed with prior arrangement (in 3 cabins). **Smoking:** Not allowed.

South of Lake Tahoe and north of Yosemite, the rugged, mountainous country of the High Sierra has a scenic grandeur that rivals the Alps'. In fact, it's called Alpine County and most of it is public land — a colossal park of nearly 800 square miles of lakes, meadows, rivers, mighty forests and high peaks. Just east of Carson Pass, where Kit Carson explored and mapped the territory, are the green meadows of Hope Valley and this homey resort.

Owned by the Brissenden family since 1981, Sorensen's offers a full range of activities for all ages. Favorites are fishing, fly-tying and rod building courses, hiking, river rafting, kayaking, bicycling, soaking at the hot springs, and llama trekking. In winter, the resort is a cross-country ski center, with sixty miles of trails in the peaceful valley and Toiyabe National Forest. Ski lessons, equipment rentals, and classes in winter survival skills are available.

All but three of the cabins are clustered in the woods around a central building, which houses a country café (serving three hearty meals daily) and a gift shop. Each little building and its steeply pitched roof is outlined with tiny lights, creating a charming village effect at night.

Most of the cabins, which are named for local trees and flowers, have woodstoves (wood is supplied) and kitchens. Breakfast is provided for the three with no cooking facilities (although those cabins do have refrigerators).

Piñon, next to the sauna cabin, is one of the coziest, with pecky cedar walls and an old-fashioned tub. Aspen, in 1930s knotty pine, has a homespun style with calico bedspreads. Snowshoe is a classic log cabin furnished with a pole bed, wood burning stove, a tree slab dining table, and a kitchen. Waterfir is beloved by romantics looking for a quiet spot. Nestled among the aspen trees, with a creek running by, it has a brass double bed, a kitchen in the same room, a unique shingled shower, and a woodstove with a rock hearth.

The most unusual cabin is Norway House, a replica of a 13th-century, sod-roofed Scandinavian home. The two-story cabin sleeps up to six people, and has a full kitchen. In back, there's a deck with benches under the aspen trees. Another cabin, Chapel, also has two floors, with a spiral staircase leading to a loft bedroom. The cabin, which originally was part of Santa's Village in Santa Cruz, was reconstructed on the site and remodeled. One of the off-site cabins, which sleep up to six people, is across the river, and the others are near the hot springs.

This is a great place for children. John Brissenden, a former preschool teacher, has built a cunning log playhouse and stocked a pond with fish for kids under age twelve. There are puzzles, games, a playground, and horseshoes, as well as special programs like the October Star Watch and the Husky Express sled dog tours. If you're interested in both hiking and history, sign up for the Historical Emigrant Trail Walking Tour. The tour crosses parts of the Mormon-Emigrant Trail and the early Pony Express route.

> The Sorensen family homesteaded here a century ago; in 1902 they built a cluster of cabins, the start of a resort that is still expanding. It now covers 165 acres at an elevation of 7,000 feet.

For an enchanting winter holiday, come to Sorensen's in December and cut a fragrant Christmas tree. After a day on the snowy mountain, return to the café for hot cinnamon cocoa, mulled wine, or spiced cider and shop for gifts of books, jams and jellies, watercolors, and Native American wall hangings.

IONE

The Heirloom

P.O. Box 322
214 Shakeley Lane
Ione, CA 95640
209-274-4468

> *A quaint B&B in a gold-country town*

Innkeepers: Patricia Cross and Melisande Hubbs. **Accommodations:** 6 rooms (4 with private bath). **Rates:** $60–$100, additional person $15. **Included:** Full breakfast. **Added:** 7.25% tax. **Minimum stay:** 2 nights on weekends. **Payment:** Major credit cards. **Children:** Over age 8 welcome. **Pets:** Not allowed. **Smoking:** Not allowed indoors.

The Ione Valley, southeast of Sacramento, was a supply center for miners during the gold rush, with the village of Ione (called Bedbug or Freezeout in those days) its center. The more genteel name was chosen from a popular 19th-century book, *The Last Days of Pompeii.* Later, Ione served the farmers and ranchers of the fertile valley, which is now one of Amador County's zinfandel grape-growing areas.

> **Set back from the road, the inn is reached by a lane bordered with black walnut trees. A brick path leads to the front door and a white-paneled living room filled with furnishings from the owners' collections.**

In 1863, an early settler in the valley built a home in Ione like those he'd left in Virginia. Today it's The Heirloom. On one and a half acres, the home is a classic brick Greek Revival mansion with columned porticoes and balconies entwined with wisteria.

The large living room holds a white fireplace, soft couches and chairs, tall windows, numerous books, and a rosewood piano that once belonged to the famed entertainer Lola Montez. A Chinese ivory chess set, antique dolls (including a Shirley Temple doll that belonged to one of the innkeepers when she was a child), fans, and glassware reflect the innkeepers' many interests. The 400-year-old Italian refectory table has been in Melisande's family for many years.

The guest rooms in the main house are named for the seasons and decorated accordingly. Autumn, in rust tones, has an antique double brass bed with a carved footboard, a basket of crisp apples, and a wreath of dried weeds. French doors open to a semiprivate balcony above the garden. Summer is light and colorful in seafoam green and dusty rose. This room has an Eastlake walnut bed and a twin daybed, and looks out to a 150-year-old English walnut tree.

Winter, the most popular room, has a private entrance from the balcony, and a view of the garden and pine trees. There's a lovely walnut dresser with fold out mirrors, a desk that was the first piece of furniture Melisande's mother purchased after her wedding, and a tub draped in lace. Fittingly, the room also has a fireplace. Spring is in jonquil yellow, white, and green. Its king-size walnut Eastlake bed is topped by a wedding-ring patterned quilt, while its private balcony covered in wisteria overlooking a stately magnolia tree, is reminiscent of the old South. The room shares a bath with Autumn.

A few yards from the main house is a separate cottage called Rooms For All Seasons, which was built in 1983. Made of hand-crafted adobe with a sod roof, it contains two rooms, both with private baths. One has an Early American theme; the other is done in Early California style. They're done in hand-hewn cedar, redwood, and pine, and hold intriguing collections of furniture and artifacts. Darker than the rooms in the main house, they have a more rustic feel to them.

Patricia and Melisande receive rave reviews for their gracious hospitality; the comfort of guests is their foremost concern. Without undue fanfare, they make you feel welcome and at ease. They lend bicycles, place candies, fruit, and fresh flowers in your room, and guide you to the hammock and croquet set.

In cool weather, breakfast is served in the dining room with its fine collection of cranberry glassware, and cupboards filled with Staffordshire and Willow pattern china. In summer the meal is served in the garden. The menu changes regularly, but an example of a typical meal is fresh orange juice, baked pears, orange and cheese pastry, pumpkin muffins, cheese soufflé, and excellent coffee and teas. No other meals are served, but the innkeepers will refer you to area restaurants.

JACKSON

Gate House Inn

1330 Jackson Gate Road
Jackson, CA 95642
209-223-3500
800-841-1072
Fax: 223-1299

*A country
Victorian in the
gold country*

Proprietors: Keith and Gail Sweet.
Accommodations: 4 rooms (all with private bath) and Summerhouse. **Rates:** $85–$120 single, $90–$125 double, $20 additional person. **Included:** Full breakfast. **Added:** 8% tax. **Minimum stay:** 2 nights on weekends and for special events or holidays. **Payment:** Major credit cards. **Children:** Over age 12 welcome. **Pets:** Not allowed. **Smoking:** Not allowed indoors.

On an acre of sloping land that blooms with a thousand daffodils in spring, this turn-of-the-century Victorian home stands in quiet seclusion in the heart of the gold country. It was built by the son of one of Jackson's earliest settlers, Agostino Chichizola, a merchant and rancher, and today looks much as it did when it was new.

Oriental carpets, crystal chandeliers, antique furnishings, marble fireplaces, and a leaded and stained glass window retain the home's period atmosphere. Elegant royal blue velvet settees and a French rosewood table grace the parlor. The parquet floor in the dining room cost $10,000 to install at the time the home was built — a sizeable sum in those days.

The single guest room on the main floor has a brass bed, a

marble-topped sideboard, and, in the bathroom, the home's original lion-foot tub which is so massive and ornate, it took six men to install it for the home's first owner who was reputably over six feet tall. Upstairs, the French Room features Louis XIV walnut furniture, while the Master Suite boasts an Italian tile fireplace, and a rose velvet sofa that belonged to the Chichizola family. On the rose floral wallpaper (vintage 1948) there are pictures of cherubs reflecting the inn's angelic theme, and the bed is topped by an ivory eyelet comforter and lacy pillows. It's the only room with a hall bath, just a couple of steps away.

> **Jackson is close to all the diversions Amador County offers: wineries, golf courses, historic gold mining towns, and the Indian Grinding Rocks State Historic Park.**

Woodhaven, at the top of a private staircase and under the eaves, has a country atmosphere with pine furnishings, a braided rug, and a white iron bed. The painted chest was used by Gail's grandparents when they immigrated from the Netherlands in 1919. There's a half-bath on one side of the room, and a clawfoot tub on the other. Lace-curtained windows overlook the lushly flowered garden. Woodhaven has a sitting room and can accommodate two extra adults; the inn has no cribs for young children.

A favorite among returning guests is Summerhouse, a cottage by the back gate and arbor. Built as the caretaker's residence, it has an antique wooden headboard, chintz fabrics, wicker furnishings, air conditioning, and a woodstove on a brick hearth. There's a whirlpool tub for two in the bathroom.

Next to the garden is a screened area with table tennis and a barbecue. Brick-walled flower beds and rosebushes edge a path leading to a secluded swimming pool.

Guests can choose whether to have breakfast in their rooms or in the dining room, at a single table set with fresh flowers candles, and china. The menu varies; among the Gate House specialties are caramelized French toast with pecans and apples, salmon quiche, Belgian waffles, and a fresh fruit and yogurt parfait. Guests have the use of the kitchen refrigerator, and can help themselves to complimentary soft drinks and homemade cookies.

The thorough innkeepers try to accommodate their guests needs and interests whatever they might be. For history buffs, they've prepared a detailed history of the Chichizola family who built the home — including a Chichizola family tree. For nature lovers, the informative guest book in each room has a diagram of the plants in the garden, and each guest is given a helpful packet of area sightseeing information and coupons upon arrival. The Sweets also keep a supply of area restaurant menus on hand, and can help you with dining suggestions and dinner reservations.

The Wedgewood Inn

11941 Narcissus Road
Jackson, CA 95642
209-296-4300
800-933-4393

A gracious country home

Innkeepers: Jeannine and Vic Beltz.
Accommodations: 6 rooms (all with private bath). **Rates:** $85–$140 double, $10 less for single. **Included:** Full breakfast. **Added:** Tax. **Payment:** MasterCard, Visa. **Children:** Welcome in suite only; $20 additional. **Pets:** Not allowed. **Smoking:** Not allowed indoors.

If you had saved all those toys that are now collector's items, along with your parents' and grandparents' heirlooms, you too could furnish a home like the Wedgewood. Items the Beltzes have saved and antiques they've collected fill the rooms of their gracious Victorian replica, a blue frame house in the country six miles east of Jackson, off Highway 88.

Both Vic and Jeannine have an artistic flair that is evident in the stained glass, needlework, and lace lampshades on display throughout the inn. They're gardeners, too, and have landscaped the grounds in an English country style, with flower beds, a rose arbor, a gazebo, and fountains.

Pendulum clocks tick in the quiet parlor, where there's a woodstove and a baby grand piano. In the dining room beyond, guests gather for breakfast — a memorable meal of several courses by candlelight. Baked apples, spiced pears,

368 • *Sierra Country*

quiche, and blueberry-sour cream coffee cake are a few of the dishes served. Afternoon refreshments and early morning coffee are also provided.

The Wedgewood is a comfortable home operated by kindly people with traditional values. They set out Christian books and say grace at breakfast. If this is not to your liking, you may not feel at ease, though the innkeepers handle the issue with tact and do not push their beliefs.

> With the Wedgewood as your headquarters, you can explore the gold country, shop for antiques, and tour museums. Back at the inn, you can play croquet or horseshoes or relax in the hammock under the oak trees.

The upstairs guest rooms are spacious, and have views of the garden and oak grove or the wooded hills. Their furnishings reflect the innkeeper's interests and strong family ties. Victorian Rose is the most popular, with its rose motif, wood-burning stove, English carved bedroom set, walnut table, loveseat, and tapestry chairs. Its balcony, overlooking the rose arbor, is shared with Wedgewood Cameo. As one might expect, Wedgewood Cameo holds a cameo collection.

In Heritage Oak, the smallest room, there's a four-poster bed, tapestry rocker, and an old-fashioned spinning wheel. Jeannine's wedding dress is on display, and the bath has an antique shaving stand. Country Pine, in green and peach, features an iron scroll bed, carved armoire, a family christening gown, a cradle made by Vic's father, and an antique swift used in the counting of yarn. Up on the third floor is Granny's Attic named for Jeannine's mother. A light, airy room, it has a four-poster bed, skylight, wood-burning stove, and clawfoot tub draped in peach-colored lace.

The Carriage House, a separate cottage, is a two room suite with a private patio, old iron stove, and a canopy bed. Jeannine's childhood toys are displayed in a loft over the living room, and oval picture frames preserve old photos of her great-grandparents. The Carriage House is the only guest room with a TV, and it also has its own refrigerator. Other guests are welcome to beverages from the refrigerator in the upstairs hallway in the main house.

If you like vintage automobiles, ask Vic to show you his

1921 Model-T named Henry. Vic is also an amateur gold prospector, and can demonstrate proper gold panning procedure and fill you in on gold country history.

JAMESTOWN

The National Hotel

P.O. Box 502
Main Street
Jamestown, CA 95327
209-984-3446
800-894-3446 in California
Fax: 209-984-5620

*A historic hotel in
a picturesque
gold-mining town*

Proprietor: Steven Willey. **Accommodations:** 11 rooms (5 with private bath). **Rates:** $65–$80 double; midweek discounts available. **Included:** Expanded Continental breakfast. **Added:** 8% tax. **Payment:** Major credit cards. **Children:** Under age 10 by prior arrangement only. **Pets:** Allowed by prior arrangement. **Smoking:** Allowed in saloon and on balcony.

Fortunately for those who revel in glimpses of the past, progress has bypassed Jamestown. Because it looks much as it did in the 1870s, the well-preserved gold-mining town has been used as a background for such movies as *High Noon* and *Butch Cassidy and the Sundance Kid,* and for the television series *Little House on the Prairie.*

Some two and a half hours east of San Francisco and just south of Sonora, Jamestown is considered the gateway to the

Mother Lode. Tourists love its antiques shops and the classic brick and gingerbread Emporium. One of the most historically significant buildings in Jamestown is the National Hotel, which has been open continuously since 1859. Today, as in the past, it offers comfortable accommodations, good food, and a convivial atmosphere.

If you've caught gold fever and hanker for a real nugget, you may find one in August during Gold Nugget Days. Clues, sold for one dollar each, lead modern argonauts to nuggets hidden around town.

Many a bag of gold dust has changed hands over the redwood bar in the saloon, where guests register. It's a casual, friendly spot, with a bartender who serves concoctions with such labels as Gold Rush Margarita and Miner's Punch as well as more common drinks. The guest rooms, up carpeted stairs, are furnished in country antiques, with handmade patchwork quilts and lace curtains. "They're simple, because that's the way they were in the 1800s in the gold country," says the congenial innkeeper.

Steve Willey and his brother have owned the hotel since 1974 and have been instrumental in helping Jamestown turn from slow decay to a revitalized community. They were careful in restoring the National to keep it authentic except for the plumbing. Now all the rooms contain wash basins, and five have spotlessly clean private baths. The others share two baths down the hall.

The doors to rooms that are not occupied are open, so you can peek in and select your choice. A typical example has a brass bed with a handmade quilt, lace curtains, pegs to hold hanging items, and fresh flowers. Some rooms overlook the courtyard and a century-old grape arbor covered with Virginia Creeper vines.

In the downstairs dining room, an expanded Continental breakfast is set out for guests: freshly sliced fruits, coffee, assorted juices, hard-boiled eggs, teas, cereals, fresh sourdough French bread, and homemade muffins. Victorian relics— white kid boots, a doll, long gowns—are on display here. The restaurant's meals are excellent, with a different special daily and more than eighty wines from regional wineries available. Champagne brunch, lunch, and dinner are served. In the summer, you can eat outside under the vine-shaded grape arbor.

Television does not fit the hotel's motif (though it will be provided upon request). Jigsaw puzzles, chess, checkers, and bragging at the bar are activities more in tune with the times. Jamestown also offers other forms of entertainment. You can shop for antiques, see stagecoach robberies enacted, pan for gold, ride a steam train, and in June, attend the widely acclaimed Dixieland Jazz Festival.

KIRKWOOD

Caples Lake Resort

P.O. Box 88
Kirkwood, CA 95646
209-258-8888

A lodge and cabins at the edge of a lake

Proprietors: John Voss and sons JT, Bob, Joe and Mike. **Accommodations:** 7 lodge rooms (with shared baths), 7 cabins. **Rates:** $30–$95 single or double in lodge, $65–$195 1–6 people in cabins. **Included:** Tax. **Minimum stay:** 2–5 nights in cabins depending upon season and 2–3 nights in lodge (policy is flexible). **Payment:** MasterCard, Visa. **Children:** Welcome. **Pets:** Not allowed. **Smoking:** Not allowed.

On the shore of a small, peaceful lake thirty miles south of Lake Tahoe, this rustic resort offers basic accommodations, good food, and friendly hospitality in the High Sierra. Caples Lake is just west of Carson Pass, at a 7,800-foot elevation against a rugged range of mountains that soar to 10,000 feet.

The lodge doesn't look like much from the road — a simple building behind a parking lot. The most modern thing about it is the phone booth on the broad, uneven front deck. But inside, you'll find an admirable restaurant and guest rooms with new, queen-size beds. The windows overlook the one-square-mile lake, with forested slopes and snow-tipped peaks rising behind it.

Caples Lake Resort was built in the late 1940s and bought by the Voss family in 1982. The Vosses have been gradually remodeling since then. In the small, rough-hewn dining room, fresh flowers stand on tables made of log rounds. Classical music plays while diners feast on fresh seafood and pastas, steaks, and chicken. Labels of empty wine bottles lining the window sills indicate the range of wines former guests have enjoyed. Top off your dinner with homemade cheesecake, and take in the views of the lake and mountains.

> **Hiking in the High Sierra is an incomparable wilderness experience. Trails wind through canyons and meadows, around towering peaks, and across cold rushing streams. If you follow the clearly marked Emigrant Trail, you will walk in the footsteps of early pioneers.**

Also on the main floor of the lodge is a lounge where, in the winter, guests like to warm their toes by a crackling blaze in the stone fireplace. The guest rooms upstairs are plain and small, but adequate. As this is a wilderness lodge catering to outdoorspeople, do not expect luxury. Room R5 is a good choice for picturesque views. All the lodge rooms share two bathrooms with showers.

Weathered cabins with pitched roofs stand on granite slopes a few yards from the lodge. They all have housekeeping kitchens, bedding, wall heaters, and barbecues. Number 2 is the largest and has a private deck under the trees. Number 5 features paneled walls, an old-fashioned kitchen with a gas stove, and a fine lake view. Number 3 has a sheltered wooden porch, knotty pine wainscoting, and a corner nook in the kitchen.

All the lodgings are clean and well maintained, if a bit worn at the edges, as you'd expect in the mountains where harsh winters can take their toll on buildings both inside and out. Rates vary according to the season, the length of stay, and the number of people in a room.

Behind the lodge is a sauna at water's edge and a small marina and launch facility. Here you may rent motorboats and canoes. You can fish in the stocked lake and in other small lakes and snow-fed streams in the back country, within hiking distance.

Horseback riding is offered by a nearby riding stable. Pack trips can be arranged for treks into the back country. Grover State Park hot springs are twenty-eight miles away, and white-water rafting is available on the Carson River. In winter, at the nearby Kirkwood ski area, you can glide over seventy-five kilometers of groomed cross-country tracks, through open bowls and pine forests. For downhill skiers there are eleven lifts and more than fifty-five runs, starting at a base of 7,800 feet. The mountains of the Sierra Nevada rise above Kirkwood to Thimble Peak's height of 9,876 feet.

MAMMOTH LAKES

Alpers' Owens River Ranch

Route 1, Box 232
Mammoth Lakes, CA 93546
619-648-7334 (summer)
619-873-3466 (winter)

A rustic,
historic ranch
in the Sierras

Innkeeper: Alice Alpers. **Accommodations:** 9 cottages (all with private bath). **Rates:** $40 per person; under age 14 half-price. **Minimum stay:** 2 nights. **Payment:** No credit cards. **Children:** Under age 5 free. **Pets:** Not allowed. **Smoking:** Allowed. **Open:** Late April through October.

The spring-fed waters of the upper Owens River, in the eastern Sierra Nevada range near Mammoth Lakes, create an ideal spawning ground for trout. Along a two-mile stretch of the river, the Alpers family offers an opportunity to fly-fish for the rainbows and German browns. There's also a trout pond for fishing in float tubes.

Their ranch has been in the family since 1905, when Alice Alpers' father-in-law, Fred Alpers, bought the property from the original homesteader. The original cabin, dating from the 1860s, still stands.

The riverside ranch occupies 225 acres of lush, irrigated meadowland, in one of the largest Jeffrey Pine forests in North America. It was used as a cattle ranch until 1920, when guest accommodations were added. Alice first visited the area in that year, and has lived on the ranch since 1935. Ask her for a story, and she'll share her prodigious knowledge of local history. You're likely to find her in the picturesque log lodge.

The pine log cabins are rustic but comfortable. Electricity, generated by a water wheel, is used only for electric lights. There is no television, and you do your own cooking. Each cabin has a wood-burning stove, a deck, and a screened porch. Three cabins are suitable for two or three people, five will accommodate four to six, and one is large enough for a bigger group. It has a good-size kitchen and two baths. Clubs and groups are welcome at the ranch.

When you want a break from fishing, you can hike the trails that offer breathtaking views of the Sierra Nevada and White Mountain ranges, tour the fish hatchery, go on a photography expedition, or simply relax in the peace and quiet. If you tire of cooking meals, Mammoth Lakes, a resort town twelve miles away, has several good restaurants.

Word of mouth brings guests to Alpers' Owens River Ranch, and it has become a tradition for many families to return year after year. There's a five acre lake stocked with trophy trout, and children enjoy the "Huck Finn" angling in Alpers' Creek, which is stocked with trout from the ranch's hatchery. There are also swings and a tetherball to keep the youngsters happy.

When they're old enough, they join the adults in the resort's main attraction: fly-fishing. Beyond the two-fish limit, all fishing is catch-and-release. A fishing guide service is available.

Edelweiss Lodge

P.O. Box 658
Mammoth Lakes, CA 93546
619-934-2445
Fax: 619-924-2172

> *A chalet-style inn with a quiet atmosphere*

Innkeepers: Duffy and Diane Wright. **Accommodations:** 9 units (all with private bath). **Rates:** $95–$140 in winter, $65–$105 in summer (2 to 6 people), $10 additional person. **Added:** 10% tax. **Minimum stay:** 2 nights. **Payment:** Major credit cards. **Children:** Under age 5 free. **Pets:** Not allowed. **Smoking:** Non-smoking rooms available.

Mammoth Lakes, on the slopes of Mammoth Mountain in the High Sierras, is a resort town that draws vacationers all year. In summer its environs offer great hiking, mountain biking, and fishing. But ski season, from November to July (!), is really special. And Edelweiss is one of the places where skiers like to stay.

Forest green shutters with heart cut-outs and carved porch railings decorate the alpine chalets, which cover three-quarters of an acre south of town. The personable owners, who came from the Bay Area and took over the lodge in 1987, offer clean, roomy, one- and two-bedroom accommodations with equipped kitchens. A duplex unit has honey-colored walls of knotty pine, a vaulted ceiling with hand-hewn beams, and a spiral staircase leading up to the liv-

> **After a day of skiing in crystal air, under an intense blue sky, you can luxuriate in the cedar and redwood whirlpool spa at Edelweiss. Sign up to reserve a time, and you'll have it all to yourself.**

ing room and bedroom. There's a full bath upstairs, and a half bath downstairs. Café curtains hang at the kitchen window, and there are a TV sets (with HBO) on both levels. Bedroom suites have oak interiors, a living room with an adjoining eat-in kitchen, and a king- or queen-size bed in the bedroom. A few rooms have stone fireplaces, others feature woodstoves. Area artists painted the landscapes on the walls.

At Edelweiss, you can go cross-country skiing from your door. For downhill skiers, a short drive or shuttle bus ride takes you to Mammoth's thirty-nine chairlifts and groomed slopes of powdery snow.

The lodge offers quiet relaxation under the pine trees. It's not the place to stay if you're looking for the lights, music, and action some mountain resorts provide. Duffy Wright says, "What I like best about running this place is seeing guests who arrive tired and tense leave a few days later relaxed and happy. Some people never leave their cabin. They just sit and read or look out the window and rest."

Mammoth Mountain Inn

P.O. Box 353
Mammoth Lakes, CA 93546
619-934-2581
800-228-4947
Fax: 619-934-0700

*A mountainside
resort for
all seasons*

General manager: Tom Smith. **Accommodations:** 213 rooms. **Rates:** $85–$175, 2–13 people in summer, $80–$330 winter weekdays, $99–$400 winter weekends and holidays. **Added:** 10% tax. **Payment:** Major credit cards. **Children:** age 13 and under free in room with parents. **Pets:** Not allowed. **Smoking:** Nonsmoking rooms available upon request.

Mammoth Mountain, in the eastern High Sierra south of Yosemite National Park, is one of the major ski areas in the country, drawing thousands yearly to its 3,500 acres of skiable terrain. On its broad slope, a short drive from the resort village of Mammoth Lakes, stands Mammoth Mountain Inn, the only full-service hotel in the eastern Sierra.

The redwood inn's exterior, with its steeply pitched roof and balconies with flags snapping in the wind, resembles a large mountain chalet. Inside, a stone fireplace rises to the loft lounge, where another fireplace offers warmth on winter evenings. Guests gather in the paneled lounge after a day of skiing Mammoth's powdery runs, or out on the sundeck facing the mountain slopes.

Guest rooms in the main lodge have either two queen-size beds or a queen and a twin, and portable cribs are available. The furnishings are comfortable and modern, with television, phones, plenty of closet space, and a balcony filled with flowers in summer. Some view the 11,053-foot mountain; others, the parking lot.

In the East/West annex are rooms and suites ranging from a studio that accommodates two to a two-bedroom unit with a loft that sleeps thirteen. Once privately owned, the units are now all operated by the inn. Several have kitchenettes, dining tables, and sitting areas. Ski storage is provided. Preferred for mountain views are corner rooms (515, 516, 617, or 717) and the executive suite, Room 600. The best buy is a studio with a kitchenette. The inn has covered parking available on a first-come first-served basis, laundry facilities, and three whirlpool spas.

> **Drive up to Minaret Vista to see sensational views of the 13,000-foot Ritter Range and the Ansel Adams Wilderness. Devil's Postpile National Monument, east of Mammoth, is well worth a visit. This 60-foot wall of symmetrical basalt columns is a geological wonder.**

The Mountainside Grill is the main restaurant. Recommended are the homemade soups, the teriyaki chicken, and the chef's special prawn dish — broiled jumbo shrimp wrapped in bacon and topped with a jalapeño hollandaise sauce. There's nothing rustic in this mountain retreat. You may sip a good California wine while listening to Chopin in the background. To really get into the Alpine spirit, try the Yodler Restaurant and Bar in an authentic Swiss chalet brought over from Switzerland in 1959. Fittingly, the restaurant serves European dishes such as wiener schnitzel and bockwurst in beer with sauerkraut, along with more traditional steak, seafood, and pasta.

You may rent skis and buy lift tickets at the ski area just across the road from the inn or at the front desk. The slopes are just out the door. Mammoth has 31 lifts, 150 trails, and 3,100 vertical drop. (Skis can be checked at the bell-hop stand during ski season, and bikes can be checked during the summer months.) You can also cross-country ski, go dog-sledding, snowmobiling, or bobsledding.

Skiers flock to Mammoth Lakes in winter, but the area is a fine summer destination as well. It has cool mountain air, dozens of clear alpine lakes, miles of backcountry trails, and good fishing. To encourage summer visitors, Mammoth Mountain Inn offers mountain biking, fly-fishing, horseback riding, kayaking, golf, and hiking excursions, among others. In addition, the inn offers scenic gondola rides to the summit, outdoor barbecues, a play area for children, and child care. Mammoth Lakes is only thirty-five miles south of the Tioga Pass entrance to Yosemite National Park, so Yosemite tours are also popular when weather permits.

Tamarack Lodge Resort

P.O. Box 69
Mammoth Lakes, CA 93546
619-934-2442
800-237-6879 in southern
  California
Fax: 619-934-2281

*A lakeside
wilderness resort
in the High Sierra*

Proprietors: Carol and David Watson. **Accommodations:** 10 rooms (5 with private bath) and 1 suite, 25 cabins. **Rates:** $70–$160 in rooms, $80–$380 for 1–11 persons in cabins; rates vary according to number of people and season. **Minimum stay:** 2 nights on weekends, 3 to 5 nights summer and holidays. **Payment:** Major credit cards. **Children:** Infants free. **Pets:** Not allowed. **Smoking:** Not allowed indoors.

You know you're in wild country when the sign on your cottage wall reads Bears Dwell Here. Do Not Leave Food on Your Porch or Near Windows. On the other hand, the restaurant a few steps from your door serves beef Wellington, rack of lamb, eggplant parmigiana, and the latest in colorful pasta dishes.

Tamarack Lodge is located on the shore of the Twin Lakes, the last and lowest of the Mammoth Lakes group. The lakes lie in an immense glacial basin scooped out of the eastern High Sierra.

Here in the woods, just three miles from the resort town of

Mammoth Lakes, the lodge was built in 1924 by the Foy family of Los Angeles. (Later the family gained fame through the Bob Hope movie *The Seven Little Foys*.) It has had several owners since then, and expanded into a full cross-country ski resort by the time the Watsons took over in 1986. They retained the rustic quality but have made improvements over time.

Entering the lodge, you find a knotty pine parlor where kerosene lamps stand on the mantel and skis crisscross above a stone fireplace. Sleds and snowshoes adorn the walls, a desk and phone for guest use are in one corner, and there are bookshelves stacked with games and paperbacks. A log table holds coffee and snacks, available for purchase. It's a cozy scene in winter, when skiers come in to a hot lunch and mulled wine and cider by the fire.

The lakes teem with native brown trout, brooks, and native and stocked rainbows, offering some of the best fishing in the eastern Sierra. At the lodge they'll give you maps and information on obtaining day packs, rowboats and canoes. They will also pack a lunch to take along on your adventure.

The guest rooms line the pine-paneled hall upstairs, one side viewing the forest and cabins, and the other overlooking the two lakes with mountain peaks in the background. The decor is simple but comfortable and clean. White curtains hang at the windows, and baskets of dried flowers and pastel watercolors add to the homey atmosphere. Some share well-maintained baths; others have private baths. Top of the Lodge is the two-bedroom suite, with great views of the lakes and mountain ridges. It has a living room, a dining area, and a small kitchen.

The housekeeping cabins are clustered around the lodge under pines and aspens on six wooded acres. They all have carpeting, linens, and kitchens, and a few have fireplaces. There is no daily maid service in the cabins, but you can pick up fresh towels at the lodge; weekly cleaning is provided for extended stays.

After a day of skiing or hiking, you may not want to cook. Lakefront Restaurant, at the south end of the lodge, is the only other choice; fortunately, it's excellent. The setting is rustic, but white tablecloths are topped with country floral cloths, and classical music plays in the background. California cuisine and wines are served. Breakfast is also available.

The resort rents ski equipment, offers private and group lessons, and keeps twenty-five miles of cross-country trails groomed. You can ski right from your door. The variety of terrain and beautiful forest and mountain views provide plenty of winter interest.

In summer, boating, hiking, fishing, and mountain biking are the favorite activities. Miles of trails lead to Mammoth Mountain and its pass and crest, Coldwater Canyon, and spectacular Cascade Canyon. A day's hike to the west takes you to Red's Meadow and Devil's Postpile National Monument.

MURPHYS

Dunbar House, 1880

P.O. Box 1375
271 Jones Street
Murphys, CA 95247
209-728-2897
800-225-3764 Ext. 321
Fax: 209-728-1451

*An inviting B&B
in a historic gold
mining town*

Innkeepers: Barbara and Bob Costa. **Accommodations:** 4 rooms (all with private bath). **Rates:** $115–$155. **Included:** Full breakfast. **Added:** 7.25% tax. **Minimum stay:** 2 nights on weekends. **Payment:** MasterCard, Visa. **Children:** Under age 10 not appropriate. **Pets:** Not allowed. **Smoking:** Not allowed

Murphys is a quiet little town now, drowsing in the Sierra sun, but in 1850 it bustled with action as prospectors and miners rushed in, lured by gold. Over a ten-year period, Wells Fargo shipped more than $15 million in gold dust from the Murphys office. Meanwhile, settlers looking for more than quick riches moved in.

In 1880, Willis Dunbar built an Italianate home for his bride, Ellen Roberts of Douglas Flat. A citizen of substance, he was the superintendent of the local water company, a member of the state assembly, and the head of a ranch and a lumber company. Willis and Ellen raised five sons in their big country home.

A century later, the Dunbar home became Calaveras County's first bed-and-breakfast, and in 1987 Barbara and Bob Costa took it over. They welcome guests looking for pleasant, homey accommodations with character and history. This is the sort of place where you sit in wicker chairs on the porch and sip lemonade on summer afternoons, while bees hum in the old-fashioned flower garden.

The roomy parlor is decorated in English chintz. Lace and flowers and turn-of-the-century photographs fill the house, but it's not overly fussy and the furnishings aren't all antiques. "This is our home," says Barbara. "We enjoy sharing it and treat guests as new friends."

Crowds come to Murphys and the surrounding area in fall to see the brilliant foliage against dark green pine trees. Murphys boasts six wineries, tennis courts, a community swimming pool, and three nearby golf courses. It's a short drive from the village to Mercer Caverns, Moaning Caves, and Calaveras Big Trees State Park, where ancient sequoias grow.

The hospitable innkeeper likes to serve breakfast by candlelight in the dining room or outside at white wrought-iron tables. You can also have breakfast in your room. Some of Barbara's dishes are crab and cheese delight, peach or cherry turnovers, fresh fruit with Grand Marnier sauce, and a sweet fruit spritzer. She provides appetizers in the afternoon and homemade chocolates in the evening. Each guest receives a complimentary bottle of locally produced wine.

All the guest rooms have woodstoves, refrigerators, and TV with VCR. In the Sequoia Room, on the ground floor, you can watch the birds bathe while you do the same; the clawfoot tub, screened from the bed, stands by a window overlooking the back lawn and birdbath. The bed has a lushly flowered comforter and ruffled pillows; bouquets of dried flowers hang on the wall above. By the door, a pair of high laced boots look as if they've just been left by their owner. Space for hanging clothes is limited. A basket of lemon drops, a painted globe lamp, delicate doilies, and windows overlooking the wrap-around porch and white picket fence are touches that give the inn distinction and charm.

The Cedar Room, off the dining area, is a suite with a sitting area, a two-person Jacuzzi, and a sunroom overlooking the back lawn and flowers. Champagne is served to guests who stay in the suite. Ponderosa, at the front of the house, is light and sunny in yellow. Sugar Pine faces the side yard. In addition to a clawfoot tub painted with flowers, it has a separate shower and sizable dressing area.

The Costas' love of gardening shows in their landscaped half-acre. Lilac and crape myrtle bloom in the front yard, elm trees line the fence, and baskets of blooms provide color on the veranda.

NEVADA CITY

Grandmere's Bed & Breakfast Inn

449 Broad Street
Nevada City, CA 95959
916-265-4660

A stylish B&B in a restored historic town

Innkeepers: Geri and Douglas Boka. **Accommodations:** 7 rooms (all with private baths). **Rates:** $100–$160 single or double, $20 additional person. **Included:** Full breakfast. **Added:** 10% tax. **Payment:** MasterCard, Visa. **Children:** Additional $20. **Pets:** Not allowed. **Smoking:** Not allowed.

It was in Nevada City, in 1859, that a bit of blue clay brought in to the assayer's office set off the silver mining rush to the Comstock Lode. Ott's Assay Office still stands, along with other historic structures in a town that carefully preserves its past.

One of them is the A. A. Sargent residence, built in 1856 by the owner of the first newspaper in Nevada County. Sargent was also a miner, lawyer, and United States senator. His wife, Ellen Clark, was an influential suffragist. In 1985, the Sargent home became Grandmere's.

Behind a black wrought-iron fence, the white house with dark trim has an open veranda with inviting wicker chairs. The interior is equally welcoming, with a clean and stylishly simple decor.

The guest rooms all have queen-size beds and pine chests painted with flower designs by the home's former owner. The

Master Suite boasts a private sun porch with a sofa bed overlooking the back garden. Danny's Room has a country atmosphere, with a bed of peeled pole pine, louvered shutters, and wicker chairs.

Maggie's Room contains a four-poster bed with a patchwork quilt. The roomy bath has a shower stall, and there's plenty of space in the armoire for hanging clothes. Mama & Papa's Room is in the corner, where the balcony wraps around the house. Spacious and dignified, it has a dark four-poster with puffy pillows on a floral quilt, a sofa bed, wingback chairs, and a little writing table in an alcove.

If you're traveling with a child, your best choice is Gertie's Room, which has a private garden entrance. Once the billiards room, it's now a light, bright suite with white wicker furnishings. The suite accommodates four and has a small kitchen with a sink, refrigerator, and microwave oven. All other rooms have air conditioning, but this one stays naturally cool.

> **Nevada City offers a cleaned-up view of a past era. When a freeway sliced the town in two, the citizens decided to turn their backs on it and bring history to life on either side. No trucks, no neon, no overhead wiring — nothing intrudes on the quaint mood. Gaslights cast an old-fashioned glow on twisting streets of cobblestone, and almost every shopfront has a romantic story.**

Outside the door, fragrant wisteria climbs above the umbrella tables on the patio. Early in the mornings, guests like to choose a mug in the dining room, help themselves to coffee, and wander out to the patio and garden. Here they stroll among the lilacs, redwoods, and spruce trees, along daisy-edged paths until breakfast is ready. Fruit, juice, spinach quiche, potatoes with cheese, croissants, and bread pudding are a few of Grandmere's morning options. Coffee and tea are available during the day, and the cookie jar is always full.

Nevada City has several excellent restaurants. The Creek-side offers patio dining along Deer Creek.

Red Castle Inn

109 Prospect Street
Nevada City, CA 95959
916-265-5135

An elaborate hillside mansion overlooking a gold-country town

Innkeepers: Mary Louise and Conley Weaver. **Accommodations:** 7 rooms (all with private bath). **Rates:** $105–$140 double, $5 discount for single occupancy, $20 additional person. **Included:** Full breakfast. **Added:** 10% tax. **Payment:** MasterCard, Visa. **Children:** Young children not appropriate; additional charge for rollaway. **Pets:** Not allowed. **Smoking:** Not allowed indoors.

This mansion was built in 1860 for Judge John Williams and his wife, Abigail, and eleven children — four of their own and the rest taken in as orphans. Some say their nanny, a woman in gray, can still be glimpsed occasionally in the former children's quarters.

Even without a ghost, the Red Castle is full of reminders of the past. It became an inn in 1963, after a major restoration effort. The current owners continue to put careful attention into creating a world far from the late 20th century. Mary Louise has done extensive research and insists on authenticity in the period furnishings. "This is a mixture of 'what might have been' and whimsy," she says.

The Weavers collect Renaissance Revival furniture. In the formal parlor, an Oriental carpet covers the floor and a prism chandelier flickers light on gold walls. A 19th-century burl walnut Jelliff setee, dark wicker arm chairs, a pump organ with candle sconces, and a vase of peacock feathers set the Victorian tone. Afternoon tea is served, with spiced tea, cakes, pies, and pastries, and sometimes hot cider or lemonade.

Breakfast is a buffet in the main foyer. The five-course meal artfully prepared by a pastry chef, changes daily. You may help yourself to orange juice or berry flips, homemade breads, poached pears with crème Anglaise, quiche, granola, and coffee or tea. You can take your tray to the parlor, your own room, out to the garden, or to the veranda set with white iron tables for two. Each guest room has its own character. Forest View, a honeymoon favorite, is the only room on the lower floor, one flight down from the entrance. It has a small chandelier, complete with dimmer switch inside the lacy folds of the bed's canopy, and a private entrance under old and gnarled grapevines. It also has private access to the balcony and garden.

> This red brick Gothic Revival mansion, dripping with gingerbread, has been a landmark in Nevada City for more than a century. Set high against Prospect Hill, it overlooks the little town that is a living museum of the gold rush era.

The Rose Room has a pineapple four-poster, a brass and custard glass chandelier above the bed, red velvet curtains, and tall French doors opening out to the wraparound porch. It's a pretty room; however the bathroom is small. The Garden Room, also on the main level, is big and bright and has a canopy bed and a sitting area. One of its striking features is an antique hall tree of carved walnut.

It's a steep climb to the upstairs rooms, but some guests prefer these for their charm and decor. There are two suites on the third floor, and the entire fourth floor, formerly the judge's study, is now a two-bedroom suite with a sitting room. In this private enclave, nooks under the eaves have quaint arched windows at knee level, and the private veranda has a treetop view of the town.

Gravel paths wind down the hill, under a grove of trees, from the house to the road below. From there it's a few yards to the freeway overpass and the main historic part of town. Here you'll find quaint shops, fine restaurants, and gold rush memorabilia in a preserved remnant of the Old West.

OLYMPIC VALLEY

Resort at Squaw Creek

P.O. Box 3333
400 Squaw Creek Road
Olympic Valley, CA 96146
916-583-6300
800-327-3353
Fax: 916-581-5407

An all-purpose resort in a dramatic mountain setting

General manager: John Kirk. **Accommodations:** 405 rooms and suites. **Rates:** $165–$855 single or double, $25 additional person, rates vary seasonally. **Added:** 8% tax. **Payment:** Major credit cards. **Children:** Under age 16 free in room with parents. **Pets:** Not allowed. **Smoking:** Nonsmoking rooms available.

In late 1990, this $100 million resort opened on 626 acres near Lake Tahoe. Year-round outdoor recreation is the main draw of the complex, which has a dramatic setting at the base of Squaw Valley's surrounding peaks.

In winter, skiers come for some of the nation's most challenging slopes. A triple lift links the resort with the Squaw Valley network of 33 lifts, covering 4,000 acres of ski slopes. Groomed trails on the meadows and hillsides attract the cross-country skier. There's an ice skating pavilion, and you can take bell-jingling sleigh rides over the snow.

Golfers and tennis players take over in the summer. Squaw Creek has an 18-hole championship golf course designed by Robert Trent Jones, Jr. Its scenic mountainous terrain includes wetlands, ponds, and a meandering creek. There are also putting greens, a practice range, and a pro shop.

Seven miles of walking and biking paths surround the golf course, while five miles of horseback riding trails continue through the meadows and into the hills. The all-purpose resort has three swimming pools and spas in an aquatic center with a waterfall and sandy beach, and a fitness center featuring weight training equipment, an aerobics studio, massage rooms, and beauty salon. In the winter there's a locker room for storing skis, in the summer Chuckwagon dinners are held on the Sun Plaza Deck.

The casual Cascades restaurant, serving regional American

foods and elaborate buffets, showcases a stone hearth as an open cooking area. You can eat on the balcony here, overlooking Squaw Peak. Ristorante Montagna specializes in California Italian cuisine, rotisserie cooking, fresh baked breads. Bullwackers Pub has steakhouse food, pool tables, and tabletop shuffleboard. Glissandi offers French cuisine from a seasonal menu in an elegant setting where diners linger over their meals. Midweek wine-tasting dinners are especially popular. For gigantic deli sandwiches and fresh pastries, casual Sweet Potatoes in the gift shop arcade, is the place to go.

> Although it's surrounded by forest and mountains, the atmosphere here is more suburban country club than wilderness. In addition to a nine-story, glass-faced building with guest rooms, there are the main Plaza Building and a promenade of retail shops. The Plaza holds the fitness center, a 36,000 square foot conference center, and three restaurants.

All the guest rooms have views of the valley or the forest. They contain fine-quality contemporary wood furniture and have such amenities as dimmer lights, two TVs (with movies available), polished granite sinks, coffeemakers, robes, wet bars, hair dryers, irons, and ironing boards. Cribs are available upon request, and express video checkout is another convenience. Some suites have gas fireplaces and large bay windows that draw the mountain views right into the room. Two-story penthouses have 1½ baths and a kitchen.

The resort is popular with business groups for its 33,000 square feet of meeting space and up-to-date audiovisual equipment.

Squaw Valley Lodge

P.O. Box 2364
Olympic Valley, CA 96146
916-583-5500
800-922-9970
Fax: 916-583-0326

> *A contemporary hotel in a skier's paradise*

General manager: Art Takaki. **Accommodations:** 154 rooms. **Rates:** $100–$290 (rates vary by season and number of people). **Added:** 8% tax. **Minimum stay:** 2 nights on weekends in ski season. **Payment:** Major credit cards. **Children:** Free in room with parents. **Pets:** Not allowed. **Smoking:** Nonsmoking rooms available.

In 1960, the eighth Winter Olympics was held in Squaw Valley, a wide bowl at the foot of Squaw Peak west of Lake Tahoe. Today you can step out the door of the lodge and ski the expert runs where Olympians raced. The thirty-three lifts lead to slopes with challenges for every level of skill.

Six mountain peaks, all overlooking Lake Tahoe, hold 4,000 acres of slopes. The highest is Squaw Peak, at 8,900 feet. The lodge itself is at an elevation of 6,200 feet.

Light gray with burgundy trim, the modern lodge is surrounded by pine trees and, in summer, lawns and flowers. The rooms and condominiums overlook a protected terrace and freeform outdoor swimming pool and whirlpool tub. Just off the terra cotta tile terrace is the fitness center, with a well-equipped weight room and three tiled whirlpools. Potted palms and windows that view the snowy peaks make this one of the lodge's most attractive features.

The open lobby area has a touch of the Southwest in its decor. Desert colors, rough rocks as lamp bases, leather couches, framed weavings and Indian paintings are strikingly offset by brightly colored banners.

The rooms are in three buildings connected by covered walkways — an important feature in this snowy terrain. Units are individually owned, but those in Buildings A and B are furnished in Scandinavian style, while those in C have a southwestern decor. They all have pegs, with copper troughs below, for hanging wet clothing. A typical room has a waist-high partition dividing the bed from the sitting area, generous cupboard and drawer space, and a compact kitchenette with a microwave oven, stove, dishwasher, and refrigerator. Skis may be kept in your room or stored near the rental shop. You can have minor tune-ups done at the shop as well.

The Squaw Valley resort area has the facilities you would expect in a major resort. There are restaurants and delis and malls with video stores, a beer garden, a doctor's office, and a ski school.

> **The Squaw Valley beginner's area may be unrivaled in the world because of its location — on top of the mountain instead of the bottom. It's accessible by cable car or gondola, so you don't have to ski down. If you're more adventurous and prefer a wilderness experience on undeveloped slopes, you'll find vast areas have been left untouched.**

More than 150 instructors staff the ski school, offering a wide variety of programs for all ages and abilities and several specialty clinics. Daycare for children is available. Squaw Valley makes an unusual guarantee: Register (for a nominal fee) as a beginner, intermediate, or expert, and if the wait for lifts at your skill level is longer than ten minutes, you receive a full refund and ski free the rest of the day. Another appealing feature is the first-timer's offer. Beginners are given free lift tickets, ski lessons, and equipment rentals for one day.

When the snow melts and wildflowers spring up in the meadows, the valley offers summer pleasures, such as hiking, bicycling, horseback riding, and fishing in mountain streams. You can swim and play tennis at the lodge.

Between mid-June and October, you can take the cable car to an altitude of 8,200 feet for a stunning panorama of the High Sierra and have lunch or Sunday brunch at Alexander's Bar & Grill on the mountaintop. Also at the top are a swimming lagoon and spa, mountain bike rentals, and year-round ice skating.

SACRAMENTO

Abigail's

2120 G Street
Sacramento, CA 95816
916-441-5007
800-858-1568
Fax: 916-441-0621

*A city B&B with
homey comforts*

Innkeeper: Susanne Ventura. **Accommodations:** 5 rooms (all with private bath). **Rates:** $100–$165 single or double, $35 additional person. **Included:** Full breakfast. **Added:** 12% tax. Minimum stay: 2 nights on some holidays. **Payment:** Major credit cards. **Children:** By arrangement; additional $35. **Pets:** Not allowed. **Smoking:** Not allowed indoors.

Homey hospitality is the special attraction of this Colonial Revival mansion near downtown Sacramento. Built in 1912, the big white house with teal trim fronted by lush ferns, has large rooms, and is nicely furnished with antiques, but it's Susanne Ventura's friendly personal service that makes the inn truly distinctive.

Baskets of nuts and apples are set out for snacking in the living room, and cookies and a thermos of hot water with tins of cocoa and tea are on the antique English sideboard upstairs. Robes hang in the armoires. Every room has a telephone and each bathroom contains a cabinet filled with aspirin, shaving equipment, toothpaste, Tums, and other

One of Susanne's thoughtful touches is the bulletin board near the front door, where she posts notices of art gallery shows and other events in Sacramento. She and her husband, Ken, will recommend restaurants and make reservations for you. One highly recommended spot is Biba's, where classic northern Italian food is served in a cheerful urban atmosphere.

necessities. Susanne seems to have thought of everything a pampered bed-and-breakfast guest could want, including cats

(Sabrina and Abigail) to accompany you up and down stairs.

Four of the guest rooms are on the second floor, and one is just off the landing. The morning sun floods through eleven windows in the Solarium Room, which has its own balcony and a four-poster canopy bed. Because its bathroom is across the hall, it is the least expensive. Anne's Room, at the front of the house, has a carved four-poster bed, a writing desk, couch, and a two-door, mirrored armoire. In Margaret's Room the metal canopy bed is draped with silk ivy, or other floral adornment depending upon the season. Topped with a feather bed and white down comforter the bed is inviting enough, but there's also a fainting couch perfect for curling up with a book.

The Uncle Albert Room is the most masculine of the rooms. It looks as if it belongs to someone's kindly uncle, with books piled on the armoire, a wingback chair, and a sec-retary desk. The guest book in this room is full of interesting comments, most of them directed to "Uncle Albert" — a mysterious presence that some guests claim to have sensed while staying in the room. Aunt Rose, the companion room, is more feminine in creams, greens, and pinks. It has floral pillows, a queen size brass bed, and a marble tiled bath with a whirlpool tub.

In the dining room, Susanne serves a two-course breakfast that includes entrées such as French toast stuffed with rasp-berry or blackberry jam, pancakes, sun-dried tomato and pep-per quiche, zucchini-walnut waffles, and fruit cobbler. She'll bring a Continental breakfast to your room if you prefer, but she encourages guests to get acquainted over the long table. Outside, there's a fenced patio and hot tub.

Amber House Bed & Breakfast Inn

1315 22nd Street
Sacramento, CA 95816
916-444-8085
800-755-6526
Fax: 916-552-6529

> *A stately home
> in a central
> location*

Innkeepers: Mike and Jane Richardson. **Accommodations:** 9 rooms in 2 houses (all with private bath). **Rates:** $85–$139 single, $99–$199 double. **Included:** Full breakfast. **Added:** 12% tax. **Payment:** Major credit cards. **Children:** Well-behaved children welcome. **Pets:** Not allowed. **Smoking:** Not allowed.

Only eight blocks from the state capitol and the Convention Center, Amber House is popular with business travelers, offering both easy access to the city and a relaxing retreat. It's in a residential neighborhood where elm trees line the streets, shading turn-of-the-century homes.

The inn is actually two houses, side by side, with very different styles. The main house is a 1905 Craftsman home in rich brown, with the original woodwork intact. It has stained glass windows, antique furnishings, a fireplace in the living room, and a cozy little den with books, games, and puzzles. Guests are welcome to play the banjo that rests in the corner, curl up on the windowseat with a book, peruse restaurant menus, and sip sherry in the evenings.

This house is called the Poet's Refuge, with each room named for a poet and containing examples of the poet's works. Lord Byron, on the first floor, has a queen-size canopy bed and a Jacuzzi for two in the bath. A rose motif dominates the decor in Longfellow which has a luxurious bath in rose colored marble and a skylit Jacuzzi tub. Chaucer, in deep yellow and gold, is the smallest room. Emily Dickinson, with windows on three sides, was once a sun porch, and is a good choice for sun worshippers. Its double bed has a sumptuous ivory comforter with complementing shams, and there's a small seating area off to one corner with wicker chairs. The bath is detached, but robes are provided.

> **If you're eating out, some good choices are Biba's for Italian food; Celestin's, with a Caribbean menu; and Harlow's, serving innovative California cuisine in a lively, art deco atmosphere.**

Next door is Artist's Retreat, a well-restored 1913 white stucco home with a Mediterranean look. The Monet room, with a garden ambience, lies behind beveled glass curtained in pastel fabric. For atmosphere, the stained glass window above its large, square Jacuzzi can be lighted at night. Degas features ballet prints, a queen-size canopy bed draped in lace, and a double-size Jacuzzi tub. Renoir, a semi-suite in greens and fuchsias, also has a Jacuzzi for two.

As lovely as the other rooms are, Van Gogh has to be the favorite. The bedroom is pleasant, with yellow walls, chintz fabrics, and wicker furniture, but it's the bath that makes the room extra special. The solarium bath, with an exterior wall of glass and a glass ceiling overhead, is sun-filled and almost large enough to live in on its own. There's a wicker chaise and a heart-shaped tub for two. Even on a rainy day, it's a cheerful room, and hard to leave.

The innkeepers understand that visitors' hours vary — business travelers are early risers, while vacationers like to sleep in — so breakfast is served at the hour you request it, any time from 7 A.M. to checkout, and can be brought to your room if you'd like. That's an example of the determination to meet guests' needs. "We'll accommodate in any way we can to make our guest's experience perfect," say the innkeepers. That includes supplying silver and china if you wish to have dinner delivered to your room by a restaurant. Or you can dine on the veranda or in the dining room if you prefer.

Other amenities and services the inn provides one might expect to only find at a first-rate hotel. There's nightly turn-down service, televisions (some have VCRs — all have cable) are hidden in armoires, rooms have telephones with voice mail (some rooms even have an extra phone in the bath), clock radios with cassette players, and baths have English herbal toiletries and robes. All are just further evidence of the quality of this professionally run inn.

Delta King Hotel

1000 Front Street
Sacramento, CA 95814
916-444-5464
800-825-5464
Fax: 916-444-5314

An old-fashioned stern-wheeler on the Sacramento River

General manager: Charlie Coyne. **Accommodations:** 44 staterooms and suites. **Rates:** staterooms $89–$139 single or double, suites $400. **Included:** Expanded Continental breakfast. **Added:** 12% tax. **Payment:** Major credit cards. **Children:** Welcome. **Pets:** Not allowed. **Smoking:** Allowed

If you yearn to return to the days when river travel reigned supreme, step aboard the historic *Delta King*, an authentic 1926 stern-wheel paddle steamer permanently moored along the waterfront of Old Sacramento.

The five-story, 285-foot-long paddlewheeler was built during the peak of the steam navigation period in the Sacramento Delta. Like its twin, the *Delta Queen* (now on the Mississippi River), the *King* once plied the Sacramento from the capital to San Francisco offering overnight dinner and entertainment cruises that were especially popular during prohibition because drinking and gambling were allowed. During World War II the *King* served as barracks for the troops tending the submarine nets under the Golden Gate Bridge. Following the war the ship sank twice and fell into disrepair until it was finally restored in 1984. Although the riverboat was originally built for a then-staggering sum of $1 million, the meticulous restoration has cost more than $8 million.

Now in its original condition, the *King* gleams with polished brass fittings and the patina of paneling, window trim, doors and benches. A carpeted grand staircase sweeping from the promenade deck to the observation deck is back in place. At the top of the stairs is the mahogany-paneled Delta Lounge, featuring an oyster bar and decorated with stained glass scenes of the Sacramento River of yesteryear. The lower deck lounge, the Paddlewheel Saloon, offers dancing on weekends. The gigantic revolving paddlewheel can be seen through the glass-walled stern.

> Preserved as a 28-acre historic district, Old Sacramento includes the Sacramento History Center, a State Railroad Museum (the largest of its kind), an 1860s railroad station, and shops and restaurants. All are within easy walking distance of the gleaming white *Delta King*.

Even more spacious than the originals, the staterooms are furnished with brass beds and wicker furnishings. Some of the baths have clawfoot tubs and pull-chain toilets. Other features such as air conditioning and tiled showers have been added. The Captain's Quarters is a posh bilevel suite with a queen-size bed, a wet bar, and a wheelhouse loft with an observation deck.

Morning fruit, juice, granola, yogurt, and pastries are served to overnight guests in the Pilothouse Restaurant. It also serves lunch, dinner, and a highly reputed Sunday brunch. The 43,745-square-foot vessel contains a theater showing musical revue and other productions. Weddings can be performed on board, and an outdoor plank landing is next to the boat for receptions. Valet parking is available.

The last of California's original steam paddlewheelers, the *Delta King* has been placed on the National Register of Historic Ships. It is the only lodging in old Sacramento.

Hartley House

700 22nd Street
Sacramento, CA 95816
916-447-7829
800-831-5806
Fax: 916-447-1820

> *A bed-and-breakfast*
> *in a gracious*
> *Victorian home*

Innkeeper: Randy Hartley. **Accommodations:** 5 rooms (all with private bath). **Rates:** $85–$105 single, $99–$155 double. **Included:** Full breakfast. **Added:** 12% tax. **Payment:** Major credit cards. **Children:** Not appropriate. **Pets:** Not allowed. **Smoking:** Not allowed indoors.

This Craftsman-style redwood home is in a residential area but is close to downtown, the capitol, and the Convention Center. Built by the innkeeper's grandparents in 1906 in what was then Sacramento's first subdivision, the house remained in the family until 1995 when a Mrs. Murphy purchased it and ran it as a boarding house. Randy Hartley bought it back from Mrs. Murphy in 1987, and has been operating it as a bed-and-breakfast ever since.

The home's character has been preserved inside and out. The original hitching posts still stand in front of the home, as do the elm trees planted by Randy's grandfather. Inside the hardwood floors, dark woodwork, leaded and stained glass windows, and brass light fixtures converted from gas are also original. Some of the furniture, such as the English oak sideboard in the dining room, belonged to Randy's grandparents, and other antiques and artworks were carefully selected to match the period decor — although modern comforts have been added throughout the inn to suit today's tastes. Downstairs, the large living room has a four-window bay with a window seat and a fireplace. Couches provide comfortable seating for a game of chess or lounging by the fire on a chilly night.

The rooms have English place names. Brighton, once a sunporch, is the least formal and has a light and sunny aspect with twelve windows in three walls.

Dover, the largest room, has an antique curved brass bed, and a marble sink and clawfoot tub in the bath. Canterbury, in pale green, has a mirrored armoire that the innkeeper's grandparents had made in London. The other rooms are Southampton, and Stratford.

> **Hartley House offers a Romance Package. It includes fresh flowers, chocolate truffles, and champagne or sparkling cider — you can keep the vase and wine glasses.**

During the week, most guests are business and professional travelers who appreciate rooms with private baths, telephones, cable TV, clock radios, and air conditioning, as well as fax and copy facilities. For a small daily fee, guests can use the health club down the street, and inn guests receive discounts at a number of area restaurants. Massages are available by appointment.

All guests like the lavish breakfasts. Eggs Benedict, blueberry pancakes, quiche, blintzes, or Belgian waffles are served with fruit, muffins, juice and house blend coffees in the dining room or outside in the pleasant walled courtyard. Cookies are baked daily, and lemonade is always available in the refrigerator.

Radisson Hotel Sacramento

500 Leisure Lane
Sacramento, CA 95815
916-922-2020
800-333-3333
Fax: 916-649-9463

*A comfortable
family hotel
on a lake*

Manager: Richard Williams. **Accommodations:** 314 rooms and suites. **Rates:** $89–$114; suites $189–$400. **Added:** 12% tax. **Payment:** Major credit cards. **Children:** Under age 18 free. **Pets:** Allowed. **Smoking:** Non-smoking rooms available.

Close to the American River, as it skirts the heart of Sacramento, is this pleasant, pink stucco hotel with a red tile roof. Several features make the hotel a good lodging choice in the Sacramento area, especially if you're traveling with children. It centers around a small lake, edged by a lawn and weeping willow trees; paddle boats are available for fun on the water. Bicycles can be rented for riding the comparatively flat roads, there's an outdoor swimming pool, and child care can be arranged.

The hotel has a well-designed, air-conditioned fitness room (open to adults only) and there's a par station fitness course around the sizable parking lots.

The three-tiered Palm

If you're in Sacramento in late August or early September, don't miss a visit to the State Fair, a popular annual event for more than 100 years. It has carnival rides, equestrian shows, a kids' park, horseracing, entertainment, and hundreds of exhibits.

Court Restaurant, overlooking the lake, serves three meals a day and a Sunday brunch. Next to it is the Lakeside lounge for cocktails, dancing, and live music. Java City has gourmet coffees and pastries, and Crocodiles is the hotel's nightspot open seven nights a week. At one end of the lake is a gazebo, a popular place for weddings. In the summer the hotel sponsors outdoor concerts featuring entertainers such as George Benson, Grover Washington, and Kathy Mattea, and groups make use of the Radisson's ample convention facilities year-round.

The guest rooms, all with patios or balconies, are in several two-story buildings. They have similar up-to-date furnishings and comforts, but some are more motel-like and face a parking lot. Preferred rooms are on the second floor by the lake. All rooms have coffeemakers, hair dryers, and makeup mirrors. Soaps and shampoos are provided in dispensers for ecological reasons.

The Sterling Hotel

1300 H Street
Sacramento, CA 95814
916-448-1300
800-365-7660

A small and sophisticated historic hotel

Proprietors: Richard and Sandi Kann. **Accommodations:** 12 rooms. **Rates:** $95–$225 single or double, $15 additional person. **Added:** 12% tax. **Payment:** Major credit cards. **Children:** Welcome. **Pets:** Not allowed. **Smoking:** Not allowed.

The Sterling is a small luxury hotel in central Sacramento. Its amenities and convenient downtown location — near the capitol, convention center, and county courthouse — make it a favorite of business and government travelers, while its elegance and style draw discriminating vacationers.

The three-story, century-old Victorian structure was renovated in 1987, removing all vestiges of the apartment building it had been for fifty years. Now it has a gracious facade with a generous porch entry, a lobby with a marble floor, and a lounge where guests enjoy morning coffee. Oriental simplicity is emphasized by Japanese paintings and Chinese rugs. More ornate is the lobby, mirror-framed in painted birds and flowers with a filigreed brass chandelier hanging from the open loft.

There are no ruffles or fringes in this contemporary hotel, but touches of its origins may be seen in the molding detail, lace curtains, and paintings by old masters. The spacious guest rooms, on all three floors, have four-poster, canopy, or sleigh beds and Queen Anne–style furniture. The pink marble baths contain pedestal sinks with gleaming brass taps and oversize whirlpool tubs and showers enclosed by brass and glass.

On the hotel's lower level is an exquisite little restaurant, Chanterelle. It seats only forty people in three glass-partitioned rooms of understated decor enlivened by colorful modern art prints on the walls. The Continental cuisine is expensive but is considered some of the best in Sacramento. Fresh regional ingredients are used with traditional French techniques and California creativity. A specialty is veal with chanterelle mushrooms.

Next door is the Glass Garden, a conservatory imported from England. The 40-foot-long structure, with a glass roof in three graceful tiers, is used for receptions, parties, dances, and weddings. At press time plans were in the works to add a ballroom and five additional guest rooms.

> **Among Sacramento's attractions are the lovely tree-shaded capitol grounds and the oldest public art museum in the west, Crocker Art Museum. Old Sacramento has a railroad museum, a reconstruction of Sutter's Fort, and more than 250 shops and restaurants.**

Vizcaya

2019 21st Street
Sacramento, CA 95818
916-455-5243
800-456-2019

An elegant home with antiques and contemporary comforts

Innkeepers: Sandi and Richard Kann. **Accommodations:** 9 rooms (all with private bath). **Rates:** $95–$225 single or double. **Included:** Full breakfast. **Added:** 12% tax. **Payment:** Major credit cards. **Children:** Welcome. **Pets:** Not allowed. **Smoking:** Not allowed indoors.

Formerly called the Driver Mansion Inn, Vizcaya is one of the classiest bed-and-breakfasts you'll encounter. Calico and teddy bears would definitely be out of place here. Stately antiques, thick carpeting, and fine art set the theme.

Pink, white, and red roses flank the pillared porch of the big house, which is set on a slope above a busy street. You may park on the street, and there are a few parking spaces in back. Traditional furniture faces a white brick fireplace in the parlor, where beverages are available, by request, in the afternoons.

Breakfast is served at glass-topped tables in the dining room (or in your room, for a $15 fee). Fresh fruit, juice, and excellent coffee are prepared along with Belgian waffles, French toast, quiche, or other main dishes.

The six guest rooms in the main house all have antiques or reproductions, desks, private phones, TV, and shirred white curtains at wide leaded glass windows. The baths are in modern white tile, with glass and brass showers, and most have

Jacuzzis. The Garden Suite has a large living room, and an iron and brass bed in the bedroom. Room 2 has a four-poster bed, a sofa, and an oversize roll-top desk with a brass lamp fit for an executive. Room 4 is smaller with a sleigh bed, but has a large marble bath with a two-person Jacuzzi, and rose-colored stained glass windows.

> This bed-and-breakfast inn was once a private mansion owned by Philip Driver, a prominent attorney in the late 1800s. The mansion remained in the Driver family until 1977 and now is owned by the Kanns, who are also part-owners of the luxurious Sterling Hotel.

The spacious third-floor Penthouse suite has a contemporary look with a black marble dining table that seats eight, a black marble coffee table, two comfortable sofas covered in salmon sateen, a writing desk, and a bed in a dormer window alcove in the living room. The bedroom has an iron and brass bed, a walk-in closet, and a small balcony. The suite also features a giant whirlpool tub surrounded in black marble.

The Carriage House, in a garden of brick walks edged with impatiens and shaded by oak, persimmon, and crape myrtle trees, has three rooms. One is furnished in white wicker and has a wood-burning stove; another has an Oriental feel.

The *Sacramento Bee* is supplied, and Sandi will recommend restaurants and suggest sightseeing attractions if requested. With intuitive tact, she knows when to leave people alone. "I try to be available, but not hover," she says. "We offer hotel-type accommodations but with a warmer, more personal atmosphere."

Vizcaya now offers space in an adjacent attractive pavilion fronted by gardens and a fountain for banquets and receptions for up to 400 people.

SIERRA CITY

Busch & Heringlake Country Inn

P.O. Box 68
Sierra City, CA 96125
916-862-1501

> *A mountain hideaway in a former mining town*

Innkeeper: Carlo Giuffre. **Accommodations:** 4 rooms (all with private bath). **Rates:** $90–$115 single or double. **Included:** Full breakfast. **Added:** 10% Tax. **Payment:** Major credit cards. **Children:** Not appropriate. **Pets:** Not allowed. **Smoking:** Not allowed

Tucked away in the northern Sierra Nevada range, on the North Fork of the Yuba River about an hour's drive north of Lake Tahoe, lies Sierra City, a little town of charm and historic interest. The area was opened to mining in the 1850s; saloons and churches and the Wells Fargo office inevitably followed. Wells Fargo was housed in the Busch Building, a three-story structure made of clay from a nearby brickyard in 1871. Western Union, a general store, and a third-floor dance hall were also in the building constructed by miner and entrepreneur A. C. Busch. Mr. Heringlake became his partner.

> In the summer the Kentucky Mine Museum is open for tours, and there's a concert series in July and August. Winter offers Nordic skiing, ice-fishing, and relaxing by the flickering fire.

In 1986 Carlo Giuffre bought the red brick building, which had been deteriorating for years, and began the long restoration process. He spent two and a half years meticulously returning the place to its original status, creating a beautifully crafted inn that combines the old and the new.

On the ground floor is an Italian restaurant and a conversation corner where hikers and skiers gather by the massive woodstove in the evenings. The stove, made from an old boiler, railroad ties, and miners' picks, is a conversation piece of its own.

The guest rooms upstairs, named after historic mines, have wide plank floors and pine and cedar wainscoting and furniture. The Phoenix Room is a large, sunny space in a corner, with a fireplace in blue ceramic tile, a pineapple four-poster bed, a wet bar, and a whirlpool tub. In the Young America Room there is a brass bed and a whirlpool for two in the bath. Marguerite is a comfortable corner room with a double shower, while Lusk Meadow has a queen-size bed, armoire, and views of the mountains. A hearty American breakfast — eggs, bacon, potatoes — is served in the restaurant.

The hotel is on Sierra City's main street, where the stagecoach used to stop. Across the road are private homes and shops; ask the innkeeper about access to the river below and about hiking and mountain biking trails in the Lakes Basin area, a series of crystal clear mountain lakes. You can try gold-panning or fishing in the river, and there are good picnic spots along its banks.

SONORA

Llamahall Guest Ranch

18170 Wards Ferry Road
Sonora, CA 95370
209-532-7264

A modern home in a woodland setting

Innkeeper: Cindy Hall. **Accommodations:** 2 rooms (both with private bath). **Rates:** $95 double, $15 additional person. **Included:** Full breakfast. **Added:** 8% tax on room, 7.75% tax on food. **Minimum stay:** 2 nights on holiday weekends. **Payment:** No credit cards. **Children:** Over age 1 charged as an adult if third person in room. **Pets:** Not allowed. **Smoking:** Not allowed indoors.

At Llamahall Guest Ranch, visitors are welcome to feed the llamas and take them for walks on trails that wind through the woods down to Curtis Creek. Cindy is training the animals to pull carts and takes them to hospitals and convalescent homes to cheer patients.

But there's more to the ranch than llamas. You can hike to

the Indian Grinding Rocks, swim in a nearby lake, fish at a local trout farm, pan for gold in the creek (Cindy lends placer pans), and romp with the dogs. Ride the Jamestown steam train, which runs on summer weekends, or, in winter, ski on the slopes at Ski Dodge Ridge, forty minutes away.

> **"Llamas are lovable," says Cindy Hall, as one of the long-necked, woolly creatures nuzzles her shoulder. Twelve of them (occasionally more, since they're breeding pairs) live on this 5-acre ranch in the gold country.**

Indoors there are games and toys, a piano, drums, an autoharp, and a guitar that you may borrow for musicfests. Cindy will pull out the television set if requested.

Her big modern redwood house is set against a hillside above the creek, under tall oak trees. It's quiet in this woodland scene, though it's just outside Sonora, about 120 miles east of San Francisco. The babbling of the creek and the rustle of oak leaves are the only sounds you her.

The comfortable, casual living room has a square grand piano, a stone fireplace, and windows that overlook the wooded hillside. A table is set for breakfast here, or you can sit at black wrought iron tables on the wide deck. A fruit plate, muffins or coffee cake, fresh juice, and cereals are provided, along with eggs cooked however you like them.

The guest rooms, Flora and Fauna, are on the lower level. Each has a private Dutch door entrance. Flora is decorated with Victorian brambleberry wallpaper, and the ceiling border in Fauna is a frieze of deer and other forest creatures. Fauna has plum carpeting, a black iron bed with a trundle, a desk, and windows viewing the deck and trees. Children's books lie on the shelves. In the spacious bath are a clawfoot tub with ring shower, a pedestal sink, and a chain-pull toilet.

The refrigerator downstairs is stocked with soft drinks and iced tea, which you'll enjoy as you relax on the deck under a sky full of stars.

SOUTH LAKE TAHOE

Lakeland Village Beach & Ski Resort

P.O. Box 1356
3535 Highway 50
South Lake Tahoe, CA 96156
916-541-7711
800-822-5969
Fax: 916-541-6278

*A lakeside resort
for year-round
recreation*

General manager: Patrick Ronan. **Accommodations:** 215 units. **Rates:** $75–$160 for lodge rooms, $140–$440 for townhouses. **Added:** 10% tax. **Minimum stay:** 2–4 nights in some rooms. **Payment:** Major credit cards. **Children:** Welcome. **Pets:** Not allowed. **Smoking:** Allowed.

The resort complex of Lakeland Village is on the southern shore of Lake Tahoe, facing a thousand feet of private sandy beach. Under tall pine trees, its 19 acres contain two swimming pools, two tennis courts, saunas, a spa, a lakeside clubhouse, a children's playground, and a boat dock.

Despite its proximity to Highway 50, location is the resort's major attraction. It borders the sapphire blue lake, Heavenly Valley ski area is a mile and a half away (a free shuttle is available), and the casinos of Nevada are one mile to the northeast.

More than twenty other ski areas surround the lake, many of them offering shuttle service. You can also ferry to the north shore on the Tahoe Queen paddlewheeler. Lakeland

Tahoe's slopes are famous for magnificent scenery and challenging skiing. Heavenly Valley has a network of lifts to Tahoe's highest skiing, with an elevation of 10,100 feet and a vertical drop of 3,600 feet. About half the ski area is devoted to intermediate slopes, with the other half divided between beginner and advanced runs.

Village rents skis and equipment but does not offer ski storage; several rooms have porches that may be used for storage.

During the summer, you can rent paddleboats, canoes, or kayaks, play golf at five courses in the area, or throw a private party at the clubhouse. Tennis lessons are available and other recreation includes bicycling, hiking the back country, fishing, windsurfing, rafting, and horseback riding.

The rooms in the three-story lodge range from studios with Murphy beds to one-bedroom suites; there are also privately owned three-story town houses, which go up to four bedrooms with three baths. All the rooms have cable TV with HBO, equipped kitchens, fireplaces, and phones.

The town houses, especially those on the waterfront, are recommended over the lodge rooms. Not only do they have enviable views and easy access to the beach, they're larger and better maintained. They are also farther from the highway. The furnishings in the lodge rooms are comfortable and functional, but they fall short of top resort standards.

A typical four-bedroom lakefront town house will have a bedroom with two beds and a vaulted ceiling that soars above two lofts, one with two bedrooms and the highest with windows overlooking the lake. Glass doors slide open to a deck on the beach. Plenty of closet space, an entry where wet clothing can be hung to dry, and personal touches in books and artwork make this a homelike, all-purpose family choice.

There's a coin-operated laundry on the property, and parking is free.

SUTTER CREEK

The Foxes Bed and Breakfast Inn

P.O. Box 159
77 Main Street
Sutter Creek, CA 95685
209-267-5882
Fax: 209-267-0712

*A luxurious
bed-and-breakfast
in the gold country*

Innkeepers: Pete and Min Fox.
Accommodations: 7 rooms (all with private bath). **Rates:** $100–$145 single, $110–$160 double. **Included:** Full breakfast. **Added:** 7.25% tax. **Minimum stay:** 2 nights on week-

ends. **Payment:** MasterCard and Visa. **Children:** Not appropriate. **Pets:** Not allowed. **Smoking:** Not allowed indoors.

Since the day the Foxes opened their gold country bed-and-breakfast in 1980 with a single guest room, the inn has been praised as one of the best in California. Gracious hosts with a sure sense of visitors' needs, the innkeepers go out of their way to provide every comfort. And they make it seem easy, a rare skill in this demanding business.

Their 1857 home is in the center of Sutter Creek, a pretty little town surrounded by hills studded with oak and pine trees. The town and the stream that runs through it were named for John Sutter, whose sawmill on the American River caught the sparkle of gold in 1848 and set off the great gold rush. Several mines operated in Sutter Creek, but all have long since been closed. Pete and Min Fox moved to Sutter Creek from southern California. They became antiques dealers, then opened their home as a B&B, and later expanded into the Carriage House in back. Now their inn is so well known for its consistent high quality, early reservations are a must.

Traffic noise from Highway 49 recedes when you enter the house, as the melodic strains of Chopin flood the foyer and parlor. Doors with etched glass panes lead to the parlor furnished with antiques. The windows overlook the front porch, its columns entwined with wisteria, and a yard filled with flowers and ferns.

You can have breakfast in the garden, but it's usually brought to your room on a silver tray, with items you've selected the night before: fresh juice, eggs as you like them or the house specialty of cream-poached eggs on an English muffin, fruit, and muffins and jam.

The guest rooms are air conditioned. The Honeymoon Suite, on the ground floor in the main house, is spacious and has a private entrance. Blue velvet wingback chairs face a brick fireplace, the bed has a partial canopy, the armoire has an ornate door, and there's an unusual corner cupboard. A clawfoot tub and pull-chain toilet add a nostalgic touch to the bath. The Master Suite has a separate living room with a small dining table for two and a fireplace. In the bedroom there's a half-canopy bed topped with an ivory eyelet lace coverlet and draped in floral curtains.

The Victorian Suite, upstairs, was the Foxes' first bed-and-breakfast room. It has a handsome, nine-foot headboard on the bed, a matching dresser, a gold velvet couch in the sitting area, and a small bath with a shower. The Anniversary Room features a bed with a carved headboard and a ten-foot mirrored armoire.

All three rooms in the Carriage House have private entrances and cable TV hidden behind armoire doors. The Blue Room, decorated in powder blue, has an extra-large bath and a carved bedstead with a partial canopy. The bay window in the Garden Room overlooks the garden, while Fox Den is cozy with a library, wood-burning fireplace, and foxes everywhere. There are foxes dressed in red coats, foxes dressed in plaid, foxes on the wall, and even the wallpaper has a fox motif trim.

> The innkeepers will direct you on sightseeing expeditions and make restaurant recommendations. Pick up a walking tour map of Sutter Creek, and you'll learn some history and discover more of the town's charm as you stroll.

Among the amenities the Foxes provide are clock radios, tape decks with tapes of restful music, the *Sacramento Bee* at your doorstep in the morning, plenty of storage space for clothes, a safe for valuables, covered parking, and elegant breakfast settings with wine glasses and linen napkins.

There's only one drawback here: highway 49 runs through the middle of town, and its cars and rumbling trucks are more than a mild annoyance. The Foxes have installed storm windows, and some residents are hoping for a bypass, which would rescue Sutter Creek's serenity.

Grey Gables Inn

P.O. Box 1687
161 Hanford Street
Sutter Creek, CA 95685
209-267-1039
800-GREY-GABLES

*A taste of
English country
in the heart
of California's
gold country*

Innkeepers: Roger and Sue Garlick. **Accommodations:** 8 rooms. **Rates:** $85–$125. **Included:** Full breakfast, afternoon tea, and evening refreshments. **Added:** 7.25% tax. **Minimum Stay:** 2 nights if Saturday is included. **Payment:** MasterCard and Visa. **Children:** Not appropriate. **Pets:** Not allowed. **Smoking:** Not allowed.

It is easy to spot this attractive multi-gabled home while passing through the 19th-century mining town of Sutter Creek. If the inn, with a rose trellis, fountain, and benches sitting amid a glorious cottage garden abloom with columbine, foxgloves, pansies, California poppies, and coral bells, looks more like an English country manor than the Catholic school it once was, it is due to the innkeepers' heritage and vision.

Originally from Gloucestershire, England, Sue and Roger Garlick came to this country when Roger's work in computers brought him to California. Sue had always dreamed of opening an inn, and in 1992 the Garlicks purchased this property on the edge of Sutter Creek that had originally been built as a school back in the 1870s by Bishop Patrick Manogue. The Garlicks then spent nearly two years extensively renovating and remodeling, resulting in the lovely Victorian-style structure guests see today.

Guests are welcomed in a formal parlor decorated with plush velvet furniture, English floral drapes, and an antique map of Gloucestershire — the innkeepers' homeland. A full breakfast including chicken-mushroom crêpes, poached pears, a quiche, or blackberry crepes, is served on fine china and crisp linens in the adjacent dining room, or in your guest room if you prefer.

> In keeping with the hosts' background, cakes and scones are served in the afternoon as part of a traditional English tea.

The immaculate guest rooms were designed for comfort, and have been decorated with polish and taste. Bearing the names of famous English poets, each has a private bath, gas fireplace, ceiling fan, clock radio, air conditioning, and an armoire for hanging clothes. In lavenders, mints, and creams, Browning has a country feel with pine furnishings, lace curtains, and a clawfoot tub. Byron has a French bed, rich wood armoire, and a marble fireplace. In Wordsworth, floral wreaths adorn the walls, and bay windows bring in lots of light. There's also an antique hand-painted Singer sewing machine, and a wedding dress hangs on a dressmaker's dummy in the corner.

Shelley, in blacks, tans, and plums, is more masculine than the others, and is wheelchair accessible. Keats, a personal favorite, is a pretty room overlooking a portion of the garden, and has an eye-catching English dogwood print comforter and matching pillow shams. Brontë has a king-size bed and a full sofa, and Tennyson is decorated in Laura Ashley fabrics. With a dragon motif armoire, a collection of Oriental plates, and fringed satin lamps, the Victorian Suite has an Eastern feel. Alone on the top floor, it is also the most secluded room.

Sutter Creek Inn

P.O. Box 385
75 Main Street
Sutter Creek, CA 95685
209-267-5606

*A gold country
bed-and-breakfast
of character
and charm*

Innkeeper: Jane Way. **Accommodations:** 18 rooms (all with private bath). **Rates:** $50–$88 single or double weekdays, $68–$97 weekends, $25 additional person. **Included:** Full breakfast. **Minimum stay:** 2 nights on weekends. **Payment:** No credit cards; personal checks accepted. **Children:** Over age 10 welcome, under age 15 not appropriate on weekends. **Pets:** Not allowed. **Smoking:** Allowed outdoors only.

This historic home with a breezy, friendly atmosphere was one of the first bed-and-breakfasts in California. Jane Way fell in love with the place while touring the gold country with her children in the mid-1960s. Since then she has continued to expand the inn; it's now a sizable complex that has retained its homey character.

The Greek Revival structure, built in 1859, stands on Sutter Creek's main street (Highway 49, often heavy with traffic), behind attractive lawns and gardens. Some guest rooms are in the main house; others are tucked away in outbuildings by the grape arbor and terrace.

Visitors are drawn irresistibly to the large living room, for Jane has filled it with comfortable couches and chairs, a spinet piano, games and magazines, a chess table set up for play, and many of her hundreds of books. A corner cabinet holds antique china and a grandfather clock stands in dignity against one wall, faithfully sounding the Westminster Chimes.

All the guest rooms have electric blankets and air conditioners. Nine rooms contain fireplaces, and some have swinging beds (which can be stabilized if you don't like the notion of gentle swaying all night long). There are three rooms in the main house.

The Library Room has lots of books in addition to three beds and a small deck. The East Room is cheerful in sunny yellow, with a cozy alcove painted in stenciled designs. Traffic noise can be a problem. Fortunately a sound conditioner emits the soothing murmur of rain and surf to help block any less welcome sounds. The West Room has windows under the eaves. Its yellow bath, bright with flowers and stripes, is original. This was the first house in Sutter Creek to have an indoor bathroom.

The Garden Cottage, behind the grape arbor, is fronted by a porch with wicker furniture; its interior is dark in natural woods. The Patio room has a swinging bed, window seat, and fully stocked bookshelves. The Lower Wash House has lots of windows, and Lindsay's Room, with twin beds, a fireplace, and a high pitched roof, feels like a private cottage. The Miner's Cabin, Tool Shed, and Cellar Room each have a fireplace.

> **The Amador County Museum, Chaw Se Indian Grinding Rock State Historic Park, and the Kennedy Tailing Wheels are among the historic sights. You'll find more active recreation at Mace Meadows Golf Course, Kirkwood ski area, and on Mokelumne River and Amador and Camanche lakes.**

The Carriage House is the most expensive accommodation. An old Chinese rug that represents all of the spiritual leaders of China hangs over the brick fireplace, and there's a four-poster canopy bed and two baths. One of the most romantic choices is the Loft, reached by climbing outside stairs past green clematis vines winding up the branches of a tall Chinese elm. It has a four-poster bed, a vaulted beamed ceiling, and high windows above the gardens.

The menu for the country breakfast varies, but typical of Jane's morning choices are zucchini walnut bread, Spanish omelette, fresh fruit, coffee and tea. Hot cider or cold lemonade is set out for guests along with homemade cookies each afternoon.

The personable innkeeper has a wide range of interests, most of them reflected in the book titles and items displayed in her inn. Handwriting analysis, reflexology, therapeutic massage, palm reading, and psychic experiences are often topics of conversation, for Jane also enjoys visiting with guests as time allows. She and her assistants are happy to give visitors suggestions for day trips and points of interest.

TRUCKEE

Northstar at Tahoe

P.O. Box 2499
Truckee, CA 95734
916-562-1010
800-GO-NORTH
Fax: 916-562-2215

> *A family resort
> near Lake Tahoe*

General manager: Tim Silva. **Accommodations:** Approximately 250 units. **Rates:** $129–$499 1–10 people in winter, $99–$319 in summer (rates cover a range of accommodations, from standard hotel rooms to 3–4 bedroom homes, and are priced by unit rather than level of occupancy). **Minimum stay:** 3 nights in winter, 2 nights in summer. **Payment:** Major credit cards. **Children:** Welcome. **Pets:** Not allowed. **Smoking:** Nonsmoking rooms available in hotel.

Skiing and snow play draw crowds to Northstar in winter, while summer's pleasures on the 2,500-acre resort six miles from Lake Tahoe include hiking, mountain biking, fishing, swimming in the pool, horseback riding, tennis, and golf.

The resort is ideal for family vacations because there's such a wide variety of recreation. Those who are too young for the ski slopes or tennis courts are happily ensconced in the Minors' Camp, a child-care program which accepts children ages two to six. Every day they learn songs, listen to stories, paint, take walks, and are given snacks and a hot

While the kids are busy, their parents are skiing on Mount Pluto and Lookout Mountain, which have 2,200 vertical feet of ski slopes. Lifts include a high-speed gondola, four express quad chairs, three triple chairs, and two double chairs.

lunch. If they're in the Ski Cubs program (age three and older) they receive a skiing lesson, too. In the summer, an experienced staff gives children aged two to ten tennis and swimming lessons and takes them horseback riding.

With the expansion of downhill skiing facilities, Northstar

has opened the Summit Deck & Grille at the top of Mount Pluto. The restaurant offers Mexican food and microbrewery beers.

Cross-country and telemark skiing lessons are available in the winter. There are 65 kilometers of groomed trails near the lodge. Golf is the big draw in summer, and golf packages offer a good value. The 18-hole, par 72 course has water hazards on 14 holes, a driving range, a resident pro, and a well-equipped pro shop. Tennis players appreciate the two- and five-day tennis camps. There are ten courts.

Northstar Village has several restaurants, bars, and shops. Timbercreek serves dinner in summer, and three meals a day in winter. The first floor of the Village Building holds a sport shop in winter that is a conference room in summer; its second and third floors have hotel rooms and loft suites.

The rest of Northstar's lodgings are in five clusters of privately owned condominiums scattered across the wooded hills. Each has a fireplace (firewood is provided), cable television, a covered deck, and a kitchen with microwave oven. A typical two-bedroom, two-bath condo is a split-level unit with a living room, kitchen, and bath on the upper level and two bedrooms and a laundry room downstairs.

The condos in the Indian Hills cluster are farthest from the village, high on a hill with a view of the surrounding mountains and the valley below. A free shuttle bus takes guests back and forth in winter; in summer, buses come upon request.

Winter is busier than summer at Northstar, but that is likely to change as the resort continues to entice visitors with special packages and a wide array of activities and events.

The Truckee Hotel

10007 Bridge Street
P.O. Box 884
Truckee, CA 96160
916-587-4444
800-659-6921

*A restored
historic hotel*

Owners: Jeffrey and Karen Winter. **Accommodations:** 37 rooms. **Rates:** $60–$115 for rooms with shared baths, $80–$125 for rooms with private baths. **Included:** Continental breakfast. **Added:** 10% tax. **Payment:** Major credit cards. **Children:** Age 3 and under are free. **Pets:** Not allowed. **Smoking:** Not allowed.

The town of Truckee, named for a Paiute Indian chief, began as a stage coach stop in the 1860s. Yet unlike many towns in Sierra country, Truckee's early growth was due more to the expansion of the transcontinental railroad than to prospecting. Truckee became a lumber town, providing materials for the railroad's construction. Nearby lakes and cold winters also made Truckee a center for ice production in the days before refrigeration, while the town's proximity to beautiful Lake Tahoe and surrounding mountain terrain brought tourists as early as the turn-of-the-century.

The Truckee Hotel's history mirrors that of the town itself. Built in 1868, the hotel, then known as the American Hotel, offered accommodations to lodgers traveling along the stage coach route. Then it became home to laborers working on the railroad and in the ice and timber industries. Today the hotel is frequented mainly by tourists who come to the area for outdoor recreation such as skiing, boating, fishing, hiking, or bicycling.

The current owners bought the Truckee Hotel in the early 1990s and immediately began restoring it. Their efforts won them an award for historic preservation, and resulted in a comfortable lodging that retains its historic flavor. Although the thirty-seven guest rooms are not overly luxurious, they are pleasantly furnished. Each is individually decorated, and most have a Victorian theme with lace curtains, floral comforters, and furniture original to the hotel. Eight rooms have private baths with clawfoot tubs; the rest share hall baths. Some rooms have television, and all have coffeemakers. The Whitney Room on the second floor has a television and stereo that all guests are welcome to use.

> One of Truckee's most famous visitors was Charlie Chaplin who came to the area to film his movie *The Gold Rush*.

In the afternoons guests relax over tea which is set out in the cozy common living room in front of a gaslit fireplace and green marble tile hearth. A Continental breakfast of muffins, bagels, hot cereal, fresh fruit, teas, and juices is served in the adjoining dining area. The Passage restaurant adjacent to the hotel lobby serves more substantial meals including grilled swordfish with mango salsa and black bean chili, and a focaccia sandwich with grilled eggplant, roasted red peppers, and mozzarella cheese in a tomato garlic sauce. The restaurant also boasts a fine wine list and home-baked desserts such as mixed berry cobbler and triple chocolate mousse cake. For day-trippers, picnic lunches and fresh pastries can be purchased from the Passage Way shop.

To recapture some of the spirit of the old west, many guests follow Truckee's walking tour and visit sites along the Emigrant Trail. Others prefer to window shop, or head to the ski slopes, as there are multiple ski areas within a half hour of Truckee. The hotel provides a locker room for ski equipment.

WAWONA

Wawona Hotel

Yosemite National Park
CA 95389
Reservations:
Yosemite Park Reservations
5410 East Home Street
Fresno, CA 93727
209-252-4848

*A gracious,
traditional lodge
in south Yosemite*

Manager: Judy Durr. **Accommodations:** 103 rooms (48 with private bath). **Rates:** $68.25–$91.35 single or double, $10 additional person. **Added:** Tax. **Payment:** MasterCard, Visa. **Children:** Under age 12 free in room with parents. **Pets:** Not allowed. **Smoking:** Allowed outdoors only. **Open:** Weekends year round, closed weekdays November–December.

Wawona, in the southwestern corner of a park that is one of the world's great natural wonders, resembles a fine plantation home in the South. The main hotel has a big veranda with white columns and wicker furniture overlooking an expanse of lawn and a water lily pond. The pace is slower here, compared to the midsummer rush in Yosemite Valley.

Some wilderness lodges feature rough logs and antler trophies, but not this one. Here the lobby is white and pink, with a flowered ceiling border and carpeting in teal and burgundy. Vintage furniture provides seating near the two stone fireplaces.

On one side of the lobby is a restaurant, a large white room with two walls of high windows framing views of the trees. Dinners and buffet lunches feature standard fare, good but not exceptional.

At the opposite end of the lobby is a small lounge with high ceilings, round marble tables and a grand piano. The tall windows still have the original wavy glass put in more than a century ago, when Henry Washburn and John Bruce opened the hotel. It was owned by the Washburn family until 1932. Now Wawona, like the rest of Yosemite's lodgings, is run by the Yosemite Park and Curry Company.

All the rooms at Wawona are reserved early, often as far as a year in advance. Upstairs in the main building are twenty-six guest rooms, a few with private baths but most sharing four men's and four women's baths. Modern and well maintained, they have showers and are tiled in white with tan, green, and pink accents.

Typical of the small, comfortable accommodations is Room 202, a tidy space with a white iron bed, flowered wallpaper, pegs (but no closet), and a stack of towels on the dresser. The largest rooms are 213 and 220, good choices for a family.

Other rooms are in five side buildings with one or two stories. The oldest is Clark Cottage, which dates from 1876. Cool and green under a cloak of vines, it has eight boxy rooms with windows to the wraparound porch.

> The famed Mariposa Grove is south of Wawona, just inside the southernmost park entrance. Yosemite's largest tree grows here, soaring skyward in a community of giant sequoias. Trams operate daily, and a trail winds through the awesome grove.

The Annex is ideal for golfers. Encircled by porches, it stands on the edge of a 9-hole golf course and has a golf shop on the lower level. There's a large lounge, appropriately called the Sun Room for the light that floods through glass doors on three sides of the room.

On the property there are tennis courts, a pool, a putting green, and riding stables. Near the stables is the Pioneer Yosemite History Center, a collection of historic buildings and horse-drawn wagons. A self-guiding trail and tours led by a ranger describe the people and events that led to the establishment of the park.

You can relive the days of stage travel in Yosemite with a ten-minute stage ride and hear legends and stories at evening campfire talks given regularly by park rangers.

YOSEMITE

The Ahwahnee

Yosemite National Park
CA 95389
Reservations:
Yosemite Reservations
5410 East Home Street
Fresno, CA 93727
209-372-1407
Fax: 209-372-1463

*A grand lodge in
a glorious
natural setting*

Manager: Deborah Price. **Accommodations:** 99 lodge rooms, 24 cottages. **Rates:** $208 double, $20 less for single, $20 additional person. **Payment:** MasterCard, Visa. **Children:** Under age 4 free in room with parents; $5 age 4–13. **Pets:** Not allowed. **Smoking:** Nonsmoking rooms available

The Ahwahnee, faced with native granite and concrete stained to resemble redwood, fits comfortably into its magnificent surroundings — the great granite cliffs, roaring waterfalls, and majestic forests of Yosemite Valley. The hotel stands among pine and cedar trees on the valley floor, with the Royal Arches soaring 2,000 feet behind it.

Since it opened in 1927, celebrities and unknowns alike have adored the Ahwahnee. Winston Churchill, John F. Kennedy, Will Rogers, Greta Garbo, Walt Disney, and Lucille Ball slept under its imposing roof, as have hosts of others. Queen Elizabeth and the Duke of Edinburgh stayed here, and two rooms are named for them.

Dinner at the Ahwahnee is an unforgettable experience. Two walls of floor-to-ceiling windows look over the grassy meadows to Glacier Point and the long ribbon of Yosemite Falls. Tables extend the length of the immense room, and each holds a single tall candle. Overhead, dozens of candles are suspended from pine beams in wrought-iron holders. The atmosphere is at once festive and formal, contrasting wilderness and urbanity in a single setting. Jackets and ties are requested, but no longer required. A pianist performs during dinner.

Several special events are offered during the year. The oldest is the Bracebridge Dinner, a celebration based on Washington Irving's story of a Yorkshire Christmas. The feast and theatrical production are now so in demand that five dinners are held, so that 1,800 of the 60,000 applicants can attend. They're chosen by lottery.

> **Everything in the six-story hotel is on a grand scale. Fireplaces are big enough to stand in; windows are 24 feet high; the restaurant is 130 feet long and has a 34-foot ceiling supported by pillars of sugar pine. Yet despite the size, it's not intimidating — just impressive.**

A Native American motif enlivens the hotel's heavy beams and sturdy furniture. Some of the most interesting designs are on the ceiling of the Great Lounge.

The Indian theme continues in the geometric fabric patterns in the guest rooms. The rooms are more elegant than rustic, with pastels of pale green and salmon, weathered copper, and amenities such as clock radios, phones, robes, and hair dryers. Many have king-size beds and all have private baths. The royal rooms contain a fireplace and library. The highlight of the Presidential Suite is its open balcony, from which you have a spectacular view up and down the valley.

Other rooms are in cottages in the woods, reached on lighted paths. Each has a slate front porch, chunky furniture, dark woodwork, and deep windows. For a group traveling together, a five-bedroom, five-bath cottage is ideal.

The Ahwahnee has a gift shop with Indian baskets, weavings, Ansel Adams lithographs and paintings, and books on Yosemite. There are tennis courts and a swimming pool. Stables in the park offer horseback rides. Bicycles can be rented and guided tours arranged. A twenty-six-mile, two-hour tour by bus or tram car across the valley floor will introduce you to the history, geology, and plant and animal life that abounds here.

There are times when the most abundant life appears to be human, as three million visitors a year stream through the park. That's when you may want to explore the 750 miles of trails in Yosemite's backcountry. But whether you're alone at the top of a waterfall or basking in the sun in the Ahwahnee's solarium, you're sure to feel the power of this magnificent natural wonder.

Southern
California

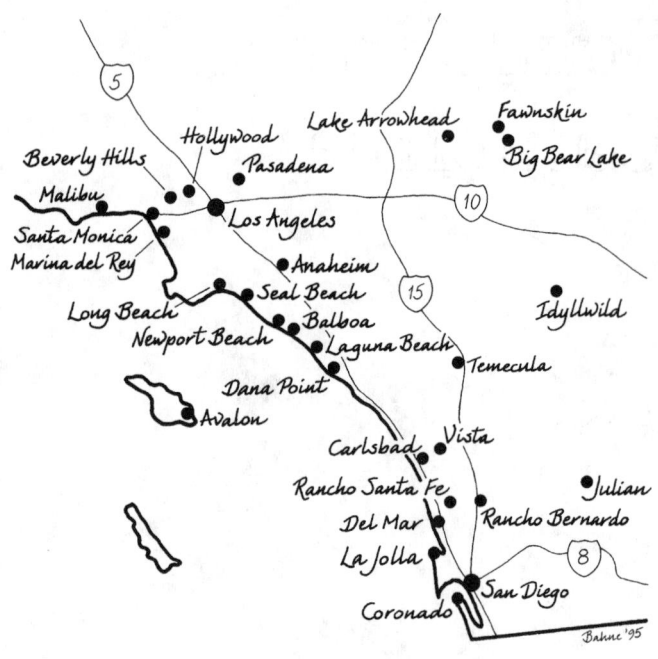

Best Intimate City Stops

Beverly Hills
The Peninsula Beverly Hills
Hollywood
La Maida House
Sunset Marquis Hotel and Villas
Los Angeles
The Argyle
The Beverly Prescott Hotel
Hotel Bel-Air
Westwood Marquis Hotel and Gardens
Wyndham Checkers Hotel
San Diego
Horton Grand Hotel
The Westgate Hotel

Best Country Inns and B&Bs

Avalon
The Inn on Mt. Ada
Zane Grey Pueblo Hotel
Idyllwild
Strawberry Creek Inn
Julian
Julian Hotel
Shadow Mountain Ranch
Temecula
Loma Vista Bed & Breakfast

Best Family Favorites

Anaheim
Disneyland Hotel
Lake Arrowhead
Lake Arrowhead Resort

Best Grand City Hotels

Beverly Hills
The Regent Beverly Wilshire

Los Angeles
 The Biltmore Hotel
 Hotel Nikko at Beverly Hills
 Hotel Sofitel
 The New Otani Hotel & Garden
San Diego
 The Pan Pacific Hotel
 U.S. Grant Hotel

Inns by the Sea

Balboa
 Balboa Inn
Carlsbad
 Pelican Cove Inn
Coronado
 Hotel Del Coronado
Dana Point
 Blue Lantern Inn
 Marriott's Laguna Cliffs Resort
Del Mar
 L'Auberge Del Mar
La Jolla
 The Bed & Breakfast Inn at La Jolla
 La Jolla Beach & Tennis Club
 La Valencia Hotel
 Prospect Park Inn
Laguna Beach
 Eiler's Inn
 Surf & Sand Hotel
Long Beach
 Hotel Queen Mary
Malibu
 Malibu Beach Inn
Marina del Rey
 Marina del Rey Hotel
Santa Monica
 Hotel Shangri-La
 Loews Santa Monica Beach Hotel
 Miramar Sheraton Hotel
 Shutters on the Beach
Seal Beach
 The Seal Beach Inn and Gardens

Best On A Budget

San Diego
   The Cottage

Best Resorts

Carlsbad
   La Costa Resort and Spa
Coronado
   Le Meridien San Diego at Coronado
   Loews Coronado Bay Resort
Laguna Beach
   The Ritz-Carlton Laguna Niguel
Pasadena
   The Ritz-Carlton Huntington
Rancho Bernardo
   Rancho Bernardo Inn
Rancho Santa Fe
   The Inn at Rancho Santa Fe
   Rancho Valencia
San Diego
   San Diego Princess

Best Romantic Hideaways

Coronado
   Coronado Victorian House
Lake Arrowhead
   Château du Lac
Newport Beach
   Doryman's Inn
San Diego
   Balboa Park Inn

Best Spas

Vista
   Cal-a-Vie

Best Wilderness Retreats

Big Bear Lake
  The Knickerbocker Mansion
Fawnskin
  Windy Point Inn

Southern California, from Malibu to San Diego, is richly diverse and full of contrast. There are gorgeous white beaches and palatial homes, mountain lakes, and simple cottages. In the metropolitan sprawl of greater **Los Angeles,** you'll find movie studios, freeways, smog, great museums, surfers, chic shops, and nine million people, all spread over 4,083 square miles. Los Angeles, founded by eleven families from Mexico in 1781, was a sleepy village until the railroad arrived in the late 1860s and a land boom began. Lured by images of a subtropical paradise, immigrants sought their fortunes in oranges. By 1889, 13,000 acres were producing oranges for shipment. Then the discovery of oil brought enormous wealth.

But it was the film industry, begun in 1910, that established the town as the glamour capital of the world. The Los Angeles area offers nonstop entertainment and numerous sporting and cultural events. Shopping is important recreation, especially in the designer boutiques of Rodeo Drive in **Beverly Hills,** and the dozens of clothing and antique shops on Melrose Avenue.

Symphony, ballet and opera companies are active, and the museums outstanding. The downtown Los Angeles County Museum of Art (LACMA) holds an important collection of pre-Columbian works, American paintings spanning two centuries, Indian and Southeast Asian art, and European and Japanese masterworks. In the Museum of Contemporary Art (MOCA), works of the postwar period are displayed under natural light in open galleries.

The Huntington is noted for its British art collection, botanical gardens, and library of rare books and manuscripts. The J. Paul Getty Museum, on a seaside hilltop in Malibu, may be the richest museum in the world. Ancient Greek and Roman sculptures and European masterpieces are displayed in a perfect replica of a Pompeiian villa.

North of Los Angeles loom the San Gabriel and San Bernardino mountains, high enough to be capped with snow in winter. Traveling south along the coast, each community has individual character, from arty **Laguna Beach** to a touch of New England in **Dana Point,** from the thoroughbred racing in **Del Mar** to **La Jolla**'s exclusive shops and stunning setting.

San Diego, the seventh largest city in the country, is best known for its ideal climate and extraordinary visitor attractions. The beach at **Coronado** and Balboa Park's marvelous zoo are not to be missed. Young and old alike are thrilled by Sea World; the orca whale show is nothing less than astonishing. The city has a major waterfront convention center, a restored Old Town with walk-through exhibitions on life in early San Diego, and a Gaslamp District of restored 19th-century buildings. In the heart of downtown is Horton Plaza, an innovative, multilevel shopping center that offers entertainment and restaurants as well as dozens of intriguing shops.

Inland from the beach and the bay, in the hills north of San Diego, are the wealthy communities of **Rancho Santa Fe** and **Rancho Bernardo.** A few miles away, tucked against the hot, dry hills, lie the peaceful enclaves of Vista, an avocado and citrus-growing center, and Escondido, the heart of San Diego County's wine industry. Farther east there's a quaint old gold-mining town, **Julian,** now known for its apple orchards and relaxed atmosphere.

ANAHEIM

Disneyland Hotel

1150 West Cerritos Avenue
Anaheim, CA 92802
714-778-6600
Fax: 714-956-6582

A jolly hotel complex near Disneyland

Manager: Hideo Amemiya. **Accommodations:** 1,136 rooms and suites.
Rates: $150–$240 single or double; suites $425–$2,000.
Added: 15% tax. **Payment:** Major credit cards. **Children:** Under age 17 free in room with parents. **Pets:** Not allowed.
Smoking: Nonsmoking rooms available.

Here's a resort to thrill the young at heart. Not only does it have all kinds of entertainment, recreation, and restaurants, it's just a short monorail ride from the Magic Kingdom itself, the fantasy playground of every kid.

The hotel was built in 1955 by Jack Wrather, a Texas oil-man who agreed with Walt Disney that the new theme park would draw enough visitors to merit a new hotel. So he acquired 60 acres adjoining Disneyland and built the "Official Hotel of the Magic Kingdom." Now it's a major attraction in its own right and an award-winning convention hotel. Most of the accommodations are in three towers, two of eleven stories and the other fourteen, surrounding Seaports of the Pacific, a marina playland and shopping and dining extravaganza.

> **The landscaping at Disneyland Hotel is extraordinary. A team of gardeners works continually to keep the floral color blazing, and the property is kept as immaculate as the clean streets of Disneyland.**

Despite the hotel's size it is easy to find your way around, helped by sign and paths that cross the villagelike grounds. There are three swimming pools, ten tennis courts, and Papeete Beach, a pseudo-Polynesian stretch of sand complete with shipwreck decor. Around the Seaports of the Pacific lagoon are remote-controlled boats, two-seater pedal boats, and a video game center.

Free entertainment adds to the hotel's considerable vacation value. Regular features are Fantasy Waters, a twice-nightly display of fountains, lights, and music, and country and western singing nightly at the Wharf Bar. The Neon Cactus Saloon features entertainment and dancing.

The restaurants range from Mazie's, a sidewalk café serving garnish-your-own hamburgers and hot dogs, to Granville's Steak House, featuring steak, prime rib, and lobster in a dressy, candlelit setting. The children's favorite is Goofy's Kitchen, with an all-you-can-eat buffet taking second place to the Disney characters who join them for breakfast. Others include Shipyard Inn, on the marina, and Stromboli's Ristorante, where Italian food is served. Special children's menus are available at all the hotel's restaurants.

Hotel facilities include car rentals, foreign currency exchange, laundry and dry cleaning, a limousine, and interpreter services.

With all this, guest rooms seem almost secondary. On the other hand, they're crucial to the hotel's appeal. A standard room is clean and comfortable and has a small stocked refrigerator, a TV with closed-circuit channel and Disney channel, and a narrow balcony overlooking the marina. On a clear day you can see from Bonita Tower to the beach. Each room has a reproduction of Disney artwork; the originals hang in the public spaces. A few rooms are in Garden Villas and Oriental Gardens, two-story buildings located apart from the center of activity and entered through attractive gardens.

With an operation as carefully orchestrated as the famous theme park, it's not a surprise to learn that as many as four weddings a day have been held in the rose garden gazebo.

AVALON

The Inn on Mt. Ada

398 Wrigley Road
Mailing address:
P.O. Box 2560
Avalon, CA 90704
310-510-2030

An elegant, historic mansion on a Santa Catalina hilltop

Innkeepers: Susie Griffin and Marlene McAdam. **Accommodations:** 6 rooms (all with private bath). **Rates:** $340–$620 June through October and weekends throughout the year, $250–$495 weekday rate November through May, single or double, $100 additional person, $3,000 per night for entire inn. **Included:** All meals and use of golf cart. **Minimum stay:** 2 nights on weekends and weekend holidays. **Payment:** Major credit cards. **Children:** Age 14 and older welcome. **Pets:** Not allowed. **Smoking:** Not allowed.

As you approach the Avalon harbor of Santa Catalina Island, you notice on your left, above the bobbing boats and pretty little town, a white Georgian Colonial mansion crowning a hillside. Once the summer estate of William Wrigley, Jr. (of chewing gum fame) and his family, now it is the Inn on Mt. Ada, one of the finest bed-and-breakfasts in California.

The house was built in 1921 for Wrigley, who also held title to the entire island. It remained in the family until the

1970s, when the land was transferred to the Santa Catalina Island Conservancy and the mansion donated to the University of Southern California for use as a conference center.

Later it was leased to a partnership dedicated to preserving the mansion and providing superb hospitality. It was opened as a bed-and-breakfast inn for guests accustomed to (or wanting a taste of) personal luxury.

Listed on the National Register of Historic Places, the mansion is as grand as it was when the Wrigleys were in residence and their visitors were Presidents Wilson and Coolidge and the Prince of Wales. Many original details have been retained, such as paneled walls, French doors, built-in bookcases, curved ceilings, and narrow planked floors. There are six fireplaces. The inn sits on 5½ acres on Mt. Ada (named for William Wrigley's wife), overlooking the harbor and town.

> **From almost every angle you see a panorama of the harbor, ocean, and mainland coast from Malibu to Oceanside. In the living room, wingback and Chippendale chairs invite you to sit by the fire or admire the view. A baby grand stands in one corner, and bookshelves line the walls beside the fireplace.**

The dining room, elegant with teal silk wallcoverings and an Austrian crystal chandelier, has French doors that open to the breeze-washed patio. A hearty breakfast is served here at tables for two or four. Tea and coffee, juice, and muffins are followed by a fruit dish such as apple crisp, and then an entrée, perhaps French toast and sausages. (If exercise seems a necessity after this meal, a trail at the edge of the property will lead you on a brisk fifteen-minute walk up the canyon and back, giving you a sense of the island's rugged back country.) A light lunch is provided, and dinner, from a set menu, includes a house wine, homemade bread, and a dessert such as chocolate mousse or individual tarts. Trays of cookies, fresh fruit, and other snacks are replenished during the day, as are beverages.

Each guest room is distinctively decorated in subtle blues and greens, the colors of the surrounding land and seascape. Most impressive is the Grand Suite, with a four-poster canopy bed, a fireplace, and French doors to a private balcony.

Next door is the Second Suite, which has a lighter touch, with ecru lace on the canopy. It also has a fireplace.

Room 3, in a corner, views both the harbor and the ocean. It too is furnished with a high four-poster and fireplace. The smallest is Number 6, a corner room that is decidedly limited in space, but the scaled-down furniture keeps it from feeling too cramped. It does have a walk-in closet and a full bath.

Portable TVs and a phone are available. Since visitors do not drive on Catalina, the inn has golf carts for guests at no extra charge. A courtesy van provides complimentary pick-up and drop-off at the boat dock.

Other amenities include nightly wine and hors d'oeuvres, early morning coffee and tea on the upstairs landing, and arrangements for island tours. All this is combined with a friendly, casual warmth that makes The Inn on Mt. Ada not just a classic mansion with a view, but a welcoming home of charm.

To get there, take one of the ferries that make daily trips from the mainland. Catalina Express is recommended for its smooth, fast (60- or 90-minute) ride.

Zane Grey Pueblo Hotel

P.O. Box 216
199 Chimes Tower Road
Avalon, CA 90704
310-510-0966
800-378-3256

A western adobe inn overlooking Santa Catalina harbor

Owner: Karen Baker. **General manager:** Laurie Carter. **Accommodations:** 17 rooms (all with private bath). **Rates:** $55–$125 single or double, $35 additional person, rates vary seasonally. **Included:** Continental breakfast. **Added:** 9% tax. Minimum stay: 2 or 3 nights on weekends. **Payment:** Major credit cards. **Children:** Charged as an additional person if more than 2 people in room. **Pets:** Not allowed. **Smoking:** Discouraged indoors.

Zane Grey, the famous author of westerns and adventure stories, was born in Ohio in 1872 but moved west after his first novel was published. His robust, romantic tales reflected his love of the outdoors and made him the foremost writer on the American West for two generations of readers.

In 1926, he and his family decided that Santa Catalina Island, twenty-six miles from the southern California coast, was the ideal location for a home. So they built "the Pueblo" on a hillside above the village of Avalon, facing east to the harbor, the sea, and the mainland. There Grey lived and worked until his death in 1939. Now the adobe home is a hotel with modern plumbing and queen-size beds; otherwise, it is much as it was when Zane Grey made it his haven.

A courtesy taxi will pick you up at the boat landing and wind up the hill to the hotel. Before you enter, you'll notice unusual artwork that deceives the eye: John Bailey's realistic wall paintings of cacti and geraniums.

> By the time you have spent a few days on lovely Catalina enjoying the dreamlike quiet and casual ambience of the Zane Grey Hotel, you may find yourself in agreement with the author's words about the place: "It is an environment that means enchantment to me. Sea and Mountain! Breeze and roar of Surf! Music of Birds! Solitude and Tranquility! A place for rest, dream, peace, sleep."

Most of the guest rooms, named for Zane Grey novels, are divided by a long hall in the hotel. Half overlook the ocean, half view the hills. The rooms are simply but comfortably furnished in a southwestern theme, with Hopi Indian designs in rugs and weavings. Some can accommodate up to four people. None have television or phones.

At the end of the hall is Zane Grey's living room with the original fireplace and log mantel, mosaic art, beam ceiling, hewn plank door, and oak dining table. Grey himself brought the teak beams from one of his fishing trips to Tahiti. Guests are welcome to play the grand piano, or you may prefer to curl up by the fire with one of Grey's books from the hotel's collection. Better yet, step from the rustic living room onto the terrace to drink in one of the island's most beautiful views of the yacht-filled harbor, rolling hills, and blue sea.

An arrowhead-shaped swimming pool lies beside gardens of

jade and pepper trees. Morning coffee and toast are served here, on the outer terrace, or in the living room.

BALBOA

Balboa Inn

105 Main Street
Balboa, CA 92661
714-675-3412
800-652-2526
Fax: 714-673-4587

A 1920s villa-style hotel near the ocean

General manager: Lalith James. **Accommodations:** 34 rooms and suites. **Rates:** $90–$140 single or double, suites $160–$250. **Added:** 10% tax. **Payment:** Major credit cards. **Children:** Free in room with parents. **Pets:** Small pets allowed. **Smoking:** Nonsmoking rooms available.

Balboa, at Newport Beach south of Los Angeles, is the image of a southern California beach scene. In the heart of the hubbub is the Balboa Inn, a historic landmark that resembles a European villa.

Built in 1928, the restored hotel has retained hints of the period. The tiled lobby is cool and usually quiet. Beyond it is a shady courtyard for outdoor dining next to the Almare restaurant, which serves Italian foods. An outdoor staircase leads to the guest rooms on the second and third floors. There are sixteen types of rooms and eight small suites, each with slight differences in decor. Typical is Room 217, with pine furniture and a view of the ocean and pier. If you're tall, Room 220 is ideal. Designed for the basketball player Kareem Abdul Jabbar, who once owned the hotel, it has high doors and an extra-long king-size bed.

There's a large pool surrounded by a sundeck. Room service is available. Activities in the area include concerts at the Balboa Pavilion a few blocks away, ferry rides to Balboa Island, and rides on the Catalina Flyer to Catalina Island, twenty-six miles away. Balboa and Newport have numerous restaurants, several specializing in fresh seafood.

> **Sun worshippers on the sand, T-shirt shops, boutiques, sidewalks crowded with tourists and roller skaters, a ferris wheel, a carousel — they're all here, creating an atmosphere of fun and perpetual summer.**

BEVERLY HILLS

The Peninsula Beverly Hills

9882 Little Santa Monica Blvd.
Beverly Hills, CA 90212
310-551-2888
800-462-7899
Fax: 310-785-0426

An elegant,
luxurious villa
in the city

General manager: Ali Kasikci. **Accommodations:** 196 rooms, includes 32 suites. **Rates:** $315–$400 single, $345–$430 double, suites $500–$3000. **Payment:** Major credit cards. **Children:** Free in room with parents. **Pets:** Small pets allowed in villas, by arrangement. **Smoking:** Nonsmoking rooms available.

Like a carefully tended residential estate, the Peninsula Beverly Hills is surrounded by lush gardens and foliage. Tiles, planters, trellises, and fountains add to the European character of this outstanding hotel's landscape. In the heart of Beverly Hills, it's an oasis of elegance and beauty, with a quality attained by very few hotels.

Only four stories high, this French Renaissance–style hotel resembles a grand private villa. The cool white narrow lobby opens to the Living Room, a salon with a fireplace and windows overlooking sculpture and greenery. Light lunches and high tea are served here while a harpist plays.

Pale apricot walls, luxurious fabrics, peach marble, and detailed woodwork are some of the design touches that create an atmosphere of a luxurious home. When you arrive in your room, you are greeted with Chinese tea or lemonade and homemade cookies — another gracious, personal touch. There are night lights by the bedside console, baskets filled with a traveler's needs such as a toothbrush and razor, and or-chids and deep soaking tubs in the bathrooms. Each room has a stocked bar and refrigerator, three phones, computer and fax hookups, and a safe.

Suites feature full sound systems, art objects from around the world, and, as a final reminder that you are staying in out-of-the-ordinary lodgings, personal stationery that states you are in residence at the Peninsula.

Separated from the main hotel, five two-story vil-

> A member of the exclusive Peninsula Group, this hotel opened in 1991 and caters mostly to a moneyed clientele of individual travelers and small groups — you'll never find convention crowds here. It's twelve miles from downtown Los Angeles and the L.A. airport.

las contain sixteen lavishly furnished rooms and suites. They range in size from 580 to 2,250 square feet. Some have kitchens, individual security systems, spas, terraces, and fire-places.

One of the hotel's best features is its rooftop garden with spa and 60-foot heated outdoor pool overlooking Beverly Hills and Century City. White poolside cabanas may be reserved for a fee, which includes a phone, fruit basket, and other amenities. The rooftop cafe serves light meals and cocktails.

The hotel's main restaurant is the Belvedere, with garden views and a classic Continental cuisine. By contrast, the Club Bar is a handsome lounge in maple and brass, with a collection of museum-quality California landscapes.

The Regent Beverly Wilshire

9500 Wilshire Blvd.
Beverly Hills, CA 90212
310-275-5200
800-421-4354
Fax: 310-274-2851

*A glamorous
landmark hotel*

Manager: John Indrieri. **Accommodations:** 220 rooms, 54 suites. **Rates:** Singles start at $275, doubles start at $295, suites start at $425. **Added:** 15.2% tax. **Payment:** Major credit cards. **Children:** Free in room with parents. **Pets:** Allowed. **Smoking:** Nonsmoking rooms available.

The rococo facade of the Beverly Wilshire Hotel has been a famous landmark since 1928. It was glamorous then, but now, after a $100 million renovation, the word has new meaning. As the Regent Beverly Wilshire, it's one of the world's grand hotels.

The lobby, with its marble columns, inlaid woods, massive bouquets, and tall palms, whispers of elegance and good taste, and is the first evidence that you're checking into a first-rate establishment. (The hotel spends thousands of dollars a month on flowers alone and employs six florists.) The brass elevators with pressed motifs from the 20s, mahogany paneling, and an elegant bench in case you want to rest on the way to your floor, add to the sense of luxury and comfort.

Through the years the hotel has hosted many famous figures including former Presidents Carter, Reagan, and Ford, Emperor Hirohito of Japan, the Dalai Lama, the Aga Kahn, Elton John, Ringo Starr, Mick Jagger, Andrew Lloyd Webber, and the royal families of Monaco and Great Britain. Many of them stayed in the five-room, three-bath presidential suite.

There's a long entrance hallway, a formal dining room, and a regal master bedroom with a high half canopy bed. The guest bedroom has an Oriental look, and each bedroom has its own sumptuous bath and formal parlor. While the suite retains the hotel's period flavor, even to the original pegwood floors and skylights, modern amenities such as a shower/steam room in the master bath have been incorporated for maximum guest comfort. Other special suites are the cabana and veranda suites.

Guest rooms are in two buildings, the Beverly and the Wilshire, which are divided by a domed entrance road lit by gas lanterns that once held court at Edinburgh Castle.

Rooms in the Wil-shire building are spacious, and are well furnished in sunny pastels. Rooms in the Beverly wing, which was constructed in 1972, are also pleasant in yellows and deep greens, with bleached wood pieces, and windows that offer fine views and lots of light. All rooms have the expected amenities of a modern luxury hotel, including three phones, and a mini-TV in the bathroom. There are hair dryers, scales, robes, shaving mirrors, high-quality toiletries, wonderfully fluffy pillows, and lots of pink marble. On each floor there's a room attendant who can be summoned with the push of a button. The attendant will mend a hem, pack your bags, produce an iron and ironing board, or bring in a basket of baby needs and a crib.

> **The Beverly Wilshire's Hollywood ties run deep. Elvis Presley often stayed in the hotel when shooting films, Warren Beatty lived in the hotel for a number of years, and motion picture deals are often struck over a meal in one of the hotel's restaurants. In recent years the hotel has become somewhat of a celebrity in its own right as the back-drop for some of the scenes in the popular movie *Pretty Woman*.**

The Regent Beverly Wilshire takes justifiable pride in all its eating spots, but the award-winning Dining Room is in a class by itself. Surrounded by lush French art, Regency furnishings, and parquet floors, you can order wood-fired veal chop with roasted pear sauce or Lake Superior whitefish with an emerald mustard sauce, and other imaginative dishes from the menu that changes daily. The lengthy wine list offers a wide range of labels and prices. Sunday brunch, with a lavish appetizer buffet, and Saturday fashion luncheons are also popular meals served by the Dining Room. The Café has an upscale diner theme and serves traditional American fare, including soda fountain milkshakes and malted milks. The Bar, with its mahogany bar and French marquetry panels, is an elegant and intimate spot to enjoy a cocktail and perhaps spot a celebrity or two.

On the second floor of the Beverly Wing is a fitness center with weight machines, saunas, hot tubs, a snack bar, and an outdoor pool (a replica of Sophia Loren's pool in Italy) surrounded by jardinieres of bougainvillea and creeping fig. Massage, facials, and manicure and pedicure treatments are available. Business travelers appreciate the secretarial, telex, copying, computer, and delivery services. Shoppers revel in the hotel's location — it's directly across the street from Rodeo Drive, the famous street of designer shops. Other nearby streets have appealing boutiques, cafés, and art galleries, while major department stores are represented on Wilshire Boulevard.

BIG BEAR LAKE

The Knickerbocker Mansion

P.O. Box 3661
869 South Knickerbocker
Big Bear Lake, CA 92315
714-866-8221

A roomy log house close to ski trails and a national forest

Innkeeper: Phyllis Knight. **Accommodations:** 10 rooms (5 with private bath; 5 share 2 baths). **Rates:** $95–$165 single or double, $10 additional person. **Included:** Full breakfast. Minimum stay: 2 nights on weekends. **Payment:** MasterCard, Visa. **Children:** Welcome. **Pets:** Not allowed. **Smoking:** Not allowed.

In the early 1920s, Bill and Rose Knickerbocker built this big, rambling, log house in the woods, near the waterside village of Big Bear Lake. They raised five children here, and Bill gained notoriety for his wild poker games — there are still bullets in the walls.

Now it's a place for romantic retreats, ski trips, and active vacations. The inn is one and a half miles from Bear Mountain and close to Snow Forest; it's a three-block walk to shops and the lake. The national forest behind the inn is webbed with hiking and mountain-biking trails. In addition, the inn offers horseshoes, croquet, darts, and table tennis.

In the dining room, a homey place with baskets of dried flowers, family photos, and a loom (Phyllis is a weaver), everyone eats at one table. Fruit, muffins, cereal, yogurt, blueberry pancakes, and crêpes filled with chicken, green peppers, and cheese, are some of the breakfast dishes.

> **You'll be greeted by Nellie, a friendly border collie, and led into the foyer and parlor, where couches wait by the stone fireplace. The room is filled with entertainment possibilities, including a piano, puzzles, games, and books. From the parlor, the front door opens to a veranda with a hammock for two, a quiet spot to relax under the ponderosa pines.**

The stairs that lead up to the guest rooms in the main house are fashioned from split logs. Blue Room, in a corner, is sunny and bright with a patchwork quilt and flowered wallpaper. Rose's Room has rustic paneling and bunk beds tucked into a closet — suitable when you're traveling with children. These rooms share a bath at the end of the hall. Calico, with a hammock on the balcony and glimpses of the lake, is nice in summer; it adjoins and shares a bath with Treasure Room.

The suite on the third floor holds four people. It has a woodstove, a TV with VCR, a CD player, a microwave, a refrigerator, and a double whirlpool. All the rooms have television, heirloom quilts, and robes and towels you can take to the outdoor Jacuzzi.

The other rooms are in the carriage house, reached by a covered walkway, past a redwood deck that is fine for lounging in the sun. Named for the four seasons, the carriage house rooms have fireplaces and Victorian accents and are good choices when you favor seclusion at the edge of the forest.

Special events and seminars are often held at the Knicker-bocker. Several weekends a year an astronomer comes in from Griffith Observatory and sets up a telescope so stargazers can scan the heavens.

CARLSBAD

La Costa Resort and Spa

Costa del Mar Road
Carlsbad, CA 92009
619-438-9111
800-854-5000
Fax: 619-438-3758

A large luxury resort in the country

Managing director: John Peto. **Accommodations:** 400 rooms, 77 suites, and 6 executive homes. **Rates:** $225–$340 single or double, $35 each additional adult, suites $395 and up, executive homes $1,050 and up. **Payment:** Major credit cards. **Children:** Under age 18 free in room with parents. **Pets:** Not allowed. **Smoking:** Nonsmoking rooms available.

La Costa combines a concern for health and fitness with luxury, fine dining, outdoor recreation, and lavish entertainment all in a resort complex that sprawls over 400 acres of hills in the southern California sun. It's just off I-5, ninety minutes south of Los Angeles and thirty minutes north of San Diego. Opened in 1965, La Costa underwent a $100 million remodeling in 1987 which gave it a softer, more romantic appearance, with rose-colored buildings, red tile roofs, and arched walkways and windows.

The guest rooms are decorated in teal, peach, and tan. The best rooms in the main building are those inside, overlooking tall ferns and eucalyptus trees. The outside rooms, which view the road and parking lots, are more susceptible to noise. The other rooms are near the spa center, golf courses, and tennis courts. Suites are twice the size of standard rooms, but all are spacious and have terrycloth robes, large mirrors, lighted vanity tables, television and phones, and baskets of individual toiletries — La Costa's brand of course. Most of La

Costa's suites have one or two bedrooms; the executive homes have two to five bedrooms and up to three and a half baths. Complimentary valet parking and transportation to your rooms are provided.

The spa facilities are extensive, featuring rock steam baths, bracing Swiss showers, facials, massages, herbal wraps, and loofah scrubs. There's a complete fitness program of exercise and nutrition classes. However, La Costa is more a worldly resort than a sequestered spa. It bustles with activity and caters to groups looking for a variety of pleasures.

The resort's conference center can hold up to a thousand people for a reception. The complex, which includes a grand ballroom and fourteen meeting rooms, boasts advanced audio-visual systems and simultaneous translation capability.

La Costa's restaurants offer a range of dining choices. The Brasserie is

> In the Clubhouse you can see the paintings of golf greats who have won the Tournament of Champions on La Costa's greens. In the evening, live entertainment is presented in the Tournament of Champions Lounge.

casual and serves health-conscious spa cuisine in addition to more traditional fare. Classical music plays in the background in Ristorante Figaro, where tapas, pastas, and meats are served with a Mediterranean slant. Pisces, with appropriate fish-patterned fabric wall coverings and shell-shaped lighting fixtures, serves seafood. There's also a snack bar adjacent to center court at the racquet club.

The resort has racquet courts, swimming pools, and two 18-hole championship golf courses, where major golf events take place. Bicycles are available to rent. A special program, Camp La Costa, is devoted to children ages five to fourteen. Arts and crafts, golf and tennis lessons, and nature walks are some of the activities pursued at the day camp.

Pelican Cove Inn

320 Walnut Avenue
Carlsbad, CA 92008
619-434-5995
Fax: 619-434-6015

*A B&B in a
beach resort town*

Innkeepers: Kris and Nancy Nayudu.
Accommodations: 8 rooms (all with private bath). **Rates:** $85–$175 single or double, $15 additional person. Included: Full breakfast. Minimum stay: 2 nights on weekends. **Payment:** Major credit cards. **Children:** Age 12 and older welcome. **Pets:** Not allowed. **Smoking:** Not allowed.

Carlsbad, once known for its mineral waters, is a comparatively little-known resort town thirty miles north of San Diego. The Nayudus are happy to tell their guests about its attractions, and their charming inn is certainly one of them.

The gray exterior with burgundy trim and white-railinged walkways that lead to rooms and decks on multilevels give the inn a boatlike appearance — appropriate for this lodging that is just two blocks from the beach. Colorful plants at the entrance are cheerful and inviting.

**Pelican Cove is just 200 yards from the beach.
Two walkways along the beachfront are popular strolling, bicycling, and jogging paths. The friendly and accommodating innkeepers will lend you beach chairs, towels, and picnic baskets for jaunts around the area.**

All the guest rooms in this comfortable bed-and-breakfast are light and airy, have private entrances, fireplaces, and ceiling fans. Each has a feather bed with a down comforter, a television, and antique furnishings. Thoughtful details include clock radios, good reading lamps, handmade herbal soaps, and candy.

Coronado in light peaches and greens, has a draped canopy pole bed and an oversize Jacuzzi tub. Laguna, with a colorful lavender and floral decor, has white wicker furniture. La Jolla, sunny in cream-colored tones, has a fainting couch. Newport, facing the street, features an unusual lofty conical ceiling of green beams beneath the inn's distinctive cupola. Carlsbad has a high bed, an antique reproduction complete with stepstool and mirrored headboard. Carlsbad adjoins Balboa, the smallest room.

Breakfast — ham and asparagus strata, cottage cheese pancakes, artichoke quiche, and Scotch eggs might be served — is set on a table in a corner of the front parlor. This small room serves as the lobby, phone room, and visiting area, so it can be cramped. Better to take a tray back to your room, to the gazebo in the garden, or up to the sundeck or rooftop deck.

The inn is close to tennis, golf, fishing, sailing, and shopping. It's within walking distance of several restaurants, such as Chin's, where Szechuan fare is served. Try Dini's for its ocean view, Neiman's for a Victorian atmosphere, and Henry's for good food and service.

CORONADO

Coronado Victorian House

1000 Eighth Street
Coronado, CA 92118
619-435-2200

> *A unique
> bed and breakfast
> in the heart of
> Coronado*

Innkeeper: Bonni Marie Kinosian. **Accommodations:** 7 rooms (all with private bath). **Rates:** Start at $200; each package is individually designed and priced accordingly. **Payment:** Personal checks. **Children:** Welcome. **Pets:** Not allowed. **Smoking:** Allowed outdoors only.

At this far from ordinary bed and breakfast you can brush up on your tap, ballet, or ballroom dancing; take an exercise class; solve a murder mystery; dine on ethnic cuisine, then learn how to cook it; or walk to the beach with a gourmet picnic basket in tow — all thanks to the efforts of the energetic innkeeper. Bonni Marie Kinosian is a woman of many talents. A longtime dance teacher, Bonni Marie's dance studio adjoins the inn, and guests often take a private dance lesson at some point during their stay.

Bonni Marie is also an excellent cook. Of Armenian descent, she incorporates ethnic dishes in the meals she prepares with many recipes coming from a simple old Armenian cookbook with family recipes tucked between the pages. At breakfast there's homemade yogurt, called lebon and pilaf, alongside fruit and more traditional breakfast items. In the afternoons zucchini salsa and sarma (rolled grape leaves) are served with homebaked Armenian bread. If you're intrigued as to how these delicacies are made, Bonni Marie can give you a cooking lesson, and supply you with the recipes so you can try your hand at replicating them at home. Since the beach is just under four blocks from the inn, she'll also make up a picnic basket for you including ethnic foods if you'd like them.

Bonni Marie put the same time and enthusiasm in creating the inn, as she does in welcoming her guests. The Victorian that houses the inn was built in 1894. Bonni Marie spent four years restoring the home before opening it as a bed-and-breakfast in 1993, and won an award for its preservation in the process. The inn is furnished with antiques and stunning Persian rugs, some of which were brought over by her father when he immigrated to the United States.

> **Holidays get special attention at the inn. The innkeeper cooks an elaborate Valentine's Day dinner, and the house is festively decorated during the holiday season. Murder mystery weekends are also offered.**

Rooms, named for famous dancers or ballets, are individually decorated. Although all of the beds are antiques, they have modern mattresses and featherbeds, and all of the rooms have small televisions and refrigerators. In burgundies and blues, Baryshnikov is handsome with twin sleigh beds that date back to 1810. Footstools are provided because the beds are high in order to accommodate trundles underneath. Nutcracker is a small room, but has its own private entrance and porch with a wicker settee. The room, in plums and silvers, has a white spool bed and a clawfoot tub.

As one might expect, a beautiful door leads out to a balcony in the romantic Romeo and Juliet suite. The high brass bed is topped with a cross-stitched quilt, and the large bath has a Jacuzzi tub, double shower, and a vanity made from a Victorian dresser. Pavlova, with pretty floral wallpaper, also has a brass bed.

On the top floor a Persian rug-lined hallway leads to guest rooms named after the legendary dancing pair Fred Astaire and Ginger Rogers. Fred, a cheerful room, has a daybed as well as a double, covered in chintz. Its bath, which is located down a flight of stairs, has a pull-chain toilet original to the home. In Ginger, cozy beds tucked under the eaves are perfect for children; and the two rooms combined might make a good choice for families.

All guests are welcome to use the living room on the second floor where seven foot windows can be opened from both the top or the bottom to bring in the ocean breeze. Here the decor includes everything from a bronze angel chandelier and a fainting couch to a table laid with a checker set. Breakfast is served in the adjoining dining room on a table elegantly set with lace, gold leaf china, and silverware with mother-of-pearl handles.

When not taking a dance class or a cooking lesson, guests can enjoy the bilevel terrace off the dining room, head to the beach, explore charming Coronado, or visit San Diego's many attractions just across the bridge.

Hotel Del Coronado

1500 Orange Avenue
Coronado, CA 92118
619-435-6611
800-HOTEL-DEL
Fax: 619-522-8262

A historic landmark resort on the beach

General manager: Dean Nelson.
Accommodations: 692 rooms. **Rates:** $169–$389 single or double, $25 additional person; suites $499 and up. **Minimum stay:** 2 nights on weekends. **Payment:** Major credit cards. **Children:** Under age 15 free in room with parents. **Pets:** Not allowed. **Smoking:** Nonsmoking rooms available.

The Del, as it's affectionately called by frequent guests, is a living legend, a significant piece of southern California's history. Here modern comforts have been added to the rich patina of past glories.

The Del Coronado opened in 1888, the result of the grand dreams of Elisha Babcock, a railroad tycoon who wanted to build a resort that would be "the talk of the Western World." The hotel he and his partner, H. L. Story, built on a peninsula in San Diego Bay was the largest structure outside New York

City to have electric lights. It's said that Thomas Edison supervised the installation of the incandescent lamps and that he pulled the switch for the hotel's first electrically lighted Christmas tree. Quickly established as a cultural oasis in the sparsely settled West, the resplendent Del drew celebrities, dignitaries, and royalty. Twelve U.S. presidents stayed at the hotel during its first hundred years. Charles Lindbergh had a reception here following his solo flight over the Atlantic. Frank L. Baum wrote part of *The Wizard of Oz* on the premises and based the Emerald City on the towered Victorian structure. The Prince of Wales — later King Edward VIII and then the Duke of Windsor — was honored at a dinner here in 1920, when he reportedly met Wallis Simpson for the first time.

> **Numerous films and television shows have been made on the grounds of the Del Coronado. The most famous and enduring was *Some Like It Hot*, filmed in 1958 with Marilyn Monroe, Jack Lemmon, and Tony Curtis.**

All this history is on display in the hotel's lower level corridors, providing glimpses of change from 1888 to the present. Today, most people arrive at the Del by car and catch their first glimpse of the red and white Victorian extravaganza while driving across a high bridge that connects San Diego to Coronado. There's a sense of quaintness in the village of Coronado, with its winding, tree-lined streets and shops tucked away in courtyards, yet the city of San Diego is just minutes across the bay. Coronado also has a municipal golf course, several small hotels, and a Navy presence.

The original five-story, amply curved structure of the Del Coronado is still in use today, along with two newer sections closer to the beach. The lobby is a throw-back to an earlier era with its oak ceiling and muted lighting, and guest rooms in the main building are grouped around a lush garden courtyard. Lawns, palm trees, and a latticed gazebo make this a favorite spot for weddings and relaxation away from the hubbub of the lobby and arcades of shops. Between the courtyard and lobby is Palm Court, where you may purchase a Continental breakfast in the morning and order coffee all day.

In the lobby, an old-fashioned birdcage elevator, still operating, stands in a corner near the door to the Crown Room, the Del's majestic dining room. Here crown-shaped chandeliers hang from one of the largest support-free structures in the country. The lofty redwood-paneled room has a 30-foot-high elliptical ceiling made of sugar pine that was crafted without a single nail. Banquets and formal state dinners are held here, though the food is less spectacular than the atmosphere.

Downstairs, the Prince of Wales restaurant, named for the Duke of Windsor, is elegant. In soft beiges and creams, the restaurant is art deco in decor and intimate in ambience. Pictures of the Duke of Windsor and Wallis Simpson hang on one wall, and the table below is considered the most romantic in honor of their relationship. (The Duke's uniform is on display just outside the restaurant.) For dinner, traditional American favorites such as broiled salmon and lamb chops are given modern treatments. The broiled salmon comes with artichokes and Port Salut ravioli in a tomato tarragon sauce, and the lamb chop is topped with mustard marmalade and served with baby beans and oven-roasted potatoes. A private dining room seating up to sixteen adjoins the restaurant and can be reserved for small functions.

The more casual Ocean Terrace is open for breakfast on weekends and lunch and cocktails daily. It overlooks the gazebo bar, the Olympic-size swimming pool, two miles of sandy beach, and tennis courts where you half expect the women to be wearing 1920s style tennis dresses. On the terrace, glass panels shield diners from the wind while maintaining the marvelous ocean view. For quick meals, you can buy snacks in the basement deli, which was carved from the hotel's original stone cistern.

Guest rooms retain their period decor while meeting the expectations of today's travelers. The large rooms with private verandas facing the sea are preferred; they have tall windows, varying configurations, comfortable couches, king- or queen-size beds with wicker headboards and floral spreads, and roomy baths with showers. Some are rumored to be haunted, and all have ceiling fans, alarm-clock radios, televisions, phones, safes, and stocked mini-bars. Movies filmed at the hotel are shown nightly on one of the TV channels.

In Ocean Towers, the newer annex, seven floors contain over 300 rooms, all redecorated. The guest rooms lack the Victorian flavor that gives the original Del its charm, but they're softer and lighter in decor and provide a retreat from the bustle across the way. The annex has its own swimming pool, and most of the rooms have balconies. All have air conditioning and king-size beds.

The service at the Del Coronado is outstanding. The award-winning staff is enthusiastic and eager to please, from the youngest valets to those who've been loyal to the Del for forty years and more. The hotel has meeting and conference rooms and a convention center that accommodates up to 1,500. Services at the hotel's spa include facials, massages, body masks, fitness instruction, and steam and whirlpool baths.

Le Meridien San Diego at Coronado

2000 Second Street
Coronado, CA 92118
619-435-3000
800-543-4300
Fax: 619-435-3032

> *An elegant resort on San Diego Bay*

Managing director: Abel Damergi. **Accommodations:** 265 rooms, 7 executive suites, 28 villa suites. **Rates:** $165–$225, suites $475–$725. **Added:** 8% tax. **Payment:** Major credit cards. **Children:** Under age 12 free in room with parents. **Pets:** Not allowed. **Smoking:** Nonsmoking rooms available.

The natural surroundings and the southern California climate provided inspiration for the design of Le Meridien, an elegant bayfront resort. Opened in 1988, it sits on 16 acres at the northeast corner of Coronado Island, facing San Diego Bay, the bridge, and the city skyline.

In the lobby and public areas, limestone flooring and walls glazed in honey tones provide a backdrop to oversize furnishings that range from large rattan settees to an antique armoire. A handsome flower arrangement is the centerpiece, and crimson ginger and palms fill corner pots.

In Marius, the softly lit formal dining room, the cuisine is French. The casual L'Escale has a country look and seafood is the specialty. With a wall of windows facing the terrace, the pool, and the bay, L'Escale is a popular setting for the Saturday jazz brunch and the restaurant's Latin extravaganza featuring South American fare and Latin music. In the cocktail lounge, La Provence, the San Diegans' passion for sailing is evident. Pictures of old schooners and the sleek, 12-meter *Stars and Stripes* grace the walls.

The guest rooms, which are spread over three floors and outlying villas, have views of the bay, lagoon, or Tidelands Park, a 22-acre community park that borders Le Meridien.

> At the dock, cruise vessels will stop to take you for a cruise of the harbor or taxi you to Seaport Village, the convention center, and other stops. Bicycling, sailing, water skiing, and windsurfing can be arranged.

The standard rooms, with pale wood furniture and seafoam colors, are comfortable and generously sized. They have mini-bars, marble-topped vanities, deep tubs, hair dryers, and Lanvin toiletries. The corner, executive suites have deeper toned furnishings and Laura Ashley designs.

The villas, named after Impressionist artists, are like private homes, each with its own terrace. The villa cluster has its own pool and whirlpool. Celebrities seeking seclusion and visitors on longer stays like these luxury lodgings with one or two bedrooms. They have French country print fabrics, kitchenettes, wet bars, VCRs, built-in cupboards, double-headed showers, and oversize Jacuzzis, along with the more usual amenities. The resort has meeting and banquet space and a business center.

Le Meridien draws raves for the high quality of its service and accommodations, but its most striking feature is the landscaping. Tropical plantings and a pond with pink flamingoes set the tone at the entrance. Ducks, swans, and geese swim in a lagoon. As you walk the path that winds through the resort and along the waterfront, you'll see a koi pond, an aviary, fountains, and irises and lilies blooming along the edge of a stream.

The resort has six tennis courts, three pools, and a spa with a wide range of services. The spa packages range from a one-day rejuvenator (massage, facial, herbal wrap, lunch) to four days of body pampering and treatments.

Loews Coronado Bay Resort

4000 Coronado Bay Road
Coronado, CA 92118
619-424-4000
800-23-LOEWS
Fax: 619-424-4400

*A waterside resort
across the bay
from San Diego*

Manager: John Thacker. **Accommodations:** 436 rooms and suites. **Rates:** $174–$245 single or double, $20 additional person,Bayside units start at $500 and can accommodate up to 6 people. **Added:** 8% tax. **Payment:** Major credit cards. **Children:** Welcome. **Pets:** Not allowed. **Smoking:** Nonsmoking rooms available.

San Diego's downtown skyline is across the bay from this lovely waterside resort. The city is only a water taxi ride away, while the marina and beach are just out the door — so visitors here get the best of both worlds. Often conventioneers meeting in San Diego stay here for a change of scene. Boaters like the fully secured 80-slip anchorage, directly in front of the hotel, which can accommodate both small cruisers and mega-yachts.

The curving, three-story buildings of the main hotel are fully connected by a hallway, and stand on a 14-acre private peninsula between Crown Isle Marina and San Diego Bay. Inside, there's a broad lobby with crystal chandeliers and a double staircase rising to a mezzanine. From here, wide, arching windows frame views of the bay and city.

The restaurants are like the rest of the hotel — informal but impeccably tasteful. Critically acclaimed Azzura Point is the resort's fine dining restaurant, romantic and candlelit in the evenings. On the second floor on the bay side, it features fresh seafood dishes such as grilled Pacific swordfish with Asian stirfry in a spicy red Thai shellfish broth, and morel-crusted Alaskan halibut with creamy braised fennel, leek, and Barola wine. For more casual meals there's the Café, overlooking the boats of the marina, and a wonderful market and deli off the lobby where you can buy box lunches as well as gourmet foods, cookbooks, and various gifts and sundries. In Cays Lounge, musicians play nightly.

Guest rooms are attractive and inviting, and every room has a balcony and a view of the bay, pool, or marina. Big windows, pastel walls, splashy floral fabrics, and touches of rattan emphasize the sunny resort atmosphere, while spacious baths with marble vanities, deep soaking tubs, separate showers, scales, hair dryers, and makeup mirrors add a note of luxury and comfort. The hotel also appeals to business travelers who need desks, phones, a business center, and lots of meeting space; and for executives that need to stay in touch with their office — all suites have their own fax machines. Loews also has one of the largest ballrooms in San Diego, as well as several breakout rooms and audiovisual equipment.

> **The resort's major appeal lies in its recreational facilities. There are five tennis courts, three pools, a small putting green, and easy access to miles of beach. Snorkeling, aerobics, and step classes are all given at the resort, and wave runners, paddleboats, sailboats, and kayaks are available for rental.**

The Bayside units are an excellent lodging choice for small groups or families traveling together because they have private entrances, kitchen areas, and separate living rooms. Stretched along the bay, the units with peach-stuccoed exteriors and red tile roofs, are nicely landscaped on the outside, and furnished in soothing pastel tones on the inside. Large bay windows accentuate the view, and San Diego bay literally laps beneath each unit's balcony. The most deluxe accommodations at the resort, their baths have double Jacuzzi tubs.

For families, the resort's Commodore Kids program has a roster of entertainment activities for children, and daycare is provided by licensed caregivers at the Commodore Kids Clubhouse. For area sightseeing, a shuttle service runs every day to Coronado and San Diego, and to Mexico on weekends.

DANA POINT

Blue Lantern Inn

34343 Street of the Blue Lantern
Dana Point, CA 92629
714-661-1304
800-950-1236
Fax: 714-496-1483

*A stylish clifftop
inn overlooking
the harbor*

Innkeeper: Nancy Teel. **Accommodations:** 29 rooms (all with private bath). **Rates:** $135–$200 single or double, suites $250–$350, $15 additional person. **Included:** Breakfast buffet and afternoon tea. **Added:** 10% tax. **Payment:** Major credit cards. **Children:** Under age 5 free in room with parents. **Pets:** Not allowed. **Smoking:** Not allowed.

High on a bluff above the Dana Point Yacht Harbor, the Blue Lantern presents panoramic views as well as comfortable accommodations and fine service. Its gabled, gray frame trimmed in white reflects the Cape Cod theme of Dana Point.

The Blue Lantern is similar to the other Four Sisters inns in its commitment to high quality, capable staff, and attention to detail. Everything here is done well. The reception area, sitting room, library, and dining room are peaceful, welcoming places where you can enjoy complimentary wine and hors d'oeuvres

Near the inn is the Cannon restaurant, where you can enjoy candlelight dining with a stunning view. For a livelier spot with festive crowds, good mesquite broiled seafood, and fast service, go to the Harbor Grill in Mariners' Village at the water's edge.

in the afternoon, talk to the concierge about Dana Point's attractions, relax in front of a fire, and pick up a cookie on your way to your room.

The guest rooms, done in coastal colors, have traditional and antique furniture, televisions, coffeemakers, phones, terry bathrobes, shuttered windows, and attractive molding detail. Some rooms have whirlpool tubs and gas fireplaces.

Pacific Edge rooms have a balcony or flower-lined terrace that overlooks the harbor where waves crash against a long stone breakwater. Although Hill view rooms don't overlook the ocean, they are still delightful; and Harbor view rooms have bay windows. Room 309, with its harbor view, has a writing desk, wicker furnishings, bay windows, and a skylight in the bath. The Tower rooms are worth the splurge. The second floor Tower room (#201), decorated in mints, creams, and lavenders, has multiple windows that bring in lots of light, a large terrace, a four-poster bed topped with plentiful pillows, and an oval Jacuzzi tub. The first floor Tower room has a step-down living room.

In the morning, the *Los Angeles Times* is delivered to your door. An ample buffet breakfast of juice, granola, muffins, and a hot dish such as baked French toast is served in the sun-room off the lobby. Downstairs is a small exercise room with a stairclimber, treadmill, lifecycle, and weight machine.

Stuffed animal lovers will be certain to notice the inn's teddy bears. The fluffy creatures climb the central staircase, and rest on each guest bed. For guests that happen to fall in love with a particular bear, adoption papers are available at the front desk.

Marriott's Laguna Cliffs Resort

25135 Park Lantern
Dana Point, CA 92629
714-661-5000
800-533-9748
Fax: 714-661-5358

> *A stylish, casual resort on a hill above the sea*

Manager: Michael Miner. **Accommodations:** 333 rooms, 17 suites. **Rates:** $149–$219 single or double, $20 additional person, suites start at $300. **Added:** 10% tax. **Payment:** Major credit cards. **Children:** Under age 16 free in room with parents. **Pets:** Not allowed. **Smoking:** Nonsmoking rooms available

South of Laguna Beach is a point of land named for Richard Henry Dana, Jr., who wrote *Two Years Before the Mast.* Dana Point has a yacht harbor, a lighthouse filled with nautical lore, a marine institute, and a complex of shops and restaurants designed to recreate the flavor of the port's 19th-century trading days. And it has, on a grassy hill above the harbor, Marriott's Laguna Cliffs Resort.

The gabled, four-story resort, painted gray with white trim, stands on landscaped grounds overlooking the 2,500-slip harbor. All the rooms have either a full or partial sea view; some have balconies, others their own terraces. They occupy four wings: Laguna, Capistrano, San Clemente, and Del Mar.

The rooms are spacious and comfortably furnished, decorated in neutral tones of beige and gray, with abstract pastel art on the walls. It's not the decor that draws the eye in these rooms; it's the gorgeous view, which makes every visitor immediately open the sliding glass doors and admire the panorama of blue sea and sky. Kimonos with a nautical design hang in the closets. Baths in warm gold marble have a tub and shower, hair dryers, and makeup mirrors.

On the first floor are two lounges beyond the light and open lobby. In Burton's, chrome chairs stand at marble tables by the dance floor. From here there's an oblique view of the harbor. Stop in on a Thursday, Friday, or Saturday night for live jazz and cocktails. Next door, in the Lantern Bay Lounge, a pianist plays mellow jazz during the day. This is a pleasant spot for lunch, as local business-folk will attest. It's a high-ceilinged, bright space, with many windows that have a good view of the resort's lawns and flowers. Water-colors Restaurant is on the lower level, near the lawn that slopes to the road and marina. It serves three meals a day and a Sunday brunch buffet.

> **The mood at Marriot's Laguna Cliff's Resort is that of a casual country club, where guests come for outdoor recreation. You can play tennis, golf at the Links course, take a fishing or whale-watching cruise, or exercise in the health center, which has stationary bicycles, weights, a rowing machine, and a sauna. Massages are available by appointment.**

At the marina, you can rent sailboards and kayaks, go rowing or parasailing, or take the five-mile walk around the harbor's edge. Jet skis and sailboats may be rented.

In the summer months the resort offers a special day program for children called Club Cowabunga. Supervised activities include flying kites in the park, playing games, and visiting the Marine Institute to explore tidepools and see the whale exhibition. In the evenings, movies and videos are shown.

DEL MAR

L'Auberge Del Mar

P.O. Box 2078
1540 Camino Del Mar
Del Mar, CA 92014
619-259-1515
800-553-1336
Fax: 619-793-6433

> *A modern, open resort in a coastal town*

General manager: Dennis Mills. **Accommodations:** 112 rooms and 8 suites. **Rates:** $150–$300 single or double, suites $300–$800. **Added:** 10% tax. **Payment:** Major credit cards. **Children:** Under age 18 free in room with parents (cribs available). **Pets:** Not allowed. **Smoking:** Nonsmoking rooms available.

On a hill overlooking the ocean, twenty minutes north of San Diego and ninety miles south of Los Angeles, L'Auberge is a stylish resort with a reputation for excellent quality. It's on the site of the old Hotel Del Mar, which was frequented by Hollywood celebrities during the '20s, '30s, and '40s. Rudolph Valentino, Bing Crosby, Jimmy Durante, Rita Hayworth, and others have suites and meeting rooms named in their honor in the hotel. The atmosphere is light and open, typical of southern California lodgings. In the marble lobby, which has a double-sided fireplace, skylights allow the sun to stream through to the potted palms and lavish bouquets. This is the heart of the resort, where guests gather for afternoon tea and weekend dinner dances. A buffet brunch is set out on Sunday. Beyond is the terrace with a fountain and flowers and, on a level above, a swimming pool.

You can eat on the terrace, by the pool, or inside in the sunny 15th Street Grille with slate floors and wicker-backed chairs. Regional California cuisine is prepared in the restaurant's demonstration kitchen. Durante's Pub has micro-brewed beer, and wine by the glass.

For recreation, L'Auberge offers two tennis courts (private lessons with a tennis pro can be arranged), two pools, a full-service spa (single and multi-day packages are available), and the attractions of Del Mar: golf (Torrey Pines, Aviara, and Whispering Palms golf courses are all nearby), shopping, bicycling, surfing, strolling to the beach, visiting the Torrey Pines Reserve, and attending the horse races at the famous Del Mar Race Track. The inn has facilities for groups up to 250 people, with nine meeting rooms and a spacious terrace, and for children ages four to fifteen there's the VIK (very important kids) program.

Many guests enjoy continuing the tradition begun when Del Mar was famous for its glamorous visitors. Old photos throughout L'Auberge pay tribute to those earlier times.

The guest rooms, tastefully decorated in appealing colors with lush floral bedspreads and checked fabric sofas in complementing tones, all have a private balcony or terrace; some have panoramic ocean views while others look out on the garden, village, or pool. There are full-length mirrors, telephones with voice mail, large marble baths, stocked mini-bars, and amenities such as hair dryers, Neutrogena toiletries, robes, coffeemakers, irons, and ironing boards. Many rooms have gas fireplaces, and third-floor rooms have elevated domed ceilings with fans.

FAWNSKIN

Windy Point Inn

P.O. Box 375
39015 North Shore Drive
Fawnskin, CA 92333
909-866-2746
Fax: 909-866-1593

> *A secluded,
> contemporary
> home on the lake*

Innkeepers: Val and Kent Kessler.
Accommodations: 3 rooms (all with private bath). **Rates:** $105–$225 single or double. Included: Full breakfast. **Minimum stay:** 2 nights on most weekends. **Payment:** Major credit cards. **Children:** Not appropriate. **Pets:** Not allowed. **Smoking:** Not allowed.

On the north shore of Big Bear Lake, in the San Bernardino Mountains east of Los Angeles, this contemporary home stands on a tiny private peninsula bordered by secluded sandy beaches. Through every window you see a different aspect of the lake, forest, and mountains.

Windy Point offers both serenity and stimulation. You can go for quiet walks, watch the sunset, and play the grand piano or snuggle up by the blazing hearth in the sunken living room. Or you can admire artworks from around the world and visit with the interesting guests who come to the inn.

The guest rooms are on three levels. In the Pines on the first floor you step down to a queen-size bed with a featherbed. The Pines has a corner fireplace in the cozy sitting area, a separate entrance, a refrigerator, and a skylit Jacuzzi. Least expensive, but intimate and romantic, is the Sands, which has a wet bar, a private deck, and a sunrise view.

The most spectacular room is the Peaks, which has glass on three sides revealing wide views through the tops of the pine trees to the lake and often snow-capped mountains. Vaulted ceilings give the suite a grand and open feel, and even the wall above the walk-through galley wet bar is cut out to take advantage of the views. An oversize sofa offers a prime viewing spot, while interesting objets d'art, and weathered driftwood pieces add a timeless style to the modern decor. Sliding glass doors open onto a large deck from which you could almost dive right into the lake, the water seems so close. In the suite's sleeping area there's a king-size platform bed, and the tiled bath has a bidet, a whirlpool tub, and a separate steam shower.

> At Windy Point you can rent a boat from a nearby marina and explore the lake (the inn has a private dock), or make the 12-minute drive to Big Bear's ski slopes.

Amenities abound: thick towels, individually controlled heat, stereo players, VCR, a barbecue. But it's style and personality that make the inn outstanding. Its whimsical sculptures, paintings, and exotic artifacts combine with a sophisticated decorating sense to create a memorable retreat.

Breakfast includes out of the ordinary treats such as bananas Foster crêpes and cinnamon French toast with sautéed fruit. The innkeepers offer afternoon appetizers in the living room or on the deck and will provide suggestions on restaurants, give directions, and even drive you where you want to go.

HOLLYWOOD

La Maida House

11159 La Maida Street
North Hollywood, CA 91601
818-769-3857
Fax: 818-753-9363

*A peaceful retreat
in residential
Hollywood*

Innkeeper: Megan Timothy. **Accommodations:** 11 rooms (7 in bungalows). **Rates:** $85–$210 single or double, discounts for stays longer than 1 week. **Included:** Expanded Continental breakfast. **Added:** 14% tax. **Minimum stay:** 2 nights. **Payment:** Major credit cards. **Children:** Not appropriate. **Pets:** Not allowed. **Smoking:** Not allowed.

This Italianate villa, built in 1926 by Antonio La Maida, exudes romance and beauty from every corner. The inn is distinctive, thanks to the talents and personality of Megan Timothy. She has put her skills at decorating, cooking, painting, sewing, gardening, and carpentry — among others — to play in creating an extraordinary retreat that is a few minutes' drive from the shopping, restaurants, and studios of Los Angeles and Hollywood.

Tropical plants grow in the glass-walled solarium, which opens to a back lawn with a fountain and magnolia trees. The small dining room is where private dinners of culinary distinction are held. If you arrange it with Megan, she'll prepare a light supper before the theater or a four-course dinner with complimentary wine.

Mediterranean in design, with white stucco walls, a red tile roof, and arched doorways and windows, the 25-room villa combines an Old World background with a fresh California outlook and Megan's inimitable style. On the main floor, off the entry hall, is a living room with two groups of chairs invitingly arranged beside the gold marble fireplace. A grand piano stands in one corner.

Windows look toward the gardens and lily pond. Also on the main floor are two dining areas, a den filled with books and soft cushions, and a solarium.

Walk up the curving mahogany staircase, past a brilliant red and gold peacock of stained glass (made by Megan, as are the other ninety-six stained glass creations throughout the inn), and you come to four bedrooms off halls displaying photographs from the innkeeper's world travels. The rooms all have phones, closets with luggage racks and robes, fresh flowers, clock radios, down comforters, and big, tiled bathrooms; some have whirlpool tubs. A thoughtful touch in each bath is the drawer full of toiletries — razors, toothpaste and toothbrush, Alka-Seltzer, and other extras often needed by travelers.

The Cipresso Suite, the largest, is an airy room overlooking the rose garden and tall cypress trees at the side of the house. It has a four-poster canopy bed and wicker chairs piled with pillows. Vigna is dark and peaceful, with vine-green walls. From the window you see over the wall. The other two rooms are equally pleasant: Fontana, in crisp blue and white with twin beds, and Magnolia, furnished in handsome whitewashed pine. Portable TVs and answering machines are available, and there's an executive conference room that accommodates twenty.

All the other guest rooms are in nearby cottages. The Streletzia Suite is the most luxurious, with a wood-burning fireplace, rattan furniture, stained glass accents, and a front porch that views a Japanese fern garden with a goldfish pond.

Among La Maida's special features are the swimming pool behind one of the cottages, an exercise room, a complimentary morning newspaper, a library of guidebooks, evening wine, cookies, and breakfasts that are artistic feasts.

Sunset Marquis Hotel and Villas

1200 N. Alta Loma Road
West Hollywood, CA 90069
310-657-1333
800-858-9758
Fax: 310-652-5300

*A secluded
group of villas
set in landscaped
gardens*

General manager: Rod Gruendyke.
Accommodations: 113 suites, 12
villas. **Rates:** suites $215–$275, villas $350–$1,200. **Payment:**
Major credit cards. **Children:** Under age 12 free in room with
parents. **Pets:** Not allowed. **Smoking:** Nonsmoking rooms
available.

This lovely retreat is ideal if you're looking for quiet luxury
in the heart of Hollywood's bustle. Close to production studios, tourist attractions, and businesses, just a half-block
south of Sunset Boule-
vard, they seem a world
away once you step into
the lobby. A few diners
may be seated in the ro-
mantic little restaurant
on your right, where soft
music plays. A cordial
staff member will show
you to your room.

**A fountain trickles in a
patio, parakeets chirp in the
trees, and rabbits can be
seen hopping among the
calla lilies and azaleas.
White lounge chairs sit by
the pool, each with its
monogrammed pink towel.
There's also an exercise
room, a spa, and sauna.**

The three-story stucco
hotel and its individual
villas stand on two acres
of cloistered gardens and
hills.

You may lunch among
the tropical plants at the poolside café or, if your villa is near
the secluded second pool, have your order delivered there by
the butler.

In the hotel building, rooms are grouped around the main
swimming pool. Decorated in peaches and teals, bedrooms
are separated from living rooms by French doors. Each suite
has two televisions, a safe, and two-line telephones. Some
rooms have VCRs and wet bars. Baths come with makeup
mirrors and hair dryers, and in addition to the usual shampoos and soaps, sunscreen lotion is provided.

If the rooms are attractive, the villas, with one or two bedrooms and baths, are grand. All are light and spacious, with hanging plants, kitchens, and well-proportioned furniture. Some have private terraces overlooking the gardens and herringbone brick walkways; villas on the street have their own parking spaces. Chocolates and wine await your arrival, and the butler will light your fireplace and bring in kitchen equipment if you need it.

Villa 2 North is one of the most deluxe. Hollywood style, with Asian accents, the villa has two gold fainting couches in front of the fireplace, and a grand piano in the living room. Corinthian columns and an arched entryway separate the living room from the dining room. In Villa 1 South a Persian rug lies on the floor before the brick fireplace in the living room, and nearby a dining table seats six. One of the bedrooms has a canopy bed, the other a brass king-size bed, a dressing area, and a garden view patio. Both bedrooms have their own baths with bidets, and separate tubs and showers.

The attentive service at Sunset Marquis equals the setting. Valet parking and shoeshines are available 24 hours a day. Self-parking in the garage under the hotel is complimentary (rare for a city hotel). At evening turndown you're given a weather report, and if you place your breakfast order on the door it will be delivered to your room in the morning. Limousine service is also available. The concierge can arrange for theater tickets, tours, flowers, and appointments with hairdressers — all with a smile.

The Sunset Marquis is where many well-known names and faces go for privacy and relaxation so you may spot a familiar face or two in the hotel's Whiskey Bar which is open only to guests and VIPs — many of them in the music business. Notes restaurant across the hall has only eight tables and an eclectic menu with Asian influences. With La Cienaga's "restaurant row" within easy walking distance, the hotel decided to keep its own eatery small and intimate.

IDYLLWILD

Strawberry Creek Inn

P.O. Box 1818
26370 Highway 243
Idyllwild, CA 92349
909-659-3202
800-262-8969
Fax: 909-659-4707

*A traditional
home in
the mountains*

Innkeepers: Diana Dugan and Jim Goff. **Accommodations:** 9 rooms and 2 cottages (all with private bath). **Rates:** $85–$155 single or double, cottages $125–$135, $20 additional person. **Included:** Full breakfast, except in cottage. **Added:** 10% tax. **Minimum stay:** 2 nights on weekends, longer on holidays. **Payment:** MasterCard, Visa. **Children:** Welcome in cottage. **Pets:** Not allowed. **Smoking:** Not allowed. **Open:** Year-round except Christmas.

In the rustic mountain village of Idyllwild, high above the desert near Palm Springs, stands Strawberry Creek Inn, a rambling, shingled home with a sense of nostalgia.

In the big, open living room, guests like to sit by the fire or browse among the ceiling-high shelves of books (including *How to Open a Country Inn*) in the cozy reading nook. Country antiques, an old-fashioned pie chest, and heirloom quilts furnish the room. On one side, next to a wall of windows, is the breakfast area.

Most of the guest rooms are fairly small. In the main house, the Evergreen room, on the

The savvy innkeepers have combined old-fashioned furnishings with modern comforts in this 1941 house, which lies on wooded grounds above Strawberry Creek. From every window there are views of tall pine and oak trees.

ground floor, has a queen-size canopy bed and a fireplace. Upstairs, the rooms are comfortably and individually furnished with patchwork quilts, ruffled cushions, fresh flowers, and good reading lamps.

Behind the main house is a separate building with rooms that face a courtyard. These are cabinlike retreats with fireplaces, refrigerators, and skylights. Santa Fe has a southwestern decor; Helen's Room is Victorian with a carved walnut bed; Autumn has a four-poster bed and the rich colors of fall, and is handicapped accessible. San Jacinto is a favorite for the stone fireplace, rag rugs, and rustic atmosphere.

The cedar shake cottage down by the creek is a quaint spot, nice for honeymooners. (It can also hold four people, using the Murphy bed and sofa bed.) The cottage, decorated in blue, has a stone fireplace, two bathrooms, and a glassed-in dining porch, as well as a kitchen with a microwave oven, a gas stove, dishes, and staples for cooking. The bedroom is upstairs under the eaves and has a deep whirlpool tub.

Most visitors have high praise for Strawberry Creek. In the guest books they write, "Beautiful memories," "Friendly atmosphere," and "All you need for a romantic weekend."

JULIAN

Julian Hotel

P.O. Box 1856
2032 Main Street
Julian, CA 92036
619-765-0201
800-734-5854 in California

*A historic hotel
in a former
mining town*

Innkeepers: Steve and Gig Ballinger. **Accommodations:** 18 rooms (5 with private bath). **Rates:** $38 single, $64–$110 double, suites $110–$145. **Included:** Full breakfast and afternoon tea. **Added:** 9% tax. **Min-**

imum stay: 2 nights on weekends. **Payment:** Major credit cards. **Children:** Welcome. **Pets:** Not allowed. **Smoking:** Allowed outdoors only.

A hundred years ago, the mining town of Julian was a two-day stage ride from San Diego and had fifteen hotels lodging prospectors with gold fever. Now the trip takes less than two hours and only one hotel is left. The town still draws visitors, but these days they're tourists looking for reminders of the Old West.

The Julian Hotel is the oldest continuously operating hotel in southern California. It was built by freed slaves, Albert and Margaret Robinson, who started with a restaurant and bakery and, as their reputation for hospitality grew, put up the two-story wood frame hotel. Albert planted the cedar and locust trees that circle the hotel today. The Robinsons' venture was a success, and so it remains. It's on the National Register of Historic Places; a landmark with a frontier flavor.

> **You're in another century as soon as you step into the large lobby. A woodstove stands in the center of the room, red velvet curtains hang at the tall windows, and a couple of cats may amble through. You'll be invited to join the other guests for tea and cakes at five o'clock.**

In the large parlor classical music plays in the evenings while guests read, browse through turn-of-the-century Sears catalogs or play Parcheesi. An ample breakfast of eggs Florentine, date nut raisin bread, fresh fruit, oats, coffee, tea, and juice is served here at tables for four.

Upstairs, the rooms are small, but pleasant, and each has space for an antique bed with a modern mattress topped by a patchwork quilt, a dresser with a mirror (some are original to the hotel), a closet, a window covered in lace curtains, and a table and chair. All beds have electric blankets — nights are chilly at Julian's misty 4,000-foot elevation. As in the old days, baths are shared (they're indoors, however; an improvement over the original).

Three rooms off the hotel's porch have private baths, and there are two cottages in back. The one-room cottage off the patio is cozy, with white muslin curtains, a white wicker chair, and a black iron bed under a flowered quilt. In the Honeymoon House, you'll have a wood-burning Franklin stove on a brick hearth, a queen-size bed with a satin spread, and a dressing alcove with clawfoot tub.

The Ballingers, who have owned the Julian Hotel since the late 1970s, have been careful to retain and restore the hotel's original decor. They have put together a walking tour that points out historic landmarks and will direct you to Julian's several antiques stores, gift shops, and a couple of good restaurants. Try Romano's, the Julian Grill, and, for lunch, Mom's Apple Pies. Julian apples are famous in the region; harvest season brings crowds of tourists and apple buyers.

To add to the memories of the time warp you're visiting, take the half-hour horse and carriage ride and then stop at the Bad Blood Studio Saloon and have your photograph taken in frontier costume. An excellent way to see more of the area is by following one of the Ballingers' detailed itineraries to nearby Cuyamaca Ranch State Park, the Anza-Borrego Desert, and Palomar Mountain.

Shadow Mountain Ranch

P.O. Box 791
2771 Frisius Road
Julian, CA 92036
619-765-0323

*A homey
bed-and-breakfast
in the country*

Innkeepers: Jim and Loretta Ketcherside. **Accommodations:** 6 rooms (all with private bath). **Rates:** $80–$100 single or double, $160 cottage for 4. **Included:** Full breakfast. **Added:** 9% tax. **Minimum stay:** 2 nights on weekends. **Payment:** Personal checks or cash. **Children:** Not appropriate. **Pets:** Not allowed. **Smoking:** Not allowed indoors.

This peaceful retreat lies in the rolling, wooded hills outside Julian, a historic mining town east of San Diego. Once an eight-acre apple orchard and cattle ranch, it is now a bed-and-breakfast, and the Ketchersides' home. Visitors can join in feeding their cows, horse, and goat.

Loretta, a former nurse, and Jim, a retired superintendent of schools, enjoy meeting people and sharing their country hideaway. If you arrive in the afternoon, you'll be in time for tea and snacks, served on the deck under the trees, or by the fire in their large, homey living room. There are games, magazines, and books, and the musically inclined hosts have a piano, violin, and guitars for guests to use.

In the Apple Pantry underneath Grandma's Attic or on an outdoor patio called the Cocina, Loretta and Jim serve a ranch-style breakfast: steak or sausage, eggs with steamed vegetables, hot cereal, orange juice, and an endless supply of coffee that will prepare you for an active day. On Sundays, the cook adds strawberry pancakes topped with whipped cream to the array of food. After a few laps in the indoor pool, fishing in the Ketchersides' catch and release pond, a game of horseshoes, croquet, or badminton, and a hike in the Pine Hills forest, you may feel like eating again. The Apple Pantry's kitchen which has a toaster oven, refrigerator, and two burners, can be used by guests, and comes in handy if you'd like to stay put rather than drive in to Julian for dinner.

Each guest room is different and often decorated with an imaginative flair. Oak room, in the main house, is the most traditional, and has a brick sitting area, wood-burning stove, country antiques, and a wonderfully shaped clawfoot tub. Grandma's Attic, across a wooden bridge from the main deck, is named for Loretta who is now a grandmother. Spacious and sunny, the room has a white iron bed with brass accents topped with a pink damask and white lace comforter, wicker furnishings, and a cozy sitting area in a bay window. Loretta's wedding dress is also on display. Outside, next to the path by the wall, is an elaborate miniature village, complete with bridges, trees, and churches. It was made by Loretta's father years ago.

The Enchanted Cottage, on a grassy knoll, is quaint and cozy. It has a wood-burning stove and cushioned seat by a mullioned window that looks into the pine trees, and rabbit motifs appear on a throw and a footstool. Manzanita is a two-bedroom cottage perfect for couples traveling together. A woodstove on a brick hearth warms the living room on chilly mornings where there's a cowhide rug, coffee table, and gameboard. One bedroom is decorated in peach tones and has its own bath, the other is paneled and opens onto a porch. The full kitchen has a breakfast nook and window seat overlooking a pasture. Each bedroom has a private entrance.

If you've always wanted to sleep in a tree or have nostalgic memories of a tree house, reserve the Tree House. In the branches of an ancient oak tree, the rustic room is reached by a stairway from the lower deck that surrounds the tree. The room contains a queen-size bed, a sitting area, and toilet facilities — the shower is located downstairs. Its windows view the treetops of the Cleveland National Forest and fields below. What could be more satisfying than falling asleep to the sighs of mountain breezes, sheltered in the arms of a great oak?

This unique lodging has much to offer the visitor — a lovely rural setting, plentiful activities, down-home hospitality, and creative accommodations that will help restore the most cherished memories of childhood.

For a true return to the fairy tales of childhood, request the Gnome Home — the most unusual and enchanting accommodation at Shadow Mountain Ranch. The charming cottage is made from cement sculpted to look like the bark of a tree. Gnome footprints are embedded in the cement at the doorstep. Inside the circular structure, the whimsical, carved furnishings were handmade by a local artist, and playful touches are everywhere. A carved tree stumps doubles as a footstool, a hand-forged wrought iron chandelier designed to resemble tree branches hangs from the central skylight, carved swinging doors of gnomes kissing shield the toilet area, the rock shower has the appearance of a forest waterfall, and even the sink has a face of its own. There is no telling what fantastic dreams may visit you in the night while sleeping in this bewitching chamber.

LA JOLLA

The Bed & Breakfast Inn at La Jolla

7753 Draper Avenue
La Jolla, CA 92037
619-456-2066

> *An inn of charm and architectural interest*

Innkeeper: Jeris Hackl. **Accommodations:** 16 rooms (15 with private bath). **Rates:** $85–$225 single or double, $25 additional person. **Included:** Continental breakfast. Minimum stay: 2 nights on weekends. **Payment:** MasterCard, Visa. **Children:** Over age 12 welcome. **Pets:** Not allowed. **Smoking:** Not allowed indoors.

La Jolla is a chic little town on the coast just north of San Diego. It's known for its scenic beaches and exclusive shops; it is also the home of the Stephen Birch Aquarium Museum, the Scripps Institution of Oceanography, and the La Jolla Museum of Contemporary Art.

Across the street from the museum, a few blocks from the sea, is the Bed & Breakfast Inn at La Jolla. Built in 1913, the boxy stucco inn is representative of the stripped-down style of the architect Irving Gill. Other examples of his influential Cubist work may be seen elsewhere in La Jolla. Now restored in a style compatible with Gill's simple plan, it is on the San Diego Historical Registry.

The guest rooms are in the two-story main building and the annex behind it, off a courtyard garden. Bird Rock, a tiny room decorated in Laura Ashley blue and white pinstripes and flowered prints, is the only room to share a bath. It's one of five rooms on the ground level. Upstairs, on a corner, Cove Room is furnished with a wicker table and rocker. A decanter of sherry sits on the table. A soft breeze blows through windows that open to a view of trumpet vines over the arbor next door. Until late in the evening, every quarter-hour you'll hear the gentle sound of chimes from a nearby church. Across the hall is Ocean Breeze, a small room with a queen-size bed and a view of the courtyard and large podocarpus tree.

> Complimentary wine and cheese are served in the afternoon. Guests may choose where to have breakfast — in the dining room of the main house, in your own room, on the sundeck, or in the garden.

In the guests' sitting room there's a small refrigerator, a television, and a 12-minute video explaining the inn's history and restoration. Shelves contain books, magazines, and games that include LaJollaopoly, in which players trade local properties instead of Park Place and Marvin Gardens. Off the lounge are a rooftop sundeck and two guest rooms: the Shores, which has antique headboards on twin beds, and Peacock Salon, a brightly decorated room with a garden view.

The largest space is the Irving Gill Penthouse, at the top of the annex. It has a sitting room with a TV and a VCR, and a small deck with a view. The most spectacular ocean view, looking over rooftops two blocks to the cove, is from Pacific View. It's furnished with antiques in a nautical theme. All rooms have fluffy robes, fresh flowers, fresh fruit, and decanters filled with sherry. Some rooms have refrigerators.

La Jolla Beach & Tennis Club

2000 Spindrift Drive
La Jolla, CA 92037
619-454-7126
800-624-2582
Fax: 619-456-3805

*A beach resort
for tennis and
swimming*

General manager: John Campbell.
Accommodations: 90 rooms and apartments. **Rates:** $99–$365
double occupancy. **Added:** 10.5% tax. **Payment:** Major credit
cards. **Children:** Over age 2 additional $15 per night. **Pets:**
Not allowed. **Smoking:** Nonsmoking rooms available.

The guest apartments at this private tennis club stretch along
a quarter-mile of beautiful beach fifteen miles north of San
Diego. About a thousand families in the well-heeled La Jolla
area belong to the club, which is located in a palm grove in a
residential district, but visitors have full membership privileges.

With twelve championship tennis courts (four of them
lighted) and a pro instructor and pro shop, the club is a favorite with tennis players. Around the 10-acre property's
tropical lagoon there's a
9-hole pitch-and-putt golf
course, which guests may
use for a nominal fee. A
heated, Junior Olympic-
size swimming pool lies
next to the patio, where
lunch is served daily. You
may also eat in the club
dining room, facing the
esplanade by the private
beach.

**The Marine Room is a
restaurant so close to the
water that cresting waves,
illuminated at night, sometimes splash against the
windows. Live seahorses
swim in the aquarium and
skylights open to the sun or
stars. A small orchestra
plays for evening dancing.**

The guest rooms and
apartments are in low
stucco buildings with red
tile roofs. Most face the
water, and some are just a step from the smooth sand. A typical room, decorated in a seaside motif, will have two double
beds with rattan headboards, comfortable seating, and an
equipped kitchenette. All the rooms are supplied with bottled
water or piped purified water.

The club's seahorse logo is everywhere: at the bottom of a pool on a seaside terrace, in a tiled fountain in the central courtyard, and on the bright yellow boards supplied as wind protection on the beach. The club also provides beach towels, chairs, and blue and white umbrellas for protection from the sun. You may rent scuba and snorkeling gear, wetsuits, and surf boards from a nearby surf shop. Snorkeling in La Jolla Cove will allow you to see coral and undersea marine life among the wavy strands of kelp.

With apartment sizes up to three bedrooms, this lodging appeals to families. It provides daily maid service, cable television, self-service laundromats, and a hair salon.

La Valencia Hotel

1132 Prospect Street
La Jolla, CA 92037
619-454-0771
800-451-0772
Fax: 619-456-3921

A vintage hotel with a Mediterranean atmosphere

Manager: Michael J. Ullman. **Accommodations:** 100 rooms and suites. **Rates:** $170–$360 single or double; suites $385–$635. **Added:** 10.5% tax. **Payment:** Major credit cards. **Children:** Welcome. **Pets:** Not allowed. **Smoking:** Allowed.

In the heart of La Jolla, ten miles north of San Diego, this pink stucco hotel has been welcoming travelers and holding social events since 1926. The hotel and the town grew up together on the California Riviera, where palms sway in gentle breezes and the sun shines beneficently on sheltered La Jolla Cove.

On the street level (which is also the fourth floor; three more stories descend a hillside toward the water, and several others rise above), you pass through a colonnade beside a palm-shaded patio to the lobby. Beyond the small, usually crowded registration area and down a few tiled stairs is a long parlor with colorful Spanish mosaics, a hand-painted ceiling, and, at the far end, a floor-to-ceiling window with a compelling view of the sea.

La Valencia boasts three restaurants. Mediterranean Room, with its pastel colors, fresh flowers, superb view, and acclaimed menu is a popular spot for breakfast, lunch, or dinner. The Tropical Patio, the outdoor section of the Mediterranean Room, is ideal for a leisurely lunch on a sunny day.

> **From the parlor you look down on tall palm trees, a green park flashing with Frisbees, a sandy shore, and the blue Pacific. Double glass doors open to a balcony above a curved swimming pool and terraced gardens that descend to the road.**

The Whaling Bar and Grill has a New England nautical decor. The bar contains New Bedford harpoons and lanterns, ivory scrimshaw, and pewter candle holders. There's a model of a full-rigged sailing ship behind the leather booths, and a mural depicting the old whaling days. The romantic tenth-floor Sky Room, an elegant, intimate space, overlooks the ocean. The imaginative dinner menu features such dishes as grilled scallops on tangerine tarragon sauce and magret of duck with sun-dried wild cherries and ginger.

The hotel has one elevator — the original, still with a human operator. It's swift but is likely to be crowded at peak times. The attractively furnished guest rooms have a traditional European flavor that combines stately lines with the softness of floral fabrics and clear colors. Each has its own climate control, television, and queen- or king-size beds.

A deluxe oceanfront room offers a panoramic view beyond double-glazed windows. A brass chandelier in the living room, mint-green carpeting, soft gold walls, potted plants, and a stocked mini-bar are among the room's furnishings. The marble and black granite bathroom has an oval whirlpool tub.

The hotel has a small fitness room with sauna. You can play table tennis or shuffleboard, lounge by the pool or on the beach, or join the vacationers shopping along Prospect Street. The La Jolla Museum of Contemporary Art is a few blocks from the hotel.

Prospect Park Inn

1110 Prospect Street
La Jolla, CA 92037
619-454-0133
800-433-1609
Fax: 619-454-2056

*A small inn in
downtown La Jolla*

Innkeeper: Jean Beazley. **Accommodations:** 23 rooms, 2 suites. **Rates:** $80–$115 single, $90–$140 double, $10 additional person; suites $200–$280. **Included:** Continental breakfast. **Added:** 10.5% tax. **Payment:** Major credit cards. **Children:** Free in room with parents. **Pets:** Not allowed. **Smoking:** Not allowed.

Like La Jolla ("The Jewel") itself, Prospect Park Inn is a jewel of a place. The small hotel has a perfect resort location, between chic, busy Prospect Street and the green parks, palm trees, and sandy beaches of La Jolla Cove.

It's easy to overlook the brick hotel, for its entrance is sandwiched between a corner shop and the showy pink La Valencia Hotel. But behind the teal awnings and small, light lobby are three floors of charming rooms, all of them furnished in Mediterranean pastels, California style.

There's a minuscule library on the ground floor, with just enough room for a couch, two chairs, and a sideboard where you may help yourself to tea, coffee, chocolate, and cookies any time of day. There are a few shelves of books and magazines and a phone for guests' use. Coke and ice machines are down the hall.

All the rooms have television. Studios and penthouses have kitchenettes with microwave and toaster ovens; the mini-suite has a full kitchen. Since the front door is locked and there's no desk clerk on duty after 2:00 A.M., your room key also opens a wrought-iron gate to a side entrance. Underground parking is available.

The Cove Suite is a penthouse that opens to a sundeck overlooking the shops and cafés on the corner of Jenner and Prospect and the park and lovely cove to the west. Continental breakfast and afternoon tea are served on the deck. The suite has a spacious bedroom, a living area with a fold-down queen-size bed and a self-contained kitchenette. The Village Suite has similar features. The two penthouses share an entry foyer that may be closed off if a family or couples traveling together wish to share the hotel's upper story.

For bird's-eye views of the coastline from Oceanside to Mexico, take the scenic drive up Mount Soledad to the top. To get a close look at some of California's most exciting surfing action, go to Windansea Beach. Boomer Beach is also a favorite of experienced surfers.

A few steps away from the inn are the famed attractions of La Jolla: beaches, art galleries, boutiques, and restaurants. Highly recommended for dinner is George's At The Cove.

LAGUNA BEACH

Eiler's Inn

741 South Coast Highway
Laguna Beach, CA 92651
714-494-3004
Fax: 714-497-2215

> *A small inn
> with a courtyard
> in the heart of
> Laguna Beach*

Innkeepers: Henk and Annette Wirtz. **Accommodations:** 11 rooms, 1 suite. **Rates:** $100–$200 single or double; $20 additional person. **Included:** Expanded Continental breakfast. **Added:** 10% tax. **Minimum stay:** 2 nights on weekends. **Payment:** Major credit cards. **Children:** Additional $20 if third person in room. **Pets:** Not allowed. **Smoking:** Allowed.

Eiler Larsen was a character in Laguna Beach's past, a colorful Dane who regularly walked the streets and greeted people as they came to town. For many residents and visitors he epitomized the friendly, relaxed attitude of the coastal community. Eiler's Inn represents the same hospitable tradition. The inn, half a block from the sea, stands in the center of Laguna Beach and faces busy Highway 101. Once you enter the front door, however, the outside world seems far removed. Classical music drifts from the living room, where sectional couches face a corner fireplace and a tableful of books and magazines. The cinnamon scent of freshly baked coffeecake is likely to waft from the kitchen.

You're greeted by a welcoming innkeeper who will take you through the brick courtyard, with its trailing bougainvillea and bubbling fountain, to your room where champagne is chilling. Two floors of guest rooms form a U around the courtyard. Each room has a different decor — though all are furnished with handsome antiques — and is named for a place of significance in the area.

The single suite is the only one named for a person: Eiler Larsen. It's also the preferred room, in an upstairs corner next to the sundeck, with a view of the sea. The suite has a woodstove, a queen-size sofa bed in the sitting area, an equipped kitchen, and a bedroom with a king-size bed. The guest book in the suite is full of raves. A sample: "Cozy by the fire, awakened by sounds of the ocean, all tension is gone — what a romantic and peaceful place."

The next best rooms are those upstairs overlooking the courtyard or sundeck. Main-floor rooms tend to be boxy and less inviting, with no view. All the bathrooms have good showers but some are very small.

> **Laguna Beach is an artists' colony as well as a resort town. You'll find more than seventy art galleries, along with quaint shops and several good restaurants.**

In the evenings, you're invited to join the other guests for wine and appetizers in the flowery courtyard. On Saturdays a classical guitarist will play. Breakfast is served here or, in cool weather, by the fire in the parlor. Orange juice, boiled eggs, fresh fruits, granola, and probably that fragrant coffeecake will make up the morning meal.

Eiler's Inn keeps menus on nearby restaurants, and the innkeepers are happy to recommend their favorites. One of the best and most unusual is Five Feet, which specializes in "nouvelle Chinese." Examples of this happy culinary combination are escargots with blackbean red wine sauce and artichoke stuffed with tiger prawns, with Cajun pineapple dressing. Also popular, with excellent food, are Kachina Restaurant and Monique's.

Surf & Sand Hotel

1555 South Coast Highway
Laguna Beach, CA 92651
714-497-4477
800-524-8621
Fax: 714-494-7653

> *A sophisticated beachside hotel*

General manager: Rushton Hayes. **Accommodations:** 157 rooms and suites. **Rates:** $195–$325 single or double, $10 additional person, suites. $500–$750; winter discounts available. **Added:** 10% tax.**Minimum stay:** 2 nights in July, 3 nights in August. **Payment:** Major credit cards. **Children:**

Under age 12 free in room with parents. **Pets:** Not allowed. **Smoking:** Nonsmoking rooms available.

A $25 million renovation, which took place in the early 1990s, turned the Surf & Sand from quaint to elegant. Now it occupies four buildings of varying heights, and all but three guest rooms have ocean views from private balconies. Directly above the sandy beach, south of the shops and restaurants and crowds of Laguna Beach, this hotel has one of southern California's prime locations.

> The Towers restaurant, on the ninth floor of Surf and Sand's main building, is one of the most interesting and stylish in southern California. Towers has a sophisticated art deco theme, with curved glass partitions, mirrored walls, and a wall of windows overlooking the Pacific.

The rooms vary in size but have the same Mediterranean decor and the same amenities: phones, radios, television, cotton and silk fabrics, original art, and hair dryers and robes in bathrooms of beige marble. They were refurbished in a contemporary style by the noted designer, James Northcutt. Guests find a split of champagne when they arrive, and returning guests receive Godiva chocolates as well. The most luxurious rooms are the two-bedroom penthouses, both with stunning panoramic views.

In the center of the complex is a terrace with a pool; below it, overlooking the surf, is Splashes restaurant, the hotel's attempt to prove that fine food and a beachfront location can go together. The Mediterranean-influenced menu changes daily. Examples of the provocative dishes are butternut squash bisque with roasted shrimp, sautéed scallops with sun-dried tomatoes and fennel chutney, and roast chicken with almond and thyme crust, caramelized onions, and balsamic sauce. In the more formal Towers restaurant, you can have cocktails by the granite fireplace and glass-topped grand piano in the lounge. Contemporary cuisine is served and there's a brunch on weekends.

Surf & Sand has facilities for groups up to 250 people, but individuals also receive attentive care. Attendants will set up umbrellas on the beach and serve cocktails and lunch by the pool.

The Ritz-Carlton Laguna Niguel

33533 Shoreline Drive
Laguna Niguel, CA 92677
714-240-2000
800-241-3333
Fax: 714-240-0829

An opulent resort on the coast

General manager: John Dravinski. **Accommodations:** 362 rooms, 31 suites, and 27 Ritz-Carlton Club rooms. **Rates:** $215–$495 single or double, suites $500–$2,750, $50 additional person. **Added:** Tax. **Payment:** Major credit cards. **Children:** Under age 17 free in room with parents. **Pets:** Not allowed. **Smoking:** Nonsmoking rooms available.

On a 150-foot shoreline bluff, five miles south of the resort and art community of Laguna Beach, the Ritz-Carlton stands like a Mediterranean aristocrat transplanted to southern California. Outside the surf crashes and the beach beckons, while four tennis courts, an 18-hole golf course, and two swimming pools sprawl enticingly over the landscaped grounds. Indoors, Old World tradition takes over.

With crystal chandeliers, marble fireplaces, beveled mirrors, richly paneled walls, and custom-made furniture, the hotel is the epitome of the Ritz tradition begun in 1898 by the legendary French hotelier, Caesar Ritz. Since 1927, when the first Ritz-Carlton opened in Boston, the hotels have been noted for their high standards.

The guest services include same-day valet service, airport transportation, secretarial and babysitting services, valet parking, golf bag and luggage storage, twice-daily maid service, a shuttle to and from the golf course and beach, and a multilingual

This hotel, like the others in the Ritz-Carlton collection, is an example of first-class opulence, with a formality unusual in casual California. Those who prefer subdued, classic elegance and strict dress codes to more laid-back lifestyles find it a perfect retreat.

staff. In addition to golf, tennis, and swimming, there is a fitness center with exercise and weight equipment, a sauna, and exercise classes. Individual fitness assessment programs and massage are also available.

Many of these facilities are offered by other luxury resorts. What makes this one different is its standard of consistent quality and service — and its art collection. Museum-quality European paintings, prints, and tapestries hang throughout the hotel, each cataloged and photographed by an arts conservator.

The artwork starts at the porte-cochere with a fountain full of bronze dolphins, sculpted by California artist John Edward Svenson, and continues through the long lobby, with its Italian marble and handloomed carpets, to the maritime theme of the library. In the library are portraits of Early American naval officers. A model sailing ship encased in glass stands on a mahogany table before a window that frames a magnificent view of the sea. Shelves of leatherbound books stand beside the black marble fireplace, completing the atmosphere of a peaceful refuge. The seagoing motif continues with paintings of clipper ships and steamers in the bar. Opposite the bar is the formal Dining Room, where French art complements the pricey Continental cuisine such as filet of Rouget with eggplant, caviar and basil oil, or veal piccata with crayfish and soft polenta. The Club Grill is livelier, with a menu dominated by à la carte seafood, steak, and pasta. The food is well sauced and the mode is hunting-club sporty. Music from the up-tempo combo will entice you into a whirl on the dance floor. Have breakfast or Sunday brunch in the café above the south side swimming pool and terrace; in warm months, enjoy light lunches and cocktails at the pool bar. High tea, a Ritz tradition, is served in the lobby lounge.

Each guest room has its own balcony overlooking the curving beach or the gardens and courtyards. Rare ferns, sycamore trees, weeping willows, palms, and native plants surround fountains and lawns. When you can tear yourself away from the view, you'll see that your room has a classical look, and antique reproduction furniture. Stocked honor bars, TVs with complimentary movies, armoires, safes, terrycloth robes, and marble bathrooms are standard in all guest rooms. Suites are extra spacious with separate living rooms, and wet bars; and some even have fireplaces.

There is enough at the resort to keep any vacationer occupied, but if you wish to explore, Laguna Beach is a short drive away. The charming village, long known for its devotion to the arts, would be idyllic if a highway didn't slice through the center. The shops are delightful, and there are several good restaurants.

LAKE ARROWHEAD

Château du Lac

911 Hospital Road
Lake Arrowhead, CA 92352
909-337-6488
Fax: 909-337-6746

*A gracious
modern home
above the lake*

Innkeepers: Jody and Oscar Wilson.
Accommodations: 5 rooms (all with private bath). **Rates:** $125–$215. **Included:** Full breakfast and afternoon tea. **Added:** Tax. **Minimum stay;** 2 nights on weekends. **Payment:** Major credit cards. **Children:** Over age 14 welcome. **Pets:** Not allowed. **Smoking:** Not allowed

On a bluff overlooking Lake Arrowhead, in the San Bernardino mountains, the Wilsons welcome guests who want to enjoy the tranquility of the area and their large, attractive home. Château du Lac is a place to sleep late, enjoy an excellent breakfast, relax during the day, and be back in time for afternoon tea and hors d'oeuvres. "This is a do-nothing area," Oscar Wilson says. Formerly in the television industry in Los Angeles, he makes birdhouses, helps run the B&B, and plays the role of gracious host to perfection.

There's a touch of Queen Anne style in the contemporary cedar house, which Oscar and his wife Jody completed in 1988. Built around an atrium with oak trees, it has more than 100 windows that flood each room with light. You enter to a living room with a brick fireplace and high ceilings. Beyond is the dining area with doors to a deck and spectacular view of the lake and mountains. The deck curves around to a gazebo and stairs that lead to a balcony upstairs. From every angle there's another pan-oramic vista to admire.

Jody, who serves breakfast by the dining room windows, is an expert cook who once had a catering company. She prepares eggs Benedict, potato casserole, quiche, pancakes, sausages in cider, and other entrées that are accompanied with fruit, juice, and hot breads.

> **In the winter you can cross-country ski near Lake Arrowhead; in summer walk wooded trails or go to the lake. The Wilsons are beach club members, so their guests have access to the beaches.**

Upstairs the spacious Lakeview room is often reserved months in advance by honeymooning couples. The room has high vaulted ceilings, a brick fireplace, and a mirrored antique armoire — the only antique in the house, other furnishings are reproductions. A dried floral sway hangs over the bed topped with a white eyelet lace comforter, teddy bear, and lots of pillows. The private balcony offers fine views of the lake and the San Gabriel Mountains in the distance, as does the Jacuzzi tub in the bath set beneath a bay window. Downstairs there's a suite with a bedroom and separate living room with a sleeper sofa.

The Loft suite is another good choice for those seeking privacy as it is set off from the other rooms, and has its own entrance. Decorated in blue and rose tones, it has a four-poster bed, and a loveseat in front of a gas fireplace. A dressing table is set in a dormer windows as is a rolltop writing desk in another dormer. The large bath has a Jacuzzi and separate shower. Room 4 has a romantic iron and brass bed, floral wallpaper, a cushioned window seat, and a sofa tucked away in an alcove. Room 3 is the least expensive room because it has a shower only. All rooms have TVs and VCRs, and guests can borrow movies from the Wilson's video library.

Throughout, the house is full of angles and nooks. Make your way to the upper level to see Jody's gift corner and on up the stairs to the tiny garret room at the top of the house which looks out over pine trees for seclusion, listening to music, or reading.

Lake Arrowhead Resort

P.O. Box 1699
27984 Highway 189
Lake Arrowhead, CA 92352
909-336-1511
800-800-6792
Fax: 909-336-3300

> *A family resort
> on a mountain
> lake*

Managing director: Ray Serafin. **Accommodations:** 261 rooms and suites. **Rates:** $100–$399. **Payment:** Major credit cards. **Children:** Free in room with parents ($15 fee for rollaway bed). **Pets:** Allowed in villas only with $50 deposit. **Smoking:** Nonsmoking rooms available.

On the shores of Lake Arrowhead, east of Los Angeles in the San Bernardino Mountains, lies a lakefront resort that offers almost anything a vacationing family could want. There are two restaurants, a lounge, an extensive fitness center, tennis courts, racquetball, a private beach and dock, a lakeside pool, and whirlpool tubs.

The guest rooms in the chaletlike lodge are furnished in contemporary style and have televisions and honor bars. Some have balconies, and those with views of the pool or lake are the best. Suites have a separate living room with a fireplace, and baths with a Jacuzzi.

> **In addition to the outdoor recreation, the resort offers a Kids Club, which entertains children with movies and cartoons, arts and crafts, games, sports, visits to Santa's Village, and includes meals and snacks. Babysitting is available with 24-hour advance notice.**

The most outstanding feature of the hotel is its array of activities. The staff is friendly and eager to help, and the guest services desk is set up specifically to assist in arranging the recreation you prefer. There's hiking, bicycling, and fishing. You can ice skate on the Olympic-size rink in nearby Blue Jay, and, in winter, ski at Snow Valley.

Seasons is the resort's restaurant for Continental dining and has a lake view. In summer it's open for dinner nightly except Monday, and for brunch on Sunday; in winter it is open Thursday through Sunday. The Barkley offers informal meals off the open, spacious lobby, and Rodney's Bar has entertainment in the evenings. Within walking distance of the lodge is Lake Arrowhead Village, a waterside complex of shops and restaurants.

Seminars and conventions are often held at the lodge. It can accommodate up to 400 people in nineteen banquet and meeting rooms. A full-time staff assists in coordinating groups, and audiovisual equipment is available.

LONG BEACH

Hotel Queen Mary

1126 Queens Highway
Long Beach, CA 90802
310-435-3511
800-437-2934
Fax: 310-437-4531

A historic cruise ship docked in Long Beach harbor

President: Joseph F. Prevratil. **Accommodations:** 365 staterooms and suites. **Rates:** $75–$180 single or double, suites $190–$575. **Payment:** Major credit cards. **Children:** Under age 18 free in room with adult. **Pets:** Not allowed. **Smoking:** Nonsmoking rooms available.

The last and most luxurious of the great ocean liners, the *Queen Mary* is now permanently docked at Long Beach. Her first voyage was in 1936, her last in 1967, when first-class passengers paid a top rate of $1,282 to travel from Southampton around Cape Horn to Long Beach Harbor. Now owned by the City of Long Beach, the ship is open for tours and to overnight guests who want a cruise experience without leaving the wharf. Called "the ship of beautiful woods," its paneling and inlaid decoration of rare woods create a warm and beautiful interior.

The *Queen Mary* is immense. Taller than Niagara Falls, longer than the Eiffel Tower is high, weighing 81,000 tons, she's a majestic sight, even anchored next to a parking lot. Thousands of visitors troop aboard all year round, some to spend a night, others to dine in one of the three restaurants or dance in the art deco lounge, and many who want simply to tour the historic curiosity.

It's like visiting a theme park. There are marching jazz bands, lifeboat demonstrations, weddings (600 a year), and shops selling English imports. Exhibits show the history of the *Queen Mary*. From royal cruises to World War II transport, the story is fascinating.

The staterooms, in what was once the first-class section, are the largest ever built on a ship. They are on three of the vessel's twelve decks and have the authentic decor of a stylish, if somewhat worn, '30s ship — paneled walls, portholes, the original bathtub spigots for fresh or salt water. The most preferred staterooms are the Duke of Edinburgh, King George, and Queen Mary suites, and the Churchill Suite where Sir Winston himself stayed.

Sir Winston's, dimly lit and with a view of Long Beach Harbor, is the ship's top restaurant, serving California nouvelle cuisine with dishes such as venison portobello and beef phyllo and Sir Winston's beef tenderloin foie gras wrapped in phyllo. The Promenade Café, also with a view of the harbor, is more casual. The Chelsea features a buffet breakfast and lunch, and a seafood menu for dinner. On Sunday mornings, the Grand Salon is open for champagne brunch. You can help yourself to fifty-odd entrées — just as you're likely to find on a real cruise. The Observation Bar is a stunning art deco cocktail lounge. Live entertainment performs here Monday through Saturday.

> **Despite knowing that you can walk off anytime, and despite the fact that the portholes (2,000 of them) view the lights of Los Angeles and the oil refineries of Long Beach, there's a distinct sense of being in an enclosed world, far out at sea, that lends a festive atmosphere to the *Queen Mary*.**

The *Queen Mary* is part of the Queen Mary Seaport, a complex that includes the ship, the Dome (former home of Howard Hughes' Spruce Goose airplane), the shops at Queen's Marketplace, and a children's playground called the Queen's Playland.

LOS ANGELES

The Argyle

8358 Sunset Boulevard
Los Angeles, CA 90069
213-654-7100
800-225-2637
Fax: 213-654-9287

*An elegant
city hotel with art
deco ambience*

General manager: Michael Gaedeke. **Accommodations:** 63 rooms and suites. **Rates:** $170 single, $225 double, suites $325–$1200. **Added:** 12.5% tax. **Payment:** Major credit cards. **Children:** Free in room with parents. **Pets:** With prior approval only. **Smoking:** Nonsmoking rooms available.

In the 1930s, this opulent hotel was the Sunset Towers, the first all-electric apartment building in California and the tallest (14 stories) building on Sunset Boulevard. Charlie Chaplin, Errol Flynn, Clark Gable, Jean Harlow, and other screen stars called it home. Now extensively restored and a member of the Lancaster Hotel Group, it's an art deco landmark on the National Registry of Historic Places, and a stunning example of its period.

The Argyle's white fanciful exterior is easy to spot as you travel along Hollywood's famed Sunset Boulevard. Inside the front door the '30s theme continues with white marble, frosted glass light fixtures, and metal railings with art deco motifs.

In silvers, blacks, and golds, guest rooms are delightful throwbacks to Hollywood's heyday. Deco originals and reproductions grace every room, showcasing furniture with walnut burl veneer, and replicas of Emile Ruhl-mann's classic gondola beds. Marble baths have European fixtures and individual heaters, and some have Jacuzzi tubs.

Although the rooms have the distinctive flavor of an earlier era, modern conveniences have not been forgotten. In fact, cutting edge technology can be found next to the bed where a computer keypad lets you control your lights, room temperature, music, and TV without ever having to get up. All rooms have mini-bars, VCRs, and stereos. For a homey touch, freshly baked cookies are left at bedside during nightly turndown.

Single rooms are the smallest, with only a twin bed, but still have ample living space for one. Some Tower suites

Close to the hotel are such landmark restaurants as Hollywood's oldest, Musso & Frank Grill, which opened in 1919; Engine Co. No. 28, a restored firehouse; and the oldest eatery in Los Angeles, Philippe, known for its French dip sandwiches and pickled eggs.

have two baths, but for a real treat rent one of the Penthouses. The two Penthouse suites share the entire 15th floor, and each has a terrace that wraps around half the building affording some of the best views of Los Angeles and the Hollywood Hills you'll find. The spacious suites have a separate living room with dining area, a large bedroom, and a bath fit for even the most finicky Hollywood idol with marbleized black tile, an oversize steam shower, deep whirlpool tub, double sinks, and a bidet.

The fenix restaurant has Los Angeles talking about chef Ken Frank's French/Californian cuisine. He incorporates French inspired sauces — many of them vegetable based — with fresh California produce. Signature dishes include spinach soup with Maine Lobster, rosti potato with caviar, and filet mignon with red wine, shallots, bone marrow, and cepes. In fenix, you can enjoy fine cuisine and a city view, and then move on to the Argyle's lounge where there's live entertainment.

The hotel has a well-equipped health club and a heated outdoor swimming pool. (You may recognize the pool area with its city views and wrought iron palm tree sculptures from the movie *The Player.*) If you're looking for more celebrity oriented entertainment, Thunder Roadhouse, owned by Peter Fonda, Dennis Hopper, and Dwight Yoakum is just across the street, the Comedy Store in on the same block, and Dan Ackroyd's House of Blues, one block from the hotel, is always jammed.

The Beverly Prescott Hotel

P.O. Box 3065
1224 S. Beverwil Drive
Los Angeles, CA 90035
310-277-2800
800-421-3212
Fax: 310-203-9537

> *A romantic hilltop hotel with a central location*

Manager: David Smith. **Accommodations:** 140 rooms and suites. **Rates:** $185–$350. **Added:** 14% tax. **Payment:** Major credit cards. **Children:** Under age 16 free in room with parents. **Pets:** Not allowed. **Smoking:** Nonsmoking rooms available.

The former Beverly Hillcrest hotel, an aging West Los Angeles landmark, has joined the impressive collection of Kimpton Hotels — this after a name change and $12.5 million remodeling job. Like the other Kimpton properties in San Francisco, Portland, and Seattle, the Beverly Prescott follows Bill Kimpton's successful formula: affordable rooms, individual — sometimes playful — design, and convenient location.

The hotel, overlooking Beverly Hills, Century City, and West Hollywood, has the sophisticated yet casual charm of a private residence, evident as you enter through wrought-iron gates to a gardenlike loggia with a gossamer-draped day bed. Off the lobby is a living room with warm colors, flowered fabrics, fat yellow hassocks, and a fireplace. Complimentary wine is served here every evening, and coffee and tea in the morning. Adjoining the lobby is a meeting room that accommodates up to eighty; audiovisual equipment is available. Up on the 12th floor there's a banquet room with a stunning, 360-degree view of the Los Angeles area.

Guest rooms, which have a balcony with a view, are furnished in bold, sprightly colors and mahogany and cherry woods. There are honor bars, safes, an outdoor swimming pool, a health club, and 24-hour room service; and a newspaper is delivered to your door. If you set your shoes out at night, they'll be returned with a shine in the morning. Shuttle service is provided to shopping districts.

In contrast to the whimsical decor and plush warmth of much of the hotel, Sylvie, the hotel's restaurant, has a neutral background in the tones of the southern California landscape, with splashes of color in the lights and glass chandeliers. The restaurant specializes in French Mediterranean cuisine.

When you want to dine more formally, L'Escoffier is a short cab ride from the Beverly Prescott. The penthouse restaurant in the Beverly Hilton hotel has won numerous awards for its innovative French cuisine. And it's one of the city's few nightspots where you can dine and dance in an elegant setting.

The Biltmore Hotel

506 South Grand Avenue
Los Angeles, CA 90071
213-624-1011
800-245-8673
Fax: 213-612-1545

A grand hotel of traditional grace and elegance

Manager: Randy Villereal. **Accommodations:** 683 rooms and suites. **Rates:** $185–$275 single, $215–$275 double, $30 additional person, suites $325–$2,000. **Payment:** Major credit cards. **Children:** Under age 18 free in room with parents. **Pets:** Not allowed. **Smoking:** Nonsmoking rooms available.

When the Biltmore opened in 1923, it was the largest and most elaborate hotel west of Chicago. Constructed in Spanish-Italian Renaissance style, with lavish interior ceilings and wall paintings by Italian artist Giovanni Smeraldi, the hotel was — and is — splendid. It has hosted presidents, kings, and Hollywood stars, as well as mere travelers, and along the way it has become a historic landmark.

> It's worth visiting the Biltmore just to see the wonderfully ornate Rendezvous Court, where you may take afternoon tea, cocktails, or dessert as you listen to the melodic strains of a piano.

It's been refurbished several times, most recently with a $40 million restoration that spruced up all the public spaces and guest rooms. Furnishings and bathrooms now reflect contemporary luxury, but the artistry that made the Biltmore famous in the '20s may still be seen in the hand-oiled paneling, fine moldings and millwork, carvings, vivid frescoes, and stately columns and pilasters.

Next to the beautiful Rendezvous Court lounge is Bernard's, a classic, where the lighting is subdued and creatively prepared grilled seafood and meats are expensive. Each table is set with a single salmon rose, starched blue linens, crystal and silver. Much of the 1923 silver set, designed exclusively for the Biltmore, had never been used until it was discovered during the restoration. Lighter and less formal is Ristorante Smereldi's, serving northern Italian and California cuisine. It's open for three meals a day.

The Grand Avenue Bar, off the main lobby, is noted for its weekday lunch buffet, wines, and jazz, while the European-style Gallery Bar and Cognac Room features beer and liquors. Yet another restaurant is Sai Sai, with a menu of Japanese dishes. The hotel has sixteen grand banquet and meeting rooms.

The Biltmore's concierge desk will handle almost any request: theater tickets, reservations, tours, laundry, and clothes pressing are a few. Room service is available all day. Several languages are spoken by the staff; in this world crossroads, they're all needed.

The guest rooms are spacious and comfortable, if somewhat bland in their furnishings. They have modern or traditional French furniture, including writing tables, armoires that house television sets, and extender reading lamps. You can choose a king- or queen-size or two double beds. There are twenty-six room configurations, with three pastel color schemes, and Jim Dine's heart engravings hang on the walls. Each room has a mini-bar stocked with pricey snacks and drinks. Toiletries in the baths are beautifully packaged with scenes of the hotel. All guests have the use of the Biltmore's art deco spa equipped with a Roman-style indoor swimming pool, steam room, sauna, whirlpool, Nautilus equipment, and massage service.

To attract the affluent business traveler, the Biltmore offers corporate packages that include an array of special services and amenities. The Club Floor features the hotel's most luxurious accommodations, express check-in and departure, daily newspaper, shoeshine, and twice-daily maid service. On the Club Floor, you have access to the Club Lounge, where a concierge, copy machines, translators, and a small library are available. Complimentary tea, cocktails, and a Continental breakfast are served in the Lounge. Business travelers who need fewer amenities like the Executive Floor, which has no concierge or lounge but does offer such services as computer hookups.

The Biltmore represents opulence on the grand scale. It's a fine old hotel that has fortunately been revived with style and a genuine sense of tradition.

Hotel Bel-Air

701 Stone Canyon Road
Los Angeles, CA 90077
310-472-1211
800-648-4097
Fax: 310-476-5890

A luxurious inn of charm and style

Managing director: Frank Bowling.
Accommodations: 92 rooms and suites. **Rates:** $315–$455 single or double, suites $550–$2,500. **Added:** 14% tax. **Payment:** Major credit cards. **Children:** Welcome. **Pets:** Not allowed. **Smoking:** Allowed.

In 1922, the oil millionaire Alonzo E. Bell created a subdivision of estates in the foothills and canyons north of Sunset Boulevard, where palatial homes lie off winding, tree-shaded roads. Named Bel-Air, it became one of the most prestigious residential areas in Los Angeles.

Bell's planning and sales offices were in a Mission-style building which was later converted to hotel accommodations — the centerpiece of the present Hotel Bel-Air. Now considerably expanded and renowned for its luxury, celebrated guests, and sequestered location, the hotel is also close to city shopping, restaurants, and offices.

The one- and two-story pink buildings are set on 11½ acres of towering ferns, palms, California sycamores, and native live oaks that shade fountain courtyards, a tumbling stream, and a tranquil pond. In the pond, beautiful (but cranky) swans float regally.

In season the gardens glow with color. Jasmine and gardenia scent the balmy air; red bougainvillea climbs to terra cotta tiled roofs. The lush grounds are tended by a team of ten gardeners. One of the plantings in their expert care is a 50-foot pink-flowering silk floss tree, largest of its kind in California. It was planted by Alonzo Bell.

When you arrive in the parlorlike lobby, you are asked which newspaper you'd like to have delivered to your door in the morning and then are escorted through the gardens to your room. Classical music plays softly on your radio when you arrive, and the lamps are lit.

Most of the rooms and suites are on the ground level, with glimpses of gardens through their rose-draped windows. They vary widely in size and decor; most have a patio or fireplace or both. Some are furnished in a French country style that is light, simple, and classic. Others are traditional American or have a California mission theme. The white tiled baths have brass fixtures.

The best choices in the old section are the suites. For consistency in size and style, request a room in the newer section. Each is elegant in pastels and floral fabrics, and has its own fountain and whirlpool in a private patio. A few have small kitchens. All guests receive tea service upon arrival and nightly turndown service. Some of the amenities available are same-day laundry and dry cleaning, 24-hour room service, and a complimentary shoe shine.

> To enter the hotel you cross an arched bridge and walk past a waterfall and Swan Lake. The main building is crowned by a tower that is partly obscured by the brilliant red of flowering trumpet vines.

The restaurant, at the end of a graceful arcade, has banquettes and romantic tables for two by the windows, which face tropical plantings and a terrace that is set for outdoor dining. Contemporary California cuisine is served, using fresh regional ingredients with herbs from the hotel's gardens. Breakfasts are outstanding, and the presentation is stylish. You may have breakfast, lunch, dinner, and afternoon tea in the restaurant or, for a change, eat lightly in the bar next door. With a pianist and vocalist performing nightly, the cozy bar is a favorite evening gathering place for Bel-Air residents as well as hotel guests.

Although the Bel-Air is mostly a place to retreat and relax, and maybe take a stroll through the quiet, sun-dappled gardens before dinner, there is a heated swimming pool and fitness center with cardiovascular equipment on the property, and tennis and golf are easily accessible. And don't forget the shopping opportunities — you're close to Beverly Hills and Rodeo Drive, where glamorous boutiques and designer displays draw shoppers who can afford the best.

Hotel Nikko at Beverly Hills

465 S. La Cienega Blvd.
Los Angeles, CA 90048
310-247-0400
800-645-5687
Fax: 310-247-0315

> *A city hotel
> with understated
> luxury and a
> touch of Japan*

General manager: Moenick Man-fred. **Accommodations:** 304 rooms, 40 suites. **Rates:** $275–$395 single or double, suites $450–$1600. **Added:** Tax. **Payment:** Major credit cards. **Children:** Under age 12 free in room with parents. **Pets:** By prior arrangement; $25 cleaning fee required. **Smoking:** Nonsmoking rooms available.

The Nikko is sleek, modern, quiet, and very comfortable. Business travelers love this hotel for its high-tech amenities, elegant simplicity, and top-quality service. In the center of the lobby, under a skylight, a stream flows over stone and a fountain plays. Black marble floors with soft leather chairs surround the water; it's a serene place, inviting contemplation when the day's work is done. At the far end of the lobby is the Hana Lounge, with music nightly, and beyond it, windows overlooking the swimming pool. There's one restaurant, the Matrixx, which is open all day serving California and Japanese cuisine.

> **When you enter the blocky, seven-story hotel, which stands across the street from Cedars Sinai Medical Center, the sense of purpose is apparent. No one rushes and voices are low, but few of the people in the beautiful lobby are relaxed vacationers. Most guests are here to get things done.**

The guest rooms have king-size beds or two doubles and are outfitted with useful items such as hair dryers, complimentary coffee and tea, satin padded hangers, and robes. The black and ivory baths have deep soaking tubs, one of the reminders of Japan. Another is the rice paper screen used as a window shade. The most unusual features are the state-of-the-art communications systems. A computer connected to the phone can, on command, provide the room temperature and world time zones, control room lighting, operate the CD stereo, and order a wake-up call. Every room has an executive desk and two-line speaker phone with voice mail. Preferred rooms are those with patios. The Executive Suite is largest and has a separate sitting room.

On the ground floor there's a business center with computers and fax and copy machines; secretarial services are available. The Nikko has conference and meeting facilities and an exercise room and sauna.

Hotel Sofitel

8555 Beverly Blvd.
Los Angeles, CA 90048
310-278-5444
800-221-4542
Fax: 310-657-2816

A contemporary hotel with a convenient location

Manager: Cindy Johnson. **Accommodations:** 311 rooms and suites. **Rates:** $195–$240 single or double, $25 each additional person, suites $300–$450. **Added:** Tax. **Payment:** Major credit cards. **Children:** Under age 18 free in room with parent. **Pets:** Allowed by prior arrangement. **Smoking:** Nonsmoking rooms available.

This sleek ten-story hotel occupies a choice spot in West Los Angeles. It's close to the Pacific Design Center and Cedars Sinai Hospital, and across the street from the famed shops of Beverly Center. It's also convenient to Beverly Hills, westside offices, and Melrose Avenue boutiques. Part of a French chain, the hotel is functional and attractive, with a Mediterranean ambience. The lobby has stone floors, a sweeping staircase, and textured walls and columns. Colors are muted throughout.

The rooms, too, reflect a southern European style with French country fabrics and decor. The color schemes include flowered bedspreads and drapes, and walls of soft brick or green with matching carpeting. Upper-floor rooms have French doors leading to outside terraces where one can sit and sip a drink or watch the world pass by below. The hotel was designed primarily to serve business travelers with conveniences such as 24-hour room service, three phones per room with fax/modem capability and voice-activated message centers, minibars, and morning newspapers. Hair dryers and Nina Ricci toiletries are amenities that women travelers will especially appreciate.

> La Cajole Brasserie is a copy of a popular French restaurant in Paris. Wooden cutouts of people reading *Le Monde* add to the eatery's genial atmosphere, while French favorites such as crêpes and escargot can be found on the menu.

Since some rooms are quite small and lack workable desk space, an Executive King room is a good choice if you plan to work during your visit. It has separate areas for sitting, sleeping, and dressing and includes a desk. The partial suite can be used as one large space or the areas can be separated by drapes for privacy. The closets are ample, but drawer space is very limited. The best rooms are on the north side, facing what residents call the Blue Whale (Pacific Design Center) and the Hollywood Hills beyond. The nighttime view, when it's clear, is spectacular.

The hotel's conference facilities consist of seven rooms that vary in capacity from 12 to 240. There's a health club for guests' use, with Nautilus machines and a sauna, and an outdoor pool surrounded by decking, lounge chairs, and umbrella tables.

Setting Hotel Sofitel above many city hotels are its constant room service, babysitting, and same-day valet service. Also worth noting, if you're bored with airline food, is the box lunch prepared for air travelers and available upon request. Rushed travelers appreciate the Three-Minute Breakfast, a selection of beverages, croissants, pastries, and seasonal fruit set up buffet-style in the lobby. All guests receive a freshly baked French baguette upon check-out.

The New Otani Hotel & Garden

120 South Los Angeles Street
Los Angeles, CA 90012
213-629-1200
800-273-2294 in California
800-421-8795 in U.S. and Canada
Fax: 213-620-0980

*A Western city
hotel with
Japanese character*

General manager: Kenji Yoshimoto. **Accommodations:** 435 rooms. **Rates:** $155–$225 single, $180–$250 double, suites $440–1500. **Added:** Tax. **Payment:** Major credit cards. **Children:** Under age 12 free in room with parents. **Pets:** Not allowed. **Smoking:** Nonsmoking rooms available

When the New Otani opened in 1977, the management did not stress its Japanese heritage and connections. "We didn't want Americans to feel we were simply a Japanese hotel where they could not get by in English or find their eggs and bacon," says Kenji Yoshimoto, the hotel's general manager. But it soon became clear that the touch of Japan was one of the hotel's main attractions. Now it's strongly emphasized, though all employees speak English; in fact, front desk personnel collectively speak nineteen languages.

When you leave your car with the valet and enter the three-story lobby, you'll see a dramatic glass sculpture, and behind it the Rendezvous Lounge. In this raised, open area a pianist plays on weekdays. To the left is a shopping arcade; on the right a sweeping staircase winds up to a mezzanine and guest rooms above it.

The Azalea Restaurant and Bar, on the lobby level, offers a contemporary version of classic Continental cuisine. Upstairs, A Thousand Cranes features Japanese meals at standard tables or in private tatami rooms. This is the place to try sushi, uni (fresh sea urchin), awabi (abalone cooked with sake wine), and tempura in a traditional setting. The restaurant overlooks the "garden in the sky," a tranquil half-acre roof garden of pathways, ponds, and waterfalls bordered with azaleas. Also with a view of the garden is the contemporary Garden Grill, open for Teppan Yaki dining.

Each guest room has a television, refrigerator, and desk in a lacquer red or pastel curved cabinet. Bedside tables match the dramatic red and gray or pastel decor. Shoji screens at the windows and a single flower or delicate piece of art complete the Oriental accent. The bathrooms have phones, hand-held showers, and thick white towels with the hotel's name handsomely embroidered in red. Yukatas (Japanese kimonos) are available, as well as standard robes.

> **East meets West in this 21-story hotel, where you may dine on New York steaks or yakitori, sleep on an American bed or a futon, and listen to cocktail piano music or a Koto player.**

For the most interesting experience the New Otani offers, reserve one of the Japanese suites. The parlor is Western, with modern couches and soft chairs, while the sleeping area behind sliding shoji doors is a large, elevated tatami room with a futon. The bath has a sunken tub, traditional in Japan.

At the Sanwa Health Spa, you may relax in a sauna or herb-scented Jacuzzi and enjoy a shiatsu massage. Other features are room service, same-day cleaning, a beauty salon, and concierge services.

Special events and cultural programs exploring Japanese culture take place throughout the year. You can learn about the tea ceremony, take a calligraphy lesson, or study one of the many forms of ikebana (flower arranging). Traditional celebrations include Setsubun (the end of winter), the Hina Doll Festival, and Temari, a demonstration of a 1,400-year-old folk art in which colorful silk balls are created.

The New Otani, in Little Tokyo, is close to Los Angeles City Hall, the Music Center, city and county courthouses, and the *Los Angeles Times* building. Across the street is St. Vibiana Cathedral, one of L.A.'s oldest.

Westwood Marquis Hotel and Gardens

930 Hilgard Avenue
Los Angeles, CA 90024
310-208-8765
800-421-2317
Fax: 310-824-0355

*A gracious hotel
of charm near
the university*

Managing director: John Strozdas.
Accommodations: 258 suites. **Rates:** $220–$650, single or double. **Added:** Tax. **Payment:** Major credit cards. **Children:** Welcome. **Pets:** Allowed. **Smoking:** Nonsmoking rooms available.

In a typical California blend of urban elegance and unpretentious warmth, the Westwood Marquis strikes a fine balance that is less than grandeur but more than mere good taste. Behind its ivied walls are excellent restaurants, a plush little lobby, an unflappable concierge, a lounge where tea is served every day but Sunday, and sixteen floors of exquisite suites.

In a residential area near the trendy shops of Westwood Village and virtually next to UCLA, the hotel was built in 1969 as a dormitory for university students and later became a retirement home. Since 1979 it has been an exclusive hotel, noted for its polish and personal service.

A valet will park your car. Then, from the sidewalk setting of luxuriant greenery, you step into a lobby of Persian rugs, tapestries, and marble. Light from wide windows sparkles on the prisms of glass chandeliers, and fresh flowers add color to every corner.

The tasteful appointments are continued in the suites, which are equally appealing in salmons, grays, and rusts. With one, two, or three bedrooms, they all have separate living rooms and plenty of space in which to work or relax. The baths are in pink or beige marble and have oversize terrycloth robes and towels, hair dryers, two-line telephones, and vanity tables. In the living room you'll find another phone, a sofa with fluffy pillows, a refrigerator, TV with Nintendo, writing table, and black and white lithographs or English hunt scenes. All the suites have views of the San Gabriel Mountains or the pool and gardens.

If you're in one of the eighteen lavish penthouse suites, you'll have the services of a butler who serves coffee or cocktails, brings in mail, and generally caters to your every whim.

For those needing a lot of space, there's a grand three-bedroom bi-level suite connected by a spiral staircase.

Executive Business Suites are one- or two-bedroom suites that have speaker phones with data ports and voice mail, fax machines, and assorted business publications. Another aspect of the hotel's effort to reach the international business traveler is Business with Breakfast. Portable telephones, hand-held computers, and stock market reports are brought to your breakfast table, so you won't waste a moment.

> Hollywood stars stay here when in Los Angeles, as do many top executives in the entertainment, financial, and communications industries. Like other discriminating travelers, they seek integrity, top quality, and an atmosphere pleasing to the senses — and the well-run Westwood Marquis delivers in each area.

The gardens lend a touch of the country to this city hotel. A lawn rises up a slope from street level to a shell-shaped swimming pool surrounded by flowering plants. Colorful bougainvillea spills over a pink stucco wall nearby, and the scent of star jasmine fills the air. On one side of the pool are cabanas and changing rooms; on the other, a terrace for outdoor dining. Café Perroquet, named for the wild parrots that fly through the gardens, offers light fare, grilled over an open fire. There's also an outdoor lap pool surrounded by ferns on the second level, and the hotel has an exercise room, saunas, a Jacuzzi, and steam rooms.

Breakfast, lunch, and a lavish Sunday champagne breakfast are served in the Garden Terrace Restaurant, under white and green trellises and hanging ferns. Around the corner is the Erté Room for up to twenty-four guests' private dining. It was named after the noted artist and designer whose famous Alphabet lithographs adorn the red walls. The more formal Dynasty Room has a regal setting of porcelain artifacts, exotic plants, and softly lit tables and cushioned booths. Continental cuisine with a California flair is served.

Afternoon tea in the Westwood Lounge is to be savored. To the delicate strains of a harp, you may enjoy sherry or a choice of Twining's teas. A trolley will be brought with sandwiches, golden caviar, scones, petits fours, and pastries that are baked daily on the premises.

You'll find few flaws in this lovely enclave. Traffic noise could be a problem but can be avoided by requesting a suite away from the street. You can hear the steady, annoying hum of a roof generator in some penthouse suites; again, it's avoidable by request. More pleasant are the church bells that ring nightly from across the street, a sound that only adds to the sense of harmony in this fine hotel.

Wyndham Checkers Hotel

535 South Grand Avenue
Los Angeles, CA 90071
213-624-0000
800-WYNDHAM
Fax: 213-626-9906

A classic, small hotel of urban elegance

General manager: Guy Hensley.
Accommodations: 188 rooms, 17 suites. **Rates:** $185–$205 single or double, $20 additional person, suites $450–$1000. **Added:** 14% tax. **Payment:** Major credit cards. **Children:** Free in room with parents. **Pets:** Allowed. **Smoking:** Nonsmoking rooms available.

In the heart of downtown Los Angeles, near Pershing Square, the Museum of Contemporary Art, and the remodeled public library, this posh little hotel offers a tranquil and elegant retreat. Built as the Mayflower Hotel in 1927, the 14-story building underwent a $50 million restoration to be reborn as Checkers, which opened in 1989 with the finest in residential furnishings, antiques, artworks, accommodations, and service. The building's creamy stone exterior with intricate ornamentation is as lovely as it was when the hotel first opened back in the '20s.

The lobby is divided into three sections, each displaying beautiful pieces of contemporary and antique art. Among them are rare old Japanese vases, a Chinese red lacquer screen, and a German armoire of ebony and rosewood that dates from 1725. On the mezzanine above are meeting rooms and a library/sitting room in soft gray, with more Oriental antiques including two 19th-century mother-of-pearl elephants. It's a favored gathering place for small groups, ideal when the lobby is too public and a guest room too private.

All the guest rooms, furnished alike, are decorated in light woods and soothing, soft colors. They have clock radios, TVs with movie and sports channels, Belgian linens, mini-bars, writing tables, and phones with voice mail and international signs on the buttons, in deference to the hotel's many foreign visitors. Suites have separate living rooms and two baths, but orchids in the marble bathrooms, tub thermometers, makeup mirrors, coffeemakers, closets that light when the door opens, and padded satin hangers are a few of the special touches common to all rooms.

> **Near the rooftop lap pool there's an equipped weight room and Jacuzzi. Some guests like to work out in the mornings, read the paper, and order a light breakfast here. Sweatsuits and robes are provided.**

Attention to detail in appointments and service makes Checkers exceptional. The well-trained staff can respond to almost any need: valet assistance, same-day laundry service, secretarial help, and 24-hour room service are routine. Guests receive complimentary limousine service to any downtown business area.

Near the rooftop lap pool there's an equipped weight room and Jacuzzi; some guests like to work out in the mornings, read the paper, and order a light breakfast here. Sweatsuits and robes are provided.

Checkers' restaurant, serene and elegant, fits in well with the hotel's overall intimate tone. Dinner is served on lovely Wedgwood china bearing an Oriental motif, and the glassware is crystal. Lentil and caraway crusted pork tenderloin with white beans, savoy cabbage, and caramelized Bermuda onions, and filet of Atlantic salmon with corn and leek fondue with semolina crème fraîche rounds and a red roasted chili sauce are examples of chef Andreas Kisler's inventive cuisine.

MALIBU

Malibu Beach Inn

22878 Pacific Coast Highway
Malibu, CA 90265
310-456-6444
800-4-MALIBU
Fax: 310-456-1499

*An oceanside hotel
with a festive air*

Innkeeper: Lorraine Irving. **Accommodations:** 47 rooms. **Rates:** $156–$275 single or double, $15–$25 additional person; rates vary seasonally. **Included:** Continental breakfast. **Added:** 12% tax. **Minimum stay:** 2 nights on summer weekends. **Payment:** Major credit cards. **Children:** Additional $15 per day. **Pets:** Not allowed. **Smoking:** Allowed.

Ideally located just north of Los Angeles on the famous coastal strip of celebrities' homes and interesting shops, this pink stucco, Spanish-style inn on the beach will have you smiling the minute you walk in the front entrance. You're bound to love the colorfully painted tiles, Mexican paver tiled floors, fountain, and wondrous ocean breezes and views.

There are all kinds of recreation options nearby: golf, tennis, parasailing, surfing, and scuba diving. The incomparable J. Paul Getty Museum is ten minutes from the inn.

The three-level inn has a small, open lobby with a fireplace in the sitting area and doors that open to a terrace above the beach. The view extends from Point Dume to Palos Verdes.

The rooms, in pinks and aquas, have a beachy feel with a touch of Mexico thrown in for good measure. Waves lap below each room's balcony, and furniture from the Philippines, and painted tile murals complete the look. Television, a stocked refrigerator, tableware, and a coffeemaker are provided. Baths have makeup mirrors and hair dryers. Except for four rooms on the ground floor, all rooms have fireplaces, and six have Jacuzzis on their terrace.

Continental breakfast is included in the room rate, and the front desk sells beer and wine for picnics on the beach. Room service is provided by a local restaurant. For more dining options, recommended restaurants in the area include La Scala, Beaurivage, Pier View Café, Granita's, Tradinoi, and Monroe's.

MARINA DEL REY

Marina del Rey Hotel

13534 Bali Way
Marina del Rey, CA 90292
310-301-1000
800-8-MARINA in California
800-882-4000 in U.S.
Fax: 310-301-8167

A harborside hotel between downtown and the airport

General manager: Ira Kleinrock.
Accommodations: 150 rooms, 6 suites. **Rates:** $120–$190 single, $140–$210 double, suites $250 and up. **Added:** 12% tax.
Payment: Major credit cards. **Children:** Under age 18 free in room with parents. **Pets:** Allowed. **Smoking:** Nonsmoking rooms available.

Sitting on your shaded balcony, watching the sun set over the Pacific and the yachts and sailboats come and go, you can hardly believe that Los Angeles International Airport is just a ten-minute drive. But that's the beauty of this hotel. The hotel convenient to the freeway and the airport, yet is a sunny retreat where you can fish from the piers, take a harbor cruise, stroll a sandy beach, watch windsurfers dart across the channel, or shop in a New England–style fishing village.

The hotel provides 24-hour complimentary transportation to and from the airport, and cars are available to rent if you need to drive the ten miles to downtown L.A. or elsewhere.

Jaunty in white with blue awnings, the three-story hotel stands at the tip of one of the harbor's peninsulas, allowing for good views from most guest rooms (though some overlook the parking lot). Large windows and open spaces bring the outdoors in. Boats dock at the doorstep, here in the world's largest manmade yacht harbor. The location is this hotel's best feature.

> **Marina del Rey offers all kinds of outdoor recreation. There are four parks where you can jog, ride bicycles, fish from a jetty, barbecue, or listen to free outdoor concerts. Mother's Beach is a favorite spot for swimming and boating and has a ramp that accommodates wheelchairs.**

A restaurant and cocktail lounge offer views of the harbor and sea from picture windows. The Crystal Seahorse is a dining room specializing in California cuisine and seafood dishes such as crab and clams in dill sauce and mussel soup with lime and saffron. Desserts are light, focusing on fresh fruits prepared in tempting ways. If you want to be even closer to the sound of the waves, you may dine outside on the terrace, which has seating for twenty.

The spacious rooms, emphasizing simplicity and comfort, have a Mediterranean atmosphere. A recent renovation considerably brightened the decor of the hotel, which was the first in Marina del Rey when it was built some thirty years ago. Outriggers Lodging Services, which began managing the hotel in mid-1993, has spruced the place up and added more meeting space.

The suites have king-size beds, contemporary couches, console TVs, dining areas and wet bars, and big closets with full mirrors. For the best view in the hotel, reserve Suite 3139. At times it seems that all the thousands of boats moored at Marina del Rey are sailing just below the suite's balcony, which extends along two sides of the corner room. And the view of the sunset over the main channel is spellbinding.

NEWPORT BEACH

Doryman's Inn

2102 West Ocean Front
Newport Beach, CA 92663
714-675-7300
800-634-3303
Fax: 714-675-7300

*A small,
romantic hotel
by the beach.*

General manager: Michael Palitz.
Accommodations: 10 rooms. **Rates:** $135,–$275 single or double, $15 additional person. **Included:** Expanded Continental breakfast. **Added:** 10% tax. **Payment:** Major credit cards. **Children:** Over age 10 $15 additional. **Pets:** Not allowed. **Smoking:** Allowed on patio only.

This spot on the Pacific shore is unabashedly romantic; the guest rooms have been designed for lovers. Canopy beds piled with ruffled pillows are topped with silk rosettes, lush tropical plants stand in the corners, and fireplaces light at the touch of a switch (these are gas fireplaces, of course, lacking the crackle and character of the real thing; but as a substitute they're not bad.) Most of the beds are backed by wide mirrors. All the bathrooms have marble sunken tubs.

Other than the beach, points of interest in the area are the 1904 Balboa Pavilion, which has been restored as a restaurant and boat terminal for Catalina Island; the Balboa Island ferry; and Lido Isle, or "Fashion Isle," as it's called for its many shops.

The rooms are lavishly furnished with antiques that recall the 1890s period when the brick hotel was built. The small lobby and rooms are on the second floor, off paneled halls with skylights and hanging ferns. Room 1 is a corner room with a three-door armoire and a down comforter on a brass and white iron bed. Lighter and larger is Room 2, which has an ocean view. Four others also have ocean views. The largest, most expensive, and probably the most romantic is the Master Suite, which has an ocean view, a bed with a draped canopy, and a sunken whirlpool tub.

Coffee is always available in the little breakfast room, where morning pastries, boiled eggs, sliced fruits, and yogurt are set out. You may have breakfast here, in your room, or on the rooftop terrace, with its view of Santa Catalina Island.

Parking and a morning paper are provided at Doryman's. The manager is glad to help with any other needs, from an aspirin to a boat reservation to Catalina.

The inn is a seaside retreat for holidays and romance, not a place to do business. The rooms have phones, but as antique reproductions they're not convenient, and the hall telephone is squeezed into a tiny booth.

The only real flaw here is not in the inn itself. Since this is a beach resort town, summer brings noisy crowds and traffic.

PASADENA

The Ritz-Carlton Huntington Hotel

1401 South Oak Knoll Avenue
Pasadena, CA 91106
818-568-3900
800-241-3333
Fax: 818-568-3700

*A luxurious hotel
of classic elegance
and style*

Manager: William Hall. **Accommodations:** 383 rooms and suites. **Rates:** $165–$265, suites $275–$1,500. **Added:** 11.49% tax. **Payment:** Major credit cards. **Children:** Under age 18 free with parents. **Pets:** Not allowed. **Smoking:** Nonsmoking rooms available.

Combining resort and hotel amenities, the Ritz-Carlton Huntington offers tennis courts and a tennis pro, a swimming pool, and a fitness center with saunas and steam rooms. The complex is set on 23 acres at the base of the San Gabriel Mountains, a 15-minute drive from downtown Los Angeles.

The hotel opened in 1991, a reconstructed version of the Huntington, a grand and famous hotel built in 1906. The rebuilt version closely follows the original architecture, with its tiled roof and imposing design. Two rooms were kept intact: the elegant Viennese Ballroom and the lovely Georgian

Room. The genteel ambience was also retained. Guests at the Ritz-Carlton recognize, appreciate, and can afford the finest.

A typical room has a king-size or two double beds, yellow damask walls, three telephones, and an honor bar. The distinctive black and white marble bathroom has gray walls of shot silk and assorted toiletries. Guests receive twice-daily maid service, robes, evening turndown, and devoted attention from the staff. Those who want even more amenities stay on the concierge floors and enjoy a private lounge and complimentary breakfast, afternoon tea, hors d'oeuvres, and cocktails. The hotel also has six cottages.

> **Tasteful art objects are displayed and 18th- and 19th-century oil paintings hang on the walls. Overstuffed sofas, fresh flowers, and Oriental carpets add to the atmosphere of comfort and graciousness.**

A major draw for business groups are the eight handsomely appointed meeting rooms, a large ballroom, and computer and secretarial facilities.

You can dine in style in the Grill and, for casual fare, the Café Restaurant. Lunch and cocktails are available both indoors and out at the Pool Bar, and Continental breakfast, cocktails, and traditional afternoon tea are served in the Lobby Lounge.

The swimming pool is a restoration of California's first Olympic-size pool. A whirlpool has been added, and a pool lounge offering tropical drinks and light fare. To reach the Health Club, you cross the Picture Bridge, a part of the original hotel. Under its peaked roof are carefully restored triangular panels, each painted with a California scene.

Such reminders of its origins give the Ritz-Carlton a timeless atmosphere. Fostering this sense of continuity, the hotel participates in the annual Rose Parade with a float, as it has for seventy-five years.

RANCHO BERNARDO

Rancho Bernardo Inn

17550 Bernardo Oaks Drive
San Diego, CA 92128
619-487-1611
800-542-6096
Fax: 619-487-1423

> *A Spanish-style resort in the hills*

General manager: Rick Mansur. **Accommodations:** 287 rooms and suites. **Rates:** $135–$210 single or double, $10 additional person, suites $160–$600. **Payment:** Major credit cards. **Children:** Under age 12 free in room with parents. **Pets:** Not allowed. **Smoking:** Nonsmoking rooms available.

Balmy days and cool nights; tennis, golf, and fine dining; broad loggias and pathways that wind through courtyards with gardens and antique fountains — these are a few of the pleasures at Rancho Bernardo Inn, one of California's outstanding resorts. The setting is lovely, a green valley in the sepia-toned San Pasqual Mountains thirty miles from San Diego.

The hotel was built in 1962, as part of a development of Spanish-style homes for commuters and retirees. The main building, stucco with a red tile roof, shelters a warm, quiet lobby with low beamed ceilings of limed wood and adobe walls etched with straw. To the left of the entrance is the Music Room, where antique musical instruments are displayed. Piano music begins at four o'clock every afternoon, announcing tea time. Complimentary tea, sandwiches, port and sherry are brought in on silver trays. For lunch, guests dine on the Veranda, and El Bizcocho, with its extensive wine list, is the inn's gourmet dining spot for dinner.

The guest rooms and suites are in eight low haciendas, each by a courtyard of palm trees and flowers. The rooms are furnished similarly in color schemes of earthtones, gold, and red and have stocked honor bars, television, and patios overlooking the golf course or a courtyard. In the white tile bathrooms are phones, magnifying makeup mirrors, and hair dryers. Robes hang in the closets, and there are safes for your valuables.

Original artwork graces the guest room walls, while artifacts from Mexico and early California are displayed throughout the inn. The museum-quality works begin at the entrance, near the porte cochere, where a Zuniga bronze statue stands in a grove of sycamore and pine.

The original lobby is now the Fireside Room, where you may relax by a fire with board games or cards. On Friday nights, meet the staff over complimentary cocktails at the general manager's reception.

The swimming pools have adjoining hydrospas, and there are three other whirlpools on the property. A sports fitness center offers training equipment, steam rooms, and a juice bar. The inn's twelve tennis courts are a major recreational draw, as are the special tennis packages. The Tennis College, begun in 1971, has a team of five pros who offer courses in improving your stroke, strategy, and game. Also available are video critiques, tournament arrangements, partner match-ups, tennis movies, and demonstrations.

If you prefer golf, you have several choices. The 72-par West Course unrolls down the valley for 6,400 yards of tricky play. Under the olive and eucalyptus trees are two lakes, a stream, doglegs, and numerous bunkers. Five pros are on hand to help with instruction or arrange tournaments. Two other courses are open to guests: the Temecula Creek Inn course and the 27-hole Oaks North.

RANCHO SANTA FE

The Inn at Rancho Santa Fe

P.O. Box 869
5951 Linea del Cielo
Rancho Santa Fe, Ca 92067
619-756-1131
800-654-2928
Fax: 619-759-1604

> *A resort
> of quiet charm
> and luxury*

General manager: Duncan Royce Hadden. **Accommodations:** 90 rooms, suites and cottages. **Rates:** $95–$195 rooms and suites, single or double, cottages $285–$500. **Added:** 9% tax. **Minimum stay:** 2–5 nights on some holidays and weekends. **Payment:** Major credit cards. **Children:** Under age 17 free; cot or crib $20 per night. **Pets:** Allowed in certain cottages. **Smoking:** Allowed.

The scent of money, old and new, is an integral part of Rancho Santa Fe, a quietly wealthy community set in the eucalyptus-covered hills twenty-seven miles north of San Diego. The Spanish-style village, known for its attractive shops, restaurants, and two golf courses, began in 1923 with a guest house for prospective landowners. The Santa Fe Railroad had imported three million eucalyptus trees from Australia and planted them on 10,000 acres, planning to use them as railroad ties. It didn't work out — the gum trees just weren't suitable — so the railroad turned the land over to residential development. Eventually the adobe guest house became the Inn at Rancho Santa Fe, and cottages and gardens were added.

Steve Royce bought the place in 1958, and it's been a family operation ever since, with daughters and sons, nephews and cousins involved.

The low cottages, containing from two to ten guest rooms, are placed on twenty acres of landscaped grounds and terraced gardens. The main building, the original guest house, has eight rooms and a suite, restaurants, a communal library and comfortable living room. In the Garden Room, guests dine on breakfast and lunch surrounded by walls painted with floral vistas. Beyond it is the Vintage Room (actually comprised of several rooms including a cheerful sunroom), where American and Continental dishes are served at lunch and dinner, and cocktails are available in the evening. The Patio Terrace is open for dancing under the stars on summer weekends. Lunches and beverages are served by the long outdoor pool.

> One of the inn's special features is not in Rancho Santa Fe: it's a beach cottage seven miles away on the coast at Del Mar. If you want to spend an afternoon by the sea, you'll have a place to shower, dress, and borrow beach equipment.

Jackets are suggested for dinner, but the atmosphere at the inn is unpretentious and casual. The service, however, is not at all casual, though it may be unhurried. The staff seems genuinely interested in meeting the guests' needs promptly and with a smile. The inn is the type of place where couples and families return year after year, and the staff knows many of the guests by name. Evidence that it's a well-loved place is obvious in everything from the attentive service to the inn's rose garden.

Croquet, tennis, and golf are major diversions. The Rancho Santa Fe Croquet Club plays regularly at the inn, while golfers may choose between two private 18-hole courses. The inn has three tennis courts, and lessons may be arranged. For indoor relaxation there are hundreds of books in the library, backgammon, and chess.

Guest rooms are traditionally furnished and have air conditioning, television, and writing desks; most have patios with views of the gardens. Some rooms have fireplaces and kitchens or wet bars. The baths are roomy, with dressing areas and separate showers. There are several private cottages with one, two and three bedrooms and baths. The largest has its own patio and swimming pool.

Airport limousine service is available for a fee.

Rancho Valencia

P.O. Box 9126
5921 Valencia Circle
Rancho Santa Fe, CA 92067
619-756-1123
800-548-3664
Fax: 619-756-0165

A luxurious tennis resort near San Diego

General manager: Michael Ullman. **Accommodations:** 43 suites. **Rates:** $315–$450 1 bedroom suites, 2-bedroom casita $710–$825, 3-suite Hacienda $2000. **Added:** Tax. **Payment:** Major credit cards. **Children:** Welcome. **Pets:** Not allowed. **Smoking:** Nonsmoking rooms available.

Like a grand private estate, this tranquil resort lies on a hill among terraced gardens and citrus orchards. Twenty miles from the San Diego airport, it's one of the loveliest places in southern California. The resort opened in 1989, but it has the atmosphere of a long-established hacienda, with red tile roofs, scuffed Mexican pavers in the lobby, wicker furniture, a tile fireplace, and bleached beams. Fountains splash in the courtyards and arches over cool walkways are smothered in bougainvillea. The courtyard by the lobby is open for dining and, on Thursday nights, dancing under the stars.

The suites, housed in twenty casitas, are gems of comfort and country luxury. The Rancho Santa Fe suites are the largest. Each has a fireplace, a tiled bath, a walk-in closet and dressing room, shuttered windows, hand-painted tiles on the walls, and a garden terrace. Smaller, but with similar amenities and southwestern decor, are the Del Mar Suites. In the morning, fresh orange juice from the trees on the grounds is brought to your door on a tray, with a newspaper and a single red rose.

The stone Hacienda Suite is a former private home with

three bedrooms, four baths, a central living room, a large kitchen with a fireside sitting area, and outdoor private pool and Jacuzzi surrounded by gardens, palm and fruit trees. Each of the three bedrooms has its own bath and patio, and one has its own sitting room. Exposed adobe walls, Mexican tiles, pottery, and decor throughout gives the Hacienda a distinct south-of-the-border flavor. Used mainly for VIPs and hospitality events, it would also be a lovely spot to hold a family reunion or small wedding.

> **The resort's widely acclaimed, elegant little restaurant overlooks the hills and serves Mediterranean and southwestern cuisine. Next to the restaurant is the Sunrise Room, with brilliant blue and yellow painted tiles, and a patio for outdoor dining. A terrace runs the length of the building, overlooking the tennis courts.**

The focus of activity here is tennis; about 25 percent of the resort's guests come for the eighteen courts, lessons, clinics, and tennis packages. But many other activities are offered. You can swim in the 25-meter pool, relax in two Jacuzzis, jog on the trails, golf, go deep sea fishing or hot air ballooning, play polo and croquet, or head for the horse races in nearby Del Mar (a limited number of Turf Club passes are available for resort guests).

If you didn't bring your own car, Rancho Valencia provides complimentary transportation to the beach and Del Mar and shuttle access to the airport and train station.

SAN DIEGO

Balboa Park Inn

3402 Park Blvd.
San Diego, CA 92103
619-298-0823

> *A comfortable
> inn near
> Balboa Park*

General manager: Ed Wilcox. **Accommodations:** 26 suites (all with private bath). **Rates:** $80–$190 1–4 people. **Included:** Continental breakfast. **Added:** Tax. **Payment:** Major credit cards. **Children:** Welcome in family suites. **Pets:** Not allowed. **Smoking:** Allowed.

Four pink stucco Spanish Colonial buildings on a corner near Balboa Park, form this complex of suites, courtyards, gardens, and terraces. Originally built in the teens as guesthouses for dignitaries that came to San Diego for the first World's Fair, the buildings now house imaginatively furnished suites — each with a special theme.

In Greystoke, for example, you'll sleep in the jungle beside a painting of Tarzan; in Nouveau Ritz you'll enter the glamour of Hollywood in the 1940s with its curved black deco couches backed by a glittery cityscape, and a bathroom in violet and black. Marianne's Southwest has a Hopi Indian motif, Paris in the Thirties is furnished in deep greens and has a wood-burning fireplace, and Las Palmas is an exuberant splash of tropical color. The Courtyard Suite, with a double Jacuzzi tub and an ice bucket, two champagne glasses, and a candelabra standing at the ready nearby, is the most recent addition to the inn.

Tara is a roomy, tastefully furnished, residential-style apartment. It has an old-fashioned kitchen and a separate bedroom with a deep whirlpool tub. In the living room, a *Gone with the Wind* painting hangs on the wall. There's a wet bar, and a fire is laid in the fireplace. Tara is often used as a reception suite for groups up to twenty-five people. It connects to the west courtyard and sun terrace. You can rent the suite alone or add the courtyard and terrace if you have a larger party. The sun terrace has lounge chairs and a bar overlooking a lower courtyard. All suites have refrigerators, cable TV with HBO, phones (local calls are free), and daily maid service.

> **Talmadge, on the ground floor, is a favorite of honeymooners. Off the inn's small lobby, it has white satin fabrics, a heart-shaped mirror behind the bed, a bar, a sizable kitchen with a gas stove, and a bathroom in pink.**

The service here is welcoming. A friendly staff member escorts you to your room where the lights have been turned on. In the morning, you're served a breakfast in your suite that includes muffins, bagels, fruit, and juice, along with the local paper. Parking is on the street, with no restrictions.

Catamaran Resort Hotel

3999 Mission Boulevard
San Diego, CA 92109
619-488-1081
800-288-0770 in U.S.
800-233-8172 in Canada
Fax: 619-488-1387

> *A casual resort on the water*

General manager: Luis Barrios. **Accommodations:** 312 rooms. **Rates:** $140–$265. **Added:** 10.5% tax. **Minimum stay:** 2 nights on weekends July and August. **Payment:** Major credit cards. **Children:** Under age 18 free in room with parents. **Pets:** Not allowed. **Smoking:** Nonsmoking rooms available.

Polynesia comes to San Diego at the Catamaran, where the grounds are filled with palm trees, exotic birds, flowers, and streams. In the skylighted reception area, a waterfall cascades over stone into a pool of koi. A tapa cloth hangs behind the counter, and a full-size catamaran is suspended from the ceiling. The decor sets the mood for the casual atmosphere at this seaside resort, which faces a long stretch of sandy beach.

Water sports predominate. You can ride a pedalboat, take a sailboard or catamaran lesson, or rent a kayak. Two stern-wheelers cruise Mission Bay for private parties or cocktails and dancing.

The guest rooms are in two-story motel units that surround a swimming pool or edge the beach, and in a 14-story tower. Each room in the tower has a balcony with a view; the higher your room the more expansive the view of Mission Bay and the San Diego skyline. You can see the colorful sails of outriggers waiting by the pier on the beach below, and joggers and skaters on the path. The tower rooms are furnished in a basic, contemporary style with no embellishments — nothing can compete with the glorious views. Even the penthouse suite is simple, though comfortable, with good reading lamps, textured tan walls and a crisp white bathroom. There's a kitchen suitable for cooking light meals. Drapes cover a wall of sliding glass doors that open to a balcony.

The rooms in lower buildings have balconies and patios, but their views are of the lush, well-tended gardens or the freeform pool. There's also a whirlpool spa and an equipped exercise room.

The Catamaran has several meeting rooms and is popular as a site for small conferences and seminars. You can eat well in the Atoll restaurant or on its patio, and enjoy drinks and dancing in the Cannibal Bar, one of San Diego's favorite night clubs. It has an oval bar of koa wood on one level and a large cabaret a few steps below.

The Cottage

3829 Albatross Street
San Diego, Ca 92103
619-299-1564
Fax: 619-299-6213

*A secluded cottage
in a residential
neighborhood*

Innkeepers: Carol and Bob Emerick. **Accommodations:** 1 room and 1 cottage (both with private bath). **Rates:** $55–$95 single or double, $10 additional person. **Included:** Continental breakfast. **Added:** 10.5% tax. **Minimum stay:** 2 nights. **Payment:** MasterCard, Visa. **Children:** Additional $10 per night. **Pets:** Not allowed. **Smoking:** Not allowed.

The old homes and undeveloped canyons in the Hillcrest section of San Diego make it a quiet part of the city, with an unhurried atmosphere. The Cottage, built in 1913 behind the Emericks' homestead-style residence, fits well with the peaceful mood, along with its sense of a bygone day. When you arrive, Carol greets you at the front door of the main house and guides you past the herb garden and hibiscus hedge, under the rose-covered trellis to the cozy cottage in back.

In the cottage, a woodstove (wood is supplied), a sofa bed, and an oak pump organ stand in the living room. An Austrian carved breakfront holds books along with menus of San Diego restaurants, in a rack by the rocker. There's a small gas stove in the kitchen, and fresh coffee beans in the refrigerator.

With the sofa bed, three people will fit nicely in the cottage; any more would be crowding it. A king-size bed almost fills the snug bedroom with fabric covered walls. Corner windows view a tiny, fenced garden. A television is hidden in a wall niche; the room also has reading lamps, a phone, and clock radio. Travelers appreciate the padded hangers and the iron and ironing board in the closet. The immaculate blue and white bathroom, with vibrant touches of red, has both a tub and shower.

> Carol brings a hot breakfast from her kitchen in the mornings. Fresh bread, blueberry muffins, and apple cake are a few of her specialties that accompany coffee and juice or fresh fruit.

The Emericks have also opened a room in the main house to guests. The Garden Room has a private entrance, TV, and a refrigerator. If you stay in the Garden Room you'll have breakfast in the Emericks' pleasant, homey dining room. You're welcome to relax in the parlor, too, listening to the stereo and tape deck or looking through the books on opera. Other interesting items from the couple's collection include old bottles, a stereopticon, and a working player organ that dates from 1875. Bob is an expert on piano and organ restoration; the pump organ in the Cottage is an example of his work.

Most of the furnishings here come from the owners' previous business as antiques dealers. Now Bob teaches sociology at San Diego State College and, with their two daughters grown and gone, Carol manages the guest house.

Horton Grand Hotel

311 Island Avenue
San Diego, CA 92101
619-544-1886
800-542-1886
Fax: 619-239-3823

> *An updated
> historic landmark
> of old San Diego*

Owners: John and Dori Rose. **Accommodations:** 110 rooms and 24 suites. **Rates:** $109–$129, suites $159–$210. **Added:** Tax. **Payment:** Major credit cards. **Children:** Welcome. **Pets:** Allowed. **Smoking:** Nonsmoking rooms available.

The Horton Grand is in San Diego's historic Gaslamp District, once a downtown core gone to seed but now prime urban property. The ornate hotel, two Victorian buildings joined by a courtyard and atrium, stands as a well-restored tribute to comforts past and present. The district is not yet the showcase planners envision, but restaurants and nightspots have sprouted, there's a new convention center, and Horton Plaza, an open-air, multilevel complex of shops and theaters, draws hordes of curious visitors. It's lively and interesting, a cultural as well as a shopping experience.

> **The brick courtyard is one of the hotel's most charming features. Four floors of guest rooms surround it, their balconies overlooking white garden furniture, birds that dart among the potted ficus, and vines climbing over lattices.**

When the site for Horton Plaza was announced in the 1970s, the Horton Grand — built in 1886 as a replica of the Innsbruck Hotel in Vienna and the oldest hotel in San Diego — was in danger of being razed. So in 1980 it was purchased from the city by a group of historical preservationists for $1, dismantled, and rebuilt on its present location two blocks from the Plaza. The Horton Grand was connected by an atrium to another historic hotel, the Kahle Saddlery Hotel, which was reconstructed next door. In 1986, 100 years after the two hotels originally opened their doors, they reopened in style under one name — the Horton Grand Hotel. Now, when you drive up to the front door, energetic young valets whisk your car and luggage away and you step into a conservatory that turns out to be the lobby. Skylights, white wicker furniture, and a cage of chirping finches create a bright and cheerful atmosphere. The clerks at the front desk, dressed in period costume, add to the turn-of-the-century ambience. Despite its monumental sounding name, the hotel is more an example of intimate Victorian charm than of imposing grandeur.

On one side of the lobby there's a tea room where high tea is served Tuesday through Saturday. On the other is a beautifully carved staircase, and the Palace Bar — a combination parlor and saloon where renowned jazz artists play on weekends. Next to the bar is the Palace Café.

The rather small rooms are decorated individually, though they all have gas fireplaces and antique furniture. The best, and quietest, are the rooms overlooking the courtyard. The King Kalakana suite has a Hawaiian theme, while the Bridal suite has a canopied antique bed. All have small sitting areas, rich Victorian draperies, lace curtains, and television sets hidden in wall niches behind mirrors.

One room, 309, is supposedly haunted. Guests and chambermaids have felt an unusual presence there, and some speculate that it's the ghost of Roger Whitaker, who was killed in the hotel a hundred years ago by a gambling associate. The room has been booked solid since the phenomena was investigated by psychics. "The ghost is harmless," they said. "He's really very nice."

As the hotel now stands in the section of the city that was once San Diego's Chinatown, it has a suite dedicated to Ah Quin — Chinatown's unofficial mayor. The most Asian of all the rooms, it has an ornately carved Chinese opium bed with hand-painted murals, and Ah Quin's photograph hangs on the wall.

There's also a third building, which provides large, deluxe suites geared to corporate travelers on extended stays. The Horton Grand offers several special packages, such as a Jazz Special, the Victorian Grand Tradition (including afternoon tea, breakfast in bed, and a sightseeing tour on San Diego's quaint trolley), and one "For Hopeless Romantics."

The Pan Pacific Hotel

400 West Broadway
San Diego, CA 92101
619-239-4500
800-626-3988
Fax: 619-239-3274

> *A contemporary
> downtown hotel*

General manager: Martin Astengo. **Accommodations:** 436 rooms and suites. **Rates:** $160–$180 single, $180–$200 double; suites $320–2000. **Added:** 10.5% tax. **Payment:** Major credit cards. **Children:** Under age 18 free in room with parent. **Pets:** Not allowed. **Smoking:** Nonsmoking rooms available.

The Pan Pacific, which opened in 1991, is an example of the redevelopment that has sparked San Diego's urban renaissance, creating a busy district of office towers, restaurants, hotels, nightclubs, and stores. Part of the Emerald-Shapery Center (a complex that includes offices and shops), the glittery hotel, with its hexagonal glass towers is one of the most highly visible and distinctive buildings in downtown San Diego. A 100-foot atrium rises from the lobby and lounge, and glass elevators soar 25 stories. The centerpiece of the atrium is "Flying Emeralds," an immense sculpture of hanging green glass. Beneath this canopy is a lounge featuring cocktails, appetizers, and piano music.

There are two restaurants: the Grill, with California cuisine that includes heart healthy entrées, and Romeo Cucina, serving contemporary Italian cuisine. You can watch the cooking action at The Grill, which has an open-display kitchen, or take a table on the outdoor patio. When you want a quick, light breakfast, stop in at Creative Croissants on the corner for coffee and rolls.

The hotel occupies three towers (called pods) of the complex's eight. It has a health club on the third level, adjacent to the lap pool, Jacuzzi, and sundeck. Sauna, aerobics classes, and massage are on the fitness program. Business and corporate travelers are well served at the Pan Pacific. They have the use of the most extensive business-support system of any hotel in the region. Secretarial and courier services, telephone, fax, telex, word processing, office supplies, meeting rooms, computers, a notary public, and desktop publishing are available. There's even a law library. Ballrooms and conference facilities total 22,000 square feet.

> **The hotel is close to San Diego's splashy convention center, the performing arts center, Horton Plaza's shopping complex, and the Paladion fashion center. The Museum of Contemporary Art is just a few blocks away.**

The guest rooms start at the fourth floor and go up to the presidential suite on the 25th floor. Because of each pod's hexagonal shape, rooms have interesting configurations. They're furnished comfortably in beige tones, in modern hotel style, and have atrium or city (and some bay) views. They all have multi-line phones, TV, mini-bars, desks, and express check-out. Standard rooms have two doubles or one queen-size, parlor suites have a sleeper sofa in the sitting room and a queen-size bed in the bedroom, and executive suites have separate bed and living rooms, and marble baths with whirlpools and Neutrogena toiletries.

Part of an Asian hotel chain, the Pan Pacific has numerous features that appeal to travelers in the city — the best one is the service. The staff is outstanding. Virtually everyone is courteous, knowledgeable, and eager to help. They're glad to recommend and provide directions to nightspots, visitor attractions, and restaurants. If you like to arrive in style, there's a helipad on top of the hotel. For in-town transportation, a courtesy van will take you to close destinations, and buses and bright red trolley cars provide service to a wider area.

San Diego Princess

1404 West Vacation Road
San Diego, Ca 92109
619-274-4630
800-542-6275
Fax: 619-581-5929

A sprawling resort complex with tropical gardens

General manager: Thomas C. Vincent. **Accommodations:** 359 rooms and 103 suites. **Rates:** $110–$195 single or double, $15 additional person; suites $215–$345. **Added:** Tax. **Payment:** Major credit cards. **Children:** Under age 12 free. **Pets:** Allowed with permission. **Smoking:** Nonsmoking rooms available.

In Mission Bay, north of San Diego Bay, is a 44-acre manmade island that was formed in 1962 from marshland and developed into Vacation Village Resort. The resort's one-level bungalows, surrounded by tropical plants and lagoons and the Mission Bay beachfront, along with numerous recreational facilities, made it a favored San Diego destination. Now it's owned by Princess Cruises Resorts and Hotels, and renamed the San Diego Princess.

There are six tennis courts, five swimming pools, a fitness center, and a new marina. You can play shuffleboard, go bicycling, jog on paths or a mile of beach, and rent sailboats and motorboats.

Like its namesake cruise line, the hotel offers comfortable accommodations and vacation fun in the company of like-minded people.

More than half of the hotel's guests are leisure travelers, while the rest are visiting on business or staying with a group. It's an excellent choice for a group trip if you want to be near the water. The resort is a ten-minute drive from the airport and accessible by bridge from San Diego. It's convenient to the area's major attractions: Sea World, Balboa Park and the San Diego Zoo, and Old Town. Seventy golf courses are within easy driving distance and there's an 18-hole putting course on the property. You can drive or be taken by golf cart to one of the bungalows that lie along the property's curving roads. The spacious guest rooms, two to six to each white brick bungalow, have garden, lagoon, or bay views. Most have sliding glass doors to private patios or the sandy white beach that borders the island. Each room has a dressing area, refrigerator, stocked ServiBar, television, clock radio, and air conditioning. Some contain kitchens.

The suites include eight Executive Suites with movable, soundproof walls, surrounding a lawn suitable for outdoor meetings, a Governor's Suite, and a grand 4,500-square-foot Presidential Bay Suite. Meeting facilities are ample and have been recently expanded with a ballroom.

The most expensive restaurant, Dockside Broiler, features seafood and a view of Mission Bay. The Barefoot Bar & Grill is more casual.

The service throughout the hotel is exemplary, with that special quality of sunny cheerfulness that seems to be a southern California trademark.

The most appealing aspect of San Diego Princess, the one that makes it different from other, similar resorts, is its beautifully landscaped grounds. Paths wind among gardens lush with palm trees, ferns, pine trees, birds of paradise and banana trees. Many of the plantings are neatly labeled. Ducks paddle on a blue lagoon that is centered by a fountain and crossed by small, arching bridges. You can climb a high observation tower for a 360-degree view of the island, the waters around it, and the busy mainland on the other side of the bridge.

U.S. Grant Hotel

326 Broadway
San Diego, Ca 92101
619-232-3121
800-HERITAGE
Fax: 619-232-3626

*A classic historic
hotel in downtown
San Diego*

Manager: Joe Duncalfe. **Accommodations:** 218 rooms, 62 suites. **Rates:** $135–$155 single, $155–$175 double, $20 additional person, suites $245–$1000. **Added:** Tax. **Payment:** Major credit cards. **Children:** Under age 18 free in room with parents. **Pets:** Allowed by prior arrangement. **Smoking:** Nonsmoking rooms available.

In 1985, the historic U.S. Grant Hotel underwent a four-year, $80 million restoration. The hotel had become rundown and closed for nine years, a far cry from its illustrious beginnings in 1910, when it was built by Ulysses S. Grant, Jr., in honor of his father. It had been a San Diego landmark for decades, before it fell into disrepair. A striking building on the outside, the expensive restoration returned the hotel's interior to classic grandeur, with a palatial lobby marked by Palladian columns, a series of crystal chandeliers, 18th-century reproduction furnishings, Dutch and Venetian oil paintings, and Chinese porcelains.

The U.S. Grant takes up a full block in the heart of San Diego's renewed downtown district, across from Horton Plaza, a multilevel shopping center. However, when you drive up to the hotel you don't enter at this front door, but at the parking lot entrance to the lobby, where a valet will take your car to the hotel garage.

The guest rooms, though small, are well furnished with Queen Anne mahogany two-poster beds, armoires, and wing-back chairs. Each has television with cable, and movies are available. Baths of travertine marble and ceramic tile have hand-milled soaps and terrycloth robes. The suites feature decorative fireplaces and built-in bars. Their decor is comfortably traditional, and their large casement windows open to views of the city and downtown redevelopment. There are few complaints about the service at U.S. Grant. Not only is it prompt and courteous, it is given with genuine warmth.

> In the large lobby, a concierge is on duty, prepared to obtain tickets for any cultural, theatrical, or recreational event or to arrange for secretarial and other business services. A wide marble staircase leads to the meeting rooms on the mezzanine.

The cocktail lounge is a congenial room with polished paneling, high ceilings, and a fireplace. Next door is the Grant Grill where grilled steaks, chops, and seafood are served in a men's club atmosphere of rich wood and brass, with fresh flowers on crisp linens, and cozy booth seating. The hotel's sidewalk café is busy during the noon hour serving gourmet pizzas, pastas, and sandwiches. Afternoon tea is served in the lobby to the strains of harp or violin music.

The Westgate Hotel

1055 Second Avenue
San Diego, CA 92101
619-238-1818
800-221-3802
Fax: 619-557-3737

A touch of Versailles in downtown San Diego

General manager: Joe Wancha. **Accommodations:** 223 rooms. **Rates:** $154–$184 single, $164–$194 double; $10 each additional person; suites $325–$1200. **Added:** Tax. **Payment:** Major credit cards. **Children:** Under age 18 free in room with parents. **Pets:** Not allowed. **Smoking:** Nonsmoking rooms available.

From the outside, there isn't much to set the Westgate Hotel apart from its neighbors. Construction on the hotel began in 1969, and the 20-story structure blends in easily with the surrounding office buildings of downtown San Diego. Yet any resemblance to a typical city office building fades as soon as you step inside the Westgate's front door.

> In the heart of downtown, the Westgate is within easy walking distance of the convention center, Horton Plaza, and the Gaslamp district. The hotel provides complimentary limousine service to the airport, as well as a number of tourist and downtown business locations.

In the lobby, Baccarat crystal chandeliers, 18th-century furnishings trimmed in gold, one of the first Steinway pianos ever built, Aubusson tapestries, paintings by Utrillo and Velazquez, polished parquet floors topped by expansive Persian rugs, creamy paneled walls with fanciful moldings, and chairs crafted by Marie Antoinette's personal furniture maker, create an opulent ambience. The ornate decor is deliberate, as the room was designed as a re-creation of the anteroom at Versailles.

Guest rooms, each individually decorated in the Louis XV, Louis XVI, and Regency periods with reproduction furniture and fine fabrics, are also elegant. Standard rooms have either a king-size bed or two oversize doubles, two-line speaker phones with computer capabilities, and an Italian marble bath with brass fixtures. The most regal accommodations are the Governor's and Presidential suites with antique furnishings, a large living room, two bedrooms, two baths, and a full kitchen.

White glove service, crystal chandeliers, and French cuisine are all part of the experience when dining in the Westgate's Fountainebleau restaurant. The Westgate Room, cheerful in lime greens, is more casual and serves both American and Continental cuisine. In the afternoons, high tea is served in the lobby.

SANTA MONICA

Hotel Shangri-La

1301 Ocean Avenue
Santa Monica, CA 90401
310-394-2791
800-345-STAY
Fax: 310-451-3351

A deco hotel
facing the beach

General manager: Dino Nanni. **Accommodations:** 55 rooms and suites. **Rates:** $110–$450, 1 to 4 people, $15 additional person. **Included:** Continental breakfast and afternoon refreshments. **Added:** 12% tax. **Payment:** Major credit cards. **Children:** Under age 16 free in room with parents. **Pets:** Not allowed. **Smoking:** Nonsmoking rooms available.

Like the setting for a Hollywood movie of the 1930s, the Shangri-La has an art deco motif that is skillfully accomplished. It's rare to find a theme carried through as well while keeping guests' comfort a priority. The small lobby contains soft green couches, torch lamps, and a large version of the hotel's signature design: stylized palm trees and a vast blue ocean, viewed from behind a pink balcony railing.

For updated comfort with a touch of vintage L.A. in a light, bright setting by the beach, the Shangri-La is an excellent choice for those traveling on a budget.

The rooms on the first six floors range from studios to two- bedroom, two-bath suites. The seventh floor is reserved for two penthouse suites with sundecks. All the rooms have television, phones, and movie posters that are reminders of the period the decor evokes. Most rooms, except for those on the fifth and sixth floors, come with equipped kitchens. The open-gallery design of the building, with exterior hallways, provides cross-ventilation and ocean views.

One typical studio room contains curved chrome chairs and a painting of pink flamingoes. There's a dressing area near the white tile bath and a kitchen with a gas stove. At this location, $110 is not a bad price. And you get breakfast and afternoon tea, served in a pretty little breakfast room off the courtyard.

A one-bedroom suite on the sixth floor will have its own wraparound deck and sleek gray furniture striped with burgundy in the spacious living room and bedroom. All rooms on the sixth floor have private sundecks facing west. The Shangri-La has no restaurant and no recreational facilities. There's a tiled terrace with lounge chairs in back in the large courtyard, which has the only thing out of scale with the art deco flavor of the hotel — a chunky, oversize gazebo.

The artfully curved seven-story hotel stands on a busy corner in Santa Monica, directly across the street from Palisades Park and the beach. Several fine restaurants and Santa Monica's Third Street Promenade are within walking distance, and a major shopping mall is close by.

Loews Santa Monica Beach Hotel

1700 Ocean Avenue
Santa Monica, CA 90401
310-458-6700
800-23-LOEWS
Fax: 310-458-6761

One of L.A.'s only luxury hotels near the beach

General manager: Richard Cassale. **Accommodations:** 350 rooms, includes 31 suites. **Rates:** $255–$315 single, $275–$335 double, $20 additional person, suites up to $2500. **Added:** Tax. **Payment:** Major credit cards. **Children:** Under age 18 free in room with adult. **Pets:** Not allowed. **Smoking:** Nonsmoking rooms available.

Facing a broad stretch of Santa Monica sand, but not directly on the beach, this eight-story hotel has a light, open atmosphere befitting its oceanfront location. Sunshine streams through Palladian windows and the skylight over a an extensive five-story atrium lobby. Couches and chairs are grouped in conversation areas in the lobby, which has a cheerful array of fountains, palms, orchids, and even a koi pond.

Off the lobby are United Airline and Hertz car rental counters. The hotel offers valet and self-parking, multilingual concierge service, a business center, dry cleaning, laundry, and shoe shines. Guests can rent bicycles, skates and rollerblades.

You're likely to see people in the film and television industries here; Santa Monica has become a popular site for production companies. Once the area was a getaway for movie stars. Charlie Chaplin and Mary Pickford built homes that still stand on the beach directly below the hotel. Two blocks away is the historic Santa Monica pier, with its famous restored carousel and other rides.

Most guest rooms have partial ocean views. Location makes the difference in rates; all rooms are spacious and have the

> **There are several restaurants and cafés on Third Street Promenade, a tree-lined plaza closed to traffic. Busy and festive, it has three blocks of shops, eateries, nightclubs, and theaters.**

same decor. They're furnished in California-casual style, with bleached rattan, wicker, and fabrics in sand tones. They have narrow balconies, mini-bars, hair dryers, robes, irons and ironing boards, and small TVs in marble baths in addition to large televisions with all channels in the room. Most suites are corner rooms, so they enjoy both a pool view and full ocean view. The pool, thirty feet above the beach, is designed for both indoor and outdoor use. Near it is the Jackson Sousa Fitness Facility. This excellent fitness center provides state-of-the-art equipment, classrooms, Jacuzzi, sauna and steam, massage, and personal training sessions.

The bewildering array of restaurants in Santa Monica — some 400 within eight square miles — makes dining choices a pleasant dilemma. In the hotel, you have two choices (plus 24-hour room service and a lobby bar that serves snacks). Riva features California-Italian cookery in an informal atmosphere, while the Coast Cafe offers casual meals all day on the terrace. Both are relaxing spots with ocean views.

Miramar Sheraton Hotel

101 Wilshire Boulevard
Santa Monica, CA 90401
310-576-7777
800-325-3535
Fax: 310-458-7912

> *Ocean views, comfort, and elegance are all features of this Santa Monica hotel*

General manager: William T. Worcester. **Accommodations:** 302 rooms and suites. **Rates:** $220–$295 doubles; bungalows $325–$800. **Added:** 12% tax. **Payment:** Major credit cards. **Children:** Welcome. **Pets:** Not Allowed. **Smoking:** Nonsmoking rooms available.

The lobby's polished marble floors, bamboo furniture, and potted palms are the first clues that the Miramar Sheraton offers sophisticated lodging in a relaxed atmosphere. From there a friendly staff member will lead you to your room or suite in either the Palisades building, Ocean tower, or a 1930s bungalow — each representing a different stage of the hotel's development.

The present day hotel stands on what was once John P. Jones's private estate. Jones, who made his fortune in silver, was the founder of Santa Monica. His mansion was constructed on the site in 1889, and for a short while the home belonged to King C. Gillette of razor fame, and was a military academy before becoming a hotel in 1921. In the late 1930s the mansion was torn down to make way for guest bungalows and a hotel building. The ten-story Ocean tower was added in 1959.

The guest rooms in the Ocean tower are the least formal. Decorated in a California style with light wood furnishings, they have mini-bars, alarm-clock radios, hair dryers, coffeemakers, makeup mirrors, and irons and ironing boards. Angled to take advantage of the ocean views on the upper floors, the rooms also have balconies. The Palisades building has a more classic look with paneled hallways, antique replica furniture in rich woods, and larger rooms with roomier baths.

The cream colored stuccoed bungalows provide the most private and deluxe accommodations at the hotel. Each with its own entrance, they are sunny with large windows, hardwood floors, and high ceilings. In addition to the standard amenities, they have scales, heat lamps, Swiss toiletries, and marble vanities in the baths, as well as in-room safes, extra feather pillows, three telephones, and a entertainment center complete with a VCR, stereo, and built-in bath speaker. The list of celebrities who have stayed at the Miramar over the years is a long one (it includes Garbo, JFK, Marilyn Monroe, Eleanor Roosevelt, and Charles Lindbergh), and bungalows bear the names of former famous guests.

> **The Miramar is well situated. The Pacific is just across the street, and the Santa Monica Pier and Third Street Promenade are both within walking distance.**

The buildings all surround a garden courtyard with palms, a lush lawn, fountain, and swimming pool. The Miramar also has a good fitness center with a covered outdoor Jacuzzi, sundeck, locker rooms with sauna and steam rooms, and a pleasant workout room where you can see the ocean while you exercise.

The Miramar Grille and the Miramar Café are the hotel's restaurants. A Pacific-style grill, the Grille has a demonstration kitchen which serves up meals such as seared boneless trout over spaghettied vegetables and rice noodles spiced with shiitaki broth, and shrimp and lobster tail over fennel and spinach risotto. A good wine selection, tapas, and tasty desserts round out the menu. The cuisine is Continental and the mood is casual at the Café, which serves all three meals. As Santa Monica boasts some 400 restaurants, additional dining choices are close at hand.

Shutters on the Beach

One Pico Boulevard
Santa Monica, CA 90405
310-458-0030
800-334-9000
Fax: 310-458-4589

> *A classy
> beachfront hotel*

General manager: Klaus Mennekes. **Accommodations:** 198 rooms including 12 suites. **Rates:** $245–$400 single or double, suites $550–$1900. **Added:** Tax. **Payment:** Major credit cards. **Children:** Free in room with parents. **Pets:** Not allowed. **Smoking:** Nonsmoking rooms available.

Although the gray and white hotel looks as though it could have been built in the 1920s, Shutters on the Beach, which opened in 1993, is one of Santa Monica's newest lodgings. Shutters is also one of the closest oceanside hotels to Los Angeles, making it ideal for a quick weekend escape from the city.

Urban cares and pressures seem to dissipate as soon as you step into the understated elegance of the lobby — a long room with a light stenciled ceiling and beautiful parquet floors set with comfortable sitting areas, plants, and fresh flowers. Artwork on the walls bear the names of artists such as David Hockney, William Wegman, Jasper Johns, Roy Lichtenstein, and Robert Motherwell. At the far end of the room, glass doors open onto a white railinged terrace overlooking the sandy beach dotted with palms and the ocean beyond.

The best seats in the house can be found in One Pico, the hotel's fine dining restaurant which adjoins the lobby. Every table has an ocean view, and seafood and fresh California cuisine are emphasized in dishes such as applewood smoked salmon with creamed spinach, and wide ribbon pasta with shredded duck and snap peas. You can watch the roller bladers and bicyclists zip by downstairs in the aptly named Pedals, a casual bistro serving Italian-influenced pizza, pasta, salads, and sandwiches from an exhibition kitchen. The adjacent Handlebars, which is bright for a bar because of its beachside location, has the same view.

The preferred guest rooms and suites are those located in this main three-story building that skirts the beach. With balconies that practically open out to the edge of the sand, they are priced accordingly. (The rooms on the upper two floors are better, as first-floor balconies are a little too close to the bike path for comfort.) Bright sunlight and the blue of the ocean fill these spacious rooms, and white shutters — hence the hotel's name — can be drawn closed to keep the sun's rays from disturbing late sleepers.

Rooms have a crisp clean look with color schemes and decor appropriate for the oceanside location — blue trimmed white linens on two-poster beds, fish prints on the walls, and comfortable sofas and easy chairs covered in cool mint, blue, and white stripes. Televisions are hidden behind lattice work doors in armoires, and baths are luxurious with whirlpool tubs, white marble floors, and handsome green marble vanities. Other comforts include terry robes, three two-line telephones with computer capabilities, complimentary in-room movies with additional videos available for rental, mini-bars, safes, makeup mirrors, and natural soaps. Some suites have extras such as large oceanview Jacuzzis, separate living rooms, and fireplaces. Guest rooms in the rear five-story building without views, or with partial ocean views, are less expensive.

> **Attentive service, fine dining, and comfortably elegant decor all add to the appeal of this attractive seaside lodging.**

A brick pool deck and lower terrace that extends toward the beach, connect the two lodging buildings. Chaise longues topped with blue and white cushions for soaking up the rays are plentiful, and there's a heated whirlpool and an outdoor fireplace to warm chillier days. Poolside service means you needn't interrupt your siesta to dine if you don't wish to. If you crave more active recreation, you can work out in the hotel's fitness center, or rent a bike and cycle to nearby Santa Monica Pier or down the shore to offbeat Venice Beach.

SEAL BEACH

The Seal Beach Inn and Gardens

212 5th Street
Seal Beach, CA 90740
310-493-2416
800-HIDEAWAY
Fax: 310-799-0483

> *A colorful inn surrounded by flowers*

Innkeeper: Marjorie Bettenhausen-Schmaehl. **Accommodations:** 23 rooms (all with private bath). **Rates:** $118–$185 single or double, $10 additional person, penthouse suite $255. **Included:** Full breakfast and afternoon refreshments. **Added:** 9% tax. **Payment:** Major credit cards. **Children:** Discouraged, $10 additional per night. **Pets:** Not allowed. **Smoking:** Not allowed.

Seal Beach is a pleasant, friendly, quiet town on Highway 1, south of Long Beach. Busy in summer, it's a popular place for surfing, sailboarding, and strolling on the beach, though it doesn't have the glamour of some southern California resort areas. Go to Seal Beach to enjoy the fresh ocean breezes, some good casual restaurants, the shops of Old Town and Seaport Village, fishing off the pier, bicycle riding, and maybe a gondola ride through the canals. And when you're here, stay at the charming Seal Beach Inn, a block from the sea.

The first thing you notice about the inn is color. The brick terrace in front of the two-story inn is overflowing with bright flowers. Bougainvillea cascades over wrought-iron railings; Boston ivy climbs the walls. Blue canopies and old-fashioned red street lamps add further touches of color.

Built in the 1920s, the long-neglected inn was restored in the mid-1970s by Marjorie Bettenhausen. She created a showplace reminiscent of the inns along the Mediterranean coast of France. Antiques from her travels are in all the rooms and gardens. They include a 300-year-old French fountain, an oak fireplace mantel and altar from a historic Chicago church, a Persian tile mural four centuries old, and numerous frescoes and marble pieces. The bed from John Barrymore's estate is here, along with a French armoire that was part of a trousseau in 1839.

> **Marjorie wants contented guests, and she goes out of her way to make sure they're happy. You'll find homemade chocolate chip cookies in your room at night and a list of local points of interest. You can order a picnic basket or get a restaurant recommendation from the innkeeper or her staff.**

The rooms, named for flowers, have TVs and phones. Fourteen have kitchens and one has a fireplace. The suites have sitting areas with antiques, lacy curtains, and lots of chintz and ruffles that are almost — but not quite — too fussy for comfort. Most expensive and largest are the interior Imperial Suites, all eight of them considered honeymoon suites. Some rooms have paneled walls and ceilings. They can be quite dark, so if you prefer a lighter atmosphere you may want to request it.

Vienna Woods is a favorite for its elaborately carved bed from pre–Civil War Virginia. Mexican pavers form the floor and German lace curtains hang at the windows. Black and white glass tiles from France give the bathroom a dramatic look.

A buffet breakfast is provided in the cozy tearoom; if you're like most guests, you'll want to enjoy it by the pool or on the terrace. The fare includes homemade breads, granola, a quiche or casserole, juice, and coffee or tea. Afternoon wine and cheese are served by the fire in the dining room.

TEMECULA

Loma Vista Bed & Breakfast

33350 La Serena Way
Temecula, CA 92390
909-676-7047

A Mission-style hilltop home overlooking vineyards

Innkeepers: Betty and Dick Ryan. **Accommodations:** 6 rooms (private baths). **Rates:** $95–$125. **Included:** Full champagne breakfast. **Added:** 10% tax. **Minimum stay:** 2 nights on holiday weekends. **Payment:** MasterCard, Visa. **Children:** $25 for rollaway. **Pets:** Not allowed. **Smoking:** Not allowed. **Open:** Year-round except Thanksgiving, Christmas, and New Year's.

When the Ryans designed Loma Vista in 1987, they chose Betty Ryan's favorite architecture: Spanish Mission–style, with its curved archways, red tile roofs, and cool courtyards. The interior of their imposing hilltop home is light and spacious, but the decor is more American traditional than early California, with a carpeted living room and white and flower-patterned couches by a brick fireplace. The windows overlook the vineyards of Temecula Valley, a wine production region north of San Diego.

Betty and Dick are relaxed, friendly hosts who know how to keep guests happy. You'll find sherry and a basket of fruit in your room and evening wine and cheese on the patio. Afterward there's an outdoor hot tub to soak in.

Loma Vista's guest rooms, named after wine grapes, are air conditioned and have queen- or king-size beds and clock radios. Each is decorated distinctively. Fumé Blanc is light and airy, with white wicker and plants; Sauvignon Blanc features the desert hues and white pine of the Southwest. Zinfandel has gracious Queen Anne furnishings and a balcony with a view of Palomar Observatory.

The most striking room is Champagne. Though it has no

balcony or view, it's a glamorous retreat with curved black lacquer furniture, a satin quilt, and framed photos of Fred Astaire and Marilyn Monroe lending a Hollywood/art deco flavor.

In the morning a champagne breakfast is served family style in the dining room. It includes hot entrées such as chicken mushroom crêpes or Huevos Loma Vista (half an avocado is topped with poached eggs and nestled in refried beans), as well as sundaes made from fresh fruit, muffins, yogurt, and granola.

The Ryans will urge you to explore the historic Temecula area. The village was a stagecoach stop 150 years ago, on the Butterfield State Line between St. Louis and San Francisco, and has retained some of its Old West atmosphere. You can shop for antiques, tour the wineries, go hot air ballooning, play golf, fish at Lake Skinner, and try the local restaurants the innkeepers recommend.

VISTA

Cal-a-Vie

2249 Somerset Road
Vista, CA 92084
619-945-2055
Fax: 619-630-0074

A country inn with a focus on fitness

Owners: William and Marlene Power. **Accommodations:** 24 cottages. **Rates:** $4,250 per person per week, European plan; $3,750 per week American plan. **Included:** All meals. **Added:** Tax. **Minimum stay:** 7 days. **Payment:** MasterCard, Visa.

Children: Age 18 and older welcome. **Pets:** Not allowed. **Smoking:** Allowed in designated smoking rooms. **Open:** Year-round except Christmas/New Year holidays.

Forty miles north of San Diego, this exclusive spa nestles against a rural hillside like a Mediterranean village. From the tile-roofed stucco cottages, the view is of citrus and avocado orchards, mountains, and blue sky. The air is clean, and the climate balmy. It's an ideal setting for a retreat into self-improvement.

> Throughout the year, Cal-a-Vie offers women's sessions, men's sessions, and coed sessions; they begin on Sunday afternoon and end the following Sunday morning. Transportation to and from the San Diego International Airport is provided at no charge.

At Cal-a-Vie you'll find an emphasis on balance, combining the American approach to fitness with a European focus on skin and body care. Heavy exercise takes place in the mornings; the afternoons are devoted to rest, relaxation, and therapeutic treatments. The day begins with a brisk walk in the adjacent hills; then it's breakfast and a series of warmups, aerobics, and exercise classes. Since the spa never has more than twenty-four people at a time, each guest receives attention and instruction.

Afternoon skin and body treatments include facials, Swedish and shiatsu massage, seaweed wraps, hydrotherapy, aromatherapy, and the highlight, a one-hour Body-glo treatment that sloughs dead skin cells and leaves you feeling rejuvenated.

In this busy schedule, time is allotted for lounging by the pool and relaxing in the gardens of oleander, lavender, and agapanthus. There's no television and no piped-in music, just the rustle of vines, the sound of a trickling waterfall, and a few bird songs. The spicy scent of eucalyptus mingles with the inviting smells of good foods baking, and you begin to think of dinner.

Three meals and two snacks a day add up to just 900 calories that don't leave you hungry. The Cal-a-Vie cuisine features fresh ingredients and a variety of spices and herbs. Examples of the light and elegant fare are grilled swordfish with papaya salsa, mango sorbet with raspberries, Italian pear cake, and even strawberry cheesecake.

The spa provides the gear and clothing you'll need and launders it daily; all you need to pack are your swimsuit, underwear, shoes, and toothbrush. Your room, in one of the four buildings around the swimming pool, will have a clock radio, phone, armoire, a duvet on the bed, and a closet with an umbrella for the occasional rain sprinkle. All the units are the same size, with slightly different decorating schemes, and have private patios.

Wine Country

Best Country Inns and Bed and Breakfasts

Calistoga
Brannan Cottage Inn
Foothill House
Meadowlark Country House
Mount View Hotel
Scott Courtyard
Silver Rose Inn

Geyserville
Campbell Ranch Inn
Hope-Merrill House

Glen Ellen
Beltane Ranch
Gaige House Inn

Guerneville
Applewood

Healdsburg
Belle de Jour Inn
The George Alexander House
Madrona Manor

Kenwood
The Kenwood Inn

Napa
Churchill Manor
La Residence Country Inn
The Old World Inn

Rutherford
Auberge du Soleil
Rancho Caymus Inn

St. Helena
Bartels Ranch and Country Inn
Deer Run
The Wine Country Inn
Zinfandel Inn

Santa Rosa
The Gables
Vintners Inn

Sonoma
El Dorado Hotel
Sonoma Hotel
Victorian Garden Inn

Yountville
  Burgundy House
  Maison Fleurie
  Oleander House
  The Webber Place

Best on a Budget

Guerneville
  Creekside Inn & Resort

Best Resorts

Napa
  Silverado Country Club & Resort
St. Helena
  Meadowood

Best Romantic Hideaways

St. Helena
  Villa St. Helena

Best Spas

Boyes Hot Springs
  Sonoma Mission Inn & Spa

Although there are small pockets of wine growing regions in other parts of the state, the Napa and Sonoma valleys north of San Francisco is the area that people generally refer to as the California wine country. Between the towns of **Napa** and **Healdsburg,** some of the state's finest and best-known wines are produced. Vineyards cover the valley floor, border the Russian River, climb almost every hillside, and grow between farmlands and towns near historic **Sonoma** where wineries have been producing wines for over a hundred years. The lesser-known Alexander Valley near **Geyserville** is also worth exploring, and adds even greater depth to the famed wine-growing region.

The highest concentration of wineries, including some of California's largest, face Highway 29 which runs right through the heart of the Napa valley. For this reason the route is often crammed with traffic and weekend wine tasters. Hence Sonoma tends to be somewhat less crowded with tourists than the Napa valley, while Napa has a slight edge when it comes to acclaimed eateries that incorporate the region's natural bounty in their creative cuisine. Both valleys have charming towns such as Sonoma with its town central plaza surrounded by historic buildings, **St. Helena** and **Yountville** with their smart shops and first-rate restaurants, and **Boyes Hot Springs** and **Calistoga** where visitors have been coming for decades to soak in health-giving mineral waters. In recent years, hot air balloon companies have sprung up to offer travelers the chance to soar over the region's abundant beauty.

Ultimately whether you decide to focus your attention on either Napa or Sonoma, both are lovely and have a wide selection of good wineries, restaurants, and fine inns. Best of all each valley is easily accessible from the other, no matter where you stay in the area.

BOYES HOT SPRINGS

Sonoma Mission Inn & Spa

18140 Sonoma Highway 12
Boyes Hot Springs, CA
Mailing Address: P.O. Box 1447
Sonoma, CA 95476
707-938-9000
800-862-4945
Fax: 707-996-5358

A Mission-style hotel with spa facilities

General manager: Jack Burkham. **Accommodations:** 167 rooms, 3 suites. **Rates:** $185–$395 single or double, $30 for additional person, suites $350–$690. **Added:** 9% tax. **Minimum stay:** 2 nights on weekends. **Payment:** Major credit cards.

Children: Under age 12 free in room with parents. **Pets:** Not allowed. **Smoking:** Nonsmoking rooms available.

In 1895, an enterprising young Englishman, Captain H. E. Boyes, built a bathhouse and hotel. That later burned to the ground, and in 1927 the present Sonoma Mission Inn was con-structed. Typifying the romantic revivalism of the era, the new building was designed as a California mission, complete with arcade and bell tower.

> Since the mid-1800s, San Franciscans have been traveling 40 miles north to the Boyes Hot Springs site for the curative mineral waters of its underground springs. The area was long considered a sacred healing ground by Native Americans.

The inn's fortunes waxed and waned over the years, until, in the 1980s, it was restored and brought to its present state of luxury as a top resort. The rambling beige hotel stands on seven acres of grounds shaded by big maple and eucalyptus trees in the thriving little town of Boyes Hot Springs, two miles north of Sonoma.

The mission motif stops at the front door. Inside, the big open lobby has white walls, a beamed ceiling, tiled floors, and comfy sofas and chairs situated in front of a large fireplace topped by a wreath of dried flowers.

Adjacent to the lobby are a bar and The Grille, a restaurant in pinks and greens, soft linens, and fresh orchids on the tables, all glowing in candlelight. The Grille features mesquite specialties and California cookery. Examples include a mesquite-grilled veal chop with sun-dried tomato butter and grilled lamb chops with hazelnut mint pesto. Fresh local ingredients are emphasized. The menu includes imaginative and tasty spa cuisine for those monitoring calories. Another restaurant, the Café, is located on a corner at the north end of the property. It has a wine bar and an adjoining market selling a variety of wines, gifts, kitchenware, and T-shirts.

The guest rooms are in the three-story main hotel and in newer, separate buildings. The older rooms are smaller but have the most charm and character, with half-canopy beds, pretty floral fabrics, and walk-in closets. Stocked bars hold complimentary wine. The air-conditioned rooms have similar furnishings and contain writing tables, TV sets, digital clocks, and phones. Rates are based on room size. Deluxe rooms are largest. In the Wine Country section of the resort, some rooms have fireplaces and overlook the inner courtyard and landscaped grounds. Carneros Suite, which opens to a patio, is a good choice for small group meetings. It has a granite fireplace, comfortable couches, and a wet bar. The rooms closest to the spa are in North Building.

The resort's much-touted spa and fitness facility occupies a smaller space than you might expect, but it's attractively designed and the services seem unending. You can get at least four kinds of massage, a seaweed body wrap, a salt scrub, clay packs, facials, waxings, and numerous hair, nail, and skin treatments. There's an extra charge for spa use.

The inn offers aerobics classes, a weight room, and an Olympic-size swimming pool, heated in winter, that is open to guests and supervised children. Another, smaller exercise pool is for adults only. There are also two tennis courts on the property.

CALISTOGA

Brannan Cottage Inn

P.O Box 81
109 Wapoo Avenue
Calistoga, CA 94515
707-942-4200

A small, historic inn close to Calistoga's attractions

Innkeepers: Dieter and Ruth Back. **Accommodations:** 6 rooms (all with private bath). **Rates:** $115 single, $140 double, $160 suite. **Included:** Full breakfast. **Added:** 12% tax. **Payment:** MasterCard, Visa. **Children:** Over age 10 welcome. **Pets:** Not allowed. **Smoking:** Not allowed.

Sam Brannan was one of the first people to recognize the commercial potential in the hot springs at the northern end of the Napa Valley. In 1859, he purchased 2,000 acres surrounding the hot springs and named the area Calistoga (a combination of California and Saratoga, New York's famous mineral water spa). The elaborate resort he built included twenty-five guest cottages. The only one remaining is now a bed-and-breakfast inn. Its Greek Revival architecture, with an intricate gingerbread gableboard and scalloped ridge-cresting, was intended to bring a sense of civilization to Calistoga in the rugged 1860s. The building has been completely restored and is on the National Register of Historic Places. In 1985 it received the prestigious Napa Landmarks award for its contribution to historic preservation in Napa County.

> A breakfast that varies daily is served in the dining room, though with the Napa Valley's benign weather, guests can often eat outdoors in an enclosed, lemon-fragrant courtyard.

The charming white cottage with green trim stands behind a white picket fence, roses, and a palm tree that was planted by Sam Brannan. Robert Louis Stevenson referred to it as a "weedy palm" in Silverado Squatters. Now the tree is tall and stately. The rooms are light and simple, with oak floors, cozy loveseats, primitive pine antiques, and white wicker furnishings. Fresh flowers and wall border stencils provide touches of color in the cheerful and uncluttered surroundings. Each room is named for the wildflower stencil that decorates its walls: sweet pea, poppy, morning glory, wild rose, wood violet, and iris. Poppy is a favorite and has a clawfoot tub in the bath. The carriage house can accommodate up to four people. All rooms have private entrances, ceiling fans, and air conditioning. They do not have telephones, but there is one centrally located for guest use. Several rooms have televisions.

In the parlor, furnished with pink velvet loveseats near a brick fireplace, stenciled clusters of grapes and leaves decorate the walls, and bunches of flowers from the surrounding garden brighten every corner. Sherry and tea are available all day in the parlor.

Foothill House

3037 Foothill Boulevard
Calistoga, CA 94515
707-942-6933
800-942-6933
Fax: 707-942-5692

> *A well-run B&B near wineries and mineral baths*

Innkeepers: Doris and Gus Beckert. **Accommodations:** 3 suites plus cottage (all with private bath, 3 will Jacuzzi tubs). **Rates:** $140–$275 single or double, $35 additional person. **Included:** Full breakfast and afternoon hors d'oeuvres. **Minimum stay:** 2 nights weekends, 3 nights holiday weekends. **Payment:** Major credit cards. **Children:** Not appropriate. **Pets:** Not allowed. **Smoking:** Not allowed indoors.

Everything is done well at this fine inn, but when guests leave Foothill House, they always rave about the food. Doris Beckert, a longtime culinary student, loves to prepare breakfast specialties and afternoon appetizers, artistically presented, for her guests. Appetizers such as chunky marinara sauce topped with brie cheese and toasted pine nuts accompanied by French bread and roasted garlic, or feta cheese in a garlic cream base with fresh basil, pine nuts, and roasted red peppers are tied to the wine selection for the day. Breakfast could be a frittata or soufflé served in individual ramekins and adorned with edible flowers from the inn's front garden. Doris serves them in the sunroom or on a terrace, in the shade of an immense redwood tree. Some guests like to take their coffee up the grassy slope to the pretty white gazebo.

The small inn also offers well-furnished, attractive, spacious rooms with good reading lamps and stacks of books and magazines. Bottles of valley wine and Calistoga mineral water chill in each refrigerator. Sherry is provided at bedtime, and a teddy bear or other stuffed animal holds freshly baked cookies. Most rooms have neither a telephone or television, but each has a phone jack and the house phone may be borrowed. Wood is laid and the fire is ready to light. Other amenities include coffeemakers, irons and ironing boards, terry robes, tape decks and cassettes, extra pillows in each room; and in the baths, hair dryers, makeup mirrors, Q-tips, cotton balls, and soaps wrapped in calico. Three suites have Jacuzzi tubs.

The Evergreen suite, in green and peach tones, has an elegant country look. A blanket chest stands at the foot of the four-poster canopy bed topped by a patchwork quilt, and there's a calico print sofa. Other features include a fainting couch, an art deco armoire, an easy chair, a dining table for two in front of a window with a view of Mount St. Helena, a deck with a fountain, and a twin bed in an alcove with drapes surrounding it that can be closed to shield light from a sleeping traveling companion if one decides to stay up late reading a book.

> The innkeepers will arrange for winery and sightseeing tours and make reservations at Calistoga's famed mud and mineral baths. Recommended nearby restaurants include Catahoula's, in the Mount View Hotel, and Terra in nearby St. Helena.

The Lupine, in blues and greens, is also pleasant. A small dining table divides the bedroom room from the living room, and there's a cozy sitting area in front of a wood-burning stove. The Redwood room is the smallest, but particularly attractive, and mirrors have been used to make the space appear larger. It's decorated with red velvet sofas, grape print wallpaper, and Laura Ashley's fruit pattern fabric in rich burgundies, golds, dark greens, and olives.

Quail's Roost is the inn's largest suite in a separate, hillside cottage with a full kitchen, a wet bar, a four-poster bed, and a smaller bed by a bay window. A quail made from driftwood stands on a dresser, and even the china in the kitchen has a quail motif. There's a large entertainment center housing a TV and VCR with many videos to choose from, and the fireplace is visible from the living room, bedroom, and bath. A two-person whirlpool tub and double-headed shower are in a very private glass-walled bathroom that faces a waterfall flowing down a rocky slope. The Roost makes a great retreat for those seeking both space and privacy.

Meadowlark Country House

601 Petrified Forest Road
Calistoga, CA 94515
707-942-5651
Fax: 707-942-5023

> *A quiet country home in the Napa valley*

Innkeeper: Kurt Stevens. **Accommodations:** 4 rooms (all with private bath). **Rates:** $125–$150 single or double. **Included:** Breakfast. **Added:** 10.5% tax. **Minimum stay:** 2 nights on weekends. **Payment:** Major credit cards. **Children:** Not appropriate. **Pets:** Allowed by prior arrangement. **Smoking:** Not allowed.

This country home, set on twenty acres of rolling wooded hills outside Calistoga, at the northern end of the Napa Valley, began as a small cabin in 1886. Space was added in the ensuing years, and when Kurt Stevens purchased the property he remodeled it into a light, bright, airy inn that is a pleasure to visit.

Meadowlark's property includes a hill of oak groves behind the house, and walking paths and a swimming pool off to one side of the driveway. The tan house with white trim, surrounded by perky red geraniums, is set well back from the road making it a quiet refuge from the world beyond.

The innkeeper welcomes guests hospitably and turns the house over to them. "I treat them as my friends," he says. "I hope they feel that this is their own temporary home." With that aim, he fills the refrigerator with soft drinks, juice, and ice, and a basket with fruit. In the morning he serves a substantial California-style breakfast of English muffins, turkey ham, an egg dish such as quiche or frittata, coffee, and yogurt, granola, or fruit on a rustic table in the dining room. The adjoining living room has overstuffed chairs perfect for relaxing in, and from there French doors lead to a veranda — a pleasant spot for enjoying a cup of coffee and the garden.

After a day spent exploring, sightseeing, and wine tasting, you can relax on the peaceful veranda or enjoy a picnic by the murmuring creek.

Upstairs, the guest rooms offer views of the forest, garden, or meadow. They're furnished in a mixture of antique and contemporary styles done with fine taste, and an awareness of travelers' needs for space and amenities. Each is decorated with objects from Kurt's personal collections. The well-traveled host, who came to California from Germany in the early 1970s, has collected Oriental perfume bottles, old English prints, antique doorknobs, and jade and porcelain horses. (He has live horses as well, kept on another part of the estate.)

There are no phones in the rooms, but guests may use the house phone (with no charge for local calls). Guests are also welcome to use the inn kitchen when Kurt is not whipping up one of his ample breakfasts. He lives in a separate home a few yards down a path from the main house, and is easy to reach in an emergency.

Meadowlark is just a short distance from Calistoga's mineral baths, the town center, and the valley's numerous wineries and restaurants. Yet it's truly a retreat from the crowds and traffic that can clog Highway 29.

Mount View Hotel

1457 Lincoln Avenue
Calistoga, CA 94515
707-942-6877
Fax: 707-942-6904

A wine country hotel with deco style

General manager: Mitch Jaffuel.
Accommodations: 33 rooms. **Rates:**
$85–$125 single or double, suites $140–$190, cottages $189.
Added: Tax. **Minimum stay:** 2 nights on weekends and holidays. **Payment:** Major credit cards. **Children:** Under age 10
free in room with parents. **Pets:** Not allowed. **Smoking:** Nonsmoking rooms available.

The first owner of the Mount View was Johnny Ghisolfo, an
Italian immigrant with little education but a keen business
sense. He became the first mayor of Calistoga, a village at the
north end of the Napa Valley known then and now for its
mineral waters. In 1917 Ghisolfo built the hotel on the
town's main street. Additional wings were added in 1939, and
a complete restoration of the Mount View to its original art
deco style was completed in 1980. Two years later it was
placed on the National Register of Historic Places.

Some of the original furnishings are still in place in the
two-story stucco building. Graceful palms stand in the corners of the busy lobby, designed to capture a 1930s European
flavor. Overstuffed sofas, a fireplace, and bouquets of flowers
make it a pleasant gathering place for conversation and games
of backgammon.

On one side of the lobby is a lounge, where you can hear
jazz or light rock music on Friday and Saturday nights. On the

other is Catahoula's, serving California cuisine spiced with a touch of Louisiana. The chef is Jan Birnbaum, formerly of San Francisco's famed Campton Place. Rock shrimp cakes with yellow pepper coulis, oven-roasted squid salad with honey caramelized endive, and grilled salmon with white beans and maple cap mushrooms, are just a few of the dishes Birnbaum's open kitchen turns out.

> In back of the hotel is a terrace and a swimming pool bordered with fan palms, daisies, aloe in terra cotta pots, and a row of elk fountains. Poolside dining is provided by the hotel's acclaimed restaurant so in addition to traditional burgers and sandwiches, you can get inventive entrées that are a cut above standard poolside fare.

The guest rooms are in two parallel wings that extend back toward the pool area. In a typical corner room in back you'll have a glimpse of palm trees and the pool and terrace from one casement window, and a hotel wall view from the other. All rooms are air conditioned and have phones and TV. Patterns painted on guest room walls complement the colors and designs of other furnishings in the room which include matching antique bed and armoire sets.

Balcony suites, which are at the front of the building overlooking Calistoga's main street, can be subject to street noise — although the town does tend to be pretty quiet after dark. The Presidential Suite has a clawfoot tub in its bath, and a separate bedroom. In the living room there's a velvet sofa, and a beautiful coffee table inlaid with mother-of-pearl. The Jacob Schram Suite, named for the founder of Schramsberg winery, is a handsome suite with an ornate carved bed and matching armoire. Flamboyant Sam Brannan, the San Franciscan who founded Calistoga, would likely be pleased with his namesake suite, which is richly furnished in Victorian style.

Most in keeping with the hotel's theme is the Carole Lombard Suite. The actress never stayed at the Mount View, but she would have been comfortable in the large and airy rooms, with their French deco furniture. Framed photographs of the Lombard era hang on pink walls. The bed has a stunning mirror headboard of smoked, beveled glass. Matching end tables hold French porcelain lamps. The tile bath has a shower only, no tub.

Across the driveway in back of the hotel are three deluxe cottages. Clematis vines and private patios shield hot tubs outside each cottage, and inside, high ceilings and skylights only add to the cheerful decor. Comforters have cut-out patterns reminiscent of Matisse's playful designs, and sun motifs are stenciled on the walls in gold. Cottages have wet bars, televisions, clock radios, and refrigerators stocked with a split of champagne. Their blue and white checkerboard tiled baths have hair dryers, brass fixtures, and botanical toiletries from the hotel's spa. The spa offers services such as mud baths, facials, massages, and body wraps to all guests.

Scott Courtyard

1443 Second Street
Calistoga, CA 94515
707-942-0948
800-942-1515
Fax: 707-942-5102

A secluded inn of suites in a historic town

Innkeepers: Joe and Lauren Scott.
Accommodations: 6 suites (all with private bath). **Rates:** $125–$135 single or double, $20–$25 for rollaway. **Included:** Full breakfast. **Added:** 12% tax. **Payment:** MasterCard, Visa. **Minimum stay:** 2 nights on weekends. **Children:** Welcome in bungalows. **Pets:** Not allowed. **Smoking:** Not allowed.

Courtyard is an apt name for this complex of four pale yellow buildings; they surround a latticed courtyard and garden that gives guests a sense of privacy and seclusion, though the inn is within walking distance of most of Calistoga's attractions — restaurants, shops, spas, the glider port, and the Sharpsteen Museum.

The Scotts, who came from San Francisco and opened their inn in 1990, have created a relaxing haven with an aviary, garden, pool, three suites in the main house, and three separate bungalows with kitchens suitable for light cooking.

Each of the 1930s-era bungalows has its own entrance and a

theme such as Tropical, Philadelphia, and Hollywood. Two have fireplaces. Furnishings are eclectic with vintage chenille bedspreads and tropical-style art deco antiques the Scotts selected from curio and antiques shops in the bay area. Burgundy Suite is the smallest, but still quite comfortable, with a separate sitting room, and an iron and brass bed in the bedroom. Philadelphia Suite has light terra cotta walls and a sleigh day bed in the living room bursting with pillows. Rose Suite, on the ground floor of the main house, is like a residential apartment, with a private entrance, rattan furniture, and peach walls. If you take the Palisades Suite upstairs, you have exclusive use of the upper floor. All the rooms have queen-size beds and air conditioning.

> **At Scott Courtyard you can be as sociable or secluded as you wish. There's plenty to do, with Calistoga's pleasures nearby and the Scotts' art studio seminars; or you can relax in the sauna or in your spacious room.**

In the social room, the innkeepers serve evening refreshments, and invite guests to enjoy their books and CD player or play chess with an elaborate chess set. This high-ceilinged, airy room has a gorgeous Oriental rug on the floor before a brick fireplace, and French doors that open to the courtyard and swimming pool.

Eggs pesto, dijon dill quiche, freshly baked banana bread, lemon poppyseed French toast, and chicken apple sausage are some of the items that might appear in the morning breakfast buffet. The menu changes everyday, and Lauren tries to concentrate on healthy ingredients. It is served at umbrella tables by the pool or in a dining area with bistro-style tables for two.

Silver Rose Inn

351 Rosedale Road
Calistoga, CA 94515
707-942-9581
800-995-9381
Fax: 707-942-0841

*A top-quality
romantic country
inn near the
vineyards*

Innkeepers: Sally, J. Paul, and Derrick Dumont. **Accommodations:** 9 rooms (all with private bath). **Rates:** $125–$145 single or double; suites $190 weekdays, $210 weekends. **Included:** Breakfast and afternoon refreshments. **Added:** 12% tax. **Minimum stay:** 2 nights on weekends. **Payment:** Major credit cards. **Children:** Not appropriate. **Pets:** Not allowed. **Smoking:** Not allowed.

If you want more from the Napa Valley than winery tours, the Silver Rose offers appealing options. Once you're settled in this outstanding bed-and-breakfast inn, you may be reluctant to leave for anything but dinner. It's tempting to sit by the pool all day, or relax on your private balcony and watch the lambs at play and the grapes grow.

The big redwood home on a hill was built as a B&B, with the owners' quarters separate from the side used by guests. The Dumonts' favorite flower, the rose, pervades the inn, from the etched glass rose on the front oak door to the private Silver Rose wine label and the masses of roses in the lovely garden.

Guests enjoy complimentary wine and cheese in the large living room, which has a stone fireplace, dark beams, and tile flooring. Breakfast — a rose-garnished fruit plate and homemade breads and muffins — is served here or can be taken to your room or out on the terrace.

Each guest room has a theme. Turn of the Century is romantic, in old rose and lace, with a half-canopy bed topped with a floral swag, antique dolls atop a mirrored armoire, and a clawfoot tub. Peach Delight, which gets morning sun, has a four-poster bed and calico wallpaper. Cat-lovers will appreciate the collection of stuffed cats in this room.

> If you decide to venture beyond this lovely enclave, the Dumonts can provide suggestions on places to go. They will make restaurant or wine tour reservations for you, or arrange for a hot air balloon trip over nearby vineyards.

Country Blue has a country motif, and Bears in Burgundy features approximately thirty teddy bears. There are bears in a hot air balloon basket, bears of brass, stuffed bears, a Beefeater bear, a "Bogie" bear, and bears in formal dress. The Oriental Suite is the largest and has shoji screens, hardwood floors, Oriental rugs, rattan furniture, and Japanese lacquered wood. The good size bath has two sinks, a Jacuzzi tub, and a bidet.

Western, fittingly furnished with cowboy wrought-iron lamps, horseshoes, a saddle, and southwestern prints, has high ceilings, a gas fireplace, and a patio overlooking the pool. Safari is Sally's personal favorite. Cuddly stuffed animals are perched above the closet, African masks hang above the fireplace, and a papier-mâché zebra and giraffe stand on the mantel. Leopard print wallpaper, a zebra-striped comforter on the half-canopy bed, and rattan furnishings complete the exotic look. The Dumonts plan to add on eleven additional individually decorated suites in a separate building with its own swimming pool.

At Silver Rose, the hospitality is generous, and personal thought and care went into every aspect of the inn's design. Soft music makes the perfect accompaniment to a soothing moonlit soak in the inn's mineral water fed hot tub and adjoining swimming pool. Throughout the lovely grounds, there are plenty of nooks and corners that make ideal spots to relax in a chaise and admire the surrounding vineyards and riot of color in the flowerbeds.

For a relatively small inn, the Silver Rose offers many ser-

vices one would only expect to find at a much larger resort —
such as the inn's "Heavenly Spa" where angels adorn walls
and attractive shoji screens separate the treatment rooms
from one another. Spa treatments include massage, facials,
body wraps, and hydrotherapy. The inn also provides fax,
laundry, and wine shipping services.

The Dumonts originally settled in Calistoga with the idea
of becoming vintners, and they hope to have producing vineyards on the 20 acres that surround the inn within five years.
If their professionalism in running the Silver Rose is any indication, their wine will most likely be a terrific success as
well.

GEYSERVILLE

Campbell Ranch Inn

1475 Canyon Road
Geyserville, CA 95441
707-857-3476
800-959-3878
Fax: 707-857-3239

A casual country home in the wine country

Innkeepers: Mary Jane and Jerry
Campbell. **Accommodations:** 5 rooms (all with private bath).
Rates: $90–$155 single, $100–$165 double, $25 additional per-
son. **Included:** Full breakfast and evening dessert. **Added:** 9%
tax. **Minimum stay:** 2 nights on weekends. **Payment:** Major
credit cards. **Children:** Welcome in cottage by prior arrangement, $25 additional if third person. **Pets:** Not allowed.
Smoking: Not allowed indoors.

This ranch-style home in the Alexander Valley wine country,
seventy-five miles north of San Francisco, provides a quiet,
relaxing base for exploring Sonoma County. If you're not interested in wine tasting, the Campbells have provided other
options. On their 35-acre ranch there are walking trails, a tennis court, a 40-foot swimming pool, a hot tub spa, bicycles
and a horseshoe pit. Lake Sonoma, where you may boat and
fish, is four miles away, and you're just three miles from the
Russian River.

Indoor activities include table tennis, checkers, chess, and reading by the two-sided brick fireplace in the family room or living room. There's always a puzzle in progress. Guests have the run of the house. You're welcome to use the refrigerator, watch Jerry work on his model train sets, turn on the stereo, watch television, turn on the VCR, or iron your clothes in the laundry room.

> **Breakfast is served on the terrace or at the family dining table next to the open kitchen counter. In this friendly, homey atmosphere, the hosts make it a point to spend time with their guests.**

Three spacious, air-conditioned rooms are upstairs in the split-level home, all with king-size beds. One has a Baldwin piano. Balconies off the rooms face the hills and Pedroncelli and Gallo vineyards, green-leaved in summer and flaming red in fall. The one downstairs guest room offers the most privacy, though less of a view. The paneled room has a large closet, a writing table, a tiny TV, and shelves full of books and magazines. There are no antiques here; the traditional furnishings and decor are reminders that you've joined a family in their home.

The fifth lodging is a well-furnished, two-room cottage a few steps from the main house. It holds four people and has a refrigerator, fireplace, and a redwood deck overlooking the vineyards. The cottage is rented as a single unit to a family.

The Campbells provide brochures, maps, and menus to help you find your way around. Good-humored Mary Jane is an excellent cook who knows how to make guests feel at home. Even if it's a second dessert, don't miss the delicious pie she serves with coffee or tea at bedtime. Your breakfast choices, which you select the night before, include fruits and juices, cereal, omelettes, and an egg puff filled with sautéed mushrooms or chiles. Breads may be bran or blueberry muffins or raspberry cream cheese coffeecake, among others.

Hope-Merrill House

P.O. Box 42
21253 Geyserville Avenue
Geyserville, CA 95441
707-857-3356
800-825-4233
Fax: 707-857-4673

*A superbly
restored example
of Eastlake Stick
architecture*

Innkeeper: Rosalie Hope. **Accommodations:** 8 rooms (all with private bath). **Rates:** $95–$140 single or double, $20 additional person. **Included:** Full breakfast. **Added:** 8.5% tax. **Minimum stay:** April–November, 2 nights on weekends, 3 nights on holiday weekends. **Payment:** MasterCard, Visa. **Children:** Additional $20 if third person in room. **Pets:** Not allowed. **Smoking:** Not allowed indoors.

More than one hundred years ago, J.P. and Martha Merrill settled in Geyserville, a small town seventy-four miles north of San Francisco. The grand redwood home they built, a striking example of Eastlake Stick architecture, is now an inn.

The Hope-Merrill House opened to guests in 1981. Since then, hundreds of visitors have come to see Rosalie Hopes' stunning restoration efforts and to enjoy her brand of informal hospitality.

The inn is furnished with treasures collected by Rosalie. Most outstanding are the wallpapers, silkscreened by the designer Bruce Bradbury as replicas of the bold Victorian papers used a hundred years ago. Intricate and fanciful, they cover the walls with exotic designs.

The guest rooms are individually decorated. The Victorian Room has an antique double bed, as well as a chaise longue in the bay alcove window and a clawfoot tub. The Peacock

Room features a fireplace and a whirlpool tub for two, set in old marble. Briar Rose, Carpenter Gothic, and Bachelor Button all take their names from their motifs.

Bradbury and Vineyard View both have fireplaces and double showers. Bradbury displays an amazing array of wallpapers — nine separate designs, swirling around the room in brilliant color.

> Geyserville lies in the fertile Alexander Valley, where the vineyards produce some of California's finest wines. Several wineries along the Russian River Wine Trail are open for tours and tastings. From the inn you have a view of Geyser Peak and the steam clouds rising from a geothermal field.

Vineyard View, in colors of plum and wine, has long narrow windows overlooking the vineyard and grape arbor. Sterling Suite is the largest room and has a fireplace, a sitting area, and a queen-size bed.

Downstairs in the front parlor is a collection of Victoriana — baskets, eggs, ceramics, plates, tureens. The sunroom, by contrast, is casual and light, with wide windows and tables strewn with magazines. Here guests look over restaurant menus and discuss their sightseeing plans.

Continuing the Victorian theme, the backyard is fenced with a stone wall and wrought iron fence. There are raised flower beds, a kiwi arbor, rhododendrons, and persimmon and fig trees on the grounds, as well as a deck and swimming pool.

Rosalie serves a country breakfast of juice, fruit, homemade breads and pastries, and egg dishes. Later in the day, if you want soft drinks or local wine, they're available for purchase.

Rosalie also offers lodging in the Hope-Bosworth House, a historic landmark across the street. Furnished in a sophisticated country style, it is quite different from its impressive Victorian sister, with a cozy atmosphere. The Hope-Bosworth has four rooms and is slightly less expensive. It stands behind tall palm trees and a picket fence covered with old roses. Concord grapes grow over the arbor in the back yard; from them, Rosalie makes and sells spicy grape jelly.

GLEN ELLEN

Beltane Ranch

P.O. Box 395
11775 Highway 12
Glen Ellen, CA 95442
707-996-6501

*A country inn
overlooking
vineyards*

Innkeeper: Rosemary Wood. **Accommodations:** 4 rooms (all with private bath). **Rates:** $110–$160 single or double, $15 additional person. **Included:** Full breakfast. **Payment:** No credit cards. **Children:** Welcome by arrangement. **Pets:** Not allowed. **Smoking:** Not allowed indoors.

This century-old, sunny yellow ranch house with white gingerbread trim and wraparound veranda and balcony stands on a hill above Highway 12 in the Sonoma Valley wine country north of San Francisco. Rosemary Wood restored the old place in the 1970s and opened it as a bed-and-breakfast for wine country travelers in 1981. In this peaceful country setting she has created a quiet retreat, complete with a tennis court under the oak trees. Behind a low white picket fence are the two-story house where fragrant jasmine vines grow on porch railings and well-tended gardens bursting with California poppies, iris, and roses. Ever-bearing raspberry bushes supply breakfast fruit.

Indoors, there's a dining area by the front door, where breakfast is served in cool weather. On sunny days breakfast is brought to your own table on the balcony or, if you're traveling with a group, to a table under the trees. On Sundays a chef who used to have his own local restaurant, prepares creative breakfasts for inn guests. Pancakes and waffles are topped with homemade raspberry syrup, and frittatas and omelettes use fresh ingredients such as leeks and fennel from Rosemary's garden.

Built in the 1890s as a bunkhouse when the place was a working ranch, the ranch house was purchased in the 1930s by the present owner's aunt and uncle. They raised turkeys, sheep and cattle on acreage where Rosemary now grows chardonnay and cabernet grapes for local wineries and olives for her own label olive oil.

The one room guest room on the ground floor is the smallest, but is pleasant with a cozy wicker rocking chair, hooked rug, and ceiling fan. The upstairs rooms, off the long balcony, are larger and airier. One suite, which extends the width of the house, has a fireplace and daybed in the sitting area and, in the bedroom, a double bed of black iron and gracefully curved brass. Fresh flowers are on the dresser. Books by the noted Glen Ellen author M.F.K. Fisher mingle with travel guidebooks on the table. Works by Jack London, another author who lived in Glen Ellen, are in the opposite corner suite. This suite has a daybed and a settee.

Out on the balcony a hammock swings in the gentle breeze, inviting you to relax while the ranch's cat snoozes on the railing beside you. Or head for the swing on the veranda below, a restful perch for viewing the garden and valley, vineyards, fields, and the shadowed hills against the horizon.

Gaige House Inn

13540 Arnold Drive
Glen Ellen, CA 95442
707-935-0237
800-935-0237
Fax: 707-935-6411

> *A bed-and-breakfast
> in a historic home*

Innkeeper: Ardath Rouas. **Accommodations:** 9 rooms (all with private bath). **Rates:** $125–$245 single or double. **Included:** Full breakfast. **Added:** 9% tax. **Minimum stay:** 2 nights on weekends. **Payment:** Major credit cards. **Children:** Over age 12 welcome. **Pets:** Not allowed. **Smoking:** Not allowed.

Glen Ellen is a tree-shaded village in the Sonoma Valley north of San Francisco. The Gaige House is one of its historic homes, set on 1.2 acres near Calabezas Creek and surrounded by the wooded hills of the California Coast Range. The Italianate Queen Anne home on Glen Ellen's main street was built in about 1890 for A. E. Gaige, the town's butcher. As the years passed, the large Victorian was used as a boarding house and school and finally, after falling into disrepair, was restored as a small inn in 1980.

Jasmine climbs the porch columns, its sweet scent wafting in the front door as you enter. Two parlors offer seating on hot summer days, where you can enjoy the owner's collection of art from around the world including a striking Balinese armoire. The owner, one of the originating partners of the acclaimed Auberge du Soliel, is highly qualified to create a lodging offering guests both comfort and style, and she has succeeded admirably.

Beyond the parlors is the kitchen, with a big open space where guests eat breakfast at several tables. When the weather permits, breakfast is served outside either on a deck overlooking the lawn and 40-foot heated swimming pool edged with brick, or another deck built over Calabezas Creek. The meal is prepared by a professional chef. While the menu changes daily, Gaige House sunrise scrambled eggs served with smoked salmon and balsamic tomato slices and asparagus, or rum brioche French toast with apples and walnuts and served with chicken apple sausage, are examples of the tempting fare.

The guest rooms are furnished with an eclectic accumulation of antiques and art, reflecting the owner's background in design. They all have air conditioning, and two have fireplaces. One first floor room is spacious with a fireplace and features a clawfoot tub, and two queen-size beds topped with fluffy comforters and pig stuffed animals — the owner's favorite animal that you'll see in toy or picture form throughout the house.

Gaige House is a comfortable place to relax after touring the Valley of the Moon. A major attraction is Jack London State Historic Park, about a mile from the inn. The author's former home is now a Jack London museum. Also in the park are the ruins of London's fabulous Wolf House and walking and horse trails.

On the second floor the Gaige Suite is popular for its immense blue tile bath with a whirlpool tub, and a private wraparound balcony that overlooks the pool and backyard lawn. The suite is equally well done including a king-size canopy bed with carved posters, and a daybed covered in creamy canvas and plump pillows. Also on the second floor are two rooms with seating by the bay windows and four-poster beds. In room Two an old-fashioned radio sits on the bedside table, and lace curtains hang in the windows. Room One has a red velveteen sofa in its bay window, and a walk-in closet. Up two stairs from the second floor is cozy room Four with a fireplace, floors of polished oak, and watercolors of Sonoma scenes painted by a local artist. Room Three has a handsome marble-topped dresser.

Three rooms on the lower level have private entrances from a backyard porch. Room Seven is popular in the summer because its location off the shaded vine covered porch is cool and dark, but pale blue and ivory tones lighten up the room's interior. Room Six is the least expensive because it has a shower only in its bath. Room Eight is the quietest room. Television is available in some rooms, and all have phones.

Glen Ellen is a few miles from Sonoma, where you may see several restored buildings from California's Spanish and Mexican history. The Sonoma area has wineries that are open for touring and tastings, and there are several excellent restaurants.

GUERNEVILLE

Applewood

13555 Highway 116
Pocket Canyon
Guerneville, CA 95446
707-869-9093

A luxurious mansion near the Russian River

Owner: Jim Caron. **Accommodations:** 16 rooms (all with private bath). **Rates:** $125–$250 single or double. **Included:** Full breakfast. **Added:** 9% tax. **Minimum stay:** 2 nights on weekends, 3 nights on some holidays. **Payment:** Major credit cards. **Children:** Not appropriate. **Pets:** Not allowed. **Smoking:** Not allowed.

The Russian River between Highway 101 and the coast has long been a scenic playground for vacationers.
 One of the grand homes built during the 1920s was the Belden Mansion, intended to be a "centerpiece of elegant living." Today it's a bed-and-breakfast of great quality and charm. Jim Caron brought his experience in business and interior decorating to the venture when he purchased the home in 1985. His goal was to achieve the ideal country inn, which he has done with style and warm hospitality.
 When you enter the stucco, tile-roofed B&B, which sits on a knoll outside Guerneville, you're in a large common room with a stone fireplace, dark woodwork, and comfortable couches. Around the corner is the solarium which is used for dining. Curved walls, lots of glass and views of the trees, leaf patterns against green walls, and tall palms in terra cotta pots give this room an outdoor atmosphere. The stone fireplace makes it cozy. Coffee and tea and the newspaper are provided here in the morning.
 All the guest rooms, which are on various levels, have phones, television, fresh flowers, down comforters, and a harmonious blend of family heirlooms, antique botanical prints, books, and art. One room has a covered porch, another a walled patio where roses and camellias grow. One room on the ground level, has a secretary desk against apple green walls and a sitting area overlooking the trees.
 Applewood's largest rooms are six luxurious suites which

were added to the inn in 1995. Occupying three floors in the Mediterranean-style "piccola casa," the airy suites have fireplaces, double showers, individually controlled heat and air conditioning, and have courtyard or orchard views. Two have Jacuzzi tubs, and the honeymoon suite has its own rooftop sundeck.

> In the 1920s, San Franciscans would ferry across the bay and take the train north to Guerneville to fish, swim, ride horses through the redwoods, and dance to swing bands.

Dinners are available five nights a week (not on Tuesday and Wednesday); Jim has gained renown for his cooking as well as his innkeeping. A typical meal might include hot onion rolls, minestrone, a salad of thinly sliced roast beef and capers, lamb Florentine or pasta with bacon, tomato, and basil, and apple tart with crème frâiche. You can purchase wine or bring your own (a corkage fee is charged).

When you return to your room you'll find chocolates, the bedclothes turned down, and your clothing neatly folded or hung in the closet. In the morning, another outstanding meal is served in the dining room or solarium.

The inn has a swimming pool behind a wrought-iron gate; beyond is a small vineyard, the garden, and the wooded hills. You can tour nearby wineries, buy the region's famous apples, fish for steelhead, taste fresh jam at Koslowski's, or take a Japanese enzyme bath at Osmosis Company. In Armstrong Park, walk among majestic giants — some of the redwood trees are more than 300 feet high and one thousand years old.

Creekside Inn & Resort

P.O. Box 2185
16180 Neeley Road
Guerneville, CA 95446
707-869-3623
800-776-6586
Fax: 707-869-1417

*A casual resort
that's easy on
the budget*

Innkeepers: Lynn and Mark Crescione. **Accommodations:** 6
rooms (2 with private bath) and 9 cottages. **Rates:** $60–$150
single or double per night, $300–$600 per week. **Included:** Expanded Continental breakfast in B&B rooms. **Added:** 9% tax.
Minimum stay: 1 week in cottages in July and August. **Payment:** Major credit cards. **Children:** Welcome. **Pets:** Not allowed. **Smoking:** Not allowed in B&B rooms.

A stroll away from Guerneville, over the bridge that crosses
the Russian River, is the Creekside, an unpretentious resort
on three acres. It's bordered by redwood and bay trees and dotted with colorful flower beds.

The homey inn, a lively, busy spot, has rooms furnished
with simple charm in individual themes. The Victorian
Room is a spacious suite with a fireplace, a four-poster
canopy bed and a private
balcony, while the Iron
Room, the least expensive, has a bent-iron bedframe and whimsical decorations. The Oak and
Walnut rooms are furnished in those woods,
while the Wicker Room
contains white wicker
and has a Victorian motif.

**In the Guerneville area, you
can taste local wines, shop
at roadside stands, walk in
deep redwood forests, rent
canoes and bicycles, and
browse through shops and
galleries.**

There's a cheerful living room with a fireplace, a deco-style
dining room where a breakfast of fruit, cereals, and cheese is
set out, and a lounge next to a patio with umbrella tables.
Books, TV, and a VCR are available.

The cottages have a rustic appearance. Each has a kitchen,
and several have a fireplace or private deck. The largest is the
Tree House, which accommodates ten. It has a large living
room with a fireplace and a sleeping loft under skylights.

Packages and special rates are available. At one end of the property there are RV spaces.

Creekside has billiards, a swimming pool, barbecue facilities, and pinball and video games. Guests must use public access to reach the river.

The resort's policy of "welcoming well-behaved guests of any age or attitude" draws a mixed clientele and many repeat guests who appreciate the casual atmosphere, reasonable rates, and proximity to the attractions of the Russian River.

HEALDSBURG

Belle de Jour Inn

16276 Healdsburg Avenue
Healdsburg, CA 95448
707-431-9777
Fax: 707-431-7412

A romantic bed-and-breakfast near wineries

Innkeepers: Tom and Brenda Hearn. **Accommodations:** 4 cottages. **Rates:** $125–$185 single or double. **Included:** Full breakfast. **Added:** 10% tax. **Minimum stay:** 2 nights on weekends, 3 nights some holidays. **Payment:** MasterCard, Visa. **Children:** Not appropriate. **Pets:** Not allowed. **Smoking:** Not allowed.

At Belle de Jour, an Italianate farmhouse built around 1873 stands on a hill surrounded by six acres of gardens and fields. This is the owners' residence; a few yards up the slope are the white, rough-hewn guest cottages.

All the rooms have woodstoves or fireplaces, with wood supplied and a fire laid. They're decorated in a light French country theme and have refrigerators, air conditioning, hair dryers, and robes.

Atelier, once used as a studio, has rattan furnishings and a bed with a muslin canopy. Posters of France hang on the walls. There's a streamlined pedestal sink and a whirlpool tub in the white tile bath. More sophisticated is the Terrace Room, with a fireplace, a king-size brass bed, colors of mauve, deep green, and rose, and a terrace with views of an expansive lawn and the Alexander Valley beyond. The rosy-hued bath has a shower and a whirlpool tub for two.

The Caretaker's Suite, which was the caretaker's quarters for many years (the other cottages were built in the 1970s), is a large, barnlike room in buff, white, and tan. It boasts a bed with a lacy canopy and crisp white linens and a sitting area with a Franklin fireplace. This suite also has an oversize whirlpool tub. Double doors lead to a trellised deck that overlooks rolling hills and vineyards.

A favorite among repeat guests for its lovely view is Morning Hill.

> The little town of Healdsburg lies in the Alexander Valley wine country 70 miles north of San Francisco. On its outskirts, directly across the road from Simi Winery, is this romantic country getaway.

Green pine walls, dark green shutters, and throw rugs on wood floors add rustic atmosphere to the comfortable room. Floral watercolors above the bed echo the gardens outside.

The breakfast menu changes daily. "Guests are at my mercy," Brenda says with a laugh. She may prepare mushroom-chive omelettes, eggs Benedict, or Parmesan eggs and bacon to accompany her sour cream cinnamon swirl bread or blueberry muffins, orange juice, fresh fruit, and coffee. Breakfast is served in the farmhouse or on the deck.

Brenda and Tom came to Healdsburg and Belle de Jour in 1986 from Los Angeles. "We had the house, the exotic cars, the toys," says Brenda. "Then one day we were in freeway traffic, talking to each other on our car phones, and decided we didn't want to live that way anymore." Now they happily tend vegetable and herb gardens, hang linens to dry in the sun, and welcome travelers looking for a secluded wine country retreat.

The George Alexander House

423 Matheson Street
Healdsbury, CA 95448
707-433-1358

> *A well-run
> bed and breakfast
> in a wine country
> town*

Innkeepers: Christian and Phyllis Baldenholder. **Accommodations:** 4 rooms (all with private baths). **Rates:** $80–$130. **Included:** Full breakfast. **Added:** Tax. **Payment:** MasterCard or Visa. **Children:** Welcome. **Pets:** Not allowed. **Smoking:** Not allowed.

The George Alexander House is a solid, turn-of-the-century home with quatrefoil windows, while shaker blue and maroon trim add cheer to its deep taupe exterior. Birch trees and lively gardens provide even more color and appeal to this handsome inn. The home was built in 1905 by George Alexander, the son of Cyrus Alexander who founded the Alexander Valley, and was turned into a bed and breakfast by San Franciscans Phylllis and Christian Baldenhofer in 1991.

Two of the inn's guest rooms are named for the Alexanders. The Mr. and Mrs. George Alexander room has a bay window, fireplace, and antique queen-size bed. The Lucille Alexander room is named for the Alexanders' daughter. It is furnished in greens and blacks, with a four-poster spool bed, wicker chairs, and a clawfoot tub in the bath. The Butler's Room has hardwood floors, and a lovely antique bed topped by a cotton spread. The Back Porch is the most expensive room. It has a private entrance, a wood-burning stove, a king-size bed, and a two person Jacuzzi. All rooms have private baths, line-dried sheets, and down comforters. All are located on the ground floor.

Guests gather in the two front parlors. The first is illuminated by stained glass windows original to the home, and has a sunny corner window seat, and Victorian furnishings. The second parlor is more casual with a wicker sofa, fireplace, and stereo system. African artifacts stand on display on the mantel, and both parlors have exceptional Oriental rugs.

> Like other towns in the wine country, Healdsburg has no shortage of tempting eateries. The Kendall-Jackson tasting room is also here. Only four blocks from Healdsburg's plaza, the George Alexander House is convenient to all.

Breakfast is served in the formal dining room. The innkeepers focus on light California cuisine, but the breakfast is always filling, with items such as lemon ricotta pancakes, poached pears, scones, and shortbreads. Since the innkeepers were once in the gourmet coffee business, good coffee is always available.

Madrona Manor

1001 Westside Road
Healdsburg, CA 95448
707-433-4231
800-258-4003
Fax: 707-433-0703

> *A historic mansion on a wine country estate*

Innkeepers: Carol and John Muir.
Accommodations: 21 rooms. **Rates:** $140–$195 single or double, suites $190–$240, $30 additional person. **Included:** Full breakfast. **Added:** 9% tax. **Payment:**

Major credit cards. **Children:** Welcome. **Pets:** Allowed by prior arrangement. **Smoking:** Allowed in designated areas.

West of the Napa Valley lies the Sonoma Valley, a less touristed wine region with a rural ambience and calm that many visitors prefer. At the north end of the valley, near the village of Healdsburg, an elaborate three-story, seventeen-room mansion was built in 1880 by John Paxton, a wealthy businessman, state legislator, and promoter of Sonoma County's wine industry. The house remained in the Paxton family until 1913. Purchased and restored by the Muirs in the 1980s, the inn and restaurant have been receiving acclaim since they opened.

The inn is against a hillside on eight landscaped acres, under eucalyptus, oaks, and the tall madrones that give the place its name. A large garden of vegetables, herbs, roses and dozens of other flowers is overseen by Carol, who arranges the bouquets throughout the homelike hotel. If you arrive at dinnertime you may see a member of the kitchen staff picking fresh herbs from the garden for use in that evening's meal.

Staying at Madrona Manor is like visiting a friend with a country estate — a friend from another century. Victorian antiques fill the spacious rooms. The music room, with a square rosewood grand piano, an ongoing jigsaw puzzle, and books and scrapbooks, is a genteel gathering place to sip wine before dinner.

Next to it is the restaurant, noted for its California cuisine with a Mediterranean flair. The Muirs' son, Todd, is the chef, a graduate of the California Culinary Academy. He prepares such delicacies as veal ravioli with Gorgonzola cream, and rack of lamb stuffed with chicken basil farce. For dessert you can treat yourself to chocolate-cherry mousse cake or orange-almond crêpes with caramel ice cream. The menu changes seasonally to reflect Sonoma County's fresh products.

Nine guest rooms are in the main house. Their fireplaces, antiques, and decor create the atmosphere of an earlier day, while private baths and individual climate control provide modern comforts. The furnishings are impressive: intricately carved four-poster beds, dressing tables with beveled glass mirrors, paintings, and tall armoires.

The most popular is Paxton's Room, with a tile fireplace, a curtained alcove with bay windows, and a fine view of Mount St. Helena and Fitch Mountain from the balcony. This is one of two rooms with French doors opening to private balconies.

The third floor, formerly the servant's quarters, has ornate beds and Victorian wallpapers. The other rooms are in separate cottages: nine in the Carriage House, two in Meadow Wood, and one Garden Cottage. These are less formal and more "countrified" than those in the main house. The Carriage House was built for the Paxton family's carriages; it now houses visitors in luxury with a Far Eastern touch. The front door and filigreed rosewood interior trim were brought from Nepal. One room in the Carriage House is furnished with reproduction antiques, while the rest are contemporary.

> A morning newspaper and coffee are set out before breakfast. Then it's fresh orange juice, toast, granola, and an assortment of meat, cheese, and fruit. Finish it all off with a spoonful of the inn's prize-winning kiwi or dwarf mandarin orange marmalade on homemade toast.

Farther up the hill, near the terraced garden and under oak trees, is the Garden Cottage. It has its own deck and yard, a marble fireplace, and a tub for two. All guests are welcome to use the swimming pool on the hill behind the manor.

There are phones in all the rooms, but no television at Madrona Manor.

KENWOOD

The Kenwood Inn

10400 Sonoma Highway
Kenwood, CA 95452
707-833-1293

> *A luxurious inn offering spa services*

Proprietor: Terry Grimm. **Accommodations:** 12 suites (all with private bath). **Rates:** $225–$315. **Included:** Gourmet breakfast. **Added:** Tax. **Payment:** Major credit cards. **Children:** Not appropriate. **Pets:** Not allowed. **Smoking:** Not allowed.

This charming inn and spa is located on Highway 12 just north of Glen Ellen. A wall shields the inn compound from the busy road, and once inside the enclosure you'll quickly recognize a lodging of comfort and taste. For an inn of its size, the Kenwood offers a surprising number of amenities.

> **Only fifteen minutes from Sonoma, the Kenwood Inn makes a good base for exploring wine country wineries. The Kunde Estate vineyard is just across the street from the inn.**

The lobby is adjacent to the spa treatment rooms where guests can indulge themselves in seaweed masks and herbal wraps. From the reception area, a shady ramada leads to the heart of the complex where gardens, fountains, a swimming pool and hot tub are surrounded by the four remaining buildings that comprise the inn. On one side there are two stucco duplexes housing two guest rooms each, and across the garden there's a similarly constructed fourplex. Although they were built in 1995, care went into their design so as to give them an ageless European look.

From the duplexes, flower-lined stone walkways lead to the main house, which was built in the 1930s. Covered in ivy, it too looks as though it could be centuries old. Here there's a wonderful country farmhouse kitchen with colorful pottery used for decoration, slate floors, and baskets, herbs, and chiles hanging from the ceiling. In the adjoining dining room, guests dine on three-course breakfasts such as crostini with prosciutto, poached eggs in a basil cream sauce, croissants, and a fruit parfait at tables for two. There's also a central living room which serves as a gathering spot if you're feeling social, or if you want to peruse menus from the area's many fine restaurants.

There are four guest suites in the main house. Suite Seven, which is smaller than most, is furnished in golds and greens, and has a grape motif bedspread and pillow shams. Suite Eight, with its ivy framed windows, dried leaf wreath, and slate hearth, has an autumnal feel. Another suite in the main house has a separate living room. Dark and masculine, it has rich velvet sofas and a model ship.

Plaster walls in the newer buildings have been stained to give the look of age. Outside the fourplex, a pyramid of wooden wine barrels stand as a reminder of the inn's locale, and a fountain trickles at the base of the stairs. Upstairs rooms have balconies. In Suite Three, fringed gold velvet chairs offer seating in front of the fireplace, while a gargoyle carved tapestry upholstered chair stands in a corner. The bed is covered with a fluffy striped duvet and matching pillows, and the bath has an antique washstand.

No matter which room you choose, it will be elegantly furnished with antiques, coordinating armoire and bed sets, a fireplace, and a queen-size bed topped by a feather bed and down comforter. Rooms also have stereos with CD players, and baths with marble-topped wooden washstands and brass fixtures. Just to make sure you feel welcome, fresh flowers and a bottle of wine are placed in your room before your arrival.

NAPA

Churchill Manor

485 Brown Street
Napa, CA 94559
707-253-7733
Fax: 707-253-8836

*A grand wine
country mansion*

Innkeepers: Joanna Guidotti and Brian Jensen. **Accommodations:** 10 rooms (all with private bath). **Rates:** $85–$155 single or double, $15 additional person. **Included:** Full breakfast. **Added:** 12% tax. **Minimum stay:** 2 nights on weekends. **Payment:** Major credit cards. **Children:** Over age 12 welcome, $15 if third person in room. **Pets:** Not allowed. **Smoking:** Not allowed indoors.

One of the grand old mansions of the wine country has been turned into a bed-and-breakfast that is a wonderful romantic retreat. The stately, three-story house, a National Historic Landmark, was built in 1889 and restored with loving care one hundred years later.

Joanna Guidotti's husband, Brian Jensen, is a builder who has recreated the original style of the mansion even while modernizing it. The original gas light fixtures have been rewired and hang in the front parlor. Leaded glass, Oriental carpets, intricately carved woodwork, and Victorian furnishings add period atmosphere to the large (10,000 square feet) B&B. "This is our hobby," Joanna says. Once a tax lawyer in San Francisco, she moved to Napa to restore and run the inn.

Thousands of daffodils and tulips bloom in spring. There are rose beds, boxwood hedges, and an herb garden. Guests enjoy playing croquet in the side garden, exploring the area on a tandem bicycle borrowed from the innkeepers, and relaxing on the wide veranda.

There are fireplaces in all four parlors and in three of the guest rooms. Each room is decorated individually, from cheery little Amy's Room on the third floor to Edward's Room, the original master bedroom, which has an elegant French king-size bed, an armoire with three mirrors, and an oversize clawfoot tub in the bath. Granny's Room has a treadle sewing machine. The most unusual (and maybe the most fun for lovers) is the Bordello Room, with its big brass bed, ten-foot carved armoire, Victorian nude painting, and red Jacuzzi tub for two. The phone in this room is the shape of bright red lips.

A breakfast of muffins, croissants, fruit, and hot dishes such as omelettes or French toast is served in the enclosed sunroom, overlooking the colorful garden.

Churchill Manor is in a historic residential district of Napa, close to restaurants and the valley's wineries.

La Residence Country Inn

4066 St. Helena Highway North
Napa, CA 94558
707-253-0337

*A country inn
with luxurious
amenities*

Innkeepers: David Jackson and
Craig Claussen. **Accommodations:**
20 rooms (18 with private bath).
Rates: $125–$225 single or double, $20 additional person. **Included:** Full breakfast. **Minimum stay:** 2 nights weekends.
Payment: MasterCard, Visa. **Children:** Welcome. **Pets:** Not allowed. **Smoking:** Not allowed indoors.

This sophisticated country inn is one of a growing number of small inns that combine the personal touch of a bed-and-breakfast with the luxuries of a larger hotel.

La Residence, north of the city of Napa, is set back from the rush of Highway 29. Its two buildings stand on two acres of fields, vineyards, and oak and acacia trees. One is the Mansion, an 1870 Gothic Revival home. The other is Cabernet Hall, built in 1987 in the style of a French barn. Between them are the parking lot and a heated swimming

Out the back door, pear trees shade a brick patio. Across the way, on the patio by Cabernet Hall, wine is served in the late afternoon under a 200-year-old oak tree.

pool surrounded by gazebos, trellises, brick patios, and pots of flowers.

There are nine rooms in the Mansion, all furnished with American antiques. On the main floor, left of the entrance, is a suite with a marble fireplace and a Victrola, ready to be wound up for playing old Decca records. Fruit garlands border the walls, and louvered shutters cover the windows. There's a white iron bed, an armoire, and a bath of white and green tile. Across the hall is a similar room, this one in plum and peach.

All the suites in Cabernet Hall have working fireplaces and access to a balcony or the ground-floor veranda. Comforters, wicker chairs, flowered wallpapers, and painted tiles are in most rooms. Pine antiques from France and England were imported for the inn.

The dining room by the patio is a cheery breakfast spot where David Jackson, who handles the inn's cooking, sees that guests receive their fill of fresh fruit, pastries, and an egg dish, as well as hot coffee or tea and the morning newspaper.

The Old World Inn

1301 Jefferson Street
Napa, CA 94559
707-257-0112
800-966-6624

A wine country bed-and-breakfast with distinctive style

Innkeeper: Diane Dumaine. **Accommodations:** 8 rooms (all with private bath). **Rates:** $115–$150 single or double. **Included:** Full breakfast, afternoon tea, wine and cheese, and evening dessert buffet. **Added:** 12% tax. **Payment:** Major credit cards. **Minimum stay:** 2 nights on weekends, April through November. **Children:** Not appropriate. **Pets:** Not allowed. **Smoking:** Not allowed.

The room rate for the Old World Inn includes much more than a breakfast of crêpes or frittatas, fruits, and freshly baked breads. Guests are treated to a lavish afternoon tea, a wine and cheese hour, and a late evening dessert buffet of homemade treats. This inn is a food-lover's delight.

To showcase the builder's skills, he combined several architectural styles — Shingle-style in the sweeping roof line, Craftsman in the use of rough cinder brick, Colonial Revival in the porch columns, and Queen Anne in the two-story corner tower.

The innkeeper pampers her guests in other ways, with fresh flowers, soft music, restaurant reservations, a bubbling outdoor hot tub in a fenced courtyard, and rooms furnished in fresh Scandinavian style. The curly redwood used in the living and dining rooms glows with the patina of finely crafted woodwork. The Swedish artist Carl Larsson inspired the decor, which is bright with color and unusual designs. Homilies and fanciful bows are painted on the walls above the moldings, and linens and fabrics are all in coordinated colors. Most of the antiques-furnished rooms have Victorian clawfoot tubs, and one has a private Jacuzzi.

The historic inn was built in 1906 by Napa's foremost builder, E. W. Doughty, as his own residence. You can see other examples of Doughty's work on a walking tour through Old Town Napa, where vintage buildings have been restored. Diane will direct you to nearby antiques shops, restaurants, and wineries.

Silverado Country Club & Resort

1600 Atlas Peak Road
Napa, CA 94558
707-257-0200
800-532-0500
Fax: 707-257-2867

A gracious golf resort in the wine country

General manager: Kirk Candland.
Accommodations: 290 condominium units. **Rates:** $135–$150 single or double, junior suites $190, 1 bedroom condo for 2 people $250, 2 bedroom condo for up to 4 people $360, and 3 bedroom condo for up to 6 people $460, presidential suite $1200. **Payment:** Major credit cards. **Children:** $15 for rollaway. **Pets:** Not allowed. **Smoking:** Nonsmoking rooms available.

In an idyllic grove of trees above Milliken Creek, Silverado began as a classic 14-room mansion. Built in the 1870s, it was the estate of John F. Miller, a Civil War general who moved to California and became influential in state politics. He and his wife wanted their house to reflect the Italian and French architecture they had admired on their travels abroad.

Now their home, with its Palladian windows, two-story columns, white railings, and flower-filled urns, is the main lodge of a 1,200-acre luxury resort. It's forty-five minutes north of San Francisco, just outside Napa in the Napa Valley wine country.

Beyond the small lobby is a lounge with a sunken bar of

polished granite. Windows overlook a sunroom and terrace. An 18-hole golf course, one of two on the property, lies across the creek from the terrace. The 250-foot-long stone wall bordering the terrace is a remarkable example of the masonry skills common when the house was built. Today, trimmed ivy grows over the low wall and roses bloom beside it. This is a choice spot for lingering over cocktails while you watch the golfers and listen to the birds warbling in the great oak trees that arch over the fairways.

> Immense old eucalyptus trees line the road to the entrance, perfuming the air with their pungent oil. Passing a circle of lawn with tall palm trees, you reach a curving driveway where a valet relieves you of your car and smiling bellmen help with your luggage. It's a busy place, as the resort is frequently used for meetings and conferences.

Silverado has twenty tennis courts, three of them with lights, as well as pro shops and instructors. There are eight swimming pools, one of them a lap pool. Three restaurants offer varying degrees of formality. The casual Bar & Grill, overlooking the North Course, serves breakfast and lunch. Royal Oak is a pseudo-rustic steak house with a mesquite grill, open beams, and copper pans on the walls.

California cuisine is presented in Vintner's Court, a pretty salon with white and pink linens, pink roses on a white grand piano, and candlelight on the tables. On Sundays, elaborate ice sculptures decorate brunch buffet tables. A seafood buffet is served on Fridays.

The guest rooms, most of them private condominiums furnished and decorated by their owners, are in clusters called Mansion Cottages, Silverado Cottages, and Oak Creek East. They range from standard rooms with no kitchens to three-bedroom units. Studio rooms combine sitting and sleeping areas and have kitchenettes. A typical one-bedroom lodging has contemporary rattan furnishings, mirrored sliding doors on a roomy closet, television, phone, and a corner fireplace. The kitchen is fully equipped and the bath has both a tub and shower. The two- and three-bedroom apartments are in Oak Creek East, the most secluded cluster. They border quiet cul-de-sacs and have private patios and balconies overlooking the fairways.

Special holiday packages are available at Silverado. Most include a round of golf and unlimited tennis, along with seasonal festivities.

RUTHERFORD

Auberge du Soleil

180 Rutherford Hill Road
Rutherford, CA 94573
707-963-1211
800-348-5406
Fax: 707-963-8764

> *A sophisticated country inn with a valley view*

General manager: George Goeggel.
Accommodations: 50 rooms. **Rates:** $175–$475 singe or double, suites $375–$800 depending on season. **Added:** Tax. **Minimum stay:** 2 nights on weekends. **Payment:** Major credit cards. **Children:** Not appropriate. **Pets:** Not allowed. **Smoking:** Allowed.

First the inn was a restaurant, set against a steep hillside above Napa Valley's grape-growing heartland. The venture of a renowned San Francisco restaurateur, Claude Rouas, Auberge du Soleil opened in 1981 to great acclaim. It wasn't long before its visitors, impressed with the stunning location and cuisine, yearned for lodging, as well. So, in the mid-1980s, some of the valley's most exclusive lodgings joined one of its most fashionable eateries. The views are spectacular from the inn's 33 acres of olive and oak groves, similar to inland country vistas of the French Riviera.

One- and two-bedroom suites combine the sophisticated and the rustic to create a luxurious country French decor. Each has a fireplace, television, and wet bar. The floors are polished terra cotta tile, the furniture of natural wood and leather. The mood is light, the colors pastel. Near the villas and below the restaurant terrace is a large swimming pool with lounge chairs. There are three tennis courts. Room service is available, and the restaurant is open for breakfast.

The Auberge du Soleil menu, showcasing locally grown ingredients, is labeled "wine country cuisine." Lunch may be taken inside or out, on the sun-dappled terrace at umbrella tables. Dinners include Peking duck with red cabbage salad, roast poussin filled with wild rice and Sonoma foie gras on roast corn coulis, and grilled bass on fennel and red pepper rouille. A pianist plays on weekends in the bar and lounge across the lobby from the restaurant. The round room has a southwestern flavor, with a single pole in the center reaching to a cone ceiling. A high circular shelf holds firewood for the adobe fireplace. Windows look out on a curving deck and over the treetops to the countryside.

> The restaurant, lounge, and terrace all face a panorama of valley and hills that sprawls to the horizon. Terraced against the hillside, reached by winding paths bordered with sweet-scented flowering shrubs, are the guest villas, named for French wine-growing regions.

The inn also has meeting and audiovisual facilities. The White Room, lined with mirrors to reflect the light and panoramic view, seats up to eighty. Next to it is the more intimate Club Room, seating up to twenty. A secluded conference room, decorated with light leather, wood, and oil paintings, is off the lower terrace.

Auberge du Soleil retains the chic cachet it has had since it opened. This is not the place to go for cozy warmth. A cool professionalism best characterizes most of the staff, and the well-dressed clientele is here to see and be seen as well as to dine and enjoy the beautiful setting.

Rancho Caymus Inn

P.O. Box 78
Rutherford, CA 94573
707-963-1777

A wine-country inn with eclectic style

Innkeeper: Otto Komes. **Accommodations:** 26 rooms and suites. **Rates:** $125–$295 single or double, $15 additional person; winter rates $15–$30 less. **Included:** Continental breakfast. **Added:** Tax. **Minimum stay:** 2 nights on weekends. **Payment:** Major credit cards. **Children:** Not appropriate. **Pets:** Not allowed. **Smoking:** Allowed.

This Spanish-style inn, its walls encircling a courtyard of flowers, vines, and trees, is a showplace for the artists and craftspeople who have created it. Mary Tilden Morton, a third-generation Californian and a professional sculptor, built Rancho Caymus in 1985 to provide lodging for visitors to the Napa Valley and to create a stunning setting for handcrafts she'd collected from California, Mexico, and South America.

It's easy to understand why Rancho Caymus is popular for wedding receptions. At night, when a guitarist plays and hundreds of lights cast wavery shadows from the shrubbery, this seems one of the most romantic places on Earth.

The inn stands on part of the original land grant given by the Mexican general Vallejo to George Yount more than a century ago. Rutherford, sixty miles north of San Francisco, is known for its wineries and Rutherford Square, a complex of cafés and Beaulieu Vineyard's tasting room. Within walking distance of the square are the white stucco buildings and red tile roofs of Rancho Caymus.

All the spacious suites are named for locally famous people and historic places. They contain furnishings that are both beautiful and unusual. Most have plaster beehive fireplaces, and all have wet bars, stocked refrigerators, telephones, television, and a complimentary bottle of wine. Four split-level master suites have whirlpool tubs and full kitchens. Hastings Suite, with two bedrooms, accommodates larger parties.

The dressers, chairs, and tables were carved in Guadalajara; the black walnut beds, colorful handwoven bedspreads, llama blankets, and rare leather paintings came from Ecuador. Wrought-iron door straps and railings, tile murals, stained glass windows, stoneware basins, and oaken countertops — all were made by noted regional artists and carpenters. The white oak and pine doors and beams came from an eighty-year-old barn in Ohio.

The General Vallejo Room is a suite with a daybed in the sitting area and a private balcony that views the pine trees of Beaulieu Winery next door. The Major Tilden Suite has a kitchen, a sitting area with a fireplace, a private balcony, and the skin of a grizzly bear on the wall. The bed is one of the few antiques in the inn. Beside it stands an elaborate cupboard with spindle columns and arched doors carved with birds, garlands, and a royal crest.

All the rooms are off the ground-floor breezeway or long upper balcony, overlooking the courtyard. Here umbrella tables are grouped near a stone fountain under drooping wisteria, bougainvillea, and pepper trees. The gardens are designed so well, with succulents and cacti, that they were awarded first place in a competition for landscaping with drought-tolerant or native plant materials.

A breakfast buffet of fresh breads, orange juice, and coffee is served in the courtyard or in the function room, which can also be used by groups.

ST. HELENA

Bartels Ranch and Country Inn

1200 Conn Valley Road
St. Helena, CA 94574
707-963-4001
800-225-5288
Fax: 707-963-5100

*A friendly home
in the wine
country hills*

Innkeeper: Jami Bartels. **Accommodations:** 4 rooms (all with private bath). **Rates:** $115–$225 single or double, suites $275–$315. **Included:** Full breakfast. **Added:** 10.5% tax. **Minimum stay:** 2 nights on weekends.

Payment: Major credit cards. **Children:** Allowed by prior arrangement, additional $25. **Pets:** Not allowed. **Smoking:** Not allowed in guest rooms.

Conn Valley lies four miles east of St. Helena, in the Napa Valley wine country about sixty miles north of San Francisco. Vineyards line the road that winds through oak-covered hills leading to Jami Bartels's 60-acre estate. The sprawling stone ranch house stands on a hilltop that overlooks pastures and sloping fields of grape vines. Its landscaped grounds include fig trees, flowering plums, cypress, and magnificent old oaks.

Jami Bartels is the energetic force who created this unusual inn. She designed all 7,000 square feet of her home, from the formal dining room, where she serves catered dinners, to the thirteen-sided game room with a brick fireplace and diagonal redwood walls. The huge room holds an amazing array of entertainment possibilities, including table tennis, a pool table, CD sound system, and shelves crammed with books and magazines. There are also games, puzzles, an organ, exercise equipment, and even a Wurlitzer jukebox. Throughout the house are examples of Jami's collections and artworks: butterflies, Chinese perfume bottles, glassware, baskets, and watercolors.

If you want a complete itinerary for your wine country tour, Jami will plan it. She'll make arrangements for hot air ballooning, glider flights, and limousine and helicopter service. You may borrow her bicycles for a ride to Lake Hennessey or just relax by the pool.

The Blue Valley guest room, with a private terrace overlooking the valley, has a queen-size canopy bed and a Victorian table for two, while the Brass Room features an Empire brass bed dating from the 1850s. Its glass doors open to a terrace by the pool. The Sunset Hillside Room has a king-size canopy bed, alcohol fireplace, and an etagere with a TV/VCR for watching movies. The newest room is the lavishly appointed Heart of the Valley Suite. It has a king-size bed, a sunken heart-shaped Jacuzzi, a huge fireplace, a TV and stereo, and a private deck.

The innkeeper's hospitality adds the crowning touch that makes her B&B exceptional. She's an expert at pampering, yet you will never feel stifled by all the attention. In the laundry room, an ironing board is always set up. "You know the fancy French restaurants around here; you can't show up wrinkled," Jami says. Fresh flowers abound, bubble bath awaits in the bathrooms, wine and cheese are served every evening, and breakfast is available at any time you like.

Breakfast, often served on the terrace, includes a heaping plate of fresh fruit, almond croissants, banana bread, granola, and yogurt. An egg entrée is also served, but Jami's specialty is Iowa raisin bread pudding ("I'm from Iowa, can you tell?" she asks with a laugh).

Bartels Ranch is well known as a superb place to stay in the valley, away from the mainstream of tourism, but everyone who comes here considers it a private find. The inn has attracted the orchestra conductor at La Scala, concert violinists, movie producers, chefs, artists, and the cast from *A Chorus Line*, among others.

Deer Run

3995 Spring Mountain Road
St. Helena, CA 94574
707-963-3794
800-843-3408
Fax: 707-963-9026

> *A quiet, woodsy retreat above the Napa Valley*

Innkeepers: Tom and Carol Wilson. **Accommodations:** 4 rooms (all with private bath). **Rates:** $125–$155 single or double. **Included:** Full breakfast. **Added:** 10.5% tax. **Minimum stay:** 2 nights weekends, April 1–November 1. **Payment:** Major credit cards. **Children:** Age 6 months and under welcome. **Pets:** Not allowed. **Smoking:** Not allowed.

Imagine a fifty-year-old cedar bungalow with a stone chimney and a washporch, back in the hills among tall pine trees. Picture it with rough paneling, a fireplace, and a king-size bed with a down quilt, and you've visualized the master bedroom in this woodsy bed-and-breakfast on Spring Mountain, in the Napa Valley.

The original cabin is only part of this delightful B&B, however. For the most seclusion, reserve the Cottage. A good honeymooners' choice, it has white-washed pine, an open beam ceiling in the living room, and Laura Ashley decor. Breakfast is brought to the cabin in the morning.

Another private spot is the Carriage Room, an odd-angled building with a large guest room decorated in forest green and burgundy. A vaulted ceiling of bleached pine with charcoal-stained beams covers part of the room. On the other side, sliding glass doors open to a porch under the trees. It's a quiet place; all you hear are crickets. There's also

> It's quiet here on Spring Mountain. You can hike a one-mile trail, walk to a winery, or swim in the pool. In every nook and corner, strawberry pots overflow with blue lobelia, marigolds flame yellow, and orange and lemon trees glow in sun or shade.

a separate studio with a large bedroom and bath, beamed ceilings, and Ralph Lauren fabrics.

But all is not as rustic as you might expect. A lot of expansion has taken place since the home was built in the 1930s. There are large living and dining areas and a wraparound deck that looks right into the treetops. Guests in the main house have breakfast at a round oak table near a buffet set with coffee, fresh fruit, nut breads, quiche or frittata, granola, and berries from the garden.

In the comfortable, casual living/dining room, collections on display reveal the Wilsons' interests: antiques, silver, German helmets, electric insulators, spoons, and salt cellars. They like the whimsical, too. A cabbage-shaped teapot with rabbit handle perches on the sideboard, and a ceramic rabbit tureen stands on an antique sewing machine table.

Tom is wonderfully creative. A watercolorist, his paintings hang in the residence as well as the guest rooms. On the deck, along with barrels of flowers and a picnic table, are examples of his work with tree twigs. He makes baskets and tiny chairs as holders for pots and dried flowers or as ornamentation. The wood comes from hazelnut trees on the 4-acre property, which also has walnut and maple trees. Yet another interest of Tom's — and his pride and joy — is a shiny yellow and black Model A automobile. It's kept under shelter, but he's happy to show it off if you ask.

The Wilsons opened Deer Run in 1981. Since then a good

many venturesome travelers have followed the winding, 4½-mile road in search of the romantic inn, and most are not disappointed with what they find.

Meadowood

900 Meadowood Lane
St. Helena, CA 94574
707-963-3646
800-458-8080
Fax: 707-963-3532

An exclusive resort in the country

General manager: Jorg Lippuner.
Accommodations: 99 rooms and suites. **Rates:** $305–$500 single or double, $25 additional person; $1375–$1875 for a 4 bedroom suite. **Added:** 10.5% tax. **Minimum stay:** 2 nights on weekends. **Payment:** Major credit cards. **Children:** Under age 12 free in room with parents. **Pets:** Not allowed. **Smoking:** Allowed.

On 250 acres of oak groves and green meadows in the Napa Valley, outside the village of St. Helena, this luxurious resort welcomes discriminating travelers. Formerly an exclusive private club, it opened to the public in 1985. Driving up the quiet, shady entrance road is like approaching a country estate, with vineyards on one side and walnut orchards on the other. After the guarded entry, you wind past madrone and oak trees sheltering guest houses, tennis courts, and a swimming pool to the main lodge. The three-story, white and gray gabled building and the clubhouse on a hill above the golf course resemble the grand New England resorts of the early 20th century.

Inside is a large, bright room with registration and concierge desks and couches by a stone fireplace. Pillows are piled on the window seat of one curving alcove, a comfortable spot to retreat with an apple from the basket on the table and a book from the array of classic novels in the glass-covered bookshelves.

Up in the clubhouse are two restaurants and an executive conference center with 4,000 square feet of meeting space.

The formal restaurant serves California cuisine with a Provençal influence and has a wine list that reads like a catalogue of the finest vineyards in the valley. More casual is the Grill, serving light meals indoors and on the terrace.

The guest rooms are in Croquet Lodge and in cottages tucked away in the woods above the pool, near the tennis courts, and by the golf course. Croquet Lodge directly faces a carpet of perfectly manicured grass — English regulation croquet courts. From your balcony or patio you can watch the white-clad players intent on a game

> Other than winery tours, activities include bicycling on country roads, fishing at Conn Dam and Lake Berryessa, shopping in the boutiques of St. Helena and Yountville, floating above the valley in a hot air balloon or soaring in a glider, and soaking in the mud baths of Calistoga.

or instruction from the resident pro. Beyond the croquet courts, among the cedar, oak, and tall pine trees are the sweeping fairways of the 9-hole golf course. Seven championship tennis courts lie on the other side of the property, between the main lodge and the entrance, not far from the swimming pool. Light meals and bar service are available by the pool.

Each cottage has four one-bedroom suites and a studio. They have private entrances, king-size beds, TV, ample closet space, and skylights that open with the press of a button. Cool luxury combined with great comfort is the motif — nothing flowery here. Walls are gray with white woodwork, the vaulted ceilings have rough white beams, and the artwork is minimal (winery maps and wine labels).

Most suites have stone fireplaces, with baskets of wood supplied. Other amenities include stocked refrigerators, coffeemakers, terrycloth robes, baskets of fresh fruit, down comforters with lots of pillows, room service, and a daily newspaper at your door.

Wine tastings and classes are an important part of the activities at Meadowood. John Thoreen, a winemaker, writer, and educator, teaches regular courses in wine appreciation. If you wish to go farther afield to explore regional wines, the concierge will arrange tours. Walking in the woods around

Meadowood is an experience in serenity and dreamlike natural beauty. Just be sure to stick to the paths to avoid contact with poison oak.

Villa St. Helena

2727 Sulphur Springs Avenue
St. Helena, CA 94574
707-963-2514

*A secluded
mansion above
Napa Valley
vineyards*

Owners: Ralph and Carolyn Cotton. **Accommodations:** 3 suites (all with private bath). **Rates:** $145–$245. **Included:** Expanded Continental breakfast. **Added:** 10.5% tax. **Minimum stay:** 2 nights on weekends. **Payment:** Major credit cards. **Children:** Age 12 and older welcome. **Pets:** Not allowed. **Smoking:** Not allowed in public spaces.

Secluded among California live oaks, bay trees, and madrones in the foothills of the Mayacamas Mountains of the Napa Valley, this expansive villa has a commanding view of vineyards and the village of St. Helena. From the hilltop at the end of a long, winding road, the inn looks over the valley to Mount St. Helena, high in the distance.

This is an ideal retreat for relaxing with a book in the library or under the avocado tree in the courtyard. And when you want to explore the countryside and perhaps taste what Robert Louis Stevenson called "bottled poetry," dozens of wineries are waiting.

The red brick structure was designed in 1941 by the architect Robert M. Carrere. Carrere designed only two California homes, though he created and restored numerous castles, mansions, and châteaux in Europe and the eastern United States.

Villa St. Helena stands on 20 acres of wooded hillside, its

three levels blending into the landscape rather than sitting atop it like a fortress. Two wings extend from a central section that contains a stone fireplace and dark beamed ceiling, a pleasing contrast to the white walls and glass and brass table.

Wide, high glass doors lead to a sunroom, where a buffet breakfast of breads, cheese, fresh fruit, and juice is set out in the morning. The sunroom's windows, framed by wisteria and bougainvillea vines, look toward a swath of lawn ending at a 60-foot pool and brick barbecue pit. On either side of this grassy enclave are suites simply labeled A, B, and C.

A Suite, at the end of the west wing, was the original master bedroom. The spacious room has a bed with an antique headboard, a marble fireplace (with fire laid), a turquoise and white tile bath, and several closets, including one just for shoes. Parquet floors and high-backed maroon leather chairs lend a sense of traditional dignity, while several windows and French doors leading to a private balcony keep it light and sunny. On one antique table there's a tray with a complimentary bottle of local white wine — replaced daily.

B Suite, smaller than A, has a two-poster bed with a tapestry hanging above it, large corner windows, and brass accents. There's no television, but each room has a phone jack, and a phone will be provided if you request it.

Most charming, and most private, is C Suite, across the lawn in the east wing. Up a tile staircase from the breezeway, it has two bedrooms, a sitting room with a white brick fireplace, wicker furniture, and a wet bar. It's a perfectly furnished apartment, complete with fold-down ironing board in the little hall.

There are few lodgings in the Napa Valley that can compare with Villa St. Helena for peace, quiet, and exclusive privacy.

The Wine Country Inn

1152 Lodi Lane
St. Helena, CA 94574
707-963-7077
Fax: 707-963-9018

> *A comfortable
> inn with a
> vineyard view*

Innkeepers: Jim Smith and Diane Horkheimer. **Accommodations:** 24 rooms (all with private bath). **Rates:** $118–$238 double, $20 less for single, $20 additional person; winter and midweek rates available. **Included:** Full breakfast and afternoon wine and appetizers. **Added:** 10.5% tax. **Minimum stay:** 2 nights on weekends in some rooms. **Payment:** Major credit cards. **Children:** Over age 6 charged as an additional person. **Pets:** Not allowed. **Smoking:** Allowed.

The Wine Country Inn's gray-brown siding has a look of weathered age, and the mansard roof above the central stone section creates the Old World impression the builders, Ned and Marge Smith, wanted. Now the inn is run by Marge and her son, Jim.

In the 1970s, when the Napa Valley was rapidly becoming the major tourist destination it is today, this inn was built on three acres above a country lane. Its landscaped grounds are bright with roses and other seasonal flowers, and a sweep of lawn descends to a swimming pool and spa.

The guest rooms are divided among three buildings. Most of them are in the main lodge; six are behind it, in Brandy Barn, and four are in Hastings House. Each room is furnished distinctly, with country antiques, handmade quilts, and color schemes reflecting the valley's seasonal changes. Most have patios or balconies. Fifteen have fireplaces that can be used from October to April; plenty of wood is supplied.

All the rooms are comfortable, but those upstairs are preferred if you're bothered by the sounds of drain pipes and footsteps overhead. Also, if you have a downstairs room with patio you must open the doors for ventilation, which could create a privacy problem. There are phones but no TVs in the rooms. A breakfast buffet is presented in the large common room in the main house. You can sit at one of several tables here or in a neighboring smaller room by a deck overlooking lawns and vineyards. Coffee, tea, fruit, granola, a choice of juices, a hot egg dish, and a variety of fresh breads such as pecan rolls, poppyseed bread, and strawberry bread constitute a typical breakfast, enough to start you on a tour of the countryside. The inn has a refrigerator for chilling your wine purchases and a stock of wine glasses.

In addition to tasting wine at the dozens of wineries nearby, the inn offers a private wine tasting for guests each afternoon. Appetizers are provided, and a different local winery is featured each day. For additional activities, you can visit Bale Grist Mill Historic Park, climb Mt. St. Helena, and see Robert Louis Stevenson memorabilia at the Silverado Museum. Or go shopping in the many boutiques and galleries and, at the top of everyone's list, eat at wonderful restaurants. Some outstanding valley favorites are TraVigne, Mustard's Grill, Showley's, Brava Terrace, and Terra.

Zinfandel Inn

800 Zinfandel Lane
St. Helena, CA 94574
707-963-3512
Fax: 707-963-5310

*A wine country
bed-and-breakfast*

Innkeeper: Diane Payton. **Accommodations:** 3 rooms (all with private bath). **Rates:** $150–$250 single or double, $25 additional person. **Included:** Full breakfast. **Added:** 10.5% tax. **Minimum stay:** 2 nights on weekends. **Payment:** Major credit cards. **Children:** Not appropriate. **Pets:** Not allowed. **Smoking:** Not allowed indoors.

On the outside, this bed-and-breakfast inn in the heart of the Napa Valley wine country resembles a European manor house, with a stone facade, towers, and a curving driveway with a fountain in the center. Inside, it's a comfortable, casual family home.

The inn is on a quiet road off Highway 29, south of St. Helena, a 90-minute drive from San Francisco. It was built in the early 1980s on two acres and has been open to guests since 1988.

"I want visitors to feel at home here," says Diane. She encourages guests to relax and watch TV in the big living room and help themselves to ice from the refrigerator.

The Chardonnay Room, on the main floor, has a brass and white iron bed facing an immense stone fireplace. A small TV rests on the corner of the hearth. In shades of blue, Chardonnay has a vaulted beamed ceiling, a curving bay window, and double doors leading to the back deck. Romantic touches include candles on the ledge of the oversize bathtub and a basket with fruit, candy, and wine.

> Diane will book balloon flights, make restaurant reservations, and arrange for mud baths at Calistoga's spas. If you request flowers or champagne for a special occasion, she'll see that they are in your room when you arrive.

Upstairs, past a landing where guests enjoy perching on the curved windowseat to watch hot air balloons floating over nearby vineyards, are the other two rooms. Petite Sirah is the smallest. It has a 19th-century French feather bed and a view of the vineyards. Zinfandel, which accommodates four, is furnished with velvet boudoir chairs, a fireplace, and a private balcony above the landscaped yard. As you relax on the balcony, you can enjoy the view of Mount St. Helena and the surrounding hills. The tile bath has a whirlpool tub and double-headed shower.

The balcony is a pleasant place to enjoy a breakfast of fresh fruits and a hot dish such as Belgian waffles, "gringo" ranchero eggs, pesto eggs, eggs Benedict, or banana pancakes; or you may eat at the formal dining table downstairs.

In the back garden, pepper trees grow by a curving lawn, a bubbling hot tub, and a lagoon with a fish pond and waterfall. There's also a natural-looking free-form swimming pool and a gazebo.

With only three rooms, the inn can fill up quickly. If there is no space available, you may want to ask Diane if she has room at her other bed and breakfast — the Glass Mountain Inn. The shingled Victorian inn has several suites and an obsidian wine cave built in the 1800s.

SANTA ROSA

The Gables

4257 Petaluma Hill Road
Santa Rosa, CA 95404
707-585-7777
800-GABLES-N
Fax: 707-584-5634

*A Victorian
country mansion*

Innkeepers: Michael and Judy Ogne. **Accommodations:** 8
rooms and cottage (all with private bath). **Rates:** $95–$115
single or double; suites $125–$195. **Included:** Full breakfast
and afternoon tea. **Added:** 9% tax. **Minimum stay:** 2 nights on
weekends. **Payment:** Major credit cards. **Children:** Allowed in
suitable rooms, $25 additional. **Pets:** Not allowed. **Smoking:**
Not allowed.

In 1877, William and Mary Jane Roberts built one of the most
interesting homes in Sonoma County — a Gothic Revival
mansion with fifteen gables above keyhole-shaped windows.
Inside there are 12-foot ceilings, marble fireplaces, and a spiral staircase of mahogany.

The Roberts' home is now a bed-and-breakfast, a graceful
combination of formal elegance and country comforts. It's
only 3½ miles from downtown Santa Rosa, but with wooded
acreage, a 150-year-old barn, a creek, and chickens providing
breakfast eggs, its atmosphere is one of rural tranquility.

Soft music plays in the parlor, where tea is served in the afternoon. You climb the curved staircase to reach the spacious
guest rooms with antique furnishings, brass beds with down
comforters, and literary classics to read in bed or by the windows that overlook the countryside. No two rooms are alike,
and there's a gable at every angle. Sunrise is filled with light
from bay windows; Sunset has a view of the hills and lights of
Sebastopol in the distance, and on the south overlooks the
pasture.

Meadow, crisp in blue and white, is furnished in bird's-eye
maple. Garden View is a favorite for its flowery decor, clawfoot tub in an arched alcove, and sunset view. The Parlor
Suite is luxurious with a king-size four-poster, an Italian marble fireplace, and a clawfoot tub.

Behind the main house is a separate, romantic cottage with

a roomy living room, a woodstove, a wet bar, and a Jacuzzi for two. In this trim little home, built in the 1850s, the Robertses raised seven children and worked to build their estate. Now completely restored, it's a cozy spot for a honeymoon or a small family. It has a loft with just enough space for a queen-size bed and a trunk. The loft has a pitched ceiling, so the only place you can stand upright is in the center of the room.

> In the dining room, a fire burns on cool mornings while guests enjoy a breakfast that varies daily. It might include apricot cobbler with cream or a frittata, as well as coffee cake, muffins, and fruit.

Michael and Judy are gracious innkeepers, happy to make suggestions for dining and sightseeing. They'll direct you to award-winning wineries, antiques shops, the Luther Burbank gardens, and the coast. Recommended restaurants in Santa Rosa include La Gare, Mixx, and John Ash & Co.

If you'd like to take a cup of coffee to the inn's back deck and join the snoozing cats, you're welcome to do so. You'll have a view of the rose garden, lilacs, grapevines, the weathered barn, and the old outhouse, now covered with roses.

Vintners Inn

4350 Barnes Road
Santa Rosa, CA 95403
707-575-7350
800-421-2584
Fax: 707-575-1426

> *A Mediterranean village in California wine country*

General manager: Cindy Duffy. **Accommodations:** 44 rooms. **Rates:** $128–$178 single or double, $10 additional person; suites $185–$205. **Included:** Expanded Continental breakfast. **Added:** 9% tax. **Minimum stay:** 2 nights on weekends, May through October. **Payment:** Major credit cards. **Children:** Under age 6 free in room with parents. **Pets:** Not allowed.

Smoking: Not allowed in restaurant or conference rooms; nonsmoking rooms are available.

Santa Rosa is a sprawling town sixty miles from San Francisco, between the vineyards of Sonoma on the south and Alexander Valley on the north. Just north of town and adjacent to Highway 101, Vintners Inn stands in the center of 45 acres of chardonnay, and sauvignon blanc grapes. Some of the vinifera grapes are sold to local wineries, while some are bottled under the inn's own label.

> **Jeffrey Madura is a talented, award-winning chef who works culinary magic with fresh local produce, the bounty of regional ranches and vineyards, and herbs grown just outside the window.**

Like a luxury complex transplanted from the south of France, the country inn is composed of stucco buildings centered around lawns and a fountain courtyard. Red tile roofs, arched doorways and windows, and wrought-iron railings add to the Mediterranean theme. Because the owners want an authentic village atmosphere, there are no swimming pools or tennis courts. However, nearby country clubs and health clubs are accessible to guests.

The rooms, divided among three two-story buildings, are furnished with European antiques. They all have air conditioning as well as French doors that open to a patio or balcony. In a typical mid-range room, you will find wingback chairs by tall windows overlooking the landscaped grounds, an armoire concealing a television set, phones, and matching pine night stands, a desk, and a refrigerator. The well-lighted bath has an oversize tub and shower. Five junior suites are larger and have wet bars, refrigerators, and fireplaces. Beer and wine will be delivered to your room upon request.

The library off the lobby in the main building is a comfortable place to relax by the fire. Across the lobby is the breakfast room, where croissants, waffles, homemade breakfast breads, fruits, and cereals are served. In the lobby itself, sun streams through high, curving windows to light walls and tiled floors, creating a welcoming entrance. For the area's few rainy days, a basket of umbrellas stands by the door.

Next to the inn is John Ash & Co., a restaurant that is one

of the best reasons for lodging at Vintners Inn. The restaurant has three dining areas separated by graceful arches and furnished with Spanish antiques.

An after-dinner stroll among the vineyards, a soak in the whirlpool tub by the sundeck, and you may be ready for a book or movie from the library — or the bed that has been turned down while you were out. VCRs are available for $10, which includes the rental fee for your first videotape.

SONOMA

El Dorado Hotel

405 First Street West
Sonoma, CA 95476
707-996-3030
800-289-3031
Fax: 707-996-3148

*A historic hotel
in a historic wine
country town*

General manager: Jana Trout. **Accommodation:** 27 rooms. **Rates:** $155–$145 single or double in summer, $85–$110 in winter. **Included:** Continental breakfast. **Added:** 10% tax. **Minimum stay:** 2 nights on weekends. **Children:** Under age 7 free. **Pets:** Not allowed. **Smoking:** Allowed.

Old Mexico meets contemporary California, with a colorful dash of Italy, at the El Dorado in historic Sonoma. The two-story mission revival hotel, overlooking the town's shady plaza, has an interesting past. Built in 1843 as a home for Don Salvador Vallejo (brother of the Mexican commandante), it was a refuge during the Bear Flag uprising of 1846 and became a hotel in 1851. Later it was a literary college, a wine-making shop, a home, and finally a hotel again.

Grape leaves are handpainted on guest rooms doors, and each pale taupe room is simply furnished with a steel four-poster bed, a peach duvet, and a dresser. Bedside tables are covered with floral tablecloths, and there's a wicker chair in the corner. There are no curtains, and the walls are plain except for one mirror, artfully framed with twigs. A woven throw rug lies on the tile floor; a TV is on the dresser. White louvered doors slide open to reveal a narrow balcony overlooking the courtyard or the town plaza. Baths have Mexican tile floors and oversize showers.

A breakfast of orange juice, Italian cheese, fruit, and fresh breads and muffins is served in a lounge off the white, open lobby. Each guest also receives a split of Sonoma Valley wine. The hotel's acclaimed restaurant, Ristorante Piatti, is noted for

> **The restaurant has a latticed courtyard with an old fig tree in the center. Here you can sit at umbrella tables, swim in the heated lap pool, or have a party for 100 people.**

its innovative Italian cookery. Artichokes, asparagus, and other foods are painted on the walls in this casual setting.

The obliging staff at the El Dorado will advise you on winery tours and nearby attractions.

Sonoma Hotel

110 West Spain Street
Sonoma, CA 95476
707-996-2996
800-468-6016
Fax: 707-996-7014

> *A historic*
> *Old West hotel*
> *by a shady plaza*

Innkeepers: John and Dorene Musilli. **Accommodations:** 17 rooms (5 with private bath). **Rates:** $75–$120 single or double. **Included:** Continental breakfast. **Added:** 10% tax. **Payment:** Major credit cards. **Children:** Not appropriate. **Pets:** Not allowed. **Smoking:** Allowed.

More than a century ago, a bar and dance hall were built across the street from the plaza in Sonoma, a town of significance in California history. This was where the state's wine industry was founded, where the short-lived Bear Flag Revolt took place, and where the northernmost (and last) of the twenty-one missions was built in 1823. Part of the adobe mission still stands.

In the early 1900s, the two-story dance hall gained a third floor and was converted to a hotel. The Sonoma Hotel has been providing rooms to travelers since then, in an atmosphere that is still turn-of-the-century. The Musilli family works hard to keep it that way with items such as an old fashioned baby carriage, clothes wringer, trunk, coffee mill, and sewing machine adding a nostalgic tone to the hotel's hallways.

> Mexican-era adobes surround the grassy, shaded plaza, which was laid out by General Vallejo in 1835 and is now the largest in California. It has flower gardens, picnic tables, a playground, a duck pond, and an outdoor theater.

If the hotel is not yet full when you check in you can go upstairs and pick the room you like the best. Each is individually decorated, but all are pleasantly furnished in antiques such as brass or intricately carved wooden beds, carved armoires, dressers with beveled mirrors, and marble-topped nightstands. The grandest is the Bear Flag Room, which boasts a bedroom suite of carved rosewood furnishings. Many rooms are quite small, often with an antique bed angled against a corner. Only five rooms have private baths; the others, on the upper two floors, have washbasins but share baths down the hall.

A breakfast of juice, croissants, and coffee is served in the small lobby/parlor, a bit of frontier elegance with velvet Victorian settees, puckered sheer curtains, and a rough stone fireplace.

Adjoining the lobby is a saloon with genuine Old West flavor. It has wooden floors, a battered piano, a gleaming old oak and mahogany bar, and even a bullet hole in the mirrored back bar to add authenticity. Ask the friendly bartender to tell you about the hotel's ghost. Some guests and staff members swear they've seen a Chinese spirit — perhaps from the days when there was a Chinese laundry on the back patio.

Victorian Garden Inn

316 East Napa Street
Sonoma, CA 95476
707-996-5339
800-543-5339
Fax: 707-996-1689

*A stylish
Victorian home
in town*

Innkeeper: Donna Lewis. **Accommodations:** 4 rooms (3 with private bath). **Rates:** $79–$139 single or double, $20 additional person. **Included:** California breakfast. **Added:** 10% tax. **Minimum stay:** 2 nights on weekends, 3 nights on holiday weekends. **Payment:** Major credit cards. **Children:** Discouraged. **Pets:** Not allowed. **Smoking:** Outside only.

Follow the path past lavish flower gardens and you'll come to this charming Victorian home built in the 1870s. It's on a comparatively busy street in Sonoma, but because it is set back, the atmosphere is one of seclusion. Guests will find lots of cozy sitting areas amidst the well-established gardens.

Donna Lewis, once an interior decorator, has furnished and decorated the rooms with flair. The most popular is Top o'

Donna will organize winery tours, pack a picnic basket, and recommend Sonoma's best restaurants. Breakfast, prepared by a professional chef, is served on the patio, in the dining room, or can be brought on a wicker tray to your room.

the Tower, with its own entrance. Decorated in blue and

white and wicker, it has the country charm of painted floors and braided rugs. The tower overlooks the maze of gardens and the swimming pool. Below it, with a door to the garden, is the Garden Room, which has a high bed with crisp white linens, a wicker rocker in front of the fireplace, and a claw-foot tub draped in battenburg lace.

Woodcutter's Cottage, next to the pool and brick patio, is cool and dark in green with peach accents. It has a fireplace, window seat, country antiques, a brass bed piled with pillows, a ceiling fan and skylight in the pitched roof, and a clawfoot tub and stained glass in the bath. This room can accommodate three. The least expensive accommodations are two antiques-furnished rooms in the main house; together they are called the Classic. You have a choice of a room with twin beds or one with a queen-size iron bed. A basket of towels is provided to use in the adjacent bathroom.

Laundry facilities and a refrigerator are available.

YOUNTVILLE

Burgundy House

P.O. Box 3156
6711 Washington Street
Yountville, CA 94599
707-944-0889

A picturesque stone inn with a country flavor

Innkeepers: Dieter and Ruth Back. **Accommodations:** 5 rooms (all with private bath). **Rates:** $110 single, $125 double, $25 additional person. **Included:** Breakfast. **Added:** 10% tax. **Minimum stay:** 2 nights on weekends. **Payment:** MasterCard, Visa; personal checks required to secure room reservation. **Children:** Over age 12 welcome. **Pets:** Not allowed. **Smoking:** Not allowed indoors.

Like an old stone house in the French countryside, this Napa Valley inn built in 1891 has 22-inch thick walls, hand-hewn posts and lintels, and rustic masonry. Originally a brandy distillery, it also housed a winery, a hotel, and a warehouse before becoming the bed-and-breakfast it is today.

There are five guest rooms named for cities in Burgundy: Beaune, Autun, Dijon, Pommard, and Cluny. Although they've been recently remodeled, you can see traces of the old stone walls in each. The rooms are quiet, as the inn is off the main highway. Beaune and Autun occupy the front corners of the inn. Dijon, in a back corner, has a cozy window seat with a view of the lovely rose garden. Pommard, with its own entrance off the garden, has a fireplace, a white

> **When you arrive, perhaps after a day of touring the wineries that make the valley famous, you'll find fresh flowers and a decanter of wine in your room.**

iron bed, and white walls and rustic beams. Outside the door is a patio under a sweet-scented orange tree.

The ebullient innkeeper, Dieter Back, serves breakfast in the comfortable little parlor or on the patio. He'll assist you in planning winery tours, balloon and glider rides, and selecting one of the many highly rated restaurants in the area.

Maison Fleurie

6529 Yount Street
Yountville, CA 94599
707-944-2056
800-788-0369

> *A French-style inn in wine country*

Owners: Roger and Sally Post. **Innkeeper:** Roger Asbill. **Accommodations:** 13 rooms. **Rates:** $110–$190. **Included:** Full breakfast. **Added:** Tax. **Payment:** Major credit cards. **Children:** Welcome. **Pets:** Not allowed. **Smoking:** Not allowed.

If traveling through the California wine country puts you in the mood for a European sojourn, then a night or two at Maison Fleurie may be just what you need. The charming inn, consisting of three ivy-covered brick and stone buildings, feels as if it belongs in the countryside of Provence. The main building was built as a small hotel and saloon back in 1872. The two adjacent buildings are the old carriage house, and the bakery building, which housed a bakery called the "Court of Three Sisters" until the mid-1970s. In 1994 the Four Sisters Inns, a small group known for their high-quality lodgings, opened Maison Fleurie as a bed-and-breakfast.

In the lobby of the main building, there's a cozy sitting area with a fruit-patterned sofa and comfortable chairs in front of a fireplace guarded by the Four Sisters Inns' signature teddy bears. The breakfast room, with its exposed brick walls, terra cotta floor tiles, and antique French thatched-backed chairs, was added on to the original structure about 1901. Here a full breakfast of bagels, English muffins, muesli, coffeecake, and a hot dish such as Spanish eggs is served each morning. Vegetarians will be pleased to know that meat is not a breakfast staple at this inn.

> The vineyards and grapevine-covered hills of the Napa Valley are often best explored at a leisurely pace. Maison Fleurie has bicycles available to help facilitate such a tour of the lovely surrounding countryside.

There are seven guest rooms in the main building — one on the first floor, four on the second floor, and two rooms on the top floor. Rooms are attractively decorated with floral carpeting and a mixture of original antiques and French country furniture. Hand-painted designs by a Monterey artist in each of the guest rooms is an appealing personal touch. All rooms have terry robes and private baths.

The bakery building has four guest rooms each with a fireplace and king-size bed. Room 10, upstairs, opens onto a terrace overlooking the backyard gardens and swimming pool. A floral bouquet painted above the fabric headboard is the crowning stroke to the bed, with its floral comforter, red-checked pillows, and cuddly teddy bear.

The two remaining guest rooms are in the carriage house. One has a queen-size bed with vineyard views, and the other has a king-size bed and a fireplace. All rooms have extra-large beach towels for lounging by the pool or soaking in the outdoor spa surrounded by teak furniture and blooming pots of flowers.

Wine and hors d'oeuvres are set out each evening between five o'clock and seven o'clock. There is always a cheese board along with another appetizer such as pumpkin surprise or a chocolatey Texas sheetcake. For other meals, the fine restaurants of Yountville are within easy walking distance.

Oleander House

7433 St. Helena Highway
Yountville, CA 94599
707-944-8315
800-788-0357
Fax: 707-944-2279

A bed-and-breakfast within walking distance of wineries

Innkeepers: Louise and John Packard. **Accommodations:** 4 rooms (all with private bath). **Rates:** $130–$175 single or double. **Included:** Full breakfast. **Added:** 10.5% tax. **Minimum stay:** 2 nights on weekends and holidays. **Payment:** MasterCard, Visa. **Children:** Not appropriate. **Pets:** Not allowed. **Smoking:** Not allowed indoors.

Bordered by the oleander hedges that give the place its name, this bed-and-breakfast inn offers numerous amenities and (despite facing the heavily used Highway 29) a fine location. It's set back from the road, behind a garden of strawberries, herbs, and roses, and is within walking distance of two wineries and one of the Napa Valley's best restaurants, Mustard's Grill.

The Packards, who have owned the inn since 1989, have created a haven for their guests. The rooms are furnished in a contemporary style, each with a fireplace, a balcony, Laura Ashley wallpaper and fabrics, and a basket of brochures and choco-

In the evening, you can watch the sun set from the patio and sample your wine purchases as you enjoy the romantic fragrance of star jasmine and the tempting scents that waft over from Mustard's Grill.

late kisses. The quietest rooms, in the back of the house, have brass beds and views of the hills and Carmelite monastery.

On the second-floor landing there's a sitting area with a TV, wet bar, bookshelves, and refrigerator. You can help yourself to soft drinks or chill your wine. Guests are welcome to use the spa on the back patio.

Breakfast is served at a long table in the dining room, which has items the Packards brought home from their two-year stay in Japan. Among them are a Nakayama painting and an antique kitchen ton-su, used as a sideboard. Strawberries from the garden are used in a sauce for the baked pancakes and French toast; breakfast dishes vary daily and are served along with juice, coffee, and fruit.

The Webber Place

P.O. Box 2873
6610 Webber Street
Yountville, CA 94599
707-944-8384
800-647-7177

A classic farm-house close to valley vineyards

Innkeeper: Diane Bartholomew.
Accommodations: 4 rooms (2 with private bath). **Rates:** $69–$119 single or double. **Included:** Breakfast. **Added:** 10% tax. **Minimum stay:** 2 nights on summer weekends. **Payment:** Major credit cards. **Children:** Over age 12 welcome, $15 additional. **Pets:** Allowed by arrangement. **Smoking:** Not allowed.

If you've ever longed to visit Grandma's house in the country, where you're welcomed with a smile, a cup of tea, and an invitation to rest in the rocker on the veranda, you will be happy at The Webber Place.

The old-fashioned red farmhouse stands on a quiet corner, behind a flower garden marked by a white picket fence and rose-covered trellis. Built in the 1850s by early settlers, the house was moved from a ranch site east of town to its present location by John Lee Webber. Reconstruction began in 1971, with careful attention paid to details in the woodwork, wallpapers, brass fittings, and porcelain fixtures. The original tongue-and-groove redwood paneling had been painted so many times that it was simply removed, turned, and replaced to create the desired effect.

> **A nice place to end an afternoon of touring wineries, bicycling, or ballooning is at the picnic table in the front yard. Pick up a snack at a deli to enjoy with the wine you have purchased or the complimentary beverage Diane provides.**

Diane Bartholomew, a painter and sculptor, has furnished her home for simple comfort. "Classic Victorian is too elegant and formal for this country farmhouse," she says, arranging a big bouquet of sweet peas on the coffee table. "I want the style to fit the place."

Diane lives in a cottage next door, where she has a studio, and is back and forth regularly. Between the houses is her "art yard," with sculptures and other works of art. On the main floor is a cozy living room with a brick hearth and woodstove, a small dining area, and one guest room with a private entrance off the side veranda. The Veranda Room has a white wicker rocker, a clawfoot tub, and a down duvet on the bed. Double doors lead to a latticed porch where a big hammock sways, perfect for lazing away an idle afternoon.

The three rooms upstairs contain double beds. The East Room has its own bath; Redwood and the Sun Room share a white tile bath. Rose café curtains hang at long windows in the Sun Room. Fluttering leaves on the valley oak outside cast intricate shadows on the bare wood floor. None of the rooms has television or a phone, but guests may use the phone in the living room.

If you visit at harvest time, you'll see an amazing array of jack-o'-lanterns at The Webber Place. They perch on posts, grin from railings, and peek out from cornstalks and piles of hay. Each October, Diane invites all the children in town to carve pumpkins. For every twelve faces, she gives the carver a T-shirt commemorating the occasion. You're welcome to join in the fun.

Recommended Reading

2 to 22 Days in California, Roger Rapoport (John Muir Publications), $11.95. Detailed itineraries, maps, daily plans, and sightseeing highlights. Small print, no illustrations, but useful information.

Adventuring in the California Desert, Lynne Foster (Sierra Club Books), $14.00. Part of the Sierra Club series focusing on outdoor activities, camping facilities, natural history. How to best enjoy the Great Basin, Mojave, and Colorado Desert regions. A few drawings and maps. Carefully crafted, lots of information.

California: The Ultimate Guidebook, by Ray Riegert (Ulysses Press), $13.95. Riegert knows California well and is a trustworthy guide. His book divides the state by area and includes restaurants, lodging, nightlife, shopping, beaches and parks, and offbeat attractions. It covers so much ground the information is limited. Contains simple maps.

Fielding's California: The Mission Trail, San Diego to San Francisco, Lynn Foster, $10.95. For the history buff. Contains practical tips and suggestions for activities and explains historical events along the mission trail.

Fishing in Northern California and *Fishing in Southern California,* Ken Albert (Marketscope Books), $14.95 each. Everything you need to know about fishing California's 5,000 lakes and 30,000 miles of streams. Clear format.

Fodor's Pocket San Francisco: The Best of the City, Fodor's Travel Publications, $7.00. Pocket size, readable, covers highlights for short visits.

The Great Family Getaway Guide, Bill Gleeson (Chronicle Books), $8.95. Includes 180 California adventures — resorts, motels, theme parks, museums, and attractions with special appeal to kids. Personal, chatty style. Black and white photographs, no maps.

The Hiker's Guide to California, Ron Adkison (Falcon Press), $11.95. Detailed information on 100 hikes in the backcountry. Some maps and photographs.

Inside San Francisco, Don and Betty Martin (Pine Cone Press), $8.95. Detailed, witty, opinionated city guide. Convenient size.

Insight Guide: California (Houghton Mifflin Co.), $19.95. Grand overview of the state, with essays on its history, social fabric, ethnic cultures, and geography. Includes maps and superb color photographs.

Los Angeles Access, Richard S. Wurman (Access Press), $11.95. Divides the L.A. area by neighborhood and reviews the hotels, restaurants, and attractions in each. Color-coded and mapped. Intriguing, workable system, once you figure it out. Strong architectural focus.

Northern California Handbook, Kim Weir (Moon Publications), $16.95. Crammed with information but well organized. Contains thoughtful commentaries, maps, and some color photographs.

San Francisco Access, Richard S. Wurman (Access Press), $12.95. Divides the San Francisco area by neighborhood; color-coded (see Los Angeles Access.)

What's What

Bicycling

American River Inn, 357
Bartels Ranch and Country Inn, 594
The Bayberry Inn, 199
Beach House, 131
Campbell Ranch Inn, 567
Carmel Valley Ranch, 154
Cobblestone Inn, 138
Coloma Country Inn, 347
La Costa Resort and Spa, 444
Four Seasons Biltmore, 202
The Gingerbread Mansion, 283
La Mancha, 245
Masion Fleurie, 613
Ojai Valley Inn, 183
The Old Yacht Club Inn, 206
San Diego Princess, 530
The Sandpiper Inn, 147
Secret Garden Inn & Cottages, 208
Simpson House Inn, 209
The Stanford Inn by the Sea, 319

Boating

The Alisal Guest Ranch, 220
Caples Lake Resort, 371
Dockside Boat & Bed, 22
Disneyland Hotel, 430
Edelweiss Lodge, 375
Lakeland Village Beach & Ski Resort, 407
Marriott's Laguna Cliffs Resort, 459
Otter Bar Lodge, 286
San Diego Princess, 530
The Stanford Inn by the Sea, 319

Business Services

Croquet

Fine Dining

Golf

The Alisal Guest Ranch, 220
Carmel Valley Ranch, 154
La Costa Resort and Spa, 444
Furnace Creek Inn, 232
The Inn at Spanish Bay, 195
The Lodge at Pebble Beach, 197
Meadowood, 598
Ojai Valley Inn, 183
Quail Lodge, 156
La Quinta Hotel Golf & Tennis Resort, 238
Rancho Bernardo Inn, 515
Resort at Squaw Creek, 387
The Ritz-Carlton Laguna Niguel, 485
The Ritz-Carlton Rancho Mirage, 254
The Sea Ranch, 329
Silverado Country Club & Resort, 589
Wawona Hotel, 419
Westin Mission Hills Resort, 257

Historic Hotels

City Hotel, 349
Fallon Hotel, 351
Horton Grand Hotel, 526
The Hotel Jeffery, 352
Imperial Hotel, 343
Julian Hotel, 470
Mount View Hotel, 561
The National Hotel, 369
Sheraton Palace Hotel, 91
Sonoma Hotel, 609
The Union Hotel (Benicia), 8
U.S. Grant Hotel, 532
Westin St. Francis Hotel, 99

Horseback Riding

The Alisal Guest Ranch, 220
Circle Bar B Guest Ranch, 165

Kitchen/Cooking Facilities

Pets Allowed with Permission

The Bayberry Inn, 199
The Clift, 44
Cypress Inn (Carmel), 140
Drakesbad Guest Ranch, 269
Four Seasons Biltmore, 202
Golden Gate Hotel, 51
The Inn at Rancho Santa Fe, 517
The Lodge at Pebble Beach, 197
Meadowlark, 559
Quail Lodge, 156
Radisson Hotel Sacramento, 399
The Regent Beverly Wilshire, 440
San Diego Princess, 530
San Ysidro Ranch, 173
Sorensen's, 360
Stillwater Cove Ranch, 293
Trinity Alps Resort, 295
Vagabond's House, 152

Restaurant Open to Public

The Ahwahnee, 421
Auberge du Soleil, 591
Beverly Prescott Hotel, 494
The Biltmore Hotel, 496
Campton Place, 41
Caples Lake Resort, 371
Carmel Valley Ranch Resort, 154
Casa Madrona Hotel, 106
La Casa del Zorro, 230
Catamaran Resort Hotel, 522
Chaminade, 217
Circle Bar B Guest Ranch, 165
The Claremont Resort and Spa, 20
The Cliffs at Shell Beach, 219
The Clift, 44
La Costa Resort and Spa, 444
Crystal Rose Inn, 121
The Delta King Hotel, 395
Disneyland Hotel, 430
El Dorado Hotel, 608
The Fairmont Hotel, 47

Tennis

Wheelchair Access

Index

Best Places Report

Authors of the Best Places to Stay series travel extensively in their research to find the best places for all budgets, styles, and interests. However, if we've missed an establishment that you find worthy, please write to us with your suggestion. Detailed information about the service, food, setting, and nearby activities or sights is most important. Finally, let us know how you heard about the place and how long you've been going there.

Send suggestions to:

> The Harvard Common Press
> Best Places to Stay Suggestions
> 535 Albany Street
> Boston, Massachusetts 02118

NAME OF HOTEL _____ _____

TELEPHONE _____ _____

ADDRESS _____

_____ ZIP _____

DESCRIPTION _____

_____

_____

_____

_____

_____

_____

_____

YOUR NAME _____

TELEPHONE _____

ADDRESS _____

_____ ZIP _____

Best Places Report

Authors of the Best Places to Stay series travel extensively in their research to find the best places for all budgets, styles, and interests. However, if we've missed an establishment that you find worthy, please write to us with your suggestion. Detailed information about the service, food, setting, and nearby activities or sights is most important. Finally, let us know how you heard about the place and how long you've been going there.

Send suggestions to:

The Harvard Common Press
Best Places to Stay Suggestions
535 Albany Street
Boston, Massachusetts 02118

NAME OF HOTEL _____

TELEPHONE _____

ADDRESS _____

_____ ZIP _____

DESCRIPTION _____

_____

_____

_____

_____

_____

_____

_____

YOUR NAME _____

TELEPHONE _____

ADDRESS _____

_____ ZIP _____

Best Places Report

Authors of the Best Places to Stay series travel extensively in their research to find the best places for all budgets, styles, and interests. However, if we've missed an establishment that you find worthy, please write to us with your suggestion. Detailed information about the service, food, setting, and nearby activities or sights is most important. Finally, let us know how you heard about the place and how long you've been going there.

Send suggestions to:

The Harvard Common Press
Best Places to Stay Suggestions
535 Albany Street
Boston, Massachusetts 02118

NAME OF HOTEL _____

TELEPHONE _____

ADDRESS _____

_____ ZIP _____

DESCRIPTION _____

_____

_____

_____

_____

_____

_____

YOUR NAME _____

TELEPHONE _____

ADDRESS _____

_____ ZIP _____